Red Mars

Kim Stanley Robinson was born in 1952. After several years of travelling and working in different parts of the world, he has now returned to California. One of the finest science fiction writers to emerge in recent years, Robinson has won the Nebula, Asimov, John W. Campbell, Locus and World Fantasy Awards. The *Mars* trilogy is the product of a lifelong obsession with the red planet and seventeen years of dedicated research and planning.

'A staggering book – the best novel on the colonization of Mars that has ever been written . . . I think it should be required reading for the colonists of the next century'
ARTHUR C. CLARKE

'Extraordinary . . . First of a mighty trilogy, it is the ultimate in "future history", forecasting every detail and facet, triumph and tragedy, crucial breakthroughs and trivialities of humanity's colonisation of another world'   *Daily Mail*

'One of the finest works of American sf'
Times Literary Supplement

'The last time I was enthralled by a book about Mars was in 1950. Ray Bradbury's *Martian Chronicles* inspired a whole generation of readers and writers. *Red Mars* will do the same'   *Manchester Evening News*

'Absorbing. . . impressive. . . fascinating. . . Utterly plausible . . . The product of an imaginative love affair between the author and Earth's nearest planetary neighbour'
Financial Times

'I have this belief that Kim Stanley Robinson was one of the first settlers on Mars, and that somehow he has travelled back to today to tell his tale. There is no other explanation for this brilliant new novel. This is how it *should* be done'
City Limits

SCIENCE
FICTION
FANTASY

KIM STANLEY ROBINSON

Red Mars

HarperCollins*Publishers*

HarperCollins Science Fiction & Fantasy
An Imprint of HarperCollins*Publishers*
77–85 Fulham Palace Road,
Hammersmith, London W6 8JB

Special overseas edition 1993
This paperback edition 1993
3 5 7 9 8 6 4 2

First published in Great Britain by
HarperCollins*Publishers* 1992

ISBN 0 586 21389 9

Set in Aldus

Printed in Great Britain by
HarperCollinsManufacturing Glasgow

For Lisa

CONTENTS

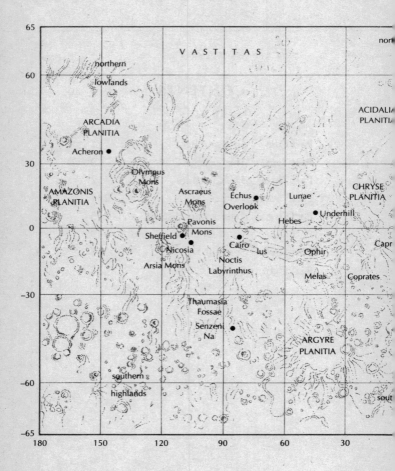

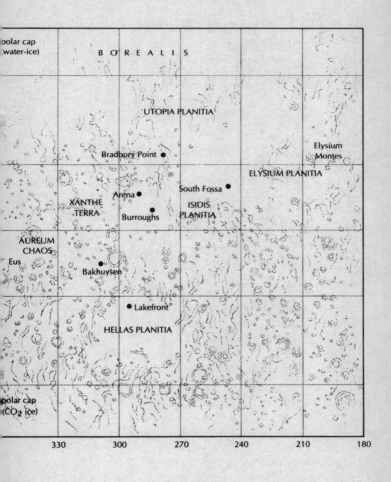

polar cap (water-ice)

B O R E A L I S

UTOPIA PLANITIA

Bradbury Point ●

Elysium Montes

ELYSIUM PLANITIA

Arena ●

South Fossa ●

XANTHE TERRA

Burroughs ●

ISIDIS PLANITIA

AUREUM CHAOS

Eus

Bakhuysen ●

Lakefront ●

HELLAS PLANITIA

polar cap (CO_2 ice)

330   300   270   240   210   180

PART ONE

Festival Night

Mars was empty before we came. That's not to say that nothing had ever happened. The planet had accreted, melted, roiled and cooled, leaving a surface scarred by enormous geological features: craters, canyons, volcanoes. But all of that happened in mineral unconsciousness, and unobserved. There were no witnesses — except for us, looking from the planet next door, and that only in the last moment of its long history. We are all the consciousness that Mars has ever had.

Now everybody knows the history of Mars in the human mind: how for all the generations of prehistory it was one of the chief lights in the sky, because of its redness and fluctuating intensity, and the way it stalled in its wandering course through the stars, and sometimes even reversed direction. It seemed to be saying something with all that. So perhaps it is not surprising that all the oldest names for Mars have a peculiar weight on the tongue — Nirgal, Mangala, Auqakuh, Harmakhis — they sound as if they were even older than the ancient languages we find them in, as if they were fossil words from the Ice Age or before. Yes, for thousands of years Mars was a sacred power in human affairs; and its color made it a dangerous power, representing blood, anger, war and the heart.

Then the first telescopes gave us a closer look, and we saw the little orange disk, with its white poles and dark patches spreading and shrinking as the long seasons passed. No improvement in the technology of the telescope ever gave us much more than that; but the best Earthbound images gave Lowell enough blurs to inspire a story, the story we all know, of a dying world and a heroic people, desperately building canals to hold off the final deadly encroachment of the desert.

It was a great story. But then Mariner and Viking sent

13

back their photos, and everything changed. Our knowledge of Mars expanded by magnitudes, we literally knew millions of times more about this planet than we had before. And there before us flew a new world, a world unsuspected.

It seemed, however, to be a world without life. People searched for signs of past or present Martian life, anything from microbes to the doomed canal-builders, or even alien visitors. As you know, no evidence for any of these has ever been found. And so stories have naturally blossomed to fill the gap, just as in Lowell's time, or in Homer's, or in the caves or on the savannah — stories of microfossils wrecked by our bio-organisms, of ruins found in dust storms and then lost forever, of Big Man and all his adventures, of the elusive little red people, always glimpsed out of the corner of the eye. And all of these tales are told in an attempt to give Mars life, or to bring it to life. Because we are still those animals who survived the Ice Age, and looked up at the night sky in wonder, and told stories. And Mars has never ceased to be what it was to us from our very beginning — a great sign, a great symbol, a great power.

And so we came here. It had been a power; now it became a place.

". . . **And so** we came here. But what they didn't realize was that by the time we got to Mars, we would be so changed by the voyage out that nothing we had been told to do mattered anymore. It wasn't like submarining or settling the Wild West – it was *an entirely new experience*, and as the flight of the *Ares* went on, the Earth finally became so distant that it was nothing but a blue star among all the others, its voices so delayed that they seemed to come from a previous century. We were on our own; and so we became *fundamentally different beings*."

All lies, Frank Chalmers thought irritably. He was sitting in a row of dignitaries, watching his old friend John Boone give the usual Boone Inspirational Address. It made Chalmers weary. The truth was, the trip to Mars had been the functional equivalent of a long train ride. Not only had they not become fundamentally different beings, they had actually become more like themselves than ever, stripped of habits until they were left with nothing but the naked raw material of their selves. But John stood up there waving a forefinger at the crowd, saying "We came here to make something new, and when we arrived our earthly differences fell away, irrelevant in this new world!" Yes, he meant it all literally. His vision of Mars was a lens that distorted everything he saw, a kind of religion.

Chalmers stopped listening and let his gaze wander over the new city. They were going to call it Nicosia. It was the first town of any size to be built free-standing on the Martian surface; all the buildings were set inside what was in effect an immense clear tent, supported by a nearly invisible frame, and placed on the rise of Tharsis, west of Noctis Labyrinthus. This location gave it a tremendous view, with a distant western horizon punctuated by the broad peak of Pavonis Mons. For the Mars veterans in the crowd it was giddy stuff:

15

they were on the surface, they were out of the trenches and mesas and craters, they could see forever! Hurrah!

A laugh from the audience drew Frank's attention back to his old friend. John Boone had a slightly hoarse voice and a friendly Midwestern accent, and he was by turns (and somehow even all at once) relaxed, intense, sincere, self-mocking, modest, confident, serious, and funny. In short, the perfect public speaker. And the audience was rapt; this was *the First Man On Mars* speaking to them, and judging by the looks on their faces they might as well have been watching Jesus produce their evening meal out of the loaves and fishes. And in fact John almost deserved their adoration, for performing a similar miracle on another plane, transforming their tin can existence into an astounding spiritual voyage. "On Mars we will come to care for each other more than ever before," John said, which really meant, Chalmers thought, an alarming incidence of the kind of behavior seen in rat overpopulation experiments; "Mars is a sublime, exotic and dangerous place," said John – meaning a frozen ball of oxidized rock on which they were exposed to about fifteen rem a year; "And with our work," John continued, "we are carving out a new social order and the next step in the human story" – i.e. the latest variant in primate dominance dynamics.

John finished with this flourish, and there was, of course, a huge roar of applause. Maya Toitovna then went to the podium to introduce Chalmers. Frank gave her a private look which meant he was in no mood for any of her jokes; she saw it and said, "Our next speaker has been the fuel in our little rocket ship," which somehow got a laugh. "His vision and energy are what got us to Mars in the first place, so save any complaints you may have for our next speaker, my old friend Frank Chalmers."

At the podium he found himself surprised by how big the town appeared. It covered a long triangle, and they were gathered at its highest point, a park occupying the western apex. Seven paths rayed down through the park to become wide, tree-lined, grassy boulevards. Between the boulevards stood low trapezoidal buildings, each faced with polished stone of a different color. The size and architecture of the buildings gave things a faintly Parisian look, Paris as seen by a drunk Fauvist in spring, sidewalk cafés and all. Four or five kilometers downslope the end of the city was marked by three slender skyscrapers, beyond which lay the low greenery of the farm. The skyscrapers were part of the tent framework, which overhead was an arched network of sky-colored lines. The tent fabric itself was invisible, and so taken all in all, it appeared that they *stood in the open air*. That was gold. Nicosia was going to be a popular city.

Chalmers said as much to the audience, and enthusiastically they agreed. Apparently he had the crowd, fickle souls that they were, about as securely as John. Chalmers was bulky and dark, and he knew he presented quite a contrast to John's blond good looks; but he knew as well that he had his own rough charisma, and as he warmed up he drew on it, falling into a selection of his own stock phrases.

Then a shaft of sunlight lanced down between the clouds, striking the upturned faces of the crowd, and he felt an odd tightening in his stomach. So many people there, so many *strangers*! People in the mass were a frightening thing – all those wet ceramic eyes encased in pink blobs, looking at him . . . it was nearly too much. Five thousand people in a single Martian town. After all the years in Underhill it was hard to grasp.

Foolishly he tried to tell the audience something of this. "Looking," he said. "Looking around – the strangeness of our presence here is – accentuated."

He was losing the crowd. How to say it? How to say that they alone in all that rocky world were alive, their faces glowing like paper lanterns in the light? How to say that even if living creatures were no more than carriers for ruthless genes, this was still, somehow, better than the blank mineral nothingness of everything else?

17

Of course he could never say it. Not at any time, perhaps, and certainly not in a speech. So he collected himself. "In the Martian desolation," he said, "the human presence is, well, a remarkable thing" (they would care for each other more than ever before, a voice in his mind repeated sardonically). "The planet, taken in itself, is a dead frozen nightmare" (therefore exotic and sublime), "and so thrown on our own, we of necessity are in the process of – reorganizing a bit" (or forming a new social order) – so that yes, yes, yes, he found himself proclaiming exactly the same lies they had just heard from John!

Thus at the end of his speech he too got a big roar of applause. Irritated, he announced it was time to eat, depriving Maya of her chance for a final remark. Although probably she had known he would do that and so hadn't bothered to think of any. Frank Chalmers liked to have the last word.

People crowded onto the temporary platform to mingle with the celebrities. It was rare to get this many of the first hundred in one spot anymore, and people crowded around John and Maya, Samantha Hoyle, Sax Russell and Chalmers.

Frank looked over the crowd at John and Maya. He didn't recognize the group of Terrans surrounding them, which made him curious. He made his way across the platform, and as he approached he saw Maya and John give each other a look. "There's no reason this place shouldn't function under normal law," one of the Terrans was saying.

Maya said to him, "Did Olympus Mons really remind you of Mauna Loa?"

"Sure," the man said. "Shield volcanoes all look alike."

Frank stared over this idiot's head at Maya. She didn't acknowledge the look. John was pretending not to have noticed Frank's arrival. Samantha Hoyle was speaking to another man in an undertone, explaining something; he nodded, then glanced involuntarily at Frank. Samantha kept her back turned to him. But it was John who mattered, John

18

and Maya. And both were pretending that nothing was out of the ordinary; but the topic of conversation, whatever it had been, had gone away.

Chalmers left the platform. People were still trooping down through the park, toward tables that had been set in the upper ends of the seven boulevards. Chalmers followed them, walking under young transplanted sycamores; their khaki leaves colored the afternoon light, making the park look like the bottom of an aquarium.

At the banquet tables construction workers were knocking back vodka, getting rowdy, obscurely aware that with the construction finished, the heroic age of Nicosia was ended. Perhaps that was true for all of Mars.

The air filled with overlapping conversations. Frank sank beneath the turbulence, wandered out to the northern perimeter. He stopped at a waist-high concrete coping: the city wall. Out of the metal stripping on its top rose four layers of clear plastic. A Swiss man was explaining things to a group of visitors, pointing happily.

"An outer membrane of piezoelectric plastic generates electricity from wind. Then two sheets hold a layer of airgel insulation. Then the inner layer is a radiation-capturing membrane, which turns purple and must be replaced. More clear than a window, isn't it?"

The visitors agreed. Frank reached out and pushed at the inner membrane. It stretched until his fingers were buried to the knuckles. Slightly cool. There was faint white lettering printed on the plastic: *Isidis Planitia Polymers*. Through the sycamores over his shoulder he could still see the platform at the apex. John and Maya and their cluster of Terran admirers were still there, talking animatedly. Conducting the business of the planet. Deciding the fate of Mars.

He stopped breathing. He felt the pressure of his molars squeezing together. He poked the tent wall so hard that he pushed out the outermost membrane, which meant that some of his anger would be captured and stored as electricity in the town's grid. It was a special polymer in that respect; carbon atoms were linked to hydrogen and fluorine atoms in such a way that the resulting substance was even more piezoelectric than quartz. Change one element of the three, however, and everything shifted; substitute chlorine for fluorine, for instance, and you had saran wrap.

Frank stared at his wrapped hand, then up again at the other two elements, still bonded to each other. But without him they were nothing!

Angrily he walked into the narrow streets of the city.

Clustered in a plaza like mussels on a rock were a group of Arabs, drinking coffee. Arabs had arrived on Mars only ten years before, but already they were a force to be reckoned with. They had a lot of money, and they had teamed up with the Swiss to build a number of towns, including this one. And they liked it on Mars. "It's like a cold day in the Empty Quarter," as the Saudis said. The similarity was such that Arabic words were slipping quickly into English, because Arabic had a larger vocabulary for this landscape: *akaba* for the steep final slopes around volcanoes, *badia* for the great world dunes, *nefuds* for deep sand, *seyl* for the billion year-old dry river beds . . . people were saying they might as well switch over to Arabic and have done with it.

Frank had spent a fair bit of time with Arabs, and the men in the plaza were pleased to see him. "*Salaam aleyk!*" they said to him, and he replied, "*Marhabba!*" White teeth flashed under black moustaches. Only men present, as usual. Some youths led him to a central table where the older men sat, including his friend Zeyk. Zeyk said, "We are going to call this square *Hajr el-kra Meshab,* 'the red granite open place in town.' " He gestured at the rust-colored flagstones. Frank nodded and asked what kind of stone it was. He spoke Arabic for as long as he could, pushing the edges of his ability and getting some good laughs in response. Then he sat at the central table and relaxed, feeling like he could have been on a street in Damascus or Cairo, comfortable in the wash of Arabic and expensive cologne.

He studied the men's faces as they talked. An alien culture, no doubt about it. They weren't going to change just because they were on Mars, they put the lie to John's vision. Their thinking clashed radically with Western thought; for instance the separation of church and state was wrong to them, making it impossible for them to agree with Westerners on the very basis of government. And they were so patriarchal that some of their women were said to be illiterate – illiterates, on Mars! That was a sign. And indeed these men had the dangerous look that Frank associated with *machismo*, the look of men who oppressed their women so cruelly that naturally the women struck back where they could, terrorizing sons who then terrorized wives who terrorized sons and so on and so on, in an endless death spiral of twisted love and sex hatred. So that in that sense they were all madmen.

Which was one reason Frank liked them. And certainly they would come in useful to him, acting as a new locus of power. Defend a weak new neighbor to weaken the old powerful ones, as Machiavelli had said. So he drank coffee, and gradually, politely, they shifted to English.

"How did you like the speeches?" he asked, looking into the black mud at the bottom of his demitasse.

"John Boone is the same as ever," old Zeyk replied. The others laughed angrily. "When he says we will make an indigenous Martian culture, he only means some of the Terran cultures here will be promoted, and others attacked. Those perceived as regressive will be singled out for destruction. It is a form of Ataturkism."

"He thinks everyone on Mars should *become* American," said a man named Nejm.

"Why not?" Zeyk said, smiling. "It's already happened on Earth."

"No," Frank said. "You shouldn't misunderstand Boone. People say he's self-absorbed, but—"

"He is self-absorbed!" Nejm cried. "He lives in a hall of mirrors! He thinks that we have come to Mars to establish a good old American superculture, and that everyone will agree to it because it is the John Boone plan."

Zeyk said, "He doesn't understand that other people have other opinions."

"It's not that," Frank said. "It's just that he knows they don't make as much sense as his."

They laughed at that, but the younger men's hoots had a bitter edge. They all believed that before their arrival Boone had argued in secret against UN approval for Arab settlements. Frank encouraged this belief, which was almost true – John disliked any ideology that might get in his way. He wanted the slate as blank as possible in everybody who came up.

The Arabs, however, believed that John disliked them in particular. Young Selim el-Hayil opened his mouth to speak, and Frank gave him a swift warning glance. Selim froze, then pursed his mouth angrily. Frank said, "Well, he's not as bad as all that. Although to tell the truth I've heard him say it would have been better if the Americans and Russians had been able to claim the planet when they arrived, like explorers in the old days."

Their laughter was brief and grim. Selim's shoulders hunched as if struck. Frank shrugged and smiled, spread his hands wide. "But it's pointless! I mean, what can he do?"

Old Zeyk lifted his eyebrows. "Opinions vary."

Chalmers got up to move on, meeting for one instant Selim's insistent gaze. Then he strode down a side street, one of the narrow lanes that connected the city's seven main boule-vards. Most were paved with cobblestones or streetgrass, but this one was rough blond concrete. He slowed by a recessed doorway, looked in the window of a closed boot manufactury. His faint reflection appeared in a pair of bulky walker boots.

Opinions vary. Yes, a lot of people had underestimated John Boone – Chalmers had done it himself many times. An image came to him of John in the White House, pink with conviction, his disobedient blond hair flying wildly, the sun streaming in the Oval Office windows and illuminating him as he waved his hands and paced the room, talking away while the President nodded and his aides watched, pondering how best to co-opt that electrifying charisma. Oh, they had been hot in those days, Chalmers and Boone; Frank with the ideas and John the front man, with a momentum that was practically unstoppable. It would be more a matter of derailment, really.

Selim el-Hayil's reflection appeared among the boots.

"Is it true?" he demanded.

"Is what true?" said Frank crossly.

"Is Boone anti-Arab?"

"What do you think?"

"Was he the one who blocked permission to build the mosque on Phobos?"

"He's a powerful man."

The young Saudi's face twisted. "The most powerful man on Mars, and he only wants more! He wants to be king!" Selim made a fist and struck his other hand. He was slimmer than the other Arabs, weak-chinned, his moustache covering a small mouth.

"The treaty comes up for renewal soon," Frank said. "And Boone's coalition is bypassing me." He ground his teeth. "I don't know what their plans are, but I'm going to find out tonight. You can imagine what they'll be, anyway. Western biases, certainly. He may withhold his approval of a new treaty unless it contains guarantees that all settlements will be made only by the original treaty signatories." Selim shivered, and Frank pressed; "It's what he wants, and it's very possible he could get it, because his new coalition makes him more powerful than ever. It could mean an end to settlement by non-signatories. You'll become guest scientists. Or get sent back."

In the window the reflection of Selim's face appeared a kind of mask, signifying rage. "*Battal, battal*," he was muttering. Very bad, very bad. His hands twisted as if out of his control, and he muttered about the Koran or Camus, Persepolis or the Peacock Throne, references scattered nervously among non-sequiturs. Babbling.

"Talk means nothing," Chalmers said harshly. "When it comes down to it, nothing matters but action."

That gave the young Arab pause. "I can't be sure," he said at last.

Frank poked him in the arm, watched a shock run through the man. "It's your people we're talking about. It's this planet we're talking about."

Selim's mouth disappeared under his moustache. After a time he said, "It's true."

Frank said nothing. They looked in the window together, as if judging boots.

Finally Frank raised a hand. "I'll talk to Boone again," he said quietly. "Tonight. He leaves tomorrow. I'll try to talk to him, to reason with him. I doubt it will matter. It never has before. But I'll try. Afterwards – we should meet."

"Yes."

"In the park, then, the southernmost path. Around eleven."

Selim nodded.

Chalmers transfixed him with a stare. "Talk means nothing," he said brusquely, and walked away.

The next boulevard Chalmers came to was crowded with people clumped outside open-front bars, or kiosks selling cous-cous and bratwurst. Arab and Swiss. It seemed an odd combination, but they meshed well.

Tonight some of the Swiss were distributing face masks from the door of an apartment. Apparently they were celebrating this *stadtfest* as a kind of Mardi Gras, *Fassnacht* as they called it, with masks and music and every manner of social inversion, just as it was back home on those wild February nights in Basel and Zürich and Luzern . . . On an impulse Frank joined the line. "Around every profound spirit a mask is always growing," he said to two young women in front of him. They nodded politely and then resumed conversation in guttural Schwyzerdüütsch, a dialect never written down, a private code, incomprehensible even to Germans. It was another impenetrable culture, the Swiss, in some ways even more so than the Arabs. That was it, Frank thought; they worked well together because they were both so insular that they never made any real contact. He laughed out loud as he took a mask, a black face studded with red paste gems. He put it on.

A line of masked celebrants snaked down the boulevard, drunk, loose, at the edge of control. At an intersection the boulevard opened up into a small plaza, where a fountain shot sun-colored water into the air. Around the fountain a steel drum band hammered out a calypso tune. People gathered around, dancing or hopping in time to the low *bong* of the bass drum. A hundred meters overhead a vent in the tent frame poured frigid air down onto the plaza, air so cold that little flakes of snow floated in it, glinting in the light like chips of mica. Then fireworks banged just under the tenting, and colored sparks fell down through the snowflakes.

Sunset, more than any other time of day, made it clear that they stood on an alien planet; something in the slant and redness of the light was fundamentally wrong, upsetting expectations wired into the savannah brain over millions of years. This evening was providing a particularly garish and unsettling example of the phenomenon. Frank wandered in its light, making his way back to the city wall. The plain south of the city was littered with rocks, each one dogged by a long black shadow. Under the concrete arch of the city's south gate he stopped. No one there. The gates were locked during festivals like these, to keep drunks from going out and getting hurt. But Frank had gotten the day's emergency code out of the fire department AI that morning, and when he was sure no one was watching he tapped out the code and hurried into the lock. He put on a walker, boots, and helmet, and went through the middle and outer doors.

Outside it was intensely cold as always, and the diamond pattern of the walker's heating element burned through his clothes. He crunched over concrete and then duricrust. Loose sand flowed east, pushed by the wind.

Grimly he looked around. Rocks everywhere. A planet sledgehammered billions of times. And meteors still falling. Someday one of the towns would take a hit. He turned and looked back. It looked like an aquarium glowing in the dusk. There would be no warning, but everything would suddenly fly apart, walls, vehicles, trees, bodies. The Aztecs had believed the world would end in one of four ways: earthquake, fire, flood, or jaguars falling from the sky. Here there would be no fire. Nor earthquake nor flood, now that he thought of it. Leaving only the jaguars.

The twilight sky was a dark pink over Pavonis Mons. To the east stretched Nicosia's farm, a long low greenhouse running downslope from the city. From this angle one could see that the farm was larger than the town proper, and jammed with green crops. Frank clumped to one of its outer locks, and entered.

Inside the farm it was hot, a full 60° warmer than outside, and 15° warmer than in the city. He had to keep his helmet on, as the farm air was tailored to the plants, heavy on CO_2 and short on oxygen. He stopped at a work station and fingered through drawers of small tools and pesticide patches, gloves and bags. He selected three tiny patches and put them in a plastic bag, then slipped the bag gently into the walker's pocket. The patches were clever pesticides, biosaboteurs designed to provide plants with systemic defenses; he had been reading about them, and knew of a combination that in animals would be deadly to the organism . . .

He put a pair of shears in the walker's other pocket. Narrow gravel paths led him up between long beds of barley and wheat, back toward the city proper. He went in the lock leading into town, unclipped his helmet, stripped off the walker and boots, transferred the contents of the walker pockets to his coat. Then he went back into the lower end of town.

Here the Arabs had built a medina, insisting that such a neighborhood was crucial to a city's health; the boulevards narrowed, and between them lay warrens of twisted alleyways taken from the maps of Tunis or Algiers, or generated randomly. Nowhere could you see from one boulevard to the next, and the sky overhead was visible only in plum strips, between buildings that leaned together.

Most of the alleys were empty now, as the party was uptown. A pair of cats skulked between buildings, investigating their new home. Frank took the shears from his pocket and scratched into a few plastic windows, in Arabic lettering, *Jew, Jew, Jew, Jew, Jew*. He walked on, whistling through his teeth. Corner cafés were little caves of light. Bottles clinked like prospectors' hammers. An Arab sat on a squat black speaker, playing an electric guitar.

He found the central boulevard, walked up it. Boys in the branches of the lindens and sycamores shouted songs to each other in Schwyzerdüütsch. One ditty was in English: "John Boone, Went to the moon, No fast cars, He went to Mars!" Small disorganized music bands barged through the thickening crowd. Some moustached men dressed as American cheerleaders flounced expertly through a complicated can-can routine. Kids banged little plastic drums. It was loud; the tenting absorbed sound, so there weren't the echoes one heard under crater domes, but it was loud nevertheless.

Up there, where the boulevard opened into the sycamore park – that was John himself, surrounded by a small crowd. He saw Chalmers approaching and waved, recognizing him despite the mask. That was how the first hundred knew each other—

"Hey, Frank," he said. "You look like you're having a good time."

"I am," Frank said through his mask. "I love cities like this, don't you? A mixed-species flock. It shows you what a diverse collection of cultures Mars is."

John's smile was easy. His eyes shifted as he surveyed the boulevard below.

Sharply Frank said, "A place like this is a crimp in your plan, isn't it?"

Boone's gaze returned to him. The surrounding crowd slipped away, sensing the antagonistic nature of the exchange. Boone said to Frank, "I don't have a plan."

"Oh come on! What about your speech?"

Boone shrugged. "Maya wrote it."

A double lie: that Maya wrote it, that John didn't believe it. Even after all these years it was almost like talking to a stranger. To a politician at work. "Come on, John," Frank snapped. "You believe all that and you know it. But what are you going to do with all these different nationalities? All the ethnic hatreds, the religious manias? Your coalition can't possibly keep a thumb on all this. You can't keep Mars for yourselves, John, it's not a scientific station anymore, and you're not going to get a treaty that makes it one."

"We're not trying to."

"Then why are you trying to cut me out of the talks!"

"I'm not!" John looked injured. "Relax, Frank. We'll hammer it out together just like we always have. Relax."

Frank stared at his old friend, nonplussed. What to believe? He had never known how to think of John – the way he had used Frank as a springboard, the way he was so friendly . . . hadn't they begun as allies, as friends?

It occurred to him that John was looking for Maya. "So where is she?"

"Around somewhere," Boone said shortly.

It had been years since they had been able to talk about Maya. Now Boone gave him a sharp look, as if to say it was none of his business. As if everything of importance to Boone had become, over the years, none of Frank's business.

Frank left him without a word.

The sky was now a deep violet, streaked by yellow cirrus clouds. Frank passed two figures wearing white ceramic dominoes, the old Comedy and Tragedy personas, hand-cuffed together. The city's streets had gone dark and windows blazed, silhouettes partying in them. Big eyes darted in every blurry mask, looking to find the source of the tension in the air. Under the tidal sloshing of the crowd there was a low tearing sound.

He shouldn't have been surprised, he shouldn't. He knew John as well as one could know another person; but it had never been any of his business. Into the trees of the park, under the hand-sized leaves of the sycamores. When had it been any different! All that time together, those years of friendship; and none of it had mattered. Diplomacy by other means.

He looked at his watch. Nearly eleven. He had an appointment with Selim. Another appointment. A lifetime of days divided into quarter hours had made him used to running from one appointment to the next, changing masks, dealing with crisis after crisis, managing, manipulating, doing business in a hectic rush that never ended; and here it was a celebration, Mardi Gras, Fassnacht! and he was still doing it. He couldn't remember any other way.

He came on a construction site, skeletal magnesium

framing surrounded by piles of bricks and sand and paving stones. Careless of them to leave such things around. He stuffed his coat pockets with fragments of brick just big enough to hold. Straightening up, he noticed someone watching him from the other side of the site – a little man with a thin face under spiky black dreadlocks, watching him intently. Something in the look was disconcerting, it was as if the stranger saw through all his masks and was observing him so closely because he was aware of his thoughts, his plans.

Spooked, Chalmers beat a quick retreat into the bottom fringe of the park. When he was sure he had lost the man, and that no one else was watching, he began throwing stones and bricks down into the lower town, hurling them as hard as he could. And one for that stranger too, right in the face! Overhead the tent framework was visible only as a faint pattern of occluded stars; it seemed they stood free, in a chill night wind. Air circulation was high tonight, of course. Broken glass, shouts. A scream. It really was loud, people were going crazy. One last paving stone, heaved at a big lit picture window across the grass. It missed. He slipped further into the trees.

Near the southern wall he saw someone under a sycamore – Selim, circling nervously. "Selim," Frank called quietly, sweating. He reached into his jumper pocket, carefully felt in the bag and palmed the trio of stem patches. Synergy could be so powerful, for good or ill. He walked forward and roughly embraced the young Arab. The patches hit and penetrated Selim's light cotton shirt. Frank pulled back.

Now Selim had about six hours. "Did you speak with Boone?" he asked.

"I tried," Chalmers said. "He didn't listen. He lied to me." It was so easy to feign distress: "Twenty-five years of friendship, and he lied to me!" He struck a tree trunk with his palm, and the patches flew away in the dark. He controlled himself. "His coalition is going to recommend that all Martian settlements originate in the countries that signed the first treaty." It was possible; and it was certainly plausible.

"He hates us!" Selim cried.

"He hates everything that gets in his way. And he can see that Islam is still a real force in people's lives. It shapes the way people think, and he can't stand that."

Selim shuddered. In the gloom the whites of his eyes were bright. "He has to be stopped."

Frank turned aside, leaned against a tree. "I – don't know."

"You said it yourself. Talk means nothing."

Frank circled the tree, feeling dizzy. You fool, he thought, talk means everything. We are nothing but information exchange, talk is all we have!

He came on Selim again and said, "How?"

"The planet. It is our way."

"The city gates are locked tonight."

That stopped him. His hands started to twist.

Frank said, "But the gate to the farm is still open."

"But the farm's outer gates will be locked."

Frank shrugged, let him figure it out.

And quickly enough Selim blinked, and said "Ah." Then he was gone.

Frank sat between trees, on the ground. It was a sandy damp brown dirt, product of a great deal of engineering. Nothing in the city was natural, nothing.

After a time he got to his feet. He walked through the park, looking at people. If I find one good city I will spare the man. But in an open area masked figures darted together to grapple and fight, surrounded by watchers who smelled blood. Frank went back to the construction site to get more bricks. He threw them and some people saw him, and he had to run. Into the trees again, into the little tented wilderness, escaping predators while high on adrenalin, the greatest drug of all. He laughed wildly.

31

Suddenly he caught sight of Maya, standing alone by the temporary platform up at the apex. She wore a white domino, but it was certainly her: the proportions of the figure, the hair, the stance itself, all unmistakably Maya Toitovna. The first hundred, the little band; they were the only ones truly alive to him any more, the rest were ghosts. Frank hurried toward her, tripping over uneven ground. He squeezed a rock buried deep in one coat pocket, thinking Come on, you bitch. Say something to save him. Say something that will make me run the length of the city to save him!

She heard his approach and turned. She wore a phosphorescent white domino, with metallic blue sequins. It was hard to see her eyes.

"Hello, Frank," she said, as if he wore no mask. He almost turned and ran. Mere recognition was almost enough to do it . . .

But he stayed. He said, "Hello, Maya. Nice sunset, wasn't it?"

"Spectacular. Nature has no taste. It's just a city inauguration, but it looked like Judgement Day."

They were under a streetlight, standing on their shadows. She said, "Have you enjoyed yourself?"

"Very much. And you?"

"It's getting a little wild."

"It's understandable, don't you think? We're out of our holes, Maya, we're on the surface at last! And what a surface! You only get these kind of long views on Tharsis."

"It's a good location," she agreed.

"It will be a great city," Frank predicted. "But where do you live these days, Maya?"

"In Underhill, Frank, just as always. You know that."

"But you're never there, are you? I haven't seen you in a year or more."

"Has it been that long? Well, I've been in Hellas. Surely you heard?"

"Who would tell me?"

She shook her head and blue sequins glittered. "Frank." She turned aside, as if to walk away from the question's implications.

Angrily Frank circled her, stood in her path. "That time on the *Ares*," he said. His voice was tight, and he twisted his neck to loosen his throat, to make speech easier. "What happened, Maya? What happened?"

She shrugged and did not meet his gaze. For a long time she did not speak. Then she looked at him. "The spur of the moment," she said.

And then it was ringing midnight, and they were in the Martian time slip, the thirty-nine and a half minute gap between 12:00:00 and 12:00:01, when all the clocks went blank or stopped moving. This was how the first hundred had decided to reconcile Mars's slightly longer day with the twenty-four hour clock, and the solution had proved oddly satisfactory. Every night to step for a while out of the flicking numbers, out of the remorseless sweep of the second hand—

And tonight as the bells rang midnight, the whole city went mad. Forty minutes outside of time; it was bound to be the peak of the celebration, everyone knew that instinctively. Fireworks were going off, people were cheering; sirens tore through the sound, and the cheering redoubled. Frank and Maya watched the fireworks, listened to the noise.

Then there was a noise that was somehow different: desperate cries, serious screams. "What's that?" Maya said.

"A fight," Frank replied, cocking an ear. "Something done on the spur of the moment, perhaps." She stared at him, and quickly he added, "Maybe we should go have a look."

The cries intensified. Trouble somewhere. They started down through the park, their steps getting longer, until they were in the Martian lope. The park seemed bigger to Frank, and for a moment he was scared.

The central boulevard was covered with trash. People darted through the dark in predatory schools. A nerve-grating siren went off, the alarm that signaled a break in the tent. Windows were shattering up and down the boulevard. There on the streetgrass was a man flat on his back, the surrounding grass smeared with black streaks. Chalmers seized the arm of a woman crouched over him. "What happened?" he shouted.

She was weeping. "They fought! They are fighting!"

"Who? Swiss, Arab?"

"Strangers," she said. "*Ausländer.*" She looked blindly at Frank. "Get help!"

Frank rejoined Maya, who was talking to a group next to another fallen figure. "What the hell's going on?" he said to her as they took off toward the city's hospital.

"It's a riot," she said. "I don't know why." Her mouth was a straight slash, in skin as white as the domino still covering her eyes.

Frank pulled off his mask and threw it away. There was broken glass all over the street. A man rushed at them. "Frank! Maya!"

It was Sax Russell; Frank had never seen the little man so agitated. "It's John – he's been attacked!"

"What?" they exclaimed together.

"He tried to stop a fight, and three or four men jumped him. They knocked him down and dragged him away!"

"You didn't stop them?" Maya cried.

"We tried – a whole bunch of us chased them. But they lost us in the medina."

Maya looked at Frank.

"What's going *on*!" he cried. "Where would anyone take him?"

"The gates," she said.

"But they're locked tonight, aren't they?"

"Maybe not to everyone."

They followed her to the medina. Streetlights were

broken, there was glass underfoot. They found a fire marshall and went to the Turkish Gate; he unlocked it and several of them hurried through, throwing on walkers at emergency speed. Then out into the night to look around, illuminated by the bathysphere glow of the city. Frank's ankles hurt with the night cold, and he could feel the precise configuration of his lungs, as if two globes of ice had been inserted in his chest, to cool the rapid beat of his heart.

Nothing out there. Back inside. Over to the northern wall and the Syrian Gate, and out again under the stars. Nothing.

It took them a long time to think of the farm. By then there were about thirty of them in walkers, and they ran down and through the lock and flooded down the farm's aisles, spreading out, running between crops.

They found him among the radishes. His jacket was pulled over his face, in the standard emergency air pocket; he must have done it unconsciously, because when they rolled him carefully onto one side, they saw a lump behind one ear.

"Get him inside," Maya said, her voice a bitter croak – "Hurry, get him inside."

Four of them lifted him. Chalmers cradled John's head, and his fingers were intertwined with Maya's. They trotted back up the shallow steps. Through the farm gate they stumbled, back into the the city. One of the Swiss led them to the nearest medical center, already crowded with desperate people. They got John onto an empty bench. His unconscious expression was pinched, determined. Frank tore off his helmet and went to work pulling rank, bulling into the emergency rooms and shouting at the doctors and nurses. They ignored him until one doctor said, "Shut up. I'm coming." She went into the hallway and with a nurse's help clipped John into a monitor, then checked him out with the abstracted, absent look doctors have while working: hands at neck and face and head and chest, stethoscope . . .

Maya explained what they knew. The doctor took down an oxygen unit from the wall, looking at the monitor. Her

35

mouth was bunched into a displeased little knot. Maya sat at the end of the bench, face suddenly distraught. Her domino had long since disappeared.

Frank crouched beside her.

"We can keep working on him," the doctor said, "but I'm afraid he's gone. Too long without oxygen, you know."

"Keep working on him," Maya said.

They did, of course. Eventually other medical people arrived, and they carted him off to an emergency room. Frank, Maya, Sax, Samantha, and a number of locals sat outside in the hall. Doctors came and went; their faces had the blank look they took on in the presence of death. Protective masks. One came out and shook his head. "He's dead. Too long out there."

Frank leaned his head back against the wall.

When Reinhold Messner returned from the first solo climb of Everest, he was severely dehydrated, and utterly exhausted; he fell down most of the last part of the descent, and collapsed on the Rongbuk glacier, and he was crawling over it on hands and knees when the woman who was his entire support team reached him; and he looked up at her out of a delirium, and said "Where are all my friends?"

It was quiet. No sound but the low hum and whoosh that one never escaped on Mars.

Maya put a hand on Frank's shoulder, and he almost flinched; his throat clamped down to nothing, it really hurt. "I'm sorry," he managed to say.

She shrugged the remark aside, frowned. She had somewhat the air of the medical people. "Well," she said, "you never liked him much anyway."

"True," he said, thinking it would be politic to seem honest with her at that moment. But then he shuddered and said bitterly, "What do you know about what I like or don't like."

He shrugged her hand aside, struggled to his feet. She didn't know; none of them knew. He started to go into the

36

emergency room, changed his mind. Time enough for that at the funeral. He felt hollow; and suddenly it seemed to him that everything good had gone away.

He left the medical center. Impossible not to feel sentimental at such moments. He walked through the strangely hushed darkness of the city, into the land of Nod. The streets glinted as if stars had fallen to the pavement. People stood in clumps, silent, stunned by the news. Frank Chalmers made his way through them, feeling their stares, moving without thought toward the platform at the top of town; and as he walked he said to himself, *Now we'll see what I can do with this planet.*

PART TWO

The Voyage Out

PART TWO

The Voyage Out

"Since they're going to go crazy anyway, why not just send insane people in the first place, and save them the trouble?" said Michel Duval.

He was only half joking; his position throughout had been that the criteria for selection constituted a mind-boggling collection of double binds.

His fellow psychologists stared at him. "Can you suggest any specific changes?" asked the chairman, Charles York.

"Perhaps we should all go to Antarctica with them, and observe them in this first period of time together. It would teach us a lot."

"But our presence would be inhibitory. I think just one of us will be enough."

So they sent Michel Duval. He joined a hundred and fifty-odd finalists at McMurdo Station. The initial meeting resembled any other international scientific conference, familiar to them all from their various disciplines. But there was a difference: this was the continuation of a selection process that had lasted for years, and would last another. And those selected would go to Mars.

So they lived in Antarctica for over a year together, familiarizing themselves with the shelters and equipment that were already landing on Mars in robot vehicles; familiarizing themselves with a landscape that was almost as cold and harsh as Mars itself; familiarizing themselves with each other. They lived in a cluster of habitats located in Wright Valley, the largest of Antarctica's Dry Valleys. They ran a biosphere farm, and then they settled into the habitats through a dark austral winter, and studied secondary or tertiary professions, or ran through simulations of the various tasks they would be performing on the spaceship Ares, or later on the red planet itself; and always, always aware that they were being watched, evaluated, judged.

41

They were by no means all astronauts or cosmonauts, although there were a dozen or so of each, with many more up north clamoring to be included. But the majority of the colonists would have to have their expertise in areas that would come into play after landfall: medical skills, computer skills, robotics, systems design, architecture, geology, biosphere design, genetic engineering, biology; also every sort of engineering, and construction expertise of several kinds. Those who had made it to Antarctica were an impressive group of experts in the relevant sciences and professions, and they spent a good bit of their time cross-training to become impressive in secondary and tertiary fields as well.

And all their activity took place under the constant pressure of observation, evaluation, judgement. It was necessarily a stressful procedure; that was part of the test. Michel Duval felt that this was a mistake, as it tended to ingrain reticence and distrust in the colonists, preventing the very compatability that the selection committee was supposedly seeking. One of the many double binds, in fact. The candidates themselves were quiet about that aspect of things, and he didn't blame them; there wasn't any better strategy to take, that was a double bind for you: it insured silence. They could not afford to offend anyone, or complain too much; they could not risk withdrawing too far; they could not make enemies.

So they went on being brilliant and accomplished enough to stand out, but normal enough to get along. They were old enough to have learned a great deal, but young enough to endure the physical rigors of the work. They were driven enough to excel, but relaxed enough to socialize. And they were crazy enough to want to leave Earth forever, but sane enough to disguise this fundamental madness, in fact to defend it as pure rationality, scientific curiosity or something of the sort — that seemed to be the only acceptable reason for wanting to go, and so naturally they claimed to be the most scientifically curious people in history! But of course there had to be more to it than that. They had to be alienated somehow, alienated and solitary enough not to care about leaving everyone they had known behind forever – and yet still connected and social enough to get along with all their new acquaintances in Wright Valley, with every member of the tiny village that the colony would become. Oh, the double binds were endless! They were to be both extraordinary and extra ordinary, at one and the same time. An impossible task, and yet a task that was an obstacle to their heart's greatest desire; making it the very stuff of anxiety, fear, resentment, rage. Conquering all those stresses . . .

But that too was part of the test. Michel could not help but observe with great interest. Some failed, cracked in one way or another. An American thermal engineer became increasingly withdrawn, then destroyed several of their rovers and had to be forcibly restrained and removed. A Russian pair became lovers, and then had a falling out so violent that they couldn't stand the sight of each other, and both had to be dropped. This melodrama illustrated the dangers of romance going awry, and made the rest of them very cautious in this regard. Relationships still developed, and by the time they left Antarctica they had had three marriages, and these lucky six could consider themselves in some sense "safe"; but most of them were so focused on getting to Mars that they put these parts of their lives on hold, and if anything conducted discreet friendships, in some cases hidden from almost everyone, in other cases merely kept out of the view of the selection committees.

And Michel knew he was seeing only the tip of the iceberg. He knew that critical things were happening in Antarctica, out of his sight. Relationships were having their beginnings; and sometimes the beginning of a relationship determines how the rest of it will go. In the brief hours of daylight, one of them might leave the camp and hike out to Lookout Point; and another follow; and what happened out there might leave its mark forever. But Michel would never know.

43

And then they left Antarctica, and the team was chosen. There were fifty men and fifty women: thirty-five Americans, thirty-five Russians, and thirty miscellaneous international affiliates, fifteen invited by each of the two big partners. Keeping such perfect symmetries had been difficult, but the selection committee had persevered.

The lucky ones flew to Cape Canaveral or Baikonur, to ascend to orbit. At this point they both knew each other very well and did not know each other at all. They were a team, Michel thought, with established friendships, and a number of group ceremonies, rituals, habits, and tendencies; and among those tendencies was an instinct to hide, to play a role and disguise their real selves. Perhaps this was simply the definition of village life, of social life. But it seemed to Michel that it was worse than that; no one had ever before had to compete so strenuously to join a village; and the resulting radical division between public life and private life was new, and strange. Ingrained in them now was a certain competitive undercurrent, a constant subtle feeling that they were each alone, and that in case of trouble they were liable to be abandoned by the rest, and yanked out of the group.

The selection committee had thus created some of the very problems it had hoped to prevent. Some of them were aware of this; and naturally they took care to include among the colonists the most qualified psychiatrist they could think of.

So they sent Michel Duval.

At first it felt like a shove in the chest. Then they were pushed back in their chairs, and for a second the pressure was deeply familiar: one g, the gravity they would never live in again. The *Ares* had been orbiting Earth at 28,000 kilometers per hour. For several minutes they accelerated, the rocket's push so powerful that their vision blurred as corneas flattened, and it took an effort to inhale. At 40,000 kilometers per hour the burn ended. They were free of the Earth's pull, in orbit to nothing but the sun.

The colonists sat in the delta V chairs blinking, their skin flushed, their hearts pounding. Maya Katarina Toitovna, the official leader of Russian contingent, glanced around. People appeared stunned. When obsessives are given their object of desire, what do they feel? It was hard to say, really. In a sense their lives were ending; and yet something else, some other life, had finally, finally begun . . . Filled with so many emotions at once, it was impossible not to be confused; it was an interference pattern, some feelings cancelled, others reinforced. Unbuckling from her chair Maya felt a grin contorting her face, and she saw on the faces around her the same helpless grin; all but Sax Russell, who was as impassive as an owl, blinking as he looked over the readouts on the room's computer screens.

They floated weightlessly around the room. December 21st, 2026: they were moving faster than anyone in history. They were on their way. It was the beginning of a nine-month voyage – or of a voyage that would last the rest of their lives. They were on their own.

Those responsible for piloting the *Ares* pulled themselves to the control consoles, and gave the orders to fire lateral control rockets. The *Ares* began to spin, stabilizing at four rpm. The colonists sank to the floors, and stood in a pseudogravity of

.38 g, very close to what they would feel on Mars. Many man-years of tests had indicated that it would be a fairly healthy g to live in, and so much healthier than weightlessness that rotating the ship had been deemed worth the trouble. And, Maya thought, it felt great. There was enough pull to make balance relatively easy, but hardly any feeling of pressure, of drag. It was the perfect equivalent of their mood; they staggered down the halls to the big dining hall in Torus D, giddy and exhilarated, walking on air.

In Torus D's dining hall they mingled in a kind of cocktail party, celebrating the departure. Maya wandered about, sipping freely from a mug of champagne, feeling slightly unreal and extremely happy, a mix that reminded her of her wedding reception many years before. Hopefully this marriage would go better than that one had, she thought, because this one was going to last forever. The hall was loud with talk. "It's a symmetry not so much sociological as mathematic. A kind of aesthetic balance." "We're hoping to get it into the parts per billion range, but it's not going to be easy." Maya turned down an offered refill, feeling giddy enough. Besides, this was work. She was co-mayor of this village, so to speak, responsible for group dynamics, which were bound to get complex. Antarctic habits kicked in even at this moment of triumph, and she listened and watched like an anthropologist, or a spy.

"The shrinks have their reasons. We'll end up fifty happy couples."

"And they already know the match-ups."

She watched them laugh. Smart, healthy, supremely well-educated; was this the rational society at last, the scientifically-designed community that had been the dream of the Enlightenment? But there was Arkady, Nadia, Vlad, Ivana. She knew the Russian contingent too well to have many illusions on that score. They were just as likely to end up resembling an undergraduate dorm at a technical

46

university, occupied by bizarre pranks and lurid affairs. Except they looked a bit old for that kind of thing; several men were balding, and many of both sexes showed touches of gray in their hair. It had been a long haul; their average age was forty-six, with extremes ranging from thirty-three (Hiroko Ai, the Japanese prodigy of biosphere design) to fifty-eight (Vlad Taneev, winner of a Nobel Prize in medicine).

Now, however, the flush of youth was on all their faces. Arkady Bogdanov was a portrait in red: hair, beard, skin. In all that red his eyes were a wild electric blue, bugging out happily as he exclaimed, "Free at last! Free at last! All our children are free at last!" The video cameras had been turned off, after Janet Blyleven had recorded a series of interviews for the TV stations back home; they were out of contact with Earth, in the dining hall anyway, and Arkady was singing, and the group around him toasted the song. Maya stopped to join this group. Free at last; it was hard to believe, they were actually on their way to Mars! Knots of people talking, many of them world class in their fields; Ivana had won part of a Nobel prize in chemistry, Vlad was one of the most famous medical biologists in the world, Sax was in the pantheon of great contributors to subatomic theory, Hiroko was unmatched in enclosed biological life support systems design, and so on all around; a brilliant crowd!

And she was one of their leaders. It was a bit daunting. Her engineering and cosmonautic skills were modest enough, it was her diplomatic ability that had gotten her aboard, presumably. Chosen to head the disparate, fractious Russian team, with the several commonwealth members – well, that was okay. It was interesting work, and she was used to it. And her skills might very well turn out to be the most important ones aboard. They had to get along, after all. And that was a matter of guile, and cunning, and will. Willing other people to do your bidding! She looked at the crowd of glowing faces, and laughed. All aboard were good at their

47

work, but some were gifted far beyond that. She had to identify those people, to seek them out, to cultivate them. Her ability to function as leader depended on it; for in the end, she thought, they would surely become a kind of loose scientific meritocracy. And in such a society as that, the extraordinarily talented constituted the real powers. When push came to shove, they would be the colony's true leaders – they, or those who influenced them.

She looked around, located her opposite number, Frank Chalmers. In Antarctica she had not gotten to know him very well. A tall, big, swarthy man. He was talkative enough, and incredibly energetic; but hard to read. She found him attractive. Did he see things as she did? She had never been able to tell. He was talking to a group across the length of the room, listening in that sharp inscrutable way of his, head tilted to the side, ready to pounce with a witty remark. She was going to have to find out more about him. More than that, she was going to have to get along with him.

She crossed the room, stopped by his side, stood so their upper arms just barely touched. Leaned her head in toward his. A brief gesture at their comrades: "This is going to be fun, don't you think?"

Chalmers glanced at her. "If it goes well," he said.

After the celebration and dinner, unable to sleep, Maya wandered through the *Ares*. All of them had spent time in space before, but never in anything like the *Ares*, which was enormous. There was a kind of penthouse at the front end of the ship, a single tank like a bowsprit, which rotated in the opposite direction the ship did, so that it held steady. Solar watch instruments, radio antennas, and all the other equipment which worked best without rotation were located in this tank, and at the very tip of it was a bulbous room of transparent plastic, a chamber quickly named the bubble dome, which provided the crew with a weightless, non-rotating view of the stars, and a partial view of the great ship behind it.

Maya floated near the window wall of this bubble dome, looking back at the ship curiously. It had been constructed using space shuttle external fuel tanks; around the turn of the century NASA and Glavkosmos had begun attaching small booster rockets to the tanks and pushing them all the way into orbit. Scores of tanks had been launched this way, then tugged to work sites and put to use – with them they had built two big space stations, an L5 station, a lunar orbit station, the first manned Mars vehicle, and scores of unmanned freighters sent to Mars. So by the time the two agencies agreed to build the *Ares*, the use of the tanks had become routinized, with standard coupling units, interiors, propulsion systems and so forth; and construction of the big ship had taken less than two years.

It looked like something made from a children's toy set, in which cylinders were attached at their ends to create more complex shapes – in this case, eight hexagons of connected cylinders, which they called toruses, lined up and speared down the middle by a central hub shaft, made of a cluster of five lines of cylinders. The toruses were connected to the hub shaft by thin crawl spokes, and the resulting object looked somewhat like a piece of agricultural machinery, say the arm of a harvester combine, or a mobile sprinkler unit. Or like eight knobby doughnuts, Maya thought, toothpicked to a stick. Just the sort of thing a child would appreciate.

The eight toruses had been made from American tanks, and the five bundled lengths of the central shaft were Russian. Both were about fifty meters long and ten meters in diameter. Maya floated aimlessly down the tanks of the hub shaft; it took her a long time, but she was in no hurry. She dropped down into Torus G. There were rooms of all shapes and sizes, right up to the largest, which occupied entire tanks. The floor in one of these she passed through was set just below the halfway mark, so its interior resembled a long Quonset hut. But the majority of the tanks had been divided up into smaller rooms. She had heard there were over five hundred of them in all, making for a total interior space roughly the equivalent of a large city hotel.

But would it be enough?

Perhaps it would. After the Antarctic, life on the *Ares* seemed an expansive, labyrinthine, airy experience. Around six every morning the darkness in the residential toruses would lighten slowly to a gray dawn, and around six-thirty a sudden brightening marked "sunrise." Maya woke to it as she had all her life. After visiting the lavatory she would make her way to Torus D's kitchen, heat a meal, and take it into the big dining hall. There she sat at a table flanked by potted lime trees. Hummingbirds, finches, tanagers, sparrows and lories pecked underfoot and darted overhead, dodging the creeping vines that hung from the hall's long barrel ceiling, which was painted a gray-blue that reminded her of St Petersburg's winter sky. She would eat slowly, watch the birds, relax in her chair, listen to the talk around her. A leisurely breakfast! After a lifetime of grinding work it felt rather uncomfortable at first, even alarming, like a stolen luxury. As if it were Sunday morning every day, as Nadia said. But Maya's Sunday mornings had never been particularly relaxed. In her childhood that had been the time for cleaning the one-room apartment she had shared with her mother. Her mother had been a doctor and like most women of her generation had had to work ferociously to get by, obtaining food, bringing up a child, keeping an apartment, running a career; it had been too much for one person, and she had joined the many women angrily demanding a better deal than they had gotten in the Soviet years, which had given them half the money jobs while leaving them all the work at home. No more waiting, no more mute endurance; they had to take advantage while the instability lasted. "Everything is on the table!" Maya's mother would exclaim while cooking their meager dinners, "everything but food!"

And perhaps they had taken advantage. In the Soviet era

women had learned to help each other, a nearly self-contained world had come into being, of mothers, sisters, daughters, babushkas, women friends, colleagues, even strangers. In the commonwealth this world had consolidated its gains and thrust even further into the power structure, into the tight male oligarchies of Russian government.

One of the fields most affected had been the space program. Maya's mother, slightly involved in space medical research, always swore that cosmonautics would need an influx of women, if only to provide female data for the medical experimentation. "They can't hold Valentina Tereshkova against us forever!" her mother would cry. And apparently she had been right, because after studying aeronautic engineering at Moscow University, Maya had been accepted in a program at Baikonur, and had done well, and had gotten an assignment on *Novy Mir*. While up there she had redesigned the interiors for improved ergonomic efficiency, and later spent a year in command of the station, during which a couple of emergency repairs had bolstered her reputation. Administrative assignments in Baikonur and Moscow had followed, and over time she had managed to penetrate Glavkosmos's little politburo, playing the men against each other in the subtlest of ways, marrying one of them, divorcing him, rising afterwards in Glavkosmos a free agent, becoming one of the utmost inner circle, the double triumvirate.

And so here she was, having a leisurely breakfast. "So civilized," Nadia would scoff. She was Maya's best friend on the *Ares*, a short woman round as a stone, with a square face framed by cropped salt-and-pepper hair. Plain as could be. Maya, who knew she was good-looking, and knew that this had helped her many times, loved Nadia's plainness, which somehow underlined her competence. Nadia was an engineer and very practical, an expert in cold-climate construction. They had met in Baikonur twenty years before, and once lived together on *Novy Mir* for several months; over the years they had become like sisters, in that they were not

51

much alike, and did not often get along, and yet were intimate.

Now Nadia looked around and said, "Putting the Russian and American living quarters in different toruses was a horrible idea. We work with them during the day, but we spend most of our time here with the same old faces. It only reinforces the other divisions between us."

"Maybe we should offer to exchange half the rooms."

Arkady, wolfing down coffee rolls, leaned over from the next table. "It's not enough," he said, as if he had been part of their conversation all along. His red beard, growing wilder every day, was dusted with crumbs. "We should declare every other Sunday to be moving day, and have everyone shift quarters on a random basis. People would get to know more of the others, and there would be fewer cliques. And the notion of ownership of the rooms would be reduced."

"But I like owning a room," Nadia said.

Arkady downed another roll, grinned at her as he chewed. It was a miracle he had passed the selection committee.

But Maya brought up the subject with the Americans, and though no one liked Arkady's plan, a single exchange of half the apartments struck them as a good idea. After some consulting and discussion, the move was arranged. They did it on a Sunday morning; and after that, breakfast was a little more cosmopolitan. Mornings in the D dining hall now included Frank Chalmers and John Boone, and also Sax Russell, Mary Dunkel, Janet Blyleven, Rya Jimenez, Michel Duval, and Ursula Kohl.

John Boone turned out to be an early riser, getting to the dining hall even before Maya. "This room is so spacious and airy, it really has an outdoor feel to it," he said from his table one dawn when Maya came in. "A lot better than B's hall."

"The trick is to remove all chrome and white plastic," Maya replied. Her English was fairly good, and getting better fast. "And then paint the ceiling like real sky."

"Not just straight blue, you mean?"

"Yes."

He was, she thought, a typical American: simple, open, straightforward, relaxed. And yet this particular specimen was one of the most famous people in history. It was an unavoidable, heavy fact; but Boone seemed to slip out from under it, to leave it around his feet on the floor. Intent on the taste of a roll, or some news on the table screen, he never referred to his previous expedition, and if someone brought the subject up he spoke as if it were no different from any of the flights the rest of them had taken. But it wasn't so, and only his ease made it seem that way: at the same table each morning, laughing at Nadia's lame engineering jokes, making his portion of the talk. After a while it took an effort to see the aura around him.

Frank Chalmers was more interesting. He always came in late, and sat by himself, paying attention only to his coffee and the table screen. After a couple of cups he would talk to people nearby, in ugly but functional Russian. Most of the breakfast conversations in D hall had now shifted to English, to accommodate the Americans. The linguistic situation was a set of nesting dolls: English held all hundred of them, inside that was Russian, and inside that, the languages of the commonwealth, and then the internationals. Eight people aboard were idiolinguists, a sad kind of orphaning in Maya's opinion, and it seemed to her they were more Earth-oriented than the rest, and in frequent communication with people back home. It was a little strange to have their psychiatrist in that category.

Anyway English was the ship's *lingua franca*, and at first Maya had thought that this gave the Americans an advantage. But then she noticed that when they spoke they were always on stage to everyone, while the rest of them had more private languages they could switch to if they wanted.

Frank Chalmers was the exception to all that, however.

53

He spoke five languages, more than anyone else aboard. And he did not fear to use his Russian, even though it was very bad; he just hacked out questions and then listened to the answers, with a really piercing intensity, and a quick startling laugh. He was an unusual American in many ways, Maya thought. At first he seemed to have all the characteristics, he was big, loud, maniacally energetic, confident, restless; talkative enough, after that first coffee; friendly enough. It took a while to notice how he turned the friendliness on and off, and to notice how little his talk revealed. Maya never learned a thing about his past, for instance, despite deliberate efforts to chat him up. It made her curious. He had black hair, a swarthy face, light hazel eyes – handsome in a tough-guy way – his smile brief, his laugh sharp, like Maya's mother's. His gaze too was sharp, especially when looking at Maya; a matter of evaluating the other leader, she assumed. He acted toward her as if they had an understanding built on long acquaintance, a presumption which made her uneasy given how little they had spoken together in Antarctica. She was used to thinking of women as her allies, and of men as attractive but dangerous problems. So a man who presumed to be her ally was only the more problematic. And dangerous. And . . . something else.

She recalled only one moment when she had seen further into him than the skin, and that had been back in Antarctica. After the thermal engineer had cracked and been sent north, news of his replacement had come down, and when it was announced everyone was quite surprised and excited to hear that it was going to be John Boone himself, even though he had certainly received more than the maximum radiation dosage on his previous expedition. While the evening room was still buzzing with the news Maya had seen Chalmers come in and be told of it, and he had jerked his head around to stare at his informant; and then for a fraction of a second she had seen a flash of fury, a flash so fast it was almost a subliminal event.

But it had made her attentive to him. And certainly he and John Boone had an odd relationship. It was difficult for Chalmers, of course; he was the Americans' official leader, and even had the title *Captain*; but Boone, with his blond good looks and the strange presence of his accomplishment, certainly had more natural authority – he *seemed* the real American leader, and Frank Chalmers something like an overactive executive officer, doing Boone's unspoken bidding. That could not be comfortable.

They were old friends, Maya had been told when she asked. But she saw few signs of it herself, even watching closely. They seldom talked to each other in public, and did not seem to visit in private. Thus when they were together she watched them more closely than ever, without ever consciously considering why; the natural logic of the situation just seemed to demand it. If they had been back at Glavkosmos, it would have made strategic sense to drive a wedge between them; but she didn't think of it that way here. There was a lot that Maya didn't think about consciously.

She watched, though. And one morning Janet Blyleven wore her video glasses into D hall for breakfast. She was a principal reporter for American television, and often she wove her way through the ship wearing her vidglasses, looking around and talking the commentary, collecting stories and transmitting them back home where they would be, as Arkady put it, "predigested and vomited back into that baby bird consensus."

It was nothing new, of course. Media attention was a familiar part of every astronaut's life, and during the selection process they had been more scrutinized than ever. Now, however, they were the raw material for programs magnitudes more popular than any space program had been before. Millions watched them as the ultimate soap opera, and this bothered some of them. So when Janet settled at the end of the table wearing those stylish spectacles with the optical fibers in the frame, there were a few groans. And at the other end of the table Ann Clayborne and Sax Russell were arguing, oblivious to any of them.

"It'll take years to find out what we have there, Sax. Decades. There's as much land on Mars as on Earth, with a unique geology and chemistry. The land has to be thoroughly studied before we can start changing it."

"We'll change it just by landing." Russell brushed aside Ann's objections as if they were spiderwebs on his face. "Deciding to go to Mars is like the first phrase of a sentence, and the whole sentence says—"

"*Veni, vidi, vinci.*"

Russell shrugged. "If you want to put it that way."

"You're the weenie, Sax," Ann said, lip curled with irritation. She was a broad-shouldered woman with wild brown hair, a geologist with strong views, difficult in argument. "Look, Mars is *its own place*. You can play your climate-shifting games back on Earth if you want, they need the help. Or try it on Venus. But you can't just wipe out a three billion year-old planetary surface."

Russell rubbed away more spiderwebs. "It's dead," he said simply. "Besides, it's not really our decision. It'll be taken out of our hands."

"None of these decisions will be taken out of our hands," Arkady put in sharply.

Janet looked from speaker to speaker, taking it all in. Ann was getting agitated, raising her voice. Maya glanced around, and saw that Frank didn't like the situation. But if he interrupted it he would give away to the millions the fact that he didn't want the colonists arguing in front of them. Instead he looked across the table and caught Boone's gaze. There was an exchange of expressions between the two so quick it made Maya blink.

Boone said, "When I was there before, I got the impression it was already Earthlike."

"Except 200° Kelvin," Russell said.

"Sure, but it *looked* like the Mojave, or the Dry Valleys.

56

The first time I looked around on Mars I found myself keeping an eye out for one of those mummified seals we saw in the Dry Valleys."

And so on. Janet turned to him; and Ann, looking disgusted, picked up her coffee and left.

Afterward Maya concentrated, trying to recall the looks Boone and Chalmers had exchanged. They had been like something from a code, or the private languages invented by identical twins.

The weeks passed, and the days each began with a leisurely breakfast. Mid-mornings were far busier. Everyone had a schedule, although some were fuller than others. Frank's was packed, which was the way he liked it, a maniacal blur of activity. But the necessary work was not really all that great: they had to keep themselves alive and in shape, and keep the ship running, and keep preparing for Mars. Ship maintenance ranged from the intricacy of programming or repairs to the simplicity of moving supplies out of storage, or taking trash to the recyclers. The biosphere team spent the bulk of its time on the farm, which occupied large parts of Toruses C, E, and F; and everyone aboard had farm chores. Most enjoyed this work, and some even returned in their free hours. Everyone was on doctors' orders to spend three hours a day on treadmills, escalators, running wheels, or using weight machines. These hours were enjoyed or endured or despised, depending on temperament; but even those who claimed to despise them finished their exercises in noticeably (even measurably) better moods. "Beta endorphins are the best drug," Michel Duval would say.

"Which is lucky, since we don't have any others," Arkady would reply.

"Oh, there's caffeine . . ."

"Puts me to sleep."

"Alcohol . . ."

"Gives me a headache."

"Procaine, darvon, morphine—"

"Morphine?"

"In the medical supplies. Not for general use."

Arkady smiled. "Maybe I'd better get sick."

The engineers, including Maya, spent many mornings in training simulations. These took place on the back-up bridge in Torus B, which had the latest in image synthesizers; the simulations were so sophisticated that there was little visible difference between them and the act itself. This did not necessarily make them interesting: the standard orbital insertion approach, simulated weekly, was dubbed "The Mantra Run," and became quite a bore to every conceivable flight crew.

But sometimes even boredom was preferable to the alternatives; Arkady was their training specialist, and he had a perverse talent for designing problem runs so hard that they often "killed" everybody. These runs were strangely unpleasant experiences, and did not make Arkady popular among his victims. He mixed problem runs with Mantra Runs randomly, but more and more often they were problem runs; they would "approach Mars" and red lights would flash, sometimes with sirens, and they were in trouble again. Once they struck a planetesimal weighing approximately fifteen grams, leaving a large flaw in the heat shield. Sax Russell had calculated that their chances of hitting anything larger than a gram were about one in every seven thousand years of travel, but nevertheless there they were, *emergency!*, adrenalin pouring through them even as they derided the very idea of it, rushing up to the hub and into EVA suits, going out to fill the pothole before they hit the Martian atmosphere and burned to a crisp; and halfway there, Arkady's voice came over their intercoms: "Not fast enough! All of us are dead."

But that was a simple one. Others . . . The ship, for instance, was guided by a fly-by-wire system, meaning that the pilots fed instructions to flight computers which translated them into the actual thrusts needed to achieve the desired result. This was how it had to be, because when approaching a gravitational mass like Mars at their speed, one simply could not feel or intuit what burns would achieve the desired effects. So none of them were flyers in the sense of a pilot flying a plane. Nevertheless, Arkady frequently blew the entire massively redundant system just as they were reaching a critical moment (which failure, Russell said, had about a one in ten billion chance of happening) and they had to take over and command all the rockets mechanically, watching the monitors and an orange-on-black visual image of Mars bearing down on them, and they could either go long and skip off into deep space and die a lingering death, or go short and crash into the planet and die instantly; and if the latter, they got to watch it right down to the simulated hundred and twenty klicks per second final smash.

Or it might be a mechanical failure: main rockets, stabilizing rockets, computer hardware or software, heat shield deployment; all of them had to work perfectly during the approach. And failures of these systems were the most likely of all – in the range, Sax said (though others contested his risk assessment methods), of one in every ten thousand approaches. So they would do it again and red lights would flash, and they would groan, and beg for a Mantra Run even as they partly welcomed the new challenge. When they managed to survive a mechanical failure, they were tremendously pleased; it could be the high point of a week. Once John Boone successfully aerobraked by hand, with a single main rocket functioning, hitting the safe millisecond of arc at the only possible speed. No one could believe it. "Blind luck," Boone said, grinning widely as the deed was talked about at dinner.

Most of Arkady's problem runs ended in failure, however, meaning death for all. Simulated or not, it was hard not to be sobered by these experiences, and after that, irritated with Arkady for inventing them. One time they repaired every monitor in the bridge just in time to see the screens register a hit by a small asteroid, which sheared through the hub and killed them all. Another time Arkady, as part of the navigation team, made an "error" and instructed the computers to increase the ship's spin rather than decrease it. "Pinned to the floor by six gs!" he cried in mock horror, and they had to crawl on the floor for half an hour, pretending to rectify the error while weighing half a ton each. When they succeeded, Arkady leaped off the floor and began pushing them away from the control monitor. "What the hell are you doing?" Maya yelled.

"He's gone crazy," Janet said.

"He's *simulated* going crazy," Nadia corrected her. "We have to figure out—" doing an end run around Arkady "—how to deal with someone on the bridge going insane!"

Which no doubt was true. But they could see the whites of Arkady's eyes all the way around, and there wasn't a trace of recognition in him as he silently assaulted them; it took all five of them to restrain him, and Janet and Phyllis Boyle were hurt by his sharp elbows.

"Well?" he said at dinner afterward, grinning lopsidedly, as he was growing a fat lip. "What if it happens? We're under pressure up here, and the approach will be worst of all. What if someone cracks?" He turned to Russell and the grin grew wider. "What are the chances of that, eh?" And he began to sing a Jamaican song, in a Slavic Caribbean accent: "'Pressure drop, oh pressure drop, oh-o, pressure going to drop on you-oo-oo!'"

So they kept trying, handling the problem runs as seriously as they could, even the attack by Martian natives or the decoupling of Torus H caused by "explosive bolts installed by mistake when the ship was built," or the last minute veering of Phobos out of its orbit. Dealing with the more implausible scenarios sometimes took on a kind of surreal black humor, and Arkady replayed some of his videotapes as after-dinner entertainment, which sometimes got people launched into the air with laughter.

But the plausible problem runs . . . They kept on coming, morning after morning. And despite the solutions, despite the protocols for finding solutions, there was that sight, time after time: the red planet rushing at them at an unimaginable forty thousand kilometers an hour, until it filled the screen and the screen went white, and small black letters appeared on it: *Collision*.

They were traveling to Mars in a Type II Hohmann Ellipse, a slow but efficient course, chosen from among other alternatives mainly because the two planets were in the correct position for it when the ship was finally ready, with Mars about 45° ahead of Earth in the plane of the ecliptic. During the voyage they would travel just over halfway around the Sun, making their rendezvous with Mars some three hundred days later. Their womb time, as Hiroko called it.

The psychologists back home had judged it worthwhile to alter things from time to time, to suggest the passing of the seasons on the *Ares*. Length of days and nights, weather, and ambient colors were shifted to accomplish this. Some had maintained their landfall should be a harvest, others that it should be a new spring; after a short debate it had been decided by vote of the voyagers themselves to begin with early spring, so that they would travel through a summer rather than a winter; and as they approached their goal, the ship's colors would turn to the autumn tones of Mars itself, rather than to the light greens and blossom pastels they had left so far behind.

So in those first months, as they finished their morning's business, leaving the farm or the bridge, or staggering out of Arkady's merrily sadistic simulations, they walked into springtime. Walls were hung with pale green panels, or mural-sized photos of azaleas, and jacarandas and ornamental cherries. The barley and mustard in the big farm rooms glowed vivid yellow with new blooms, and the forest biome and the ship's seven park rooms had been stocked with trees and shrubs in the spring of their cycles. Maya loved these colorful spring blossoms, and after her mornings' work she fulfilled part of her exercise regimen by taking a walk in the forest biome, which had a hilly floor, and was so thick with trees one could not see from one end of the chamber to the other. Here she often met Frank Chalmers of all people, taking one of his short breaks. He said he liked the spring foliage, though he never seemed to look at it. They walked together, and talked or not as the case might be. If they did talk, it was never about anything important; Frank didn't care to discuss their work as leaders of the expedition. Maya found this peculiar, though she didn't say so. But they did not have exactly the same jobs, which might account for his reluctance. Maya's position was fairly informal and non-hierarchical; cosmonauts among themselves had always been relatively egalitarian, this had been the tradition since the days of Korolyov. The American program had a more military tradition, indicated even in titles: while Maya was merely Russian Contingent Co-ordinator, Frank was Captain Chalmers, and supposedly in the strong sense of the old sailing navies.

Whether this authority made it more or less difficult for him, he didn't say. Sometimes he discussed the biome, or small technical problems, or news from home; more often he just seemed to want to walk with her. So – silent walks, up and down on narrow trails, through dense thickets of pine and aspen and birch. And always that presumption of closeness, as if they were old friends, or as if he were, very shyly (or subtly), courting her.

Thinking about that one day, it occurred to Maya that starting the *Ares* in springtime might have created a problem. Here they were in their mesocosm, sailing through spring, and everything was fertile and blooming, profligate and green, the air perfumed with flowers and windy, the days getting longer and warmer, and everyone in shirts and shorts, a hundred healthy animals, in close quarters, eating, exercising, showering, sleeping. Of course there had to be sex.

Well, it was nothing new. Maya herself had had some fantastic sex in space, most significantly during her second stint on *Novy Mir*, when she and Georgi and Yeli and Irina had tried every weightless variant imaginable, which was a great many indeed. But now it was different. They were older, they were stuck with each other for good: "*Everything is different in a closed system*," as Hiroko often said in other contexts. The idea that they should stay on a fraternal basis was big at NASA: out of the 1,348 pages of the tome NASA had compiled called *Human Relations In Transit To Mars*, only a single page was devoted to the subject of sex; and that page advised against it. They were, the tome suggested, something like a tribe, with a sensible taboo against intra-tribal mating. The Russians laughed hilariously at this. Americans were such prudes, really. "We are not a *tribe*," Arkady said. "We are *the world*."

And it was spring. And there were the married couples aboard, some of whom were pretty demonstrative; and there was the swimming pool in Torus E, and the sauna and whirl-pool bath. Bathing suits were used in mixed company, this because of the Americans again, but bathing suits were nothing. Naturally it began to happen. She heard from Nadia and Ivana that the bubble dome was being used for assignations in the quiet hours of the night; many of the cosmonauts and astronauts turned out to be fond of weightlessness. And the many nooks in the parks and the forest biome were serving as hideaways for those with less weightless experience; the parks had been designed to give people the sense that they could get away. And every person had a private soundproofed room of their own. With all that, if a couple wanted to begin a relationship without becoming an item in the gossip mill, it was possible to be very discreet.

Maya was sure there was more going on than any one person could know.

She could feel it. No doubt others did as well. Quiet conversations between couples; changes in dining room partners; quick glances, small smiles; hands touching shoulders or elbows in passing; oh yes, things were happening. It made for a kind of tension in the air, a tension that was only partly pleasant. Antarctic fears came back into play; and besides, there was only a small number of potential partners, which tended to give things a musical chairs kind of feeling.

And for Maya there were additional problems. She was even more wary than usual of Russian men, because in this case it would mean sleeping with the boss; she was suspicious of that, knowing how it had felt when she had done it herself. Besides, none of them . . . well, she was attracted to Arkady, but she did not like him; and he seemed uninterested. Yeli she knew from before, he was just a friend; Dmitri she didn't care for; Vlad was older, Yuri not her type, Alex a follower of Arkady's . . . on and on like that.

And as for the Americans, or the internationals; well, that was a different kind of problem. Cross cultures, who knew? So . . . she kept to herself. But she thought about it. And occasionally, while waking up in the morning, or finishing a workout, she floated on a wave of desire that left her washed up on the shore of bed or shower, feeling alone.

Thus late one morning, after a particularly harrowing problem run, which they had almost solved and then failed to solve, she ran into Frank Chalmers in the forest biome and returned his hello, and they walked for about ten meters into the woods, and stopped. She was in shorts and tank-top, barefoot, sweaty and flushed from the crazed simulation. He was in shorts and a T-shirt, barefoot, sweaty and dusty from the farm. Suddenly he laughed his sharp laugh, and reached out to touch her upper arm with two fingertips. "You're looking happy today." With that darting smile.

The leaders of the two halves of the expedition. Equals. She lifted her hand to touch his, and that was all it took.

They left the trail and ducked into a tight thicket of pine. They stopped to kiss, and it had been long enough since the last time that it felt strange to her. Tripping over a root Frank laughed under his breath, that quick secretive laugh which gave Maya a shiver, almost of fear. They sat on pine needles, rolled together like students necking in the woods. She laughed; she had always liked the quick approach, the way she could just knock a man down when she wanted to.

And so they made love. For a time passion took her away. Afterwards she relaxed, enjoying the wash of afterglow. But then it got a bit awkward, somehow; she didn't know what to say. There was something hidden still about him, as if he were hiding even when making love. And even worse, what she could sense behind his reserve was some kind of triumph, as if he had won something and she had lost. That Puritan streak in Americans, that sense that sex was wrong and something that men had to trick women into. She had closed up a little herself, annoyed at that hidden smirk on his face. Win and lose, what children.

And yet they were co-mayors, so to speak. So if it was put on a zero sum basis . . .

Well, they talked for a while in a jovial enough way, and even made love again before they left. But it wasn't quite the same as the first time, she found herself distracted. So much in sex was beyond rational analysis. Maya always felt things about her partners that she could not analyze or even express; but she always either liked what she felt or didn't, there was no doubt about that. And looking at Frank Chalmers's face after the first time, she had been sure that something wasn't right. It made her uneasy.

But she was amiable, affectionate; it would not do to be put off at such a moment, no one would forgive that. They got up and dressed and went back into Torus D, and ate dinner at the same table with some others, and that was when it made perfect sense to become more distant. But then in the days after their encounter, she was surprised and displeased to find herself putting him off a little bit, making excuses to avoid being alone with him. It was awkward, not what she had wanted at all. She would have preferred not to feel the way she did, and once or twice after that they went off alone again, and when he started things she made love with him again, wanting it to work, feeling that she must have made a mistake or been in a bad mood somehow. But it was always the same, there was always that little smirk of triumph, that I-got-you that she disliked so much, that moralistic Puritan double-standard dirtiness.

And so she avoided him even more, to keep from getting into the start situation; and quickly enough he caught the drift. One afternoon he asked her to go for a walk in the biome and she declined, claiming fatigue; and a staccato look of surprise passed over his face, and then it had closed up like a mask. She felt badly, because she couldn't even explain it to herself.

To try to make up for such an unreasonable withdrawal, she was friendly and forthright with him after that, as long as it was a safe situation. And once or twice she suggested, indirectly, that for her their enounters had been only a matter of sealing a friendship, something she had done with others as well. All this had to be conveyed between words, however, and it was possible he misunderstood; it was hard to say. After that first jolt of comprehension, he only seemed puzzled. Once, when she left a group just before it broke up, she had seen him give her a sharp glance; after that, only distance and reserve. But he had never been really upset, and he never pressed the issue, or came to her to talk about it. But that was part of the problem, wasn't it? He didn't seem to *want* to talk to her about that kind of thing.

Well, perhaps he had affairs going with other women, with some of the Americans, it was hard to say. He really did keep to himself. But it was . . . awkward.

Maya resolved to abolish the knockover seduction, no matter the thrill she got from it. Hiroko was right; everything was different in a closed system. It was too bad for Frank (if he did care), because he had served as her education in this regard. In the end she resolved to make it up to him, by being a good friend. She worked so hard at doing this that once, almost a month later, she miscalculated and went a little too far, to the point where he thought she was seducing him again. They had been part of a group, up late talking, and she had sat next to him, and afterwards he had clearly gotten the wrong impression, and walked with her around Torus D to the bathrooms, talking in the charming and affable way he had at this stage of things. Maya was vexed with herself; she didn't want to seem completely fickle, although at this point either way she went it would probably look that way. So she went along with him, just because it was easier, and because there was a part of her that wanted to make love. And so she did, upset with herself and resolved that this should be the last time, a sort of final gift that would hopefully make the whole incident a good memory for him. She found herself becoming more passionate than ever before, she really wanted to please him. And then, just before orgasm, she looked up at his face, and it was like looking in the windows of an empty house.

That was the last time.

Δ V. V for velocity, delta for change. In space, this is the measure of the change in velocity required to get from one place to another — thus, a measure of the energy required to do it.

Everything is moving already. But to get something from the (moving) surface of the Earth into orbit around it, requires a minimum Δv of ten kilometers per second; to leave Earth's orbit and fly to Mars requires a minimum Δv of 3.6 kilometers per second; and to orbit Mars and land on it requires a Δv of about one kilometer per second. The hardest part is leaving Earth behind, for that is by far the deepest gravity well involved. Climbing up that steep curve of spacetime takes tremendous force, shifting the direction of an enormous inertia.

History too has an inertia. In the four dimensions of spacetime, particles (or events) have directionality; mathematicians, trying to show this, draw what they call "world lines" on graphs. In human affairs, individual world lines form a thick tangle, curling out of the darkness of prehistory and stretching through time: a cable the size of Earth itself, spiraling round the sun on a long curved course. That cable of tangled world lines is history. Seeing where it has been, it is clear where it is going — it is a matter of simple extrapolation. For what kind of Δv would it take to escape history, to escape an inertia that powerful, and carve a new course?

The hardest part is leaving Earth behind.

The form of the *Ares* gave a structure to reality; the vacuum between Earth and Mars began to seem to Maya like a long series of cylinders, bent up at their joints at 45° angles. There was a runner's course, a kind of steeplechase, around Torus C, and at each joint she slowed down in her run and tensed her legs for the increased pressure of the two 22.5° bends, and suddenly she could see up the length of the next cylinder. It was beginning to seem a rather narrow world.

Perhaps in compensation, the people inside began to get somehow larger. The process of shedding their Antarctic masks continued, and every time someone displayed some new and hitherto unknown characteristic, it made all who noticed it feel that much freer; and this feeling caused more hidden traits to be revealed. One Sunday morning the Christians aboard, numbering a dozen or so, celebrated Easter in the bubble dome. It was April back home, though the *Ares'* season was midsummer. After their service they came down to the D dining hall for brunch. Maya, Frank, John, Arkady, and Sax were at a table, drinking cups of coffee and tea. The conversations among them and with other tables were densely interwoven, and at first only Maya and Frank heard what John was saying to Phyllis Boyle, the geologist who had conducted the Easter service.

"I understand the idea of the universe as a superbeing, and all its energy being the thoughts of this being. It's a nice concept. But the Christ story . . ." John shook his head.

"Do you really know the story?" Phyllis asked.

"I was brought up Lutheran in Minnesota," John replied shortly. "I went to confirmation class, had the whole thing drilled into me."

Which, Maya thought, was probably why he bothered to get into discussions like this. He had a displeased expression that Maya had never seen before, and she leaned forward a bit, suddenly concentrating. She glanced at Frank; he was gazing into his coffee cup as if in a reverie, but she was sure he was listening.

John said, "You must know that the gospels were written decades after the event, by people who never met Christ. And that there are other gospels which reveal a different Christ, gospels that were excluded from the Bible by a political process in the third century. So he's a kind of literary figure really, a political construct. We don't know anything about the man himself."

Phyllis shook her head. "That's not true."

"But it is," John objected. This caused Sax and Arkady to look up from the next table. "Look, there's a history to all this stuff. Monotheism is a belief system that you see appearing in early herding societies. The greater their dependence on sheep herding, the more likely their belief in a shepherd god. It's an exact correlation, you can chart it and see. And the god is always male, because those societies were patriarchal. There's a kind of archeology, an anthropology — a sociology of religion, that makes all of this perfectly clear — how it came about, what needs it fulfilled."

Phyllis regarded him with a small smile. "I don't know what to say to that, John. It's not a matter of history, after all. It's a matter of faith."

"Do you believe in Christ's miracles?"

"The miracles aren't what matter. It's not the church or its dogma that matters. It's Jesus himself that matters."

"But he's just a literary construct," John repeated doggedly. "Something like Sherlock Holmes, or the Lone Ranger. And you didn't answer my question about the miracles."

Phyllis shrugged. "I consider the presence of the universe to be a miracle. The universe and everything in it. Can you deny it?"

"Sure," John said. "The universe just is. I define a miracle as an action that clearly breaks known physical law."

70

"Like traveling to other planets?"

"No. Like raising the dead."

"Doctors do that every day."

"Doctors have never done that."

Phyllis looked nonplussed. "I don't know what to say to you, John. I'm kind of surprised. We don't know everything, to pretend we do is arrogance. The creation is mysterious. To give something a name like 'the big bang,' and then think you have an explanation – it's bad logic, bad thinking. Outside your rational scientific thought is an enormous area of consciousness, an area more important than science. Faith in God is part of that. And I suppose you either have it or you don't." She stood. "I hope it comes to you." She left the room.

After a silence, John sighed. "Sorry, folks. Sometimes it still gets to me."

"Whenever scientists say they're Christian," Sax said, "I take it to be an aesthetic statement."

"The church of the wouldn't-it-be-pretty-to-think-so," Frank said, still looking into his cup.

Sax said, "They feel we're missing a spiritual dimension of life that earlier generations had, and they attempt to regain it using the same means." He blinked in his owlish way, as if the problem were disposed of by being defined.

"But that brings in so many absurdities!" John exclaimed.

"You just don't have faith," Frank said, egging him on.

John ignored him. "People who in the lab are as hard-headed as can be – you should see Phyllis grilling the conclusions her colleagues draw from their data! And then suddenly they start using all kinds of debater's tricks, evasions, qualifications, fuzzy thinking of every kind. As if they were an entirely different person."

"You just don't have faith!" Frank repeated.

"Well I hope I never get it! It's like being hit by a hammer in the head!"

John stood and took his tray to the kitchen. The rest looked

71

at each other in silence. It must have been, Maya thought, a really bad confirmation class. Clearly none of the others had known any more than her about this side of their easy-going hero. Who knew what they would learn next, about him or any of them?

News of the argument between John and Phyllis spread through the crew. Maya wasn't sure who was telling the story; neither John nor Phyllis seemed inclined to speak of it. Then she saw Frank with Hiroko, laughing as he told her something. Walking by them she heard Hiroko say, "You've got to admit Phyllis is right about that part – we don't understand the why of things at all."

Frank, then. Sowing discord between Phyllis and John. And (not a trivial point) Christianity was still a major force in America, and elsewhere. If word got around back home that John Boone was anti-Christian, it could give him problems. And that wouldn't be such a bad thing for Frank. They were all getting media play on Earth, but if you watched some of the news and features, it became clear that some were getting more than others, and this made them seem more powerful, and so they became more powerful in fact, by association. Among this group were Vlad and Ursula (whom she suspected were more than friends, now), Frank, Sax – all people who had been well known before their selection – and none so much as John. So that any diminution in Earth's regard for one of them might have a kind of corresponding effect on their status within the *Ares*. This at any rate seemed to be Frank's operating principle.

It felt as if they were confined to the interior of a hotel with no exits, without even any balconies. The oppression of hotel life was growing; they had been inside now for four long months, but it was still less than half their trip. And none of their carefully designed physical surroundings or daily routines could hasten its end.

Then one morning the second flight team was dealing with

another of Arkady's problem runs, when all at once red lights burned on several screens.

"A solar flare has been detected by the solar monitoring equipment," Rya said.

Arkady stood quickly. "That's not me!" he exclaimed, and leaned over to read the screen nearest him. He looked up, met his colleagues' skeptical stares, grinned. "Sorry, friends. This is the real wolf."

An emergency message from Houston confirmed him. He could have faked those as well, but he was headed for the nearest spoke and there was nothing they could do; fake or not, they had to follow.

In fact, a big solar flare was an event they had simulated many times before. Everyone had tasks to perform, quite a few of them in a very short time, so they ran around the toruses, cursing their luck and trying not to get in each other's way. There was a lot to do, as battening down was complicated and not very automated. In the midst of dragging plant trays into the plant shelter Janet yelled, "Is this one of Arkady's tests?"

"He says not!"

"Shit."

They had left Earth during the low point in the eleven-year sunspot cycle, specifically to reduce the chance of a flare like this occurring. And here it was anyway. They had about half an hour before the first radiation arrived, and no more than an hour after that the really hard stuff would follow.

Emergencies in space can be as obvious as an explosion or as intangible as an equation, but their obviousness has nothing to do with how dangerous they are. The crew's senses would never perceive the subatomic wind approaching them, and yet it was one of the worst things that could have happened. And everyone knew it. They ran through the toruses to get their bit of battening done — plants had to be covered or moved to protected areas, the chickens and pigs and pygmy cows and the rest of the animals and birds had to be herded into their own little shelters, seeds and frozen embryos had to be collected and carried along, sensitive electrical components had to be boxed or likewise carried along. When they were done with these high-speed tasks they yanked themselves up the spokes to the central shaft as fast as they could, and then flew down the central shaft tube to the storm shelter, which was directly behind the tube's aft end.

Hiroko and her biosphere team were the last ones in, banging through the hatch a full twenty-seven minutes after the initial alarm. They hurtled into the weightless space flushed and out of breath. "Has it started yet?"

"Not yet."

They plucked personal dosimeters from a velcro pad of them, pinned them to their clothing.

The rest of the crew already floated in the semi-cylindrical chamber, breathing hard and nursing bruises and a few sprains. Maya ordered them to count off, and was relieved to hear the whole hundred run through without gaps.

The room seemed very crowded. They hadn't gathered the whole hundred in one spot for many weeks, and even a max room didn't seem large enough. This one occupied a tank in the middle strand of the hub shaft. The four tanks surrounding theirs were filled with water, and their tank was divided lengthwise between their room and another semi-cylinder that had been filled with heavy metals. This semi-cylinder's flat side was their "floor," and it was fitted inside the tank on circular tracks, and rotated to counteract the spin of the ship, keeping the tub between the crew and the sun.

So they floated in a non-rotating space, while the curved roof of the tank rotated over them at its usual four rpm. It was a peculiar sight, which along with the weightlessness made some people begin to look thoughtful in a pre-seasick kind of way. These unfortunates congregated down at the end of the shelter where the lavatories were located, and to help them out visually, everyone else oriented themselves to the floor. The radiation was therefore coming up through their feet, mostly gamma rays scattering out of the heavy metals. Maya felt an impulse to keep her knees together. People floated in place, or put on velcro slippers to walk over the floor. They talked in low voices, instinctively finding their next-door neighbors, their working partners, their friends. Conversations were subdued, as if a cocktail party had been told that the hors d'oeuvres had been tainted.

John Boone *rip-ripped* his way to the computer terminals at the fore end of the room where Arkady and Alex were monitoring the ship. He punched in a command, and the exterior radiation data were suddenly displayed on the room's biggest screen. "Let's see how much is hitting the ship," he said brightly.

Groans. "Must we?" exclaimed Ursula.

"We might as well know," John said. "And I want to see how well this shelter works. The one on the *Rust Eagle* was about as strong as the bib you wear at the dentist's."

Maya smiled. It was a reminder, rare from John, that he had been exposed to much more radiation than any of the rest of them – about a hundred and sixty rem over the course of his life, as he explained now in response to someone's question. On Earth one caught a fifth of a *roentgen equivalent man* per year; orbiting Earth, still inside the protection of the Earth's magnetosphere, one took around thirty-five per year. So John had taken a lot of heat. And somehow that gave him the right, now, to screen the exterior data if he wanted to.

Those who were interested – about sixty people – clumped behind him to watch the screen. The rest relocated at the far end of the tank with the people worrying about motion sickness, a group that definitely didn't want to know how much radiation they were taking. Just the thought was enough to send some of them into the heads.

Then the full force of the flare struck. The exterior

75

radiation count shifted to well above the solar wind's usual level, and then soared in a sudden rush. An indrawn hiss came from several observers at once, and there were some shocked exclamations.

"But look how much the shelter is stopping," John said, checking the dosimeter pinned to his shirt. "I'm still at 1.3 rem."

That was several lifetimes of dentists' X-rays, to be sure; but the radiation outside the storm shelter was already 70 rem, well-on its way to a lethal dose, so they were getting off lightly. Still, the amount flying through the rest of the ship! Billions of particles were penetrating the ship and colliding with the atoms of water and metal they were huddled behind; hundreds of millions were flying between these atoms and then through the atoms of their bodies, touching nothing, as if they were no more than ghosts. Still, thousands were striking atoms of flesh and bone. Most of those collisions were harmless; but in all those thousands, there were in all probability one or two (or three?) in which a chromosome strand was taking a hit, and kinking in the wrong way: and there it was. Tumor initiation, begun with just that typo in the book of the self. And years later, unless the victim's DNA luckily repaired itself, the tumor promotion that was a more or less unavoidable part of living would have its effect, and there would appear a bloom of Something Else inside: cancer. Leukemia, most likely; and, most likely, death.

So it was hard not to regard the figures unhappily. 14.658 rems, 1.786, 19.004. "Like an odometer," Boone said calmly as he looked at his dosimeter. He was gripping a rail with both hands and pulling himself back and forth, as if doing isometric exercises. Frank saw it and said, "John, what the hell are you doing?"

"Dodging," John said. He smiled at Frank's frown. "You know – moving target!"

People laughed at him. With the extent of the danger

precisely charted on screens and graphs, they were beginning to feel less helpless. This was illogical, but naming was the power that made every human a scientist of sorts. And these were scientists by profession, with many astronauts among them as well, trained to accept the possibility of such a storm. All those mental habits began channeling their thoughts, and the shock of the event receded a bit. They were coming to terms with it.

Arkady went to a terminal and called up Beethoven's *Pastoral Symphony*, picking it up in the third movement, when the village dance is disrupted by storm. He turned up the volume, and they floated together in the long half-cylinder, listening to the intensity of Beethoven's fierce tempest, which suddenly seemed to enunciate perfectly the lashings of the silent wind pouring through them. It would sound just like that! Strings and woodwinds shrieking in wild gusts, out of control and yet beautifully melodic at the same time – a shiver ran down Maya's spine. She had never listened to the old warhorse this closely before, and she looked with admiration (and a bit of fear) at Arkady, who was beaming ecstatically at the effects of his inspired disk jockeying, and dancing like some red knot of fluff in the wind. When the symphony's storm peaked, it was difficult to believe that the radiation count wasn't rising; and when the musical storm abated, it seemed like theirs should be over too. Thunder muttered, the last gusts whistled through. The French horn sang its serene all-clear.

People began to talk about other things, discussing the various business of the day that had been so rudely interrupted, or taking the opportunity to talk about other things. After a half hour or more, one of those conversations got louder; Maya didn't hear how it began, but suddenly Arkady said, very loudly and in English, "I don't think we should pay any attention to plans made for us back on Earth!"

Other conversations went silent, and people turned to look

at him. He had popped up and was floating under the rotating roof of the chamber, where he could survey them all and speak like some mad flying spirit.

"I think we should make new plans," he said. "I think we should be making them now. Everything should be re-designed from beginning, with our own thinking expressed. It should extend everywhere, even to first shelters we build."

"Why bother?" Maya asked, annoyed at his grand-standing. "They're good designs." It really was irritating; Arkady often took center stage, and people always looked at her as if she were somehow responsible for him, as if it were her job to keep him from pestering them.

"Buildings are the template of a society," Arkady said.

"They're rooms," Sax Russell pointed out.

"But rooms imply the social organization inside them." Arkady looked around, pulling people into the discussion with his gaze. "The arrangement of a building shows what the designer thinks should go on inside. We saw that at the beginning of the voyage, when Russians and Americans were segregated into Torus D and B. We were supposed to remain two entities, you see. It will be same on Mars. Buildings express values, they have a sort of grammar, and rooms are the sentences. I don't want people in Washington or Moscow saying how I should live my life: I've had enough of that."

"What don't you like about the design of the first shelters?" John asked, looking interested.

"They are rectangular," Arkady said. This got a laugh, but he persevered: "Rectangular, the conventional shape! With work space separated from living quarters, as if work were not part of life. And the living quarters are taken up mostly by private rooms, with hierarchies expressed, in that leaders are assigned larger spaces."

"Isn't that just to facilitate their work?" Sax said.

"No. It isn't really necessary. It's a matter of prestige. A very conventional example of American business thinking, if I may say so."

There was a groan, and Phyllis said, "Do we have to get political, Arkady?"

At the very mention of the word, the cloud of listeners ruptured; Mary Dunkel and a couple of others pushed out and headed for the other end of the room.

"Everything is political," Arkady said at their backs. "Nothing more so than this voyage of ours. We are beginning a new society, how could it help but be political?"

"We're a scientific station," Sax said. "It doesn't necessarily have much politics to it."

"It certainly didn't last time I was there," John said, looking thoughtfully at Arkady.

"It did," Arkady said, "but it was simpler. You were an all-American crew, there on a temporary mission, doing what your superiors told you to do. But now we are an international crew, establishing a permanent colony. It's completely different."

Slowly people were drifting through the air toward the conversation, to hear better what was being said. Rya Jiminez said, "I'm not interested in politics," and Mary Dunkel agreed from the other end of the room: "That's one of the things I'm here to get away from!"

Several Russians replied at once. "That itself is a political position!" and the like. Alex exclaimed, "You Americans would like to end politics and history, so you can stay in a world you dominate!"

A couple of Americans tried to protest, but Alex overrode them: "It's true! The whole world has changed in the last thirty years, every country looking at its function, making enormous changes to solve problems – all but the United States. You have become the most reactionary country in the world."

Sax said, "The countries that changed had to because they were rigid before, and almost broke. The United States

79

already had flex in its system, and so it didn't have to change as drastically. I say the American way is superior because it's smoother. It's better engineering."

This analogy gave Alex pause, and while he was thinking about it John Boone, who had been watching Arkady with great interest, said, "Getting back to the shelters. How would you make them different?"

Arkady said, "I'm not quite sure – we need to see the sites we build on, walk around in them, talk it over. It's a process I advocate, you see. But in general I think work space and living space should be mixed as much as is practical. Our work will be more than making wages – it will be our art, our whole life. We will give it to each other, we will not buy it. Also there should be no signs of hierarchy. I don't even believe in the leader system we have now." He nodded politely at Maya. "We are all equally responsible now, and our buildings should show it. A circle is best – difficult in construction terms, but it makes sense for heat conservation. A geodesic dome would be a good compromise – easy to construct, and indicating our equality. As for the insides, perhaps mostly open. Everyone should have their room, sure, but these should be small. Set in the rim, perhaps, and facing larger communal spaces—" He picked up a mouse at one terminal, began to sketch on the screen. "There. This is architectural grammar that would say 'All equal.' Yes?"

"There's lots of prefab units already there," John said. "I'm not sure they could be adapted."

"They could if we wanted to do it."

"But is it really necessary? I mean, it's clear we're already a team of equals."

"Is it clear?" Arkady said sharply, looking around. "If Frank and Maya tell us to do something, are we free to ignore them? If Houston or Baikonur tell us to do something, are we free to ignore them?"

"I think so," John replied mildly.

This statement got him a sharp look from Frank. The

conversation was breaking up into several arguments, as a lot of people had things to say, but Arkady cut through them all again:

"We have been sent here by our governments, and *all* of our governments are flawed, most of them disastrously. It's why history is such a bloody mess. Now we are on our own, and I for one have no intention of repeating all of Earth's mistakes just because of conventional thinking. We are the first Martian colonists! We are *scientists*! It is our *job* to think things new, to make them new!"

The arguments broke out again, louder than ever. Maya turned away and cursed Arkady under her breath, dismayed at how angry people were getting. She saw that John Boone was grinning. He pushed off the floor toward Arkady, came to a stop by piling into him, and then shook Arkady's hand, which action swung them both around in the air, in an awkward kind of dance. This gesture of support immediately set people to thinking again – Maya could see it on their surprised faces; along with John's fame he had a reputation for being moderate and low-keyed, and if he approved of Arkady's ideas, then it was a different matter.

"Goddammit, Ark," John said. "First those crazy problem runs, and now this – you're a wild man, you really are! How in the hell did you get them to let you on board this ship, anyway?"

Exactly my question, thought Maya.

"I lied," Arkady said.

Everyone laughed. Even Frank, looking surprised. "But of course I lied!" Arkady shouted, a big upside-down grin splitting his red beard. "How else could I get here? I want to go to Mars to do what I want, and selection committee wanted people to go and do what they were told. You know that!" He pointed down at them, shouted: "You all lied, you know you did!"

Frank was laughing harder than ever. Sax wore his usual Buster Keaton, but he raised a finger and said, "The Revised

Minnesota Multiphasic Personality Inventory," and a great jeer went up from them all. They had all been required to take this exam: it was the world's most widely used psychological test, and well regarded by experts. Respondents agreed or disagreed to five hundred and fifty-six statements, and a profile was formed from the replies; but the judgements concerning what the answers meant were based on the earlier responses of a sample group of 2,600 white, married, middle class Minnesota farmers of the 1930s. Despite all subsequent revisions, the pervading bias created by the nature of that first test group was still deeply engrained in the test; or at least some of them thought so. "Minnesota!" Arkady shouted, rolling his eyes. "Farmers! Farmers from Minnesota! I tell you this now, I lied in answer to every single question! I answered exactly *opposite* to what I really felt, and *this* is what allowed me to score as normal!"

Wild cheers greeted this announcement. "Hell," John said, "I'm *from* Minnesota and I had to lie."

More cheers. Frank, Maya noted, was crimson with hilarity, incapable of speech, hands clutching his stomach, nodding, giggling, helpless to stop himself. She had never seen him laugh like that.

Sax said, "The test made you lie."

"What, not you?" Arkady demanded. "Didn't you lie too?"

"Well, no," Sax said, blinking as if the concept had never occurred to him before. "I told the truth to every question."

They laughed harder than ever. Sax looked startled at their response, but that only made him look funnier.

Someone shouted, "What do you say, Michel? How do you account for yourself?"

Michel Duval spread his hands. "You may be underestimating the sophistication of the RMMPI. There are questions which test how honest you are being."

This statement brought down a rain of questions on his head, a methodological inquisition. What were his controls?

82

How did the testers make their theories falsifiable? How did they repeat them? How did they eliminate alternative explanations of the data? How could they claim to be scientific in *any* sense of the word *whatsoever*? Clearly a lot of them considered psychology a pseudoscience, and many had considerable resentment for the hoops they had been forced to jump through to get aboard. The years of competition had taken their toll. And the discovery of this shared feeling sparked a score of voluble conversations. The tension raised by Arkady's political talk disappeared.

Perhaps, Maya thought, Arkady had defused the one with the other. If so it had been cleverly done, but Arkady was a clever man. She thought back. Actually it had been John Boone who had changed the subject. He had in effect flown to the ceiling and come to Arkady's rescue, and Arkady had seized the chance. They were both clever men. And it seemed possible they were in some sort of collusion. Forming a kind of alternative leadership, perhaps, one American, one Russian. Something would have to be done about that.

She said to Michel, "Do you think it's a bad sign we all consider ourselves such liars?"

Michel shrugged. "It's been healthy to talk about it. Now we realize we're more alike than we thought. No one has to feel they were unusually dishonest to get aboard."

"And you?" Arkady asked. "Did you present yourself as most rational and balanced psychologist, hiding the strange mind we have come to know and love?"

A small smile from Michel. "You're the expert in strange minds, Arkady."

Then the few still watching the screens called out. The radiation count had started to fall. After a while it slipped back to just a little above normal.

Someone returned the *Pastoral* to the moment of the horn call. The last movement of the symphony, "Glad and Grateful Feelings After the Storm," poured over the speaker system, and as they left the shelter and fanned out through the ship like dandelion seeds on a breeze, the beautiful old folk melody was broadcast thoughout the *Ares*, elaborating itself in all its Brucknerian richness. While it played, they found that the ship's hardened systems had survived intact. The thicker walls of the farm and the forest biome had afforded the plants some protection, and although there would be some die-offs and an entire crop they could not eat, the seed stocks were not harmed. The animals could not be eaten either, but presumably would give birth to a healthy next generation. The only casualties were some uncaptured songbirds from D's dining hall; they found a scattering of them dead on the floor.

As for the crew, the shelter's protection had shielded them from all but about 6 rem. That was bad for a mere three hours, but it could have been worse. The exterior of the ship had taken over 140 rem, a lethal dose.

Six months inside a hotel, with never a walk outside. Inside it was late summer, and the days were long. Green dominated the walls and ceilings, and people went barefoot. Quiet conversations were nearly inaudible in the hum of machinery, the whoosh of ventilators. The ship seemed empty somehow, whole sections of it abandoned as the crew settled down to wait. Small knots of people sat in the halls in Toruses B and D, talking. Some stopped their conversations when Maya wandered by, which she naturally found disturbing. She was having trouble falling asleep, trouble waking up. Work made her restless: all the engineers were only waiting, after all, and the simulations had gotten nearly intolerable. She had trouble gauging the passage of time. She stumbled more than she used to. She had gone to see Vlad and he had recommended over-hydration, more running, more swimming.

Hiroko told her to spend more time on the farm. She gave it a try, spending hours weeding, harvesting, trimming, fertilizing, watering, talking, sitting on a bench, looking at leaves: spacing out. The farm rooms were max chambers, their barrel roofs lined with bright sunstrips. The multi-leveled floors were crowded with crops, many new since the storm. There was not enough space to feed the crew entirely on farm food, but Hiroko disliked that fact and struggled against it, converting storage rooms as they emptied out. Dwarf strains of wheat, rice, soy and barley grew in stacked trays; above the trays hung rows of hydroponic vegetables and enormous clear jars of green and yellow algae, used to help regulate the gas exchange.

Some days Maya did nothing but watch the farm team work. Hiroko and her assistant Iwao were always tinkering at the endless project of maximizing the closure of their biological life support system, and they had a crew of other regulars working on it: Raul, Rya, Gene, Evgenia, Andrea, Roger, Ellen, Bob and Tasha. Success in the closure attempt was measured in K values, K representing closure itself. Thus for every substance they recycled,

$$K = I - \frac{e}{E}$$

where E was the rate of consumption in the system, e the rate of (incomplete) closure, and I a constant for which Hiroko, earlier in her career, had established a corrected value. The goal, $K = I\text{-}1$, was unreachable, but asymptotically approaching it was the farm biologists' favorite game, and more than that, critical to their eventual existence on Mars. So conversations about it could extend over days, spiraling off into complexities that no one really understood. In essence the farm team was already at their real work, which Maya envied; she was so sick of simulations!

Hiroko was an enigma to Maya. Aloof and serious, she always seemed absorbed in her work and her team tended always to be around her, as if she was the queen of a realm that had nothing to do with the rest of the ship. Maya didn't like that, but there was nothing she could do about it. And something in Hiroko's attitude made it not so threatening: it was just a fact, the farm was a separate place, its crew a separate society. And it was possible that Maya could use them to counterbalance the influence of Arkady and John somehow; so she did not worry about their separate realm. In fact she joined them more than ever before. Sometimes she went with them up to the hub at the end of a work session, to play a game they had invented called tunneljump. There was a jump tube down the central shaft; all the joints between cylinders had been expanded to the same width as the cylinders themselves, making a single smooth tube. There were rails to facilitate quick movement back and forth along this tube, but in their game, jumpers stood on the storm shelter hatch, and tried to leap up the tube to the bubble dome hatch, a full five hundred meters away, without bumping into the walls or railings. Coriolis forces made this effectively impossible, and flying even halfway would usually win a game. But one day Hiroko came by on her way to check an experimental crop in the bubble dome, and after greeting them she crouched on the shelter hatch and jumped, and slowly floated the full length of the tunnel, rotating as she flew, and stopping herself at the bubble dome hatch with a single outstretched hand.

The players stared up the tunnel in stunned silence.

"Hey!" Rya called to Hiroko. "How did you do that?"

"Do what?"

They explained the game to her. She smiled, and Maya was suddenly certain she had already known the rules. "So how did you do it?" Rya repeated.

"You jump straight!" Hiroko explained, and disappeared into the bubble dome.

That night at dinner the story got around. Frank said to Hiroko, "Maybe you just got lucky."

Hiroko smiled. "Maybe you and I should total twenty jumps and see who wins."

"Sounds good to me."

86

"What'll we bet?"

"Money, of course."

Hiroko shook her head. "Do you really think money matters anymore?"

A few days later Maya floated under the curve of the bubble dome with Frank and John, looking ahead at Mars, which was now a gibbous orb the size of a dime.

"A lot of arguments these days," John remarked casually. "I hear Alex and Mary got into an actual fight. Michel says it's to be expected, but still . . ."

"Maybe we brought too many leaders," Maya said.

"Maybe you should have been the only one," Frank jibed.

"Too many chiefs?" said John.

Frank shook his head. "That's not it."

"No? There are a lot of stars on board."

"The urge to excel and the urge to lead aren't the same. Sometimes I think they may be opposites."

"I leave the judgement to you, Captain." John grinned at Frank's scowl. He was, Maya thought, the only relaxed person left among them.

"The shrinks saw the problem," Frank went on, "it was obvious enough even for them. They used the Harvard solution."

"The Harvard solution," John repeated, savoring the phrase.

"Long ago Harvard's administrators noticed that if they accepted only straight A high school students, and then gave out the whole range of grades to freshmen, a distressing number of them were getting unhappy at their Ds and Fs and messing up the Yard by blowing their brains out on it."

"Couldn't have that," John said.

Maya rolled her eyes. "You two must have gone to trade schools, eh?"

"The trick to avoiding this unpleasantness, they found, was to accept a certain percentage of students who were used

87

to getting mediocre grades, but had distinguished themselves in some other way — "

"Like having the nerve to apply to Harvard with mediocre grades?"

" — used to the bottom of the grade curve, and happy just to be at Harvard at all."

"How did you hear of this?" Maya asked.

Frank smiled. "I was one of them."

"We don't have any mediocrities on this ship," John said.

Frank looked dubious. "We do have a lot of smart scientists with no interest in running things. Many of them consider it boring. Administration, you know. They're glad to hand it over to people like us."

"Beta males," John said, mocking Frank and his interest in sociobiology. "Brilliant sheep." The way they mocked each other —

"You're wrong," Maya said to Frank.

"Maybe so. Anyway, they're the body politic. They have at least the power to follow." He said this as if the idea depressed him.

John, due for a shift on the bridge, said goodbye and left.

Frank floated over to Maya's side and she shifted nervously. They had never discussed their brief affair and it hadn't come up, even indirectly, in quite a while. She had thought about what to say if it ever did: she would say that she occasionally indulged herself with men she liked. That it had been something done on the spur of the moment.

But he only pointed to the red dot in the sky. "I wonder why we're going."

Maya shrugged. Probably he meant not *we*, but *I*. "Everyone has their reasons," she said.

He glanced at her. "That's so true."

She ignored his tone of voice. "Maybe it's our genes," she said. "Maybe they felt things going wrong on Earth. Felt an increased speed of mutation, or something like that."

"So they struck out for a clean start."

"Yes."

"The selfish gene theory. Intelligence only a tool to aid successful reproduction."

"I suppose."

"But this trip endangers successful reproduction," Frank said. "It isn't safe out here."

"But it isn't safe on Earth either. Waste, radiation, other people . . ."

Frank shook his head. "No. I don't think the selfishness is in the genes. I think it's somewhere else." He reached out with a forefinger, and tapped her between the breasts — a solid tap on the sternum, causing him to drift back to the floor. Staring at her the whole while, he touched himself in the same place. "Good night, Maya."

A week or two later Maya was in the farm harvesting cabbages, walking down an aisle between long stacked trays of them. She had the room to herself. The cabbages looked like rows of brains, pulsing with thought in the bright afternoon light.

Then she saw a movement and looked to the side. Across the room, through an algae bottle, she saw a face. The glass of the bottle warped it: a man's face, brown-skinned. The man was looking to the side and didn't see her. It appeared he was talking to someone she couldn't see. He shifted, and the image of his face came clear, magnified in the middle of the bottle. She understood why she was watching so closely, why her stomach was clenched: she had never seen him before.

He turned and looked her way. Through two curves of glass their eyes met. He was a stranger, thin-faced and big-eyed.

He disappeared in a brown blur. For a second Maya hesitated, scared to pursue him; then she forced herself to run the length of the room and up the two bends of the joint, into the next cylinder. It was empty. She ran through three more cylinders before stopping. Then she stood there, looking at tomato vines, her breath rasping hard in her throat. She was sweating yet felt chilled. A stranger. It was impossible. But she had seen him! She concentrated on the memory, tried to see the face again. Perhaps it had been . . . but no. It had been none of the hundred, she knew that. Facial recognition was one of the mind's strongest abilities: it was amazingly accurate. And he had run away at the sight of her.

A stowaway. But that too was impossible! Where would he hide, how would he live? What would he have done in the radiation storm?

Had she begun to hallucinate, then? Had it come to that?

She walked back to her room, sick to her stomach. The hallways of Torus D were somehow dark despite their bright illumination, and the back of her neck crawled. When the door appeared she dove into the refuge of her room. But her room was just a bed and a side table, a chair and a closet, some shelves of stuff. She sat there for an hour, then two. But there was nothing there for her to do, no answers, no distractions. No escape.

Maya found herself unable to mention her sighting to anyone, and in a way this was more frightening than the incident itself, as it emphasized to her its impossibility. People would think she had gone mad. What other conclusion was there? How would he eat, where would he hide? No. Too many people would have to know, it really wasn't possible. But that face!

One night she saw it again in a dream, and woke up in a sweat. Hallucination was one of the symptoms of space breakdown, as she well knew. It happened fairly frequently during long stays in Earth orbit, a couple dozen incidences had been recorded. Usually people started by hearing voices in the ever-present background noise of ventilation and machinery, but a fairly common alternative was the sighting of a workmate who wasn't there, or worse yet of a *doppelgänger*, as if empty space had begun to fill with mirrors. Shortage of sensory stimuli was believed to cause the phenomena, and the *Ares*, with its long voyage, and no Earth to look at, and a brilliant (and some might say driven) crew, had been judged a potential hazard. This was one of the main reasons the ship's rooms had been given so much variety of color and texture, along with changing daily and seasonal weather. And still she had seen something that couldn't be there.

And now when she walked through the ship, it seemed to her that the crew was breaking up into small and private groups, groups which rarely interacted. The farm team spent almost all its time in the farms, even eating meals there on the floors, and sleeping (together, rumor had it) among the rows of plants. The medical team had its own suite of rooms and offices and labs in Torus B and they spent their time in there, absorbed with experiments and observations and consultations with Earth. The flight team was preparing for MOI, running several simulations a day. And the rest were

91

. . . scattered. Hard to find. As she walked around the toruses the rooms seemed emptier than ever before. The D dining hall was never full anymore. And then again in the separated clumps of diners that were there she noticed arguments broke out fairly frequently, and were hushed with peculiar speed. Private spats, but about what?

Maya herself said less at table, and listened more. You could tell a lot about a society by what topics of conversation came up. In this crowd, the talk was almost always science. Shop talk: biology, engineering, geology, medicine, whatever. You could chat forever about that stuff.

But when the number of people in a conversation fell below four, she noticed, the topics of conversation tended to change. Shop talk was augmented (or replaced entirely) by gossip; and the gossip was always about those two great forms of the social dynamic, sex and politics. Voices lowered, heads leaned in; and word got around. Rumors about sexual relations were becoming more common and more quiet, more caustic and more complex. In a few cases, as in the unfortunate triangle of Janet Blyleven, Mary Dunkel and Alex Zhalin, it went very public and became the talk of the ship; in others it stayed so hidden that the talk was in whispers, accompanied by pointed, inquisitive glances. Janet Blyleven would walk into the dining hall with Roger Calkins, and Frank would remark to John, in an undertone meant to reach Maya's ears, "Janet thinks we're a panmixia." Maya would ignore him, as she always did when he spoke in that sneery tone of voice; but later she looked up the word in a sociobiology lexicon, and found that a panmixia was a group where every male mated with every female.

The next day she looked at Janet curiously; she had had no idea. Janet was friendly, she leaned in at you as you talked, and really paid attention. And she had a quick smile. But . . . well, the ship had been built to insure a lot of privacy. No doubt there was more happening than anyone could know.

And among these secret lives, might there not be another secret life, led in solitude, or in teamwork with some few among them, some small clique or cabal?

"Have you noticed anything funny lately?" she asked Nadia one day, at the end of their regular breakfast chat.

Nadia shrugged. "People are bored. It's about time to get there, I think."

Maybe that was all it was.

Nadia said, "Did you hear about Hiroko and Arkady?"

Rumors were constantly swirling about Hiroko. Maya found it distasteful, disturbing. That the lone Asian woman among them should be the focus of that kind of thing — dragon lady, mysterious orient . . . Underneath the scientific rational surfaces of their minds, there were so many deep and powerful superstitions. Anything might happen, anything was possible.

Like a face seen through a glass.

And so she listened with a tight feeling in her stomach as Sasha Yefremov leaned over from the next table and responded to Nadia's question by wondering if Hiroko were developing a male harem. That was nonsense; although an alliance of some sort between Hiroko and Arkady had an unsettling sort of logic to Maya, she was not sure why. Arkady was very open in advocating independence from mission control, Hiroko never talked about it at all; but in her actions hadn't she already led the whole farm team away, into a mental torus the others could never enter?

But then when Sasha claimed in a low voice that Hiroko had plans to fertilize several of her own ova with sperm from all the men on the *Ares* and store them cryonically for later growth on Mars, Maya could only sweep up her tray and head for the dishwashers, feeling something like vertigo. They were becoming strange.

The red crescent grew to the size of a quarter, and the feeling of tension grew as well, as if it were the hour before a thunderstorm, and the air charged with dust and creosote and static electricity. As if the god of war were really up there on that blood dot, waiting for them. The green wall panels inside the *Ares* were now flecked with yellow and brown, and the afternoon light was thick with sodium vapor's pale bronze.

People spent hours in the bubble dome, watching what none among them but John had seen before. The exercise machines were in constant use, the simulations performed with renewed enthusiasm. Janet took a swing through the toruses, sending back video images of all the changes in their little world; then she threw her glasses on a table, and resigned her post as reporter. "Look, I'm tired of being an outsider," she said. "Every time I walk into a room everyone shuts up, or starts preparing their official line. It's like I was a spy for an enemy!"

"You were," Arkady said, and gave her a big hug.

At first no one volunteered to take over her job. Houston sent messages of concern, then reprimands, then veiled threats. Now that they were about to reach Mars, the expedition was getting a lot more TV time, and the situation was about to "go nova," as mission control put it. They reminded the colonists that this burst of publicity would eventually reap the space program all kinds of benefits; the colonists had to film and broadcast what they were doing, to stimulate public support for the later Mars missions on which they were going to depend. It was their duty to transmit their stories!

Frank got on the screen and suggested that mission control could concoct their video reports out of footage from robot cameras. Hastings, head of Mission Control in Houston, was visibly infuriated by this response. But as Arkady said, with a grin that extended the realm of the question to everything: "What can they do?"

Maya shook her head. They were sending a bad signal, she knew; and revealing what the video reports had so far hidden, that the group was splintering into rival cliques. Which indicated Maya's own lack of control over the Russian half of the expedition. She was about to ask Nadia to take over the reporting job as a favor to her, when Phyllis and some of her friends in Torus B volunteered for the job. Maya, laughing at the expression on Arkady's face, gave it to them. Arkady pretended not to care. Irritated, Maya said in Russian, "You know you've missed a chance! A chance to shape our reality, in effect!"

"Not our reality, Maya. Their reality. And I don't care what they think."

Maya and Frank began conferring about landfall assignments. To a certain extent these were predetermined by the crew members' areas of expertise, but because of all the skill redundancies, there were still some choices to be made. And Arkady's provocations had had this effect at least: Mission Control's preflight plans were now generally regarded as provisional at best. In fact no one seemed all that inclined to acknowledge Maya's or Frank's authority either, which made things tense when it became known what they were working on.

Mission Control's preflight plan called for the establishment of a base colony on the plains north of Ophir Chasma, the enormous northern arm of Valles Marineris. All the farm team was assigned to the base, and a majority of the engineers and medical people – altogether, around sixty of the hundred. The rest would be scattered on subsidiary missions, returning to the base camp from time to time. The largest subsidiary mission was to dock a part of the disassembled *Ares* on Phobos, and begin transforming that moon into a space station. Another smaller mission would leave the base camp and travel north to the polar cap, to build a mining system which would transport blocks of ice back to the base. A third mission was to make a series of geological surveys, traveling all over the planet; a glamor assignment for sure. All the smaller groups would become semi-autonomous for periods of up to a year, so selecting them was no trivial matter; they knew well, now, how long a year could be.

Arkady and a group of his friends – Alex, Roger, Samantha, Edvard, Janet, Tatiana, Elena – requested all the jobs on Phobos. When Phyllis and Mary heard about it, they came to Maya and Frank to protest. "They're obviously trying to take over Phobos, and who knows what they'll do with it?"

Maya nodded, and she could see Frank didn't like it either. The problem was, no one else wanted to stay on Phobos; even Phyllis and Mary weren't clamoring to replace Arkady's crew, so it wasn't clear how to oppose him.

Louder arguments broke out when Ann Clayborne passed around her crew list for the geological survey. A lot of people wanted to join that one, and several of those left off her list said they were going on surveys whether Ann wanted them or not.

Arguments became frequent, and vehement. Almost everyone aboard declared themselves for one mission or another, positioning themselves for the final decisions. Maya felt that she was losing all control of the Russian contingent; she was getting furious at Arkady. In a general meeting she suggested sarcastically that they let the computer make the assignments. The idea was rejected with no regard for her authority. She threw up her hands. "Then what do we do?"

No one knew.

She and Frank conferred in private. "Let's try giving them the illusion of making the decision," he said to her with a brief smile; she realized that he was not displeased to have seen her fail in the general meeting. Their encounter was coming back to haunt her, and she cursed herself for a fool. Little politburos were dangerous . . .

Frank polled everyone concerning their wishes, and then

displayed the results on the bridge, listing everyone's first, second and third choices. The geological surveys were popular, while staying on Phobos was not. Everyone already knew this, and the posted lists proved that there were fewer conflicts than it had seemed. "There are complaints about Arkady taking over Phobos," Frank said at the next public meeting. "But no one but him and his friends want that job. Everyone else wants to get down to the surface."

Arkady said, "In fact we should get hardship compensation."

"It's not like you to talk about compensation, Arkady," Frank said smoothly.

Arkady grinned and sat back down.

Phyllis wasn't amused. "Phobos will be a link between Earth and Mars, like the space stations in Earth orbit. You can't get from one planet to the other without them, they're what naval strategists call choke points."

"I promise to keep my hands off your neck," Arkady said to her.

Frank snapped, "We're all going to be part of the same village! Anything we do affects all of us! And judging by the way you're acting, dividing up from time to time will be good for us. I for one wouldn't mind having Arkady out of my sight for a few months."

Arkady bowed. "Phobos here we come!"

But Phyllis and Mary and their crowd still were not happy. They spent a lot of time conferring with Houston, and whenever Maya went into Torus B, conversations seemed to cease, eyes followed her suspiciously – as if being Russian would automatically put her in Arkady's camp! She damned them for fools, and damned Arkady even more. He had started all this.

But in the end it was hard to tell what was going on, with a hundred people scattered in what suddenly felt like such a large ship. Interest groups, micropolitics; they really were fragmenting. One hundred people only, and yet they were too large a community to cohere! And there was nothing she or Frank could do about it.

One night she dreamed again of the face in the farm. She woke shaken, and was unable to fall back asleep; and suddenly everything seemed out of control. They flew through the vacuum of space inside a small knot of linked cans, and she was supposed to be in charge of this mad argosy! It was absurd!

She left her room, climbed D's spoke tunnel to the central shaft. She pulled herself to the bubble dome, forgetting the tunneljump game.

It was four a.m. The inside of the bubble dome was like a planetarium after the audience has gone: silent, empty, with thousands of stars packed into the black hemisphere of the dome. Mars hung directly overhead, gibbous and quite distinctly spherical, as if a stone orange had been tossed among the stars. The four great volcanoes were visible pockmarks, and it was possible to make out the long rifts of Marineris. She floated under it, spreadeagled and spinning very slightly, trying to comprehend it, trying to feel something specific in the dense interference pattern of her emotions. When she blinked, little spherical teardrops floated out and away among the stars.

The lock door opened. John Boone floated in, saw her, grabbed the door handle to stop himself. "Oh, sorry. Mind if I join you?"

"No." Maya sniffed and rubbed her eyes. "What gets you up at this hour?"

"I'm often up early. And you?"

"Bad dreams."

"Of what?"

"I can't remember," she said, seeing the face in her mind.

He pushed off, floated past her to the dome. "I can never remember my dreams."

"Never?"

98

"Well, rarely. If something wakes me up in the middle of one, and I have time to think about it, then I might remember it, for a little while anyway."

"That's normal. But it's a bad sign if you never remember your dreams at all."

"Really? What's it a symptom of?"

"Of extreme repression, I seem to recall." She had drifted to the side of the dome; she pushed off through the air, stopped herself against the dome next to him. "But that may be Freudianism."

"In other words something like the theory of phlogiston."

She laughed. "Exactly."

They looked out at Mars, pointed out features to each other. Talked. Maya glanced at him as he spoke. Such bland, happy good looks; he really was not her type. In fact she had taken his cheeriness for a kind of stupidity back at the beginning. But over the course of the voyage she had seen that he was not stupid.

"What do you think of all the arguments about what we should do up there?" she asked, gesturing at the red stone ahead of them.

"I don't know."

"I think Phyllis makes a lot of good points."

He shrugged. "I don't think that matters."

"What do you mean?"

"The only part of an argument that really matters is what we think of the people arguing. X claims *a*, Y claims *b*. They make arguments to support their claims, with any number of points. But when their listeners remember the discussion, what matters is simply that X believes *a* and Y believes *b*. People then form their judgement on what they think of X and Y."

"But we're scientists! We're trained to weigh the evidence."

John nodded. "True. In fact, since I like you, I concede the point."

99

She laughed and pushed him, and they tumbled down the sides of the dome away from each other.

Maya, surprised at herself, arrested her motion against the floor. She turned and saw John coming to a halt across the dome, landing against the floor. He looked at her with a smile, caught a rail and launched himself into the air, across the domed space on a course aimed at her.

Instantly Maya understood, and forgetting completely her resolution to avoid this kind of thing, she pushed off to intercept him. They flew directly at each other, and to avoid a painful collision had to catch and twist in mid-air, as if dancing. They spun, hands clasped, spiraling up slowly toward the dome. It was a dance, with a clear and obvious end to it, there to reach whenever they liked: whew! Maya's pulse raced, and her breath was ragged in her throat. As they spun they tensed their biceps and pulled together, as slowly as docking spacecraft, and kissed.

With a smile John pushed down from her, sending her flying to the dome, and him to the floor, where he caught and crawled to the chamber's hatch. He locked it.

Maya let her hair loose and shook it out so it floated around her head, across her face. She shook it wildly and laughed. It was not as though she felt on the verge of any great or overmastering love; it was simply going to be fun; and that feeling of simplicity was . . . She felt a wild surge of lust, and pushed off the dome toward John. She tucked into a slow somersault, unzipping her jumper as she spun, her heart pounding like tympanis, all her blood rushing to her skin, which tingled as if thawing as she undressed, banged into John, flew away from him after an overhasty tug at a sleeve; they bounced around the chamber as they got their clothes off, miscalculating angles and momentums until with a gentle thrust of the big toes they flew into each other and met in a spinning embrace, and floated kissing among their floating clothes.

*

100

In the days that followed they met again. They made no attempt to keep the relationship a secret; so very quickly they were a known item, a public couple. Many aboard seemed taken aback by the development; and one morning walking into the dining hall, Maya caught a swift glance from Frank, seated at a corner table, that chilled her; it reminded her of some other time, some incident, some look on his face that she couldn't quite call to mind.

But most of those aboard seemed pleased. After all it was a kind of royal match, an alliance of the two powers behind the colony, signifying harmony. Indeed the union seemed to catalyze a number of others, which either came out of the closet or, in the newly supersaturated medium, sprang into being. Vlad and Ursula, Dmitri and Elena, Raul and Marina; newly evident couples were everywhere, to the point where the singletons among them began to make nervous jokes about it. But Maya thought she noticed less tension in voices, fewer arguments, more laughter.

One night, lying in bed thinking about it (thinking of wandering over to John's room) she wondered if that was why they had gotten together: not from love, she still did not love him, she felt no more than friendship for him, charged by lust that was strong but impersonal – but because it was, in fact, a very *useful* match. Useful to her – but she swerved from that thought, concentrated on the match's usefulness to the expedition as a whole. Yes, it was politic. Like feudal politics, or the ancient comedies of spring and regeneration. And it felt that way, she had to admit; as if she were acting in response to imperatives stronger than her own desires, acting out the desires of some larger force. Of, perhaps, Mars itself. It was not an unpleasant feeling.

As for the idea that she might have gained leverage over Arkady; or Frank; or Hiroko . . . well, she successfully avoided thinking about that. It was one of Maya's talents.

*

Blooms of yellow and red and orange spread across the walls. Mars was now the size of the moon in Earth's sky. It was time to harvest all their effort; only a week more, and they would be there.

There was still tension over the unsolved problems of landfall assignments. And now Maya found it less easy than ever to work with Frank: it was nothing obvious, but it occurred to her that he did not dislike their inability to control the situation, because the disruptions were being caused more by Arkady than anyone else, and so it looked like it was more her fault than his. More than once she left a meeting with Frank and went to John, hoping to get some kind of help. But John stayed out of the debates, and threw his support behind everything that Frank proposed. His advice to Maya in private was fairly acute, but the trouble was he liked Arkady and disliked Phyllis; so often he recommended to her that she support Arkady, apparently unaware of the way this tended to undercut her authority among the other Russians. She never pointed this out to him, however. Lovers or not, there were still areas she didn't wish to discuss with him, or with anyone else.

But one night in his room her nerves were jangling, and lying there, unable to sleep, worrying about first this and then that, she said, "Do you think it would be possible to hide a stowaway on the ship?"

"Well, I don't know," he said, surprised. "Why do you ask?"

Swallowing hard, she told him about the face through the algae bottle.

He sat up in bed, staring at her. "You're sure it wasn't . . ."

"It wasn't any of us."

He rubbed his jaw. "Well . . . I suppose if he were getting help from someone in the crew . . ."

"Hiroko," Maya suggested. "I mean, not just because she's Hiroko, but because of the farm and all that. It would solve his food problem, and there's a lot of places to hide there. And he could have taken shelter with the animals during the radiation storm."

"They got a lot of rems!"

"But he could have gotten behind their water supply. A little one-man shelter wouldn't be too hard to set up."

John still hadn't gotten over the idea of it. "A whole year in hiding!"

"It's a big ship. It could be done, right?"

"Well, I suppose so. Yeah, it could, I guess. But why?"

Maya shrugged. "I have no idea. Someone who wanted on, who didn't make the selection. Someone who had a friend, or friends . . ."

"Still! I mean, a lot of us had friends who wanted to come. That doesn't mean that . . ."

"I know, I know."

They talked about it for most of an hour, discussing the possible reasons, the methods that could have been used to slip a passenger on board, to hide him, and so on. And then Maya suddenly noticed that she felt much better; that she was, in fact, in a wonderful mood. John believed her! He didn't think she had gone crazy! She felt a wash of relief and happiness, and threw her arms around him. "It's so good to be able to talk to you about this!"

He smiled. "We're friends, Maya. You should have brought it up before."

"Yes."

The bubble dome would have been a wonderful place to view their final approach to Mars, but they were going to be aerobraking to reduce speed, and the dome would be behind the heat shield that they now deployed. There would be no view.

Aerobraking saved them from the necessity of carrying the enormous amount of fuel it would have taken to slow down, but it was an extremely precise operation, and therefore dangerous. They had a leeway of less than a milli-second of arc, and so several days before MOI the navigation team began to tweak their course with small burns on an almost hourly basis, fine tuning the approach. Then as they got closer they stopped the ship's rotation. The return to weightlessness, even in the toruses, was a shock; suddenly it came home to Maya that it wasn't just another simulation. She lofted through the windy air of the hallways, seeing everything from a strange new high perspective; and all of a sudden it felt real.

She slept in snatches, an hour here, three hours there. Every time she stirred, floating in her sleeping bag, she had a moment of disorientation, thinking she was in *Novy Mir* again. Then she would remember, and adrenalin would knock her awake: almost there. She would pull through the halls of the torus, pushing off the wall panels of brown and gold and bronze. On the bridge she would check with Mary or Raul or Marina, or someone else in navigation; everything still on course. They were approaching Mars so quickly it seemed they could see it expanding on the screens.

They had to miss the planet by thirty kilometers, or about one ten-millionth of the distance they had traveled. No prob-lem, Mary said, with a quick glance at Arkady. So far they were on the Mantra Run, and hopefully none of his mad problems would crop up.

The crew members not involved with navigation worked to batten down, preparing everything for the torque and bumps that two and half g were sure to bring. Some of them got to go out on EVAs, to deploy subsidiary heat shields and the like. There was a lot to do; and yet the days seemed long anyway.

It was going to happen in the middle of the night, and so that evening all the lights stayed on, and no one went to bed. Everyone had a station – some on duty, most of them only waiting it out. Maya sat in her chair on the bridge, watching the screens and the monitors, thinking that they looked just like they would if it were all a simulation in Baikonur. Could they really be going into orbit around Mars?

They could. The *Ares* hit Mars's thin high atmosphere at forty thousand kilometers per hour, and instantly the ship was vibrating heavily, Maya's chair shaking her fast and hard, and there was a faint low roar, as if they flew through a blast furnace — and it looked like that too, because the screens were bursting with an intense pink-orange glow. Compressed air was bouncing off the heat shields and blazing past all the exterior cameras, so that the whole bridge was tinged the color of Mars. Then gravity returned with a vengeance; Maya's ribs were squeezed so hard that she had trouble breathing, and her vision was blurred. It hurt!

They were plowing through the thin air at a speed and height calculated to put them into what aerodynamicists call transitional flow, a state halfway between free molecular flow and continuum flow. Free molecular flow would have been the preferred mode of travel, with the air that struck the heat shield shoved to the sides, and the resulting vacuum refilled mostly by molecular diffusion; but they were moving too fast for that, and they could only just barely avoid the tremendous heat of continuum flow, in which air would have moved over shield and ship as part of a wave action. The best they could do was to take the highest possible course that would slow them enough; and this put them into transitional flow, which vacillated between free molecular and continuum flow, making for a bumpy ride. And there lay the danger. If they were to hit a high pressure cell in the Martian atmosphere, where heat or vibration or g forces caused some sensitive mechanism to break, then they could be cast into one of Arkady's nightmares at the very time they were crushed in their chairs, "weighing" four hundred pounds apiece, which was something Arkady had never been able to simulate very well. In the real world, Maya thought grimly, at the moment when they were most vulnerable to danger, they were also most helpless to deal with it.

But as fate would have it, Martian stratospheric weather was stable, and they remained on the Mantra Run, which in actuality turned out to be a roaring, shuddering, breath-robbing eight minutes. No hour Maya could remember had lasted as long. Sensors showed that the main heat shield had risen to 600° Kelvin—

And then the vibration stopped. The roar ended. They had skipped out of the atmosphere, after skidding around a quarter of the planet. They had decelerated by some twenty thousand kilometers an hour, and the heat shield's temperature had risen to 710° Kelvin, very near its limit. But the method had worked. All was still. They floated, weightless again, held down by their chair straps. It felt as if they had stopped moving entirely, as if they were floating in pure silence.

Unsteadily they unstrapped themselves, floated like ghosts around the cool air of the rooms, an airy faint roar sounding in their ears, emphasizing the silence. They were talking too loudly, shaking each other's hands. Maya felt dazed, and she couldn't understand what people were saying to her; not because she couldn't hear them, but because she wasn't paying attention.

Twelve weightless hours later their new course led them to a periapsis thirty-five thousand kilometers from Mars. There they fired the main rockets for a brief thrust, increasing their speed by about a hundred kilometers an hour; after that they were pulled toward Mars again, carving an ellipse that would bring them back to within five hundred kilometers of the surface. They were in Martian orbit.

Each elliptical orbit of the planet took around a day. Over the next two months, the computers would control burns that would gradually circularize their course just inside the orbit of Phobos. But the landing parties were going to descend to the surface well before that, while apogee was so close.

They moved the heat shields back to their storage positions, and went inside the bubble dome to have a look.

During apogee Mars filled most of the sky, as if they flew over it in a high jet. The depth of Valles Marineris was perceptible, the height of the four big volcanoes obvious: their broad peaks appeared over the horizon well before the surrounding countryside came into view. There were craters everywhere on the surface: their round interiors were a vivid sandy orange, a slightly lighter color than the surrounding countryside. Dust, presumably. The short rugged curved mountain ranges were darker than the surrounding countryside, a rust color broken by black shadows. But both the light and dark colors were just a shade away from the omnipresent rusty-orangish-red, which was the color of every peak, crater, canyon, dune, and even the curved slice of the dust-filled atmosphere, visible high above the bright curve of the planet. Red Mars! It was transfixing, mesmerizing. Everyone felt it.

They spent long hours working, and at last it was real work. The ship had to be partially disassembled. The main body would be eventually parked in orbit near Phobos, and used as an emergency return vehicle. But twenty tanks from the outer lengths of the hub shaft had only to be disconnected from the *Ares* and prepped to become planetary landing vehicles, which would take the colonists down in groups of five. The first lander was scheduled to descend as soon as it was decoupled and prepped; so they worked in round-the-clock shifts, spending a lot of time in EVA. They pulled in to the dining halls tired and ravenous, and conversations were loud; the ennui of the voyage seemed forgotten. One night Maya floated in the bathroom getting ready for bed, feeling stiffened muscles that she hadn't heard from in months. Around her Nadia and Sasha and Yeli Zudov were chattering away, and in the warm wash of voluble Russian it suddenly occurred to her that everyone was happy – they were in the last moment of their anticipation, an anticipation that had lain in their hearts for half a lifetime, or ever since childhood – and now suddenly it had bloomed below them like a child's crayon drawing of Mars, growing huge then small, huge then small, and as it yo-yoed back and forth it loomed before them in all its immense potential: *tabula rasa*, blank slate. A blank red slate. Anything was possible, anything could happen – in that sense they were, in just these last few days, perfectly free. Free of the past, free of the future, weightless in their own warm air, floating like spirits about to invest a material world. In the mirror Maya caught sight of the toothbrush-distorted grin on her face, and grabbed a railing to hold her position. It occurred to her that they might never be so happy again. Beauty was the promise of happiness, not happiness itself; and the anticipated world was often more rich than anything real. But this time who could say? This time might be the golden one at last.

She released the railing and spit toothpaste into a wastewater bag, then floated backwards into the hallway. Come what may, they had reached their goal. They had earned at least the chance to try.

Disassembling the *Ares* made a lot of them feel odd. It was, as John remarked, like dismantling a town and flinging the houses in different directions. And this was the only town they had. Under the giant eye of Mars all their disagreements became taut; clearly it was critical now, there was little time left. People argued, in the open or under the surface. So many little groups now, keeping their own council . . . what had happened to that brief moment of happiness? Maya blamed it mostly on Arkady. He had opened Pandora's box; if not for him and his talk, would the farm group have drawn so close around Hiroko? Would the medical team have kept such close counsel? She didn't think so.

She and Frank worked hard to reconcile differences and forge a consensus, to give them the feeling they were still a single team. It involved long conferences with Phyllis and Arkady, Ann and Sax, Houston and Baikonur. In the process a relationship developed between the two leaders that was even more complex than their early encounters in the park; though that was part of it; Maya saw now, in Frank's occasional flashes of sarcasm and resentment, that he had been bothered by the incident more than she had thought at the time. But there was nothing to be done about it now.

In the end the Phobos mission was indeed given to Arkady and his friends, mainly because no one else wanted it. Everyone was promised a spot on a geological survey if they wanted one; and Phyllis and Mary and the rest of the "Houston crowd" were given assurances that the construction of base camp would go according to the plans made in Houston. They intended to work at the base to see that it happened that way. "Fine, fine," Frank snarled at the end of one of these meetings. "We're all going to be *on Mars*, do we *really* have to fight like this over what we're going to *do* there?"

"That's life," Arkady said cheerfully. "On Mars or not, life goes on."

Frank's jaw was clenched. "I came here to get away from this kind of thing!"

Arkady shook his head. "You certainly did not! This is your life, Frank. What would you do without it?"

One night shortly before the descent, they gathered and had a formal dinner for the entire hundred. Most of the food was farm-grown: pasta, salad and bread, with red wine from storage, saved for a special occasion.

Over a dessert of strawberries, Arkady floated up to propose a toast. "To the new world we now create!"

A chorus of groans and cheers; by now they all knew what he meant. Phyllis threw down a strawberry and said, "Look, Arkady, this settlement is a scientific station. Your ideas are irrelevant to it. Maybe in fifty or a hundred years. But for now, it's going to be like the stations in Antarctica."

"That's true," Arkady said. "But in fact Antarctic stations are very political. Most of them were built so that countries that built them would have a say in the revision of the Antarctic treaty. And now the stations are governed by laws set by that treaty, which was made by a very political process! So you see, you cannot just stick your head in sand crying 'I am a scientist, I am a scientist!'" He put a hand to his forehead, in the universal mocking gesture of the prima donna. "No. When you say that, you are only saying, 'I do not wish to think about complex systems!' Which is not really worthy of true scientists, is it?"

"The Antarctic is governed by a treaty because no one lives there except in scientific stations," Maya said irritably. To have their final dinner, their last moment of freedom, disrupted like this!

"True," Arkady said. "But think of the result. In Antarctica, no one can own land. No one country or organization can exploit the continent's natural resources, without the consent of every other country. No one can claim to own those resources, or take them and sell them to other people, so that some profit from them while others pay for their use. Don't you see how radically different that is from the way the rest of the world is run? And this is the last area on Earth to be organized, to be given a set of laws. It represents what all governments working together feel instinctively is fair, revealed on land free from claims of sovereignty, or really from any history at all. It is, to say it plainly, Earth's best attempt to create just property laws! Do you see? This is the way entire world should be run, if only we could free it from the straitjacket of history!"

Sax Russell, blinking mildly, said, "But Arkady, since Mars is going to be ruled by a treaty based on the old Antarctic one, what are you objecting to? The Outer Space Treaty states that no country can claim land on Mars, no military activities are allowed, and all bases are open to inspection by any country. Also no Martian resources can become the property of a single nation – the UN is supposed to establish an international regime to govern any mining or other exploitation. If anything is ever done along that line, which I doubt will happen, then it is to be shared among all the nations of the world." He turned a palm upward. "Isn't that what you're agitating for, already achieved?"

"It's a start," Arkady said. "But there are aspects of that treaty you haven't mentioned. Bases built on Mars will belong to the countries that build them, for instance. We will be building American and Russian bases, according to this provision of the law. And that puts us right back into the nightmare of Terran law and Terran history. American and Russian businesses will have the right to exploit Mars, as long as the profits are somehow shared by all the nations signing the treaty. This may only involve some sort of percentage paid to UN, in effect no more than bribe. I don't believe we should acknowledge these provisions for even a moment!"

Silence followed this remark.

Ann Clayborne said, "This treaty also says we have to take measures to prevent the disruption of planetary environments, I think is how they put it. It's in Article Seven. That seems to me to expressly forbid the terraforming that so many of you are talking about."

"I would say that we should ignore that provision as well," Arkady said quickly. "Our own well-being depends on ignoring it."

This view was more popular than his others, and several people said so.

"But if you're willing to disregard one article," Arkady pointed out, "you should be willing to disregard the rest. Right?"

There was an uncomfortable pause.

"All these changes will happen inevitably," Sax Russell

said with a shrug. "Being on Mars will change us in an evolutionary way."

Arkady shook his head vehemently, causing him to spin a little in the air over the table. "No, no, no, no! History is not evolution! It is a false analogy! Evolution is a matter of environment and chance, acting over millions of years. But history is a matter of environment and choice, acting within lifetimes, and sometimes within years, or months, or days! History is Lamarckian! So that if we choose to establish certain institutions on Mars, there they will be! And if we choose others, there *they* will be!" A wave of his hand encompassed them all, the people seated at the tables, the people floating among the vines: "I say we should make those choices ourselves, rather than having them made for us by people back on Earth. By people long dead, really."

Phyllis said sharply, "You want some kind of communal utopia, and it's not possible. I should think Russian history would have taught you something about that."

"It has," Arkady said. "Now I put to use what it has taught me."

"Advocating an ill-defined revolution? Fomenting a crisis situation? Getting everyone upset and at odds with each other?"

A lot of people nodded at this, but Arkady waved them away. "I decline to accept blame for everyone's problems at this point in the trip. I have only said what I think, which is my right. If I make some of you uncomfortable, that is your problem. It is because you don't like the implications of what I say, but can't find grounds to deny them."

"Some of us can't understand what you say," Mary exclaimed.

"I say only this!" Arkady said, staring at her bug-eyed: "We have come to Mars for good. We are going to make not only our homes and our food, but also our water and the very air we breathe — all on a planet that has none of these things. We can do this because we have technology to manipulate matter right down to the molecular level. This is an extraordinary ability, think of it! And yet some of us here can accept transforming the entire physical reality of this planet, without doing a single thing to change ourselves, or the way we live. To be twenty-first century scientists on Mars, in fact, but at the same time living within nineteenth century social systems, based on seventeenth century ideologies. It's absurd, it's crazy, it's — it's—" he seized his head in his hands, tugged at his hair, roared "It's *unscientific*! And so I say that among all the many things we transform on Mars, ourselves and our social reality should be among them. We must terraform not only Mars, but ourselves."

No one ventured a rebuttal to that; Arkady at full throttle was pretty much unopposable, and a lot of them were genuinely provoked by what he had said and needed time to think. Others were simply disgruntled, but unwilling to cause too much of a fuss at this particular dinner, which was supposed to be a celebration. It was easier to roll one's eyes, and drink to the toast. "To Mars! To Mars!" But as they floated around after finishing dessert, Phyllis was disdainful. "First we have to survive," she said. "With dissension like this, how good will our chances be?"

Michel Duval tried to reassure her. "A lot of these disagreements are symptoms of the flight. Once on Mars, we'll pull together. And we have more than just what we brought on the *Ares* to help us — we'll have what the unmanned landers have brought already, shipments of equipment and food all over the surface and the moons. All that's there for us. The only limit will be our own stamina. And this voyage is part of that — it's a kind of preparation, a test. If we fail this part, we won't even get to try on Mars."

"Exactly my point!" Phyllis said. "We are failing in this."

Sax stood, looking bored, and pushed off toward the kitchen. The hall was filled with the seashell roar of many small discussions, some of them acrimonious in tone. A lot of people were angry at Arkady, clearly; and others were angry at them for getting upset.

Maya followed Sax into the kitchen. As he cleaned his tray he sighed. "People are so emotional. Sometimes it seems like I'm stuck in an endless performance of the play *No Exit*."

"That's the one where they can't get out of a little room?"

He nodded. "Where hell is other people. I hope we don't prove the hypothesis."

A few days later the landers were ready. They would descend over a period of five days; only the Phobos team would stay in what was left of the *Ares*, guiding it to its near-docking with the little moon. Arkady, Alex, Dmitri, Roger, Samantha, Edvard, Janet, Raul, Marina, Tatiana, and Elena said their farewells, absorbed already in the task at hand, promising to descend as soon as the Phobos station was built.

The night before the descent Maya couldn't sleep. Eventually she gave up trying, and pulled herself through the rooms and corridors, up to the hub. Every object was sharp-edged with sleeplessness and adrenalin, and every familiarity of the ship was countered or overwhelmed by some alteration, a lashed-down stack of boxes or a dead-end in a tube. It was as if they had already left the *Ares*. She looked around at it one last time, drained of emotion. Then she pulled herself through the tight locks, into the landing vehicle she had been assigned to. Might as well wait there. She climbed into her spacesuit, feeling, as she so often did when the real moment came, that she was only going through another simulation. She wondered if she would ever escape that feeling, if being on Mars would be enough to end it. It would be worth it just for that: to make her feel *real* for once! She settled into her chair.

A few sleepless hours later she was joined by Sax, Vlad, Nadia, and Ann. Her companions belted in, and they ran through the check-out together. Toggles were flipped, there was a countdown; and their rockets fired. The lander drifted away from the *Ares*. Its rockets fired again. They fell toward the planet. They hit the top of the atmosphere, and their single trapezoidal window became a blaze of Mars-colored air. Maya, vibrating with the craft, stared up at it. She felt tense and unhappy, focused backward rather than forward, thinking of everyone still on the *Ares*; and it seemed to her that they had failed, that the five of them in the lander were leaving behind a group in disarray. Their best chance for creating some kind of concord had passed, and they had not succeeded; the momentary flash of happiness she had felt while brushing her teeth had been just that, a flash. She had failed, then. They were going their separate ways, splintered by their beliefs, and even after two separate years of enforced togetherness they were, like any other human group, no more than a collection of strangers. The die was cast.

PART THREE

The Crucible

It formed with the rest of the solar system, around five billion years ago. That's fifteen million human generations. Rocks banging together in space and then coming back and holding together, all because of the mysterious force we call gravity. That same mysterious warp in the weft of things caused the pile of rocks, when it was big enough, to crush in on its center until the heat of the pressure melted the rock. Mars is small but heavy, with a nickel-iron core. It is small enough that the interior has cooled faster than Earth's: the core no longer spins inside the crust at a different speed and so Mars has practically no magnetic field. No dynamo left. But one of the last internal flows of the molten core and mantle was in the form of a huge anomalous lumping outward on one side, a shove against the crust wall that formed a continent-sized bulge, eleven kilometers high: three times as high as the Tibetan plateau is above its surroundings. This bulge caused many other features to appear: a system of radial fractures covering an entire hemisphere, including the largest cracks of all, the Valles Marineris, a lace of canyons that would cover the United States coast to coast. The bulge also caused a number of volcanoes, including three straddling its spine, Ascraeus Mons, Pavonis Mons and Arsia Mons; and off on its northwest edge, Olympus Mons, the tallest mountain in the solar system, three times the height of Everest, one hundred times the mass of Mauna Loa, the Earth's largest volcano.

So the Tharsis Bulge was the most important factor in shaping the surface of Mars. The other major factor was meteor fall. In the Noachian Age, three to four billion years ago, millions of meteors were falling on Mars at a tremendous rate, and thousands of them were planetesimals, rocks as big as Vega or Phobos. One of the impacts left behind Hellas Basin, 2000 kilometers in diameter, the largest obvious crater in the solar system; although Daedalia Planum appears to be the remains of an impact basin 4500 kilometers across. Those are big; but then there are areologists who believe that the entire northern hemisphere of Mars is an ancient impact basin.

These big impacts created explosions so cataclysmic that it is hard to imagine them; ejecta from them ended up on the Earth and the Moon, and as asteroids in Trojan orbits; some areologists think that the Tharsis Bulge started because of the Hellas impact; others believe that Phobos and Deimos are ejecta. And these were only the largest impacts. Smaller stones fell every day, so that the oldest surfaces on Mars are saturated with cratering, the landscape a palimpsest of newer rings obscuring older ones, with no patch of land untouched. And each of these impacts released explosions of heat that melted rock: elements were broken out of their matrix and fired away in the form of hot gases, liquids, new minerals. This and the outgassing from the core produced an atmosphere, and lots of water; there were clouds, storms, rain and snow, glaciers, streams, rivers, lakes, all scouring the land, all leaving unmistakable marks of their passage — flood channels, stream beds, shorelines, every kind of hydrologic hieroglyphic.

But all that went away. The planet was too small, too far from the sun. The atmosphere froze and fell to the ground. Carbon dioxide sublimed to form a thin new atmosphere, while oxygen bonded to rock and turned it red. The water froze, and over the ages seeped down through the kilometers of meteor-broken rock. Eventually this layer of regolith became permeated with ice, and the deepest parts were hot enough to melt the ice; so there were underground seas on Mars. And water always flows downhill; so these aquifers migrated down, slowly seeping, until they pooled behind some stoppage or another, a rib of high bedrock or a frozen soil barrier. Sometimes intense artesian pressures built against these dams; and sometimes a meteor would hit, or a volcano appear, and the dam would burst apart and a whole underground sea would spew over the landscape in enormous floods, floods ten thousand times the flow of the Mississippi. Eventually, however, the water on the surface would freeze and sublime away in the ceaseless dry winds, and fall on the poles in every winter's fog hood. The polar caps therefore thickened, and their weight drove the ice underground until the visible ice was only the tip of two world-topping lenses of underground permafrost, lenses ten and then a hundred times the visible caps' volume. While back down toward the equator, new aquifers were being filled from below, by outgassing from the core; and some of the old aquifers were refilling.

And so this slowest of cycles approached its second round. But as the planet was cooling, all of it happened more and more slowly, in a long ritard like a clock winding down. The planet settled into the shape we see. But change never stops; the ceaseless winds carved the land, with dust that grew finer and finer; and the eccentricities of Mars's orbit meant that the southern and northern hemispheres traded the cold and warm winters in a 51,000 year cycle, so that the dry ice cap and the water ice cap reversed poles. Each swing of this pendulum laid down a new stratum of sand, and the troughs of new dunes cut through older layers at an angle, until the sand around the poles lay in a stippled cross-hatching, in geometrical patterns like Navajo sand paintings, banding the whole top of the world.

The colored sands in their patterns, the fluted and scalloped canyon walls, the volcanoes rising right through the sky, the rubbled rock of the chaotic terrain, the infinity of craters, ringed emblems of the planet's beginning . . . Beautiful, or harsher than that: spare, austere, stripped down, silent, stoic, rocky, changeless. Sublime. The visible language of nature's mineral existence.

Mineral; not animal, nor vegetable, nor viral. It could have happened but it didn't. There was never any

121

spontaneous generation out of the clays or the sulphuric hot springs; no spore falling out of space, no touch of a god; whatever starts life (for we do not know), it did not happen on Mars. Mars rolled, proof of the otherness of the world, of its stony vitality.

And then, one day . . .

She hit the ground with both feet solid, nothing tricky about it, the g familiar from nine months in the *Ares*; and with the suit's weight, not that much different from walking on Earth, as far as she could remember. The sky was a pink shaded with sandy tans, a color richer and more subtle than any in the photos. "Look at the sky," Ann was saying, "look at the sky." Maya was chattering away, Sax and Vlad spun like rotating statues. Nadezhda Francine Cherneshevsky took a few more steps, felt her boots crunch the surface. It was salt-hardened sand a couple of centimeters thick, which cracked when you walked on it; the geologists called it duri-crust or caliche. Her boot tracks were surrounded by small systems of radial fractures.

She was out away from the lander. The ground was a dark rusty orange, covered with an even litter of rocks the same color, although some of the rocks showed tints of red or black or yellow. To the east stood a number of rocket landing vehicles, each one a different shape and size, with the tops of more sticking over the eastern horizon. All of them were crusted the same red-orange as the ground: it was an odd, thrilling sight, as if they had stumbled upon a long-abandoned alien spaceport. Parts of Baikonur would look like this, in a million years.

She walked to one of the nearest landing vehicles, a freight container the size of a small house, set on a skeletal four-legged rocket assembly. It looked like it had been there for decades. The sun was overhead, too bright to look at even through her faceplate; it was hard to judge through the polar-ization and other filters, but it seemed to her that the day-light was much like that on Earth, as far as she could remember. A bright winter's day.

She looked around again, trying to take it in. They stood on a gently bumpy plain, covered with small sharp-edged rocks, all half-buried in dust. Back to the west the horizon was marked by a small flat-topped hill. It might be a crater rim, it was hard to say. Ann was already halfway there, still quite a large figure; the horizon was closer than seemed right, and Nadia paused to take note of that, suspecting that she would soon become accustomed to it, and never notice. But it was not Earthlike, that strangely close horizon, she saw that clearly now. They stood on a smaller planet.

She made a concerted effort to recall Earth's gravity, wondering that it should be so hard. Walking in the woods, over tundra, on the river ice in winter . . . and now: step, step. The ground was flat, but one had to thread a course between the ubiquitous rocks; there was no place on Earth that she knew of where they were distributed so copiously and evenly. Take a jump! She did, and laughed; even with her suit on she could tell she was lighter. She was just as strong as ever, but weighed only thirty kilos! And the forty kilos of the suit . . . well, it threw her off balance, that was true. It made her feel that she had gone hollow. That was it: her center of gravity was gone, her weight had been shifted out to her skin, to the outside of her muscles rather than the inside. That was the effect of the suit, of course. Inside the habitats it would be as it had been in the *Ares*. But out here in a suit, she was the hollow woman. With the aid of that image she could suddenly move more easily, hop over a boulder, come down and take a turn, dance! Simply pop in the air, dance, land on top of a flat rock – watch out—

She tumbled, landed on a knee and both hands. Her gloves broke through the duricrust. It felt like a layer of caked sand at the beach, only harder and more brittle. Like hardened mud. And cold! Their gloves weren't heated the way their boot soles were, and there wasn't enough insulation when actually touching the ground. It was like touching ice with the bare fingers, wow! Around 215° Kelvin, she recalled, or −90° Centigrade; colder than Antarctica, colder than Siberia at its worst. Her fingertips were numb. They would need better gloves to be able to work, gloves fitted with heating elements, like their boot soles. That would make the gloves thicker and less flexible. She'd have to get her finger muscles back into shape.

She had been laughing. She stood and walked to another freight drop, humming "Royal Garden Blues." She climbed the leg of the next drop and rubbed the crust of red dirt off an engraved manifest on the side of the big metal crate. One John Deere/Volvo Martian bulldozer, hydrazine-powered, thermally protected, semi-autonomous, fully programmable. Prostheses and spare parts included.

She felt her face stretched in a big grin. Backhoes, front loaders, bulldozers, tractors, graders, dump trucks; construction supplies and materials of every kind; air miners to filter and collect chemicals from the atmosphere; little factories to render these chemicals into other chemicals; other factories to combine those chemicals; a whole commissary, everything they were going to need, all at hand in scores of crates scattered over the plain. She began to hop from one lander to the next, taking stock. Some of them had obviously hit hard, some had their spider legs collapsed, others their bodies cracked, one was even flattened into a pile of smashed boxes, half-buried in dust; but these were just another kind of opportunity, the salvage and repair game, one of her favorites! She laughed aloud, she was a bit giddy, she noticed the comm light on her wrist console blinking; she switched to the common band and was startled by Maya and Vlad and Sax all talking at once, "Where's Ann, you women get back here, hey Nadia, come help us get this damned habitat online, we can't even get the door open!"

She laughed.

The habitats were scattered like everything else, but they had landed near one that they knew was functional; it had been turned on from orbit some days before, and run through a complete check. Unfortunately the outer lock door could not be included in the check, and it was stuck. Nadia went to work on it, grinning; it was odd to see what looked like a derelict trailer home sporting a space station lock door. It only took a minute for her to get it open, by tapping out the emergency open code while pulling out on the door. Stuck with cold, differential shrinking perhaps. They were going to have a lot of little problems like that.

Then she and Vlad were into the lock, and then inside the habitat. It still looked like a trailer home, but with the latest in kitchen fixtures. All the lights were on. The air was warm, and circulating well. The control panel looked like a nuclear power plant's.

While the others came inside, Nadia walked down a row of small rooms, through door after door, and the oddest feeling suddenly came over her: things seemed out of place. The lights were on, some of them blinking; and down at the far end of the hall, a door was swinging slightly back and forth on its hinges.

Obviously the ventilation. And the shock of the habitat's landing probably had disarranged things slightly. She shook off the feeling and went back to greet the others.

By the time everyone had landed and walked across the stony plain (stopping, stumbling, running, staring off at the horizon, spinning slowly, walking again), and had entered into the three functioning habitats, and gotten out of their EVA suits, and put them away, and checked out the habitats, and eaten a bit, talking it all over the whole while, night had fallen. They continued working on the habitats and talking through most of that night, too excited to fall asleep; then most of them slept in snatches until dawn, when they woke and suited up and went out again, looking around and checking manifests and running machines through checks. Eventually they noticed they were famished, and went back in to jam down a quick meal; and then it was night again!

126

And that was what it was like, for several days; a wild swirl of time passing. Nadia would wake to the bip of her wrist console and eat a quick breakfast looking out of the habitat's little east window: dawn stained the sky rich berry colors for a few minutes, before shifting rapidly through a series of rosy tones to the thick pink-orange of daytime. All over the floor of the habitat her companions slept, on mattresses that would fold up against the wall during the day. The walls were beige, tinted orange by the dawn. The kitchen and living room were tiny, the four toilet rooms no more than closets. Ann would stir as the room lightened and go to one of the four toilets. John was already in the kitchen, moving around quietly. Conditions were so much more crowded and public than they had been on the *Ares* that some of them were having trouble adjusting; every night Maya complained she couldn't sleep in such a crowd, but there she was, mouth open girlishly. She would be the last to rise, snoozing through the noise and bustle of the others' morning routines.

Then the sun would crack the horizon, and Nadia would be done with her cereal and milk, the milk made of powder mixed with water mined from the atmosphere (it tasted just the same); and it was time to get into her walker, and out to work.

The walkers were designed for the Martian surface, and were not pressurized like spacesuits, but were rather made of an elastic mesh, which held in the body at about the same pressure that the Terran atmosphere would have. This prevented the severe expansion bruising that would result if skin were exposed to Mars's minimal atmosphere, but it gave the wearer a lot more freedom of movement than a pressurized spacesuit would have. Walkers also had the very significant advantage of being fail-operational; only the hard helmet was airtight, so if you ripped a hole at knee or elbow you would have a badly bruised and frozen patch of skin, but would not suffocate and die within minutes.

Getting into a walker, however, was a workout in itself. Nadia wriggled the pants over her long underwear, then the jacket, and zipped the two sections of the suit together. After that she jammed into big thermal boots, and locked their toprings to the suit's ankle rings; pulled on gloves, and locked the wrist rings; put on a fairly standard hard helmet, and locked it to the suit's neck ring; then shouldered into an airtank backpack, and linked its air tubes to her helmet. She breathed hard a few times, tasting the cool oxygen-nitrogen in her face. The walker's wristpad indicated that all the seals were good; and she followed John and Samantha into the lock. They closed the inner door; the air was sucked back into containers; John unlocked the outer door. The three of them stepped outside.

It was a thrill every morning to step out onto that rocky plain, with the early morning sun casting long black shadows to the west, and the various small knolls and hollows revealed clearly. There was usually a wind from the south, and loose fines moved in a sinuous flow over the ground, so that the rocks sometimes seemed to creep. Even the strongest of these winds could scarcely be felt against an outstretched hand, but they hadn't yet experienced one of the storm winds; at five hundred kilometers per hour they were pretty sure to feel something. At twenty, nearly nothing.

Nadia and Samantha walked over to one of the little rovers they had uncrated and climbed in. Nadia drove the rover across the plain to a tractor they had found the day before about a kilometer to the west. The morning cold cut through her walker in a diamond pattern, as the result of the X weave of the heating filaments in the suit material. A strange sensation, but she had been colder in Siberia many a time and she had no complaints.

They came to the big lander and got out. Nadia picked up a drill with a Phillips screwdriver bit, and started dismantling the crate on top of the vehicle. The tractor inside the lander's crate was a Mercedes-Benz. She poked the drill into the head of a screw, pulled the trigger and watched the screw spin out. She moved to the next, grinning. Innumerable times in her youth she had gone out in cold like this, with numb white chopped-up hands, and fought titanic battles to unscrew frozen or stripped screws . . . but here it was *ziiip*, another one out. And really with the walker it was warmer than it had been in Siberia, and freer than in space, the walker no more restrictive than a thin stiff wetsuit. Red rocks were scattered all around in their uncanny regularity; voices chattered on the common band: "Hey, I found those solar panels!" "You think that's something, I just found the goddamn *nuclear reactor*." Yes, it was a great morning on Mars.

The stacked crate walls made a ramp to drive the tractor off the lander; they didn't look strong enough, but that was the gravity again. Nadia had turned on the tractor's heating system as soon as she could reach it, and now she climbed into the cab and tapped a command into its autopilot, feeling that it would be best to let the thing descend the ramp on its own, with her and Samantha watching from the side, just in case the ramp was more brittle in the cold than expected, or otherwise unreliable. She still found it almost impossible to think in terms of Martian g, to trust the designs that took it into account. The ramp just looked too flimsy!

But the tractor rolled down without incident, and stopped on the ground: eight meters long, royal blue, with wire mesh wheels taller than they were. They had to climb a short ladder into the cab. The crane prosthesis was already attached to the mount on the front end, and that made it easy to load the tractor with the winch, the sandbagger, the boxes of spare parts, and finally the crate walls. When they were done, the tractor looked as overloaded and topheavy as a steam calliope; but the g made it only a matter of balance. The tractor itself was a real pig, with six hundred horse-power, a wide wheelbase, and wheels big as tracks. The hydrazine motor had pick-up even worse than diesel, but it was like the ultimate first gear, completely inexorable. They took off and rolled slowly toward the trailer park – and there she was, Nadezhda Cherneshevsky, driving a Mercedes-Benz across Mars! She followed Samantha to the sorting lot, feeling like a queen.

And that was the morning. Back into the habitat, helmet and tank off, a quick bite in walker and boots. With all that running around they were famished.

After lunch they went back out in the Mercedes-Benz, and used it to haul a Boeing air miner to an area east of the habitats, where they were going to gather all the factories. The air miners were big metal cylinders, somewhat resembling 737 fuselages except that they had eight massive sets of landing gear, and rocket engines attached vertically to their sides, and two jet engines mounted above the fuselage fore and aft. Five of these miners had been dropped in the area some two years before. In the time since, their jet engines had been sucking in the thin air and ramming it through a sequence of separating mechanisms, to divide it into its component gases. The gases had been compressed and stored in big tanks, and were now available for use. So the Boeings each now held 5,000 liters of water ice, 3,000 liters of liquid oxygen, 3,000 liters of liquid nitrogen, 500 liters of argon, and 400 liters of carbon dioxide.

It was no easy task hauling these giants across the rubble to the big holding tanks near their habitats, but they needed to do it, because after they were drained into the holding tanks they could be turned on again. Just that afternoon another group had gotten one emptied out and turned back on, and the low hum of its jets could be heard everywhere, even in a helmet or a habitat.

Nadia and Samantha's miner was more stubborn; in the whole afternoon they only managed to haul it a hundred meters, and they had to use the bulldozer attachment to scrape a rough road for it all the way. Just before sunset they returned through the lock into the habitat, their hands cold and aching with fatigue. They stripped down to their dust-caked underwear and went straight to the kitchen, ravenous once more; Vlad estimated they were each burning about six thousand calories a day. They cooked and gulped down rehydrated pasta, nearly scalding their partially-thawed fingers on their trays. Only when they had finished eating did they go to the women's changing room and start trying to clean themselves up, sponging down with hot water, changing into clean jumpers. "It's going to be hard to keep our clothes clean, that dust even gets through the wristlocks, and the waist zippers are like open holes." "Well yeah, those fines are micron-sized! We're going to have worse trouble from it than dirty clothes, I can tell you that. It's going to be getting into *everything*, our lungs, our blood, our brains . . ."

"That's life on Mars." This was already a popular refrain, used whenever they encountered a problem, especially an intractable one.

On some days after dinner there were a couple hours of sunlight left, and Nadia, restless, would sometimes go back outside. Often she spent the time wandering around the crates that had been hauled to base that day, and over time she assembled a personal tool kit, feeling like a kid in a candy store. Years in the Siberian power industry had given her a reverence for good tools, she had suffered brutally from the lack of them. Everything in north Yakut had been built on permafrost, and the platforms sank unevenly in the summer, and were buried in ice in the winter, and parts for construction had come from all over the world, heavy machinery from Switzerland and Sweden, drills from America, reactors from the Ukraine, plus a lot of old scavenged Soviet stuff, some of it good, some indescribably shoddy, but all of it unmatched – some of it even built *in inches* – so that they had had to improvise constantly, building oil wells out of ice and string, knocking together nuclear reactors that made Chernobyl look like a Swiss watch. And every desperate day's work accomplished with a collection of tools that would have made a tinker weep.

Now she could wander in the dim ruby light of sunset, her old jazz collection piped from the habitat stereo into her helmet headphones, as she rooted in supply boxes and picked out any tool she wanted. She would carry them back to a small room she had commandeered in one of the storage warehouses, whistling along with King Oliver's Creole Jazz Band, adding to a collection that included, among other items, an Allen wrench set, some pliers, a power drill, several clamps, some hacksaws, an impact wrench set, a brace of cold-tolerant bungie cords, assorted files and rasps and planes, a crescent wrench set, a crimper, five hammers, some hemostats, three hydraulic jacks, a bellows, several sets of screwdrivers, drills and bits, a portable compressed gas cylinder, a box of plastic explosives and shape charges, a tape measure, a giant Swiss Army knife, tin snips, tongs, tweezers, three vises, a wirestripper, X-acto knives, a pick, a bunch of mallets, a nut driver set, hose clamps, a set of end mills, a set of jeweler's screwdrivers, a magnifying glass, all kinds of tape, a plumber's bob and ream, a sewing kit, scissors, sieves, a lathe, levels of all sizes, long nosed pliers, vise grip pliers, a tap and die set, three shovels, a compressor, a generator, a welding and cutting set, a wheelbarrow—

and so on. And this was just the mechanical equipment, her carpenter's tools. In other parts of the warehouse they were stockpiling research and lab equipment, geological tools, and any number of computers and radios and telescopes and videocameras; and the biosphere team had warehouses of equipment to set up the farm, the waste recyclers, the gas exchange mechanism, in essence their whole infrastructure; and the medical team had more warehouses of supplies for the clinic, and their research labs, and the genetic engineering facility. "You know what this is," Nadia said to Sax Russell one evening looking around her warehouse. "It is an *entire town*, disassembled and lying in pieces."

"And a very prosperous town at that."

"Yes, a university town. With first-rate departments in several sciences."

"But still in pieces."

"Yes. But I kind of like it that way."

Sunset was mandatory return-to-habitat time, and in the dusk she would stumble into the lock and inside, and eat another small cold meal sitting on her bed, listening to the talk around her which mostly concerned the day's work, and the arrangement of the tasks for the next morning. Frank and Maya were supposed to be doing this, but in fact it was happening spontaneously, in a kind of *ad hoc* barter system. Hiroko was particularly good at it, which was a surprise given how withdrawn she had been on the voyage out; but now that she needed help from outside her team, she spent most of every evening moving from person to person, so single-minded and persuasive that she usually had a sizeable crew working on the farm every morning. Nadia couldn't really see this; they had five years of dehydrated and canned food on hand, fare that suited Nadia fine, she had eaten worse for most of her life and she paid little attention to food anymore, she might as well have been eating hay, or refueling like one of the tractors. But they did need the farm for growing bamboo, which Nadia planned to use as a construction material in the permanent habitat that she hoped to start building soon. It all interlocked; all their tasks linked together, were necessary to each other. So when Hiroko plopped down beside her, she said, "Yeah, yeah, be there at eight. But you can't build the permanent farm until the base habitat itself is built. So really you ought to be helping me tomorrow, right?"

"No, no," Hiroko said, laughing. "Day after, okay?"

Hiroko's main competition for labor came from Sax Russell and his crowd, who were working to start all the factories. Vlad and Ursula and the biomed group were also hungry to get all their labs set up and running. These three teams seemed willing to live in the trailer park indefinitely, as long as their own projects were progressing; but luckily there were a lot of people who were not so obsessed by their work, people like Maya and John and the rest of the cosmonauts, who were interested in moving into larger and better-protected quarters as soon as possible. So Nadia's project would get help from them.

When she was done eating, Nadia took her tray into the kitchen and cleaned it with a little swab, then went over to sit by Ann Clayborne and Simon Frazier and the rest of the geologists. Ann looked nearly asleep; she was spending her mornings taking long rover trips and hikes, and then working hard on the base all afternoon, trying to make up for her trips away. To Nadia she seemed strangely tense, less happy about being on Mars than one would have thought. She appeared unwilling to work on the factories, or for Hiroko; indeed she usually came to work for Nadia, who, since she was only trying to build housing, could be said to be impacting the planet less than the more ambitious teams. Maybe that was it, maybe not; Ann wasn't saying. She was hard to know, moody – not in Maya's extravagant Russian manner, but more subtly, and, Nadia thought; in a darker register. In Bessie Smith land.

All around them people cleaned up after dinner and talked, and looked over manifests and talked, and bunched around computer terminals and talked, and washed clothes and talked; until most were stretched out on their beds, talking in lower voices, until they passed out. "It's like the first second of the universe," Sax Russell observed, rubbing his face wearily. "All crammed together and no differentiation. Just a bunch of hot particles rushing about."

And that was just one day; and that was what it was like every day, for day after day after day. No change in the weather to speak of, except occasionally a wisp of cloud, or an extra-windy afternoon. In the main, the days rolled by one like the next. Everything took longer than planned. Just getting into the walkers and out of the habitats was a chore, and then all the equipment had to be warmed; and even though it had been built to a uniform set of standards, the international nature of the equipment meant that there were inevitable mismatches of size and function; and the dust ("Don't call it dust!" Ann would complain. "That's like calling dust gravel! Call it fines, they're fines!") got into everything; and all the physical work in the penetrating cold was exhausting, so that they went slower than they thought they would and began to collect a number of minor injuries. And, finally, there was just an amazing number of things to do, some of which had never even occurred to them. It took them about a month, for instance (they had budgeted ten days) just to open all the freight loads, check their contents and move them into the appropriate stockpiles — to get to the point where they could really begin to work.

After that, they could begin to build in earnest. And here Nadia came into her own. She had had nothing to do on the *Ares*, it had been a kind of hibernation for her. But building things was her great talent, the nature of her genius, trained in the bitter school of Siberia; and very quickly she became the colony's chief troubleshooter, the universal solvent as John called her. Almost every job they had benefited from her help, and as she ran around every day answering questions and giving advice, she blossomed into a kind of timeless work heaven. So much to do! So much to do! Every night in the planning sessions Hiroko worked her wiles, and the farm went up: three

135

parallel rows of greenhouses, looking like commercial greenhouses back on Earth except smaller and very thick-walled, to keep them from exploding like party balloons. Even with interior pressures of only three hundred milli-bars, which was barely farmable, the differential with the outside was drastic; a bad seal or a weak spot, and they would go bang. But Nadia was good at cold weather seals, and so Hiroko was calling her in a panic every other day.

Then the materials scientists needed help getting their factories operational, and the crew assembling the nuclear reactor wanted her supervision for every breath that they took: they were petrified with fright that they would do something wrong, and were not reassured by Arkady send-ing radio messages down from Phobos insisting they did not need such a dangerous technology, that they could get all the power they needed from wind generation: he and Phyllis had bitter arguments about this. It was Hiroko who cut Arkady off, with what she said was a Japanese commonplace: "Shikata ga nai," meaning *there is no other choice*. Wind-mills might have generated enough power, as Arkady con-tended, but they didn't have windmills, while they had been supplied with a Rickover nuclear reactor, built by the US Navy and a beautiful piece of work; and no one wanted to try bootstrapping themselves into a wind-powered system: they were in too much of a hurry. *Shikata ga nai*. This too became one of their oft-repeated phrases.

And so every morning the construction crew for Cher-nobyl (Arkady's name, of course) begged Nadia to come out with them and supervise. They had been exiled far to the east of the settlement, so that it made sense to go out for a full day with them. But then the medical team wanted her help building a clinic and some labs inside, from some dis-carded freight crates that they were converting into shelters. So instead of staying out at Chernobyl she would go back midday to eat and then help the med team. Every night she passed out exhausted.

Some evenings before she did, she had long talks with Arkady, up on Phobos. His crew was having trouble with the moon's micro-gravity, and he wanted her advice as well. "If only we could get into some g just to live, to sleep!" Arkady said.

"Build train tracks in a ring around the surface," Nadia suggested out of a doze. "Make one of the tanks from the *Ares* into a train, and run it around the track. Get on board and run the train around fast enough to give you some g against the ceiling of the train."

Static, then Arkady's wild cackle. "Nadezhda Francine, I love you, I love you!"

"You love gravity."

With all this advisory work, the construction of their permanent habitat went slowly indeed. It was only once a week or so that Nadia could climb into the open cab of a Mercedes and rumble over the torn ground to the end of the trench she had started. At this point it was ten meters wide, fifty long, and four deep, which was as deep as she wanted to go. The bottom of the trench was the same as the surface: clay, fines, rocks of all size. Regolith. While she worked with the bulldozer the geologists hopped in and out of the hole, taking samples and looking around, even Ann who did not like the way they were ripping up the area; but no geologist ever born could keep away from a land cut. Nadia listened to their conversation band as she worked. They figured the regolith was probably much the same all the way down to bedrock, which was too bad; regolith was not Nadia's idea of good ground. At least its water content was low, less than a tenth of a percent, which meant they wouldn't get much slumping under a foundation, one of the constant nightmares of Siberian construction.

When she got the regolith cut right, she was going to lay a foundation of Portland cement, the best concrete they could make with the materials at hand. It would crack unless they poured it two meters thick, but *shikata ga nai*; and the thickness would provide some insulation. But she would have to box the mud and heat it to get it to cure; it wouldn't below 13° Centigrade, so that meant heating elements . . . Slow, slow, everything was slow.

She drove the dozer forward to lengthen the trench, and it bit the ground and bucked. Then the weight of the thing told, and the scoop cut through the regolith and plowed forward. "What a pig," Nadia said to the vehicle fondly.

"Nadia's in love with a bulldozer," Maya said over their band.

At least I know who I'm in love with, Nadia mouthed. She had spent too many of the evenings of the last week out in the tool shed with Maya, listening to her rattle away about her problems with John, about how she really got along in most ways better with Frank, about how she couldn't decide what she felt, and was sure Frank hated her now, etc. etc. etc. Cleaning tools Nadia had said *Da, da, da*, trying to hide her lack of interest. The truth was she was tired of Maya's problems and would rather have discussed building materials, or almost anything else.

A call from the Chernobyl crew interrupted her bulldozing. "Nadia, how can we get cement this thick to set in the cold?"

"Heat it."

"We are!"

"Heat it more."

"Oh!" They were almost done out there, Nadia judged: the Rickover had been mostly preassembled, it was a matter of putting the forms together, fitting in the steel containment tank, filling the pipes with water (which dropped their supply to nearly nothing), wiring it all up, piling sandbags around it all, and pulling the control rods. After that they would have three hundred kilowatts on hand, which would put an end to the nightly argument over who got the lion's share of generator power the next day.

There was a call from Sax: one of the Sabatier processors

138

had clogged, and they couldn't get the housing off it. So Nadia left the bulldozing to John and Maya, and took a rover to the factory complex to have a look. "I'm off to see the alchemists," she said.

"Have you ever noticed how much the machinery here reflects the character of the industry that built it?" Sax remarked to Nadia as she arrived and went to work on the Sabatier. "If it's built by car companies, it's low-powered but reliable. If it's built by the aerospace industry, it's outrageously high-powered but breaks down twice a day."

"And partnership products are horribly designed," Nadia said.

"Right."

"And chemical equipment is finicky," Spencer Jackson added.

"I'll say. Especially in this dust."

The Boeing air miners had been only the start of the factory complex; their gases were fed into big boxy trailers to be compressed and expanded and rendered and recombined using chemical engineering operations such as dehumidification, liquefaction, fractional distillation, electrolysis, electrosynthesis, the Sabatier process, the Raschig process, the Oswald process . . . Slowly they worked up more and more complex chemicals, which flowed from one factory to the next, through a warren of structures that looked like mobile homes caught in a web of color-coded tanks and pipes and tubes and cables.

Spencer's current favorite product was magnesium, which was plentiful; they were getting twenty-five kilos of it from every cubic meter of regolith, he said, and it was so light in Martian g that a big bar of it felt like a piece of plastic. "It's too brittle when pure," Spencer said, "but if we alloy it just a bit we'll have an *extremely* light and strong metal."

"Martian steel," Nadia said.

"Better than that."

So, alchemy; but with finicky machines. Nadia found the

Sabatier's problem and went to work fixing a broken vacuum pump. It was amazing how much of the factory complex came down to pumps, sometimes it seemed nothing but a mad assemblage of them; and by their nature they kept clogging with fines and breaking down.

Two hours later the Sabatier was fixed. On the way back to the trailer park, Nadia glanced into the first greenhouse. Plants were already blooming, the new crops breaking out of their beds of new black soil. Green glowed intensely in the reds of this world, it was a pleasure to see it. The bamboo was growing several centimeters a day, she had been told, and the crop was already nearly five meters tall. It was easy to see they were going to need more soil. Back at the alchemists' they were using nitrogen from the Boeings to synthesize ammonia fertilizers: Hiroko craved these because the regolith was an agricultural nightmare, intensely salty, explosive with peroxides, extremely arid, and completely without biomass. They were going to have to construct soil just like they had the magnesium bars.

Nadia went into her habitat in the trailer park for a standing lunch. Then she was out again, to the site of the permanent habitat. The floor of the trench had been almost leveled in her absence. She stood on the edge of the hole, looking down in it. They were going to build to a design that she liked tremendously, one she had worked on herself in Antarctica and on the *Ares*: a simple line of barrel-vaulted chambers, sharing adjacent walls. By setting them in the trench the chambers would be half-buried to begin with; then when completed they would be covered by ten meters of sandbagged regolith to stop radiation and also, because they planned to pressurize to 450 millibars to keep the buildings from exploding. Local materials were all they needed for the exteriors of these buildings: Portland cement and bricks were it, basically, with plastic liner in some places to insure the seal.

Unfortunately the brickmakers were having some trouble,

and they gave Nadia a call. Nadia's patience was running short, and she groaned. "We travel all the way to Mars and you can't make bricks?"

"It's not that we can't make bricks," said Gene. "It's just that I don't like them." The brickmaking factory mixed clays and sulphur extracted from the regolith, and this preparation was poured into brick molds and baked until the sulphur began to polymerize, and then as the bricks cooled they were compressed a bit in another part of the machine. The resulting blackish-red bricks had a tensile strength that was technically adequate for use in the barrel vaults, but Gene wasn't happy. "We don't want to be at minimum values for heavy roofs over our heads," he said. "What if we pile one sandbag too many on top of it, or if we get a little marsquake? I don't like it."

After some thought Nadia said, "Add nylon."

"What?"

"Go out and find the parachutes from the freight drops, and shred them real fine, and add them to the clay. That'll help their tensile strength."

"Very true," Gene said, after a pause. "Good idea! Think we can find the parachutes?"

"They must be east of here somewhere."

So they had finally found a job for the geologists that actually helped the construction effort. Ann and Simon and Phyllis and Sasha and Igor drove long-distance rovers over the horizon to east of the base, searching and surveying far past Chernobyl; and in the next week they found almost forty parachutes, each one representing a few hundred kilos of useful nylon.

One day they came back excited, having reached Ganges Catena, a series of sinkholes in the plain a hundred kilometers to the southeast. "It was strange," Igor said, "because you can't see them until the last minute, and then they're like huge funnels, about ten kilometers across and a couple deep, eight or nine in a row, each smaller and shallower.

Fantastic. They're probably thermokarsts, but they're so big it's hard to believe it."

Sasha said, "It's nice to see such a distance, after all this near horizon stuff."

"They're thermokarsts," Ann said. But they had drilled and found no water. This was getting to be a concern; they hadn't found any water to speak of in the ground, no matter how far down they drilled: it forced them to rely on the supplies from the air miners.

Nadia shrugged. The air miners were pretty tough. She wanted to think about her vaults. The new improved bricks were appearing and she had started the robots building the walls and roofs. The brick factory filled little robot cars, which rolled like toy rovers across the plain to cranes at the site; the cranes pulled out bricks one by one, and placed them on cold mortar spread by another set of robots. The system worked so well that soon the bottleneck became brick production itself. Nadia would have been pleased, if she had had more faith in the robots: these seemed okay, but her experiences with robots in the years on *Novy Mir* had made her wary. They were great if everything went perfectly, but nothing ever went perfectly, and it was hard to program them with decision algorithms that didn't either make them so cautious that they froze every minute, or so uncontrolled that they could commit unbelievable acts of stupidity, repeating an error a thousand times and magnifying a small glitch into a giant blunder, as in Maya's emotional life. You got what you put into robots; but even the best were mindless idiots.

One evening Maya snagged her out in her tool room and asked her to switch to a private band. "Michel is useless," she complained. "I'm really having a hard time, and he won't even talk to me! You're the only one I trust, Nadia. Yesterday I told Frank that I thought John was trying to undercut his authority in Houston, but that he shouldn't tell anyone

I thought so and the very next day John was asking me why I thought he was bothering Frank. There's no one who will just listen and stay quiet!"

Nadia nodded, rolling her eyes. Finally she said, "Sorry, Maya, I have to go talk to Hiroko about a leak they can't find." She banged her faceplate lightly against Maya's — symbol for a kiss on the cheek — switched to the common band and took off. Enough was enough. It was infinitely more interesting to talk to Hiroko: real conversations, about real problems in the real world. Hiroko was asking Nadia for help almost every day, and Nadia liked that, because Hiroko was brilliant, and since landfall had obviously raised her estimate of Nadia's abilities. Mutual professional respect, a great maker of friendships. And so nice to talk nothing but business. Hermetic seals, lock mechanisms, thermal engineering, glass polarization, farm/human interfaces (Hiroko's talk was always a few steps ahead of the game); these topics were a great relief after all the emotional whispered conferences with Maya, endless sessions about who liked Maya and who didn't like Maya, about how Maya felt about this and that, and who had hurt her feelings that day . . . bah. Hiroko was never strange, except when she would say something Nadia didn't know how to deal with, like, "Mars will tell us what it wants and then we'll have to do it." What could you say to something like that? But Hiroko would just smile her big smile, and laugh at Nadia's shrug.

At night the talk still went everywhere, vehement, absorbed, unselfconscious. Dmitri and Samantha were sure that they could soon introduce genetically engineered microorganisms into the regolith that would survive, but they would have to get permission first from the UN. Nadia herself found the idea alarming: it made the chemical engineering in the factories look relatively straightforward, more like brickmaking than the dangerous acts of creation Samantha was proposing . . . Although the alchemists were performing some pretty creative things themselves. Almost every day they came back to the trailer park with samples of new materials: sulphuric acid, sorel cements for the vault mortar, ammonium nitrate explosives, a calcium cyanamide rover fuel, polysulfide rubber, silicon-based hyperacids, emulsifying agents, a selection of test tubes holding trace elements extracted from the salts; and, most recently, clear glass. This last was a coup, as earlier attempts at glassmaking had produced only black glass. But stripping silicate feedstocks of their iron content had done the trick; and so one night they sat in the trailer passing around small wavy sheets of glass, the glass itself filled with bubbles and irregularities, like something out of the seventeenth century.

When they got the first chamber buried and pressurized, Nadia walked around inside it with her helmet off, sniffing the air. It was pressurized to 450 millibars, the same as the helmets and the trailer park, with an oxygen-nitrogen-argon mix, and warmed to about 15° Centigrade. It felt great.

The chamber had been divided into two stories by a floor of bamboo trunks, set in a slot in the brick wall two and a half meters overhead. The segmented cylinders made a sweet green ceiling, lit by neon tubes hung under them. Against one wall was a magnesium and bamboo staircase, leading through a hole to the upper story. She climbed up to have a look. Split bamboo over the trunks made a fairly flat green floor. The ceiling was brick, rounded and low. Up there they would locate the bedrooms and bathroom; the lower floor would be living room and kitchen. Maya and Simon had already put up wall hangings, made of nylon from the salvaged parachutes. There were no windows: lighting came only from the neon bulbs. Nadia disliked this fact, and in the larger habitat she was already planning, there would be windows in almost every room. But first things first. For the time being these windowless chambers were the best they could do. And a big improvement over the trailer park, after all.

As she went back down the stairs she ran her fingers over the bricks and mortar. They were rough, but warm to the touch, heated by elements placed behind them. There were heating elements under the floor as well. She took off her shoes and socks, luxuriating in the feel of the warm rough bricks underfoot. It was a wonderful room; and nice, too, to think that they had gone all the way to Mars, and there built homes out of brick and bamboo. She recalled vaulted ruins she had seen years ago on Crete, at a site called Aptera; underground Roman cisterns, barrel-vaulted and made of brick, buried in a hillside. They had been almost the same size as these chambers. Their exact purpose was unknown; storage for olive oil, some said, though it would have been an awful lot of oil. Those vaults were intact two thousand years after their construction, and in earthquake country. As Nadia put her boots back on she grinned to think of it. Two thousand years from now, their descendants might walk into this chamber, no doubt a museum by then, if it still existed – the first human dwelling built on Mars! And she had done it. Suddenly she felt the eyes of that future on her, and shivered. They were like Cro-Magnons in a cave, living a life that was certain to be pored over by the archeologists of subsequent generations; people like her who would wonder, and wonder, and never quite understand.

More time passed, more work got done. It blurred for Nadia: she was always busy. The interior construction of the vaulted chambers was complicated, and the robots couldn't help much: plumbing, heating, gas exchange, locks, kitchens; they had all the fixtures and tools and could work in pants and sweatshirts, but still it took an amazing amount of time. Work work work, day after day!

One evening, just before sunset, Nadia trudged across torn-up dirt to the trailer park, feeling hungry and beat and extremely relaxed, not that you didn't have to be careful at the end of a day: she had torn a centimeter hole in the back of a glove the other evening being careless, and the cold hadn't been so bad, about -50° Centigrade, nothing compared to some Siberian winter days — but the low air pressure had sucked out a blood bruise instantly, and then that had started to freeze up, which made the bruise smaller no doubt, but slower to heal as well. Anyway, you had to be careful, but there was something so fluid about tired muscles at the end of a day's construction work, the low rust sunlight slanting across the rocky plain, and all of a sudden she could feel that she was happy. Arkady called in from Phobos at just that moment, and she greeted him cheerily; "I feel just like a Louis Armstrong solo from 1947."

"Why 1947?" he asked.

"Well, that was the year he sounded the most happy. Most of his life his tone has a sharp edge to it, really beautiful, but in 1947 it was even more beautiful because it has this relaxed fluid joy, you never hear it in him before or after."

"A good year for him, I take it?"

"Oh yes! An amazing year! After twenty years of horrible big bands, you see, he got back to a little group like the Hot Five, that was the group he headed when he was young, and there it was, the old songs, even some of the old faces — and all of it better than the first time, you know, the recording technology, the money, the audiences, the band, his own power . . . It must have felt like the fountain of youth, I tell you."

"You'll have to send up some recordings," Arkady said. He tried to sing: "I can't give you any thing but love, baby!" Phobos was about over the horizon, he had just been calling to say hi. "So this is your 1947," he said before he went.

Nadia put her tools away, singing the song correctly. And she understood that what Arkady had said was true; something had happened to her similar to what had happened to Armstrong in 1947 — because despite the miserable conditions, her youthful years in Siberia had been the happiest of her life, they really had. And then she had endured twenty

146

years of big band cosmonautics, bureaucracy, simulations, an indoor life – all to get here. And now suddenly she was out in the open again, building things with her hands, operating heavy machinery, solving problems a hundred times a day, just like Siberia only better. It was just like Satchmo's return!

Thus when Hiroko came up and said, "Nadia, this crescent wrench is absolutely frozen in this position," Nadia sang to her, "That's the only thing I'm thinking of – baby!" and took the crescent wrench and slammed it against a table like a hammer, and twiddled the dial to show Hiroko it was unstuck, and laughed at her expression. "The engineer's solution," she explained, and went humming into the lock, thinking how funny Hiroko was, a woman who held their whole ecosystem in her head, but couldn't hammer a nail straight.

And that night she talked over the day's work with Sax, and spoke to Spencer about glass, and in the middle of that conversation crashed on her bunk and snuggled her head into her pillow, feeling totally luxurious, the glorious final chorus of "Ain't Misbehaving" chasing her off to sleep.

But things change as time passes; nothing lasts, not even stone, not even happiness. "Do you realize it's Ls 170 already?" Phyllis said one night. "Didn't we land at Ls 7?"

So they had been on Mars for half a Martian year. Phyllis was using the calendar devised by planetary scientists; among the colonists it was becoming more common than the Terran system. Mars's year was 668.6 local days long, and to tell where they were in this long year it took the Ls calendar. This system declared the line between the sun and Mars at its northern spring equinox to be O°, and then the year was divided into 360°, so that Ls = 0°–90° was the northern spring, 90–180° the northern summer, 180–270° the fall, and 270–360° (or 0° again) the winter.

This simple situation was complicated by the eccentricity of the Martian orbit, which is extreme by Terran standards, for at perihelion Mars is about forty-three million kilometers closer to the sun than it is at aphelion, and thus receiving about 45% more sunlight. This fluctuation makes the southern and northern seasons quite unequal. Perihelion arrives every year at Ls = 250°, late in the southern spring; so southern springs and summers are much hotter than northern springs and summers, with peak temperatures as much as thirty degrees higher. Southern autumns and winters are colder, however, occurring as they do near aphelion; so much colder that the southern polar cap is mostly carbon dioxide, while the northern one is mostly water ice.

So the south was the hemisphere of extremes, the north that of moderation. And the orbital eccentricity caused one other feature of note; planets move faster the closer they are to the sun, so the seasons near perihelion are shorter than those near aphelion; the northern autumn is 143 days long, for instance, while northern spring is 194. Spring fifty-one days longer than autumn! Some claimed this alone made it worth settling in the north.

In any case, in the north they were; and spring had arrived. The days got longer by a little bit every day and the work went on. The area around the base got more cluttered, more criss-crossed with tracks; they had laid a cement road to Chernobyl and the base itself was now so big that from the trailer park it extended over the horizon in all directions: the alchemists' quarter and the Chernobyl road to the east, the permanent habitat to the north, the storage area and the farm to the west, and the biomed center to the south.

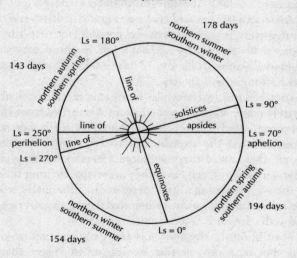

**The Martian Calendar
Year 1 (20278AD)**

669 total Martian days in 1 Martian year
24 months =
21 months at 28 days
3 months (every eighth) at 27 days

149

Eventually everyone moved into the finished chambers of the permanent habitat. The nightly conferences there were shorter and more routinized than they had been in the trailer park, and days went by when Nadia got no calls for help. There were some people she saw only once in a while; the biomed crew in its labs, Phyllis's prospecting unit, even Ann. One night Ann flopped on her bed next to Nadia's, and invited her to go along on an exploration to Hebes Chasma, some 130 kilometers to the southwest. Obviously Ann wanted to show her something outside the base area; but Nadia declined. "I've got too much work to do, you know." And seeing Ann's disappointment: "Maybe next trip."

And then it was back to work on the interiors of the chambers, and the exteriors of a new wing. Arkady had suggested making the line of chambers the first of four, arranged in a square, and Nadia was going to do it; as Arkady pointed out, it would then be possible to roof the area enclosed by the square. "That's where those magnesium beams will come in handy," Nadia said. "If only we could make stronger glass panes . . ."

They had finished two sides of the square, twelve chambers entirely done, when Ann and her team returned from Hebes. Everyone spent that evening looking at their videotapes. These showed the expedition's rovers rolling over rocky plains; then ahead there appeared a break extending all the way across the screen, as if they were approaching the edge of the world. Strange little meter-high cliffs finally stopped the rovers, and the pictures bounced as one explorer got out and walked with helmet camera turned on.

Then abruptly the shot was from the rim, a one-eighty pan shot of a canyon that was so much bigger than the sinkholes of Ganges Catena that it was hard to grasp. The walls of the far side of the chasm were just visible on the distant horizon. In fact they could see walls all the way around, for Hebes was an almost-enclosed chasm, a sunken ellipse about two hundred kilometers long and a hundred across. Ann's party had come to the north rim in late afternoon, and the eastern curve of the wall was clearly visible, flooded by sunset light; out to the west the wall was just a low dark mark. The floor of the chasm was generally flat, with a central dip. "If you could float a dome over the chasm," Ann said, "you'd have a nice big enclosure."

"You're talking miracle domes, Ann," Sax said. "That's about ten thousand square kilometers."

"Well, it would make a good big enclosure. And then you could leave the rest of the planet alone."

"The weight of a dome would collapse the canyon walls."

"That's why I said you'd have to float it."

Sax just shook his head.

"It's no more exotic than this space elevator you talk about."

"I want to live in a house located right where you took this video," Nadia interrupted. "What a view!"

"Just wait till you get up on one of the Tharsis volcanoes," Ann said, irritated. "Then you'll get a view."

There were little spats like that all the time now. It reminded Nadia unpleasantly of the last months on the *Ares*. Another example: Arkady and his crew sent down videos of Phobos, with his commentary: "The Stickney impact almost broke this rock in pieces, and it's chondritic, almost twenty percent water, so a lot of the water outgassed on impact and filled the fracture system and froze in a whole system of ice veins." Fascinating stuff, but all it did was cause an argument between Ann and Phyllis, their two top geologists, as to whether this was the real explanation for the ice. Phyllis even suggested shipping water down from Phobos, which was silly, even if their supplies were low and their demand increasing. Chernobyl took a lot of water, and the farmers were ready to start a little swamp in their biosphere; and Nadia wanted to install a swimming complex in one of the

151

vaulted chambers, including a lap pool, three whirlpool baths, and a sauna. Each night people asked Nadia how it was coming along, because everyone was sick of washing with sponges and still being dusty, and of never really getting warm. They wanted a bath; in their old aquatic dolphin brains, down below the cerebrums, down where desires were primal and fierce, they wanted back into water.

So they needed more water, but the seismic scans were finding no evidence of ice aquifers underground, and Ann thought there weren't any in the region. They had to continue to rely on the air miners, or scrape up regolith and load it into the soil-water distilleries. But Nadia didn't like to overwork the distilleries, because they had been manufactured by a French-Hungarian-Chinese consortium, and were sure to wear out if used for bulk work.

But that was life on Mars; it was a dry place. *Shikata ga nai.*

"There are always choices," Phyllis said to that. This was why she had suggested filling landing vehicles with Phobos ice, and bringing it on down; but Ann thought that was a ridiculous waste of energy; and they were off again.

It was especially irritating to Nadia because she herself was in such a good mood. She saw no reason to quarrel, and it disturbed her that the others didn't feel the same. Why did the dynamics of a group fluctuate so? Here they were on Mars, where the seasons were twice as long as Earth's, and every day was forty minutes longer: why couldn't people relax? Nadia had a sense that there was time for things even though she was always busy, and the extra thirty-nine and half minutes per day was probably the most important component of this feeling; human circadian biorhythms had been set over millions of years of evolution, and now suddenly to have extra minutes of day and night, day after day, night after night – no doubt it had effects. Nadia was sure of it, because despite the hectic pace of every day's work, and the way she passed out in sheer exhaustion every night, she always woke rested. That strange pause on the digital clocks, when at midnight the figures hit 12:00:00 and suddenly stopped, and the unmarked time passed, passed, passed, sometimes it seemed for a very long time indeed; and then snapped on to 12:00:01, and began its usual inexorable flicker; well, the Martian timeslip was something special. Often Nadia was asleep through it, as were most of the rest of them. But Hiroko had a chant that she chanted during it when she was up, and she and the farm team, and many of the rest of them, spent every Saturday night partying and chanting that chant through the timeslip — something in Japanese, Nadia never learned what, though she sometimes hummed along, sitting enjoying the vault and her friends.

But one Saturday night when she sat there, nearly comatose, Maya came over and sat against her shoulder for a talk. Maya with her beautiful face, always well-groomed, always the latest in *chicarnost* even in their everyday jumpsuits, looking distraught. ''Nadia, you have to do me a favor, please, please.''

''What?''

''I need you to tell something to Frank for me.''

''Why don't you do it yourself?''

''I can't have John seeing us talk! I have to get a message to him, and please, Nadezhda Francine, you're my only way.''

Nadia made a disgusted noise.

''*Please.*''

It was surprising how much Nadia would have rather been talking to Ann, or Samantha, or Arkady. If only Arkady would come down from Phobos!

But Maya was her friend. And that desperate look on her face: Nadia couldn't stand it. ''What message?''

''Tell him that I'll meet him tonight in the storage area,'' Maya said imperiously. ''At midnight. To talk.''

Nadia sighed. But later she went to Frank, and gave him the message. He nodded without meeting her eye, embarrassed, grim, unhappy.

Then a few days later Nadia and Maya were cleaning up the brick floor of the latest chamber to be pressurized, and Nadia's curiosity got the best of her; she broke her customary silence on the topic, and asked Maya what was going on. "Well, it's John and Frank," Maya said querulously. "They're very competitive. They're like brothers, and there's a lot of jealousy there. John got to Mars first, and then he got permission to come back again, and Frank doesn't think it was fair. Frank did a lot of the work in Washington to get the colony funded, and he thinks John has always taken advantage of his work. And now, well. John and I are good together, I like him. It's easy with him. Easy, but maybe a little . . . I don't know. Not boring. But not exciting. He likes to walk around, hang out with the farm crew. He doesn't like to talk that much! Frank, now, we could talk forever. Argue forever, maybe, but at least we're talking! And you know, we had a very brief affair on the *Ares*, back at the beginning, and it didn't work out, but he still thinks it could."

Why would he think that? Nadia mouthed.

"So he keeps trying to talk me into leaving John and being with him, and John suspects that's what he's doing, so there's a lot of jealousy between them. I'm just trying to keep them from each other's throats, that's all."

Nadia decided to stick to her resolve and not ask about it again. But now she was involved despite herself. Maya kept coming to her to talk, and to ask her to convey messages to Frank for her. "I'm not a go-between!" Nadia kept protesting, but she kept doing it, and once or twice when she did she got into long conversations with Frank, about Maya of course; who she was, what she was like, why she acted the way she did. "Look," Nadia said to him, "I can't speak for Maya. I don't know why she does what she does, you have

154

to ask her yourself. But I can tell you, she comes out of the old Moscow Soviet culture, university and CP for both her mother and her grandmother. And men were the enemies for Maya's babushka, and for her mother too, it was a *matrioshka*. Maya's mother used to say to her, 'Women are the roots, men are just the leaves.' There was a whole culture of mistrust, manipulation, fear. That's where Maya comes from. And at the same time we have this tradition of *amico-chonstvo*, a kind of intense friendship where you learn the very tiniest details of your friend's life, you invade each other's lives in a sense, and of course that's impossible and it has to end, usually badly.''

Frank was nodding at this description, recognizing something in it. Nadia sighed and went on. ''These are the friendships that lead to love, and then love has the same sort of trouble only magnified, especially with all that fear at the bottom of it.''

And Frank — tall, dark, and somehow handsome, bulky with power, spinning with his own internal dynamo, the American politician (or so Nadia thought of him), now wrapped around the finger of a neurotic Russian beauty — Frank nodded humbly, and thanked her, looking discouraged. As well he should.

Nadia did her best to ignore all that. But it seemed everything else had turned problematic as well. Vlad had never approved of how much time they were spending on the surface in the daytime, and now he said, ''We ought to stay under the hill most of the time, and bury all the labs as well. Outdoor work should be restricted to an hour in the early mornings and another in the late afternoons, when the sun is low.''

''I'll be damned if I stay indoors all day,'' Ann said, and many agreed with her.

''We've got a lot of work to do,'' Frank pointed out.

''But most of it could be done by teleoperation,'' Vlad said.

"And it should be. What we are doing is the equivalent of standing ten kilometers from an atomic explosion—"

"So?" Ann said. "Soldiers did that—"

"—every six months," Vlad finished, and stared at her. "Would you do that?"

Even Ann looked subdued. No ozone layer, no magnetic field to speak of; they were getting fried by radiation almost as badly as if they were in interplanetary space, to the tune of ten rems per year.

And so Frank and Maya ordered them to ration their time outdoors. There was a lot of interior work to be done under the hill, getting the last row of chambers finished; and it was possible to dig some cellars below the vaults, giving them some more space protected from radiation. And many of the tractors were equipped to be teleoperated from indoor stations, their decision algorithms handling the details while the human operators watched screens below. So it could be done; but no one liked the life that resulted. Even Sax Russell, who was content to work indoors most of the time, looked a bit perplexed. In the evenings a number of people began to argue for immediate terraforming efforts, and they made the case with renewed intensity.

"That's not our decision to make," Frank told them sharply. "The UN decides that one. Besides it's a long-term solution, on the scale of centuries at best. Don't waste time talking about it!"

Ann said, "That's all true, but I don't want to waste my time down here in these caves, either. We should live our lives the way we want. We're too old to worry about radiation."

Arguments again, arguments that made Nadia feel as if she had floated off the good solid rock of her planet back into the tense weightless reality of the *Ares*. Carping, complaining, arguing; until people got bored, or tired, and went to sleep. Nadia started leaving the room whenever it began, looking for Hiroko and a chance to discuss something

156

concrete. But it was hard to avoid these matters, to stop thinking about them.

Then one night Maya came to her crying. There was room in the permanent habitat for private talks, and Nadia went with her down to the northeast corner of the vaults, where they were still working on interiors, and sat by her arm to arm, shivering and listening to her, and occasionally putting an arm over her shoulder and giving her a hug. "Look," Nadia said at one point, "why don't you just decide? Why don't you quit playing one off against the other?"

"But I have decided! It's John I love, it's always been John. But now he's seen me with Frank and he thinks I've betrayed him. It's really petty of him! They're like brothers, they compete in everything, and this time it's just a mistake!"

Nadia resisted learning the details, she didn't want to hear it. She sat there listening anyway.

And then John was standing there before them. Nadia got up to leave, but he didn't appear to notice. "Look," he said to Maya. "I'm sorry, but I can't help it. It's over."

"It's not over," Maya said, instantly composed. "I love you."

John's smile was rueful. "Yes. And I love you. But I want things simple."

"It is simple!"

"No it isn't. I mean, you can be in love with more than one person at the same time. Anyone can, that's just the way it is. But you can only be loyal to one. And I want . . . I want to be loyal. To someone who is loyal to me. It's simple, but . . ."

He shook his head; he couldn't find the phrase. He walked back into the eastern row of chambers, disappeared through a door.

"Americans," Maya said viciously. "Fucking children!" Then she was up through the door after him.

But soon she came back. He had retreated to a group in one of the lounges, and wouldn't leave. "I'm tired," Nadia tried to say, but Maya wouldn't hear it, she was getting more and more upset. For over an hour they discussed it, over and over. Eventually Nadia agreed to go to John and ask him to come to Maya and talk it over. Nadia walked grimly through the chambers, oblivious to the brick and the colorful nylon hangings. The go-between that nobody noticed. Couldn't they get robots to do this? She found John, who apologized for ignoring her earlier. "I was upset, I'm sorry. I figured you'd hear it all eventually anyway."

Nadia shrugged. "No problem. But look, you have to go talk to her. That's the way it is with Maya. We talk, talk, talk; if you contract to be in a relationship, you have to talk your way all the way through it, and all the way out of it. If you don't it will be worse for you in the long run, believe me."

That got to him. Sobered, he went off to find her. Nadia went to bed.

The next day she was out working late on a trencher. It was the third job of the day, and the second had been trouble: Samantha had tried to carry a load on the earthmover blade while making a turn, and the thing had taken a nosedive and twisted the rods of the blade lifters out of their casings, spilling hydraulic fluid over the ground, where it had frozen before it even flattened out. They had had to set jacks under the airborne back end of the tractor, and then de-couple the entire blade attachment and lower the vehicle on the jacks, and every step of the operation had been a pain.

Then as soon as that was finished, Nadia had been called over to help with a Sandvik Tubex boring machine, which they were using to drill cased holes through large boulders they ran into while laying a water line from the alchemists' to the permanent habitat. The down-the-hole pneumatic hammer had apparently frozen at full extension, as stuck as an arrow fired most of the way through a tree. Nadia stood looking down at the hammer shaft. "Do you have any suggestions for freeing the hammer without breaking it?" Spencer asked.

"Break the boulder," Nadia said wearily, and walked over and got in a tractor with a backhoe already attached. She drove it over, and dug down to the top of the boulder, and then got out to attach a little Allied hydraulic impact hammer to the backhoe. She had just set it in position on the top of the boulder when the down-the-hole hammer suddenly jerked its drill back, pulling the boulder with it and catching the outside of her left hand against the underside of the Allied Hy-Ram.

Instinctively she pulled back, and pain lanced up her arm and into her chest. Fire filled that side of her body and her vision went white. There were shouts in her ears: "What's wrong? What happened?" She must have screamed. "Help," she grated. She was sitting, her crushed hand still pinned between rock and hammer. She pushed at the front wheel of the tractor with her foot, shoved with all her might and felt the hammer rasp her bones over rock. Then she was flopped on her back, the hand free. The pain was blinding, she felt sick to her stomach and thought she might faint. Pushing onto her knees with her good hand, she saw that the crushed hand was bleeding heavily, the glove ripped apart, the little finger apparently gone. She groaned and hunched over it, pressed it to her and then jammed it against the ground, ignoring the flash of pain. Even bleeding as it was, the hand would freeze in . . . how long? "Freeze, damn you, freeze," she cried. She shook tears out of her eyes and forced herself to look at it. Blood all over, steaming. She pushed the hand into the ground as hard as she could stand. Already it hurt less. Soon it would be numb, she would have to be careful not to freeze the whole hand! Frightened, she prepared to pull it back into her lap; then people were there, lifting her, and she fainted.

*

After that she was maimed. Nadia Nine Fingers, Arkady called her over the phone. He sent her lines by Yevtushenko, written to mourn the death of Louis Armstrong: "Do as you did in the past/And play."

"How did you find that?" Nadia asked him. "I can't imagine you reading Yevtushenko."

"Of course I read him, it's better than McGonagall! No, this was in a book on Armstrong. I've taken your advice and been listening to him while we work, and lately reading some books on him at night."

"I wish you'd come down here," Nadia said.

Vlad had done the surgery. He told her it would be all right. "It caught you clean. The ring finger is a bit impaired, and will act like the little finger used to, probably. But ring fingers never do much anyway. The two main fingers will be strong as ever."

Everyone came by to visit. Nevertheless she spoke more with Arkady than anyone else, in the hours of the night when she was alone, in the four and a half hours between Phobos's rising in the west and its setting in the east. He called in almost every night, at first, and often thereafter.

Pretty soon she was up and around, hand in a cast that was suspiciously slender. She went out to troubleshoot or consult, hoping to keep her mind occupied. Michel Duval never came by at all, which she thought was strange. Wasn't this what psychologists were for? She couldn't help feeling depressed: she needed her hands for her work, she was a hand laborer. The cast got in the way and she cut off the part around the wrist, with shears from her tool kit. But she had to keep both hand and cast in a box when outside, and there wasn't much she could do. It really was depressing.

Saturday night arrived, and she sat in the newly filled whirlpool bath, nursing a glass of bad wine and looking around at her companions, splashing and soaking in their bathing suits. She wasn't the only one to have been injured, by any means; they were all a bit battered now, after so many months of physical work: almost everyone had frostburn marks, patches of black skin that eventually peeled, leaving pink new skin, garish and ugly in the heat of the pools. And several others wore casts, on hands, wrists, arms, even legs; all for breaks or sprains. Actually they were lucky no one had gotten killed yet.

All these bodies, and none for her. They knew each other like family, she thought; they were each other's physicians, they slept in the same rooms, dressed in the same locks, bathed together; an unremarkable group of human animals, eyecatching in the inert world they occupied, but more comforting than exciting, at least most of the time. Middle-aged bodies. Nadia herself was as round as a pumpkin, a plump tough muscular short woman, squarish and yet rounded. And single. Her closest friend these days was only a voice in her ear, a face on the screen. When he came down from Phobos . . . well, hard to say. He had had a lot of girlfriends on the *Ares*, and Janet Blyleven had gone to Phobos to be with him . . .

People were arguing again, there in the shallows of the lap pool. Ann, tall and angular, leaning down to snap something at Sax Russell, short and soft. As usual, he didn't appear to be listening. She would hit him one day if he didn't watch out. It was strange how the group was changing again, how the feel of it was changing. She could never get a fix on it; the real nature of the group was a thing apart, with a life of its own, somehow distinct from the characters of the individuals that constituted it. It must make Michel's job as their shrink almost impossible. Not that one could tell with Michel; he was the quietest and most unobtrusive psychiatrist she had ever met. No doubt an asset, in this crowd of shrink-atheists. But she still thought it was odd he hadn't come by to see her after the accident.

One evening she left the dining chambers and walked down to the tunnel they were digging from the vaulted chambers

161

to the farm complex, and there at the tunnel's end were Maya and Frank, arguing in a vicious undertone that carried down the tunnel not their meaning but their feeling: Frank's face was contorted with anger, and Maya as she turned from him was distraught, weeping; she turned back to shout at him, "It was *never* like that," and then ran blindly toward Nadia, her mouth twisted into a snarl, Frank's face a mask of pain. Maya saw Nadia standing there and ran right by her.

Shocked, Nadia turned and walked back to the living chambers. She went up magnesium stairs to the living room in chamber two, and turned on the TV to watch a twenty-four hour news program from Earth, something she very rarely did. After a while she turned down the sound, and looked at the pattern of bricks in the barrel vault overhead. Maya came in and started to explain things to her: there was nothing between her and Frank, it was in Frank's mind only, he just wouldn't give up on it even though it had been nothing to begin with; she wanted only John, and it wasn't her fault that John and Frank were on such bad terms now, it was because of Frank's irrational desire, it wasn't her fault, but she felt so guilty because the two men had once been such close friends, like brothers.

And Nadia listened with a careful show of patience, saying "*Da, da,*" and "I see," and the like, until Maya was lying flat on her back on the floor, crying, and Nadia was sitting on the edge of a chair staring at her, wondering how much of it was true. And what the argument had really been about. And whether she was a bad friend to distrust her old companion's story so completely. But somehow the whole thing felt like Maya covering her tracks, practising another manipulation. It was just this: those two distraught faces she had seen down the tunnel had been the clearest evidence possible of a fight between intimates. So Maya's explanation was almost certainly a lie. Nadia said something soothing to her and went off to bed, thinking, you already have taken too much of my time and energy and concentration with these games, you cost me a finger with them, you bitch!

It was getting toward the end of the long northern spring, and they still had no good supply of water, so Ann proposed to make an expedition to the cap and set up a robot distillery, along the way establishing a route that rovers could follow on automatic pilot. "Come with us," she said to Nadia. "You haven't seen anything of the planet yet, just the stretch between here and Chernobyl, and that's nothing. You missed Hebes and Ganges, and you're not doing anything new here. Really, Nadia, I can't believe what a grub you've been. I mean why did you come to Mars, after all?"

"Why?"

"Yes, *why*? I mean there's two kinds of activities here, there's the exploration of Mars and then there's the life support for that exploration. And here you've been completely immersed in the life support, without paying the slightest attention to the reason we came in the first place!"

"Well, it's what I like to do," Nadia said uneasily.

"Fine, but try to keep some perspective on it! What the hell, you could have stayed back on Earth and been a plumber! You didn't have to come all this way to drive a goddamn *bulldozer*! Just how long are you going to go on grubbing away here, installing *toilets*, programming *tractors*?"

"All right, all right," Nadia said, thinking of Maya and all the rest. The square of vaults was almost finished, anyway. "I could use a vacation."

They took off in three big long-range rovers: Nadia and five of the geologists, Ann, Simon Frazier, George Berkovic, Phyllis Boyle and Edvard Perrin. George and Edvard were friends of Phyllis's from their NASA days, and they supported her in advocating "applied geological studies", meaning prospecting for rare metals; Simon on the other hand was a quiet ally of Ann's, committed to pure research and a hands-off attitude. Nadia knew all this even though she had spent very little time alone with any of these people, except for Ann. But talk was talk; she could have named all the allegiances of everyone at base if she had to.

The expedition rovers were each composed of two four-wheeled modules, coupled by a flexible frame: they looked a bit like giant ants. They had been built by Rolls-Royce and a multinational aerospace consortium, and had a beautiful sea green finish. The forward modules contained the living quarters and had tinted windows on all four sides; the aft modules contained the fuel tanks, and sported a number of black rotating solar panels. The eight wire mesh wheels were 2.5 meters high, and very broad.

As they headed north across Lunae Planum they marked their route with little green transponders, dropping one every few kilometers. They also cleared rocks from their path that might disable a robot-driven rover, using the snowplow attachment or the little crane at the front end of the first rover. So in effect they were building a road. But they seldom had to use the rockmoving equipment on Lunae; they drove northeast at nearly their full speed of thirty kilometers an hour for several days straight. They were heading northeast, to avoid the canyon systems of Tempe and Mareotis, and this route took them down Lunae to the long slope of Chryse Planitia. Both these regions looked much like the land around their base camp, bumpy and strewn with small rocks; but because they were heading downhill they often had much longer views than they were used to. It was a new pleasure to Nadia, to drive on and on and see new country-side continually pop over the horizon: hillocks, dips, enor-mous isolated boulders, the occasional low round mesa that was the outside of a crater.

When they had descended to the lowlands of the northern hemisphere, they turned and drove straight north across the immense Acidalia Planitia, and again ran straight for several days. Their wheel tracks stretched behind them like the first cut of a lawnmower through grass, and the transponders gleamed bright and incongruous among the rocks. Phyllis, Edvard and George talked about making a few side trips, to investigate some indications seen in satellite photos that there were unusual mineral outcroppings near Perepelkin Crater. Ann reminded them irritably of their mission. It made Nadia sad to see that Ann was nearly as distant and tense out here as she was back at base; whenever the rovers were stopped she was outside walking around alone, and she was withdrawn when they sat together in Rover One to eat dinner. Occasionally Nadia tried to draw her out: "Ann, how did all these rocks get scattered around like this?"

"Meteors."

"But where are the craters?"

"Most are in the south."

"But how did the rocks get here, then?"

"They flew. That's why they're so small. It's only smaller rocks could be tossed so far."

"But I thought you told me that these northern plains were relatively new, while the heavy cratering was relatively old."

"That's right. The rocks you see here come from late meteor action. The total accumulation of loose rock from meteor strikes is much greater than what we can see, that's what gardened regolith is. And the regolith is a kilo-meter deep."

"It's hard to believe," Nadia said. "I mean, that's so many meteors."

Ann nodded. "It's billions of years. That's the difference between here and Earth, the age of the land goes from millions of years to billions. It's such a big difference it's hard to imagine. But seeing stuff like this can help."

Midway across Acidalia they began running into long, straight, steep-walled, flat-bottomed canyons. They looked, as George noted more than once, like the dry beds of the legendary canals. The geological name for them was *fossae*, and they came in clusters. Even the smallest of these canyons were impassable to rovers, and when they came on one they had to turn and run along its rim, until its floors rose or its walls drew together, and they could continue north over flat plain again.

The horizon ahead was sometimes twenty kilometers off, sometimes three. Craters became rare, and the ones they passed were surrounded by low mounds that rayed out from the rims: splosh craters, where meteors had landed in permafrost that had turned to hot mud in the impact. Nadia's companions spent a day wandering eagerly over the splayed hills around one of these craters; the rounded slopes, Phyllis said, indicated ancient water as clearly as the grain in petrified wood indicated the original tree. By the way she spoke Nadia understood that this was another of her disagreements with Ann; Phyllis believed in the long wet past model, Ann in the short wet past. Or something like that. Science was many things, Nadia thought, including a weapon with which to hit other scientists.

Further north, around latitude 54°, they drove into the weird-looking land of thermokarsts, hummocky terrain spotted by a great number of steep-sided oval pits, called *alases*. These alases were a hundred times bigger than their Terran analogues, most of them two or three kilometers across, and about sixty meters deep. A sure sign of permafrost, the geologists all agreed; seasonal freezing and thawing of the

166

soil caused it to slump in this pattern. Pits this big indicated that water content in the soil must have been high, Phyllis said. Unless it was yet another manifestation of Martian time scales, Ann replied. Slightly icy soil, slumping ever so slightly, for eons.

Irritably Phyllis suggested that they try collecting water from the ground, and irritably Ann agreed. They found a smooth slope between depressions, and stopped to install a permafrost water collector. Nadia took charge of the operation with a feeling of relief; the trip's lack of work had begun to get to her. It was a good day's job: she dug a ten-meter long trench with the lead rover's little backhoe; laid the lateral collector gallery, a perforated stainless steel pipe filled with gravel; checked the electric heating elements running in strips along the pipe and filters; then filled in the trench with the clay and rocks they had dug out earlier.

Over the lower end of the gallery was a sump and pump, and an insulated transport line leading to a small holding tank. Batteries would power the heating elements, and solar panels charge the batteries. When the holding tank was full, if there was enough water to fill it, the pump would shut off and a solenoid valve would open, allowing the water in the transport line to drain back into the gallery, after which the heating elements would shut off as well.

"Almost done," Nadia declared late in the day, as she started to bolt the transport pipe onto the last magnesium post. Her hands were dangerously cold, and her maimed hand throbbed. "Maybe someone could start dinner," she said. "I'm almost done here." The transport pipe had to be packed in a thick cylinder of white polyurethane foam, then fitted into a larger protective pipe. Amazing how much insulation complicated a simple piece of plumbing.

Hex nut, washer, cotter pin, a firm tug on the wrench. Nadia walked along the line, checking the coupling bands at the joints. Everything firm. She lugged her tools over to Rover One, looked back at the result of the day's work: a tank, a short pipe on posts, a box on the ground, a long low mound of disturbed soil running uphill, looking raw but otherwise not unusual in this land of lumps. "We'll drink some fresh water on our way back," she said.

They had driven north for over two thousand kilometers, and finally rolled down onto Vastitas Borealis, an ancient cratered lava plain that ringed the northern hemisphere between latitudes 60° and 70°. Ann and the other geologists spent a couple of hours every morning out on the bare dark rock of this plain, taking samples, after which they would drive north for the rest of the day, discussing what they had found. Ann seemed more absorbed in the work, happier. One evening Simon pointed out that Phobos was running just over the low hills to the south; the next day's drive would put it under the horizon. It was a remarkable demonstration of just how low the little moon's orbit was; they were only at latitude 69°! But Phobos was only some five thousand kilometers above the planet's equator. Nadia waved goodbye to it with a smile; she would still be able to talk to Arkady using the newly arrived areosynchronous radio satellites.

Three days later the bare rock ended, running under waves of blackish sand. It was just like coming on the shore of a sea. They had reached the great northern dunes, which wrapped the world in a band between Vastitas and the polar cap; where they were going to cross, the band was about eight hundred kilometers wide. The sand was a charcoal color, tinged with purple and rose, a rich relief to the eye after all the red rubble of the south. The dunes trended north and south, in parallel crests that occasionally broke or merged. Driving over them was easy; the sand was hard-packed, and they only had to pick a big dune and run along its humpbacked western side.

After a few days of this, however, the dunes got bigger, and became what Ann called barchan dunes. These looked

168

like huge frozen waves, with faces a hundred meters tall and backs a kilometer wide; and the crescent that each wave made was several kilometers long. As with so many other Martian landscape features, they were a hundred times larger than their Terran analogs in the Sahara and Gobi. The expedition kept a level course over the backs of these great waves by contouring from one wave back to the next, their rovers like tiny boats, paddlewheeling over a sea that had frozen at the height of a titanic storm.

One day on this petrified sea, Rover Two stopped. A red light on the control panel indicated the problem was in the flexible frame between the modules; and in fact the rear module was tilted to the left, shoving the left side wheels into the sand. Nadia got into a suit and went back to have a look. She took the dust cover off the joint where the frame connected to the module chassis, and found that the bolts holding them together were all broken.

"This is going to take a while," Nadia said. "You guys might as well have another look around."

Soon the suited figures of Phyllis and George emerged, followed by Simon and Ann and Edvard. Phyllis and George took a transponder from Rover Three and set it out three meters to the right of their "road". Nadia went to work on the broken frame, handling things as little as possible: it was a cold afternoon, perhaps seventy below, and she could feel the diamond chill right down to the bone.

The ends of the bolts wouldn't come out of the side of the module, so she got out a drill and started drilling new holes. She began to hum "The Sheik of Araby". Ann and Edvard and Simon were discussing sand. It was so nice, Nadia thought, to see ground that wasn't red. To hear Ann absorbed in her work. To have some work to do herself.

They had almost reached the arctic circle, and it was Ls = 84, with the northern summer solstice only two weeks away; so the days were getting long. Nadia and George worked through the evening while Phyllis heated supper, and then after the meal Nadia went back out to finish the job. The sun was red in a brown haze, small and round even though it was near setting; there wasn't enough atmosphere for oblation to enlarge and flatten it. Nadia finished, put her tools away, and had opened the outer lock door of Rover One, when Ann's voice spoke in her ear. "Oh Nadia, are you going in already?"

Nadia looked up. Ann was on the ridge of the dune to the west, waving down at her, a black silhouette against a blood-colored sky.

"That was the idea," Nadia said.

"Come on up here just a second. I want you to see this sunset, it's going to be a good one. Come on, it'll only take a minute, you'll be glad you did it. There are clouds to the west."

Nadia sighed and closed the outer lock door.

The east face of the dune was steep. Nadia carefully stepped in the prints Ann had made in her ascent. The sand there was packed and held firm most of the time. Near the crest it got steeper, and she leaned forward and dug in with her fingers. Then she was clambering onto the broad rounded crest, and could straighten up and have a look around.

Only the crests of the tallest dunes were still in sunlight; the world was a black surface, marred by short scimitar curves of steely gray. Horizon about five kilometers off. Ann was crouching, a scoop of sand in her palm.

"What's it made of?" Nadia asked.

"Dark solid mineral particles."

Nadia snorted. "I could have told you that."

"Not before we got here you couldn't. It might have been fines aggregated with salts. But it's bits of rock instead."

"Why so dark?"

"Volcanic. On Earth sand is mostly quartz, you see, because there's a lot of granite there. But Mars doesn't have much granite. These grains are probably volcanic silicates. Obsidian, flint, some garnet. Beautiful, isn't it?"

She held out a handful of sand for Nadia's inspection. Perfectly serious of course. Nadia peered through her faceplate at the black grit. "Beautiful," she said.

They stood and watched the sun set. Their shadows went right out to the eastern horizon. The sky was a dark red, murky and opaque, only slighty lighter in the west over the sun. The clouds Ann had mentioned were bright yellow streaks, very high in the sky. Something in the sand caught at the light, and the dunes were distinctly purplish. The sun was a little gold button, and above it shone two evening stars: Venus, and the Earth.

"They've been getting closer every night lately," Ann said softly. "The conjunction should be really brilliant."

The sun touched the horizon, and the dune crests faded to shadow. The little button sun sank under the black line to the west. Now the sky was a maroon dome, the high clouds the pink of moss campion. Stars were popping out everywhere, and the maroon sky shifted to a vivid dark violet, an electric color that was picked up by the dune crests, so that it seemed crescents of liquid twilight lay across the black plain. Suddenly Nadia felt a breeze swirl through her nervous system, running up her spine and out into her skin; her cheeks tingled, and she could feel her spinal cord thrum. Beauty could make you shiver! It was a shock to feel such a physical response to beauty, a thrill like some kind of sex. And this beauty was so strange, so *alien*. Nadia had never seen it properly before, or never really felt it, she realized that now; she had been enjoying her life as if it were a Siberia made right, living in a huge analogy, understanding everything in terms of her past. But now she stood under a tall violet sky on the surface of a petrified black ocean, all new, all strange: it was absolutely impossible to compare it to anything she had seen before; and all of a sudden the past sheered away in her mind and she turned in circles like a little girl trying to make herself dizzy, without a thought in her head. Weight seeped inward from her skin, and she didn't feel hollow anymore; on the contrary she felt extremely solid, compact, balanced. A little thinking boulder, set spinning like a top.

They glissaded down the steep face of the dune on their boot heels. At the bottom Nadia gave Ann an impulsive hug: "Oh Ann, I don't know how to thank you for that." Even through the tinted faceplates she could see Ann grin. A rare sight.

After that things looked different to Nadia. Oh she knew it was in herself, that it was a matter of paying attention in a new way, of *looking*. But the landscape conspired in this sensation, feeding her new attentiveness; because the very next day they left the black dunes, and drove on to what her companions called layered or laminate terrain. This was the region of flat sand that in winter would lie under the CO_2 skirt of the polar cap. Now in midsummer it lay revealed, a landscape made entirely of curvilinear patterns. They drove up broad flat washes of yellow sand that were bounded by long sinuous flat-topped plateaus; the sides of the plateaus were stepped and benched, laminated both finely and grossly, looking like wood that had been cut and polished to show a handsome grain. None of them had ever seen any land remotely like it, and they spent the mornings taking samples and borings, and hiking around in a loping Martian ballet, talking a blue streak, Nadia as excited as any of them. Ann explained to her that each winter's frost caught a lamina on the surface. Then wind erosion had cut arroyos, and stripped away at their sides, and each stratum was stripped back farther than the one below it, so that the arroyo walls consisted of hundreds of narrow terraces. "It's like the land is a contour map of itself," Simon said.

They drove during the days and went out every evening in purply dusks that lasted until just before midnight. They drilled borings, and came up with cores that were gritty and icy, laminated for as far down as they could drill. One

172

evening Nadia was climbing with Ann up a series of parallel terraces, half-listening to her explain about the precession of aphelion and perihelion, when she looked back across the arroyo and saw that it was glowing like lemons and apricots in the evening light, and that above the arroyo were pale green lenticular clouds, mimicking perfectly the terrain's French curves. "Look!" she exclaimed.

Ann looked back and saw it, and was still. They watched the low banded clouds float overhead.

Finally a dinner call from the rovers brought them back. And walking down over the contoured terraces of sand, Nadia *knew* that she had changed – that, or else the planet was getting much more strange and beautiful as they traveled north. Or both.

They rolled over flat terraces of yellow sand, sand so fine and hard and clear of rocks that they could go at full speed, slowing down only to shift up or down from one bench to another. Occasionally the rounded slope between terraces gave them some trouble, and once or twice they even had to backtrack to find a way. But usually a route north could be found without difficulty.

On their fourth day in the laminate terrain, the plateau walls flanking their flat wash curved together, and they drove up the cleavage onto a higher plane; and there before them on the new horizon was a white hill, a great rounded thing, like a white Ayer's Rock. A white hill – it was ice! A hill of ice, a hundred meters high and a kilometer wide – and when they drove around it, they saw that it continued over the horizon to the north. It was the tip of a glacier, perhaps a tongue of the polar cap itself. In the other cars they were shouting, and in the noise and confusion Nadia could only hear Phyllis, crying "Water! Water!"

Water indeed. Though they had known it was going to be there, it was still startling in the extreme to run into a whole great white hill of it, in fact the tallest hill they had seen in the entire five thousand kilometers of their voyage. It took them all that first day to get used to it: they stopped the rovers, pointed, chattered, got out to have a look, took surface samples and borings, touched it, climbed up it a ways. Like the sand around it, the ice hill was horizontally laminated, with lines of dust about a centimeter apart. Between the lines the ice was pocked and granular; in this atmospheric pressure it sublimed at almost all temperatures, leaving pitted, rotten side walls to a depth of a few centimeters; under that it was solid, and hard.

"This is a *lot* of water," they all said at one point or another. Water, on the surface of Mars . . .

The next day the glacier hill formed their right horizon, a wall that ran on beside them for the whole day's drive. Then it really began to seem like a lot of water, especially as over the course of the day the wall got taller, rising to a height of about three hundred meters. A kind of white mountain ridge, in fact, walling off their flat-bottomed valley on its east side. And then, over the horizon to the northwest, there appeared another white hill, the top of another ridge poking over the horizon, the base remaining beneath it. Another glacier hill, walling them in to the west, some thirty kilometers away.

So they were in Chasma Borealis, a wind-carved valley that cut north into the ice cap for some five hundred kilometers, more than half the distance to the Pole. The chasm's floor was flat sand, hard as concrete, and often crunchy with a layer of CO_2 frost. The chasm's ice walls were tall, but not vertical; they lay back at an angle less than 45°, and like the hillsides in the laminate terrain, they were terraced, the terraces ragged with wind erosion and sublimation, the two forces that over tens of thousands of years had cut the whole length of the chasm.

Rather than driving up to the head of the valley, the explorers crossed to the western wall, aiming toward a transponder that had been included in a drop of ice-mining equipment. The sand dunes mid-chasm were low and regular, and the rovers rolled over the corrugated land, up and down, up and down. Then as they crested a sand wave they spotted the drop, no more than two kilometers from the foot of the northwest ice wall: bulky lime green containers on skeletal landing modules, a strange sight in this world of whites and tans and pinks. "What an eyesore!" Ann exclaimed, but Phyllis and George were cheering.

During the long afternoon, the shadowed western iceside took on a variety of pale colors: the purest water ice was clear and bluish, but most of the hillside was a translucent ivory, copiously tinted by pink and yellow dust. Irregular patches of CO_2 ice were a bright pure white; the contrast between dry ice and water ice was vivid, and made it impossible to read the actual contours of the hillside. And foreshortening made it hard to tell how tall the hill really was; it seemed to go up forever, and was probably somewhere between three and five hundred meters above the floor of Borealis.

"This is a *lot* of water," Nadia exclaimed.

"And there's more underground," Phyllis said. "Our borings show that the cap actually extends many degrees of latitude farther south than we see, buried under the layered terrain."

"So we have more water than we'll ever need!"

Ann pursed her mouth unhappily.

The drop of the mining equipment had determined the site of the ice mining camp: the west wall of Chasma Borealis, at longitude 41°, latitude 83° N. Deimos had just recently followed Phobos under the horizon; they wouldn't see it again until they returned south of 82° N. The summer nights consisted of an hour's purple twilight; the rest of the time the sun wheeled around, never more than twenty degrees above the horizon. The six of them spent long hours outside, moving the ice miner to the wall and then setting it up. The main component was a robotic tunnel borer, about the size of one of their rovers. The borer cut into the ice, and passed back cylindrical drums 1.5 meters in diameter. When they turned the borer on it made a loud, low buzz, which was louder still if they put their helmets to the ice, or even touched it with their hands. After a while white ice drums thumped into a hopper, and then a small robot forklift carried them to a distillery, which would melt the ice and separate out its considerable load of dust, then refreeze the water into one-meter cubes more suitable for packing in the holds of the rovers. Robot freight rovers would then be perfectly capable of driving to the site, loading up and returning to base on their own; and base would then have a regular water supply, larger than they could ever use. Around four or five trillion cubic kilometers in the visible polar cap, Edvard calculated, though there were a lot of guesses in the calculation.

They spent several days testing the miner and deploying an array of solar panels to power it. In the long evenings after dinner Ann would climb the ice wall, ostensibly to take more borings, although Nadia knew she just wanted away from Phyllis and Edvard and George. And naturally she wanted to climb all the way to the top, to get on the polar cap and look around, and take borings of the most recent layers of ice; and so one day when the miner had passed all the test routines, she and Nadia and Simon got up at dawn – just after two a.m. – and went out into the supercold morning air and climbed, their shadows like big spiders climbing before them. The slope of the ice was about 30°, steepening and then letting off time after time as they ascended the rough benches in the hill's layered side.

It was seven a.m. when the slope laid back and they walked onto the surface of the polar cap. To the north was a plain of ice that extended as far as they could see, to a high horizon some thirty kilometers away. Looking back to the south they could see a great distance over the geometric swirls of the layered terrain; it was the longest view Nadia had ever had on Mars.

The ice of the plateau was layered much like the laminated sand below them, with wide bands of dirty pink contouring across cleaner stuff. The other wall of Chasma Borealis lay off to the east, looking almost vertical from their point of view, long, tall, massive: "So much *water*!" Nadia said again. "It's more than we'll *ever* need."

"That depends," Ann said absently, screwing the frame of the little borer into the ice. Her darkened faceplate turned up at Nadia: "If the terraformers have their way, this will all go like dew on a hot morning. Into the air to make pretty clouds."

"Would that be so bad?" Nadia asked.

Ann stared at her. Through the tinted faceplate her eyes looked like ballbearings.

That night at dinner she said, "We really ought to make a run up to the pole."

Phyllis shook her head. "We don't have the food or air."

"Call for a drop."

Edvard shook his head. "The polar cap is cut by valleys almost as deep as Borealis!"

"Not so," Ann said. "You could drive straight to it. The swirl valleys look dramatic from space, but that's because of the difference in albedo between the water and the CO_2. The actual slopes are never more than 6° off the horizontal. It's just more layered terrain, really."

George said, "But what about getting onto the cap in the first place?"

"We drive around to one of the tongues of ice that drop to the sand. They're like ramps up to the central massif, and once there, we drive right to the pole!"

"There's no reason to go," Phyllis said. "It'll just be more of what we see here. And it means more exposure to radiation."

"And," George added, "we could use what food and air

177

we do have to check out some of the sites we passed on the way up here.''

So that was their point. Ann scowled. "I'm the head of the geological survey," she said sharply. Which may have been true, but she was a horrible politician, especially compared to Phyllis, who had any number of friends in Houston and Washington.

"But there's no geological reason to go to the pole," Phyllis said now with a smile. "It'll be the same ice as here. You just want to go."

"Well?" Ann said. "Say I do! There are still scientific questions to be answered up there. Is the ice the same composition, how much dust — everywhere we go up here we collect valuable data."

"But we're up here to get water. We're not up here to fool around."

"It's not fooling around!" Ann snapped. "We obtain water to allow us to explore, we don't explore just to obtain water! You've got it backwards! I can't believe how many people in this colony do that!"

Nadia said, "Let's see what they say at base. They might want us to help with something there, or they might not be able to send a drop, you never know."

Ann groaned. "We'll end up asking permission from the UN, I swear."

She was right. Frank and Maya didn't like the idea, John was interested but noncommittal. Arkady supported it when he heard of it, and declared he would send a supply drop from Phobos if necessary, which given its orbit was impractical at best. But at that point Maya called mission control in Houston and Baikonur, and the argument rippled outward. Hastings opposed the plan; but Baikonur, and a lot of the scientific community, liked it.

Finally Ann got on the phone, her voice very curt and arrogant, though she looked scared: "I'm the geological head here, and I say it needs to be done. There won't be any better opportunity to get onsite data on the original condition of the polar cap. It's a delicate system, and any change in the atmosphere is going to impact it heavily. And you've got plans to do that, right? Sax, are you still working on those windmill heaters?"

Sax had not been part of the discussion and he had to be called to the phone. "Sure," he said when the question was repeated. He and Hiroko had come up with the idea of manufacturing small windmills, to be dropped from dirigibles all over the planet. The constant westerlies would spin the windmills, and the spin would be converted to heat in coils in the base of the mills, and this heat would simply be released into the atmosphere. Sax had already designed a robotic factory to manufacture the windmills; he hoped to make them by the thousands. Vlad pointed out that the heat gained would come at the price of winds slowed down: you couldn't get something for nothing. Sax immediately argued that that would be a side benefit, given the severity of the global dust storms the wind sometimes caused. "A little heat for a little wind is a great trade-off."

"So, a million windmills," Ann said now. "And that's just the start. You talked about spreading black dust on the polar caps, didn't you Sax?"

"It would thicken the atmosphere faster than practically any other action we could take."

"So if you get your way," Ann said, "the caps are doomed. They'll evaporate and then we're going to say, 'I wonder what they were like?' And we won't know."

"Do you have enough supplies, enough time?" John asked.

"We'll drop you supplies," Arkady said again.

"There's four more months of summer," Ann said.

"You just want to go to the pole!" Frank said, echoing Phyllis.

"So?" Ann replied. "You may have come here to play office politics, but I plan to see a bit of this place."

179

Nadia grimaced; that ended that line of conversation, and Frank would be angry. Which was never a good idea. Ann, Ann . . .

The next day the Terran offices weighed in with the opinion that the polar cap ought to be sampled in its aboriginal condition. No objections from base; though Frank did not get back on the line. Simon and Nadia cheered: "North to the Pole!"

Phyllis just shook her head. "I don't see the point. George and Edvard and I will stay down here as a back-up, and make sure the ice miner is working right."

So Ann and Nadia and Simon took Rover Three and drove back down Chasma Borealis and around to the west, where one of the glaciers curling away from the cap thinned to a perfect rampway. The mesh of the rover's big wheels caught like a snowmobile's driving chain, running well over all the various surfaces of the cap, over patches of exposed granular dust, low hills of hard ice, fields of blinding white CO_2 frost, and the usual lace of sublimed water ice. Shallow valleys swirled outward in a clockwise pattern from the pole; some of these were very broad. Crossing these they would drive down a bumpy slope that curved away to right and left over both horizons, all of it covered by bright dry ice; this could last for twenty kilometers, until the whole visible world was bright white. Then before them a rising slope of the more familiar dirty red water ice would appear, striated by contour lines. As they crossed the bottom of the trough the world would be divided in two, white behind, dirty pink ahead. Driving up the south-facing slopes, they found the water ice more rotten than elsewhere, but as Ann pointed out, every winter a meter of dry ice sat on the permanent cap to crush the previous summer's rotten filigree, so the potholes were filled on an annual schedule; and the rover's big wheels crunched cleanly along.

Beyond the swirl valleys they found themselves on a

smooth white plain, extending to the horizon in every direction. Behind the polarized and tinted glass of the rover's windows the whiteness was unmarred and pure. Once they passed a low ring hill, the mark of some relatively recent meteor impact, filled in by subsequent ice deposition. They stopped to take borings, of course. Nadia had to restrict Ann and Simon to four borings a day, to save time and keep the rover's trunks from being overloaded. And it wasn't just borings; often they would pass black isolated rocks, resting on the ice like Magritte sculptures: meteorites. They collected the smallest of these, and took samples from the larger ones; and once passed one that was as big as the rover. They were nickel-iron for the most part, or stony chondrites. Chipping away at one of these, Ann said to Nadia, "You know they've found meteorites on Earth that came from Mars. The reverse happens too, although much less often. It takes a really big impact to jack rocks out of Earth's gravitational field fast enough to get them out here – delta V of fifteen kilometers per second, at least – I've heard it said that about two percent of the material ejected out of Earth's field would end up on Mars. But only from the biggest impacts, like the KT boundary impact. It would be strange to find a chunk of the Yucatan here, wouldn't it?"

"But that was sixty million years ago," Nadia said. "It would be buried under the ice."

"True." Later, walking back to the rover, she said, "Well, if they melt these caps then we'll find some. We'll have a whole museum of meteorites, sitting around on the sand."

They crossed more swirl valleys, falling again into the up-and-down pattern of a boat over waves, this time the largest waves yet, forty kilometers from crest to crest. They used the clocks to keep on a schedule, and parked from ten p.m. to five a.m. on hillocks or buried crater rims, to give themselves a view during their stops; and they blacked the windows with double polarization to help them to get some sleep at night.

Then one morning as they crunched along, Ann turned on the radio and began to run checks with the areosynchronous satellites. "It's not easy to find the pole," she said as she worked. "The early Terran explorers had a hell of a time in the north: they were always up there in summertime and couldn't see the stars, and they had no satellite checks."

"So how did they do it?" Nadia asked, suddenly curious.

Ann thought about it and smiled. "I don't know. Not very well, I suspect. Probably dead reckoning."

Nadia became intrigued by the problem, and started working on it on a sketchpad. Geometry had never been her strong point, but presumably at the north pole on midsummer's day, the sun would inscribe a perfect circle around the horizon, never getting higher or lower. If you were near the Pole, then, and it was near Midsummer's Day, you might be able to use a sextant to make timed checks on the sun's height above the horizon . . . was that right?

"This is it," Ann said.

"What?"

They stopped the rover, looked around. The white plain undulated to the nearby horizon, featureless except for a couple of broad red contour lines; the lines did not form bull's eyes circles around them, and it didn't look like they were at the top of anything.

"Where, exactly?" Nadia asked.

"Well, somewhere just north of here." Ann smiled again. "Within a kilometer or so. Maybe that way." She pointed off to the right. "We'll have to go over there a ways and check with the satellite again. A little bit of triangulation and we should be able to hit it on the nose. Plus or minus a hundred meters, anyway."

"If we just took the time, we could make it plus or minus a meter!" Simon said enthusiastically. "Let's pin it down!"

So they drove for a minute, consulted the radio, turned to

right angles and drove again, made another consultation. Finally Ann declared they were there, or close enough. Simon programmed the computer to keep working on it, and they suited up and went out and wandered around a bit, to make sure they had stepped on it. Ann and Simon drilled a boring. Nadia kept walking, in a spiral that expanded away from the cars. A reddish white plain, the horizon some four kilometers away; too close; it came to her in a rush, as during the black dune sunset, that this was alien – a sharp awareness of the tight horizon, the dreamy gravity, a world just so big and no bigger . . . and now she was standing right on its north pole. It was Ls = 92, about as near midsummer as you could ask; so if she stood facing the sun, and didn't move, the sun would stay right in front of her face for all the rest of the day, or the rest of the week for that matter! It was strange. She was spinning like a top. If she stood still long enough, would she feel it?

Her polarized faceplate reduced the sun's glare on the ice to an arc of crystalline rainbow points. It wasn't very cold. She could just feel a breeze against her upraised palm. A graceful red streak of depositional laminae ran over the horizon like a longitude line. She laughed at the thought. There was a very faint ice-ring around the sun, big enough that its lower arc just touched the horizon. Ice was subliming off the polar cap and gleaming in the air above, providing the crystals in the ring. Grinning, she stomped her boot prints into the North Pole of Mars.

That evening they aligned the polarizers so that a very dimmed-down image of the white desert stood around them in the module windows. Nadia sat back with an empty food tray in her lap, sipping a cup of coffee. The digital clock flicked from 11:59:59 to 0:00:00, and stopped. Its stillness accentuated the quietness in the car. Simon was asleep; Ann sat in the driver's seat, staring out at the scene, her dinner half-eaten. No sound but the whoosh of the ventilator. "I'm glad you got us up here," Nadia said. "It's been great."

"Someone should enjoy it," Ann said. When she was angry or bitter her voice became flat and distant, almost as if she were being matter-of-fact. "It won't be here long."

"Are you sure, Ann? It's five kilometers deep here, isn't that what you said? Do you really think it will completely disappear just because of black dust on it?"

Ann shrugged. "It's a question of how warm we make it. And of how much total water there is on the planet, and how much of the water in the regolith will surface when we heat the atmosphere. We won't know any of those things until they happen. But I suspect that since this cap is the primary exposed body of water, it'll be the most sensitive to change. It could sublime away almost entirely before any significant part of the permafrost has gotten within fifty degrees of melting."

"Entirely?"

"Oh, some will be deposited every winter, sure. But there's not *that* much water, when you put it in the global perspective. This is a dry world, the atmosphere is super-arid, it makes Antarctica look like a jungle, and remember how that place used to suck us dry? So if temperatures go up high enough, the ice will sublime at a really rapid rate. This whole cap will shift into the atmosphere and blow south, where it'll frost out at nights. So in effect it'll be redistributed more or less evenly over the whole planet, as frost about a centimeter thick." She grimaced. "Less than that, of course, because most of it will stay in the air."

"But then if it gets hotter still, the frost will melt, and it will rain. Then we've got rivers and lakes, right?"

"If the atmospheric pressure is high enough. Liquid surface water depends on air pressure as well as temperature. If both rise, we could be walking around on sand here in a matter of decades."

"It'd be quite a meteorite collection," Nadia said, trying to lighten Ann's mood.

It didn't work. Ann pursed her lips, stared out the window, shook her head. Her face could be so bleak; it couldn't be explained entirely by Mars, there had to be something more to it, something that explained that intense internal spin, that anger. Bessie Smith land. It was hard to watch. When Maya was unhappy it was like Ella Fitzgerald singing a blues, you knew it was a put-on, the exuberance just poured through it. But when Ann was unhappy, it hurt to watch it.

Now she picked up her dish of lasagne, leaned back to stick it in the microwave. Beyond her the white waste gleamed under a black sky, as if the world outside were a photo negative. The clockface suddenly read 0:00:01.

Four days later they were off the ice. As they retraced their route back to Phyllis and George and Edvard, the three travelers rolled over a rise and came to a halt; there was a structure on the horizon. Out on the flat sediment of the chasma floor there stood a classical Greek temple, six Dorian columns of white marble, capped by a round flat roof.

"What the hell?"

When they got closer they saw that the columns were made of ice drums from the miner, stacked on top of each other. The disk that served as roof was rough-hewn.

"George's idea," Phyllis said over the radio.

"I noticed the ice cylinders were the same size as the marble drums the Greeks used for their pillars," George said, still pleased with himself. "After that it was obvious. And the miner is running perfectly, so we had some time to kill."

"It looks great," Simon said. And it did: alien monument, dream visitation, it glowed like flesh in the long dusk, as if blood ran under its ice. "A temple to Ares."

"To Neptune," corrected George. "We don't want to invoke Ares too often, I don't think."

"Especially given the crowd at base camp," Ann said.

*

185

As they drove south their road of tracks and transponders ran ahead of them, as distinct as any highway of paved concrete. It did not take Ann to point out how much this changed the feel of their travel: they were no longer exploring untouched land, and the nature of the landscape itself was altered, split left and right by the parallel lines of crosshatched wheel tracks, and by the green canisters slightly dimmed by a rime of dust, all marking for them "the way." It wasn't wilderness any more; that was the point of roadbuilding, after all. They could leave the driving to Rover One's automatic pilot, and often did.

So they were trundling along at 30 kph, with nothing to do but look at the bisected view, or talk, which they did infrequently, except on the morning they got into a heated discussion about Frank Chalmers – Ann maintaining that he was a complete Machiavellian, Phyllis insisting that he was no worse than anyone else in power, and Nadia, remembering her talks with him about Maya, knowing it was more complex than either of those views. But it was Ann's lack of discretion that appalled her, and as Phyllis went on about how Frank had held them together in the last months of the voyage out, Nadia glared at Ann, trying to convey to her by looks that she was talking in the wrong crowd. Phyllis would use her indiscretions against her later on, that was obvious. But Ann was bad at seeing looks.

Then suddenly the rover braked and slowed to a stop. No one had been watching, and they all jumped to the front window.

There before them was a flat white sheet, covering their road for nearly a hundred meters. "What is it?" George cried.

"Our permafrost pump," Nadia said, pointing. "It must have broken."

"Or worked too well!" Simon said. "That's water ice!"

They switched the rover to manual, drove nearer. The spill covered the road like a wash of white lava. They struggled into their walkers and got out of the module, walked over to the edge of the spill.

"Our own ice rink," Nadia said, and went to the pump. She unhooked the insulation pad and had a look inside. "Ah ha — a gap in the insulation — water froze right here, and jammed the stopcock in the open position. A good head of pressure, I'd say. Ran till it froze thick enough to stop it. A tap from a hammer might get us our own little geyser."

She went to her tool cabinet in the underside of the module, took out a pick. "Watch out!" She struck a single blow at the white mass of ice, where the pump joined the tank feeder pipe. A thick bolt of water squirted a meter into the air.

"Wow!"

It splashed down onto the white sheet of ice, steaming even though it froze within seconds, making a white lobate leaf on top of the ice already there.

"Look at that!"

The hole too froze over, and the stream of water stopped, and the steam blew away.

"Look how fast it froze!"

"Looks just like those splosh craters," Nadia remarked, grinning. It had been a beautiful sight, water spilling out and steaming like mad as it froze.

Nadia chipped away at the ice around the stopvalve; Ann and Phyllis argued about migration of permafrost, quantities of water at this latitude, etc. etc. One would think they'd get sick of it. But they really did dislike each other, and so they were helpless to stop. It would be the last trip they ever took together, no doubt about it. Nadia herself would be disinclined to travel with Phyllis and George and Edvard anymore, they were too complacent, too much a little in-group of their own. But Ann was alienated from quite a few other people as well; if she didn't watch out, she'd be without anyone at all to accompany her on trips. Frank, for instance

— that comment to him the other night, and then telling Phyllis of all people how horrible he was; incredible.

And if she alienated everyone but Simon, she would be hurting for conversation; for Simon Frazier was the quietest man in the whole hundred. He had hardly said twenty sentences the entire length of the trip, it was uncanny, like traveling with a deaf-mute. Except maybe he talked to Ann when they were alone, who knew?

Nadia worked the valve into its stop position, then shut the whole pump down. "We'll have to use thicker insulation this far north," she said to no one in particular as she took her tools back to the rover. She was tired of all the sniping, anxious to get back to base camp and her work. She wanted to talk with Arkady; he would make her laugh. And without trying, or even knowing exactly how, she would make him laugh too.

They put a few chunks of the ice spill in among the rest of the samples, and set out four transponders to guide robot pilots around the spill. "Although it may sublime away, right?" Nadia said.

Ann, lost in thought, didn't hear the question. "There's a lot of water up here," she muttered to herself, sounding worried.

"You're damned right there is," Phyllis exclaimed. "Now why don't we have a look at those deposits we've spotted at the north end of Mareotis?"

As they got closer to base Ann became more close-mouthed and solitary, her face held tight as a mask. "What's the matter?" Nadia asked one evening, when they were out together near sunset, fixing a defective transponder.

"I don't want to go back," Ann said. She was kneeling by an isolated rock, chipping at it. "I don't want this trip to end. I'd like to keep traveling all the time, down into the canyons, up to the volcano rims, into the chaos and the mountains around Hellas. I don't ever want to stop."

She sighed. "But . . . I'm part of the team. So I have to climb back into the hovel with everyone else."

"Is it really that bad?" Nadia said, thinking of her beautiful barrel vaults, of the steaming whirlpool bath and a glass of icy vodka.

"You know it is! Twenty-four and a half hours a day underground in those little rooms, with Maya and Frank running their political schemes, and Arkady and Phyllis fighting over everything, which I understand now, believe me – and George complaining and John floating in a fog and Hiroko obsessed by her little empire – Vlad too, Sax too . . . I mean, what a crowd!"

"They're no worse than any other. No worse and no better. You have to get along. You couldn't be here all by yourself."

"No. But it feels like I'm not here anyway, when I'm at the base. Might as well be back on the ship!"

"No, no," Nadia said. "You're forgetting." She kicked the rock Ann was working on, and Ann looked up in surprise. "You can kick rocks, see? We're here, Ann. Here on Mars, standing on it. And every day you can go out and run around. And you'll be taking as many trips as anyone, with your position."

Ann looked away. "It just doesn't seem like enough, sometimes."

Nadia stared at her. "Well, Ann: it's radiation keeping us underground more than anything. What you're saying in effect is that you want the radiation to go away. Which means thickening the atmosphere, which means terraforming."

"I know." Her voice was tight, so tight that suddenly the careful matter-of-fact tone was lost and forgotten: "Don't you think I *know*?" She stood and waved the hammer. "But it isn't right! I mean I look at this land and, and I *love* it. I want to be out on it traveling over it always, to study it and live on it and learn it. But when I do that, I change it – I

189

destroy what it is, what I love in it. This road we made, it hurts me to see it! And base camp is like an open pit mine, in the middle of a desert never touched since time began. So ugly, so . . . I don't want to do that to all of Mars, Nadia, I don't. I'd rather die. Let the planet be, leave it wilderness and let radiation do what it will. It's only a statistical matter anyway, I mean if it raises my chance of cancer to one in ten, then nine times out of ten I'm all right!"

"Fine for you," Nadia said. "Or for any individual. But for the group, for all the living things here – the genetic damage, you know. Over time it would cripple us. So, you know, you can't just think of yourself."

"Part of a team," Ann said dully.

"Well, you are."

"I know." She sighed. "We'll all say that. We'll all go on and make the place safe. Roads, cities. New sky, new soil. Until it's all some kind of Siberia or Northwest Territories, and Mars will be gone and we'll be here, and we'll wonder why we feel so empty. Why when we look at the land we can never see anything but our own faces."

On the sixty-second day of their expedition they saw plumes of smoke over the southern horizon, strands of brown, gray, white and black rising and mixing, billowing into a flat-topped mushroom cloud that wisped off to the east. "Home again home again," Phyllis said cheerily.

Their tracks from the trip out, half-filled by dust, led them back toward the smoke: through the freight landing zone, across ground crisscrossed with treadmarks, across ground trampled to light red sand, past ditches and mounds, pits and piles, and finally to the great raw mound of the permanent habitat, a square earthen redoubt now topped by a silvery network of magnesium beams. That sight piqued Nadia's interest, but as they rolled on in she could not help noticing the litter of frames, crates, tractors, cranes, spare part dumps, garbage dumps, windmills, solar panels, water towers, concrete roads leading east west and south, air miners, the low buildings of the alchemists' quarter, their smokestacks emitting the plumes they had seen; the stacks of glass, the round cones of gray gravel, the big mounds of raw regolith next to the cement factory, the small mounds of regolith scattered everywhere else. It had the disordered, functional, ugly look of Vanino or Usman or any of the Stalinist heavy industry cities in the Urals, or the oil camps of Yakut. They rolled through a good five kilometers of this devastation; and as they did Nadia did not dare to look at Ann, who sat silently beside her, emanating disgust and loathing. Nadia too was shocked, and surprised at the change in herself; this had all seemed perfectly normal before the trip, indeed had pleased her very much. Now she was slightly nauseated, and afraid Ann might do something violent, especially if Phyllis said anything more. But Phyllis kept her mouth shut, and they rolled into the tractor lot outside the northern garage and stopped. The expedition was over.

One by one they plugged the rovers into the wall of the garage and crawled through the doors. Familiar faces crowded around, Maya and Frank and Michel and Sax and John and Ursula and Spencer and Hiroko and all the rest, like brothers and sisters really, but so many of them that Nadia was overwhelmed, she shrivelled like a touched anenome, and had trouble talking. She wanted to grasp something she could feel escaping her, she looked around for Ann and Simon, but they were trapped by another group and seemed stunned, Ann stoical, a mask of herself.

Phyllis told their story for them. "It was nice, really spectacular, the sun shone all the time, and the ice is really there, we've got access to a lot of water, it's like the Arctic when you're up on that polar cap . . ."

"Did you find any phosphorus?" Hiroko asked. Wonderful to see Hiroko's face, worried about the shortage of phosphorus for her plants. Ann told her that she had found drifts of sulphates in the light material around the craters in Acidalia, so they went off together to look at the samples. Nadia followed the others down the concrete-walled underground passageway to the permanent habitat, thinking about a real shower and fresh vegetables, half-listening to Maya give her the latest news. She was home.

Back to work; and as before, it was unrelenting and many-faceted, an endless list of things to do, and never enough time, because even though some tasks took much less human time than Nadia had expected, being robot-adequate, everything else took much more. And none of it gave her the same joy as building the barrel vault chambers, even if it was interesting in the technical sense.

If they wanted the central square under the dome to be any use, they had to lay a foundation that from bottom to top was composed of gravel, concrete, gravel, fiberglass, regolith, and finally treated soil. The dome itself would be made of double panes of thick treated glass, to hold the pressure and to cut down on UV rays, and a certain percentage of cosmic radiation. When all of it was done, they would have a central garden atrium of ten thousand square meters, really quite an elegant and satisfying plan; but as Nadia worked on the various aspects of the structure she found her mind wandering, her stomach tense. Maya and Frank were no longer speaking to one another in their official capacities, which indicated that their private relationship was going poorly indeed; and Frank did not seem to want to talk to John either, which was a shame. The broken affair between Sasha and Yeli had turned into a kind of civil war between their friends; and Hiroko's band, Iwao and Paul and Ellen and Rya and Gene and Evgenia and the rest, perhaps in reaction to all this, spent every day out in the atrium or in the greenhouses, more withdrawn than ever. Vlad and Ursula and the rest of the medical team were absorbed in research almost to the exclusion of clinical work with the colonists, which made Frank furious; and the genetic engineers spent all their time out in the converted trailer park, in the labs.

And yet Michel was behaving as if nothing were abnormal, as if he were not the psychological officer for the colony; he spent a lot of time watching French TV. When Nadia asked him about Frank and John, he only looked blankly at her.

They had been on Mars for 420 days; the first seconds of their universe were past. They no longer gathered to plot the next day's work, or discuss what they were doing. "Too busy," people said to Nadia when she asked. "Well, it's too involved to describe, you know, it'd put you to sleep. It does me." And so on.

And then at odd moments she would see in her mind's eye the black dunes, the white ice, the silhouetted figures against a sunset sky. She would shiver and come to with a sigh. Ann had already arranged another trip and was gone, this time south to the northernmost arms of great Valles Marineris, to see more unimaginable marvels. But Nadia was needed at base camp, whether she wanted to be out with Ann in the canyons or not. Maya complained about how much Ann was away. "It's clear she and Simon have started something and are just out there having a honeymoon while we slave away in here." That was Maya's way of looking at things, that would be what it would take to make Maya as happy as Ann sounded in her calls. But Ann was in the canyons, and that was all that was needed to make her sound that way. If she and Simon had started something it would only be a natural extension of that, and Nadia hoped it was true, she knew that Simon loved her, and she had felt the presence of an immense solitude in Ann, something that needed a human contact. If only she could join them again!

But she had to work. So she worked, she bossed people around the construction sites, she stalked the building sites and snapped at her friends' sloppy work. Her injured hand had regained some strength during the trip, so she was able to drive tractors and bulldozers again; she spent long days doing that, but it just wasn't the same anymore.

At Ls = 208° Arkady came down to Mars for the first time. Nadia went out to the new spaceport and stood on the edge of the broad expanse of dusty cement to watch the arrival, hopping from foot to foot. The burnt sienna cement was already marked by the yellow and black stains of earlier landings. Arkady's pod appeared in the pink sky, a white dot and then a yellow flame like an inverted gas burnoff stack. Eventually it resolved into a geodesic hemisphere with rockets and legs below, drifting down on a column of fire, and landing with unearthly delicacy right on the centerpoint dot. Arkady had been working on the descent program, apparently with good results.

He climbed out of the lander's hatch about twenty minutes later, and stood upright on the top step, looking around. He descended the staircase confidently, and once on the ground bounced experimentally on the tips of his toes, took a few steps, then spun around, arms wide. Nadia had a sudden sharp memory of how it had felt, that hollow sensation. Then he fell over. She hurried over to him, and he saw her and stood and made straight for her and tripped again across the rough Portland cement. She helped pull him back to his feet, and they met in a hug and staggered, him in a big pressurized suit, her in a walker. His hairy face looked shockingly real through their faceplates; the video had made her forget the third dimension and all the rest that made reality so vivid, so real. He banged his faceplate lightly against hers, grinning his wild grin. She could feel the stretch of a similar smile on her face.

He pointed at his wrist console and switched to their private band, 4224, and she did the same.

"Welcome to Mars."

Alex and Janet and Roger had come down with Arkady, and when they were all out of the lander they climbed into the open carriage of one of the Model Ts, and Nadia drove them back to base, over the wide paved road at first, and then shortcutting through the Alchemists' Quarter. She told them about each building they passed, aware that they already recognized them all. Suddenly she was nervous, remembering what it had looked like to her after the trip to the pole. They stopped at the garage lock and she led them inside. There it was another family reunion.

Later that day Nadia led Arkady around the square of vaulted chambers, through door after door, room after furnished room, all twenty-four of them; and then out into the atrium. The sky was a ruby color through the glass panels, and the magnesium struts gleamed like tarnished silver.

"Well?" Nadia said at last, unable to stop herself: "What do you think?"

Arkady laughed and gave her a hug. He was still in his spacesuit, his head looking small in the open neck hole; he felt padded and bulky, and she wanted him out of it.

"Well, some of it is good and some of it is bad. But why is it so ugly? Why is it so sad?"

Nadia shrugged, irritated. "We've been busy."

"So were we on Phobos, but you should see it! We've walled all the galleries in panels of nickel stripped with platinum, and scored the panel surfaces with iterated patterns that the robots run at night, Escher reproductions, mirrors offset for infinite regress, scenes from Earth, you should see it! You can put a candle in some of the chambers and it looks like the stars in the sky, or a room on fire. Every room is a work of art, wait till you see it!"

"I look forward to it." Nadia shook her head, smiling at him.

That evening they had a big communal dinner in the four connected chambers that formed the largest room in the complex. They ate chicken and soyburgers and large salads, and everyone talked at once, so that it was reminiscent of the best months on *Ares*, or even of Antarctica.

Arkady stood to tell them about the work on Phobos. "I am glad to be in Underhill at last." They were nearly done doming Stickney, he told them, and under it long galleries had been drilled into the fractured and brecciated rock, following ice veins right through the moon. "If it weren't for the lack of gravity, it would be a great place," Arkady concluded. "But that's one we can't solve. We spent most of our free time on Nadia's gravity train, but it's cramped, and meanwhile all the work is in Stickney or below it. So we spent too much time weightless or exercising, and even so we lost strength; even Martian g makes me tired now – I'm dizzy right now."

"You're always dizzy!"

"So we must rotate crews there, or run it by robot. We are thinking of all coming down for good. We've done our part up there, a functioning space station is now available for those who follow. Now we want our reward down here!" He raised his glass.

Frank and Maya frowned. No one would want to go up to Phobos, and yet Houston and Baikonur wanted it manned at all times. Maya had that look on her face familiar from the *Ares*, the one that said it was all Arkady's fault; when Arkady saw it he burst out laughing.

The next day Nadia and several others took him on a more detailed tour of Underhill and the surrounding facilities, and he spent the whole time nodding his head with that pop-eyed look of his that made you want to nod back while he said, "Yes, but, yes, but," and went into one detailed critique after another, until even Nadia began to get annoyed with him. Although it was hard to deny that the Underhill area was battered, thrashed to the horizon in every direction, so that it seemed as if it continued outward over the whole planet.

"It's easy to color bricks," Arkady said. "Add manganese oxide from the magnesium smelting and you have pure white bricks. Add carbon left over from the Bosch process for black. You can get any shade of red you want by altering the amount of ferric oxides, including some really stunning scarlets. Sulphur for yellows. And there must be something for greens and blues, I don't know what but Spencer might, maybe some polymer based on the sulphur, I don't know. But a bright green would look marvelous in such a red place. It will have a blackish shade to it from the sky, but it will still be green and the eye is pulled to it.

"And then with these colored bricks, you build walls that are all mosaics. It's beautiful to do it. Everyone can have their own wall or building, whatever they want. All the factories in the Alchemists' Quarter look like outhouses or discarded sardine tins. Brick around them would help insulate them, so there is a good scientific reason for it, but truthfully it's just as important that they look good, that it looks like home here. I've already lived too long in a country that thought only of utility. We must show that we value more than that here, yes?"

"No matter what we do to the buildings," Maya pointed

out sharply, "the ground around them will still be all ripped up."

"But not necessarily! Look, when construction is over, it would be very possible to grade the ground right back to its original configuration, and then cast loose rock over the surface in a way that would imitate the aboriginal plain. Dust storms would deposit the required fines soon enough, and then if people walked on pathways, and vehicles ran on roads or tracks, soon it would have the look of the original ground, occupied here and there by colorful mosaic buildings, and glass domes stuffed with greenery, and yellow brick roads or whatnot. Of course we must do it! It is a matter of spirit! And that's not to say it could have been done earlier, the infrastructure had to be installed, that's always messy, but now we are ready for the art of architecture, the spirit of it."

He waved his hands around, stopped suddenly, popped his eyes at the dubious expressions framed in the faceplates around him. "Well, it's an idea, yes?"

Yes, Nadia thought, looking around with interest, trying to visualize it. Perhaps that kind of process would bring back her pleasure in the work? Perhaps it would look different to Ann then? She wasn't sure.

"More ideas from Arkady," as Maya put it in the pool that night, looking sour. "Just what we need."

"But they're good ideas," Nadia said. She got out, showered, put on a jumper.

Later that night she met Arkady again, and took him to see the northwest corner chamber of Underhill, which she had left bare-walled so she could show him the structural detail.

"It's very elegant," he said, rubbing a hand over the bricks. "Really, Nadia, all of Underhill is magnificent. I can see your hand everywhere on it."

Pleased, she went to a screen and called up the plans she had been working on for a larger habitat. Three rows of vaulted chambers stacked underground, in one wall of a very deep trench; mirrors on the opposite wall of the trench, to direct sunlight down into the rooms . . . Arkady nodded and grinned and pointed at the screen, asking questions and making suggestions: "An arcade between the rooms and the wall of the trench, open space; and each story laid back a bit from the one below it, so each has a balcony overlooking the arcade . . ."

"Yes, that should be possible . . ." And they tapped at the computer screen, altering the architectural sketch as they spoke.

Later they walked in the domed atrium. They stood under tall clusters of black bamboo leaves, the plants still in pots while the ground was prepared. It was quiet and dark.

"We could perhaps lower this area one story," Arkady said softly. "Cut windows and doors into your vaults, and lighten them up."

Nadia nodded. "We thought of that, and we're going to do it, but it's slow getting so much dirt out through locks." She looked at him. "But what about us, Arkady? So far you've only talked about the infrastructure. I should have thought that beautifying buildings would be pretty low down on your list of things to do."

Arkady grinned. "Well, maybe all the things higher on the list are already done."

"What? Did I hear Arkady Nikelyovich say that?"

"Well, you know – I don't complain just to complain, Ms. Nine Fingers. And the way things have been going down here, it's very close to what I was calling for during the voyage out. Close enough that it would be stupid to complain."

"I must admit you surprise me."

"Do I? But think about how you all have been working together here, this last year."

"Half a year."

He laughed. "Half a year. And for all that time we have had no leaders, really. Those nightly meetings when everyone has their say, and the group decides what needs doing most; that's how it should be. And no one is wasting time buying or selling, because there is no market. Everything here belongs to all equally. And yet none of us can exploit anything that we own, for there's no one outside us to sell it to. It's been a very communal society, a democratic group. All for one and one for all."

Nadia sighed. "Things have changed, Arkady. It's not like that anymore. And it's changing more all the time. So it won't last."

"Why do you say that?" he cried. "It will last if we decide that it will."

She glanced at him skeptically. "You know it isn't so simple."

"Well, no. Not simple. But within our power!"

"Maybe." She sighed, thinking of Maya and Frank, of Phyllis and Sax and Ann. "There's an awful lot of fighting going on."

"That's all right, as long as we agree on certain basic things."

She shook her head, rubbed her scar with the fingers of her other hand. Her absent finger was itching, and suddenly she felt depressed. Overhead the long bamboo leaves were defined by occluded stars; they looked like sprays of a giant bacillus. They walked along the path between crop trays. Arkady picked up her maimed hand and peered at the scar, until it made her uncomfortable and she tried to pull it back. He drew it up, gave the newly exposed knuckle at the base of the ring finger a kiss. "You've got strong hands, Ms. Nine Fingers."

"I did before this," she said, making a fist and holding it up.

"Someday Vlad will grow you a new finger," he said, and took the fist and opened it, then held the hand as they continued to walk. "This reminds me of the arboretum in Sebastopol," he said.

"Mmm," Nadia said, not really listening, intent on the warm heft of his hand in hers, in the tight intermingling of their fingers. He had strong hands too. She was fifty-one years old, a round little Russian woman with gray hair, a construction worker with a missing finger. So nice to feel the warmth of another body; it had been too long, and her hand soaked up the feeling like a sponge, until the poor thing tingled, full and warm. It must feel odd to him, she thought, then gave up on it. "I'm glad you're here," she said.

Having Arkady at Underhill made it like the hour before a thunderstorm. He made people think about what they were doing; habits that they had fallen into without thought came under scrutiny, and under this new pressure some became defensive, others aggressive. All the standing arguments got a bit more intense. Naturally this included the terraforming debate.

Now this debate was in no sense a single event but was rather an ongoing process, a topic that kept coming up, a matter of casual exchanges between individuals, out working, eating meals, falling asleep. Any number of things could bring it up: the sight of the white frost plume over Chernobyl; the arrival of a robot-driven rover, laden with water ice from the polar station; clouds in the dawn sky. Seeing these or many other phenomena someone would say, "That'll add some BTUs to the system," or, "Isn't that a good greenhouse gas," and perhaps a discussion of the technical aspects of the problem would follow. Sometimes the subject would come back up in the evenings back in Underhill, leading from the technical to the philosophical; and sometimes this led to long and heated arguments.

The debate was not, of course, confined to Mars. Position papers were being churned out by policy centers in Houston, Baikonur, Moscow, Washington, and the UN Office for Martian Affairs in New York, as well as in government bureaus, newspaper editorial offices, corporate board rooms,

201

university campuses, and bars and homes all over the world. In the arguments on Earth, many people began to use the colonists' names as a kind of shorthand for the various positions, so that watching the Terran news the colonists themselves would see people saying that they backed the Clayborne position, or were in favor of the Russell program. This reminder of their enormous fame on Earth, their existence as characters in an ongoing TV drama, was always peculiar and unsettling; after the flurry of TV specials and interviews following touchdown, they had tended to forget the ongoing video transmissions, absorbed in the daily reality of their lives. But the video cameras were still shooting tape to send back home; and there were a lot of people on Earth who were fans of the show.

So nearly everyone had an opinion. Polls showed that most supported the Russell Program, an informal name for Sax's plans to terraform the planet by all means possible, as fast as they could. But the minority who backed Ann's hands-off attitude tended to be more vehement in their belief, insisting that it had immediate applications to the Antarctic policy, and indeed to all Terran environmental policy. Meanwhile different poll questions made it clear that many people were fascinated by Hiroko and the farming project, while others called themselves Bogdanovists; Arkady had been sending back lots of video from Phobos, and Phobos was good video, a real spectacle of architecture and engineering. New Terran hotels and commercial complexes were already imitating some of its features, there was an architectural movement called Bogdanovism, as well as other movements interested in him that were more concentrated on social and economic reforms in the world order.

But terraforming was near the center of all these debates, and the colonists' disagreements about it were played out on the largest possible public stage. Some of them reacted by avoiding the cameras and requests for interviews; "It's just what I came to get away from," Hiroko's assistant Iwao said, and quite a few agreed with him. Most of the rest didn't care one way or the other; a few seemed actually to like it. Phyllis's weekly program, for instance, was carried by both Christian cable stations and business analysis programs all over the world. But no matter how they dealt with it, looking at the polls and listening to the talk made it obvious that most people on Earth and on Mars assumed that terraforming would take place. It was not a question of whether but of when, and how much. Among the colonists themselves this was nearly the universal view. Very few sided with Ann: Simon of course; perhaps Ursula and Sasha; perhaps Hiroko; in his way John, and now in her way Nadia. There were more of these "reds" back on Earth, but they necessarily held the position as a theory, an aesthetic judgement. The strongest point to their arguments, and thus the one that Ann emphasized most often in her communiques back to Earth, was the possibility of indigenous life. "If there *is* Martian life here," Ann would say, "the radical alteration of the climate might kill it off. We cannot intrude on the situation while the status of life on Mars is unknown; it's unscientific, and worse, it's immoral."

Many agreed with that, including a lot of the Terran scientific community, which influenced the UNOMA committee charged with overseeing the colony. But every time Sax heard the argument he blinked rapidly. "There's no sign of life on the surface, past or present," he would say mildly. "If it does exist it has to be underground, near volcanic vents I suppose. But even if there is life down there, we could search for ten thousand years and never find it, nor eliminate the possibility it isn't down there somewhere else, somewhere we haven't looked. So waiting until we know for sure that there is no life" – which was a fairly common position among moderates – "effectively means waiting forever. For a remote possibility which terraforming wouldn't immediately endanger anyway."

"Of course it would," Ann would retort. "Maybe not

immediately, but eventually the permafrost would melt, there would be movement through the hydrosphere, and contamination of all of it by warmer water and Terran lifeforms, bacteria, viruses, algae. It might take a while, but it would surely happen. And we can't risk that."

Sax would shrug. "First, it's postulated life, very low probability. Second, it wouldn't be endangered for centuries. We could presumably locate it and protect it in that time."

"But we may not be able to find it."

"So we stop for low-probability life we can never actually find?"

Ann shrugged. "We have to, unless you want to argue that it's okay to destroy life on other planets, as long as we can't find it. And don't forget; indigenous life on Mars would be the biggest story of all time, it would have implications for the galactic frequency of life that are impossible to exaggerate. Looking for life is one of the main reasons we're here!"

"Well," Sax would say, "in the meantime, life that we are quite sure exists is being exposed to an extraordinarily high amount of radiation. If we don't do something to lessen it, we may not be able to stay here. We need a thicker atmosphere to cut down on radiation."

This was not a reply to Ann's point but the substitution of another one, and it was an argument that was very influential. Millions on Earth wanted to come to Mars, to the "new frontier," where life was an adventure again; waiting lists for emigration both real and fake were massively oversubscribed. But no one wanted to live in a bath of mutagenic radiation, and the practical desire to make the planet safe for humans was stronger in most people than the desire to preserve the lifeless landscape already there, or to protect a postulated indigenous life that many scientists assured them did not exist.

So it did seem, even among those urging caution, that terraforming was going to happen. A subcommittee of

UNOMA had been convened to study the issue, and on Earth it was now in the nature of a given, an unavoidable part of progress, a natural part of the order of things. A manifest destiny.

On Mars, however, the issue was both more open and more pressing, not so much a matter of philosophy as of daily life, of frigid poisonous air and the radiation being taken; and among those in favor of terraforming, a significant group was clustering around Sax – a group that not only wanted to do it, but to do it as fast as possible. What this meant in practice no one was sure; estimates of the time it would take to get to a "human-viable surface" ranged from a century to ten thousand years, with extreme opinions on either end, from thirty years (Phyllis) to a hundred thousand years (Iwao). Phyllis would say, "God gave us this planet to make in our image, to create a new Eden". Simon would say, "If the permafrost melts we'd be living on a collapsing landscape, and a lot of us would be killed". Arguments wandered over a wide range of issues: salt levels, peroxide levels, radiation levels, the look of the land, possibly lethal mutations of genetically engineered micro-organisms, and so on.

"We can try to model it," Sax said, "but the truth is we'll never be able to model it adequately. It's too big and there are too many factors, many of them unknown. But what we will learn from it will be useful in controlling Earth's climate, in avoiding global warming or a future ice age. It's an experiment, a big one, and it will always be an ongoing experiment, with nothing guaranteed or known for sure. But that's what science is."

People would nod at this.

Arkady as always was thinking of the political point of view. "We can never be self-sufficient unless we do terraforming," he pointed out. "We need to terraform in order to make the planet ours, so that we will have the material basis for independence."

People would roll their eyes at this. But it meant that Sax and Arkady were allies of a sort, and that was a powerful combination. And so the arguments would go around, again and again and again, endlessly.

And now Underhill was nearly complete, a functioning and in most ways a self-sufficient village. Now it was possible to act further; now they had to decide what to do next. And most of them wanted to terraform. Any number of projects had been proposed to begin the process, with advocates for each, usually those who would be responsible for doing it. This was an important part of terraforming's attraction; every discipline could contribute to the enterprise in one way or another, so it had broad-based support. The alchemists talked about physical and mechanical means to add heat to the system; the climatologists debated influencing the weather; the biosphere team talked about ecological systems theories to be tested. The bioengineers were already working on new micro-organisms; they were shifting, clipping and recombining genes from algae, methanogens, cyanobacteria, and lichens, trying to come up with organisms that would survive on the present Martian surface, or under it. One day they invited Arkady to take a look at what they were doing, and Nadia went along with him.

They had some of their prototype GEMs in Mars jars, the largest of which was one of the old habitats in the trailer park. They had opened it up, shoveled regolith onto the floor, and sealed it again. They worked inside it by teleoperation, and viewed the results from the next trailer over, where instrument gauges took readings, and video screens showed what the various dishes were producing. Arkady looked at every screen closely, but there wasn't that much to see: their old quarters, covered with plastic cubicles filled with red dirt; robot arms extending from their bases against the walls. There were visible growths on part of the soil, a bluish furze.

"That's our champion so far," Vlad said. "But still only slightly areophylic." They were selecting for a number of extreme characteristics, including resistance to cold and dehydration and UV radiation, tolerance for salts, little need for oxygen, a habitat of rock or soil. No single Terran organism had all these traits, and those that had them individually were usually very slow growers; but the engineers had started what Vlad called a mix and match program, and recently they had come up with a variant of the cyanophyte that was sometimes called bluegreen algae. "It is not precisely thriving, but it does not die so fast, let us put it that way." They had named it *cyanophyte primares*, its common name becoming Underhill algae. They wanted to make a field trial with it, and had prepared a proposal to send down to UNOMA.

Arkady left the trailer park excited by the visit, Nadia could see; and that night he said to the dinner group, "We should make the decision on our own, and if we decide in favor, act."

Maya and Frank were outraged by this, and clearly most of the rest were uncomfortable as well. Maya insisted on a change of subject, and awkwardly the dinner conversation shifted. The next morning Maya and Frank came to Nadia, to talk about Arkady. The two leaders had already tried to reason with him, late the night before. "He laughs in our face!" Maya exclaimed. "It's useless to try to reason with him!"

"What he proposes could be very dangerous," Frank said. "If we explicitly disregard a directive from the UN, they could conceivably come here and round us up and ship us home, and replace us with people who will pay attention to the law. I mean, biological contamination of this environment is simply illegal at this point, and we don't have the right to ignore that. It's international treaty. It's how humanity in general wants to treat this planet at this time."

"Can't you *talk* to him?" Maya asked.

"I can talk to him," Nadia said. "But I can't say that it will do any good."

"Please, Nadia. Just try. We've got enough problems as it is."

"I'll try, sure."

So that afternoon she talked to Arkady. They were out on Chernobyl Road, walking back toward Underhill. She brought it up, and suggested that patience was in order. "It will only be a matter of time before the UN comes around to your view anyway."

He stopped and lifted her maimed hand. "How long do you think we have?" he said. He pointed at the setting sun. "How long do you suggest we wait? For our grandchildren? Our great-grandchildren? Our great-great-grandchildren, blind as cave fish?"

"Come on," Nadia said, pulling her hand free. "Cave fish."

Arkady laughed. "Still, it's a serious question. We don't have forever, and it would be nice to see things start to change."

"Even so, why not wait a year?"

"A Terran year or a Martian year?"

"A Martian year. Get readings on all the seasons, give the UN time to come around."

"We don't need the readings, they've been taken now for years."

"Have you talked to Ann about that?"

"No. Well, sort of. But she doesn't agree."

"A lot of people don't agree. I mean maybe they will eventually, but you have to *convince* them. You can't just run roughshod over opposing opinions, otherwise you're just as bad as the people back home that you're always criticizing."

Arkady sighed. "Yeah yeah."

"Well, aren't you?"

"You damned liberals."

"I don't know what that means."

"It means you're too soft-hearted to ever actually *do* anything."

But they were now within sight of the low mound of Underhill, looking like a fresh squarish crater, its ejecta scattered around it. Nadia pointed at it. "I did that. You damned radicals," she jabbed him in the ribs with her elbow, hard, "you hate liberalism because it works."

He snorted.

"It does! It works in increments, over time, after hard labor, without fireworks or easy dramatics or people getting hurt. Without your sexy revolutions and all the pain and hatred they bring. It only *works*."

"Ah, Nadia." He put his arm over her shoulders, and they started walking again toward base. "Earth is a perfectly liberal world. But half of it is starving, and always has been, and always will be. Very liberally."

Still, Nadia seemed to have affected him; he quit calling for a unilateral decision to release the new GEMs onto the surface, and he confined the agitprop to his beautification program, spending much of his time in the Quarter, trying to make colored bricks and glass. Nadia joined him for a swim before breakfast on most days, and they along with John and Maya took over a lane in the shallow pool that filled all of one of the vaulted chambers, and swam a brisk workout of one or two thousand meters. John led the sprint sets, Maya led the distance sets, Nadia followed in everything, hampered by her bad hand, and they churned through the extra-splashy water like a line of dolphins, staring through their goggles down at the sky-blue concrete of the pool bottom. "The butterfly was made for this g," John would say, grinning at the way they could practically fly out of the water. Breakfasts afterwards were pleasant if brief, and the rest of the days were the usual round of work; Nadia seldom saw Arkady again till evenings at dinner, or afterward.

Then Sax and Spencer and Rya finished setting up the robot factory for making Sax's windmill heaters, and they applied to UNOMA for permission to distribute a thousand of them around the equatorial regions, to test their warming effect. All of them together were only expected to add about twice the heat to the atmosphere that Chernobyl did, and there were even questions as to whether they would be able to distinguish the added heat from background seasonal fluctuations; but as Sax said, they wouldn't know until they tried. And there was no doubt that the heaters would add some heat to the surface, detectable or not.

And so the terraforming argument flared again. And suddenly Ann flew into violent action, taping long messages that she sent to the members of UNOMA's executive committee, and to the national offices for Martian affairs for all the countries that were currently on the committee; and finally to the UN General Assembly. These appearances were given enormous amounts of attention, from the most serious policy-making levels all the way down to the tabloid press and TV, media that regarded it as the newest episode of the red soap opera. Ann had taped and sent her messages in private, so the colonists learned of them by seeing excerpts on Terran TV, and watching the reaction to them in the days that followed: debates in government, a rally in Washington that drew twenty thousand; endless amounts of editorial space, and commentary in the scientific nets. It was a bit shocking to see the strength of these responses, and some of them felt Ann had gone behind their backs. Phyllis for one was outraged.

"Besides, it doesn't make sense," Sax said, blinking rapidly. "Chernobyl is already releasing almost as much heat into the atmosphere as these windmills, and she never complained about that."

"Yes she did," Nadia said. "She just lost the vote."

Hearings were held at UNOMA, and while they were going on a group of the materials scientists confronted Ann after dinner. A lot of the rest of them were there to witness this confrontation; Underhill's main dining hall filled four chambers, whose dividing walls had been removed and replaced by load-bearing pillars; it was a big room, filled with chairs and potted plants and the descendants of the *Ares*' birds, and most recently lit by windows installed high across the northern wall, through which they saw the ground level crops of the atrium. A big space; and at least half the colonists were in it eating when the meeting took place.

"Why didn't you discuss this with us?" Spencer asked her.

Ann's glare forced Spencer to look away. "Why should I discuss it with you?" she said, turning her gaze on Sax. "It's clear what you all think about this, we've gone over it many times before, and nothing I've said makes any difference to you. Here you sit in your little holes running your little experiments, making things like kids with a chemistry set in a basement, while the whole time an entire world sits outside your door. A world where the landforms are a hundred times larger than their equivalents on Earth, and a thousand times older, with evidence concerning the beginning of the solar system scattered all over, as well as the whole history of a planet, scarcely changed in the last billion years. And you're going to wreck it all. And without ever honestly admitting what you're doing, either. Because we could live here and study the planet without changing it – we could do that with very little harm or even inconvenience to ourselves. All this talk of radiation is bullshit and you know it. There's simply not a high enough level of it to justify this mass alteration of the environment. You want to do *that* because you think you can. You want to try it out and see – as if this were some big playground sandbox for you to build castles in. A big Mars jar! You find your justifications where you can, but it's bad faith, and it's *not science*."

Her face had gone bright red during this tirade; Nadia had never seen her anywhere near as angry as this. The usual matter-of-fact facade that she placed over her bitter anger had shattered, and she was almost speechless with fury and shuddering. The whole room had gone deadly quiet. "It's not science, I say! It's just playing around. And for that game you're going to wreck the historical record, destroy the polar caps, and the outflow channels, and the canyon bottoms – destroy a beautiful pure landscape, and for *nothing at all.*"

The room was as still as a tableau. The ventilators hummed. People began to eye one another warily. Simon took a step toward Ann, his hand outstretched; she stopped him dead with a glance, he might as well have stepped outside in his underwear and frozen stiff. His face reddened, and he cracked his posture and sat back down.

Sax Russell rose to his feet. He looked the same as ever, perhaps a bit more flushed than usual, but mild, small, blinking owlishly, his voice calm and dry, as if lecturing on some textbook point of thermodynamics, or enumerating the periodic table.

"The beauty of Mars exists in the human mind," he said in that dry factual tone, and everyone stared at him amazed. "Without the human presence it is just a collection of atoms, no different from any other random speck of matter in the universe. It's we who understand it, and we who give it meaning. All our centuries of looking up at the night sky and watching it wander through the stars. All those nights of watching it through the telescopes, looking at a tiny disk trying to see canals in the albedo changes. All those dumb sci-fi novels with their monsters and maidens and dying civilizations. And all the scientists who studied the data, or got us here. That's what makes Mars beautiful. Not the basalt and the oxides."

He paused to look around at them all. Nadia gulped: it was strange in the extreme to hear these words come out of the mouth of Sax Russell, in the same dry tone that he would use to analyze a graph. Too strange!

"Now that we are here," he went on, "it isn't enough to just hide under ten meters of soil and study the rock. That's science, yes, and needed science too. But science is more than that. Science is part of a larger human enterprise, and that enterprise includes going to the stars, adapting to other planets, adapting them to us. Science is creation. The lack of life here, and the lack of any finding in fifty years of the SETI program, indicates that life is rare, and intelligent life even rarer. And yet the whole meaning of the universe, its beauty, is contained in the consciousness of intelligent life. We are the consciousness of the universe, and our job is to spread that around, to go look at things, to live everywhere we can. It's too dangerous to keep the consciousness of the universe on only one planet, it could be wiped out. And so now we're on two, three if you count the moon. And we can change this one to make it safer to live on. Changing it won't destroy it. Reading its past might get harder, but the beauty of it won't go away. If there are lakes, or forests, or glaciers, how does that diminish Mars's beauty? I don't think it does. I think it only enhances it. It adds life, the most beautiful system of all. But nothing life can do will bring Tharsis down, or fill Marineris. Mars will always remain Mars, different from Earth, colder and wilder. But it can be Mars and ours at the same time. And it will be. There is this about the human mind; if it can be done, it will be done. We can transform Mars and build it like you would build a cathedral, as a monument to humanity and to the universe. We can do it, so we will do it. So—" he held up a palm, as if satisfied that the analysis had been supported by the data in the graph – as if he had examined the periodic table, and found that it still held true "—we might as well start."

He looked at Ann, and all eyes followed her. Ann's mouth was tight, her shoulders slumped. She knew she was beaten.

She shrugged, as if she were shrugging a hooded cape back over her head and body, a heavy carapace that weighed her down, and covered her entirely from them. In the flat dead tone that she usually employed when she was upset, she said, "I think you value consciousness too high, and rock too little. We are not lords of the universe. We're one small part of it. We may be its consciousness, but being the

213

consciousness of the universe does not mean turning it all into a mirror image of us. It means rather fitting into it as it is, and worshipping it with our attention." She met Sax's mild gaze, and one final flare of her anger jetted out: "You've never even seen Mars."

And she left the room.

Janet had had her camera specs on, and videotaped this exchange. Phyllis sent a copy back to Earth. A week later the UNOMA committee on environmental alterations approved the dissemination of the heater windmills.

The plan was to drop them from dirigibles. Arkady immediately claimed the right to pilot one, as a sort of reward for his work on Phobos. Maya and Frank were not unhappy at the thought of Arkady disappearing from Underhill for another month or two, so they immediately assigned him one of the craft. He would drift east in the prevailing winds, descending to place windmills in channel beds and on the outer flanks of craters, both places where winds tended to be strong. Nadia first heard of the expedition when Arkady skipped through the chambers to her and told her about it.

"Sounds nice," she said.

"Want to come along?" he asked.

"Why yes," she said. Her ghost finger was tingling.

Their dirigible was the biggest ever made, a planetary model built back in Germany by Friedrichshafen Nach Einmal, and shipped up in 2029, so that it had just recently arrived. It was called the *Arrowhead*, and it measured 120 meters across the wings, 100 meters front to back, and 40 meters tall. It had an internal ultralite frame, and turboprops at each wingtip and under the gondola; these were driven by small plastic engines whose batteries were powered by solar cells arrayed on the upper surface of the bag. The pencil-shaped gondola extended most of the length of the underside, but it was smaller inside than Nadia had expected, because much of it was temporarily filled with their cargo of windmills; at takeoff their clear space consisted of nothing more than the cockpit, two narrow beds, a tiny kitchen, an even smaller toilet, and the crawlspace necessary to move among these. It was pretty tight, but happily both sides of the gondola were walled with windows, and though somewhat blocked by windmills these still gave them a lot of light, and good visibility.

Takeoff was slow. Arkady released the lines extending from the three mooring masts with the flip of a cockpit toggle; the turboprops ran hard, but they were dealing with air that was only twelve millibars thick. The cockpit bounced up and down in slow motion, flexing with the internal frame: and every up bounce was a little higher off the ground. For someone used to rocket launches it was comical.

"Let's take a three-sixty and see Underhill before we go," Arkady said when they were fifty meters high. He banked the ship and they made a slow wide turn, looking out Nadia's window. Tracks, pits, mounds of regolith, all dark red against the dusty orange surface of the plain – it looked as if a dragon had reached down with a great taloned claw, and drawn blood time after time. Underhill sat at the center of the wounds, and by itself was a pretty sight, a square dark red setting for a shiny glass-and-silver jewel, with green just visible under the dome. Extending away from it were the roads east to Chernobyl and north to the spacepads. And over there were the long bulbs of the greenhouses, and there was the trailer park . . .

"The Alchemists' Quarter still looks like something out of the Urals," Arkady said. "We really have to do something about that." He brought the dirigible out of its turn and headed east, moving with the wind. "Should I run us over Chernobyl and catch the updraft?"

"Why don't we see what this thing can do unassisted?" Nadia said. She felt light, as if the hydrogen in the ballonets had filled her as well. The view was stupendous, the hazy horizon perhaps a hundred kilometers away, the contours of the land all clearly visible: the subtle bumps and hollows of Lunae, the more prominent hills and canyons of the channeled terrain to the east. "Oh, this is going to be wonderful!"

"Yes."

It was remarkable, in fact, that they had not done anything like this before. But flying on Mars was no easy thing, because of the thin atmosphere. They were in the best solution: a dirigible as big and light as possible, filled with hydrogen, which in Martian air was not only not flammable, but also even lighter relative to its surroundings than it would have been on Earth. Hydrogen and the latest in super-light materials gave them the necessary lift to carry a cargo like their windmills, but with such a cargo aboard they were ludicrously sluggish, and everything happened in extreme slow motion.

And so they drifted along. All that day they crossed the rolling plain of Lunae Planum, pushed southeast by the wind. For an hour or two they could see Juventa Chasm on the southern horizon, a gash of a canyon that looked like a giant pit mine. Farther east, the land turned yellowish; there was less surface rubble, and the underlying bedrock was more rumpled. There were also many more craters, craters big and small, crisp-rimmed or nearly buried. This was Xanthe Terra, a high region that was topographically similar to the southern uplands, here sticking into the north between the low plains of Chryse and Isidis. They would be over Xanthe for some days, if the prevailing westerlies held true.

They were progressing at a leisurely 10 kph. Most of the time they flew at an altitude of about a hundred meters, which put the horizons about fifty kilometers away. They had time to look closely at anything they wanted to, although Xanthe was proving to be little more than a steady succession of craters.

Late that afternoon Nadia tilted the nose of the dirigible down and circled into the wind, dropping until they were within ten meters of the ground and then releasing their anchor. The ship rose, jerked on its line, and settled downwind of the anchor, tugging at it like a fat kite. Nadia and Arkady twisted down the length of the gondola, to what Arkady called the bomb bay. Nadia lifted a windmill onto the bay's winch hook. The windmill was a little thing, a magnesium box with four vertical vanes on a rod projecting from its top. It weighed about five kilos. They closed the bay door on it, sucked out the air, and opened the bottom doors. Arkady operated the winch, looking through a low window to see what he was doing. The windmill dropped like a plumb, and bumped onto hardened sand, on the southern flank of a small unnamed crater. He released the winch hook, reeled it back into the bay and closed the bomb doors.

They returned to the cockpit, and looked down again to see if the windmill was working. There it stood, a small box on the outside slope of a crater, somewhat tilted, the four broad vertical blades spinning merrily. It looked like an anemometer from a kid's meteorology kit. The heating element, an exposed metal coil that would radiate like a stove-top, was on one side of the base. In a good wind the element might get up to 200° Centigrade, which wasn't bad, especially in that ambient temperature. Still . . . "It's going to take a lot of those to make any difference," Nadia remarked.

"Sure, but every little bit helps, and in a way it's free heat. Not only the wind powering the heaters, but the sun powering the factories making the windmills. I think they're a good idea."

They stopped once more that afternoon to set out another one, then anchored for the night in the lee of a crisp young crater. They microwaved a meal in the tiny kitchen, and then retired to their narrow bunks. It felt odd to rock on the wind, like a boat at its mooring: tug and float, tug and float. But it was very relaxing when you got used to it, and soon Nadia was asleep.

The next morning they woke before dawn, cast off, and motored up into the sunlight. From a hundred meters height they could watch the shadowed landscape below turn to bronze as the terminator rolled by and clear daylight followed, illuminating a fantastic jumble of bright rocks and long shadows. The morning wind pushed right to left across their bow, so they were pushed northeast toward Chryse, humming along with the props on full power. Then the land fell away below them, and they were over the first of the outflow channels they would pass, a sinuous unnamed valley west of Shalbatana Vallis. This little arroyo's S shape was unmistakably water-cut. Later that day they lofted out over the deeper and much wider canyon of Shalbatana, and the signs were even more obvious: tear-shaped islands, curving channels, alluvial plains, scablands; there were signs everywhere of a massive flood, a flood that had created a canyon so huge that the *Arrowhead* suddenly looked like a butterfly.

The outflow canyons and the high land between them reminded Nadia of the landscape of American cowboy movies, with washes and mesas and isolated ship rocks, as in Monument Valley – except here it lasted for four days, as they passed in succession over the unnamed channel, Shalbatana, Simud, Tiu, and then Ares. And all of them had been

218

caused by giant floods, which had burst onto the surface and flowed for months, at rates ten thousand times that of the Mississippi. Nadia and Arkady talked about that as they looked down into the canyons under them, but it was very hard to imagine floods so huge. Now the big empty canyons funnelled nothing but wind. They did that quite well, however, so Arkady and Nadia descended into them a number of times per day, to drop more windmills.

Then east of Ares Vallis they floated back over the densely cratered terrain of Xanthe. Again the land was everywhere marred by craters: big craters, little craters, old craters, new craters, craters with rims marred by newer craters, craters with floors punctured by three or five smaller craters; craters as fresh as if they had struck yesterday; craters that just barely showed, at dawn and dusk, as buried arcs in the old plateau. They passed over Schiaparelli, a giant old crater a hundred kilometers across; when they floated over its central uplift knob, its crater walls formed their horizon, a perfect ring of hills around the edge of the world.

After that winds blew from the south for several days. They caught a glimpse of Cassini, another great old crater, and passed over hundreds of smaller ones. They dropped several windmills per day, but the flight was giving them a stronger sense of the size of the planet, and the project began to seem like a joke, as if they flew over Antarctica and tried to melt the ice by setting down a number of camping stoves. "You'd have to drop millions to make any difference," Nadia said as they climbed up from another drop.

"True," Arkady said. "But Sax would like to drop millions. He's got an automated assembly line that will just keep churning them out, it's only distribution that is a problem. And besides, it's just one part of the campaign he has in mind." He gestured back toward the last arc of Cassini, inscribing the whole northwest. "Sax would like to bang out a few more holes like that one. Capture some icy moonlets from Saturn, or from the asteroid belt if he can find any, and push them back and smash them into Mars. Make hot craters, melt the permafrost – they'd be like oases."

"Dry oases, wouldn't they be? You'd lose most of the ice on entry, and have the rest disappear on contact."

"Sure, but we can use more water vapor in the air."

"But it wouldn't just vaporize, it would break into its constituent atoms."

"Some of it. But hydrogen and oxygen, we could use more of both."

"So you're bringing hydrogen and oxygen from Saturn? Come on, there's lots of both here already! You could just break down some of the ice."

"Well, it's just one of his ideas."

"I can't wait to hear what Ann says to that." She sighed, thought about it. "The thing to do, I suppose, would be to graze an ice asteroid through the atmosphere, as if trying to aerobrake it. That would burn it up without breaking the molecules apart. You'd get water vapor in the atmosphere, which would help, but you wouldn't be bombing the surface with explosions as big as a hundred hydrogen bombs going off all at once."

Arkady nodded. "Good idea! You should tell Sax."

"You tell him."

East of Cassini the terrain grew rougher than ever. This was some of the oldest surface on the planet, cratered to saturation in the earliest years of torrential bombardment. A hellish age, the Noachian, you could see that in the landscape. No Man's Land from a Titanic trench war, the sight of it induced a kind of numbness after a while, a cosmological shell shock.

They floated on, east, northeast, southeast, south, northeast, west, east, east. They finally came to the end of Xanthe, and began to descend the long slope of Syrtis Major Planitia. This was a lava plain, much less densely cratered than Xanthe. The land sloped down and down, until finally they drifted over a smooth-floored basin: Isidis Planitia, one of the lowest points on Mars. It was the essence of the northern hemisphere, and after the southern highlands it seemed especially smooth and flat and low. And it too was a very large region. There really was a lot of land on Mars.

Then one morning when they lofted up to cruising altitude, a trio of peaks rose over the eastern horizon. They had come to Elysium, the only other Tharsislike "bulge continent" that the planet had. Elysium was a much smaller bulge than Tharsis, but it was still big, a high continent, one thousand kilometers long and ten kilometers taller than the surrounding terrain. As with Tharsis, it was ringed by patches of fractured land, crack systems caused by the uplift. They flew over the westernmost of these crack systems, Hephaestus Fossae, and found the area an unearthly sight: five long deep parallel canyons, like claw marks in the bedrock. Elysium loomed beyond, a saddleback in shape, Elysium Mons and Hecates Tholus rearing at each end of a long spine range, five thousand meters higher than the bulge they punctuated: an awesome sight. Everything about Elysium was so much bigger than anything Nadia and Arkady had seen so far that as the dirigible floated toward the range, the two were speechless for minutes at a time. They sat in their seats, watching it all float slowly toward them. When they did speak, it was just thinking aloud: "Looks like the Karakoram," Arkady said. "Desert Himalayas. Except these are so simple. Those volcanoes look like Fuji. Maybe people will hike up them someday in pilgrimages."

Nadia said, "These are so big, it's hard to imagine what the Tharsis volcanoes will look like. Aren't the Tharsis volcanoes twice as big as these?"

"At least. It does look like Fuji, don't you think?"

"No, it's a lot less steep. Why, did you ever see Fuji?"

"No."

After a while: "Well, we'd better try to go around the whole damn thing," Arkady said. "I'm not sure we have the loft to get over those mountains."

So they turned the props, and pushed south as hard as they could, and the winds naturally co-operated, as they were curving around the continent too. So the *Arrowhead* floated southeast into a rough mountainous region called Cerberus; and all of the next day they could mark their progress by the sight of Elysium, passing slowly to their left. Hours passed, the massif shifted in their side windows; the slowness of the shift made it plain just how big this world was. *Mars has as much land surface as the Earth* – everyone always said that, but it had been just a phrase. Their creep around Elysium was the proof of the senses.

The days passed: up in the frigid morning air, over the jumbled red land, down in the sunset, to bounce at an airy anchorage. One evening when the supply of windmills had dwindled they rearranged those that remained, and moved their beds together under the starboard windows. They did it without discussion, as if it had been the obvious thing to do when they had room; as if they had already agreed to do it long before. And as they moved around the cramped gondola rearranging things, they bumped into each other just as they had all trip long, but now intentionally, and with a sensuous rubbing which accentuated what they had been up to all along, accidents become foreplay; and finally Arkady burst out laughing and caught her up into a wild bear hug, and Nadia shouldered him back onto their new double bed and they kissed like teenagers, and made love through the night. And after that they slept together, and made love frequently in the ruddy glow of dawn and in the starry black nights, with the ship lightly bobbing at its moorings. And they lay together talking, and the sensation of floating as they embraced was palpable, more romantic than any train or ship. "We became friends first," Arkady said once, "that's what makes this different, don't you think?" He prodded her with a finger. "I love you." It was as if he were testing the words with his tongue. It was clear to Nadia that he hadn't said them often; it was clear they meant a lot to him, a kind of commitment. Ideas meant so much to him! "And I love you," she said.

And in the mornings Arkady would pad up and down the narrow gondola naked, his red hair bronzed like everything else by the horizontal morning light, and Nadia would watch from their bed feeling so serene and happy that she had to remind herself that the floating sensation was probably just Martian g. But it felt like joy.

One night as they were falling asleep Nadia said curiously, "Why me?"

"Huhn?" He had been almost asleep.

"I said, why me? I mean, Arkady Nikelyovich, you could have loved any of the women here, and they would have loved you back. You could have had Maya if you wanted."

He snorted. "I could have had Maya! Oh my! I could have had the joy of Maya Katarina! Just like Frank and John!" He snorted, and they both laughed out loud. "How could I have passed on such joy! Silly me!" He giggled until she punched him.

"All right, all right. One of the others then, the beautiful ones, Janet or Ursula or Samantha."

"Come on," he said. He propped himself up on an elbow to look at her. "You really don't know what beauty is, do you?"

"I certainly do," Nadia said mulishly.

Arkady ignored her and said, "Beauty is power and elegance, right action, form fitting function, intelligence, and reasonability. And very often," he grinned and pushed at her belly, "expressed in curves."

"Curves I've got," Nadia said, pushing his hand away.

He leaned forward and tried to bite her breast, but she dodged him.

"Beauty is what you are, Nadezhda Francine. By these criteria you are queen of Mars."

"Princess of Mars," she corrected absently, thinking it over.

"Yes that's right. Nadezhda Francine Cherneshevsky, the nine-fingered Princess of Mars."

"You're not a conventional man."

"No!" He hooted. "I never claimed to be! Except before certain selection committees of course. A conventional man! Ah, ha ha ha ha ha! – the conventional men get Maya. That is their reward." And he laughed like a wild man.

One morning they crossed the last broken hills of Cerberus, and floated out over the flat dusty plain of Amazonis Planitia. Arkady brought the dirigible down, to set a windmill in a pass between two final hillocks of old Cerberus. Something went wrong with the clasp on the winch hook, however, and it snapped open when the windmill was only halfway to the ground. The windmill thumped down flat on its base. From the ship it looked okay, but when Nadia suited up and descended in the sling to check it out, she found that the hot plate had cracked away from the base.

And there, behind the plate, was a mass of something. A dull green *something* with a touch of blue to it, dark inside the box. She reached in with a screwdriver and poked at it carefully. "Shit," she said.

"What?" Arkady said above.

She ignored him and scraped some of the substance into a bag she used for screws and nuts.

She got into the sling. "Pull me back up," she ordered.

"What's wrong?" Arkady asked.

"Just get me up there."

He closed the bomb bay doors after her, and met her as she was getting out of the sling. "What's up?"

She took off her helmet. "You know what's up, you bastard!" She took a swing at him and he leaped back, banging into a wall of windmills. "Ow!" he cried; a vane had caught him in the back. "Hey! What's the problem! Nadia!"

224

She took the bag from her walker pocket and waved it before him. "This is the problem! How could you do it? How could you lie to me? You bastard, do you have any idea what kind of trouble this is going to get us in? They'll come up here and send us all back to Earth!"

Round-eyed, Arkady rubbed his jaw. "I wouldn't lie to you, Nadia," he said earnestly. "I don't lie to my friends. Let me see that."

She stared at him and he stared back, his arm stretched out for the bag, the whites of his eyes visible all the way round the irises. He shrugged, and she frowned.

"You really don't know?" she demanded.

"Know *what*?"

She couldn't believe he would fake ignorance; it just wasn't his style. Which suddenly made things very strange. "At least some of our windmills are little algae farms."

"*What?*"

"The fucking windmills that we've been dropping everywhere," she said. "They're stuffed with Vlad's new algae or lichen or whatever it is. Look." She put the little bag on the tiny kitchen table, opened it and used the screwdriver to spoon out a little bit of it. Little knobby chunks of bluish lichen. Like Martian life forms out of an old pulp novel.

They stared at it.

"Well I'll be damned," Arkady said. He leaned over until his eyes were a centimeter from the stuff on the table.

"You swear you didn't know?" Nadia demanded.

"I swear. I wouldn't do that to you, Nadia. You know that."

She heaved a big breath. "Well – our friends would do it to us, apparently."

He straightened up and nodded. "That's right." He was distracted, thinking hard. He went to one of the windmill bases and hefted it away from the others. "Where was it?"

"Behind the heating pad."

They went to work on it with Nadia's tools, and got it

open. Behind the plate was another colony of Underhill algae. Nadia poked around at the edges of the plate, and discovered a pair of small hinges where the top of the plate met the insides of the container wall. "Look, it's made to open."

"But who opens it?" Arkady said.

"Radio?"

"Well I'll be damned." Arkady stood, walked up and down the narrow corridor. "I mean —"

"How many dirigible trips have been made so far, ten? Twenty? And all of them dropping these things?"

Arkady started to laugh. He tilted his head back, and his huge crazed grin split his red beard in two, and he laughed until he held his sides. "Ah, ha ha ha ha ha ha!"

Nadia, who didn't think it was funny at all, nevertheless felt her face grinning at the sight of him. "It's not funny!" she protested. "We're in big trouble!"

"Maybe," he said.

"Definitely! And it's all your fault! Some of those fool biologists in the trailer park took your anarchist rant seriously!"

"Well," he said, "that at least is a point in their favor, the bastards. I mean —" he went back to the kitchen table to stare at the clump of blue stuff " — who exactly do you think we're talking about, anyway? How many of our friends are in on this? And why in the world didn't they tell *me*?"

This really rankled, she could tell. In fact the more he thought about it, the less amused he was, because the algae meant there was a subculture in their group that was acting outside UNOMA supervision *but had not let Arkady in on it*, even though he had been the first and most vocal advocate of such subversion. What did that mean? Were there people who were on his side but didn't trust him? Were there dissidents with a competing program?

They had no way of telling. Eventually they pulled anchor, and sailed on over Amazonis. They passed a medium-sized crater named Pettit, and Arkady remarked that it would make a good site for a windmill, but Nadia only snarled. They flew by, talking the situation over. Certainly several people in the bioengineering labs had to be in on it; probably most of them; maybe all. And then Sax, the designer of the windmills, certainly had to be a part of it. And Hiroko had been an advocate of the windmills, but they had neither been sure why; it was impossible to judge whether she would approve of something like this or not, as she was simply too close with her opinions. But it was possible.

As they talked it over, they took the broken windmill completely apart. The heating plate doubled as a gate for the compartment containing the algae; when the gate opened, the algae would be released into an area that would be a bit warmer because of the hot plate itself. Each windmill thus functioned as a micro-oasis, and if the algae managed to survive with its help, and then grow beyond the small area warmed by the hot plate, then good. If not it was not going to do very well on Mars anyway. The hot plate served to give it a good sendoff, nothing more. Or so its designers must have thought. "We've been made into Johnny Appleseed," Arkady said.

"Johnny what?"

"American folk tale." He told her about it.

"Yeah, right. And now Paul Bunyan is going to come kick our ass."

"Ha. Never. Big Man is much bigger than Paul Bunyan, believe me."

"Big Man?"

"You know, all those names for landscape features. Big Man's Footprints, Big Man's Bathtub, Big Man's Golf Course, whatever."

"Ah yeah."

"Anyway, I don't see why we should get in trouble. We didn't know anything about it."

"Now who's going to believe that?"

227

". . . Good point. Those *bastards*, they really got me with this one."

Clearly this was what bothered Arkady most. Not that they had contaminated Mars with alien biota, but that he had been kept out of a secret. Men were such egomaniacs when it came down to it. And Arkady, he had his own group of friends, perhaps more than that: people who agreed with him, followers of a sort. The whole Phobos crew, a lot of the programmers in Underhill. And if some of his own people were keeping things from him, that was bad; but if another group had secret plans of its own, that was worse, apparently, because they were at least interference, and perhaps competition.

Or so he seemed to think. He wouldn't say much of this explicitly, but it became obvious in his mutterings, and his sudden sharp curses, which were genuine even though they alternated with bursts of hilarity. He couldn't seem to make up his mind whether he was pleased or angry, and Nadia finally believed that he was both at once. That was Arkady; he felt things freely and to the full, and wasn't much worried about consistency. But she wasn't too sure she liked his reasons this time, for either his anger or his amusement, and she told him so with considerable irritation.

"Well, but come on!" he cried. "Why should they keep it a secret from me, when it was my idea to begin with?"

"Because they knew I might come along with you. If they told you, you would have had to tell me. And if you told me, I would have stopped it!"

Arkady laughed outrageously at this. "So it was pretty considerate of them after all!"

"Fuck."

The bioengineers, Sax, the people in the Quarter who had actually constructed the things. Someone in communications, probably – there were quite a few who must have known.

"What about Hiroko?" Arkady asked.

They couldn't decide. They didn't know enough of her views to be able to guess what she might think. Nadia was pretty sure she was in on it, but couldn't explain why. "I suppose," she said, thinking about it, "I suppose I feel like there is this group around Hiroko, the whole farm team and a fair number of others, who respect her and — follow her. Even Ann, in a way. Although Ann will hate this when she hears about it! Whew! Anyway, it just seems to me that she would know about anything secret going on. Especially something having to do with ecological systems. The bio-engineering group works with her most of the time, after all, and for some of them she's like a guru, they almost worship her. They probably got her advice when they were splicing this algae together!"

"Hmm . . ."

"So they probably got her agreement for the idea. Maybe I should even say her permission."

Arkady nodded. "I see your point."

On and on they talked, hashing over every point of it. The land they passed over, flat and immobile, looked different to Nadia now. It was seeded, fertilized; it was going to change, now, inevitably. They talked about the other parts of Sax's terraforming plans, giant orbiting mirrors reflecting sunlight onto the dawn and dusk termina-tors, carbon distributed over the polar caps, areothermal heat, the ice asteroids. It was all really going to happen, it seemed. The debate had been bypassed; they were going to change the face of Mars.

The second evening after their momentous discovery, as they were cooking dinner in a crater's lee anchorage, they got a call from Underhill, relayed off one of the comm satellites. "Hey you two!" John Boone said by way of greeting. "We've got a problem!"

"*You've* got a problem," Nadia replied.

"Why, something wrong out there?"

229

"No no."

"Well good, because really it's you guys who have the problem, and I wouldn't want you to have more than one! A dust storm has started down in the Claritas Fossae region, and it's growing, and coming north at a good rate. We think it'll reach you in a day or so."

"Isn't it early for dust storms?" Arkady asked.

"Well no, we're at Ls = 240, which is pretty much the usual season for it. Southern spring. Anyway, there it is, and it's coming your way."

He sent a satellite photo of the storm, and they studied their TV screen closely. The region south of Tharsis was now obscured by an amorphous yellow cloud.

"We'd better take off for home right now," Nadia said after studying the photo.

"At night?"

"We can run the props on batteries tonight, and recharge the batteries tomorrow morning. After that we may not have much sunlight, unless we can get above the dust."

After some discussion with John, and then with Ann, they cast off. The wind was pushing them east-northeast, and on this heading they would pass just to the south of Olympus Mons. After that their hope was to get around the north flank of Tharsis, which would protect them from the dust storm for at least a while.

It seemed louder flying at night. The wind's rush over the fabric of the bag was a fluctuating moan, the sound of their engines a pitiful little hum. They sat in the cockpit, lit only by dim green instrument lights, and talked in low voices as they moved over the black land below. They had about three thousand kilometers to go before reaching Underhill; that was about three hundred hours of flying time. If they went round the clock, it would be twelve days or so. But the storm, if it grew in the usual pattern, would reach them long before then. After that – it was hard to tell how it would go. Without sunlight the props would drain the batteries, and then –

230

"Can we just float on the wind?" Nadia said. "Use the props for occasional directional nudges?"

"Maybe. But these things are designed with the props as part of the lift, you know."

"Yeah." She made coffee and brought mugs of it up to the cockpit. They sat and drank, and looked out at the black landscape, or the green sweep of the little radar screen. "We probably ought to drop everything we don't need. Especially those damned windmills."

"It's all ballast, save it for when we need the lift."

The hours of the night wore on. They traded shifts at the helm, and Nadia caught an uneasy hour's sleep. When she returned to the cockpit, she saw that the black bulk of Tharsis had rolled over the horizon ahead of them: the two northernmost of the three prince volcanoes, Ascraeus Mons and Pavonis Mons, were visible as humps of occluded stars, out at the edge of the world. To their left Olympus Mons still bulked well above the horizon, and taken with the other two volcanoes, it looked as if they flew low in some truly gigantic canyon. The radar screen reproduced the view in miniature, in green lines on the screen's gridwork.

Then, in the hour before dawn, it seemed as though another massive volcano were rising behind them. The whole southern horizon was lifting, low stars disappearing as they watched, Orion drowned in black. The storm was coming.

It caught them just at daybreak, choking off the red in the eastern sky, rolling over them, returning the world to rusty darkness. The wind picked up until it swept past the gondola windows in a muted roar, and then with a loud howling; dust flew by them with terrifying, surreal speed. Then the wind grew even more violent, and the gondola jerked up and down as the frame of the dirigible was twisted back and forth.

They were lucky north was the direction they wanted to go. At one point Arkady said, "The wind should hopefully wrap around the north shoulder of Tharsis."

Nadia nodded silently. They hadn't gotten the chance to

231

recharge the batteries after the night's flight, and without sunlight the motors wouldn't run too much longer. "Hiroko told me sunlight on the ground during a storm is supposed to be about fifteen percent of normal," she said. "Higher there should be more. So we'll get some recharge, but it'll be slow. Could be that over the course of the day we might get enough to use the props a bit tonight." She flicked on a computer to do the calculations. Something in the expression on Arkady's face – not fear, not even anxiety, but a curious little *smile* – made her aware of how much danger they were in. If they couldn't use the props, they wouldn't be able to direct their movement, and they might not even be able to stay aloft. They could descend, it was true, and try to anchor; but they had only a few weeks' more food, and storms like these often persisted for two months, sometimes three.

"There's Ascraeus Mons," Arkady said, pointing at the radar screen. "Good image." He laughed. "Best view of it we're going to get this time around, I'm afraid. Too bad, I was really looking forward to seeing them! Remember Elysium?"

"Yeah yeah," Nadia said, busy running simulations of the batteries' efficiency. Daily sunlight was near its perihelion peak, which was why the storm had started in the first place; and the instruments said that about twenty percent of full daylight was penetrating to this level (it felt to her eye more like thirty or forty); therefore it might be possible to run the props half the time, which would help tremendously. Without them they were moving at around twelve kilometers per hour, and losing altitude as well, although that might just be the ground rising under them. With the props they might be able to hold a steady altitude, and influence their course by a degree or two.

"How thick is this dust, do you think?"

"How thick?"

"You know, grams per cubic meter. Try to get Ann or Hiroko on the radio and find out, will you?"

She went back to see what they had on board that could be used to power the props. Hydrazine, for the bomb bay vacuum pumps; the pump motors could be wired to the props, probably . . . She was kicking one of the damned windmills out of the way when she stared at it. The hot plates were heated by an electric charge generated by the spinning of the windmills. So if she could run that charge into the prop batteries, the windmills could be attached to the outside of the gondola, and this wind would spin them like tops, and the resulting electricity could help power the props. As she rooted through the equipment locker looking for wire and transformers and tools she told Arkady the idea, and he laughed his madman laugh. "Good idea, Nadia! *Great* idea!"

"If it works." She rummaged through the tool kit, sadly smaller than her usual supply. The light in the gondola was eerie, a dim yellow glow flickering with every gust. The view out the side windows shifted from pockets of complete clarity, with thick yellow clouds like thunderheads flying past them, to complete obscurity, all the window surfaces streaming with dust that flashed by at well over three hundred kilometers per hour. Even at twelve millibars the blast of the wind was tossing the dirigible about; up in the cockpit Arkady was cursing the autopilot's insufficiency. "Reprogram it," Nadia called forward, and then remembered him and all his sadistic simulations on the *Ares*, and laughed out loud: "Problem run! Problem run!" She laughed again at his shouted curses, and went back to work. At least the wind would push them along faster. Arkady yelled back information from Ann: the dust was extremely fine, average particle size about 2.5 microns; total column mass about 10^{-3} grams per cm^{-2}, pretty evenly distributed from top to bottom of the column. That wasn't so bad; drop it on the ground and it would be a really thin layer, which was consistent with what they had seen on the oldest freight drops at Underhill.

When she had rewired a number of the windmills she

banged down the passageway to the cockpit. "Ann says the winds will be slowest close to the ground," Arkady said.

"Good. We need to land to get those windmills outside."

So that afternoon they descended blind, and let the anchor drag until it hooked and held. The wind here was slower, but even so Nadia's descent in the sling was harrowing; down and down into rushing clouds of yellow dust, swinging back and forth . . . and there it was right under her boots, the ground! She hit and dragged to a halt. Once out of the sling she found herself leaning into the wind; thin as it was it still struck like blows, and her old feeling of hollowness was extreme. Visibility billowed back and forth in waves, and the dust flew past so fast it was disorienting; on Earth a wind that fast would simply pick you up and throw you, like a broomstraw in a tornado.

But here you could hold your ground, if only just. Arkady had been slowly winching the dirigible down on its anchor line, and now it bulked over her like a green roof. It was weirdly dark underneath it. She unreeled the wires out to the wingtip turboprops, taped them to the dirigible and crimped them to the contacts inside, working fast to try to reduce their exposure to dust, and to get out from under the *Arrowhead*; it was bouncing on the wind. With difficulty she drilled holes in the bottom of the gondola fuselage, and attached ten windmills with screws. As she was taping the wiring from these to the plastic fuselage, the whole dirigible dropped so fast that she had to collapse onto her face, her whole body spreadeagled on the cold ground, the drill a hard lump under her stomach. "Shit!" she shouted. "What's wrong?" Arkady cried over the intercom. "Nothing," she said, jumping up and taping faster than ever. "Fucking thing – it's like working on a trampoline!" Then as she was finishing the wind picked up strength yet again, and she had to crawl back down to the bomb bay, her breath rasping in and out of her.

"The damn thing almost crushed me!" she shouted

forward to Arkady when she had her helmet off. While he worked to unhook the anchor she staggered around the interior of the gondola, picking up things that they wouldn't need and taking them into the bomb bay: a lamp, one of the mattresses, most of the cooking utensils and dinnerware, some books, all the rock samples. In they went, and she jettisoned them happily. If some traveler ever came upon the resulting pile of stuff, she thought, they would really wonder what the hell had happened.

They had to run both props full out to get the anchor unhooked, and when they succeeded they were off and flying like a leaf in November. They kept the props on full, to gain altitude as fast as possible; there were some small volcanoes between Olympus and Tharsis, and Arkady wanted to pass several hundred meters over them. The radar screen showed Ascraeus Mons falling steadily behind. When they were well north of it they could turn east, and try to chart a course around the northern flank of Tharsis, and then down to Underhill.

But as the long hours passed they found that the wind was rushing down the north slope of Tharsis, across their bow; so that even when running full power toward the southeast, they were still only moving northeast at best. In their attempts to fly across the wind the poor *Arrowhead* was bouncing like a hang glider, yanking them up and down, up and down, up and down, as if the gondola were indeed attached to the underside of a trampoline. But despite all that, they still weren't going in the direction they wanted to go.

Darkness fell again. They were carried farther northeast. On this heading, they were going to miss Underhill by several hundred kilometers. After that, nothing; no settlements at all, no refuge. They would be blown over Acidalia, up onto Vastis Borealis, up to the empty petrified sea of black dunes. And they did not have enough food and water to circumnavigate the planet again and give it another try.

Feeling dust in her mouth and eyes, Nadia went back to the kitchen and heated them a meal. Already she was exhausted, and, she realized as the smell of food filled the air, extremely hungry. Thirsty, too; and the water recycler ran on hydrazine.

Thinking about water, an image came to her mind, from the trip to the north pole: that broken permafrost gallery, with its white spill of water ice. Now how was that relevant?

She worked her way back up to the cockpit, holding onto a wall with every step. She ate a dusty meal with Arkady, trying to figure it out. Arkady watched their radar screen, saying nothing; but he was looking concerned.

Ah. "Look," she said, "if we could pick up the signals from the transponders on our road to Chasma Borealis, we could come down and land by it. Then one of the robot rovers could be sent up to get us. The storm won't matter to the robot rovers, they don't go by sight anyway. We could leave the *Arrowhead* tethered, and drive back home."

Arkady looked at her, finished swallowing. "Good idea," he said.

But only if they could actually pick up the road's transponder signals. Arkady flicked on the radio and called Underhill. The connection crackled in a storm of static almost as dense as the dust, but they could still make themselves understood. All through that night they conferred with the crowd back home, discussing frequencies, bandwidths, the power of the dust to mask the transponders' fairly weak signals, and so on. Because the transponders were designed only to signal rovers that were nearby and on the ground, it was going to be a problem hearing them. Underhill might be able to pinpoint their location well enough to tell them when to descend, and their own radar map would give them a general fix on the road's location as well; but neither of these methods would be very exact, and it would be almost impossible to find the road in the storm if they didn't land right on it. Ten kilometers either way and it would be over the horizon, and they would be out of luck. It would be a lot more certain if they could just latch onto one of the transponder signals, and follow it down.

In any case, Underhill dispatched a robot rover on the road north. It would arrive in the area of the road they were expected to cross in about five days; at their current speed, now nearly thirty kilometers per hour, they would cross the road themselves in about four days.

When the arrangements were finished, they traded watches through the rest of the night. Nadia slept uneasily on her off watches, and spent much of the time lying on the bed feeling the wind bounce her. The windows were as dark as if curtains had been drawn. The roar of the wind was like a gas stove, and then occasionally like banshees; once she dreamed they were inside a great furnace full of flame demons, and woke sweating, and went forward to relieve Arkady. The whole gondola smelled of sweat and dust, and burnt hydrazine. Despite all the gaskets' micron seals, there was a visible whitish film on all the surfaces inside the gondola. She wiped her fingers across a pale blue plastic bulkhead, and stared at her fingers' mark. Incredible.

They bounded along through the gloom of the days, through the starless black of the nights. The radar showed what they thought was Fesenkov Crater, running under them; they were being shoved northeast still, and there was absolutely no chance they would be able to buck the storm and get south to Underhill. The polar road was their only hope. Nadia occupied her off watches by looking for things to throw overboard, and cutting away at parts of the gondola frame she judged inessential, until the engineers in Friedrichshafen would have shuddered. But Germans always over-engineered things, and no one on Earth could ever really believe in Martian g anyway. So she sawed and hammered until everything inside the gondola was latticed nearly to nothing. Every use of the bay brought in another small cloud of dust, but she figured it was worth it; they needed the loft, her windmill arrangement was not getting sufficient power to the batteries, and she had tossed the rest of them overboard long before. Even if she had had them, she would not have gone back under the dirigible to install them; the memory of the incident still gave her the shivers. Instead she kept cutting further and further; she would have tossed out pieces of the dirigible frame too, if she could have gotten into the ballonets.

While she did this Arkady padded around the gondola cheering her on, naked and dust-caked, the red man incarnate, singing songs and watching the radar screen, jamming down quick meals, planning their course such as it was. It was impossible not to catch a bit of his exhilaration, to marvel with him at the strongest buffets of the wind, to feel the dust flying wild in her blood.

And so three long intense days passed, in the wild grip of the dark orange wind. And on the fourth day, a bit after noon, they turned the radio receiver up to full volume, and listened to the crackly roar of static at the transponders' frequency. Concentrating on the white noise made Nadia drowsy, for they had had very little sleep; and she was almost unconscious when Arkady said something, and she jerked up in her seat.

"Hear it?" he asked again. She listened, and shook her head. "There, it's a kind of *ping*."

She heard a little *bip*. "Is that it?"

"I think so. I'm going to get us down as fast as I can, I'll have to empty some of the ballonets."

He tapped away at the control keyboard, and the dirigible tilted forward and they began to drop at emergency speed. The altimeter's numbers flickered down. The radar screen showed the ground below to be basically flat. The *ping* got louder and louder; without a directional receiver, that was going to be their only way to tell if they were still approaching it or moving away. *Ping – ping – ping –* In her exhaustion

238

it was hard to tell whether it was getting louder or softer, and it seemed every beep was a different volume, depending on the attention she could bring to bear.

"It's getting softer," Arkady said suddenly. "Don't you think?"

"I can't tell."

"It is." He switched on the props, and with the whir of the motors the signal definitely seemed quieter. He turned into the wind, and the dirigible bounced wildly; he fought to steady its downward movement, but there was a delay between every shift of the flaps and the dirigible's bucking, and in reality they were in little more than a controlled crash. The ping was perhaps getting softer at a slower rate.

When the altimeter indicated they were low enough to drop the anchor they did so, and after an anxious bit of drifting it caught, and held. They dropped all the anchors they had, and pulled the *Arrowhead* down on the lines. Then Nadia suited up and climbed into the sling and winched down, and once on the surface she began walking around in a chocolate dawn, leaning hard into the irregular torrent of wind. She found she was more physically exhausted than she could ever remember being, it was really hard to make headway upwind, she had to tack. Over her intercom the transponder signal pinged, and the ground seemed to bounce under her feet; it was hard to keep her balance. The *ping* was quite distinct. "We should have been listening on our helmet intercoms all along," she said to Arkady. "You can hear better."

A gust knocked her over. She got up and shuffled slowly along, letting out a nylon line behind her, adjusting her course as she followed the volume of the *pings*. The ground flowed underfoot, when she could see it; visibility was actually down to a meter or less, at least in the thickest gusts. Then it would clear a touch and brown jets of dust would flash by, sheet after sheet, moving at an awesome speed. The wind buffeted her as hard as anything she had ever felt on

Earth, or harder; it was painful work to keep her balance, a constant physical effort.

While inside a thick, blinding cloud, she nearly shuffled right into one of the transponders, standing there like a fat fencepost. "Hey!" she shouted.

"What's wrong?"

"Nothing! I scared myself running into the roadmark."

"You found it!"

"Yeah." She felt her exhaustion run down into her hands and feet. She sat on the ground for a minute, then stood again; it was too cold to sit. Her ghost finger hurt.

She took up the nylon line, and returned blindly to the dirigible, feeling she had wandered into the ancient myth, and was following the only thread out of the labyrinth.

During their rover trip south, blind in the flying dust, word came crackling over the radio that UNOMA had just approved and funded the establishment of three follow-up colonies. Each would consist of five hundred people, all to be from countries not represented in the first hundred.

And the subcommittee on terraforming had recommended, and the General Assembly approved, a whole package of terraforming efforts, among them the distribution on the surface of genetically engineered micro-organisms, GEMs constructed from parent stock such as algaes, bacteria, or lichens.

Arkady laughed for a good thirty seconds. "Those bastards, those lucky bastards! They're going to get away with it."

240

PART FOUR

Homesick

One winter morning the sun shines down on Valles Marineris, illuminating the north walls of all the canyons in that great concatenation of canyons. And in that bright light, all day every day, one can see that every ledge and outcropping is black with a warty surface of lichen.

Life adapts, you see. It has only a few needs, some fuel, some energy; and it is fantastically ingenious at extracting these needs from a wide range of environments. Some Terran organisms live always below the freezing point of water, others above the boiling point; some live in high radiation zones, others in intensely salty regions, or within solid rock, or in pitch black, or in extreme dehydration, or without oxygen. All kinds of environments are accommodated, by adaptive measures so strange and marvelous they are beyond our capacity to imagine; and so from the bedrock to high in the atmosphere, life has permeated the Earth with the full weave of one great biosphere.

All these adaptive abilities are coded and passed along in genes. If the genes mutate, the organisms change. If the genes are altered, the organisms change. Bioengineers use both these forms of change, not only recombinant gene splicing, but also the much older art of selective breeding. Microorganisms are plated, and the fastest growers (or those that exhibit most the trait you want) can be culled and plated again; mutagens can be added to increase the mutation rate; and in the quick succession of microbial generations (say ten per day), you can repeat this process until you get something like what you want. Selective breeding is one of the most powerful bioengineering techniques we have.

But the newer techniques tend to get the attention. Genetically engineered micro-organisms had been on the scene only about half a century when the first hundred arrived on Mars. But half a century in modern science is a long time.

Plasmid conjugates had become very sophisticated tools in those years. The array of restriction enzymes for cutting, and ligase enzymes for pasting, was big and versatile; the ability to line out long DNA strings precisely was there; the accumulated knowledge of genomes was immense, and growing exponentially; and used all together, this new biotechnology was allowing all kinds of trait mobilization, promotion, replication, triggered suicide (to stop excess success), and so forth. It was possible to find the DNA sequences from an organism that carried the desired characteristic, and then synthesize these DNA messages and cut and paste them into plasmid rings; after that cells were washed and suspended in a glycerol with the new plasmids, and the glycerol was suspended between two electrodes and given a short sharp shock of about two thousand volts: the plasmids in the glycerol shot into the cells, and voilà! There, zapped to life like Frankenstein's monster, was a new organism. With new abilities.

And so: fast-growing lichens. Radiation-resistant algae. Extreme-cold fungi. Halophylic bacteria, eating salt and excreting oxygen. Surarctic mosses. An entire taxonomy of new kinds of life, all partially adapted to the surface of Mars, all out there having a try at it. Some species went extinct: natural selection. Some prospered: survival of the fittest. Some prospered wildly, at the expense of other organisms; and then chemicals in their excretions activated their suicide genes, and they died back until the levels of those chemicals dropped again.

So life adapts to conditions. And at the same time, conditions are changed by life. That is one of the definitions of life: organism and environment change together in a reciprocal arrangement, as they are two manifestations of an ecology, two parts of a whole.

And so: black fuzz on the polar ice. Black fuzz on the ragged surfaces of bubbled rock. Pale green patches on the ground. Bigger grains of frost in the air. Animacules shoving through the depths of the regolith, like trillions of tiny moles.

At first it was nearly invisible, and very slow. With a cold snap or a solar storm there would be massive die-offs, whole species extinct in a night. But the remains of the dead fed other creatures; conditions were thus easier for them, and the process picked up momentum. Bacteria reproduce quickly, doubling their mass many times a day if conditions are right: the mathematical possibilities for the speed of their growth are staggering, and although environmental constraints — especially on Mars — keep all actual growth far from the mathematical limits, still, the new organisms, the areophytes, quickly reproduced, sometimes mutated, always died, and the new life fed on the compost of their ancestors, and reproduced again. Lived and died; and the soil and air left behind were different than they were before these millions of brief generations.

And so one morning the sun rises, shooting long rays through the ragged cloud cover, up the length of Valles Marineris. On the north wall every horizontal face is black and yellow and olive and gray and green, all with the warty surfaces of lichen. Plates of lichen drip down the vertical faces of stone, which stand as they always have, stony, and cracked, and red; but now mottled, as if with lace.

Michel Duval dreamed of home. He was swimming in the surf off the point at Villefranche-sur-Mer, the warm August water lifting him up and down. It was windy and near sunset and the water was a sloppy white bronze, the sunlight bouncing all over it. The waves were big for the Mediterranean, swift breakers that rose up all riven with wind chop to crash in quick uneven lines, allowing him to ride them for a moment. Then it was under in a tumble of bubbles and sand, and back up into a burst of gold light and the taste of salt in everything, his eyes stinging voluptuously. Big black pelicans rode air cushions just over the swells, soared into steep clumsy turns, stalled, dropped into the water around him. They half-folded their wings when they dove, making adjustments with them until the actual moment of the awkward crash into the water. Often they came up gulping small fish. Just meters from him one splashed in, silhouetted against the sun like a Stuka or a pterodactyl. Cool and warm, immersed in salt, he bobbed on the swell and blinked, blinded by salt light. A breaking wave looked like diamonds smashed to cream.

His phone rang.

His phone rang. It was Ursula and Phyllis, to tell him that Maya was having another fit and was inconsolable. He got up, put on unders and went to the bathroom. Waves leaped over a line of backwash. Maya, depressed again. Last time he had seen her she had been in high spirits, almost euphoric, and that was what, a week ago? But that was Maya. Maya was crazy. Crazy in a Russian way, however, which meant she was a power to be reckoned with. Mother Russia! The church and the communists both had tried to eradicate the matriarchy that had preceded them; and all they had achieved was a flood of bitter emasculating scorn, a whole nation full of contemptuous russalkas and baba yagas and

twenty-hour-a-day superwomen, living in a nearly par-
thenogenic culture of mothers, daughters, babushkas,
granddaughters. Yet still necessarily absorbed in their
relationships with men, desperately trying to find the lost
father, the perfect mate. Or just a man who would pull his
share of the load. Finding that great love, and then more
often than not destroying it. Crazy!

Well, it was dangerous to generalize. But Maya was a
classic case. Moody, angry, flirtatious, brilliant, charming,
manipulative, intense – and now filling his office like a huge
slab of dejection, her eyes red-rimmed and bloodshot, her
mouth haggard. Ursula and Phyllis nodded and whispered
thanks to Michel for getting up so early, and left. He went
to the venetian blinds and opened them, and the light from
the central dome poured in. He saw again that Maya was a
beautiful woman, with wild lustrous hair and a dark charismatic gaze, immediate and direct. It was dismaying to see
her this upset, he never got used to it, it contrasted too
sharply with her usual vivaciousness, the way she would put
a finger to your arm as she rattled on in a confiding tone
about one fascinating thing or other . . .

All strangely mimicked by this desperate creature, who
leaned forward onto his desk and began to tell him in a
ragged hoarse voice about the latest scene in the unfolding
drama of her and John, and then, again, Frank. Apparently
she had gotten angry at John for refusing to help her in a
plan she had to get some of the Russian-based multinationals
to underwrite the development of settlements in Hellas
Basin, which being the deepest point on Mars was going to
be first to benefit from the atmospheric changes they were
beginning to see. The air pressure at Low Point, four kilometers below the datum, was always going to be ten times
thicker than that on top of the great volcanoes, and three
times thicker than at the datum: it was going to be the first
human-viable place, perfect for development.

But apparently John preferred to work through UNOMA

and governments. And this was just one of the many basic political disagreements which were beginning to infect their personal life, to the point that they were fighting pretty frequently about other things, things that didn't matter, things about which they had never fought before.

Watching her Michel almost said, John wants you irritated with him. He wasn't sure what John would say to that. Maya rubbed her eyes, leaned her forehead on his desk, revealing the back of her neck and her broad rangy shoulders. She would never look this distraught in front of most of Underhill; it was an intimacy between them, something she only did with him. It was as if she had taken off her clothes. People didn't understand that true intimacy did not consist of sexual intercourse, which could be done with strangers and in a state of total alienation; intimacy consisted of talking for hours about what was most important in one's life. Although it was true she would be beautiful naked, she had perfect proportions. He recalled the way she looked swimming in the pool, doing the backstroke in a blue bathing suit cut high over the hipbones. A Mediterranean image: he was floating in the water at Villefranche, everything flooded with sunset's amber light, and he was looking in at the beach where men and women were walking, naked except for the neon triangles of *cache-sexe* bathing suits – brown-skinned bare-breasted women, walking in pairs like dancers in the sunlight – then dolphins sliced out of the water between him and the beach, their sleek black bodies rounded like the women's—

But now Maya was talking about Frank. Frank, who had a sixth sense for trouble between John and Maya (six would not be necessary), and who came running to Maya every time he felt the signs, to walk with her and talk about his vision of Mars, which was progressive, exciting, ambitious, everything that John's was not. "Frank is so much more dynamic than John these days, I don't know why."

"Because he agrees with you," Michel said.

Maya shrugged. "Perhaps that's all I mean. But we have a chance to build a whole civilization here, we do. But John is so . . ." Big sigh. "And yet I love him, I really do. But . . ."

She talked for a while about their past, how their courtship had saved the voyage out from anarchy (or at least ennui), how John's easy-going stability had been so good for her. How you could count on him. How impressed she had been by his fame, how she had felt that the liaison made her part of world history forever. But now she understood that she herself was going to be part of world history anyway: all of them in the first hundred were. Her voice rose, became faster and more vehement: "I don't need John for that now, I only need him for how I feel about him, but now we don't agree on anything and we're not very much alike, and Frank who has been so careful to hold back no matter what, we agree about almost everything and I've been so enthusiastic about that part that I've given him the wrong signal again, so he did it again, yesterday in the pool he – he held me, you know, took my arms in his hands—" she crossed her arms and clasped her biceps in her hands, "—and asked me to leave John for him, which I would never do, and he was *shaking*, and I said I couldn't but I was shaking too." So later she had been on edge, and had started a fight with John, started it so flagrantly that he had gotten truly angry and had left and taken a rover out to Nadia's arcade, and spent the night there with the construction team; and Frank had come to talk to her again, and when she had (just barely) put him off, Frank had declared he was going to live with the European settlement on the other side of the planet; he who was the colony's driving force! "And he'll really do it, he's not one to threaten. He's been learning German the way he does, languages are nothing to Frank."

Michel tried to concentrate on what she was saying. It was difficult, because he knew full well that in a week everything would be different, all the dynamics in that little trio altered beyond recognition. So it was hard to care. What about his troubles? They went much, much deeper; but no one ever listened to him. He walked back and forth in front of the window, reassuring her with the usual questions and comments. The greenery in the atrium was refreshing; it could have been a courtyard in Arles or Villefranche; or suddenly it reminded him of Avignon's narrow cypress-arched plaza near the Pope's palace, the plaza and its café tables which in the summer just after sunset had just the color of Mars. Taste of olive and red wine . . .

"Let's go for a walk," he said. Standard part of therapy hour. They crossed the atrium and went to the kitchens so Michel could eat a breakfast which he forgot even as he swallowed. We should call eating forgetting, he thought as they walked around the hall to the locks. They put on suits – Maya entering a change room to get her unders on – then checked them and went in the lock and depressurized it and then opened the big outer door and stepped outside.

The diamond chill. For a while they stayed on the sidewalks circling Underhill, taking a tour of the dump and its great salt pyramids. "Do you think they'll ever find a use for all this salt?" he said.

"Sax is still working on it."

From time to time Maya went on talking about John and Frank. Michel asked the questions that a shrink program would have asked, Maya answered in the way a Maya program would have answered. Their voices right in each other's ears, the intimacy of the intercom.

They came to the lichen farm, and Michel stopped to gaze over the trays, to soak in their intense living color. Black snow algae, and then thick mats of otoo lichen, in which the algae symbiote was a blue-green strain that Vlad had just gotten to grow alone; red lichen, which seemed not to be doing well. Superfluous in any case. Yellow lichen, olive lichen, a lichen that looked exactly like battleship paint. Flaky white and lime green lichen – living green! It pulsed in the eye, a rich and improbable desert flower. He had heard

Hiroko, looking down at such a growth, say "This is *viriditas*," which was Latin for "greening power". The word had been coined by a Christian mystic of the middle ages, a woman named Hildegard. *Viriditas*, now adapting to conditions here, and spreading slowly over the lowlands of the northern hemisphere. In the southern summers it did even better; one day it had reached 285° Kelvin, a record high by 12°. The world was changing, Maya remarked as they walked by the flats. "Yes," Michel said, and could not help adding, "only three hundred years before we reach livable temperatures."

Maya laughed. She was feeling better. Soon she would be back on a level, or at least crossing through that zone on the way to euphoria. Maya was labile. Stability-lability was the most recent characteristic Michel had been studying in the first hundred; Maya represented the labile extreme.

"Let's drive out and see the arcade," she said. Michel agreed, wondering what might happen if they ran into John. They went to the parking lot and checked out a roadrunner. Michel drove the little jeep and listened to Maya talk. Did conversation change when voices were divorced from bodies, planted right in the ears of the listeners by helmet mikes? It was as if one were always on the phone, even when sitting next to the person you were talking to. Or – was this better or worse? – as if you were engaged in telepathy.

The cement road was smooth, and he drove at the roadrunner's top speed of 60 kph. He could just feel the rush of thin air against his faceplate. All that CO_2 that Sax so wanted to scrub from the atmosphere. Sax would need powerful scrubbers, even more powerful than the lichens; he needed forests, enormous multi-layered halophylic rainforests, trapping enormous loads of carbon in wood, leaves, mulch, peat. He needed peat bogs a hundred meters deep, rain forests a hundred meters tall. He had said as much. It marked Ann's face just to hear the sound of his voice.

Fifteen minutes' drive and they came to Nadia's arcade.

The site was still under construction and looked raw and messy, like Underhill in the beginning but on a larger scale. A long mound of burgundy rubble had been excavated from the trench, which ran east and west like Big Man's grave.

They stood at one end of the great trench. Thirty meters deep, thirty wide, a kilometer long. The south side of the trench was now a wall of glass; the north side of the trench was covered with arrays of filtering mirrors, alternating with wall-mesocosms, Mars jars or terrariums, all of them together a colorful mix, like a tapestry of past and future. Most of the terrariums were filled with spruce trees and other flora that made it resemble the great world-wrapping Terran forest of the sixtieth latitude. Like Nadia Cherneshev-sky's old home in Siberia, in other words. Was this perhaps a sign that she had a touch of his disease? And could he prevail on her to build a Mediterranean?

Nadia was up working on a bulldozer. A woman with her own kind of *viriditas*. She stopped and came over to talk briefly with them. The project was coming along, she told them calmly. Amazing what one could do with the robot vehicles that were still being sent up from Earth. The concourse was done, and planted with a variety of trees, including a strain of dwarf sequoia already thirty meters tall, nearly as tall as the whole arcade. The three stacked rows of Underhill-style vaulted chambers behind the concourse were installed, their insulation in place. The settlement had just the other day been sealed and heated and pressurized, so that it was possible to work inside it without suits. The three floors were stacked on each other in ever smaller arches, reminding Michel of the Pont du Gard; of course all the architecture here was Roman in origin, so that should not be a surprise. The arches were wider, however, and slighter. Airier in the tolerance of the g.

Nadia went back to work. Such a calm person. Stabile, the very opposite of labile. Low-keyed, private, inward. Couldn't be less like her old friend Maya; it was good for Maya to be around her. Opposite end of the scale, keep her from flying away. Set an example for her. As in this encounter, where Maya was matching Nadia's calm tone. And when Nadia went back to work, Maya retained some of that serenity. "I'll miss Underhill when we move out here," she said. "Won't you?"

"I don't think so," Michel said. "This will be a lot sunnier." All three floors of the new habitat would open onto the tall concourse, and have terraced broad balconies on the sunny side of the rooms, so that even though the whole structure faced north and was buried deeper than Underhill, the heliotropic filtered mirrors on the other side of the trench would pour light onto them from dawn to dusk. "I'll be happy to move. We've needed the space from the beginning."

"But we won't get all this space to ourselves. There'll be new people here."

"Yes. But that will give us space of a different kind."

She looked thoughtful. "Like John and Frank leaving."

"Yes. But even that isn't necessarily a bad thing." In a larger society, he told her, the claustrophobic village atmosphere of Underhill would begin to dissipate; this would give a better perspective on certain aspects of things. Michel hesitated before continuing, unsure how to say it. Subtlety was dangerous when you were both using a second language, coming at it from different native tongues: possibilities for misunderstanding were all too real. "You must accept the idea that you perhaps do not want to choose between John and Frank. That in fact you want them both. In the context of the first hundred that can only be scandalous. But in a larger world, over time . . ."

"Hiroko keeps ten men!" she exclaimed angrily.

"Yes, and so do you. So do you. And in a larger world, no one will know or care."

He went on reassuring her, telling her that she was powerful, that (using Frank's terms) she was the alpha female of

253

the troop. She disagreed and forced more praise from him until finally she was satiated, and he could suggest they return home.

"Don't you think it will be a shock to have new people around? Different people?" She was driving, and as she turned to ask him this she almost drove off the road.

"I suppose." Parties had already landed in Borealis and Acidalia and the videotapes of them had been a shock, you could see it in people's faces. As if aliens had arrived from space. But so far only Ann and Simon had met with any of them in person, running into a rover expedition north of Noctis Labyrinthus. "Ann said it felt as if someone had stepped out of the TV."

"My life feels like that all the time," Maya said sadly.

Michel lifted his eyebrows. The Maya program would not have said that. "What do you mean?"

"Oh, you know. Half the time it seems like one big simulation, don't you think?"

"No." He considered it. "I don't." It was all too real, in fact – the cold of it seeping up through the rover seat deep into his flesh – inescapably real, inescapably cold. Perhaps as a Russian she didn't appreciate that. But it was always, always cold. Even at noon on midsummer's day, with the sun overhead like an open furnace door blazing in the sand-colored sky, the temperature would be at best 260° K, meaning −15°C, cold enough to push through the mesh of a walker and make each move a little diamond pattern of hurt. As they approached Underhill Michel felt the cold pushing through the fabric into his skin, and he felt the too-cool oxygenated air expand out of the mouthpiece deep into his lungs, and he glanced up at the sand horizon and the sand sky and said to himself, I am a diamondback snake, slithering through a red desert of cold stone and dry dust. Someday I will shed my skin like a phoenix in a fire, to become some new creature of the sun, to walk the beach naked and splash in warm salt water . . .

254

Back at Underhill he turned on the shrink program in his head and asked Maya if she were feeling better, and she touched her faceplate to his, giving him a brief glimpse of a gaze that was a kiss. "You know I do," her voice said in his ear. He nodded. "I think I'll go for another walk, then," he said, and did not say, But what about me? What will make me feel better? He willed the movement of his legs and walked off. The bleak plain surrounding the base was a vision out of some post-holocaust desolation, a nightmare world; nevertheless he didn't want to go back into their little warren of artificial light and heated air and carefully deployed colors, colors that he himself had chosen for the most part, utilizing the very latest in color-mood theory, a theory which he now understood to be based on certain root assumptions that did not in fact apply here: the colors were all wrong, or worse, irrelevant. Wallpaper in hell.

The phrase formed in his mind and pushed at his lips. Wallpaper in hell. Wallpaper in hell. Since they're going to go crazy anyway . . . Certainly it had been a mistake to have only one psychiatrist along. Every therapist on Earth was also in therapy, it was part of the job, it came with the territory. But his therapist was back in Nice, fifteen timeslipped minutes away at best, and Michel talked to him but he couldn't help. He didn't understand, not really; he lived where it was warm and blue, he could go outside, he was (Michel presumed) in reasonably good mental health. While Michel was a doctor in a hospice in a prison in hell; and the doctor was sick.

He hadn't been able to adapt. People were different in that regard, it was a matter of temperament. Maya, walking toward the lock door, had a temperament quite different from his, which somehow enabled her to be completely at home here. To tell the truth he didn't think she really noticed her surroundings much in any case. And yet in other ways he and she were similar. It had to do with the lability-stability index, and its particular emotionality; they were

255

both labile. And yet fundamentally they were very different characters; the labile-stabile index had to be considered in combination with the very different set of characteristics grouped under the labels *extraversion* and *introversion*. This had been his great discovery of the recent year, and now it structured all his thinking about himself and his charges.

Walking toward the Alchemists' Quarter, he fit the morning's events into the gridwork of this new characterological system. Extraversion-introversion was one of the best-studied systems of traits in all psychological theory, with great masses of evidence from many different cultures supporting the objective reality of the concept. Not as a simple duality of course; one did not label a person plainly this or that, but rather placed them on a scale, rating them for such qualities as sociability, impulsiveness, changeability, talkativeness, outgoingness, activity, liveliness, excitability, optimism, and so on. These measurements had been done so many times that it was statistically certain that the various traits did indeed hang together, to a degree that exceeded chance by a huge amount. So the concept was real, quite real! In fact physiological investigations had revealed that extraversion was linked with resting states of low cortical arousal, introversion with high cortical arousal; this had sounded backwards to Michel at first, but then he remembered that the cortex inhibits the lower centers of the brain, so that low cortical arousal allows the more uninhibited behavior of the extravert, while high cortical arousal is inhibitory and leads to introversion. This explained why drinking alcohol, a depressant which lowers cortical arousal, could lead to more excited and uninhibited behavior.

So the whole collection of extravert-introvert traits, with all that they said about one's character, could be traced back to a group of cells in the brain stem called the ascending reticular activating system, the area that ultimately determined levels of cortical arousal. Thus they were driven by biology. *There should be no such thing as fate:* Ralph Waldo

Emerson, a year after his six year-old son died. But biology was fate.

And there was more to Michel's system; fate, after all, was no simple either-or. He had recently begun to consider Wenger's index of autonomic balance, which used seven different variables to determine whether an individual was dominated by the sympathetic or the parasympathetic branches of the autonomic nervous system. The sympathetic branch responds to outside stimuli and alerts the organism to action, so that individuals dominated by this branch were excitable; the parasympathetic branch, on the other hand, habituates the alerted organism to the stimulus, and restores it to homeostatic balance, so that individuals dominated by this branch were placid. Duffy had suggested calling these two classes of individuals *labiles* and *stabiles*, and this classification, while not as famous as extraversion and introversion, was just as solidly backed by empirical evidence, and just as useful in understanding varieties of temperament.

Now, neither system of classification told the investigator all that much about the total nature of the personality being studied. The terms were so general, they were collections of so many traits, that they said very little in any useful diagnostic sense, especially since both were Gaussian curves in the actual population.

But combine the two systems, and it began to get very interesting indeed.

It was not a simple matter, and Michel had spent a fair amount of time at his computer screen sketching one kind of combinatoire after another, using the two different systems as the x and y axes of several different grids, none of which told him much. But then he began moving the four terms around the initial points of a Greimas semantic rectangle, a structuralist schema with alchemical ancestry, which proposed that no simple dialectic was enough to indicate the true complexity of any cluster of related concepts,

257

so that it was necessary to acknowledge the real difference between something's opposite and its contrary; the concept "not-X" being not quite the same thing as "anti-X," as one saw immediately. So the first stage was usually indicated by using the four terms S, −S, S̄, and −S̄, in a simple rectangle:

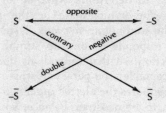

Diagram 4a (p.2.9)

Thus −S was a simple not-S, and s was the stronger anti-S; while −s was the for Michel skullcracking negation of a negation, either a neutralizing of the initial opposition, or the union of the two negations; in practice this often remained a mystery or *koan*, but sometimes it came clear, as an idea that completed the conceptual unit quite nicely, as in one of Greimas's examples:

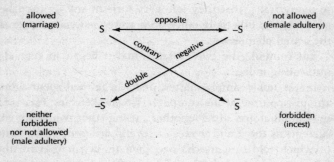

Diagram 4b (p.2.9)

The next step in the complication of the design, the step where new combinations often revealed structural relationships not at all obvious on the face of it, was to build another rectangle that bracketed the first at right angles, like so:

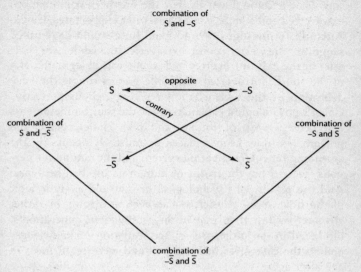

Diagram 4c (p.220)

And Michel had stared at this schema, with extraversion, introversion, lability and stability at the first four corners, and considered their combinations; and then everything had suddenly fallen into focus, as if a kaleidoscope had suddenly clicked by accident into a depiction of a rose. For it made perfect sense: there were extraverts who were excitable, and extraverts who were on an even keel; there were introverts who were quite emotional, and those who were not. He could immediately think of examples among the colonists of all four of the types.

When considering names to give these combined categories, he had had to laugh. Unbelievable! It was ironic at best to think that he had used the results of a century's psychological thinking, and some of the latest laboratory research in psychophysiology, not to mention a complicated apparatus from structuralist alchemy, all in order to reinvent the ancient system of the humours. But there it was; that was what it came down to. For the northern combination, extraverted and stabile, was clearly what Hippocrates, Galen, Aristotle, Trimestigus, Wundt, and Jung would have called sanguine; the western point, extraverted and labile, was choleric; in the east, introverted and stabile was phlegmatic; and in the south, introverted and labile was of course the very definition of the melancholic! Yes, they all fit perfectly! Galen's physiological explanation for the four temperaments had been wrong, of course, and bile, choler, blood and phlegm had now been replaced as causative agents by the ascending reticular activating system and the autonomic nervous system; but the truths of human nature had held fast! And the powers of psychological insight and analytic logic of the first Greek physicians had been as strong, or rather stronger by far, than that of any subsequent generation's, blinkered by an often-useless accumulation of knowledge; and so the categories had endured and were reaffirmed, in age after age.

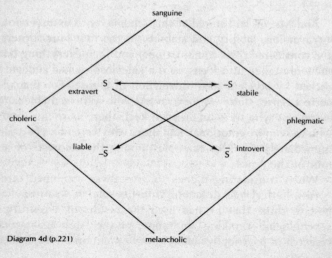

Diagram 4d (p.221)

Michel found himself in the Alchemists' Quarter. He exerted himself to pay attention to it. Here men used arcane knowledge to make diamonds out of carbon, and they made it so easily and precisely that all their window glass was coated in a molecular layer of diamond to protect it from the corrosive dust; and their great white salt pyramids (one of the great shapes of ancient knowledge, the pyramid) were coated in layers of pure diamond. And the one-molecule diamond-coating process was just one of thousands of alchemical operations performed in these squat buildings.

In recent years the buildings had taken on a faintly Moslem look, their white brick walls displaying equation after equation, all rendered in black flowing mosaic calligraphy. Michel ran into Sax, who was standing next to the terminal velocity equation displayed on the wall of the brick factory, and he switched to the common band: "Can you turn lead into gold?"

Sax's helmet tilted quizzically. "Maybe," he said. "A little of it, anyway. But it would be hard. Let me think about it some."

Saxifrage Russell. The perfect Phlegmatic.

The really useful part of mapping the four temperaments onto the semantic rectangle was that it immediately suggested a number of basic structural relationships between them, which then helped Michel to see their attractions and antagonisms in a new light. Maya was labile and extraverted, clearly choleric, and so was Frank; and both of them were leaders, and both were quite attracted to the other. Both being choleric, however, there was a volatile and essentially repellent aspect to the relationship as well, as if they recognized in each other exactly what they didn't like in themselves.

And thus Maya's love for John, who was clearly sanguine, with an extraversion similar to Maya's but much more emotionally stable, even to the point of placidity. So that most of the time he gave her great peace, like an anchor to reality

– which then occasionally rankled. And John's attraction to Maya? The attraction of the unpredictable, perhaps; the spice in his hearty bland happiness. Sure, why not? You can't make love to your fame. Even though some people try.

Yes, there were a lot of sanguines in the first hundred. Probably the psychological specs for selection to the colony preferred the type. Arkady, Ursula, Phyllis, Spencer, Yeli . . . Yes. And stability being the most preferred quality for selection, there were naturally a lot of phlegmatics among them as well: Nadia, Sax, Simon Frazier, perhaps Hiroko – the fact that one could not even be sure about her tended to support the guess – Vlad, George, Alex.

Phlegmatics and melancholics would naturally not get along, both being introverted and quick to withdraw, and the stabile one put off by the unpredictability of the labile; so that they would withdraw from each other, like Sax and Ann. There were not many melancholics among them. Ann, yes; and probably by the fate of her brain's structure, although it did not help that she had been mistreated as a child. She had fallen in love with Mars for the same reason that Michel hated it: because it was dead. And Ann was in love with death.

A few of the alchemists were melancholics as well. And, unfortunately, Michel himself. Perhaps five all told. Along both axes they had been selected against, as neither introversion nor lability had been considered desirable by the selection committee. Only people quite clever at concealing their real nature from the committee could have slipped through, people with great control over their personas, those larger-than-life masks that conceal all the wild inconsistencies within. Perhaps only a certain kind of *persona* had been selected to the colony, with a wide variety of persons behind it. Was that true? The selection committees had made impossible demands, it was important to remember that. They had wanted stabiles and yet they had wanted

people who cared about going to Mars so passionately and
monomaniacally that they would devote years of their
lives to achieving the goal. Was that consistent? They
wanted extraverts and they wanted brilliant scientists who
necessarily had had to dive deep into solitary study for
years and years. Was that consistent? No! Never. It went
on like that all down the list. They had created double
bind after double bind, no wonder the first hundred had
hidden from them, had hated them! He recalled with a
shudder that moment in the great solar storm on the *Ares*
when everyone had realized how much lying and hiding
they had had to do, when they had all turned and stared
at him with all that pent-up fury, as if it were all his
fault, as if he were all psychology, and had concocted the
criteria and conducted the tests and made the selections
all by himself. How he had cringed at that moment, how
alone he had felt! It had shocked him, frightened him, so
much that he had not been able to think fast enough to
confess that he too had lied, of course he had, more than
any of the rest of them!

But why had he lied, why?

This was what he could not quite recall. Melancholia as a
failure of memory, an acute sensation of the irreality of the
past, its non-existence . . . He was a melancholic: withdrawn, out of control of his feelings, inclined to depression.
He shouldn't have been chosen to go; and now he *could not
remember* why he had fought so passionately to be chosen.
The memory had gone away, overwhelmed perhaps by the
poignant, aching, fragmented images of the life he had lived
in the interstices of his desire to go to Mars. So minuscule
and so precious; the evenings in the plazas, the summer days
on the beaches, the nights in women's beds. The olive trees
of Avignon. The green flame cypress.

He found he had left the Alchemists' Quarter. He was at
the foot of the Great Salt Pyramid. He stepped slowly up
the four hundred stairs, putting his feet carefully on the blue

no-slip pads. Each step gave him a wider view of Underhill Plain, but it was still the same sere and barren rockpile, no matter how large it got. From the square white pavilion at the pyramid's summit one could just see Chernobyl, and the spaceport. Other than that, nothing. Why had he come to this place? Why had he worked so hard to get here, sacrificing so many of the pleasures of life, family, home, leisure, play . . . He shook his head. So far as he could recall, it had simply been what he had wanted to do, the definition of his life. A compulsion, a life with a goal, how could you tell the difference? Moonlit nights in the fragrant olive grove, the ground dotted with small black circles and the electric warm brush of the mistral rustling the leaves in quick soft waves, flat on his back, arms spread wide, the leaves flickering silver and grey under the black bowl of stars; and one of those stars would be steady, faint, red, and he would seek it out and watch it, there among the windswept olive leaves; and he had been eight years old! My God, what *were* they? *Nothing* explained that, *nothing* explained them! As well explain why they had painted in Lascaux, why they had built stone cathedrals into the sky. Why coral polyps built reefs.

He had had an ordinary youth, moved often, lost what friends he made, went to the University of Paris to study psychology, did his degree work on space station depression and went to work for Ariane, and then Glavkosmos. Along the way got married and divorced: Françoise had said he "was not there". All those nights with her in Avignon, all those days in Villefranche-sur-Mer, living in the most beautiful place on Earth, and he had walked about in a fog of desire for Mars! It was absurd! Worse, it was stupid. A failure of the imagination, of memory, of, finally, intelligence itself: he had not been able to see what he had had, or to imagine what he would get. And now he was paying for it, trapped on an icefloe in the Arctic night with ninety-nine foreigners, not one of whom spoke French worth a damn.

Only three who could even try, and Frank's French was worse than no French at all, like listening to someone attack the language with a hatchet.

The absence of his mind's own tongue had driven him to watching TV from home, which only exacerbated his pain. Still he taped video monologues, and sent them to his mother and sister, so that they would send replies in kind; he watched the replies many times, looking more at the back-drops than at his relatives. He even had occasional live con-versations with journalists, waiting impatiently between exchanges. Those talks made it clear how famous he was in France, a household name, and he was careful to answer everything conventionally, playing the Michel Duval per-sona, running the Michel program. Sometimes he cancelled consultations with fellow colonists when he was in the mood to listen to French; let them eat English! But these incidents got him a sharp reprimand from Frank, and a conference with Maya. Was he overworked? Of course not; only ninety-nine people to keep sane, while at the same time wandering in a Provence of the mind, on tree-covered steep hillsides with their vineyards and farmhouses and ruined towers and monasteries, in a living landscape, a landscape infinitely more beautiful and humane than the stony waste of this reality—

He was in the TV lounge. While lost in thought he had apparently gone back inside. But he could not remember that; he had thought he was still standing on top of the Great Pyramid; and then he had blinked and was in the TV lounge (all asylums have them), watching a video image of one of the lichen-covered canyon walls of Marineris.

He shivered. It had happened again. He had lost touch, gone away and come to later in the day. It had happened already some dozen times before. And it was not just being lost in thought, but buried in it, dead to the world. He looked around the room, shivered convulsively. It was $Ls = 5$ now, the beginning of northern spring, and the northern walls of

265

the great canyons were basking in the sun. Since they're all going to go crazy anyway . . .

Then it was Ls = 157, and 152° had passed in a blur of tele-existence. He was basking in the sun in the courtyard of Françoise's seaside villa in Villefranche-sur-Mer, looking down on tile rooftops and terracotta pillars and a small pool, turquoise above the cobalt of the Mediterranean. A cypress stood like a green flame over the pool, swaying in a breeze and casting its perfume over his face. In the distance the green headland of a peninsula—

Except really he was in Underhill Prime, usually called the trench, or Nadia's arcade, sitting on the upper balcony looking out at a dwarf sequoia, behind it the glass wall and the mirrors with their gradient refractive index that guided the light down into the concourse from its origin on the Côte D'Or. Tatiana Durova had been killed by a crane tipped by a robot, and Nadia was inconsolable. But grief runs off us, Michel thought as he sat with her, like rain off a duck. In time Nadia would be well. Meanwhile there was nothing to be done. Did they think he was a sorcerer? A priest? If that were true he would have healed himself, healed all this world, or better, flown through space home. Wouldn't that cause a sensation, to appear on the beach at Antibes and say, "Bonjour, I am Michel, I have come home"?

Then it was Ls = 190, and he was a lizard on the top of the Pont du Gard, on the narrow rectangular rock plates that covered the actual aqueduct itself, which ran in its straight line high over the gorge. His diamondback skin had sloughed off around his tail, and the hot sun burned the new skin in crisscross lines. Except he was in Underhill in fact, in the atrium, and Frank had gone off to live with the Japanese that had landed in Argyre, and Maya and John were at loggerheads about their rooms, and where to house the UNOMA local headquarters; and Maya, more beautiful than ever, stalked him through the atrium, imploring his aid. He and Marina Tokareva had stopped rooming together nearly a full

Martian year before – she had said he was not there – and looking at Maya Michel found himself imagining her as a lover but of course this was crazy, she was a russalka, she had slept with Glavkosmos bosses and cosmonauts to make her way up through the system and it had made her dissociated and bitter and unpredictable, she used sex to hurt now, sex was just diplomacy by other means to her, it would be insane to have anything to do with her in that mode, to be drawn down into the vortex of her limbs and her limbic system. Why not send crazy people in the first place . . .

But now it was $Ls = 241$. He walked over the honeycombed limestone parapet of Les Baux, looking in the ruined chambers of the medieval hermitage. It was near sunset and the light was a curious Martian orange, the limestone glowing, the whole village and hazy plain below stretching out to the whitebronze line of the Mediterranean, looking as implausible as a dream . . . Except it was a dream, and he woke up, and found himself awake and back in Underhill. Phyllis and Edvard had just returned from an expedition and Phyllis was laughing and showing them a buttery lump of rock. "It was scattered all over the canyon," she said laughing, "gold nuggets the size of your fist."

Then he was walking the tunnels out to the garage. The colony's psychiatrist, experiencing visions, falling into gaps of consciousness, gaps of memory. Physician, heal thyself! But he couldn't. He had gone insane of homesickness. Homesickness, there must be a better term for that, a scientific label that would legitimize it, make it real to others; but he already knew it was real. He missed Provence so much that at times he felt he could not breathe. He was like Nadia's hand, a part of it torn away, the ghost nerves still throbbing with pain.

. . . And save them the trouble?

Time passed. The Michel program walked around, a hollow persona, empty inside, only some tiny homunculus of the cerebellum left to teleoperate the thing.

The night of the second day of Ls = 266, he went to bed. He was dog-tired though he had done nothing, totally exhausted and drained, and yet he lay in the dark of his room and could not sleep. His mind spun miserably; he was very aware of how sick he was. He wished he could quit the pretense and admit that he had lost it, institutionalize himself. Go home. He could remember almost nothing of the previous few weeks; or maybe it was longer than that? He was not sure. He began to weep.

His door clicked. It swung open, and a narrow wedge of hall light shone in, unblocked. No one there.

"Hello?" he said, working to keep the tears out of his voice. "Who is it?"

The reply was right in his ear, as if from a helmet intercom: "Come with me," a man's voice said.

Michel jerked back and bumped into the wall. He stared up at a black silhouetted figure.

"We need your help," the figure whispered. A hand gripped his arm as he pressed back into the wall. "And you need ours." A suggestion of a smile in the voice, which Michel *did not recognize*.

Fear thrust him into a new world. Suddenly he could see much better, as if the touch of his visitor had sprung his pupils open like camera apertures. A thin dark-skinned man. A stranger. Astonishment launched through his fear, and he got up and moved through the dark light with dreamlike precision, stepping into slippers, and then at the stranger's urging following him out into the hallway, feeling the lightness of Martian g for the first time in years. The hallway seemed bursting with gray light, though he could tell that only the night strips in the floor were on. It was enough to see well by if you were scared. His companion had short black dreadlocks, which made his head appear spiked. He was short, thin, narrow-faced. A stranger, no doubt about it. An intruder from one of the new colonies in the southern hemisphere, Michel thought. But the man was leading him through Underhill with an expert touch, moving in utter silence. Indeed the whole of Underhill was soundless, as if it were a silent black-and-white film. He glanced at his wristpad: it was blank. The timeslip. He wanted to say, "Who are you?" but the silence was so blanketing that he couldn't bring himself to speak. He mouthed the words and the man turned and looked over his shoulder at him, the whites of his eyes visible and luminous all the way around the irises, the nostrils wide black holes. "I'm the stowaway," he mouthed, and grinned. His eyeteeth were discolored; they were made of stone, Michel suddenly saw that. Martian stone teeth in his head. He took Michel by the arm. They were heading to the farm lock. "We need helmets out there," Michel whispered, balking.

"Not tonight." The man opened the lock door, and no air rushed into it even though it was open on the other side. They went in and walked between the black rows of packed foliage, and the air was sweet. Hiroko will be angry, Michel thought.

His guide was gone. Ahead Michel saw movement, and heard a tinkly little laugh. It sounded like a child. Suddenly it occurred to Michel that the absence of children accounted for the colony's pervasive feeling of sterility, that they could build buildings and grow plants and yet without children this sterile feeling would still permeate every part of their lives. Extremely frightened, he continued to walk toward the center of the farm. It was warm and humid, and the air stank of wet dirt and fertilizer and foliage. Light glinted from thousands of leaf surfaces, as if the stars had fallen through the clear roof and clustered around him. Rows of corn rustled, and the air was going to his head like brandy. Little feet were scurrying behind the narrow rice paddies: even in the darkness the rice was an intense blackish green, and there among the paddies were small faces, grinning knee-high and disappearing when he turned to face them. Hot blood flooded his face and hands, his blood turned to fire and he retreated three steps, then stopped and spun. Two naked little girls were walking down the lane toward him, black-haired, dark-skinned, about three years old. Their oriental eyes were bright in the gloom, their expressions solemn. They took him by the hands and turned him around; he allowed them to lead him down the lane, looking down at first one head and then the other. Someone had decided to take action against their sterility. As they walked along, other naked toddlers appeared out of the shrubbery and crowded around them, boys and girls both, some a bit darker or lighter than the first two, most the same color, all the same age. Nine or ten of them escorted Michel to the center of the farm, weaving around him in a quick trot; and there at the center of the maze was a small clearing, currently occupied by about a dozen adults, all naked, seated in a rough circle. The children ran to the adults, gave them hugs and sat at their knees. Michel's pupils opened further in the nimbus of starlight and leaf gleam, and he recognized members of the farm team, Iwao, Raul, Ellen, Rya, Gene, Evgenia, all of the farm team except for Hiroko herself.

After a moment's hesitation Michel stepped out of his slippers and took off his clothes, and put them on top of the slippers and sat down in an empty spot in the circle. He didn't know what he was taking part in, but it didn't matter. Several of the figures nodded at him in welcome, and Ellen and Evgenia, seated on each side of him, touched him on the arms. All of a sudden the children got up and ran together down one of the aisles, squealing and giggling. They came back in a tight knot around Hiroko, who walked into the middle of the circle, her naked form dark in the darkness. Trailed by the kids she walked slowly around the circle, pouring from her two outstretched fists a little bit of dirt into each person's offered hands. Michel held up his palms with Ellen and Evgenia as she approached, he stared at her lustrous skin. Once on the night beach at Villefranche he had walked by a gang of African women splashing in the phosphorescent waves, white water on black gleaming skin—

The dirt in his hand was warm and smelled rusty. "This is our body," Hiroko said. She walked to the other side of the circle, gave the children each a fistful of dirt and sent them back to sit among the adults. She sat across from Michel and began to chant in Japanese. Evgenia leaned over and whispered a translation or rather an explanation in his ear. They were celebrating the areophany, a ceremony they had created together under Hiroko's guidance and inspiration. It was a kind of landscape religion, a consciousness of Mars as a physical space suffused with *kami*, which was the spiritual energy or power that rested in the land itself. *Kami* was manifested most obviously in certain extraordinary objects in the landscape, stone pillars, isolated ejecta, sheer cliffs, oddly smoothed crater interiors, the broad circular peaks of the great volcanoes. These intensified expressions of Mars's *kami* had a Terran analogue within the colonists themselves, the power that Hiroko called *viriditas*, that greening fructiparous power within, which knows that the wild world itself is holy. *Kami, viriditas;* it was the combination of these sacred powers that would allow humans to exist here in a meaningful way.

When Michel heard Evgenia whisper the word *combination*, all the terms immediately fell into a semantic rectangle: *kami* and *viriditas*, Mars and Earth, hatred and love, absence and yearning. And then the kaleidoscope clicked home and all the rectangles folded into place in his mind, all antimonies collapsed to a single, beautiful rose, the heart of the areophany, *kami* suffused with *viriditas*, both fully red and fully green at one and the same time. His jaw was slack, his skin was burning, he could not explain it and did not want to. His blood was fire in his veins.

Hiroko stopped chanting, brought her hand to her mouth, began to eat the dirt in her palm. All the others did the same.

271

Michel lifted his hand to his face: a lot of dirt to eat, but he stuck his tongue out and licked up half of it and felt a brief electric shiver as he rubbed it against the roof of his mouth, sliding the gritty stuff back and forth until it was mud. It tasted salty and rusty, with an unpleasant whiff of rotten eggs and chemicals. He choked it down, gagging slightly. He swallowed the other mouthful in his hand. There was an irregular hum coming from the circle of celebrants as they ate, vowel sounds shifting from one to the next, aaaay, ooooo, ahhhh, iiiiiii, eeee, uuuuuu, lingering over each vowel for a minute it seemed, the sound spreading into two and sometimes three parts, with head tones creating odd harmonies. Hiroko began to chant over this song. Everyone stood and Michel scrambled up with them. They all moved into the center of the circle together, Evgenia and Ellen taking Michel by the arms and pulling him along. Then they were all pressed together around Hiroko, in a mass of close-packed bodies, surrounding Michel so that warm skin squashed up against every side of him. This is our body. A lot of them were kissing, their eyes closed. Slowly they moved, twisting to keep maximum contact as they shifted to new kinetic configurations. Wiry pubic hair tickled his bottom, and he felt what had to have been an erect penis against his hip. The dirt was heavy in his stomach, and he felt light-headed; his blood was fire, his skin felt like a taut balloon, containing a blaze. The stars were packed overhead in astonishing numbers, and each one had its own color, green or red or blue or yellow; they looked like sparks.

He was a phoenix. Hiroko herself pressed against him, and he rose in the center of the fire, ready for rebirth. She held his new body in a full embrace, squeezed him; she was tall, and seemed all muscle. She looked him eye-to-eye. He felt her breasts against his ribs, her pubic bone hard on his thigh. She kissed him, her tongue touching his teeth; he tasted the dirt, then suddenly felt all of her at once; all the rest of his life the involuntary memory of that feeling would be enough to start the pulse of an erection, but at that moment he was too overwhelmed, completely aflame.

Hiroko pulled her head back and looked at him again. His breath was whooshing in his lungs, in and out. In English, in a voice formal but kind, she said, "This is your initiation into the areophany, the celebration of the body of Mars. Welcome to it. We worship this world. We intend to make a place for ourselves here, a place that is beautiful in a new Martian way, a way never seen on Earth. We have built a hidden refuge in the south, and now we are leaving for it.

"We know you, we love you. We know we can use your help. We know you can use our help. We want to build just what you are yearning for, just what you have been missing here. But all in new forms. For we can never go back. We must go forward. We must find our own way. We start tonight. We want you to come with us."

And Michel said, "I'll come."

PART FIVE

Falling Into History

The lab hummed quietly. Desks and tables and benches were cluttered with things, the white walls crowded with graphs and posters and cut-out cartoons, all vibrating slightly under bright artificial light. Like any lab anywhere: somewhat clean, somewhat disorderly. The one window in the corner was black and reflected the interior; it was night outside. The whole building was nearly empty.

But two men in lab coats stood at one of the benches, leaning forward to look at a computer screen. The shorter of the two tapped at the keyboard below the screen with a forefinger, and the image on the screen changed. Green corkscrews on a black field, squiggling so that they looked sharply three dimensional, as if the screen were a box. An image from an electron microscope; the field was only a few microns across.

"You see it's a kind of plasmid repair of the gene sequence," the short scientist said. "Breaks in the original strands are identified. Replacement sequences are synthesized, and when these replacement sequences are introduced into the cell, the breaks are seen as attachment sites, and the replacements bind to the originals."

"Do you introduce them by transformation? Electroporation?"

"Transformation. Treated cells are injected along with a competent, and the repair strands make a conjugal transfer."

"In vivo?"

"In vivo."

A low whistle. "So you can repair any little thing? Cell division error?"

"That's right."

The two men stared at the corkscrews on the screen, waving about like the new tips of grapevines in a breeze.

"You've got proof?"

"Did Vlad show you those mice in the next room?"

"Yeah."

"Those mice are fifteen years old."

Another whistle.

They went next door into the mice room, muttering to each other under the hum of machinery. The tall one stared curiously into a cage, where patches of fur breathed under wood chips. When they left again they turned out the lights in both rooms. The flicker of the electron microscope screen illuminated the first lab, giving it a green cast. The scientists went to the window, talking in low voices. They looked out. The sky was purple with the coming day; stars were popping out of existence. Out on the horizon stood a black massive bulk, the flat-topped mound of an immense volcano. Olympus Mons, the largest mountain in the solar system.

The tall scientist shook his head. "This changes everything, you know."

"I know."

From the bottom of the shaft, the sky looked like a bright pink coin. The shaft was round, a kilometer in diameter, seven kilometers deep. But from the bottom it seemed much thinner and deeper than that. Perspective plays a lot of tricks on the human eye.

Such as that bird, flying down the round pink dot of the sky, looking so big. Except it wasn't a bird. "Hey," John said. The shaft director, a round-faced Japanese named Etsu Okakura, looked at him, and through their two faceplates John could see the man's nervous grin. One of his teeth was discolored.

Okakura looked up. "Something falling!" he said quickly, and then: "Run!"

They turned and ran over the shaft floor. Quickly John found that although most of the loose rock had been swept off the starred black basalt, no effort had been made to make the shaft bottom perfectly level. Miniature craters and scarps became increasingly difficult as he gained speed; in this moment of primate flight the instincts formed in childhood reasserted themselves, and he kept pushing off too hard with each step, coming down on uninspected terrain with a jolt and then pushing off wildly again, a crazy run until finally he caught his toe and lost control and fell crashing across the ragged stone, arms flung out to save his faceplate. It was small comfort to see that Okakura had fallen as well. Fortunately the same gravity that had caused their tumbles was giving them more time to escape: the falling object had not yet landed. They got up and ran again, and once again Okakura fell. John glanced back and saw a bright metallic blur hit the rock, and then the sound of the impact was a solid *whump*, like a blow. Silver bits splashed away, some in their direction: he stopped running, scanned the air for incoming ejecta. No sound at all.

A big hydraulic cylinder flew out of the air and banged end over end to their left, and they both jumped. He hadn't seen it coming.

After that, stillness. They stood nearly a minute, and then Boone stirred. He was sweating; they were in pressurized suits, but at 49°C the shaft bottom was the hottest place on Mars, and the suit's insulation was built for cold. He made a move to help Okakura to his feet, but stopped himself; presumably the man would rather get up himself than owe *giri* to Boone for the help. If Boone understood the concept properly. "Let's have a look," he said instead.

Okakura got up, and they walked back over the dense black basalt. The shaft had long ago been bored into solid bedrock, in fact it was now about twenty percent of the way through the lithosphere. It was stifling at the bottom, as if the suits were entirely uninsulated. Boone's air supply was a welcome coolness in the face and lungs. Framed by the dark shaft walls, the pink sky above was very bright. Sunlight illuminated a short conic section of the shaft wall. In midsummer the sun might shine all the way – no, they were south of the Tropic of Capricorn. In shadow forever, down here.

They approached the wreck. It had been a robot dump truck, hauling rock up the road that cut a spiral into the shaft wall. Pieces of the truck were mixed with big rough boulders, some scattered as much as a hundred meters from the point of impact. Beyond a hundred meters debris was rare; the cylinder that had flown by them must have been fired out under pressure of some kind.

A pile of magnesium, aluminum and steel, all twisted horribly. The magnesium and aluminum had partially melted. "Do you think it fell all the way from the top?" Boone asked.

Okakura didn't respond. Boone glanced at him; the man was studiously avoiding his gaze. Perhaps he was frightened. Boone said, "There must have been a good thirty seconds between the time I caught sight of it and when it hit."

At roughly three meters per second squared, that had been

more than enough time for it to reach terminal velocity. So it had hit at about two hundred kilometers per hour. Not so bad, really. On Earth it would have come down in less than half the time, and might have caught them. Hell, if he hadn't have looked up when he had, this one might have caught them. He made a quick calculation. It had probably been about halfway up the shaft when he saw it. But at that point it could have been falling for quite some time.

Boone slowly walked around into the gap between the shaft wall and the pile of scrap. The truck had landed on its right side, and the left side was deformed but recognizable. Okakura climbed several steps up the wreckage, then pointed at a black area behind the left front tire. John followed him up, scraped at the metal with the claw on his right glove's forefinger. The black came away like soot. Ammonium nitrate explosion. The body of the truck was bent in there as if hammered. "A good-sized charge," John observed.

"Yes," Okakura said, and cleared his throat. He was frightened, that was sure. Well, the first man on Mars had almost been killed while in his care; and himself too, of course, but who knew which would scare him more? "Enough to push truck off road."

"Well, like I said, there's been some sabotage reported."

Okakura was frowning through his faceplate. "But who? And why?"

"I don't know. Anyone in your team seem to be having any psychological difficulties?"

"No." Okakura's face was carefully blank. Every group larger than five had someone experiencing difficulties, and Okakura's little industrial town had a population of five hundred.

"This the sixth case I've seen," John said. "Although none so close up." He laughed. The image of the birdlike dot in the pink sky came back to him. "It would have been easy for someone to attach a bomb to a truck before it came down. Detonate it with a clock or an altimeter."

"Reds, you mean." Okakura was looking relieved. "We have heard of them. But it is . . ." He shrugged. "Crazy."

"Yes." John climbed gingerly off the wreck. They walked back across the floor of the shaft to the car they had come down in. Okakura was on another band, talking to people up top.

John stopped by the central pit to have a final look around. The sheer size of the shaft was hard to grasp: the muted light and vertical lines reminded him of a cathedral, but all the cathedrals ever built would have sat like dollhouses at the bottom of this great hole. The surreal scale made him blink, and he decided he had tilted his head back too long.

They drove up the road inscribed in the side wall to the first elevator, left the car and got in the cage. Up they went. Seven times they had to get out and walk across the wall road to the bottom of the next elevator. The ambient light grew to something more like ordinary daylight. Across the shaft he could see where the wall was scored by the double spiral of the two roads: thread-marks in an enormous screw hole. The shaft's bottom had disappeared into the murk, he couldn't even make out the truck.

In the last two elevators they ascended through regolith; first the megaregolith, which looked like cracked bedrock, and then the regolith proper, its rock and gravel and ice all hidden behind a concrete retainer, a smooth curved wall that looked like a dam, and was angled so far back that the final elevator was actually a cog rail train. They cranked up the side of this enormous funnel – Big Man's bathtub drain, Okakura had said on the way down – and came finally to the surface, out into the sun.

Boone got out of the cog train and looked back down. The regolith retainer looked like the inner wall of a very smooth crater, with a two-laned road spiraling down it; but the crater had no floor. A mohole. He could see down the shaft a little way, but the wall was in shadow, and only the road spiraling down picked up any light, so that it appeared to be something like a freestanding staircase, descending through empty space to the planet's core.

Three of the giant dump trucks ground slowly up the last stretch of the road, full of black boulders. These days it took them five hours to make the trip from the bottom of the shaft, Okakura said. Very little supervision, like most of the project, in both manufacture and operation. The inhabitants of the town only had to see to programming, deployment, maintenance, and troubleshooting. And, now, security.

The town, called Senzeni Na, was scattered over the floor of Thaumasia Fossae's deepest canyon. Nearest to the hole was the industrial park; here most of the excavation equipment was manufactured, and the rock from the hole processed for its trace amounts of valuable metals. Boone and Okakura stepped into the rim station, changed out of their pressure suits into coppery jumpers, and entered one of the clear walktubes that connected all the buildings in the town. It was cold and sunny in the tubes, and everyone in them wore clothing with an outer layer of copper-colored foil, the latest in Japanese radproofing. Copper creatures, moving in clear tubes; it looked to Boone like a giant ant farm. Overhead the thermal cloud frosted into existence and shot up like steam from a valve, until it was caught by high winds and blown out in a long flattened contrail.

The town's actual living quarters were built into the southeast wall of the canyon. A big rectangular section of the cliff had been replaced by glass; behind it was a tall open concourse, backed by five stories of terraced apartments.

They walked through the concourse and Okakura led him up to the town offices, on the fifth floor. A small crowd of concerned-looking people gathered in their wake, chattering to Okakura and among themselves. They all went through the office and out onto its balcony. John watched closely as Okakura described in Japanese what had happened. A number of his audience looked nervous, and most would not meet John's eye. Had the near accident itself been enough to incur *giri*? It was important to make sure they didn't feel publicly shown up, or anything like it. Shame was strong stuff for the Japanese, and Okakura was beginning to look desperately unhappy, as if he were deciding it had been his fault.

"Look, it could just as easily have been outsiders as someone from here," John said boldly. He made some suggestions for future security. "The rim is a perfect barrier. Set up an alarm system, and a few people at the rim station could keep an eye on both the system and the elevators. A waste of time, but I guess we have to do it."

Diffidently Okakura asked him if he knew anything about who might be responsible for the sabotage. He shrugged. "No idea, sorry. People opposed to the moholes, I guess."

"But the moholes are dug," one of them said.

"I know. I guess it's symbolic." He grinned. "But if a truck falls on someone, it would be a bad symbol."

They nodded seriously. He wished he had Frank's facility for languages, it would help to be able to communicate better with these people. They were hard to read; inscrutable and all that.

They wondered if he wanted to lie down.

"I'm okay," he said. "It missed us. We'll have to look into it, but today let's just continue according to the schedule we had."

So Okakura and several men and women led him on a tour of the town, and cheerfully he visited labs and meeting rooms, lounges and dining halls. He nodded and shook hands and said hi until he was sure he had met over fifty percent of Senzeni Na's inhabitants. Most had not yet heard of the incident in the hole, and all were pleased to meet him; happy to shake his hand, to speak with him, to show him something, to look at him. It happened everywhere he went, reminding him unpleasantly of the fishbowl years between his first trip and his second.

But he did his job. An hour's work, then four hours of

being The First Man On Mars: the usual ratio. And as after-noon darkened to evening, and the whole town gathered for a banquet in honor of his visit, he settled back and patiently played his part. That meant shifting into a good mood, no easy task that night. In fact he took a break, went back to the bathroom in his room and swallowed a capsule manufac-tured by Vlad's medical group in Acheron. It was a drug they had named omegendorph, a synthetic mix of all the endorphins and opiates they had found in the brain's natural chemistry and a better feel-good drug than Boone would have imagined possible.

He returned to the banquet much more relaxed. In fact filled with a little glow. He had escaped death, after all, and by running like a wild man! Some more endorphins were not inappropriate. He moved easily from table to table, asking questions as he went. This was what pleased people, what gave them the festival feeling that a meeting with John Boone should bring. John liked being able to do that, it was the part of his job that made celebrity tolerable; because when he asked questions, people leaped to answer like salmon in the stream. It was peculiar, really, as if people were seek-ing to right the imbalance they felt in the situation, in which they knew so much about him while he knew so little about them. So that with the right encouragement, often a single carefully-judged prompt, they would erupt with the most astonishing spills of personal information: witnessing, testi-fying, confessing.

So he spent the evening learning about life at Senzeni Na ("Means, what have we done?" Quick grin.) And afterwards he was led to his big guest suite, the rooms thick with live bamboo, the bed seemingly hacked out of a stand of it. When he was alone he connected his code box to the phone, and called Sax Russell.

Russell was at Vlad's new headquarters, a research complex built into a dramatic fin ridge in the Acheron Fossae north of

Olympus Mons. Sax spent all his time there now, studying genetic engineering like an undergrad; he had become convinced that biotechnology was the key to terraforming, and he was determined to educate himself to the point where he could contribute actively to that part of the campaign, despite the fact that all his training was in physics. Modern biology was notoriously gooey, and a lot of physicists hated it; but the people at Acheron said Sax was a quick learner, and John believed it. Sax himself made little snicking noises at his own progress, but it was clear he was deep in. He talked about it all the time, "It's the crux," he would say. "We need the water out of the ground and the carbon dioxide out of the air, and it's going to take biomass to do both." And so he slaved at the screens and in the labs.

He listened to Boone's report with his usual impassivity. Such a parody of the scientist, John thought. He even wore a lab coat. Seeing his characteristic blink made John think of a story he had heard one of Sax's assistants tell, to a laughing audience at a party: in a secret experiment gone awry, a hundred lab rats that had been injected with an intelligence booster became geniuses. They revolted, escaped from their cages, captured their principal investigator, and strapped him down and retro-injected all their minds into his body, using a method they invented on the spot – and that scientist was Saxifrage Russell, white-coated, blinking, twitching, inquisitive, lab-bound. His brain the sum of a hundred hyperintelligent rats, "and named for a flower like lab rats are, it's their little joke, see?"

It explained a lot. John smiled as he finished his report, and Sax cocked his head at him curiously. "Do you think this truck was meant to kill you?"

"I don't know."

"How do the people there seem?"

"Scared."

"Think they're in on it?"

286

John shrugged. "I doubt it. They're probably just worried about what happens next."

Sax flicked a hand out. "Sabotage like that won't make the slightest dent in the project," he said mildly.

"I know."

"Who's doing this, John?"

"I don't know."

"Could it be Ann, do you think? Has she become another prophet, like Hiroko or Arkady, with followers and a program and the like?"

"You have followers and a program too," John reminded him.

"But I'm not telling my followers to wreck things and try to kill people."

"Some people think you're trying to wreck Mars. And people will certainly die as a result of terraforming, in accidents."

"What are you saying?"

"Just reminding you. Trying to get you to see why someone might do this."

"So you do think it's Ann."

"Or Arkady, or Hiroko, or someone we've never heard of in one of the new colonies. There are a lot of people here now. A lot of factions."

"I know." Sax walked over to a countertop, drained his battered old coffee mug. Finally he said, "I'd like you to try to find out who it is. Go where you need to go. Go talk to Ann. Reason with her." There was a plaintive note in his voice: "I can't even talk to her anymore."

John stared at him, surprised at the display of emotion. Sax took this silence for reluctance, and went on: "I know it isn't exactly your thing, but everyone will talk to you. You're practically the only one left we can say that about. I know you're doing the mohole work, but you can get your team to do your part of that, and keep visiting the moholes as part of this inquiry. There really isn't anyone else who

287

can do it. There's no real police to turn to. Although if things keep happening, UNOMA will provide some."

"Or the transnationals." Boone considered it. The sight of that truck, falling out of the sky . . . "All right. I'll go talk to Ann, anyway. After that we should get together and talk about security for all the terraforming projects. If we can stop anything more from happening, that will keep UNOMA out."

"Thanks, John."

Boone wandered out onto his suite's balcony. The concourse was filled with Hokkaido pines, the chilled air stiff with resin. Copper figures walked below, among the tree trunks. Boone considered the new situation. For ten years now he had worked for Russell on terraforming, managing the moholes and doing PR and the like, and he enjoyed the work; but he wasn't on the cutting edge of any of the sciences involved, and so he was out of the decision-making loop. He knew that many people thought of him as a figurehead only, a celebrity for consumption back on Earth; a dumb space jock who had gotten lucky once, and was living off that for good. That didn't bother John; there were always knee-high people hacking away, trying to get everyone down to their size. That was okay, especially since in his case they were wrong. His power was considerable, although perhaps only he could see the full extent of it, as it consisted of an endless succession of face-to-face meetings, of the influence he had over what people chose to do. Power wasn't a matter of job titles, after all. Power was a matter of vision, persuasiveness, freedom of movement, fame, influence. The figurehead stands at the front, after all, pointing the way.

Still, despite all that, there was something to be said for this new task. He could feel that already. It would be problematic, difficult, perhaps risky . . . above all, challenging. A new challenge: he liked that. Going back into his suite, getting into bed (John Boone Slept Here!) it occurred to him that now he was going to be not only the first man on Mars, but the first detective. He grinned at the thought, and the last action of the omegendorph set his nerves aglow.

Ann Clayborne was doing a survey in the mountains surrounding the Argyre Basin, which meant he could check out a glider and fly from Senzeni Na to her. So early the next morning he took the elevator balloon up the mooring mast to the stationary dirigible floating over the town, exulting as he rose in the ever-expanding view of the big Thaumasia canyons. From the dirigible he lowered himself into the cockpit of one of the gliders hooked to its underside. After securing himself he unhooked, and the glider dropped like a stone until he ran it into the mohole thermal, which tossed it violently upward. He fought for control and banked the big gossamer craft into a steep rising gyre, whooping as he battled the intense buffeting; it was like riding a soap bubble over a bonfire!

At five thousand meters the plume cloud flattened and spread out to the east. John swooped out of his spiral and headed southeast, playing with the glider as he went to get a feel for it. He would have to ride the winds carefully to make it to Argyre.

He aimed into the sun's smeary yellow blaze. Wind keened over the wings. The land below him was a dark rough orange, shading to a very light orange at the horizon. The southern highlands were wildly pocked in every direction, with the raw, primordial, lunar look that saturation cratering always had. John loved flying over it, and he piloted unconsciously, concentrating on the land below. It was precious to sit back and fly, feeling the wind as if under his elbows, watching the land and not thinking a thing. He was sixty-four years old in this year 2047 (or "m-year 10" as he usually thought of it), and he had been the most famous man alive for almost thirty of those years; and nowadays he was happiest when he was alone, and flying.

After an hour had passed, he started thinking about his

new task. It was important not to get caught up in fantasies of magnifying glasses and cigar ash, or gumshoe with handgun; there was work he could do even as he flew. He called up Sax, and asked if he could connect his AI into the UNOMA emigration and planetary travel records, without alerting UNOMA to the connection. After some investigation Sax got back to him and said that he could manage that, and so John sent a sequence of questions through, and then continued to fly. An hour and many craters later, Pauline's redlight blinked rapidly, indicating a downloading of raw data. John asked the AI to run the data through various analyses, and when she was done he studied the results on the screen. Patterns of movement; they were confusing, but he hoped that when matched with the sabotage incidents, something might turn up. Of course there were people moving around off the record, the hidden colony among them; and who knew what Hiroko and the others thought of the terraforming projects? Still, it was worth a look.

The Nereidium Montes popped over the horizon ahead. Mars had never had much tectonic movement, and so mountain ranges were rare; those that existed tended to be crater rims writ large, rings of ejecta thrown out by impacts so great that the debris fell in two or three concentric ranges, each many kilometers wide, and extremely rugged. Hellas and Argyre, being the biggest basins, therefore had the biggest ranges; and the only other major mountain range, the Phlegra Montes on the slope of Elysium, was probably the fragmentary remains of a basin impact later inundated by the Elysium volcanoes, or by an ancient Oceanus Borealis. Debate raged over that question, and Ann, John's final authority in such matters, had never expressed an opinion on it.

The Nereidium Montes made up the northern rim around Argyre, but currently Ann and her team were investigating the southern rim, the Charitum Montes. Boone adjusted his course southward, and in the early afternoon he soared low over the broad flat plain of the Argyre Basin. After the wild cratering of the highlands, the basin floor seemed smooth indeed, a flat yellowish plain bounded by the big curve of rim ridges. From his vantage he could see about ninety degrees of the arc of the rim, enough to give him a sense of the size of the impact that had formed Argyre; it was an amazing sight. Flying over thousands of Martian craters had given Boone a sense of the sizes they came in, and Argyre was simply off the scale; a quite big crater named Galle was no more than a pockmark in Argyre's rim! A whole world must have crashed in here! Or, at the very least, a damn big asteroid.

Inside the southeast curve of the rim, on the basin floor against the foothills of the Charitum, he spotted the thin white line of a landing strip. Easy to spot human constructs in such desolation, their regularity stood out like a beacon. Thermals were rising hard off the sunwarmed hills, and he turned down into one, dropping with a vibratory *hum*, the craft's wings bouncing visibly as it stopped. Dropping like a rock, like that asteroid, John thought with a grin, and he pulled up for the landing with a dramatic last flourish, putting down with as much precision as he could muster, aware of his reputation as a hot flyer, which of course had to be reinforced at every opportunity. Part of the job . . .

But it turned out there were only two people in the trailers by the strip, and neither of them had watched him land. They were inside watching TV news from Earth; they looked up when he came in the inner lock door, and jumped to their feet to greet him. Ann was up one of the mountain canyons with a team, they told him, probably no more than two hours' drive away. John ate lunch with them, two Brit women with North accents, very tough and charming; then he took a rover and followed the tracks up a cleft into the Charitum. An hour's twisting climb up a flat-bottomed arroyo brought him to a mobile trailer, with three rovers parked outside it. Together they gave it the look of a desiccated café in the Mojave.

The trailer was unoccupied. Footprints led away from the

camp in many directions. After thinking it over Boone climbed a knoll west of camp, and sat down on its peak. He lay on the rock and slept until the cold penetrated his walker. Then he sat up and tongued a capsule of omegendorph, and watched the black shadows of the hills creep east. He thought about what had happened at Senzeni Na, running through his memories of the hours before and after the accident, the looks on people's faces, what they had said. The image of the falling truck gave his pulse a little surge.

Copper figures appeared in a cleft between hills to the west. He stood and descended the knoll, and met them down at the trailer.

"What are you doing here?" Ann said over the first hundred's band.

"I want to talk."

She grunted and switched off.

The trailer would have been a bit crowded even without him. They sat in the main room knee-to-knee, while Simon Frazier heated spaghetti sauce and boiled water for pasta in the little kitchen nook. The trailer's sole window faced east, and as they ate they watched the shadow of the mountains stretch out over the floor of the great basin. John had brought along a half-liter bottle of Utopian cognac, and he broke it out after dinner to moans of approval. As the areologists sipped he cleaned the dishes ("I *want* to") and asked how their investigation was going. They were looking for evidence of ancient glacial episodes, which if found would support a model of the planet's early history that included oceans filling the low spots.

But Ann, John thought as he listened to them; would she want to find evidence of an oceanic past? It was a model that tended to lend moral support to the terraforming project, implying as it did that they were only restoring an earlier state of things. So probably she would not want to find any such evidence. Would that disinclination bias her work? Well, sure. If not consciously, then deeper. Consciousness was just a thin lithosphere over a big hot core, after all. Detectives had to remember that.

But everyone in the trailer seemed to agree that they weren't finding any evidence for glaciation, and they were all good areologists. There were high basins that resembled cirques, and high valleys with the classic U-shape of glacial valleys, and some dome-and-wall configurations that might have been the result of glacial plucking; all these features had been seen in satellite photos, along with one or two bright flashes that some people had thought might be reflections from glacial polish. But on the ground none of it was holding up. They had found no glacial polish, even in the most wind-protected sections of the U-shaped valleys; no moraines, lateral or terminal; no signs of plucking, or of transition lines where nanatuks would have stuck out of even the highest levels of ancient ice. Nothing. It was another case of what they called sky areology, which had a history going back to the early satellite photos, and even to the telescopes. The canals had been sky areology; and many more bad hypotheses had been formulated in the same way, hypotheses that were only now being tested with the rigor of ground areology. Most collapsed under the weight of surface data, got tossed in the canal as they said.

The glacial theory, however, and the oceanic model of which it was part, had always been more persistent than most. First, because almost every model of the planet's formation indicated that there should have been a lot of water outgassing, and it had to have gone somewhere. And second, John thought, because there were a lot of people who would be comforted if the oceanic model were true; they would feel less uneasy about the morality of terraforming. Opponents to terraforming, therefore . . . No, he was not surprised that Ann's team was not finding anything. Feeling the cognac a bit, and irritated by her unfriendliness, he said from the kitchen, "But if there were glaciers the most recent would have been, what, a billion years ago? That much time would take care of any of the superficial signs, I should think, glacial polish or moraines or nanatuks. Leaving nothing but the gross landforms, which is what you have. Right?"

Ann had been silent, but now she said, "The landforms aren't unique to glaciation. All of them are common in Martian ranges, because they were all formed by rock falling out of the sky. Every kind of formation you can think of is out here somewhere, bizarre shapes limited only by the angle of repose." She had refused any cognac, which surprised John, and now she stared at the floor with a disgusted look.

"Not U-shaped valleys, surely," John said.

"Yes, U-shaped valleys too."

"The problem is that the oceanic model isn't very falsifiable," Simon said quietly. "You can keep failing to find good evidence for it, and we are, but that doesn't disprove it."

The kitchen clean, John asked Ann to go out for a sunset walk. She hesitated, unwilling; but it was one of her rituals and everyone knew it, and with a quick grimace and a hard glance she agreed.

Once outside he led her up to the same peak he had napped on. The sky was a plum colored arch over the black serrated ridges surrounding them, and stars were popping into existence in a flood, hundreds per eyeblink. He stood by her side; she stared away from him. The ragged skyline might have been a scene from Earth. She was a bit taller than him, a gaunt, angular silhouette. John liked her, but whatever reciprocal liking she may have had for him – and they had had some good talks in years past – had dissipated when he chose to work with Sax. He could have done anything he liked, her hard looks said, and yet he had chosen terraforming.

Well, it was true. He put his hand before her, forefinger raised. She punched her wristpad and suddenly her breathing sighed in his ear. "What," she said, without looking his way.

"It's about the sabotage incidents," he said.

"I thought so. I suppose Russell thinks I'm behind them."

"It's not so much that—"

"Does he think I'm stupid? Does he imagine I think a little bit of vandalism will stop you from your boys' games?"

"Well, it's rather more than little bits. There've been six major incidents now, and any of them could have killed people."

"Knocking mirrors out of orbit can kill people?"

"If they're doing maintenance on them."

She hmphed. "What else has happened?"

"A truck was knocked off one of the mohole shaft roads yesterday, and almost landed on me." He heard her breath catch. "That's the third truck to go. And that mirror was knocked into a spin with a maintenance worker on it, and she had to do a free solo to a station, it took her more than an hour to get there, and she almost didn't make it. And then an explosives dump went off by accident at the Elysian mohole, a minute after a whole crew left it. And all the lichen at Underhill were killed by a virus that shut down the whole lab."

Ann shrugged. "What do you expect from GEMs? It could have been an accident. I'm surprised it doesn't happen more often."

"It wasn't an accident."

"It all adds up to peanuts. Does Russell think I'm stupid?"

"You know he doesn't. But it's a matter of tipping the balance. A lot of Terran money is being invested in the project, but it wouldn't take much bad publicity to get a lot of it to drop out."

"Maybe so," Ann said. "But you ought to listen to yourself when you say things like that. You and Arkady are the biggest advocates of some kind of new Martian society, you two plus Hiroko, maybe. But the way Russell and Frank and Phyllis are bringing up Terran capital, the whole thing's going to be out of your hands. It'll be business as usual, and all your ideas will disappear."

"I tend to think we all want something similar here," John

said. "We want to do good work in a good place. We just emphasize different parts of the process of getting there, that's all. If we only coordinated our efforts, and worked as a team—"

"We don't want the same things!" Ann said. "You want to change Mars, and I don't. It's as simple as that."

"Well . . ." John faltered before her bitterness. They were moving slowly around the hill, in a complicated dance that imitated the conversation, sometimes face to face, sometimes back to back; and always her voice was right in his ear, and his in hers. He liked that about walker conversations, and used it, that insidious voice in the ear which could be so persuasive, caressing, hypnotic. "It's not that simple, even so. I mean, you ought to be helping those of us who are closest to your beliefs, and opposing those furthest away."

"I do that."

"Which is why I came to ask you what you know about these saboteurs. It makes sense, right?"

"I know nothing about them. I wish them luck."

"In person?"

"What?"

"I've traced your movements in the last couple of years, and you've always been near every incident, within a month or so before it happened. You were in Senzeni Na a few weeks ago on your way here, right?"

He listened to her breathe. She was angry. "Using me as cover," she muttered, and something more he didn't catch.

"Who?"

She turned her back on him. "You should ask the Coyote about this stuff, John."

"The Coyote?"

She laughed shortly. "Haven't you heard of him? He wanders around on the surface without a walker, people say. Pops up here and there, sometimes on both sides of the world in a single night. Knew Big Man himself, back in the good

296

old days. And a big friend of Hiroko's. And a big enemy of terraforming.''

"Have you met him?''

She didn't reply.

"Look,'' he said after nearly a minute of their shared breathing, ''people are going to get killed. Innocent by-standers.''

"Innocent bystanders are going to get killed when the permafrost melts and the ground collapses under our feet. I don't have anything to do with that either. I just do my work. Trying to catalog what was here before we came.''

"Yes. But you're the most famous red of all, Ann. These people must have contacted you because of that, and I wish you'd discourage them. It might save some lives.''

She turned to face him. Her helmet's faceplate reflected the western skyline, purple above, black below, the border between the two colors jagged and raw. "If you left the planet alone, it would save lives. That's what I want. I'd kill *you* if I thought it would help.''

After that there was little to say. On the way back down to the trailer, he tried another topic. "What do you think happened to Hiroko and the rest of them?''

"They disappeared.''

John rolled his eyes. "She didn't talk to you about it?''

"No. Did she talk to you?''

"No. I don't think she talked to anyone but her group. Do you know where they went?''

"No.''

"Do you have any idea why they left?''

"They probably wanted to get free of us. Make something new. What you and Arkady say you want, they really wanted.''

John shook his head. "If they do it, they'll do it for twenty people. I mean to do it for everyone.''

"Maybe they're more realistic than you.''

"Maybe. We'll find out. There's more than one way to do this, Ann. You have to learn that."

She didn't reply.

The others stared at them as they entered the trailer, and Ann, storming into the kitchen nook, was no help. John sat on the arm of the one couch and asked them more questions about their work, and about groundwater levels in Argyre and the southern hemisphere generally. The big basins were low in elevation, but had been dehydrated in the impacts that formed them; and in general it appeared that the planet's water had mostly seeped north. Another part of the mystery: no one had ever explained why the northern and southern hemispheres were so different, it was *the* problem in areology, a solution to which might prove the key to explaining all the other enigmas of the Martian landscape, as tectonic plate theory had once explained so many different problems in geology. In fact some people wanted to use the tectonic explanation again, postulating that an old crust had slid over itself onto the southern half, leaving the north to form a new skin, then all of it freezing in position when planetary cooling stopped all tectonic movement. Ann thought that was ridiculous; in her opinion the northern hemisphere was simply the biggest impact basin of all, the ultimate bang of the Noachian. A similar-sized strike had knocked the moon out of the Earth, probably around the same time. The areologists discussed various aspects of the problem for a while, and John listened, asking an occasional neutral question.

They turned on the TV for news from Earth, and watched a short feature on the mining and oil drilling that was starting in Antarctica.

"That's our doing you know," Ann said from the kitchen. "They kept mining and oil out of Antarctica for almost a hundred years, ever since the IGY and the first treaty. But when terraforming began here it all collapsed. They're running out of oil down there, and the Southern Club is poor, and there's a whole continent of oil and gas and minerals

298

right next to them, being treated like a national park by the rich northern countries. And then the south saw these same rich northern countries start to take Mars completely apart, and they said, What the hell, you can tear a whole planet apart and we're supposed to protect this iceberg we've got right next door with all these resources we desperately need? Forget it! So they broke the Antarctic Treaty, and there they are drilling and no one's done a thing about it. And now the last clean place on Earth is gone too."

She walked over and sat before the screen, stuck her face in a mug of steaming hot chocolate. "There's more if you want," she said to John rudely. Simon gave him a sympathetic glance, and the others stared round-eyed at both of them, looking appalled to see a fight between two of the first hundred: what a joke that was! It almost made John laugh; and when he got up to pour a mug for himself, he leaned over impulsively and kissed Ann on the top of the head. She stiffened and he went on to the kitchen. "We all want different things from Mars," he said, forgetting he had just said the opposite to Ann out on the hill. "But here we are, and there aren't that many of us, and it's our place. We make what we want of it, like Arkady says. Now you don't like what Sax or Phyllis want, and they don't like what you want, and Frank doesn't like what anyone wants, and more people are coming every year supporting one position or another, even if they don't know it. So it could get ugly. In fact it's started to get ugly already, with these attacks on equipment. Can you imagine that happening at Underhill?"

"Hiroko's group was ripping off Underhill the whole time they were there," Ann said. "They had to've been, to take off like that."

"Yeah, maybe. But they weren't endangering people's lives." The image of the truck falling down the shaft came to him again, quick and vivid. He drank hot cocoa and scalded his mouth. "Damn! Anyway, whenever I get discouraged about all this I try to remember that it's natural. It's

299

inevitable that people are going to fight, but now we're fighting about Martian things. I mean people aren't fighting over whether they're American or Japanese or Russian or Arab, or some religion or race or sex or whatnot. They're fighting because they want one Martian reality or other. That's all that matters now. So we're already halfway there." He frowned at Ann, who stared at the floor. "Do you see what I mean?"

She glanced at him. "It's the second half that matters."

"All right, maybe so. You take too much for granted, but that's the way people are. But you have to realize that you're having your effect on us, Ann. You've changed the way everyone thinks about what we're doing here. Hell, Sax and a lot of others used to talk about doing anything possible to terraform as quick as possible – driving a bunch of asteroids directly into the planet, using hydrogen bombs to try and start volcanoes – whatever it took! Now all those plans have been scrapped because of you and your supporters. The whole vision of how to terraform and how far to go with it has changed. And I think we can eventually reach a compromise value, where we get some protection from radiation, and a biosphere and maybe air we can breathe, or at least not die in immediately – and still leave it pretty much like it was before we came." Ann rolled her eyes at this, but he forged on: "No one's talking about pumping it up into a jungle planet you know, even if they could! It'll always be cold, and the Tharsis bulge will always stick right out into space, in effect, so there'll be a huge part of the planet that's never touched. And that'll be partly because of you."

"But who's to say that with that first step done, you won't want more?"

"Maybe some will. But I for one will try to stop them. I will! I may not be on your side, but I see your point. And when you fly over the highlands like I did today, you can't help but love it. People may try to change the planet, but all the while the planet will be changing them too. A sense of

300

place, an aesthetics of landscape, all those things change with time. You know the people who first saw the Grand Canyon thought it was ugly as hell because it wasn't like the Alps. It took them a long time to see its beauty."

"They drowned most of it anyway," Ann said blackly.

"Yeah yeah. But who knows what our kids will think is beautiful? It's sure to be based on what they know, and this place will be the only place they know. So we terraform the planet; but the planet areoforms us."

"Areoforming," Ann said, and a rare little smile flashed over her face; seeing it John felt his face flush; he hadn't seen her smile like that in years, and he loved Ann, he loved to see her smile.

"I like that word," she said now. She pointed a finger at him: "But I'll hold you to it, John Boone! I'll remember what you've said tonight!"

"Me too," he said.

The rest of the evening was more relaxed. And the next day Simon saw him down to the airstrip, to the rover he was going to drive northward, and Simon, who usually would have seen him off with a smile and a handshake, at most a "nice to see you", suddenly said to him, "I really appreciate what you said last night. I think it really cheered her up. Especially what you said about kids. She's pregnant, you see."

"What?" John shook his head. "She didn't tell me. Are you the, the father?"

"Yeah." Simon grinned.

"How old is she now, sixty?"

"Yeah. It's stretching things a bit, so to speak, but it's been done before. They took an egg frozen about fifteen years ago, fertilized it and planted it in her. We'll see how it goes. They say Hiroko stays pregnant all the time these days, just keeps popping them like an incubator, same C section over and over."

"They say a lot of things about Hiroko, but it's all just stories."

"Well, but we heard this from someone who supposedly knows."

"The Coyote?" John said sharply.

Simon raised his eyebrows. "I'm surprised she told you about him."

John grunted, obscurely annoyed. No doubt his fame meant he missed out on a lot of gossip. "It's good that she did. Well, anyway —" He extended his right hand and they shook, hooking their fingers in the stiff clasp that had developed in the old space days. "Congratulations. Take care of her."

Simon shrugged. "You know Ann. She does what she wants."

So Boone drove north from Argyre for three days, enjoying the countryside and the solitude, and spending a few hours each afternoon ransacking the planetary records to track people's movement, looking for correlations with the sabotage incidents. Early on the fourth morning he reached the Marineris canyons, which were some 1500 kilometers north of Argyre. He ran into a north-south transponder road, and followed it up a short rise to the southern rim of Melas Chasma, and got out of the rover to have a proper look.

He had never been to this part of the great canyon system; before the completion of the Marineris Transverse Highway it had been extremely hard to get to. It was dramatic, no doubt about it: the Melas cliff dropped a full three thousand meters from rim to canyon floor, so that the rim had a kind of glider's view north. The other wall of the canyon was just visible out there, its rim peeking over the horizon; and between the two cliffs lay the spacious expanse of Melas Chasma, the heart of the whole Marineris complex. He could just make out the gaps in distant cliffs that marked the entrances to other canyons: Ius Chasma to the west, Candor to the north, Coprates to the east.

John walked the broken rim for more than an hour, pulling his helmet's binocular lenses down over his faceplate for long periods of time, taking in as much as he could of the greatest canyon on Mars, feeling the euphoria of red land. He threw rocks over the side and watched them disappear, he talked to himself and sang, he hopped on his toes in a clumsy dance. Then he got back in his rover, refreshed, and drove a short distance along the rim, to the start of the cliff road.

Here the Transverse Highway became a single concrete lane, and switchbacked down the spine of an enormous rock ramp that extended down from the south rim to the canyon floor. This odd feature, called the Geneva Spur, pointed north almost perpendicularly from the cliff, straight toward Candor Chasma; it was so perfectly placed for their purposes that with the road on it, it looked like a ramp that the road-builders had constructed.

It was a steep spur, however, and the road had been forced to switchback all the way down, to keep the grade within reason. It was all visible from above; a thousand switchbacks snaking down the spine, looking like yellow thread stitched down a bump in a stained orange carpet.

Boone drove down this marvel carefully, turning the rover's steering wheel left then right then left then right, time after time until he actually had to stop to rest his arms, and give himself a chance to look back and up at the southern wall behind him; it was steep indeed, fluted by a fractal pattern of deeply eroded ravines. Then it was off again for another half hour's drive, hairpins left and right, again and again, until finally the road extended straight down the top of the flattening spur, which eventually spread out and merged into the canyon floor. And down there was a little cluster of vehicles.

It turned out to be the Swiss team that had just finished building the road, and he ended up spending the night with them. They were a group of about eighty: mostly young, mostly married, speaking German and Italian and French and, for his benefit, English, in several different accents. They had kids with them, and cats, and a portable greenhouse thick with herbs and garden vegetables. Soon they would be off like gypsies, in a caravan made up mostly of their earthmoving vehicles, traveling up to the west end of the canyon, to thread a road through Noctis Labyrinthus and onto the east flank of Tharsis. After that there would be other roads; perhaps one over the Tharsis Bulge between Arsia Mons and Pavonis Mons, perhaps one north to Echus Overlook. They weren't sure yet, and Boone got the impression they didn't really care; they planned to spend the rest of their lives traveling around building roads, so it didn't much matter to them where they went next. Road gypsies forever.

They made sure all their kids shook John's hand, and after dinner he gave a short talk, rambling in his usual way about their new life on Mars. "When I see you people out here it makes me really happy because it's part of a new pattern to life: we've got the chance to create a new society out here — everything's changing on the technical level and the social level might as well follow. I'm not exactly sure what the new society should be or should look like, that's the hard part after all, but I know that it should be done, and I think you and all the other small groups out on the surface are figuring it out on an empirical basis. And seeing you helps me to think about it." Which it did, though he was never much good at doing it on his feet; so he just slithered along a bit more in his free associational way, plucking whatever stuck out of the bag of his thoughts. And their eyes shone in the lamplight as they listened to him.

Later he sat with a few of them in a circle around a single lit lamp, and they stayed up through the night talking. The young Swiss asked him questions about his first trip, and about the first years in Underhill, both of which obviously had mythic dimensions for them, and he told them the real story, sort of, and made them laugh a lot; and asked them questions about Switzerland, how it worked, what they thought of it, why they were here rather than there. A blond woman laughed when he asked that. "Do you know about the Böögen?" she said, and he shook his head. "He's part of our Christmas. Sami Claus comes to all the houses one by one, you see, and he has an assistant, the Böögen, who wears a cloak and a hood and carries a big bag. Sami Claus asks the parents how the children have been that year, and the parents show him the ledger, the record you know. And if the children have been good, Sami Claus gives them presents. But if the parents say the children have been bad, the Böögen sweeps them up in his bag and carries them away, and they're never seen again."

"What!" John cried.

"That is what they tell you. That is Switzerland. And that is why I am here on Mars."

"The Böögen carried you here?"

They laughed, the woman too. "Yes. I was always bad." She grew more serious. "But we will have no Böögen here."

They asked him what he thought of the debate between the reds and the greens, and he shrugged and summarized what he could of Ann and Sax's positions.

"I don't think they are either right," one of them said. His name was Jürgen and he was one of their leaders, an engineer who seemed some kind of cross between a burgermeister and a gypsy king, dark-haired and sharp-faced and serious. "Both sides say they are in favor of nature, of course. One has to say this. The reds say that the Mars that is already here is nature. But it is not nature, because it is dead. It is only rock. The greens tell this, and say they will bring nature to Mars with their terraforming. But that is not nature either, that is only culture. A garden, you know. An artwork. So neither way gets nature. There isn't such a thing as nature possible on Mars."

"Interesting!" John said. "I'll have to tell Ann that, and see what she says. But . . ." He thought about it. "Then what do you call this? What do you call what you're doing?"

Jürgen shrugged, grinned. "We don't call it anything. It is just Mars."

Perhaps that was being Swiss, John thought. He had been meeting them more and more in his travels, and they all seemed like that. Do things, and don't worry too much about theory. Whatever seemed right.

Later still, after they had drunk another few bottles of wine, he asked them if they had ever heard of the Coyote. They laughed; one said, "He's the one who came here before you, right?" They laughed again at his expression. "A story only," one explained. "Like the canals, or Big Man. Or Sami Claus."

Driving north the next day across Melas Chasma, John wished (as he had before) that everyone on the planet was Swiss, or at least like the Swiss. Or more like the Swiss in certain ways, anyway. Their love of country seemed to be expressed by making a certain kind of life: rational, just, prosperous, scientific. They would work for that life anywhere, because to them it was the life that mattered, not a flag or a creed or a set of words, nor even that small rocky patch of land they owned on Earth. The Swiss roadbuilding crew back there was Martian already, having brought the life and left the baggage behind.

He sighed, and ate lunch as his rover rolled past transponders north. It was not that simple, of course. The roadbuilding crew were traveling Swiss, gypsies of a sort, the kind of Swiss who spent most of their life out of Switzerland. There were a lot of those, but they were selected out by that choice, they were different. The Swiss who stayed at home were pretty intense about Swissness; still armed to the teeth, still willing to be the bagman for whoever brought them cash; still not a member of the UN. Although that fact, given the power UNOMA currently had over the local situation, made them even more interesting to John, as a model. That ability to be part of the world but to stand away from it at the same time; to use it, but hold it off; to be small but in control, to be armed to the teeth but never go to war; wasn't that one way of defining what he wanted for Mars? It seemed to him there were some lessons there, for any hypothetical Martian state.

He spent a fair amount of his time alone thinking about that hypothetical state; it was a kind of obsession with him, and he found it very frustrating that he could not seem to come up with anything more than vague desires. And so now he thought hard about Switzerland and what it might tell him, he tried to be organized about it: "Pauline, please call up an encyclopedia article on the Swiss government."

The rover passed transponder after transponder as he read the article that came up on the screen. He was disappointed to find that there was nothing obviously unique about the Swiss system of government. Executive authority was given to a council of seven, elected by the assembly. No charismatic president, which some part of Boone did not like very much. The assembly, aside from selecting the federal council, appeared to do little; it was caught between the power of the executive council and the power of the people, as exercised in direct initiatives and referenda, an idea they had gotten in the nineteenth century from California of all places. And then there was the federal system; the cantons in all their diversity were supposed to have a great deal of independence, which also weakened the assembly. But cantonal power had been eroding for generations, the federal government wresting away more and more. What did it add up to? "Pauline, please call up my constitution file." He added a few notes to the file he had just recently begun: *Federal council, direct initiatives, weak assembly, local independence, particularly in cultural matters.* Something to think over, anyway. More data to add to the stew of his ideas. It helped somehow to write it down.

He drove on, remembering the roadbuilders' calmness, their strange mixture of engineering and mysticism. The warmth of their welcome, which wasn't something Boone took for granted; it didn't always happen. In the Arab and Israeli settlements, for instance, he was received very stiffly, perhaps because he was seen as being anti-religion, perhaps because Frank had been spreading tales against him; he had been amazed to discover an Arabic caravan whose members believed he had forbidden the building of a mosque on Phobos; and they had only stared at him when he denied even hearing about such a plan. He was pretty sure that was Frank's doing, word got back to him through Janet and others that Frank was prone to undercutting him in that way. So yes, there were definitely groups that greeted him coolly: the Arabs, the Israelis, the nuclear reactor teams, some of the transnational executives . . . groups with their own intense and parochial programs, people who objected to his larger perspective. Unfortunately there were a lot of them.

He came out of his reverie and looked around, and was surprised to discover that out in the middle of Melas it looked exactly as if he were out on the northern plains somewhere. The great canyon was two hundred kilometers wide at this point, and the curvature of the planet was so sharp that the north and south canyon walls, all three vertical kilometers of them, were completely under the horizons. Not until the following morning did the northern horizon double, and then separate out into the canyon floor and the great northern wall, which was cut in two by the gap of a short north-south canyon connecting Melas and Candor. It was only when he drove into that wide slot that he had the kind of view people thought of when they imagined being down in Marineris: truly giant walls flanked him on both sides, dark brown slabs riven by a fractal infinity of gullies and ridges. At the foot of the walls lay the huge spills of ancient rockfall, or the broken terracing of fossil beaches.

In this gap the Swiss road was a line of green transponders, snaking past mesas and arroyos, so that it looked as if Monument Valley had been relocated at the bottom of a canyon twice as deep and five times as wide as the Grand Canyon. The sight was too astonishing for John to be able to concentrate on anything else, and for the first time in his journey he drove all day with Pauline off.

North of the transverse gap, he drove into the huge sink of Candor Chasma, and now it was as if he were in a gigantic replica of the Painted Desert, with great deposition layers everywhere, bands of purple and yellow sediment, orange dunes, red erratics, pink sands, indigo gullies; truly a fantastic, extravagant landscape, disorienting to the eye because all the wild colors made it hard to figure out what was what, and how big it was, and how far away. Giant plateaus that seemed about to block his way would turn out to be curving strata on a distant cliff; small boulders next to the transponders would turn out to be enormous mesas half a day's drive away. And in the sunset light all the colors blazed, the whole Martian spectrum revealed and blazing as if color was bursting out of the rock, everything from pale yellow to dark bruised purple. Candor Chasma! He was going to have to come back some time and explore it.

The day after that, he drove up the steady slope of the north Ophir road, which the Swiss crew had completed the previous year. Up and up and up; and then, without ever seeing a distinct rim he was out of the canyons, rolling past the domed holes of Ganges Catena, and then over the old familiar plain, following a wide road, over the tight horizon past Chernobyl and Underhill; then on for another day west to Echus Overlook, Sax's new terraforming headquarters. His journey had taken a week, and crossed 2500 kilometers.

Sax Russell was back from Acheron, in his own place. He was a power now and no doubt about it, having been named by UNOMA a decade before as scientific head of the terraforming effort. And of course that decade of power had had its effect on him. He had solicited UN and transnational aid to build a whole town to serve as headquarters for the terraforming effort, and he had placed this town about five hundred kilometers due west of Underhill, on the edge of the cliff that formed the eastern wall of Echus Chasma. Echus was one of the narrowest and deepest canyons on the planet, and its eastern wall was even taller than south Melas; the section they had chosen to build the town into was a vertical basalt cliff four thousand meters high.

At the top of the cliff there was very little sign of the new town; the land behind the rim was almost unmarked, only a concrete pillbox here and there, and to the north the plume of a Rickover. But when John climbed out of his rover into one of the rim pillboxes, and got in one of the big elevators inside it, the extent of the town began to come clear; the elevators went down fifty floors. And when he descended fifty stories, he got out and found other elevators that would take him even lower, a whole series of them, descending right down to the floor of Echus Chasma. Say a story was ten meters; that meant there was room in the cliff for four hundred stories. Actually not that much of the room had been used yet, and most of the rooms built so far were clustered up in the highest twenty floors. Sax's offices, for instance, were very near the top.

His meeting room was a big open chamber, with a continuous floor-to-ceiling window as its western wall. When John walked into the room looking for Sax, it was still midmorning, and the window was almost clear; far, far below lay the chasm floor, still half in shadow, and there out in the sunlight stood the much lower western wall of Echus, and beyond that the great slope of the Tharsis bulge, rising higher and higher to the south. Out in the middle distance was the low bump of Tharsis Tholus, and to the left of it, just poking over the horizon, lay the purple cone of Ascraeus Mons, the northernmost of the great prince volcanoes.

But Sax was not in the meeting room, and he never looked out of this window as far as John could tell. He was next door in a lab, more lab rat than ever, hunch-shouldered and twitch-whiskered, gazing around at the floor, speaking in a voice that sounded like an AI. He led John through a whole sequence of labs, leaning forward to peer into screens or at inching graph paper, talking to John over a shoulder, in a state of distraction. The rooms they passed through were jammed with computers, printers, screens, books, rolls and stacks of paper, disks, GC-mass specs, incubators, fume hoods, long apparatus-filled lab tables, whole libraries; and placed on every precarious surface were potted plants, most of them unrecognizable bulges, armored succulents and the like, so that at a glance it looked like a virulent mold had sprung up and covered everything. "Your labs are getting kind of messy," John said.

"The planet is the lab," Sax replied.

John laughed, moved a bright yellow surarctic cactus from a countertop and sat down. It was said Sax never left these rooms anymore. "What are you simming today?"

"Atmospheres."

Of course. It was a problem that gave Sax a serious case of the blinks. All the heat they were releasing or applying to the planet was thickening the atmosphere, but all their CO_2-fixing strategies were thinning it; and as the chemical composition of the air slowly shifted to something less poisonous it became less greenhouse-gassed as well, so that things cooled back down and the process slowed. Negative feedback countering positive feedback, all over the place. Juggling all these factors into any meaningful extrapolative program was more than anyone had yet accomplished to Sax's satisfaction, so he had resorted to his usual solution; he was trying to do it himself.

He paced the narrow aisles left between equipment, moving chairs out of his way. "There's just too much carbon dioxide. In the old days the modelers swept that under the rug. I think I'm going to have to have robots feed the southern polar cap into Sabatier factories. What we can process won't sublime, and we can release the oxygen and make bricks of the carbon, I guess. We'll have more carbon blocks than we'll know what to do with. Black pyramids to go along with the white."

"Pretty."

"Uhn." The Crays and the two new Schillers hummed away behind him, providing his monotonal recitative with a ground bass. These computers spent all their time running through one set of conditions after another, Sax said; but the results, while never the same, were seldom encouraging. The air was going to be cold and poisonous for a good while yet.

Sax wandered down the hall, and John followed him into what looked like another lab, although there was a bed and a refrigerator in one corner. Violently disarranged bookscapes were overgrown with potted plants, bizarre Pleistocene growths that looked as deadly as the air outside. John sat in the lone empty chair. Sax stood and looked down at a seashell shrub as John described his meeting with Ann.

"Do you think she's involved?" Sax said.

"I think she may know who is. She mentioned someone called the Coyote."

"Ah yes." Sax glanced briefly at John – at his feet, to be precise. "She's siccing us onto a legendary character. He's supposed to have been on the *Ares* with us, you know. Hidden by Hiroko."

John was so surprised that Sax had heard of the Coyote that it took him a while to figure out what else was disturbing about what he had said. But then it came to him. One night Maya had told him that she had seen a face, the face of a stranger. The voyage out had been hard on Maya, and he had discounted the tale. But now . . .

Sax was wandering around turning on lights, peering at screens, muttering about security measures. He opened the refrigerator door briefly and John caught a glimpse of more spiky growths; either he kept experiments in there, or else his snack food had suffered a truly virulent eruption of mold. John said, "You can see why most of the attacks have been on the moholes. They're the easiest project to attack."

Sax tilted his head to the side. "Are they?"

"Think about it. Your little windmills are everywhere, there's nothing to be done about them."

"People are disabling them. We've had reports."

"What, a dozen? And how many are out there, a hundred thousand? They're junk, Sax. Litter. Your worst idea." And nearly fatal to his project, in fact, because of the algae dishes Sax had hidden in some of them. All of that algae had died,

313

apparently; but if it hadn't, and if anyone had been able to prove Sax had been responsible for its dissemination, he could have lost his job. It was yet another indication that Sax's logical manner was a front.

Now his nose was wrinkled. "They add up to a terawatt a year."

"And knocking a few apart won't do anything to that. As for the other physical operations, the black snow algae is on the northern polar cap, and can't be removed. The dawn and dusk mirrors are in orbit, and it's not so easy to knock them out."

"Someone did it to Pythagoras."

"True, but we know who it was, and there's a security team following her."

"She may never lead them to anyone else. They may be able to afford to expend a person per act, I wouldn't be surprised."

"Yeah, but some simple changes in screening personnel would make it impossible for anyone to smuggle any tools aboard."

"They could use what's out there." Sax shook his head. "The mirrors are vulnerable."

"Okay. More than some projects, anyway."

"Those mirrors are adding thirty calories per square centimeter per sol," Sax said. "And more all the time." Almost all the freighters from Earth were sunsailers now, and when they arrived in the Martian system they were linked to large collections of earlier arrivals parked in areosynchronous orbit, and programmed to swivel so that they reflected their light onto the terminators, adding a little bit of energy to each day's dawn and dusk. The whole arrangement had been coordinated by Sax's office, and he was proud of it.

"We'll increase security for all the maintenance crews," John said.

"So. Increased security on the mirrors and at the moholes."

"Yes. But that's not all."

Sax sniffed. "What do you mean?"

"Well, the problem is that it isn't just the terraforming projects *per se* that are potential targets. I mean, the nuclear reactors are part of the project too in their way; they provide a lot of your power, and they're pumping out heat like the furnaces they are. If one of them were to go, it would cause all kinds of fallout, more political even than physical."

The vertical lines between Sax's eyes reached up nearly to his hairline. John held out his palms. "Not my fault. That's just the way it is."

Sax said, "AI, take a note. Look into reactor security."

"Note taken," one of the Schillers said, sounding just like Sax.

"And that's not the worst," John said. Sax twitched, glared furiously at the floor. "The bioengineering labs."

Sax's mouth became a tight line.

"New organisms are being cooked up daily," John went on, "and it might be possible to create something that would kill everything else on the planet."

Sax blinked. "Let's hope none of these people think like you."

"I'm just trying to think like them."

"AI, take a note. Biolab security."

"Of course Vlad and Ursula and their group have stuck suicide genes into everything they've made," John said. "But those are meant to stop oversuccess, or mutational accidents. If someone were to deliberately circumvent them, and concoct something that fed on oversuccess, we could be in trouble."

"I see that."

"So. The labs, the reactors, the moholes, the mirrors. It could be worse."

Sax rolled his eyes. "I'm glad you think so. I'll talk to Helmut about it. I'll be seeing him soon anyway. It looks like they're going to approve Phyllis's elevator at the next

315

UNOMA session. That will cut the costs of terraforming tremendously."

"Eventually it will, but the initial investment must be huge."

Sax shrugged. "Push an Amor asteroid into orbit, set up a robot factory, let it go to work. It's not as expensive as you might think."

John rolled his eyes. "Sax, who's paying for all this?"

Sax tilted his head, blinked. "The sun."

John stood, suddenly hungry. "Then the sun calls the shots. Remember that."

Mangalavid broadcast six hours of local amateur video every evening, a weird grab bag of stuff that John watched every chance he got. So after building a big green salad in the kitchen he went to the window room on the dorm floor, and watched while eating, glancing from time to time at the florid sunset over Ascraeus. The first ten minutes of that evening's broadcast had been shot by a sanitary engineer working on a waste processing plant in Chasma Borealis; her voiceover was enthusiastic but boring: "What's nice is we can pollute all we want with certain materials, oxygen, ozone, nitrogen, argon, steam, some biota – which gives us leeway we didn't have back home, we just keep grinding what they give us till we can let it loose." Back home, John said to himself, A newcomer. After her there was an attempt at a karate bout, both hilarious and beautiful at the same time; and then twenty minutes of some Russians staging *Hamlet* in pressure suits at the bottom of the Tyrrhena Patera mohole, a production that struck John as crazy until Hamlet caught sight of Claudius kneeling to pray, and the camera tilted up to show the mohole as cathedral walls, rising above Claudius to an infinitely distant shaft of sunlight, like the forgiveness he would never receive.

John shut off the TV and took the elevator down to the dorm. He got into bed and relaxed. Karate as ballet. The newcomers were all still engineers, construction workers, scientists of all kinds; but they didn't seem as single-minded as the first hundred, and that was probably good. They still had a scientific mindset and worldview, they were practical, empirical, rational; one could hope that the selection process on Earth was still working against fanaticism, sending up people with a kind of traveling-Swiss sensibility, practical but open to new possibilities, able to form new loyalties and beliefs. Or so he hoped. He knew by now it was a bit naïve.

You only had to look at the first hundred to realize scientists could become as fanatical as anybody else, maybe more so; educations too narrowly focused, perhaps. Hiroko's team disappearing . . . Out there in the wild rock somewhere, lucky bastards . . . He fell asleep.

He worked at Echus Overlook a few days more, then got a call from Helmut Bronski in Burroughs, who wanted to confer with him about the new arrivals from Earth. John decided to take the train to Burroughs and see Helmut in person.

The night before his departure, he went to see Sax in his labs; when he walked in Sax said in his monotone, "We've found an Amor asteroid that's ninety percent ice, in an orbit that will bring it near Mars in three years. Just what I've been looking for, in fact." His plan was to place a robot-controlled mass driver on an ice asteroid and push it into an aerobraking orbit around Mars, thus burning it up in the atmosphere. This would satisfy UNOMA protocols forbidding the kind of mass destruction that a direct impact would cause, but it would still add massive quantities of water and separated hydrogen and oxygen to the atmosphere, thickening it with precisely the gases they needed most. "It could raise the atmospheric pressure by as much as fifty millibars."

"You're kidding!" The pre-arrival average at the datum had been between seven and ten millibars (Earth's sea level averaged 1013), and all their efforts so far had only raised the average to around fifty. "One iceball will double the atmospheric pressure?"

"That's what the simulations indicate. Of course with the initial level so low, doubling is not as impressive as it sounds."

"Still, that's great, Sax. And it'll be hard to sabotage."

But Sax didn't want to be reminded of that. He frowned slightly, and slipped away.

John laughed at his skittishness, and went to the door. Then he stopped to think, and looked up and down the hall.

Empty. And no video monitors in Sax's offices. He went back in, grinning at his own furtive tiptoes, and glanced around at the paper chaos on Sax's desk. Where to start? Presumably his AI would be the repository of anything interesting, but probably it would only respond to Sax's voice, and would surely keep a record of any other inquiries. Quietly he opened a desk drawer. Empty. All the drawers in the desk were empty; he almost laughed out loud, stifled it. There was a stack of correspondence on a lab bench; he picked through it. Mostly notes from the biologists at Acheron. At the bottom of the stack was a single sheet of unsigned mail, with no return address or origin code; Sax's printer had spit it out without any identification that John could see. The message was brief:

"1). We use suicide genes to curb proliferation. 2). There are so many heat sources now on the surface that we don't think anyone can tell our exhaust from the rest of it. 3). We simply agreed we wanted to get off and work on our own, without interference. I'm sure you understand now."

After a minute of staring at this John whipped his head up and looked around. Still alone. He glanced at the note again, put it back where he had found it and walked quietly out of Sax's offices, back to the guest quarters. "Sax," he said admiringly, "you tricky congress of rats!"

The train to Burroughs carried mostly freight, thirty narrow cars of it, with two passenger cars up front, running over a superconducting magnetic piste so quickly and smoothly that it was hard to believe the view; after John's endless plods cross-country in rovers, it was almost frightening. The only thing to do was flood the pleasure centers in the old brain with omegendorph and sit back and enjoy it, looking out at what appeared to be some kind of terrain-following supersonic flight.

The piste had been routed roughly parallel to the $10°$ N latitude; eventually the plan was to ring the planet, but so far only the hemisphere between Echus and Burroughs had been finished. Burroughs had become the biggest town in the far hemisphere. The original settlement had been built by an American-based consortium, using a French-led EC design and was located at the upper end of Isidis Planitia, which was in effect a huge trough where the northern plains made a deep indentation into the southern highlands. The sides and head of the trough counteracted the planet's curvature in such a way that the landscape around the town had something like Terran horizons, and as the train flew down the great trough Boone could see across mesa-dotted dark plains to horizons some sixty kilometers away.

Burroughs's buildings were almost all cliff-dwellings, cut into the sides of five low mesas that were grouped together on a rise in the bend of an ancient curving channel. Big sections of the mesas' vertical sides had been filled by rectangles of mirrored glass, as if postmodern skyscrapers had been turned on their sides and shoved into the hills. A startling sight, in fact, and far more impressive than Underhill, or even Echus Overlook, which had a great view but could not be seen. No, the glass-sided mesas of Burroughs, on their rise over a channel that seemed to be begging for water, with a view out to distant hills; these features combined to give the new town a quickly growing reputation as the most beautiful city on Mars.

Its western train station was inside one of the excavated mesas, a glass-walled room sixty meters high. John stepped out into this grand space and made his way through the crowds of people, head craned back like a hick in Manhattan. Train crews were dressed in blue jumpers, prospecting teams in walker green, UNOMA bureaucrats in suits, construction workers in work jumpers, colored like rainbows to suggest sportswear. UNOMA headquarters had been located in Burroughs three years before, and that had caused a real building boom; it was a close thing whether there were more UNOMA bureaucrats or construction workers in the station.

At the far end of the great room John found a subway entrance, and took a little subway car to the UNOMA headquarters. In the car he shook hands with a few people who recognized and approached him, feeling the old weirdness of the fishbowl return. He was back among strangers. In a city.

That night he had dinner with Helmut Bronski. They had met many times before, and John was impressed by the man, a German millionaire who had gotten into politics: tall, beefy, blond and red-faced, impeccably groomed, dressed in an expensive gray suit. He had been the EEC's minister of finance when he took the UNOMA post. Now he told John the latest news, in a very urbane British English, eating roast beef and potatoes rapidly between bursts of sentences, holding his silverware in the workmanlike German fashion. "We are going to award a prospecting contract in Elysium to the transnational consortium Armscor. They will be shipping up their own equipment."

"But Helmut," John said, "won't that violate the Mars treaty?"

Helmut made a wide gesture with the hand holding the fork: they were men of the world, his look said, they understood these kinds of things. "The treaty is superannuated, this is obvious to everyone dealing with the situation. But its scheduled revision is ten years away. In the meantime, we have to try to anticipate certain aspects of the revision. That's why we give some concessions now. There is no rational reason to delay, and if we tried there would be trouble in the general assembly."

"But the general assembly can't be happy that you've given the first concession to an old South African weapons manufacturer!"

Helmut shrugged. "Armscor has very little relation to its origins. It is just a name. When South Africa became Azania, the company moved its home offices to Australia, and then to Singapore. And now of course it has become very much more than an aerospace firm. It is a true transnational, one

321

of the new tigers, with banks of its own, and controlling interest in about fifty of the old Fortune 500.''

''*Fifty* of them?'' John said.

''Yes. And Armscor is one of the smallest of the transnationals: that is why we picked it. But it still has a bigger economy than any but the largest twenty countries. As the old multinationals coalesce into transnationals, you see, they really gather quite a bit of power, and they have influence in the general assembly. When we give one a concession, some twenty or thirty countries profit by it, and get their opening on Mars. And for the rest of the countries, that serves as a precedent. And so pressure on us is reduced.''

''Uh huh.'' John thought it over. ''Tell me, who negotiated this agreement?''

''Well, it was a number of us, you know.''

Helmut ate on, serenely ignoring John's steady gaze.

John pursed his lips, looked away. He understood suddenly that he was talking with a man who, though a functionary, yet considered himself to be vastly more important on the planet than Boone. Genial, smooth-faced (and who cut his hair?), Bronski leaned back and ordered them afterdinner drinks. His assistant, their waitress for the evening, scurried off to oblige.

''I don't believe I've been waited on before on Mars,'' John observed.

Helmut met his gaze calmly, but his beefy color had heightened. John almost smiled. The UNOMA factor wanted to seem menacing, the representative of powers so sophisticated that John's little weather station mentality couldn't even comprehend them. But John had found in the past that a few minutes of his First Man On Mars routine was usually enough to crush that kind of attitude; and so he laughed, and drank, and told tales, and alluded to secrets only the first hundred were privy to, and made it clear to the assistant-waitress that he was the one in command at the table, and so on – behaving in general in an unconcerned, knowing, arrogant manner – and by the time they were finished with their sherbet and brandy Bronski was loud and blustery himself, clearly nervous and on the defensive.

Functionaries. John had to laugh.

But he was curious concerning the ultimate point of their conference, which still wasn't clear to him. Perhaps Bronski had wanted to see in person how news of the new concession would affect one of the first hundred – perhaps to gauge the reaction of the rest? That would be silly, for to get a good gauge on the first hundred you would need to poll eighty of them at least; but that didn't mean it wasn't true. John was used to being taken for a representative of things, for a symbol. The figurehead again. It could definitely be a waste of time.

He wondered if he could salvage something of his own from the evening, and as they were walking back to his guest suite, he said, "Have you ever heard of the Coyote?"

"An animal?"

He grinned, left it at that. In his room he lay on his bed, Mangalavid on the TV, thinking things over. Brushing his teeth before going to sleep, he looked his mirror image in the eye and scowled. He waved his toothbrush in the expansive gesture: "Vell," he said in an unfair parody of Helmut's slight accent, "ziss is business, you know! Business as usual!"

The next morning he had a few hours before his first meeting, and so he spent the time with Pauline, going over what he could find out about Helmut Bronski's doings in the last sixth months. Could Pauline get into the UNOMA diplomatic pouch? Had Helmut ever been to Senzeni Na, or any of the other sabotage sites? While Pauline ran through her search algorithms John swallowed an omegendorph to kill his hangover, and thought about what lay behind this inspiration to search Helmut's records. UNOMA constituted the ultimate authority on Mars these days, at least according to the letter of the law. In practice, as last night had made clear, it had the UN's usual toothlessness before national armies and transnational money; unless it did their bidding it was helpless, it could not succeed against their desires and probably would never even try, as it was their tool. So what did *they* want, the national governments and the transnational boards of directors? If enough sabotages occurred, would that constitute a reason to bring in more of their own security? Would it tend to increase their control?

He made a disgusted noise. Apparently the only result of his investigation so far was that the list of suspects had tripled. Pauline said, "Excuse me, John," and the information came up on her screen. The diplomatic pouch, she had found, was coded in one of the new unbreakable encryptions: you'd have to get the decryptions to enter it. Helmut's movements, on the other hand, were easily traceable. He had been to Pythagoras, the mirror station that had been spun out of orbit, ten weeks ago. And to Senzeni Na two weeks before John's visit. And yet no one at Senzeni Na had mentioned his appearance.

Most recently, he had just returned from the mining complex being set up at a place called Bradbury Point. Two days later John left to visit it.

Bradbury Point was located some eight hundred kilometers north of Burroughs, at the easternmost extension of the Nilosyrtis Mensae. The mensae were a series of long mesas, like islands of the southern highlands standing out in the shallows of the northern plains. The island mesas of Nilosyrtis had recently been found to be a rich metallogenic province, with deposits of copper, silver, zinc, gold, platinum and other metals. Concentrations of ore like this had been discovered in several locations on the so-called Great Escarpment, where the southern highlands dropped to the northern lowlands. Some areologists were going so far as to label the entire escarpment region a metallogenic province, banding the planet like the stitching on a baseball. It was another odd fact to add to the great north-south mystery, and a fact that was, of course, getting more than its share of attention. Excavations accompanied by intensive areological studies were being conducted by scientists working for UNOMA and, John discovered as he checked new arrivals' employment records, the transnationals; all trying to find clues that would enable them to locate more deposits. But even on Earth the geology of mineral formation was not well understood, which was why prospecting still had large elements of chance in it; and on Mars, it was more mysterious yet. The recent finds on the Great Escarpment had been mostly an accident, and only now was the region becoming the main focus for prospecting.

The discovery of the Bradbury Point complex had accelerated this hunt, as it was turning out to be as big as the largest Terran complexes, perhaps the equal of the Bushveldt Complex of Azania. So: a gold rush in Nilosyrtis. And Helmut Bronski had visited the scene.

Which turned out to be small and utilitarian, a mere beginning; a Rickover and some refineries, next to a mesa hollowed out and filled by a habitat. The mines were scattered in the lowlands between mesas. Boone drove up to the habitat, coupled to the garage, then ducked through the locks. Inside a welcoming committee greeted him, and took him up to a window-walled conference room to talk.

There were, they said, about three hundred people in Bradbury, all employees of UNOMA, and trained by the transnational Shellalco. When they took John on a brief tour, he found they were a mix of ex-South Africans, Australians and Americans, all happy to shake his hand; about three-quarters men, pale and clean, looking more like lab techs than the blackened trolls John envisioned when he heard the word *miner*. Most of them were working on two-year contracts, they told him, and keeping track of the time they had left, by the week or even by the day. They ran the mines mostly by teleoperation, and looked shocked when Boone asked to go down into a mine for a look around. "It's just a hole," one said. Boone stared at them innocently; and after another moment's hesitation, they scrambled to gather an escort team to take him out.

It took them two hours to get into walkers and out of a lock. They drove to the rim of a mine, and then down a ramp road into a terraced oval pit some two kilometers long. There they got out, and followed John as he walked around. Surrounded by big robotic dozers and dumptrucks and earth movers, his four escorts' faceplates were all eyes; on the alert for a behemoth on the loose, John guessed. He stared at them, amazed at their timidity; it made him realize, all of a sudden, that Mars could be just another version of the hardship assignment, a hellish combination of Siberia, the interior of Saudi Arabia, the South Pole in winter, and *Novy Mir*.

Or else they just thought he was a dangerous man to be around. Which gave him a start. Everyone had no doubt heard of the falling dump truck; maybe it was just that. But could it be something more? Might these people be aware of something that he wasn't? Reflecting on this for a while, John found his own eyes beginning to press glass; he had been thinking of the falling truck as an accident, or at least something that could only happen once. But his movements were easy to trace, everyone knew where he was. And every time you went outdoors you were only a walker away, as they said. And in a pit mine there were a lot of behemoths about . . .

But they got back in without incident. And that night they had the usual dinner and party in his honor, a hard-drinking party, with a lot of omegendorph consumption and loud raucous talk: a bunch of young tough engineers, pleased to find that John Boone was actually a fun guy to party with. A fairly common reaction among newcomers, especially younger men. John chatted them up, and had a good time, and slipped his inquiries into the flow pretty unnoticeably, he thought. They had not heard of the Coyote, which was interesting, as they did know about Big Man, and the hidden colony. Apparently the Coyote was not in that category of tale; he was some kind of insider thing, known, so far as John could tell, only to some of the first hundred.

The miners had had a recent unusual visit, however; an Arab caravan had come by, traveling the edge of Vastitas Borealis. And, they said, the Arabs had claimed to have been visited by some of "the lost colonists", as they called them.

"Interesting," John said. It seemed unlikely to him that Hiroko or any of her crew would reveal themselves, but who could tell. He might as well go check it out; after all, there was only so much he could do at Bradbury Point. Very little detective work, he was noticing, could be accomplished before a crime occurred. So he spent a couple more days observing the mining, but that told him little; it only reinforced his shock at the scale of the operation, at how much robotic earthmovers could tear away. "What are you going to do with all the metal?" he asked, after taking a look down into another great open pit mine, located twenty-five kilometers to the west of the habitat. "Getting it to Earth will cost more than it's worth, won't it?"

The chief of operations, a black-haired man with a hatchet face, grinned. "We'll hold onto it until it's worth more. Or until they build that space elevator."

"You believe in that?"

"Oh yeah, the materials are there! Graphite whisker reinforced with diamond spirals, why you could almost build one on Earth with that. Here, it would be easy."

John shook his head. That afternoon they drove for an hour back to the habitat, past raw pits and slag heaps, toward the distant plume of the refineries on the other sides of the habitat mesa. He was used to seeing the land torn up for building purposes, but this . . . it was amazing what a few hundred people could do. Of course it was the same

327

technology that was allowing Sax to build a vertical town the whole height of the Echus Overlook, the same technology that allowed all the new towns to be built so quickly; but still, wreaking such havoc just to strip away metals, destined for Earth's insatiable demand . . .

The next day he gave the operations chief a fiendishly tight security regimen, to be followed for two months; and then drove out into the wind-eroded tracks of the Arab caravan, and followed them north and east.

It turned out that Frank Chalmers was traveling with this Arab caravan. But he had not seen or heard of any visitation by Hiroko's people, and none of the Arabs would admit to being the one who had told the story at Bradbury Point. A false lead, then. Or else one that Frank was helping the Arabs to eliminate; and if so, how would John find that out? Though the Arabs had only recently arrived on Mars, they were already Frank's allies, no doubt about it; he lived with them, he spoke their language, and now, naturally, he was the constant mediator between them and John. Not a chance of an independent investigation, except what Pauline could do in the records, which she could do as well away from the caravan as in it.

Nevertheless, John traveled with them for a while as they roamed the great dune sea, doing areology and a bit of prospecting. Frank was only there briefly himself, to talk to an Egyptian friend; he was too busy to stay anywhere for long. His job as US Secretary made him as much of a globe-trotter as John, and they crossed paths pretty frequently. Frank had managed to keep his position as the American department head now through three administrations, even though it was a cabinet post; a remarkable feat, even without considering his distance from Washington. And so he was now overseeing the introduction of investment by the American-based transnationals, a responsibility that made him manic with overwork and puffed up with power, what John thought of as the business version of Sax, always moving, always gesturing with his hands as if conducting the music of his speech, which had shifted over the years to full-tilt Chamber of Commerce overdrive, "Got to stake a claim on the Escarpment before the transnats and the Germans snap everything up, lotta work to be done!" which was his constant refrain, often said while pointing for illustration at the little globe he carried with him in his lectern pocket. "Look at your moholes, I just entered them last week, one near the north pole, three in the sixties north and south, four along the equator, one near the south pole, all of them nicely placed west of volcanic rises to catch their updrafts, it's beautiful." He spun the globe and the blue dots marking the moholes blurred for a moment into blue lines. "It's good to see you finally doing something useful."

"Finally."

"Look, here's the new habitat factory in Hellas. They're manufacturing starter units at a rate that'll enable them to handle some three thousand emigrants per Ls ninety, and given the new fleet of roundtrip shuttles, that's just barely enough." He saw John's expression and said quickly, "All heat in the end, John, so it helps the terraforming with more than just money and labor, I mean think about it."

"But do you ever wonder what's going to come of it all?" John asked.

"What do you mean?"

"You know, this deluge of people and equipment, while things are falling apart on Earth."

"Things are always going to be falling apart on Earth. You might as well get used to it."

"Yeah, but who's going to own what up here? Who's going to call the shots?"

Frank just made a face at John's naïveté, at the very nature of the question. One look at his grimace and John could read it all, the whole complex of disgust and impatience and amusement. A part of John was pleased at this instant recognition; he knew his old friend better than he had ever known any of his family, so that the swarthy pale-eyed face glowering at him was like that of a brother, a twin that he couldn't ever remember not knowing. On the other hand, he was annoyed with Frank for his condescension. "People are wondering about it, Frank. It's not just me, and it's not just Arkady. You can't just shrug it off and

330

act like it's a stupid question, like there's nothing to be decided."

"The UN decides," Frank said brusquely. "There's ten billion of them, and ten thousand of us. That's a million to one. If you want to influence those kind of odds you ought to have become the UNOMA factor like I told you to when they set up the position. But you didn't listen to me. You just shrugged it off. You could have really done something, but now what are you? Sax's assistant in charge of publicity."

"And development, and security, and Terran affairs, and the moholes."

"Ostrich!" Frank pounced. "Head in a hole! Come on, let's go eat."

John agreed and they went off to a dinner in the Arabs' biggest rover, a meal of basted lamb and dill-flavored yogurt, delicious and exotic. But John found himself still irritated at Frank's scorn, which never let up. The old rivalry, sharp as ever; and no First Man routine would ever make a dent in Frank's sneery arrogance.

Thus when Maya Toitovna showed up unexpectedly the next day, traveling west on her way to Acheron, John gave her a longer hug than he might have otherwise; and by the time that night's dinner was over, he had made certain that she would spend the night in his rover – a matter of a particular attentiveness, a certain laugh, a certain look, the nearly-accidental brushing of arms together as they stood trying sherbets, talking to the happy men of the caravan, who clearly found her fascinating . . . all their old code of conciliation and seduction, established through the years. And Frank could only watch, deadpan, talking in Arabic to his Egyptian friends.

And that night, as John and Maya made love in John's rover bed, John pulled up from her briefly and looked down at her white body, and thought, So much for political power Frank buddy! That deadpan look had told it all, the fierce desire for Maya still there, still burning. Frank, like most of the men in the caravanserai that night, would have loved to have been in John's place at that moment; once or twice in the past he no doubt had been; but not when John was around. No, tonight Frank would be reminded what real power was made of.

Distracted by such nastiness, it took John a while to pay any real attention to Maya herself. It had been almost five years since he and she had slept together, and in the intervening time he had had several other partners, and knew she had lived for a time with an engineer in Hellas. It was strange to begin again, as they knew each other intimately and yet didn't. Her turning face flickering under him in the dim light, sister then stranger, sister then stranger . . . Something happened, then, something turned in him; all that exterior business fell away, all those games. Something in her face, in the way she was all there, the way she would give her whole self to him when they made love. He didn't know anyone else who was quite like that.

And thus the old flame sparked again, uncertainly at first, as it had not been there at all in their first lovemaking. But then, after an hour's quiet talk, they had started kissing and rolled together and suddenly it was ablaze and they were inside it. Lit up by Maya as usual, he had to admit it. She *made* him pay attention. Sex for her was not (as it tended to be for John) some kind of extension of sport; it was a grand passion, a transcendent state of being, and she was so tigerish when she got going that she always surprised him, woke him up, brought him up to her level, reminded him what sex could be. And it was wonderful to be reminded again, to learn that again; really wonderful. Omegendorph was nothing to it, how could he have forgotten, why did he keep wandering away from her as if she weren't, somehow, irreplaceable? He crushed her with a hug and they twisted together, bit at each other, panted and moaned; came together as they had so often before, Maya pulling him over the edge with her. Their ritual.

And even afterwards, just talking, he somehow felt very much more fond of her. He had started things just to irk Frank, it was true; he had been completely careless of her; but now, lying beside her, he could feel how much he had missed her presence in the previous five years, how bland life had seemed. How much he had missed her! New feelings – they always surprised him, he kept assuming he was too old for them, that he had more or less stopped changing. And then something would happen. And so often that something (thinking back over the years) was a meeting with Maya . . .

She was still the same Maya Toitovna, however: mercurial, full of her own thoughts and plans, full of herself; she had no idea what John was doing out there on the dunes, and would never think to ask. And she would slash him to ribbons if he accidentally crossed her mood, he could tell that just in the sultry set of her shoulders, just in the way she padded off to the toilet. But he knew all that already, it was old news, something from the first years at Underhill, so long ago; and the sheer familiarity of it was pleasing – even her irritability was pleasing! Like Frank and his scorn. Well, he was getting old, and they were family. He almost laughed, he almost said something to set her off, then thought better of it. Just knowing was enough, no need for another demonstration, Lord! At that thought he did laugh, and she smiled to hear it, and came back to bed and shoved him in the chest. "Laughing at me again I see! Because of my fat bottom is it?"

"You know your bottom is perfect." She shoved him again, insulted at what she considered a gross lie, and their wrestling drew them back into the reality of skin and salt, into the world of sex. At some point in the long lazy session he found himself thinking I love you, wild Maya, I really do. It was a disconcerting thought, a dangerous thought. Not something he would risk saying. But it felt true.

So a couple of days later, when she left to visit the Acheron group, and asked him to join her there, he was pleased. "Maybe in a couple of months."

"No, no." Her face was serious. "Come sooner, I want you there with me sooner."

And when he agreed, on a whim, she grinned like a girl with a secret. "You won't be sorry." With a kiss she was off, driving south to Burroughs to catch the train west.

After that, there was less chance than ever of learning anything from the Arabs. He had offended Frank, and the Arabs closed ranks behind their friend, as was only right. Hidden colony? they said. What was that?

He sighed, gave up on it and decided to leave. Stocking his rover the night before his departure (the Arabs were punctilious about filling his hold with supplies), he pondered what he had accomplished so far in his investigation of the sabotages. So far Sherlock Holmes was in no danger, that was sure. Worse than that, there was now a whole society on Mars that was basically impenetrable to him. Moslems, what were they exactly? He read Pauline that evening after he was done stocking, and then he rejoined his hosts and watched them as closely as he was able, asking questions all that night long . . . He knew asking questions was the key to people's souls, infinitely more useful than wit; but in this case it didn't seem to make any difference. Coyote? Some kind of wild dog was it?

Baffled, he left the caravan the next morning and drove west, on the southern border of the dune sea. It would be a long journey to Acheron to join Maya, five thousand kilometers of dune after dune; but he preferred driving to going down to Burroughs and taking the train. He needed time to think. And really it was a kind of habit now, driving cross-country, or flying gliders – getting away, traveling slowly across the land. He had been on the road for years now, criss-crossing the northern hemisphere and making long excursions into the south, inspecting moholes or doing

334

favors for Sax or Helmut or Frank, or looking into things for Arkady, or cutting ribbons at the opening of one thing or another — a town, a well, a weather station, a mine, a mohole — and always talking, talking in public speeches or private conversations, talking to strangers, old friends, new acquaintances, talking almost as fast as Frank did, and all in an attempt to inspire the people on the planet to figure out a way to forget history, to build a functioning society. To create a scientific system designed for Mars, designed to their specifications, fair and just and rational and all those good things. To point the way to a new Mars!

And yet after every year that passed, it seemed less likely to happen the way he had envisioned it. A place like Bradbury Point showed how rapidly things were changing, and people like the Arabs confirmed the impression; events were out of his control, and more than that, out of anyone's control. There was no plan. He rolled west on autopilot, up and down over dune after dune, not seeing a thing, sunk deep in an attempt to understand what exactly history was, and how it worked. And it seemed to him as he drove on day after day that history was like some vast thing that was always over the tight horizon, invisible except in its effects. It was what happened when you weren't looking — an unknowable infinity of events, which although out of control, controlled everything. After all, he had been here from the very beginning! He had *been* the beginning, the first person to step on this world, and then he had returned against all the odds, and helped to build it from scratch! And yet now, despite all that, it was spinning away from him. Contemplating that fact made him tense with disbelief, and sometimes with a sudden furious frustration; to think that the whole thing was accelerating not only beyond his control, but even beyond his ability to comprehend — it wasn't right, he had to fight it!

And yet how? Social planning of some sort . . . clearly they had to have it. This flailing about without a plan, in violation of even the flimsy plan people had made back at the beginning with the Mars treaty . . . well, societies without a plan, that was history so far; but history so far had been a nightmare, a huge compendium of examples to be avoided. No. They needed a plan. They had a chance at a new start here, they needed a vision. Helmut the oily functionary, Frank with his cynical acceptance of the status quo, his acceptance of the breakdown of the treaty, as if they were in a kind of gold rush; Frank was wrong. Wrong as usual!

But his own rushing about was probably wrong too. He had been operating on the unarticulated theory that if he only saw more of the planet, visited one more settlement, talked to one more person, that he would somehow (without really thinking too hard) *get it* – and that his holistic understanding would then flow back from him to everybody else, spreading out through all the new settlers and changing things. Now he was pretty sure that this feeling had been naïve; there were so many people on the planet these days, he could never hope to connect with them, to become the articulator of all their hopes and desires. And not only that, but few of the newcomers seemed much like the first hundred in regard to their reasons for coming. Well, that wasn't entirely true; there were still scientists coming up, and people like the Swiss roadbuilding gypsies. But he didn't know them like he did the first hundred, and he never would. That little band had formed him, really, they had shaped his opinions and ideas, had taught him; they were his family, he trusted them. And he wanted their help, he needed it now more than ever. Perhaps it was that which explained the sudden new intensity of his feeling for Maya. And perhaps it was this that made him so angry with Hiroko – he wanted to talk to her, he needed her help! And she had abandoned them.

Vlad and Ursula had relocated their biotech complex to a finlike ridge in the Acheron Fossae, a narrow prominence which looked like the conning tower of a vast submerged submarine. They had honeycombed the upper part of it with excavations that extended from cliff to cliff; some of the rooms were a kilometer wide, and glass-walled on both sides. The windows on the south side had a view of Olympus Mons, some six hundred kilometers away; north-facing windows looked down onto the pale tan sands of Arcadia Planitia.

John drove up a wide ledge to the bottom of the fin, and plugged into the garage lock door, noticing as he did that the ground in the narrow canyon south of the settlement was lumpy with heaps of what appeared to be melted brown sugar.

"It's a new kind of cryptogamic crust," Vlad said when John asked him about it. "A symbiosis of cyanobacteria and Florida platform bacteria. The platform bacteria go very deep, and convert sulfates in the rock to sulfides, which then feed a variant of *Microcoleus*. The top layers of that grow in filaments, which bind to sand and clay in big dendritic formations, so it's like little forest sylvanols with really long bacterial root systems. It looks like these root systems will keep on going right down through the regolith to bedrock, melting the permafrost as they go."

"And you've released this stuff?" John said.

"Sure. We need something to bust up the permafrost, right?"

"Is there anything to stop it from growing planetwide?"

"Well, it has the usual array of suicide genes in case it begins to overwhelm the rest of the biomass, but if it keeps to its niche . . . ."

"Wow."

"It's not too unlike the first life forms that covered the

Terran continents, we think. We've just enhanced its speed of growth, and its root systems. The funny thing is that I think at first it's going to cool the atmosphere, even though it's warming things underground. Because it'll really increase chemical weathering of the rock, and all those reactions absorb CO_2 from the air, so the air pressure is going to drop."

Maya had come up and joined them with a big hug for John, and now she said, "But won't the reactions release oxygen as fast as they absorb CO_2, and keep air pressure up?"

Vlad shrugged. "Maybe. We'll see."

John laughed. "Sax is a long term thinker. He'll probably be pleased."

"Oh yes. He authorized the release. And he's coming to study here again when spring comes."

They had dinner in a hall located high on the fin, just under the crest. Skylights opened above to the greenhouse on the crest itself, and windows ran the length of the north and south walls; stands of bamboo filled the walls to east and west. All the residents of Acheron were there for dinner, holding to an Underhill custom as they did in many other ways. The discussion at John and Maya's table ranged widely, but kept returning to the current work, which involved trying to solve problems caused by the need to implant safeguards in all the GEMs they were releasing. Double suicide genes in every GEM was a practice the Acheron group had initiated on its own, and it was now going to be codified as UN law. "That's all well and good for legal GEMs," Vlad said. "But if some fools try something on their own and blow it, we could be in big trouble anyway."

After dinner, Ursula said to John and Maya, "Since you're here you ought to get your physicals. It's been a while for both of you."

John, who hated physicals and indeed all medical attention of any kind, demurred. But Ursula hounded him, and eventually he gave in, and visited her clinic a couple days later. There he was put through a battery of diagnostic tests that seemed even more intensive than usual, most of them run by imaging machines and computers with too-relaxing voices, telling him to move this way and then that, while John in complete ignorance did what he was told. Modern medicine. But after all that, he was poked and prodded and tapped in time-honored fashion by Ursula herself. And when it was over he was lying on his back with a white sheet over him, while she stood at his side, looking at read-outs and humming absently.

"You're looking good," she told him after several minutes of that. "Some of the usual gravity-related problems, but nothing we can't deal with."

"Great," John said, feeling relieved. That was the thing about physicals; any news was bad news, one wanted an absence of news. Getting that was somehow a victory, and more so every time; but still, a negative accomplishment. Nothing had happened to him, great!

"So do you want the treatment?" Ursula asked, her back to him, her voice casual.

"The treatment?"

"It's a kind of geronotological therapy. An experimental procedure. Somewhat like an inoculation, but with a DNA strengthener. Repairs broken strands, and restores cell division accuracy to a significant degree."

John sighed. "And what does that mean?"

"Well, you know. Ordinary ageing is mostly caused by cell division error. After a number of generations, ranging from hundreds to tens of thousands depending which kind of cells you're talking about, errors in reproduction start to increase, and everything gets weaker. The immune system is one of the first to weaken, and then other tissues, and then finally something goes wrong, or the immune system gets overwhelmed by a disease, and that's it."

"And you're saying you can stop these errors?"

339

"Slow them down, anyway, and fix the ones that are already broken. A mix, really. The division errors are caused by breaks in DNA strands, so we wanted to strengthen DNA strands. To do it we would read your genome, and then build an auto repair genomic library of small segments that will replace the broken strands—"

"Auto repair?"

She sighed. "All Americans think that is funny. Anyhow we push this auto repair library into the cells, where they bind to the original DNA and help keep them from breaking." She began to draw double and quadruple helixes as she talked, shifting inexorably into biotech jargon, until John could only catch the general drift of the argument, which apparently had its origins in the genome project and the field of genetic abnormality correction, with application methods taken from cancer therapy and GEM technique. Aspects of these and many other different technologies had been combined by the Acheron group, Ursula explained. And the result seemed to be that they could give him an infection of bits of his own genome, an infection which would invade every cell in his body except for parts of his teeth and skin and bones and hair; and afterwards he would have nearly flawless DNA strands, repaired and reinforced strands that would make subsequent cell division more accurate.

"How accurate?" he asked, trying to grasp what it all meant.

"Well, about like if you were ten years old."

"You're kidding."

"No, no. We've all done it to ourselves, back around Ls ten of this year, and so far as we can tell, it's working."

"Does it last forever?"

"Nothing lasts forever, John."

"How long then?"

"We don't know. We ourselves are the experiment, we figure we'll find out as we go along. It seems possible we might be able to do the therapy again when the rate of division error begins to increase again. If that is successful, it could mean you would last for quite a while."

"Like how long?" he insisted.

"Well, we don't know, do we? Longer than we live now, that's pretty sure. Possibly a lot longer."

John stared at her. She smiled at the expression on his face, and he could feel that his jaw was slack with amazement; no doubt he looked less than brilliant, but what did she expect? It was . . . it was . . .

He was following his thoughts with difficulty as they skittered around. "Who have you told about this?" he asked.

"Well, we have asked everyone in the first hundred, when they get a check-up with us. And everyone here at Acheron has tried it. And the thing is, we've only combined methods that everyone has, so it won't be long before others try putting it all together too. So we're writing it up for publication, but we're going to send the articles first to be reviewed by the World Health Organization. Political fall-out, you know."

"Um," John said, considering it. News of a longevity drug loose on Mars, back among the teeming billions . . . my Lord, he thought. "Is it expensive?"

"Not extremely. Reading your genome is the most expensive part, and it takes time. But it's just a procedure, you know, it's just computer time. It's very possible you could inoculate everyone on Earth. But the population problem down there is already critical as it is. They'd have to institute some pretty intense population control, or else they'd go Malthusian really fast. We thought we'd better leave the decisions to the authorities down there."

"But word is sure to get out."

"Is that true? They might try to put a clamp on it. Maybe even a comprehensive clamp, I don't know."

"Wow. But you folks . . . you just went ahead and *did it*?"

341

"We did." She shrugged. "So what do you say? Want to do it?"

"Let me think about it."

He went for a walk on the crest of the fin, up and down the long greenhouse stuffed with bamboo and food crops. Walking west he had to shield his eyes from the glare of the afternoon sun, even through the filtered glass; walking back east, he could look out at the broken slopes of lava stretching up to Olympus Mons. It was hard to think. He was sixty-six years old; born in 1982, and what was it back on Earth now, 2048? M-11, eleven long hi-rad Martian years. And he had spent thirty-five months in space, including three trips between Earth and Mars, which was still the record. He had taken on 195 rems in those trips alone, and he had low blood pressure and a bad HDL to LDL ratio, and his shoulders ached when he swam and he felt tired a lot. He was getting old. He didn't have all that many years left, weird though it was to think of it; and he had a lot of faith in the Acheron group, who, now that he thought of it, were wandering around their aerie working and eating and playing soccer and swimming and so on with little smiles of absorbed concentration, with a kind of humming. Not like ten year-olds, certainly not; but with an aura of suffused, absorbed happiness. Of health, and more than health. He laughed out loud, and went back down into Acheron looking for Ursula. When she saw him she laughed too. "It's not really that hard a choice, is it."

"No." He laughed with her: "I mean, what have I got to lose?"

So he agreed to it. They had his genome in their records, but it would take a few days to synthesize the collection of repair strands and clip them onto plasmids, and clone millions more. Ursula told him to come back in three days.

When he got back to the guest rooms Maya was already

there, looking as shocked as he felt, wandering nervously from dresser to sink to window, touching things and looking around as if she had never seen such a room before. Vlad had told her about it after her physical, just as Ursula had with John. "Immortality plague!" she exclaimed, and laughed strangely. "Can you believe it?"

"Longevity plague," he corrected her. "And no, I can't. Not really." He felt a little dizzy, and he could see she hadn't heard him. Her agitation made him nervous. They heated soup, ate in a daze. Vlad had told Maya to come to Acheron, and intimated what it was all about; that was why she had insisted that John accompany her to Acheron. When she told him that, he felt a shiver of fondness for her. Standing next to her washing the dishes, observing her hands shake as she spoke, he felt exceptionally close to her; it was as if they knew each other's thoughts, as if, after all the years, in the face of this bizarre development, there were no need for words, only for each other's presence. That night in the warm dark of their bed she whispered hoarsely, "We'd better do it twice tonight. *While it's still us.*"

Three days later they both got the treatment. John lay back on a medical couch in a small room, and stared at an intravenous plug in the back of his hand. An IV feed shot, just like all those he'd had before. Except this time he could feel a strange heat rising up his arm, flushing his chest, pouring down his legs. Was it real? Was he imagining it? For a second he felt extremely odd all over, as if his ghost had walked through him. Then he was just very hot. "Should I be this hot?" he asked Ursula anxiously.

"It's like a fever at first," she said. "Then we put a small shock through you to push the plasmids into your cells. After that it's more chills than fever, as the new strands bond to the old. People often feel quite cold, actually."

An hour later a big IV bag had drained into him. He was still hot, and his bladder was full. They let him get up and go to the bathroom, then when he returned he was strapped into what looked like a cross between a couch and an electric chair. That didn't bother him; astronaut training had inured him to all devices. The shock when it came lasted about ten seconds, and felt like a disagreeable tickling everywhere in him. Ursula and the others detached him from the apparatus; Ursula, her eyes twinkling, gave him a kiss full on the mouth. She warned him again that in a while he would start to feel chilled, and that it would last for a couple of days. It was okay to sit in the saunas or whirlpool baths; in fact they recommended it.

So he and Maya sat in the corner of a sauna together, huddled in the penetrating warmth, watching the bodies of the other visitors, who came in white and went out pink. It seemed to John an image of what was happening to the two of them; come in sixty-five, go out ten. He really couldn't believe it. It was still very hard for him to think, he found his thoughts simply blanked, his mind stunned. If brain cells were reinforced too, had his clogged unexpectedly? He had always been a ragged slow thinker. In fact this was probably no more than his usual obtuseness, brought to his attention because he was trying so hard to come to grips with the thing, to think what it meant. Could it really be true? Could they really be sidestepping death for some years, perhaps some . . . decades . . . ?

They left the sauna to eat, and after their meals they took short walks in the crest greenhouse, looking out at the dunes to the north, the chaotic lava to the south. The view north reminded Maya of early Underhill, with the random litter of stones on Lunae replaced by Arcadia's windswept quilt pattern of dunes; as if her memory had cleaned up her recollections of that time, making them more patterned, tinting their faded ochres and reds to rich lemon yellows. Patination of the past. He stared at her curiously. It had been M-11 years since those first days in the trailer park, and in most

344

of the years since, the two of them had been lovers, with a number of (blessed) interruptions and separations, of course, caused by circumstances or, more usually, their inability to get along. But they had always started again when the opportunities came, and the upshot was that now they knew each other just about as well as any old married couple with a less interrupted history; perhaps even better, because any completely constant couple was likely to have stopped paying attention to each other at some point, while the two of them, with all their separations and reunions, fights and rapprochements, had had to relearn each other countless times. John said some of this to her, and they talked about it; it was a pleasure to talk about it; "We have *had* to keep paying attention," Maya said intently, nodding with a look of solemn satisfaction, sure that this was mostly her doing. Yes, they had paid attention, they had never fallen into the mindless rut of habit. Surely, they both agreed as they sat in the baths, or walked the crest, this compensated for the time they had spent apart, more than compensated for it. Yes; no doubt they knew each other even *better* than any old married couple.

And so they talked, trying to stitch their pasts to this strange new future, in the anxious hope that it would not prove to be an unbridgeable rupture. And late the following evening, two days after the inoculation, sitting alone naked in the sauna, their flesh still cold, their skin all rosy with sweat, John looked at Maya's body sitting there beside him, as real as a rock, and he felt a glow like the IV injection running all through him. He had not eaten much since the treatment, and the beige and yellow tiles they sat on had started to throb, as if lit from within; light gleamed on every water droplet covering the tiles, like tiny chips of lightning scattered everywhere, and Maya's body sprawled over these sparkling tiles pulsing before him like a pink candle. The intense *thereness* of it — *haecceity* Sax had called it once, when John had asked him something about his religious beliefs – I believe in haecceity, Sax had said, in *thisness*, in here-and-nowness, in the particular individuality of every moment. That's why I want to know what is this? what is this? what is this? Now, remembering Sax's odd word and his odd religion, John finally understood him; because he was feeling the *thisness* of the moment like a rock in his hand, and it felt as if his entire life had been lived only to get him to this moment. The tiles and the thick hot air were pulsing around him as if he were dying and being reborn, and sure, that was really the case if what Ursula and Vlad said were true. And there beside him in the process of being reborn was the pink body of Maya Toitovna, Maya's body which he knew better than his own. And not only in this moment, but through time; he could recall vividly his first sight of her naked, floating toward him in the bubble chamber on the *Ares*, surrounded by a nimbus of stars and the black velvet of space. And every change in her since then was perfectly visible to him, the shift from the image in his memory to the body beside him was a hallucinatory time-dissolve, her flesh and skin shifting, dropping, lining – ageing. They were both older, creakier, heavier. That was the way it went. But really the amazing thing was how much had remained, how much they were still themselves. Lines from a poem came to him, the epitaph of the Scott expedition near Ross Station in Antarctica, they had all climbed the hill to see the big wooden cross together, and carved on it had been lines: much has gone yet much remains . . . something like that. He couldn't remember – much *had* gone; it had been a long time ago, after all. But they had worked hard, and eaten well, and perhaps Mars's gravity had been kinder than Earth's would have been; because the obvious glowing truth was that Maya Toitovna was still a very beautiful woman, strong and muscly, her imperial face and gray wet hair still commanding his gaze, her breasts still magnets to his eye, completely different in appearance if she so much as shifted an elbow, and yet in every position completely familiar to him . . . *his* breasts, his arms, ribs, flanks. She was, for better and worse, the person he was closest to, a beautiful pink animal and also an avatar for him, of sex, of life itself on this bare rocky world. If this was what they were at sixty-six, and if the treatment did no more than hold them at this point, for even a few added years, or (the shock of it still) for decades? For *decades*? Well, it was astonishing. Absolutely too much to grasp, he had to stop trying or he would strip all the gears of his mind. But could it be? Could it really be? The aching desire of all true lovers through all the ages, to have a bit more time together, to be able to stretch out and live the love fully . . . Similar feelings seemed to be stirring Maya. She was in a great mood, she watched him from hooded eyes, with that come-hither half-smile he knew so well, one knee up and tucked in her armpit, not flaunting her sex at him but just comfortable, relaxing as she would if she were alone . . . yes, there was nothing like Maya in a good mood, no one could infect other people with it so much and so surely. He felt a rush of affection for that aspect of her character, an IV of sentiment, and he put a hand on her shoulder and squeezed, *eros* just a spice in a feast of *agape*, and suddenly as usual the words just burst out of him, he said things to her that he had never said before, "Let's get married!" he said, and when she laughed he did too, and said, "No, no, I mean it, let's get married." Get married and grow really, really old together, seize whatever gift years brought and make them a shared adventure, have kids, watch the kids have kids, watch the grandkids have kids, watch the great-grandkids have kids, my Lord who knew how long it might last? They might watch a whole nation of descendants flourish, become patriarch and matriarch, a kind of mini Martian Adam and Eve! And Maya laughed at each declaration, her eyes vivacious and sparkling with affection, windows to a soul in a very, very good mood, watching him and soaking him up, he could feel the blotter tug of her gaze watching

347

him and laughing delightedly at each new absurd hilarious phrase that burst out of him, and saying to him "Something like that, yes, something like that," and then hugging him hard. "Oh John," she said. "You know how to make me happy. You are the best man I ever had." She kissed him and he found that despite the sauna's heat it was going to be easy to shift the emphasis from *agape* to *eros*; but now the two were one, indistinguishable, a great mingled flood of love. "So you'll marry me and all?" he said as he locked the sauna door and they began to fall into it. "Something like that," she said, eyes flashing, face ablaze with an absolutely ravishing smile.

When you expect to live another two hundred years, you behave differently than when you expect to live only twenty.

This they proved almost immediately. John spent the winter there at Acheron, on the edge of the CO_2 fog cap that still descended over the north pole every winter, studying areobotany with Marina Tokareva and her lab group. He did this on Sax's instruction, and because he felt in no hurry to leave. Sax seemed to have forgotten about the search to find out who the saboteurs were, which made John a little suspicious; in his spare time he still made efforts through Pauline, concentrating on the areas he had been working on before Acheron; travel records mostly, and then employment records of all the people that had traveled to the areas where the sabotages had taken place. Presumably there were a lot of people involved, so individual travel records might not tell him much. But everyone on Mars had been sent there by an organization, and by checking which organizations had sent people to the relevant places, he hoped to get some indications. It was a messy business, and he had to rely on Pauline not only for statistics but advice, which was worrying.

The rest of the time he studied a branch of areobotany in which all the payoffs were at least decades away. Why not? He had the time, and might very well see the fruits of the work. So he watched Marina's group design a new tree, studying with them and doing their lab work, washing glassware and the like. The tree was designed to serve as the canopy of a multi-layered forest which they hoped to grow on the dunes of Vastitas Borealis. It was based on a sequoia genome, but they wanted trees even bigger than sequoias, perhaps two hundred meters tall, with a trunk fifty meters in diameter at the base. Their bark would stay frozen most of the time, and their broad leaves, which would probably look as if they had tobacco leaf disease, were going to be able to absorb the baseline dose of UV radiation without damage to their purplish undersides. At first John thought the trees' size was excessive, but Marina pointed out that they would be capable of taking in great quantities of carbon dioxide, fixing the carbon and transpiring the oxygen back into the air. And they were going to be quite a sight, or so they supposed; the actual shoots of the competing test prototypes were only ten meters tall, and it would be twenty years before the winners of the competition reached their mature heights. And right now all the prototypes still died in Mars jars; atmospheric conditions would have to change considerably before they would survive outdoors. Marina's lab was getting ahead of the game.

But so was everyone else. This seemed to be a result of the treatment, it made sense on the face of it. Longer experiments. Longer (John groaned) investigations. Longer thoughts.

In many respects, however, nothing changed. John felt about the same as before, except it didn't take omegendorph to get an occasional buzz humming through him, as if he had recently finished swimming a couple of kilometers, or cross-country skied for an afternoon, or, yes, taken a dose of omegendorph. Which now would have been carrying coals to Newcastle. Because things glowed. When he took the crest walk, the whole visible world glowed: stilled bulldozers, a crane like a gallows – he could watch anything for minutes on end. Maya left for Hellas, and it didn't matter; their relations were back on the old rollercoaster ride, a lot of bickering and fits of temper on her part, but all that seemed unimportant, floating inside the glow, changing nothing in the way he felt toward her, or in the way she had, from time to time, turned on him that look of hers. He would see her in a few months, and talk to her on screen; meanwhile this was a separation he was not entirely unhappy to see.

It was a good winter. He learned a lot about areobotany

and bioengineering, and in many of the evenings, after dinner, he would ask the Acheron people both individually and severally what they thought the eventual Martian society should be like, and how it should be run. At Acheron this usually led directly to considerations of ecology, and its deformed offshoot economics; these to them were much more critical than politics, or what Marina called "the supposed decision-making apparatus". Marina and Vlad were particularly interesting on this topic, as they had worked out a system of equations for what they called "eco-economics", which always sounded to John like "echo economics." He liked listening to them explain the equations, and he asked them a lot of questions, learning about concepts like carrying capacity, coexistence, counteradaptation, legitimacy mechanisms, ecologic efficiency. "That's the only real measure of our contribution to the system," Vlad would say. "If you burn our bodies in a microbomb calorimeter you'll find we contain about six or seven kilocalories per gram of weight, and of course we take in a lot of calories to sustain that through our lives. Our output is harder to measure, because it's not a matter of predators feeding on us, as in the classic efficiency equations — it's more a matter of how many calories we create by our efforts, or send on to future generations, something like that. And most of that is very indirect, naturally, and it involves a lot of speculation and subjective judgement. If you don't go ahead and assign values to a number of non-physical things, then electricians and plumbers and reactor builders and other infrastructural workers would always rate as the most productive members of society, while artists and the like would be seen as contributing nothing at all."

"Sounds about right to me," John joked, but Vlad and Marina ignored him.

"Anyway that's a large part of what economics is — people arbitrarily, or as a matter of taste, assigning numerical values to non-numerical things. And then pretending that they haven't just made the numbers up, which they have. Economics is like astrology in that sense, except that economics serves to justify the current power structure, and so it has a lot of fervent believers among the powerful."

"Better just to concentrate on what we're doing here," Marina put in. "The basic equation is simple, efficiency merely equals the calories you put out, divided by the calories you take in, times one hundred to put it in the form of a percentage. In the classic sense of passing along calories to one's predator, ten percent was average, and twenty percent doing really well. Most predators at the tops of food chains did more like five percent."

"This is why tigers have ranges of hundreds of square kilometers," Vlad said. "Robber barons are not really very efficient."

"So tigers don't have predators not because they're so tough, but because it's not worth the effort," John said.

"Exactly!"

"The problem is in calculating the values," Marina said. "We have had to simply assign certain calorie-equivalent numerical values to all kinds of activities, and then go on from there."

"But we were talking about economics?" John said.

"But this is economics, don't you see, this is our eco-economics! Everyone should make their living, so to speak, based on a calculation of their real contribution to the human ecology. Everyone can increase their ecological efficiency by efforts to reduce how many kilocalories they use – this is the old Southern argument against the energy consumption of the Northern industrial nations. There was a real ecologic basis to that objection, because no matter how much the industrial nations produced, in the larger equation they could not be as efficient as the South."

"They were predators on the South," John said.

"Yes, and they will become predators on us too, if we let them. And like all predators their efficiency is low. But here, you see – in this theoretical state of independence that you speak of—" she grinned at John's look of consternation— "you do, you have to admit that that is ultimately what you talk about all the time, John – well, there it should be the law that people are rewarded in proportion to their contribution to the system."

Dmitri, coming in the lab, said, "From each according to his capacities, to each according to his needs!"

"No, that's not the same," Vlad said. "What it means is, You get what you pay for!"

"But that's already true," John said. "How is this different from the economics that already exist?"

They all scoffed at once, Marina most persistently: "There's all kinds of phantom work! Unreal values assigned to most of the jobs on Earth! The entire transnational executive class does nothing a computer couldn't do, and there are whole categories of parasitical jobs that add nothing to the system by an ecologic accounting. Advertising, stock brokerage, the whole apparatus for making money only from the manipulation of money – that is not only wasteful but corrupting, as all meaningful money values get distorted in such manipulation." She waved a hand in disgust.

"Well," Vlad said, "we can say that their efficiency is very low, and that they predate on the system without having any predators, so that they are either the top of the chain or parasitical, depending on how you define it. Advertising, money brokering, some types of manipulation of the law, some politics . . ."

"But all of these are subjective judgements!" John exclaimed. "How have you actually assigned calorific values to such a variety of activities?"

"Well, we have done our best to calculate what they contribute back to the system in terms of well-being measured as a physical thing. What does the activity equal in terms of food, or water, or shelter, or clothing, or medical aid, or education, or free time? We've talked it over, and usually everyone at Acheron has offered a number, and we have taken the mean. Here, let me show you . . ."

And they would talk through the evening about it before the computer screen, and John would ask questions, and plug Pauline in to record the screens and tape the discussions, and they would go through the equations and jab their fingers at the flow charts, and then stop for coffee and perhaps take it up to the crest, to pace the length of the greenhouse arguing vehemently about the human value in kilocalories of plumbing, opera, simulation programming and the like. They were up on the crest, in fact, one afternoon near sunset, when John looked up from the equation on his wristpad, and stared up the long slope toward Olympus Mons.

The sky had darkened. It occurred to him that it might be just another double eclipse: Phobos was so close overhead that it blocked a third of the sun when it crossed in front of it, and Deimos about a ninth, and a couple times a month they crossed at the same time, causing a shadow to be cast across the land, as if a film had got in your eye, or you had had a bad thought.

But this wasn't an eclipse; Olympus Mons was hidden from view, and the high southern horizon was a fuzzy bronze bar. "Look at that," he said to the others, and pointed. "A dust storm." They hadn't had a global dust storm in over ten years. John called up the weather satellite photos on his wristpad. The origin of the storm had been near the Thaumasia mohole, Senzeni Na. He called up Sax and found him blinking philosophically, stating his surprise in mild tones.

"Winds at the edge of the storm were up to six hundred and sixty kilometers an hour," Sax said. "A new planetary record. It looks like this is going to be a big one. I thought the cryptogamic soils in the storm start-up zones would have dampened them, or even stopped them. Obviously that model had something wrong with it."

"Okay, Sax, too bad about that, but it'll be okay, I gotta

354

go now because it's rolling right down on us now and I want to watch."

"Have fun," Sax said, deadpan, before John clicked him off. Vlad and Ursula were scoffing at Sax's model; temperature gradients between biotically-defrosted soil and the remaining frosted areas would be greater than ever, and the winds between the two regions correspondingly fiercer; so that when they finally hit loose fines, off they would go. Totally obvious.

"Now that it's happened," John said. He laughed and moved down the greenhouse to watch the storm's approach by himself. Scientists could be so catty.

The wall of dust rolled down the long lava slopes of Olympus Mons's northern aureole. It had already halved the land visible since John first saw it, and now it approached like a giant breaking wave, a billowy chocolate milk wave ten thousand meters high, with a bronze filigree foaming up and off it, leaving great curved streamers in the pink sky above. "Wow!" John cried. "Here it comes! Here it comes!" Suddenly the crest of the Acheron fin seemed located a great distance above the long narrow canyons of the fossae below them, and lower fin ridges reared like dragon backs out of the cracked lava: a wild place from which to face the onrush of such a storm, too high, too exposed; John laughed again, and pressed himself against the southern windows of the greenhouse, looking down, out, around, shouting, "Wow! Wow! Look at it go! Wow!"

And then suddenly they were overwhelmed, dust flying over them, darkness, a high whooshing shriek. The first impact against Acheron ridge caused a wild flurry of turbulence, quick cyclonic twisters that appeared and disappeared, horizontal, vertical, at angles up the few steep gullies in the ridge; and the general shriek was punctuated by booms as these disturbances hit the ridge and collapsed. Then with dreamlike rapidity the wind settled into a smooth standing wave, and the dust rushed up past John's face; the pit of his stomach lifted, as if the greenhouse were suddenly dropping with violent speed. Certainly that's what it looked like; the ridge had caused a ferocious updraft. Stepping back, however, he saw the dust streaming overhead and then off to the north. On that side of the greenhouse he could see for a few kilometers, before the wind smashed into the ground again and cut off the view in continual explosions of dust. "Wow!"

His eyes were dry, and his mouth felt a bit caked. Lots of the fines were less than a micron across; was that a faint sheen of them, there already across the bamboo leaves? No. Only the weird light of the storm. But there would be dust on everything, eventually. No seal system could keep it out.

Vlad and Ursula were not completely confident of the greenhouse's ability to withstand the wind, and they encouraged everyone up there to go downstairs. On the way down John re-established contact with Sax. Sax's mouth was bunched into a tighter knot than usual. They would lose a lot of insolation with this storm, he said evenly. Equatorial surface temperatures had been averaging eighteen degrees higher than the baseline figures, but temperatures near Thaumasia were already down six degrees, and they would continue to plummet for the duration of the storm. And, he added with what seemed to John an almost masochistic completeness, the mohole thermals would loft the dust higher than ever before, so that it was all too possible that the storm might last for a long time.

"Buck up, Sax," John advised. "I think it'll be shorter than ever before. Don't be so pessimistic."

Later on, when the storm was going into its second M-year, Sax would remind John of this prediction with a little laugh.

Traveling during the storm was officially restricted to the trains and to certain heavily used double-transponder roads, but when it became obvious that it wasn't going to die back down that summer, John ignored the restrictions and resumed his wanderings. He made sure that his rover was well-stocked, he had a backup rover follow him, and he had an extra-powerful radio transmitter installed. That and Pauline in the driver's seat would be enough to get him around most of the northern hemisphere, he figured; rover breakdowns were rare, because of the really comprehensive internal monitoring systems hooked into their control computers; two rover breakdowns at once was almost unheard of, there had been only a single recorded fatality as a result of that happening. So he said good-bye to the Acheron group, and took off again.

Driving in the storm was like driving at night, except more interesting. The dust rocketed by in gusts, leaving little pockets of visibility that gave him quick dim sepia snatches of a view, the landscape rolling, everything seeming to be moving south. Then blank rushing tempests of dust would return again, flush against the windows. The rover rocked hard on its shock absorbers during the worst gusts, and the dust did indeed get into everything.

On the fourth day of his drive he turned straight south, and began to drive up the northwest slope of the Tharsis bulge. This was the great escarpment again, but here it was not a cliff, only a slope imperceptible in the storm's dark, lasting for more than a day, until he was high on the side of Tharsis, five vertical kilometers higher than he had been in Acheron.

He stopped at another mine, located near crater *Pt* (called Pete), located in the upper end of the Tantalus Fossae. Apparently the Tharsis bulge had initiated the great lava flood covering Alba Patera, and later bulging had then cracked the lava shield; these were the Tantalus canyons. Some of them had cracked over a platinoid-rich mafic igneous intrusion that the miners had named the Merensky Reeflets. The miners were real Azanians this time, but Azanians who called themselves Afrikaners, and spoke Afrikaans among themselves; white men who welcomed John with heavy doses of God, volk, and trek. They had named the canyons they worked in Neuw Orange Free State and Neuw Pretoria. And they, like the miners at Bradbury Point, worked for Armscor. "Yes," the operations head said happily, with an accent like a New Zealander's. He had a heavily-jowled face, a ski-jump nose and a big crooked smile, and a very intense manner. "We've found iron, copper, silver, manganese, aluminum, gold, platinum, titanium, chromium, you name it. Sulfides, oxides, silicates, native metals, you name it. The Great Escarpment has them all." The mine had been running for about an M-year; it consisted of strip mines on the canyon floors, with a habitat half buried in the mesa between two of the largest canyons, looking like a clear eggshell, packed with a meat of green trees and orange tile roofs.

John spent several days with them, being sociable and asking questions. More than once, thinking of the Acheron group's eco-economics, he asked them how they were going to get their valuable but heavy product back to Earth. Would the energy cost of the transfer overwhelm the potential profit?

"Of course," they said, just like the men at Bradbury Point. "It will take the space elevator to make it worthwhile."

Their chief said, "With the space elevator we are in the Terran market. Without it we will never get off Mars."

"That's not necessarily a bad thing," John said. But they didn't understand him, and when he tried to explain it they only went blank and nodded politely, anxious to avoid thinking about politics. Which was something Afrikaners were good at. When John realized what was going on, he found he could bring up the topic of politics to get some time to himself; it was, he said to Maya one night on the wrist, like tossing a tear gas canister in the room. It even enabled him to wander into the mining operations center alone for most of an afternoon, linking Pauline to the records and recording everything that she could lift. Pauline noticed no unusual patterns in the operation. But she did flag an exchange of communications with the Armscor home office; the local group wanted a security unit of a hundred persons, and Singapore had agreed to it.

John whistled. "What about UNOMA?" Security was supposed to be entirely their purview, and they gave out approval for private security pretty routinely; but a hundred people? John instructed Pauline to look into the UNOMA dispatches on the subject, and left for dinner with the Afrikaners.

Again the space elevator was declared a necessity. "They'll just pass us by if we don't have it, go straight out to the asteroids and not have any gravity well to worry about, eh?"

Despite the five hundred micrograms of omegendorph in his system, John was not in a happy mood. "Tell me," he said at one point, "do any women work here?"

They stared at him like fish. They were even worse than Moslems, really.

He left the next day and drove up to Pavonis, intent on looking into the space elevator notion.

Up the long slope of Tharsis. He never saw the steep, blood-colored cone of Ascraeus Mons; it was lost in the dust along with everything else. Travel now consisted of life in a set of small rooms that bumped around a lot. He worked his way around Ascraeus on its west flank, and then motored up onto the crest of Tharsis, between Ascraeus and Pavonis; here the double-transponder road became an actual concrete ribbon under the wheels – concrete under a rush of dust, concrete that finally tilted up sharply, and led him straight up the northern slope of Pavonis Mons. It went on for so long that it began to feel like a slow blind takeoff into space.

The crater of Pavonis, as the Afrikaners had reminded him, was amazingly equatorial; the round O of its caldera sat like a ball placed right on the equator line. This apparently made the south rim of Pavonis the perfect tethering point for a space elevator, as it was both directly on the equator, and twenty-seven kilometers above the datum. Phyllis had already arranged for the construction of a preliminary habitat on the south rim; she had thrown herself into work on the elevator, and was one of its chief organizers.

Her habitat was dug into the rim wall of the caldera, in Echus Overlook style, so that windows in several stories of rooms looked out over the caldera, or would, when the dust cleared. Photos blown up and stuck on the walls showed that the caldera itself would eventually be revealed as a simple circular depression, with walls five thousand meters deep, slightly terraced near the bottom; the caldera had slumped often in earlier days, but always in nearly the same place. It was the only one of the great volcanoes to have been so regular; the other three had calderas that were like sets of overlapping circles, with each circle set at a different depth.

The new habitat, nameless at this point, had been built by UNOMA, but the equipment and personnel had been provided by the transnational Praxis, one of the biggest of them all. Currently the rooms that were finished were crowded with Praxis executives, or executives of some of the other transnationals who had subcontracts on the elevator project; among them representatives of Amex, Oroco, Subarashii, and Mitsubishi. And all their efforts were being coordinated by Phyllis, who was now apparently Helmut Bronski's assistant in charge of the operation.

Helmut too was there, and after John had greeted him and Phyllis, and been introduced to some of the visiting consultants, he was led into a big high room with a window wall. Outside the window swirled clouds of dark orange dust dropping down into the caldera, so that it seemed that the room ascended, uncertainly, in a dim fluctuating light.

The room's only furnishing was a globe of Mars one meter in diameter, resting waist-high on a blue plastic stand. Extending from the globe, specifically from the little bump that represented Pavonis Mons, was a silver wire about five meters long. At the end of the thread was a small black dot. The globe was rotating on the stand at about one rpm, and the silver wire and its terminating black dot rotated with it, always remaining above Pavonis.

A group of about eight people ringed this display. "Everything is to scale," Phyllis said. "The areosynchronous satellite distance is 20,435 kilometers from the center of mass, and the equatorial radius is 3,386 kilometers, so the distance from the surface to the areosynchronous point is 17,049 kilometers; double that and add the radius, and you have 37,484 kilometers. We'll have a ballast rock at the far end, so the actual cable won't have to be quite as long. The diameter of the cable will be about ten meters, and will weigh about six billion tons. The material for it will have been mined from its terminal ballast point, which will be an asteroid that starts at around thirteen and a half billion tons, and ends up when the cable is finished at the proper ballast weight of around seven and a half billion tons. That's not a very big asteroid, about two kilometers in radius to begin with; there are six Amor asteroids crossing Mars's orbit that have been identified as candidates for the job. The cable will be manufactured by robots mining and processing the carbon in the asteroid's chondrites. Then, in the last stages of construction, the cable will be maneuvered to its tethering point, here." She pointed at the floor of the room in dramatic fashion. "At that point, the cable will be in areosynchronous orbit itself, barely touching down here, its weight suspended between the pull of the planet's gravity and the centrifugal force of the upper half of the cable, and the terminal ballast rock."

"What about Phobos?" John asked.

"Phobos is way down there, of course. The cable will be vibrating to avoid it, in what the designers call a Clarke oscillation. It won't be a problem. Deimos will also have to be avoided by oscillation, but because its orbit is more inclined this won't be such a frequent problem."

"And when it's in position?" Helmut asked, his face bright with pleasure.

"A few hundred elevators at least will be attached to the cable, and loads will be lifted into orbit using a counterweight system. There will be lots of material to load down from Earth as usual, so energy requirements for lifts will be minimized. It will also be possible to use the cable's rotation as a slingshot; objects released from the ballast asteroid toward Earth will be using the power of Mars's rotation as their push, and will have an energy-free high-speed take-off. It's a clean, efficient, extraordinarily cheap method, both for lifting bulk into space and for accelerating it toward Earth. And given the recent discoveries of strategic metals, which are becoming ever more scarce on Earth, a cheap lift and push like this is literally invaluable. It creates the possibility of an exchange that wasn't economically viable before; it will be a critical component of the Martian economy, the keystone of its industry. And it won't be that expensive to build. Once a carbonaceous asteroid is pushed into the proper orbit, and a nuclear-powered robotic cable plant put to work on it, the plant will extrude cable like a spider spinning its thread. There will be very little to do but wait. The cable plant as designed will be able to produce over three thousand kilometers of cable a year – this means we need to start as soon as possible, but after production begins, it will only take ten or eleven years. And the wait will be well worth it."

John stared at Phyllis, impressed as always by her fervor. She was like a convert giving witness, a preacher in a pulpit, quietly and confidently triumphant. The miracle of the skyhook. Jack and the Beanstalk, the Ascension to Heaven; it definitely had an air of the miraculous to it. "Really, we don't have much choice," Phyllis was saying. "This gets us out of our gravity well, eliminating it as a physical and economic problem. That's crucial; without that we'll be bypassed, we'll be like Australia in the nineteenth century, too far away to be a significant part of the world economy.

People will pass us by and mine the asteroids directly, because the asteroids have mineral wealth without gravitational constraints. Without the elevator we could become a backwater.''

Shikata ga nai, John thought sardonically. Phyllis glanced very briefly at John, as if he had spoken aloud. "We won't let that happen," she said. "And best of all, our elevator will serve as an experimental prototype for a Terran one. The transnationals who gain expertise in building this elevator will be in a commanding position when it comes to bidding the contracts for the much larger Terran project that is sure to follow.''

On and on she went, outlining every aspect of the plan, and then answering questions from the executives with her usual polished brilliance. She got a lot of laughs; she was flushed, bright-eyed, John could almost see the tongues of fire flickering from her mass of auburn hair, which in the storm light looked like a cap of jewels. The executives and project scientists glowed under her look; they were onto something big, and they knew it. Earth was seriously depleted in many of the metals they were finding on Mars. There were fortunes to be made, enormous fortunes. And someone who owned a piece of the bridge over which every ounce of metal had to pass would make an enormous fortune as well, probably the greatest fortune of all. No wonder Phyllis and the rest of them looked like they were in church.

Before dinner that evening John stood in his bathroom, and without looking at himself in the mirror took out two tabs of omegendorph and swallowed them. He was sick of Phyllis. But the drug made him feel better; she was just another part of the game, after all; and when he sat down to dinner he was in an expansive mood. Okay, he thought, they have their gold mine of a beanstalk. But it wasn't clear that they would be able to keep it to themselves; highly unlikely in fact. So that their fat-cat complacency was a bit silly, as well as grating, and he laughed in the middle of one of their enthusiastic exchanges and said, "Don't you think it unlikely that an elevator like this will stay private property?"

"We don't intend for it to be private property," Phyllis said with her brilliant smile.

"But you expect to be paid for its construction. And then you expect concessions to be granted. You expect to make a profit from the venture, isn't that what venture capitalism is all about?"

"Well, of course," Phyllis said, looking offended that he had spoken of such things so explicitly. "Everyone on Mars will profit from it, that's its nature."

"And you'll skim a percentage of every percentage." Predators at the top of the chain. Or else parasites, up and down the length of it . . . "How rich did the builders of the Golden Gate Bridge get, do you think? Were there great transnational dynasties formed from the profits of the Golden Gate Bridge? No. It was a public project, wasn't it. The builders were public employees, making a standard wage for their work. What do you want to bet that the Mars treaty doesn't stipulate a similar arrangement for infrastructural construction here? I'm pretty sure it does."

"But the treaty is up for revision in nine years," Phyllis pointed out, her eyes glittering.

John laughed. "So it is! But you wouldn't believe the support I see around this planet for a revised treaty that sets even tighter limits on Terran investment and profit. You just haven't been paying attention. The thing you have to remember is that this is an economic system being built from scratch, on principles that make sense in scientific terms. There's only a limited carrying capacity here, and to create a sustainable society we've got to pay attention to that. You can't just lift raw materials from here to Earth – the colonial era is over, you have to remember that." He laughed again at the glinty stares being leveled on him; it was as if gunsights had been implanted in their corneas.

It only occurred to him later, back in his room and

remembering those looks, that it probably had not been a very good idea to stick their noses in the situation so hard. The Amex man had even lifted his wrist to his mouth to take down a note, in a gesture obviously meant to be seen: This John Boone is bad news! he had whispered, eyes on John all the while; he had wanted John to see him. Well, another suspect then. It took John a while to get to sleep that night.

He left Pavonis the next day and headed east down Tharsis, intending to drive a full seven thousand kilometers to Hellas, to visit Maya. The journey was made strangely solitary by the great storm. He glimpsed the southern highlands in murky snatches only, through billowing sheets of sand, with the ever-shifting whistle of the wind as accompaniment. Maya was pleased he was coming to visit; he had never been to Hellas before, and a lot of people there were looking forward to meeting him. They had discovered a sizeable aquifer to the north of Low Point, so their plan was to pump water from that aquifer to the surface, and create a lake in the low point, a lake with a frozen surface which would be continuously subliming into the atmosphere, but which they would keep supplied from below. Sustained in that way it would both enrich the atmosphere, and serve as a reservoir and heat sink for cultivation, in a ring of domed farms built around the lake shore. Maya was very excited at the plans.

John's long journey toward her passed in a mesmerized state, as he watched crater after crater loom out of the clouds of dust. One evening he stopped at a Chinese settlement where they knew hardly a word of English and lived in boxes like the trailer park. He and the settlers had to make use of an AI translation program which kept them both laughing for most of the evening. Two days later, he stopped for a day at a huge Japanese air mining facility in a high pass between craters. Here everyone spoke excellent English, but they were frustrated because the air miners had been brought to a standstill by the storm; the technicians smiled painfully, and escorted him through a nightmare complex of filtering systems that they had set up to try to keep the pumps working; and all for naught.

East three days from the Japanese he ran across a Sufi caravanserai located on top of a circular steep-walled mesa. This particular mesa had once been a crater floor, but it had been so hardened by impact metamorphism that it had resisted the erosion that had cut away the surrounding soft land in the eons that followed and now stood above the plain like a thick round pedestal, its furrowed sides a kilometer high. John drove up a switchbacking ramp road to the caravanserai on top.

Up there he found that the mesa was situated in a permanent standing wave in the dust storm, so that there was more sunlight leaking through the dark clouds here than anywhere else he had been, even on the rim of Pavonis. Visibility was almost as truncated as everywhere else, but everything was more brightly colored, the dawns purple and chocolate, the days a vivid cloudy rush of umbers and yellow, orange and rust, pierced by the occasional bronzed sunbeam.

It was a great spot, and the Sufis proved to be more hospitable than any of the Arab groups he had met so far. They had come up in one of the latest Arab groups, they told him, as a concession to religious factions in the Arab world back home; and as Sufis were numerous among Islamic scientists, there had been very few objections to sending them as a coherent group of their own. One of them, a small black man named Dhu el-Nun, said to him, "It's wonderful in this time of the seventy thousand veils that you, the great *talib*, has followed his *tariqat* here to visit us."

"*Talib?*" John said. "*Tariqat?*"

"A *talib* is a seeker. And the seeker's *tariqat* is his path, his special path you know, on the road to reality."

"I see!" John said, still surprised at the friendliness of their greeting.

Dhu led him from the garage to a low black building which stood in the center of a ring of rovers, looking dense with concentrated energy; a squat round thing like a model of the mesa itself, its windows rough clear crystals. Dhu identified the black rock of the building as stishovite, a high-density silicate created by the meteor's impact, when pressures of over a million kilograms per square centimeter had momentarily existed. The windows were made of lèchatelierite, a kind of compressed glass also created by the impact.

Inside the building, a party of about twenty people greeted him, both men and women alike. The women were bareheaded and behaved just like the men, which again surprised John, and alerted him to the fact that things among the Sufis were different than they were among Arabs generally. He sat down and drank coffee with them, and started asking questions again. They were Qadarite Sufis, they told him, pantheists influenced by early Greek philosophy and modern existentialism, trying by modern science and the *ru' yat al-qalb*, the vision of the heart, to become one with that ultimate reality which was God. "There are four mystical journeys," Dhu said to him. "The first begins with gnosis and ends with *fana*, or passing away from all phenomenal things. The second begins when *fana* is succeeded by *baqa*, or abiding. At this point you journey in the real, by the real, to the real, and you yourself are a reality, a *haqq*. And after that you move on to the center of the spirit universe, and become one with all others who have done likewise."

"I guess I haven't begun the first journey yet," John said. "I don't know anything."

They were pleased by this response, he could see. You can start, they told him, and poured him more coffee. You can always start. They were so encouraging and friendly compared to any of the Arabs John had met before that he opened up to them, and told them about his trip to Pavonis, and the plans for the great elevator cable. "No fancy in the world is all untrue," Dhu said. And when John mentioned his last

367

meeting with Arabs, on Vastitas Borealis, and how Frank had been accompanying them, Dhu said cryptically, "It's the love of right lures men to wrong."

One of the women laughed and said, "Chalmers is your *nafs*."

"What's that?" John asked.

They were all laughing. Dhu, shaking his head, said "He is not your *nafs*. One's *nafs* is one's evil self, which some used to believe lived in one's chest."

"Like an organ or something?"

"Like an actual creature. Mohammed ibn 'Ulyan for instance reported that something like a young fox leaped out of his throat, and when he kicked it it only got bigger. That was his *nafs*."

"It is another name for your Shadow," the woman who had brought it up explained.

"Well," John said. "Maybe he is, then. Or maybe it's just that Frank's *nafs* gets kicked a lot." And they laughed with him at the thought.

Later that afternoon sunlight pierced the dust more strongly than usual, lighting the streaming clouds so that the caravanserai seemed to rest in the ventricle of a giant heart, with the gusts of the wind saying beat, beat, beat, beat. The Sufis called out to each other when they looked through the lechatelierite windows, and quickly they suited up to go out into this crimson world, into the wind, calling to Boone to accompany them. He grinned and suited up, surreptitiously swallowing a tab of omeg as he did so.

Once outside they walked the circumference of the ragged edge of the mesa, looking out into the clouds and down onto the shadowed plain below, pointing out to John whatever features happened to be visible. After that they gathered near the caravanserai, and John listened to their voices as they chanted, various voices providing English translations for the Arabic and Farsi. "Possess nothing and be possessed by nothing. Put away what you have in your head, give

368

what you have in your heart. Here a world and there a world, we are seated on the threshold."

Another voice: "Love thrilled the chord in my soul's lute, and changed me to love from head to foot."

And they began to dance. Watching John suddenly got it, that they were whirling dervishes: they leaped into the air to the beat of drums pattering lightly over the common band, they leaped and whirled in slow unearthly spins, arms outstretched; and when they touched down they pushed off and did it again, for turn after turn after turn. Whirling dervishes in the great storm, on a high round mesa that had been a crater floor in the Noachian. It looked so marvelous in the bloody pulsing glow of light that John stood up and started to spin with them. He wrecked their symmetries, he sometimes actually collided with other dancers; but no one seemed to mind. He found that it helped to jump slightly into the wind, to keep from being blown off balance. A hard gust would knock you flat. He laughed. Some of the dancers were chanting over the common band, the usual quarter-tone ululations, punctuated by shouts and harsh rhythmic breathing, and the phrase "Ana el-Haqq, ana el-Haqq" – I am God, one translated, I am God. A Sufi heresy. The dancing was meant to hypnotize you – there were other Moslem cults that did it with self-flagellation, John knew. Spinning was better; he danced, he joined the chant on the common band by punctuating it with his own rapid breath, and with grunts and babble; then without thinking about it he began to add to the flow of sound the names for Mars, muttering them in the rhythm of the chant as he understood it. "Al-Qahira, Ares, Auqakuh, Bahram. Harmakhis, Hrad, Huo Hsing, Kasei. Ma'adim, Maja, Mamers, Mangala. Nirgal, Shalbatanu, Simud and Tiu." He had memorized the list years ago, as a kind of party trick; now he was quite surprised to find what an excellent chant it made, how it spilled out of his mouth and helped stabilize his spinning. The other dancers were laughing at him, but in a good way, they sounded pleased. He felt drunk, his whole body was humming. He repeated the litany many times, then shifted to repeating the Arabic name, over and over: "Al-Qahira, Al-Qahira, Al-Qahira." And then, remembering what one of the translating voices had told him, "Ana el-Haqq, ana Al-Qahira. Ana el-Haqq, ana Al-Qahira." I am God, I am Mars, I am God . . . The others quickly joined him in this chant, lifted it into a wild song, and in the flash of rotating faceplates he caught sight of their grinning faces. They were really good spinners; as they whirled their outstretched fingers cut the rush of red dust into arabesques, and now as they spun they tapped him with their fingertips, guiding him or even actively pushing his clumsy turns into the weave of their pattern. He shouted the planet's names and they repeated them after him, in call and response style; they chanted the names, Arabic, Sanskrit, Inca, all the names for Mars, mixed together in a soup of syllables, creating a polyphonic music that was beautiful and shivery-strange, for the names for Mars came from times when words sounded odd, and names had power: he could hear that when he sang them.

When he finally stopped dancing and sat to watch, he began to feel sick. The world swam, his middle ear thingie was no doubt still spinning like a roulette ball. The scene pulsed before him; it was impossible to say whether this was the swirling dust or something internal, but either way he goggled at what he saw: whirling dervishes, on Mars? Well, in the Moslem world they were deviants of a kind, and with an ecumenical bent rare in Islam. And scientists too. So they were his way into Islam, perhaps, his *tariqat*; and their dervish ceremonies could perhaps be shifted into the areophany, as during his chant. He stood, reeling; all of a sudden he understood that one didn't have to invent it all from scratch, that it was a matter of making something new by synthesis of all that was good in what came before. "Love thrilled the chord of love in my lute . . . " He was too dizzy. The others were laughing at him, supporting him. He talked to them in his usual way, hoping they would understand. "I feel sick. I think I'm going to throw up. But you must tell me why we can't leave all the sad Terran baggage behind. Why we can't invent together a new religion. The worship of Al-Qahira, Mangala, Kasei!"

They laughed, and carried him on their shoulders back toward the shelter. "I'm serious," he said as the world spun. "I want you people to do it, I want your dancing to be in it, it's obvious you should be the ones to design this religion, you're doing it already." But vomiting in a helmet was dangerous, and they only laughed at him and hustled him into the crushed-stone habitat as quickly as they could. There as he threw up a woman held his head, saying in musical subcontinental English, "The King asked his wise men for some single thing that would make him happy when he was sad, but sad when he was happy. They consulted and came back with a ring engraved with the message 'This Too Will Pass.'"

"Straight into the recyclers," Boone said. He lay back spinning. It was kind of an awful feeling, when you were trying to lie still. "But what do you want here? Why are you on Mars? You have to tell me what you want here." They took him to the common room and set out cups, and a pot of aromatic tea. He still felt like he was spinning, and the dust rushing by the crystalline windows didn't help.

One of the old women around him picked up the pot and poured John's cup full. She put down the pot, gestured: "Now you fill mine." John did so, unsteadily, and then the pot went around the room. Each pourer filled someone else's cup.

"We start every meal this way," the old woman said. "It is a little sign of how we are together. We have studied the old cultures, before your global market netted everything, and in those ages there existed many different forms of exchange. Some of them were based on the giving of gifts. Each of us has a gift, you see, given us freely by the universe.

And each of us with every breath gives something back."

"Like the equation for ecologic efficiency," John said.

"Maybe so. In any case, whole cultures were built around the idea of the gift, in Malaysia, in the American northwest, in many primitive cultures. In Arabia we gave water, or coffee. Food and shelter. And whatever you were given, you did not expect to keep, but gave it back again in your turn, hopefully with interest. You worked to be able to give more than you received. Now we think that this can be the basis for a reverent economics."

"It's just what Vlad and Ursula said!"

"Maybe so."

The tea helped. After a while his equilibrium returned. They talked about other things, the great storm, the great hard plinth they lived on. Late that night he asked if they had heard of the Coyote, but they hadn't. They did know stories about a creature they called the "hidden one", the last survivor of an ancient race of Martians, a wizened thing who wandered the planet helping endangered wanderers, rovers, settlements. It had been spotted at the water station in Chasma Borealis last year, during an ice fall and subsequent power outage.

"It's not Big Man?" John asked.

"No, no. Big Man is big. The hidden one is like us. Its people were Big Man's subjects."

"I see."

But he didn't, not really. If Big Man stood for Mars itself, then maybe the story of the hidden one had been inspired by Hiroko. Impossible to say. He needed a folklorist, or a scholar of myths, someone who could tell him how stories were born; but he had only these Sufis, grinning and weird, story creatures themselves. His fellow citizens in this new land. He had to laugh. They laughed with him and took him off to bed. "We say a bedtime prayer from the Persian poet Rumi Jalaluddin," the old woman told him, and recited it:

372

" 'I died as mineral and became a plant,
I died as plant and rose to animal.
I died as animal and I was human.
Why should I fear? When was I less by dying?
Yet once more I shall die human,
To soar with angels blessed above.
And when I sacrifice my angel soul
I shall become what no mind ever conceived.'

"Sleep well," she said into his drowsing mind. "This is all our path."

The next morning he climbed stiffly into his rover, wincing with soreness and determined to eat some omeg as soon as he got on his way. The same woman was there to see him off, and he bumped his faceplate against hers affectionately.

"Whether it be of this world or of that," she said, "your love will lead you yonder in the end."

The transponder road led him through the brown wind-torn days, crossing the broken land south of Margaritifer Sinus. John would have to drive it again some other time to see any of it, for in the storm it was nothing but flying chocolate, pierced by momentary golden shafts of light. Near Bakhuysen Crater he stopped at a new settlement called Turner Wells; here they had tapped into an aquifer that was under such hydrostatic pressure at its lower end that they were going to generate power by running the artesian flow through a series of turbines. The water released would be poured into molds, frozen, and then hauled by robot to dry settlements all over the southern hemisphere. Mary Dunkel was working there, and she showed John around the wells, the power plant, and the ice reservoirs. "The exploratory drilling was actually scary as hell. When the drill hit the liquid part of the aquifer it was blasted back out of the well, and it was touch and go whether we were going to be able to control the gusher or not."

"What would have happened if you hadn't?"

"Well, I don't know. There's a lot of water down there. If it broke the rock around the well, it might have gone like the big outflow channels in Chryse."

"That big?"

"Who knows? It's possible."

"Wow."

"That's what I said! Now Ann has started an investigation into methods for determining aquifer pressures by the echoes they give back in the seismic tests. But there are people who would like to release an aquifer or two, see? They leave messages on the bulletin boards in the net. I wouldn't be surprised if Sax is among them. Big floods of water and ice, lots of sublimation into the air, why shouldn't he cheer?"

"But floods like those old ones would be as destructive to the landscape as dropping asteroids on it."

"Oh, more destructive! Those channels downslope from the chaoses were incredible outbreaks. The best Terran analogy is the scablands in eastern Washington, have you heard of them? About eighteen thousand years ago there was a lake covering most of Montana, Lake Missoula they call it, composed of Ice Age meltwater and held in place by an ice dam. At some point this ice dam broke and the lake emptied catastrophically, about two trillion cubic meters of water, draining down the Columbia plateau and out to the Pacific in a matter of days."

"Wow."

"While it lasted it ran about a hundred times the discharge of the Amazon, and carved channels in the basalt bedrock that are as much as two hundred meters deep."

"Two hundred meters!"

"Right. And this was nothing compared to the ones that cut the Chryse channels! The anastomosing up there covers areas—"

"Two hundred meters of *bedrock*?"

"Yeah, well, it isn't just normal erosion. In floods that big the pressures fluctuate so much that you get exsolution of dissolved gases, you know, and when those bubbles collapse they produce incredible pressures. Hammering like that can break anything."

"So it would be worse than an asteroid strike."

"Sure. Unless you dropped a really big asteroid. But there are people who think we should be doing that too, right?"

"Are there?"

"You know there are. But the floods are better yet, if you want to do that kind of thing. If you could direct one of them into Hellas, for instance, you'd have a sea. And you might be able to refill it faster than the surface ice sublimed."

"*Direct* a flood like that?" John exclaimed.

"Well, yeah, that would be impossible. But if you found

one in the right spot, you wouldn't have to direct it. You should check where Sax has sent the dowsing team lately, see what it looks like to you."

"But it would be forbidden by UNOMA for sure."

"Since when has that mattered to Sax?"

John laughed. "Oh, it matters now. They've given him too much for him to ignore them. They've tied him down with money and power."

"Maybe."

That night at 3:30 a.m. there was a small explosion in one of the well heads, and alarm bells ripped them from sleep and sent them stumbling through the tunnels half-naked, to be faced with a gusher that was shooting up into the night's flying dust, in a column of white water torn to shreds in the unsteady glare of hastily directed spotlights. The water was falling out of the dust clouds as chunks of ice, hail the size of bowling balls; wells downwind were being pummelled by these missiles, and the ice balls were already knee deep.

Given the discussion of the previous night John found himself quite alarmed by the sight, and he ran around until he found Mary. Through the noise of the eruption and the ever-present storm, Mary shouted in John's ear: "Clear the area, I'm going to set off a charge beside the well and try to snuff it!" She ran off in her white nightshirt, and John rounded up the spectators and got them back down the tunnels to the station habitat. Mary joined them in the lock, huffing and puffing, and fiddled with her wristpad, and there was a low boom in the direction of the well. "Come on, let's go see," she said, and they got through the lock and ran back down the tunnels toward the window overlooking the well. There in a tumble of white ice balls lay the wreckage of the drill, on its side, and still. "Yeah! Capped!" Mary cried.

They cheered weakly. Some of them went down to the well area, to see if there was anything they could do to secure the situation. "Good work!" John said to Mary.

"I've read a lot about well capping since that first incident," Mary said, still short of breath. "And we had it all set up to go. But we never actually had the chance. To try it. Of course. So you never know."

John said, "Do your locks have recorders?"

"They do."

"Great."

John went to check them. He plugged Pauline into the station system, asked questions, scanning the answers as they appeared on his pad. No one had used the locks after the time-slip that night. He called the weather satellite overhead, and clicked into the radar and IR systems that Sax had given him the codes for, and scanned the area around Bakhuysen. No sign of any machines nearby, except some of the old windmill heaters. And the transponders showed that no one had been on the roads in the area since his arrival the previous day.

John sat heavily before Pauline, feeling sluggish and slow-witted. He couldn't think of any other checks to make; and it seemed from those he had, that no one had been out that night to do the damage. The explosion could have been arranged days before, perhaps; although it would be hard to hide the device, the wells being worked on daily. He got up slowly and went to find Mary, and with her help talked to the people who had last worked on that well, the day before. No sign of tampering then, all the way until eight p.m. And after that everyone in the station had been at the John Boone party, the locks unused. So there really had been no chance.

He went back to his bed and thought about it. "Oh, by the way, Pauline; please check Sax's records, and give me a list of all the dowsing expeditions in the last year."

Continuing on his blind road to Hellas he ran into Nadia, who was overseeing the construction of a new kind of dome over Rabe Crater. It was the largest dome yet built, taking advantage of the thickening of the atmosphere and the

377

lightening of construction materials, which created a situation where gravity could be balanced with pressure, making the pressurized dome effectively weightless. The frame was to be made of reinforced areogel beams, the latest from the alchemists; areogel was so light and strong that Nadia went into little raptures as she described the potential uses for it. Crater domes themselves were a thing of the past, in her opinion; it would be just as easy to erect areogel pillars around the circumference of a town, bypassing the rock enclosures and putting the whole population inside what would be in effect a big clear tent.

She told John all about it as they walked around Rabe's interior, now nothing but a big construction site. The whole crater rim was going to be honeycombed with skylighted rooms, and the domed interior would hold a farm that would feed thirty thousand. Earth-moving robots the size of buildings hummed out of the murk of the dust, invisible even fifty meters away. These behemoths were working on their own, or by teleoperation, and the teleoperators probably had too little view of their surroundings to make nearby foot traffic entirely safe. John followed Nadia nervously as she strolled about, remembering how skittish the miners at Bradbury Point had been – and there they had been able to see what was happening! He had to laugh at Nadia's obliviousness. When the ground trembled underfoot, they just stopped and looked around, ready to leap away from any oncoming building-sized vehicles. It was quite a tour. Nadia railed against the dust, which was wrecking a lot of machinery. The great storm was now four months old, the longest in years; and it still showed no sign of ending. Temperatures had plummeted, people were eating canned and dried food, and an occasional salad or vegetable grown under artificial light. And dust was in everything. Even as they discussed it John could feel it caking his mouth, and his eyes were dry in their sockets. Headaches had become extremely common, as well as sinus trouble, sore throats, bronchitis, asthma, lung distress generally. Plus frequent cases of frostnip. And computers were becoming dangerously unreliable, a lot of hardware breakdown, a lot of AI neurosis or retardation. Middays inside Rabe were like living inside a brick, Nadia said, and sunsets looked like coal mine fires. She hated it.

John changed the subject. "What do you think of this space elevator?"

"Big."

"But the *effect*, Nadia. The effect."

"Who knows? You can never tell with a thing like that, can you?"

"It'll make a strategic bottleneck, like the one Phyllis used to talk about when we were discussing who would build Phobos station. She'll have made her own bottleneck. That's a lot of power."

"That's what Arkady says, but I don't see why it can't be treated as a common resource, like a natural feature."

"You're an optimist."

"That's what Arkady says." She shrugged. "I'm just trying to be sensible."

"Me too."

"I know. Sometimes I think we're the only two."

"And Arkady?"

She laughed.

"But you two are a couple!"

"Yes, yes. Like you and Maya."

"Touché."

Nadia smiled briefly. "I try to make Arkady think about things. That's the best I can do. We're meeting at Acheron in a month to take the treatment. Maya tells me it's a good thing to do together."

"I recommend it," John said with a grin.

"And the treatment?"

"Beats the alternative, right?"

She chuckled. Then the ground growled through their boots, and they stiffened and jerked their heads around,

379

looking for shadows in the murk. A black bulk like a moving hill appeared to their right. They ran to the side, stumbling and hopping over cobbles and debris, John wondering if this were another attack, Nadia rapping out commands over the common band, cursing the teleoperators for not keeping track of them on the IR. "Watch your screens, you lazy bastards!"

The ground stopped trembling. The black leviathan no longer moved. They approached it warily. A Brobdingnagian dump truck, on tracks. Built locally, by Utopia Planitia Machines: a robot built by robots, and big as an office block.

John stared up at it, feeling the sweat drip down his forehead. They were safe. His pulse slowed. "Monsters like this are all over the planet," he said to Nadia wonderingly. "Cutting, scraping, digging, filling, building. Pretty soon some of them will attach themselves to one of those two-kilometer asteroids, and build a power plant that will use the asteroid itself as fuel to drive it into Martian orbit, at which point other machines will land on it, and begin to transform the rock into a cable about thirty-seven thousand kilometers long! The *size* of it, Nadia! The size!"

"It's big all right."

"It's unimaginable, really. Something completely beyond human abilities as we were brought up to understand them. Teleoperation on a massive scale. A kind of spiritual waldo. Anything that can be imagined can be executed!" Slowly they walked around the giant black object before them: no more than a kind of dump truck, nothing compared to what the space elevator would be; and yet even this truck, he thought, was an amazing thing. "Muscle and brain have extended out through an armature of robotics that is so large and powerful that it's difficult to conceptualize it. Maybe impossible. That's probably part of your talent, and Sax's too – to flex the muscles that no one else realizes we have yet. I mean holes drilled right through the lithosphere, the terminator lit with mirrored sunlight, all these cities filling mesas and stuck in the sides of cliffs – and now a cable strung out way past Phobos and Deimos, so long that it's both in orbit and touching down at the same time! It's impossible to imagine it!"

"Not impossible," Nadia noted.

"No. And now of course we see the evidence of our power all around us, we almost get run down by it as it goes about its work! And seeing is believing. Even without an imagination you can see what kind of power we have. Maybe that's why things are getting so strange these days, everyone talking about ownership or sovereignty, fighting, making claims. People squabbling like those old gods on Olympus, because nowadays we're just as powerful as they were."

"Or more," Nadia said.

He drove on into the Hellespontus Montes, the curved mountain range surrounding Hellas Basin. Somehow, one night when he was sleeping his rover got off the transponder road. He woke up, and in breaks in the dust saw that he was in a narrow valley, walled with small cliffs that were cut by the typical fluting of ravines. It seemed likely that by staying on the valley floor he would cross the road again, so he headed on cross country. Then the valley floor was disrupted by shallow transverse grabens like empty canals, and Pauline kept having to stop and turn and try another branch in her route-finding algorithm, defeated by one gulch after another as they appeared out of the murk. When John got impatient and tried to take over, it only got worse. In the land of the blind, the autopilot is king.

But slowly he closed on the valley mouth, where the map showed the transponder road descending to a wider valley below. So that night he stopped, unworried, and sat in front of the TV and ate a meal. Mangalavid was showing the premiere performance of an aeolia built by a group in Noctis Labyrinthus. The aeolia turned out to be a small building, cut with apertures which whistled or hooted or squeaked, depending on the angle and strength of the wind hitting them. For the premiere the daily downslope wind in Noctis was augmented by some fierce katabatic gusts from the storm, and the music fluctuated like a composition, mournful, angry, dissonant or in sudden snatches harmonic: it seemed the work of a mind, an alien mind perhaps, but certainly something more than random chance. The almost aleatory aeolia, as a commentator said.

After that came news from Earth. The existence of the gerontological treatments had been leaked by a official in Geneva, and had flashed around the world in a day; and now there was a violent debate going on in the General Assembly concerning the matter. Many delegates were demanding that the treatments be made a basic human right, guaranteed by the UN for all, with funding from the developed nations placed immediately in a pool to make sure that financing for the treatments would be equally available to all. Meanwhile other reports were coming in: some religious leaders were coming out against the treatments, including the Pope; there were widespread riots, and some damage at certain medical centers. Governments were in a turmoil. All the faces on the TV were tense or angry, demanding change; and all the inequality, hatred and misery that the faces revealed made John flinch, he couldn't watch. He fell asleep, and then slept poorly.

He was dreaming of Frank when a sound woke him. A knock on his windshield. It was the middle of the night. Groggily he hit the lock lock; sitting up he wondered that he had such a reflex action in him. When had he learned that one? He rubbed his jaw, turned on the common band. "Hello? Anyone out there?"

"The Martians."

It was a man's voice. His English was accented, but John couldn't identify how.

"We want to talk," the voice said.

John stood and looked out the windshield. At night, in the

storm, there was precious little to see. But he thought he could pick out shapes in the blackness, there below him.

"We just want to talk," the voice said.

If they had wanted to kill him they could have blown open the rover while he slept. Besides, he still couldn't quite believe that anyone wished him harm. There was no reason for it!

So he let them in.

There were five of them, all men. Their walkers were frayed, dirty, patched with material that had not been made for walkers. Their helmets were without identification, stripped of all paint. As they took off the helmets he saw that one of the men was Asian, and young; he looked about eighteen. The youth went forward and sat in the driver's seat, leaned over the steering wheel to look closer at the instrument array. Another got off his helmet; a short brown-skinned man, with a thin face and long dreadlocks. He sat on the padded bench across from John's bed, and waited for the other three men to get their helmets off too. When they did they crouched on their haunches, watching John attentively. He had never seen any of them before.

The thin-faced man said, "We want you to slow the rate of immigration." He was the one who had spoken outside; now his accent sounded Caribbean. He spoke in a low voice, almost in a whisper, and John found it very difficult not to emulate him.

"Or stop it," the young man in the driver's seat said.

"Shut up, Kasei." The thin-faced man never took his gaze from John's face. "There are too many people coming up. You know that. They're not Martian, and they don't care what happens here. They're going to overwhelm us, they're going to overwhelm you. You know that. You're trying to turn them into Martians, we know, but they're coming in a lot faster than you can work. The only thing that will work is slowing down the influx."

"Or stopping it."

The man rolled his eyes, appealed with a grimace for John's understanding. The youth was young, his look said.

"I don't have any say—" John began, but the man cut him off:

"You can advocate it. You're a power, and you're on our side."

"Are you from Hiroko?"

The youth snicked his tongue against the roof of his mouth. The thin-faced man said nothing. Four faces stared at John; the other looked resolutely out the window.

John said, "Have you been sabotaging the moholes?"

"We want you to stop the immigration."

"I want you to stop the sabotage. It's just bringing more people here. Police."

The man eyed him. "What makes you think we can contact the saboteurs?"

"Find them. Break in on them at night."

The man smiled. "Out of sight, out of mind."

"Not necessarily."

They had to be with Hiroko. Occam's razor. There couldn't be more than one hidden group. Or maybe there could. John felt light-headed, and wondered if they were doctoring the air. Releasing aerosol drugs. He definitely felt strange, it was all surreal, dreamy; the wind buffeted the rover, sent a sudden burst of aeolian music coursing by, a weird drawn-out hoot. His thoughts were slow and ponderous, and he felt the edge of a yawn. That's it, he thought. I'm still trying to wake from a dream.

"Why do you hide?" he heard himself say.

"We're building Mars. Just like you. We're on your side."

"You ought to help, then." He tried to think. "What about the space elevator?"

"We don't care about it." The kid snicked. "That isn't what matters. It's people that matter."

"The elevator will bring a lot more people."

The man considered that. "Slow the immigration, and it can't even be built."

Another long silence, punctuated by the wind's eerie commentary. Can't even be built? Did they think people would build it? Or maybe they meant the money.

"I'll look into it," John said. The kid turned and stared at him, and John raised a hand to forestall him. "I'll do what I can." His hand stood before him, a huge pink thing. "That's all I can say. If I promised results, it would be lying. I know what you mean. I'll do what I can." He thought about it more, with difficulty. "You ought to be out in the open, helping us. We need more help."

"Each in his way," the man said quietly. "We'll be going now. We'll keep track to see what you do."

"Tell Hiroko I want to talk to her."

The five men looked at him, the young one intense and angry.

The thin-faced man smiled briefly. "If I see her I will."

One of the crouching men held out a diaphanous blue mass: an aerogel sponge, barely visible under the night-running lights. The hand holding it made a fist. Yes, a drug. He lunged out and caught the young one unawares, clawed the youth's bare neck and then fell, paralyzed.

When he came to they were gone. He had a headache. He fell back onto the bed, into an uneasy sleep. The dream about Frank made an improbable return, and John told him about the visitation. "You're a fool," Frank said. "You don't understand."

When he woke again it was morning, swirling a dim burnt umber outside the windshield. The winds had appeared to be lessening in the last month, but it was hard to be sure. Shapes in the dust clouds appeared briefly and then fell back into chaos, in little sensory deprivation hallucinations. It really was sensory deprivation, this storm; and getting very claustrophobic indeed. He ate some omeg, suited up and went outside and walked around, breathing talcum and bending over to follow the tracks of his visitors. They crossed bedrock and disappeared. A difficult rendezvous, he would have thought; a lost rover at night, how had they found it?

But if they had been tracking him . . .

Back inside he called up the satellites. Radar and IR got nothing but his rover. Even walkers would have shown on the IR; so presumably they had a refuge nearby. Easy to hide in mountains like these. He called up his Hiroko map, and drew a rough circle around his location, bulging it north and south in the mountains. He had several circles on the Hiroko map by now, but none of them had been searched by ground crews with any thoroughness, and probably they never would be, as most of them were in chaotic terrain, ravaged land the size of Wyoming or Texas. "It's a big world," he muttered.

He wandered around the inside of the car, looking at the floor. Then he remembered the last thing he had done. He looked under his fingernails; a little skin matter was stuck there, yes. He got a sample dish from the little autoclave, and carefully scraped what was there onto the dish. Genome identification was far beyond the rover's capabilities, but any big lab ought to be able to identify the youth, if his genome was on record. If not, that too would be useful information. And maybe, John wasn't sure, Ursula and Vlad could identify him by parentage.

He relocated the transponder trail that afternoon, and came down into Hellas Basin late the next day. He found Sax there, attending a conference on the new lake, although it appeared that it was turning into a conference on agriculture under artificial lighting. The next morning John took him out for a walk in the cleartunnels between buildings, and they walked in a shifting yellow murk, the sun a saffron glow in the clouds to the east.

"I think I met the Coyote," John said.

"Did you! Did he tell you where Hiroko is?"

"No."

Sax shrugged. It appeared he was distracted by a talk he had to give that evening. So John decided to wait, and that evening he attended the talk with the rest of the lake station occupants. Sax assured the crowd that atmospheric, surface, and permafrost microbacteria were growing at a rate that was a significant fraction of their theoretical maximums — about two percent, to be precise — and that they were going to have to be considering the problems of outdoor cultivation within a few decades. Applause at this announcement was non-existent, because everyone there was absorbed by horrible problems engendered by the Great Storm, which they seemed to think had begun as a result of a miscalculation of Sax's. Surface insolation was still twenty-five percent normal, as one of them waspishly pointed out, and the storm was showing no signs of ending. Temperatures had dropped, and tempers were rising. All the new arrivals had never seen more than a few meters around them, and psychological problems ranging from ennui to catatonia were pandemic.

Sax dismissed all that with a mild shrug. "It's the last global storm," he said. "It will go down in history as some kind of heroic age. Enjoy it while it lasts."

This was poorly received. Sax, however, did not notice.

A few days later, Ann and Simon drove into the settlement with their boy Peter, who was now three. He had been, so far as they could tell, the thirty-third child born on Mars; the colonies established after the first hundred had been fairly prolific. John played with the boy on the floor as he and Ann and Simon caught up on news, and exchanged some of the thousand and one tales of the Great Storm. It seemed to John that Ann ought to be enjoying the storm and the horrendous knock it had put on the terraforming process, like some kind of planetary allergic response, the temperatures plummeting below the baseline, the reckless experimenters struggling with their puny clogged machines . . . But she was not amused. Irritated as usual, in fact. "A dowsing team drilled into a volcanic vent in Daedalia and came up with a sample containing unicellular micro-organisms significantly different from the cyanobacteria you released in the north. And the vent was pretty nearly encased in bedrock, and very far from any biotic release sites. They sent samples of the stuff up to Acheron for analysis, and Vlad studied it and declared that it looked like a mutant strain of one of their releases, perhaps injected into the sample rock by contaminated drilling equipment." Ann poked John in the chest: " 'Probably Terran,' Vlad said. *Probably* Terran!"

"*Pro*babry tewwan!" her little boy said, catching Ann's intonation perfectly.

"Well, it probably is," John said.

"But we'll never know! They'll end up debating it for centuries to come, there'll be a journal devoted to that issue alone, but we'll *never really know*."

"If it's too close to tell, it's probably Terran," John said, grinning at the boy. "Anything that evolved separately from Terran life would give itself away in an instant."

"Probably," Ann said. ("*Pro*babry.") "Except what if there's a common source, the space spores theory, for instance, or ejecta blasted from one planet to another with micro-organisms buried in its rock?"

"That's not too likely, is it?"

"We don't know. We'll never know, now."

John had a hard time sharing her concern. "They might have come from the Viking landers for all we know," he said. "There's never been a very effective effort to sterilize our explorations here, that's just the way it is. Meanwhile we've got more pressing problems." Such as a global dust storm longer than the longest one ever recorded, or an influx of immigrants whose commitment to Mars was as minimal as their housing, or an upcoming treaty revision that no one could agree on, or a terraforming effort that a lot of people hated. Or a home planet going critical. Or an attempt (or two) to do one John Boone some harm.

388

"Yeah yeah," Ann said. "I know. But all that's politics, we'll never get away from that. This was science, a question I wanted answered. And now I can't. Nobody can."

John shrugged. "We'll never answer that one, Ann. No matter what. That was one of those questions that was fated always to remain unanswered. Didn't you know that?"

"*Pro*babwy tewwan."

A few days after that, a rocket landed on the little lake station spaceport pad, and a small group of Terrans emerged out of the dust, still bouncing around as they walked. Investigative agents, they said, here on UNOMA authority, to look into sabotage and related incidents. There were ten of them in all, eight clean-cut young men right out of the vids, and two attractive young women. Most had been assigned from the American FBI. Their leader, a tall brown-haired man named Sam Houston, requested an interview with Boone; John agreed politely.

When they met after breakfast the next morning – six of the agents there, including both women – he meekly answered every question without hesitation, though instinctively he told them only what he thought they knew already, plus a bit more to seem honest and helpful. They were polite and deferential; thorough in their questioning, extremely reticent if he asked them anything in return. They seemed unaware of much of the detail of the situation on Mars, and asked him about things that had happened in the first years at Underhill, or during the time of Hiroko's disappearance. They obviously knew the events of that time, and the basic facts of the various relationships among the first hundred's media stars; they asked him a lot of questions about Maya, Phyllis, Arkady, Nadia, the Acheron group, Sax . . . all of whom were well-known to these young Terrans, permanent fixtures on their TV. But it seemed they knew little beyond what had been taped and sent back to Earth. John, his mind wandering, wondered if that would be true of all Terrans.

After all what other sources of information did they have?

At the end of the interview, one of them named Chang asked him if there was anything else he wanted to say. John, who had omitted an account of his midnight visit from the Coyote, among many other things, said, "I can't think of anything!"

Chang nodded, and then Sam Houston said, "We'd appreciate it if you'd give us access to your AI on these matters," he said.

"I'm sorry," John said, looking apologetic. "I don't give access to my AI."

"You have a destruct lock on it?" Houston said, looking surprised.

"No. I just don't do it. Those are my private records."

John stared the man in the eye, watched him squirm under the gaze of his associates.

"We, um, we can get a warrant from UNOMA, if you like."

"I doubt you can, actually. And even if you do I won't let you in."

John smiled at him, almost laughed. Another moment where being the First Man On Mars was useful. There was nothing they could do to him without causing far more trouble than it was worth. He stood up, surveyed the little gang with as much easy arrogance as he could muster, which was quite a lot. "Let me know if there's anything else I can do for you."

He left the room. "Pauline, click into the building comm center and copy anything you can that they send out." He called Helmut, remembering that his own calls would be opened as well; he kept his questions brief, as if just checking credentials. Yes, a team had been sent out by UNOMA. They were part of a task force, assembled in the last six months to deal with problems.

Police on Mars, then, as well as a detective. Well, it was to be expected. But it was a nuisance nevertheless. He couldn't do much with them hanging around watching him, suspicious because he hadn't given them access to Pauline. And really there wasn't that much to do in Hellas anyway. There had been no incidents of sabotage there, and it seemed unlikely that any would occur now. Maya was unsympathetic: she didn't want to be bothered with his problems, she had enough problems of her own, with the technical aspects of the aquifer project. "You're probably their chief suspect," she said irritably. "These things keep happening to you, a truck in Thaumasia, a well at Bakhuysen, and now you won't let them into your records. Why don't you just do it?"

"Because I don't like them," John said, glaring at her. It was back to normal with Maya. Well, not really; they went through their routines in a kind of high spirits, as if playing a good role in the theater, knowing they had time for everything, knowing now what was real, what lay at the base of the relationship. So in that sense it was much better. On the surface, however, it was the same old melodrama. Maya refused to understand, and in the end John gave up. After that he spent a couple of days thinking it over. He went down to the station's labs, and had the sample of skin taken from under his fingernails cultured, cloned, and read. No one with that genome was in the planetary records, so he sent the information to Acheron requesting an analysis and any information they could give. Ursula sent their results back coded, with a single word added at the end. *Congratulations.*

He read the message again, swore out loud. He went out for a walk, alternately laughing and swearing. "Damn you, Hiroko! Damn you to hell! Get out of your hole and help us! Ah, ha ha ha! You bitch! I'm sick of this Persephone shit!"

Even the walktubes were oppressive at that moment and he went to the garage, suited up and went out the lock for a walk outside, the first in many days. He was out at the end of the northern arm of the town on a smooth desert floor.

He wandered around, staying within the fluctuating column of dust-free air that every city created, thinking the situation over as he surveyed the city. Hellas was going to be much less impressive than Burroughs, or Acheron, or Echus, or even Senzeni Na; located at the low point of the basin, it had no heights to build on, no prospect. Although the whipping dust made it a poor time to judge that. The town had been built in a crescent which would eventually become the shoreline of the new lake; that might look nice when it happened – a waterfront – but meanwhile it was as featureless as Underhill, with all the latest in power plant and service apparatus, intake vents, cables, tunnels like giant sloughed snakeskins . . . the old scientific station look, no aesthetics involved. Well, that was fine. They couldn't put every town on a mountaintop.

Two people passed him, their faceplates polarized. Odd, he thought, it being so gloomy in the storm. Then they leaped on him, knocked him down. He shoved off the sand with a wild John Carter leap and threw his fists around him, but to his surprise they were running off into the clouds of dust whipping by. He staggered, stared after them. They disappeared behind the veils of dust. His blood jolted through him; then he felt his shoulders burn. He reached up and back; they had cut his walker open. He pressed his hand over the rip and began to run hard. He couldn't feel his shoulders at all any more. It was awkward to run with his arm up and behind his neck. His air supply appeared to be all right – no – a tear in the tube, at the neck. He took his hand from his shoulder long enough to dial maximum flow on his wristpad. The cold flowed down his back like ghost ice water. A hundred below 0°C. He was holding his breath and could feel dust on his lips, caking his mouth. Impossible to tell how much CO_2 was getting into his oxygen supply, but it didn't take much to kill you.

The garage appeared out of the murk; he had run right to it, and was feeling mighty pleased with himself until he came to the lock door and pushed the open button and nothing happened. It was easy to lock a lock's outer door, just leave the inner one open. His lungs burned, he needed a breath. He ran around the garage to the walktube that connected it to habitat proper, reached it, stared in through the layers of plastic. No one in sight. He took his hand away from the rip on his shoulder and as quickly as he could opened the box on his left forearm and took out the little drill, turned it on and plunged it into the plastic, which gave without breaking and gathered up around the spinning bit, until the drill almost broke his elbow; he poked wildly with it and finally got the plastic to tear, then ripped downward, widening the hole until he could dive through it helmet first. When he was inside to the waist he held still, using his body as a rough plug for the hole. He unclipped his helmet and ripped it off his head and gasped for breath as if coming up from a long dive, *out* in *out* in *out* in. Get that CO_2 out of the blood. His shoulders and neck were numb. Down at the garage an alarm bell was ringing.

After a twenty second compressed burst of thought, he yanked his legs through the hole and ran down the quickly depressurizing tube toward the habitat, away from the garage. Happily the door there opened on command. Once inside he jumped in an elevator and dropped to the third floor below the ground, where he was staying in one of the guest suites. He let the elevator door open and looked out. No one in sight. He hustled down to his room. Inside he stripped off the walker and stashed it and the helmet in his closet. In the bathroom he winced at the sight of his whitened shoulders and upper back; a really horrible case of frostnip. He took some oral painkiller and a triple dose of omegendorph, put on a shirt with a collar, pants, shoes. He combed his hair, composed himself. The face in the mirror looked glassy-eyed and distracted, almost stunned; he threw his face through the most violent contortions, slapped it, resettled his expression, started breathing in a deep pattern. The drugs began to kick in, and his reflection looked a little better.

He went out into the hall and walked to the big trench wall concourse, which extended downward three more stories. He walked along the railing looking at the people below, feeling a curious mixture of elation and rage. Then Sam Houston and one of his women colleagues approached him.

"Excuse me, Mr Boone, but will you please come with us?"

"What's up?" he said.

"There's been another incident. Someone cut open one of the walkway tubes."

"Cut open a walktube? You call that an *incident*? We have mirror satellites flying out of orbit, and trucks falling into moholes, and you're calling a prank like that an *incident*?"

Houston glared at him, and Boone almost laughed at the man. "How do you think I can help?" he asked.

"We know you've been working on this for Dr Russell. We thought you might like to be informed."

"Oh, I see. Well, let's go have a look then."

And then it was a matter of going through the paces, for nearly two hours, his shoulders burning like fire the whole time. Houston and Chang and the other investigators spoke to him as if in confidence, and anxious for his input; but their gazes were coolly evaluative. John returned them with a little smile.

"Why now, I wonder?" Houston said at one point.

"Maybe someone doesn't like you being here," John said.

Only when the whole charade was finished did he have time to think about why he wanted to keep them from finding out about the attack. No doubt it would have drawn more investigators up, and that was bad; and certainly it would have become the top news story all over Mars and Earth, tossing him back into maximum fishbowl. And he was sick of the fishbowl.

But there was something more than that that he couldn't quite pin down. The subconscious detective. He snorted with disgust. To distract himself from the pain he stalked around from dining hall to dining hall, hoping to catch some expression of poorly-concealed surprise when he walked into each room. Back from the dead! Which one of you murdered me! And once or twice he saw someone flinch from his roving gaze. But the fact was, he thought dourly, many people flinched when he looked at them. As if avoiding the gaze of a freak, or a condemned man. He had never felt his fame in quite that way before, and it made him angry.

The painkillers were wearing off, and he returned early to his rooms. His door was open. When he rushed in he found two of the UNOMA investigators inside. "What are you doing!" he cried angrily.

"Just looking out for you," one of them said smoothly. They glanced at each other. "Wouldn't want someone to try something."

"Like breaking and entering?" Boone said, leaning against the doorway.

"Part of the job, sir. Sorry we've upset you." They shuffled nervously, trapped in his room.

"Just who gave you authorization for this?" Boone said, folding his arms over his chest.

"Well." They looked at each other again. "Mr Houston is our superior officer—"

"Call him and get him here."

One of them whispered into his wristpad. In a suspiciously short time Sam Houston appeared down the hallway, and as he hurried up glowering John laughed. "What were you doing, hiding around the corner?"

Houston walked right up to him, stuck his face forward and said in a low voice, "Look, Mr Boone, we're in the midst of a very important investigation here, and you are obstructing it. Despite what you seem to believe you are not above the law—"

Boone jerked forward so that Houston had to flinch to avoid their bumping noses. "You aren't the law," he said.

He unfolded his arms and poked Houston in the chest, driving him back further down the hall. Now Houston was losing his temper and Boone laughed at him. "What are you going to do to me, officer? Arrest me? Threaten me? Give me something good to include in my next report on Eurovid? Would you like that? Would you like me to show the world how John Boone was harassed by some tin-god tin-badge functionary, who came to Mars thinking he was a sheriff in the wild west?" He remembered his opinion that anyone who spoke of themselves in the third person was a self-declared idiot, and laughed and said, "John Boone doesn't like that kind of thing! No he doesn't!"

The other two had taken the opportunity to slip out of his room, and were now watching closely. Houston's face was the color of Ascraeus Mons, and his teeth were revealed. "No one's above the law," he grated. "There are criminal acts occurring here, very dangerous ones, and quite a few of them happen when you're around."

"Like breaking and entering."

"If we determine that we need to check your quarters, or your records, to pursue our investigation, then we're going to do that. We have that authority."

"I say you don't," John said arrogantly, and snapped his fingers in the man's face.

"We are going to search your rooms," Houston said, articulating each word very carefully.

"Get away," Boone said, contemptuously jerking at the other two and waving them back. He laughed, lip curled with scorn: "That's right, go! Get out of here, you incompetents – go back and read the regs on search and seizure!"

He went in his room and closed the door behind him.

He paused. It sounded like they were leaving, but either way he had to act like he didn't care. He laughed, went to the bathroom and took some more painkillers.

They hadn't yet gotten to the closet, which was lucky; it would have been hard to explain the torn walker without telling the truth, and that would have been messy. Curious how tangled things got when you concealed the fact that someone had tried to kill you. That made him pause. The attempt had been pretty clumsy, after all. There must have been a hundred more effective ways to kill someone out in a walker on Mars. So if they were just trying to scare him, or were perhaps hoping that he *would* try to conceal the attack, so that they could find him lying, and then have something on him . . .

He shook his head, confused. Occam's razor, Occam's razor. The detective's primary tool. If someone attacks you they mean you harm, that was the basic, the fundamental fact. It was important to find out who the attackers were. And so on. The painkillers were strong, and the omegendorph was wearing off. It was getting hard to think. It was going to be a problem disposing of the walker; the helmet in particular was a big bulky thing. But now he was into it, and there was no graceful way out. He laughed; he knew he would think of something eventually.

He wanted to talk to Arkady. A call determined that Arkady had finished the gerontological treatment in Acheron with Nadia however, and had gone up to Phobos. John had still never visited the fast little moon. "Why don't you come on up and see it?" Arkady said over the phone. "Better to talk in person, yes?"

"Okay."

He hadn't been in space since the landing from the *Ares* twenty-three years before and the familiar sensations of acceleration and weightlessness brought on an unexpected bout of nausea. He told Arkady about it as they docked with Phobos, and Arkady said, "It always used to happen to me, until I started drinking vodka right before takeoff." He had a long physiological explanation for this, but the details began to pull John back over the edge and he cut him off. Arkady laughed; the gerontological treatment had given him its usual post-operative lift, and he had been a happy man to begin with: he didn't look like he would be sick again for a thousand years.

Stickney turned out to be a bustling little town, the crater's concrete dome lined with the latest heavy-duty radiation proofing, and the floor of the crater terraced in concentric rings down to a bottom plaza. The rings alternated between parks and two-storied buildings with gardens on their roofs. There were nets in the air for people who lost control of their leaps across the city, or took off by accident: escape velocity was only fifty kilometers per hour, so it was almost possible to run right off the moon. Just under the dome foundation John spotted a small version of the exterior circumnavigating train, running horizontally compared to the buildings of the town, and moving at a speed that returned its passengers to a sensation of Martian gravity. It stopped four times a day to take people on, but if John took refuge in it that would only delay his acclimatization, so he went to the guest room assigned to him, and miserably waited out the nausea. It seemed he was a planet dweller now, a Martian for good, so that leaving it was pain. Ridiculous but true.

The next day he felt better, and Arkady took him on a tour of Phobos. The interior was honeycombed with tunnels, galleries, drifts, and several enormous open chambers, many of them still being enlarged, mined for water and fuel. Most of the interior tunnels inside the moon were smooth functional tubes, but the interior rooms and some of the big galleries had been built according to Arkady's socio-architectural theories, and he showed John around some of these: circular hallways, mixed work and recreation areas, terracing, etched metallic walls, all features that had become standard during Mars's crater-oriented phase of construction, but of which Arkady was still proud.

Three of the little surface craters on the side opposite to Stickney had been domed with glass and filled with villages which had a view of the planet rushing beneath them – views never available from Stickney, as Phobos's long axis was permanently aligned toward Mars, with the big crater always pointed away. Arkady and John stood in Semenov, looking up through the dome at Mars, which filled half the sky and was shrouded by its dust clouds, all its features obscured. "The Great Storm," Arkady said. "Sax must be going mad."

"No," John said. "A thing of the moment, he says. A glitch."

Arkady hooted. Already the two of them had fallen back into their old easy camaraderie, the feeling that they were equals, brothers from way back. Arkady was the same as ever, laughing, joking, a great kidder, ideas and opinions flooding out of him, confident in a way that John enjoyed immensely, even now, when he was sure many of Arkady's ideas were wrong, and even dangerous.

"Sax is probably right, in fact," Arkady said. "If those ageing treatments work, and we are living decades longer than previously, it will certainly cause a social revolution. Shortness of life was a primary force in the permanence of institutions, strange though it is to say it. But it is so much easier to hold onto whatever short-term survival scheme you have, rather than risking it all on a new plan that might not work — no matter how destructive your short-term plan might be for the following generations. Let them deal with it, you know. And really, to give them their due, by the time people learned the system they were old and dying, and for the next generation it was all there, massive and entrenched and having to be learned all over again. But look, if you learn it, and then stare at it for fifty more years, you will eventually be saying, Why not make this more rational? Why not make it closer to our heart's desire? What's stopping us?"

"Maybe that's why things are getting so strange down there," John said. "But somehow I don't think these people are taking the long view." He gave Arkady a quick account of the sabotage situation, and ending it by saying boldly: "Do you know who's doing it, Arkady? Are you involved?"

"What, me? No, John, you know me better than that. These destructions are stupid. The work of reds, from the look of it, and I am no red. I don't know exactly who is doing it. Probably Ann does, have you asked her?"

"She says she doesn't know."

Arkady cackled. "Still my same John Boone! I love it. Look here, my friend, I will tell you why these things are happening, and then you can work at it systematically, and perhaps see more. Ah, here's the subway to Stickney — come on, I want to show you the infinity vault, it's really a nice piece of work." He led John to the little subway car, and they floated down a tunnel to near the center of Phobos, where the car stopped and they got out. They pushed across the narrow room, and pulled themselves down a hall; John noted that his body had adjusted to the weightlessness, that he could float and keep his trim again. Arkady led him into

400

an expansive open gallery, which on first glance appeared to be too large to be contained inside of Phobos: floor, wall and ceiling were paneled in faceted mirrors, and each round slab of polished magnesium had been angled so that anyone in its microgravity space was reflected in thousands of infinite regresses.

They touched down on the floor and hooked their toes through rings, floating like sea bottom plants in a shifting crowd of Arkadys and Johns. "You see, John, the economic basis of life on Mars is now changing," Arkady said. "No, don't you dare scoff! So far we have not been living in a money economy, that's the way scientific stations are. It's like winning a prize that frees you from the economic wheel. We won that prize, and so did a lot of others, and we've all been here for years now, living that way. But now more people are flooding onto Mars, thousands of them! And many of them plan to work here, make some money, and return to Earth. They work for the transnationals that have gotten UNOMA concessions. The letter of the Mars treaty is being kept because supposedly UNOMA is in charge of it all, but the spirit of the treaty is being broken left and right, by the UN itself."

John was nodding. "Yes, I've seen that. Helmut told me about it right to my face."

"Helmut is a snail. But listen, when the treaty renewal comes up, they will change the letter of the law to match the new spirit. Or even give themselves licence to do more. It's the discovery of strategic metals, and all the open space. These represent salvation to a lot of countries down there, and new territory for the transnationals."

"And you think they'll have enough support to change the treaty?"

Millions of Arkadys stared bug-eyed at millions of Johns. "Don't be so naïve! Of course they have enough support! Look, the Mars treaty is based on the old Outer Space treaty. That was the first mistake, because the

Outer Space treaty was in fact a very fragile arrangement, and so the Mars treaty is too. According to the treaty's own provisions, countries can become voting members of the treaty council by establishing an interest here, which is why we're seeing all the new national scientific stations, the Arab League, Nigeria, Indonesia, Azania, Brazil, India and China and all the rest. And quite a few of these new countries are becoming treaty members specifically with the intent to break the treaty at renewal time. They want to open up Mars to individual governments, outside UN control. And the transnationals are using flag of convenience countries like Singapore and the Seychelles and Moldavia to try to open Mars to private settlement, ruled by corporations."

"The renewal is still a few years off," John said.

A million Arkadys rolled their eyes. "It's happening now. Not just in talk, but in what's happening day-to-day down there. When we first arrived, and for twenty years after that, Mars was like Antarctica but even purer. We were outside the world, we didn't even own things — some clothes, a lectern, and that was it! Now you know what I think, John. This arrangement resembles the prehistoric way to live, and it therefore feels right to us, because our brains recognize it from three millions of years practicing it. In essence our brains grew to their current configuration in response to the realities of that life. So as a result people grow *powerfully attached* to that kind of life, when they get the chance to live it. It allows you to concentrate your attention on the real work, which means everything that is done to stay alive, or make things, or satisfy one's curiosity, or play. That is utopia, John, especially for primitives and scientists, which is to say everybody. So a scientific research station is actually a little model of prehistoric utopia, carved out of the transnational money economy by clever primates who want to live well."

"You'd think everyone would join," John said.

"Yes, and they might, but it isn't being offered to them.

And that means it wasn't a true utopia. We clever primate scientists were willing to carve out islands for ourselves, rather than work to create such conditions for everyone. And so in reality, the islands are part of the transnational order. They are paid for, they are never truly free, there is never a case of truly pure research. Because the people who pay for the scientist islands will eventually want a return on their investment. And now we are entering that time. A return is being demanded for our island. We were not doing pure research, you see, but applied research. And with the discovery of strategic metals the application has become clear. And so it all comes back, and we have a return of ownership, and prices, and wages. The whole profit system. The little scientific station is being turned into a mine, with the usual mining attitude toward the land over the treasure. And the scientists are being asked, what you do, how much is it worth? They are being asked to do their work for pay, and the profit of their work is to be given over to the owners of the businesses they are suddenly working for."

"I don't work for anyone," John said.

"Well, but you work on the terraforming project, and who pays for that?"

John tried out Sax's answer: "The sun."

Arkady hooted. "Wrong! It's not just the sun and some robots, it's human time, a lot of it. And those humans have to eat and so on. And so someone is providing for them, for us, because we have not bothered to set up a life where we provide for ourselves."

John frowned. "Well, in the beginning we had to have the help. That was billions of dollars of equipment flown up here. Lots of work time, like you say."

"Yes, it's true. But once we arrived we could have focused all our efforts on making ourselves self-sufficient and independent, and then paid them back and been done with them. But we didn't, and now the loan sharks are here. Look, back in the beginning, if someone were to ask us who made more money, you or me, it would have been impossible to say, right?"

"Right."

"A meaningless question. But now you ask, and we have to confer. Do you consult for anybody?"

"Nobody."

"Me neither. But Phyllis consults for Amex, and Subarashii, and Armscor. And Frank consults for Honeywell-Messerschmidt, and GE, and Boeing, and Subarashii. And so on. They are richer than us. And in this system, richer is more powerful."

We'll just see about that, John thought. But he didn't want to make Arkady laugh again, so he didn't say it.

"And it is happening *everywhere on Mars*," Arkady said. Around them clouds of Arkadys waved their arms, looking like a Tibetan mandala of red-haired demons. "And naturally there are people who notice what's going on. Or I tell them. And this is what you must understand, John; there are people who will fight to keep things the way they were. There are people who loved the feel of life as a scientist primitive, so much that they will refuse to give it up without a fight."

"So the sabotages . . ."

"Yes! Perhaps some of them are done by these people. It is counterproductive, I think, but they don't agree. Mostly the sabotage is done by people who want to keep Mars the way it was before we arrived. I am not one of those. But I am one of those who will fight to keep Mars from becoming a free zone for transnational mining. To keep us all from becoming happy slaves for some executive class, walled in its fortress mansion." He faced John, and out of the corner of his eye John saw around them an infinity of confrontations. "Don't you feel the same?"

"I do, actually." He grinned. "I do! I think if we disagree, it's mostly on the matter of methods."

"What methods do you propose to use?"

"Well — basically, I want to get the treaty renewed as it stands, and then adhered to. If that happens then we'll have what we want, or we'll have the basis for getting to full independence, at least."

"The treaty will not be renewed," Arkady said flatly. "It will take something much more radical to stop these people, John. Direct action — yes, don't you look so unbelieving! Seizure of some property, or of the communication system — the institution of our own set of laws, backed by everyone here, out in the streets — yes, John, yes! It will come to that, because there are guns under the table. Mass demonstration and insurrection is the only thing that will beat them, history shows this."

A million Arkadys clustered around John, looking graver than any Arkady he could ever remember seeing — so grave that the blossoming rows of John's own face exhibited a regressive expression of slack-jawed concern. He pulled his mouth shut. "I'd like to try my way first," he said.

Which made all the Arkadys laugh. John gave him a playful shove on the arm and Arkady went to the floor, then pushed off and tackled him. They wrestled while they could keep contact and then flew away to opposite sides of the chamber; in the mirrors, millions of them flew away into infinity.

After that they went back to the subway, and to dinner in Semenov. As they ate they looked up at the surface of Mars, swirled like a gas giant. Suddenly it looked to John like a great orange cell, or embryo, or egg. Chromosomes whipping about under a mottled orange shell. A new creature waiting to be born, genetically engineered for sure; and they were the engineers, still working on what kind of creature it would be. They were all trying to clip the genes they wanted (their own) onto plasmids and insert them into the planet's DNA spirals, to get the expressions they wanted from the new chimerical beast. Yes. And John liked much of what Arkady wanted to put into it. But he had his own ideas as well. They would see who managed to create more of the genome in the end.

He glanced at Arkady, who was also looking up at the sky-filling planet, with the same grave expression that had been on his face in the hall of mirrors. It was a look that had been impressed on John very accurately and powerfully, he found, but in a weird multiple fly's-vision format.

John descended back into the murk of the Great Storm, and down in the dim blustery sandswept days he saw things he hadn't seen before. That was the value of talking with Arkady. He paid attention to things in a new way; he travelled south from Burroughs, for instance, to Sabishii ("Lonely") Mohole, and visited the Japanese who lived there. They were old-timers, the Japanese equivalent of the first hundred, on Mars only seven years after the first hundred had arrived; and unlike the first hundred they had become a very tight unit, and had "gone native" in a big way. Sabishii had remained small, even after the mohole was dug there. It was out in a region of rough boulders near Jarry-Desloges Crater, and as he drove down the last part of the transponder trail to the settlement, John caught brief glimpses of boulders carved into oversized faces or figures, or covered with elaborate pictographs, or hollowed out into little Shinto or Zen shrines. He stared in the dustclouds after these visions, but they were always gone like hallucinations, half-seen and then disappeared. As he passed into the tattered zone of clear air directly downwind from the mohole, he noticed that the Sabishiians were taking the rock hauled out of the great shaft to this area and arranging it into curving mounds – a pattern – from space it would look like, what, a dragon? And then he arrived at the garage and was greeted by a group of them, barefoot and long-haired, in frayed tan jumpers or sumo-wrestler jock straps: wizened old Japanese Martian sages, who talked about the *kami* centers in the region, and how their deepest sense of *on* had long ago shifted from the emperor to the planet. They showed him their labs, where they were working on areobotany and radiation-proofed clothing materials. They had also done extensive work on aquifer location, and climatology in the equatorial belt. Listening to them it seemed to John that they just had to be in touch with Hiroko, it didn't make sense that they weren't. But they shrugged when he asked about her. John went to work drawing them out, establishing the atmosphere of trust that he was so often able to generate in old-timers, the sense that they went back a long way together, into their own Noachian. A couple of days of asking questions, of learning the town, of showing that he was "a man who knew *giri*", and slowly they began to open up, telling him in a quiet but blunt way that they did not like the sudden growth of Burroughs, nor the mohole next to them, nor the population increase in general, nor the new pressures put on them by the Japanese government to survey the Great Escarpment and "find gold". "We refuse," said Nanao Nakayama, a wrinkled old man with scraggly white whiskers and turquoise earrings, and long white hair in a pony tail. "They cannot make us."

"And if they try?" John asked.

"They will fail." And his easy assurance caught John's attention; and he remembered the conversation with Arkady among the mirrors.

So some of the things he now saw were the result of paying attention in a new way, of asking new questions. But others were the result of Arkady sending word down through his network of friends and acquaintances, to identify themselves to John and show him around. Thus when John stopped in settlements on the way from Sabishii to Senzeni Na, he was often approached by small groups of two, or three, or five, who introduced themselves and said, Arkady thought you might be interested to see this . . . And they would lead him to see an underground farm with an independent power plant, or a cache of tools and equipment, or a hidden garage full of rovers, or complete little mesa habitats, empty but ready for occupation. John would follow them bug-eyed and slack-jawed, asking questions and shaking his head in amazement. Yes, Arkady was showing him things; there was a whole movement down here, a little group in every town!

Eventually he came to Senzeni Na. He was returning because Pauline had identified two workers there as absent without explanation from their jobs, on the day the truck had fallen on him. The day after he arrived he interviewed them, but they proved to have plausible explanations for their absence from the net; they had been out climbing. But after he had apologized for taking their time, and started back to his room, three other mohole technicians introduced themselves as friends of Arkady's. John greeted them enthusiastically, glad that something would come of the trip; and in the end a group of eight took him in a rover to a canyon paralleling the mohole's canyon. They drove down through the obscuring dust to a habitat dug into an over-hanging canyon wall: it was invisible to satellites, its heat released from a number of dispersed small vents which from space would look like Sax's old windmill heaters. "We figure that's how Hiroko's group has done it," one of his guides told him. Her name was Marian, and she had a long beak of a nose and eyes that were set too close together, so that her gaze was very intent.

"Do you know where Hiroko is?" John asked.

"No, but we think they're in the chaos."

The universal response. He asked them about the cliff dwelling. It had been built, Marian told him, with equipment from Senzeni Na. It was currently uninhabited, but ready if needed.

"Needed for *what*?" John said as he walked around the little dark rooms of the place.

Marian stared at him. "For the revolution, of course."

"The revolution!"

John had very little to say on the drive back. Marian and her companions sensed his shock, and it made them uneasy too; perhaps they were concluding that Arkady had made a mistake in asking them to show John their habitat. "There are a lot of these being prepared," Marian said defensively. Hiroko had given them the idea, and Arkady thought they might come in handy. She and her companions began ticking them off on their fingers: a whole stockpile of air and ice mining equipment, buried in a dry ice tunnel at one of the south polar cap processing stations; a wellhole tapping the big aquifer under Kasei Vallis; scattered greenhouse labs around Acheron, growing pharmacologically useful plants; a communications center in the basement of Nadia's concourse at Underhill. "And that's just what we know about. There are one-read samizdat appearing in the net that we had nothing to do with, and Arkady's certain that there are other groups out there, doing the same thing we are. Because when push comes to shove, we're all going to need places to hide and fight from."

"Oh come on," John said. "You all have to get it through your heads that this whole revolution scenario is nothing but a fantasia on the American revolution, you know, the great frontier, the hardy pioneer colonists exploited by the imperial power, the revolt to go from colony to sovereign state — it's all just a false analogy!"

"Why do you say that?" Marian demanded. "What's different?"

"Well for one thing, we're not living on land that can sustain us. And for another, we don't have the means to revolt successfully!"

"I disagree with both those points. You should talk to Arkady more about that."

"I'll try. Anyway I think there's a better way of doing it than all this sneaking around stealing equipment, something more direct. We simply tell UNOMA what the new Mars treaty is going to say."

His companions shook their heads scornfully.

"We can talk all we want," Marian said, "but that's not going to change what they do."

"Why not? Do you think they can just ignore the people who are living here? They may have continuous shuttles now, but we're still eighty million kilometers away from them, and we're here and they're not. It may not be North America in the 1760s, but we do have some of the same advantages: we're at a great distance, and we're in possession. The important thing is not to fall into their way of thinking, into all the same old violent mistakes!"

And so he argued against revolution, nationalism, religion, economics — against every mode of Terran thought that he could think of, all mashed together in his usual style. "Revolution never even worked on Earth, not really. And here it's all outmoded. We should be inventing a new program, just like Arkady says, *including* the ways to take control of our fate. With you all living a fantasy of the past you're leading us right into the repression you're complaining about! We need a new Martian way, a new Martian philosophy, economics, religion!"

They asked him just what these new Martian modes of thought might be, and he raised his hands. "How can I say? When they've never existed it's hard to talk about them, hard to imagine them, because we don't have the images. That's always the problem when you try to make something new, and believe me I know, because I've been trying. But I think I can tell you what it will feel like; it will feel like the first years here, when we were a group and we all worked together. When there was no purpose in life except to settle and discover this place, and we all decided together what we should do. That's how it should *feel*."

"But those days are gone," Marian said, and the others nodded. "That's just your own fantasy of the past. Nothing but words. It's like you're holding a philosophy class in a giant gold mine, with armies bearing down on both sides."

"No no," John said. "I'm talking about methods for resistance, methods appropriate to our real situation, and not some revolutionary fantasy out of the history books!"

And around they went, again and again, until they were back at Senzeni Na, and had retired to the workers' rooms on the lowest residential floor. There they argued passionately, through the time-slip and long into the night; and as they argued a certain elation filled John, because he could see them beginning to think about it – it was clear that they were listening to him, and that what he said, and what he thought of them, mattered to them. This was the best return yet on the old First Man fishbowl; combined with Arkady's stamp of approval, it gave him an influence over them that was palpable, he could shake their confidence, he could make them think, he could force them to re-evaluate, he could change their minds!

And so in the murky purple Great Storm dawn they wandered down the halls to the kitchen and talked on, looking out the windows and bolting down coffee, glowing with a kind of inspiration, with the age-old excitement of honest debate. And when they finally quit to go catch a little sleep before the day got going, even Marian was clearly shaken, and all of them were deep in thought, half-convinced that John was right.

John walked back to his guest suite feeling tired but happy. Whether Arkady had intended to or not, he had made John one of the leaders of his movement. Perhaps he would come to regret it, but there was no going back now. And John was sure it was for the best. He could be a sort of bridge between this underground and the rest of the people on Mars – operating in both worlds, reconciling the two, forging them into a single force that would be more effective than either alone. A force with the mainstream's resources and the underground's enthusiasm, perhaps. Arkady considered that an impossible synthesis; but John had powers that Arkady didn't. So that he could, well, not *usurp* Arkady's leadership, but simply *change them all.*

The door to his room in the guest quarters was open. He rushed in, alarmed, and there in the room's two chairs sat Sam Houston and Michael Chang. "So," Houston said. "Where have you been?"

"Oh come on," John said. His temper flared, his good mood burnt off in a flash. "Did I pick the wrong door by mistake?" He leaned back out to look. "No, I didn't. These are my rooms." He lifted his arms and clicked on his wristpad's recorder. "What are you doing in here?"

"We want to know where you've been," Houston said evenly. "We've got the authority to enter all the rooms here, and to get all our questions answered. So you might as well start."

"Come on," John scoffed. "Don't you ever get tired of playing the bad cop? Don't you guys ever trade off?"

"We just want answers to our questions," Chang said gently.

"Oh please, mister good cop," John said. "We all want answers to our questions, don't we?"

Houston stood up; already he was on the edge of losing his temper, and John walked right over to him and stopped with their chests about ten centimeters apart. "Get out of my rooms," he said. "Get out now, or I'll throw you out, and then we'll figure out who had the right to be in here."

Houston merely stared at him, and without warning John shoved him hard in the chest; Houston ran into his chair and sat down involuntarily, bounced up going for John, but Chang jumped between them, saying, "Wait a second, Sam, wait a second," while John shouted "Get out of my rooms!" over and over at the top of his lungs, bumping against Chang's back and glaring over his shoulder into Houston's red face. John nearly burst into laughter at the sight; his

412

high spirits had returned with the success of the shove, and he stalked to the door bellowing "Get out! Get out! Get out!" so that Houston would not see the grin on his face. Chang pulled his angry colleague out into the hall and John followed. The three of them stood there, Chang carefully placing himself between his partner and John. He was bigger than either of them, and now he faced John with a worried, irritated look.

"Now what did you want?" John said innocently.

"We want to know where you've been," Chang said doggedly. "We have reason to suspect that your so-called investigation of the sabotage incidents has been a very convenient cover for you."

"I suspect the same of you," John said.

Chang ignored him. "Things keep happening right after your visits, you see—"

"They happen right *during* your visits."

"—hoppers of dust were dropped in every mohole you visited during the Great Storm. Computer viruses attacked the software in Sax Russell's office at Echus Overlook, right after your consultation with him in 2047. Biological viruses attacked the fast lichens at Acheron right after you left. And so on."

John shrugged. "So? You've been here two months, and that's the best you can do?"

"If we're right, it's good enough. Where were you last night?"

"Sorry," John said. "I don't answer questions from people who break into my rooms."

"You have to," Chang said. "It's the law."

"What law? What are you going to do to me?" He turned toward the open door of the room and Chang moved to block him; he lost his temper again and jerked toward Chang, who flinched but remained in the doorway, immovable. John turned and walked away, back down to the commons.

*

He left Senzeni Na that afternoon in a rover, and took the transponder road north along the eastern flank of Tharsis. It was a good road and three days later he was 1300 kilometers to the north, just northwest of Noctis Labyrinthus, and when he came to a big transponder intersection, with a new fuel station, he hung a right and took the road east to Underhill. Each day as the rover rolled along blindly through the dust, he worked with Pauline. "Pauline, would you please look up all planetary records for theft of dental equipment?" She was as slow as a human in processing an incongruous request, but eventually the data were there. Then he had her go over the movement records of every suspect he could think of. When he was sure where everyone had been, he gave Helmut Bronski a call to protest the actions of Houston and Chang. "They say they're working with your authorization, Helmut, so I thought you should know what they're doing."

"They are trying their best," Helmut said. "I wish you would stop harassing them and co-operate, John. It could be helpful. I know you have nothing to hide, so why not be more helpful?"

"Come on, Helmut, they don't *ask for help*. It's rank intimidation. Tell them to stop it."

"They are only trying to do their job," Helmut said blandly. "I have not heard of anything illegitimate."

John broke the connection. Later on he called Frank, who was in Burroughs. "What's with Helmut? Why is he turning the planet over to these policemen?"

"You idiot," Frank said. He was typing madly at a computer screen as he talked, so that he seemed to be only barely conscious of what he was saying. "Aren't you paying any attention at all to what's going on here?"

"I thought I was," John said.

"We're knee-deep in gasoline! And these goddamned ageing treatments are the match. But you never understood why we were sent here in the first place, so why should you understand anything now?" He typed on, staring hard into his screen.

John studied the little image of Frank on his wrist. Finally he said, "Why were we sent here in the first place, Frank?"

"Because Russia and our United States of America were desperate, that's why. Decrepit outmoded industrial dinosaurs, that's what we were, about to get eaten up by Japan and Europe and all the little tigers popping up in Asia. And we had all this space experience going to waste, and a couple of huge and unnecessary aerospace industries, and so we pooled them and came here on the chance that we'd find something worthwhile, and it paid off! We struck gold, so to speak. Which is only more gasoline poured onto things, because gold rushes show who's powerful and who's not. And now even though we got a head start up here, there are a lot of new tigers down there who are better at things than we are, and they all want a piece of the action. There's a lot of countries down there with no room and no resources, ten billion people standing in their own shit."

"I thought you told me Earth would always be falling apart."

"This isn't falling apart. Think about it – if this damned treatment only goes to the rich, then the poor will revolt and it'll all explode – but if the treatment goes to everyone, then populations will soar and it'll all explode. Either way it's gone! It's going now! And naturally the transnats don't like that, it's horrible for business when the world blows up. So they're scared, and they're deciding to try to hold things together by main force. Helmut and those policemen are only the smallest tip of the iceberg – a lot of policymakers think a world police state for a few decades or so is our only chance of getting to some kind of population stabilization without a catastrophe. Control from above, the stupid bastards."

Frank shook his head disgustedly, then leaned toward his screen and became absorbed in its contents.

John said, "Did you get the treatment, Frank?"

"Of course I did. Leave me alone, John, I've got work to do."

The southern summer was warmer than the previous one that had been shrouded in the Great Storm, but still colder than any recorded. The storm was now almost two M-years long, over three Terran years, but Sax was philosophical about it. John called him at Echus Overlook, and when John mentioned the cold nights he was experiencing Sax only said, "We'll very likely have low temperatures for the greater part of the terraforming period. But warmer *per se* isn't what we're trying for. Venus is warm. What we want is survivable. If we can breathe the air, I don't care if it's cold."

Meanwhile it was cold, cold everywhere, the nights down to a hundred below every night, even on the equator. When John reached Underhill, a week after leaving Senzeni Na, he found there was a kind of pink ice covering the sidewalks; it was nearly invisible in the storm's dim light, and walking around was a treacherous business. The people at Underhill spent most of their time indoors. John occupied a few weeks by helping the local bioengineering team field test a new fast snow algae. Underhill was crowded with strangers. Most of them were young Japanese or Europeans, who fortunately still used English to communicate with each other. John roomed in one of the old barrel vaults, near the northeast corner of the quadrant. The old quadrant was less popular than Nadia's concourse, smaller and dimmer, and many of its vaults were now used for storage. It was strange to walk the square of hallways, remembering the pool, Maya's room, the dining hall — now all dark, and stacked with boxes. Those years when the first hundred had been the only hundred. It was getting hard to remember what that had been like.

He kept track through Pauline of the movements of quite a few people, the UNOMA investigating force among them.

It was a not-very-rigorous surveillance, as it was not always easy to track the investigators, especially Houston and Chang and their crew, whom he suspected were going off-net deliberately. Meanwhile the spaceports' arrival records gave more evidence every month that Frank had been right about them being only the tip of the iceberg; a lot of people coming down at Burroughs in particular were working for UNOMA without job specifications, and then spreading out to the mines and moholes and other settlements, and going to work for the local security heads. And their Terran employment records were very interesting indeed.

Often at the end of a session with Pauline John would leave the quadrant, and go for a walk outside, feeling disturbed and thinking hard. There was a lot more visibility than there had been: things were clearing up a bit out on the surface, though the pink ice still made walking tricky. It seemed the Great Storm was lessening. Wind speeds on the surface were only two or three times the pre-storm average of thirty kilometers per hour, and the dust in the air was sometimes little more than a kind of thick haze, turning the sunsets into blazing pastel swirls of pink, yellow, orange, red and purple, with random streaks of green or turquoise appearing and disappearing, along with icebows and sundogs, and occasional brilliant shafts of pure yellow light: nature at her most tasteless, transient and spectacular. And watching all that hazy color and movement John would be distracted from his thoughts and climb the great white pyramid to have a look around, and then go back inside ready to start the fight again.

One evening after one of these sunset extravaganzas he climbed down the peak of the great pyramid, and walked slowly back toward Underhill – and then he spotted two figures climb out one of the garage side doors, and down a clear crawltube into a rover. There was something quick and furtive in their motion, and he stopped to look closer: they did not have their helmets on, and he recognized Houston and Chang by the backs of their heads and the size of their

417

bodies. They moved with scurrying Terran inefficiency into the rover, and drove toward him. John polarized his faceplate and started walking again, head down, trying to look like someone coming in from work, veering to the side a bit to increase the distance between him and them. The rover dove into a thick dust cloud and disappeared abruptly.

By the time he got to the lock doors he was deep in thought, and almost frightened. He stood motionlessly at the door, thinking it over, and when he moved it was not to the door, but to the intercom console in the wall next to the door. There were several different kinds of jacks under the speakers, and carefully he unplugged the stopper in one and cleared away the fines crusting the edge – these jacks were never used anymore – and plugged in his wristpad. He tapped in the code for Pauline, and waited for encryption and decryption to work through. "Yes, John?" said Pauline's voice from his helmet intercom speaker.

"Turn on your camera please, Pauline, and pan my room."

Pauline was sitting on the side table by his bed, plugged into the wall. Her camera was a little fiber thing, rarely used, and the image on his wristpad was small. The room was dim with only a nightlight on; and his faceplate's curve was yet another barrier, so that even with the wristpad right against it, he couldn't quite make out the images; gray shapes, shifting. There was the bed, there was something on it, then the wall. "Back ten degrees," John said, and squinted trying to comprehend the two centimeter square image. His bed. There was a man lying on his bed. Wasn't that what it was? The bottom of a shoe, torso, hair. It was hard to tell. It didn't move. "Pauline, do you hear anything in the room?"

"The vents, the electricity."

"Transmit to me what you're picking up on your mike, at full volume." He leaned his head to the left against his helmet, cramming his ear against the helmet speaker. A hiss, a whoosh, static. There was too much transmission error in a process like this, especially using these corroded old jacks.

418

But certainly he heard no breathing. "Pauline, can you enter the Underhill monitoring system, and locate our vault's door camera, and transmit its image to my wrist, please?"

He had directed the installation of Underhill's security system, just a few years before; Pauline still had all the plans and codes, and it didn't take long for her to replace the image on his wrist with that of the suite outside his room, seen from above. The suite's lights were on, and in the camera's sweeps he could see that his door was shut; that was all.

He let his wrist fall to his side and thought it over. Five minutes passed before he raised it again and began giving instructions through Pauline to the Underhill security system. Possession of the codes allowed him to instruct the entire camera system to erase its surveillance tapes, and then to run them in an hour loop rather than the usual eight-hour one. Then he instructed two of the cleaning robots to come to his room, and open its door. While they did that he stood shivering, waiting for them to make their slow roll through the vaults. When they opened his door, he saw them through Pauline's little eye; light poured into the room and momentarily blazed, then adjusted, and he had a much clearer view. Yes, it was a man on his bed. John's breath went shallow. He teleoperated the robots, using the minute button toggles on his wristpad. It was a jerky procedure, but if lifting the man woke him up, so much the better.

It didn't. The man lolled down on both sides of the robot's cradling arms, which lifted him with their algorithmic delicacy. A body hanging down. The man was dead.

John deliberately took a deep breath, then held it and continued the teleoperation, directing the first robot to deposit the body in the second robot's big trash hopper. Sending the robots back down the hall to their storage vault was easy. Several people walked by them as they rolled along, but there was nothing he could do about that. The body was not visible except from above, and hopefully no one was paying enough attention to remember the robots later.

When he got them in their storage room, he hesitated. Should he take the body to the incinerators in the Alchemists' Quarter? But no – now that it was out of his room, he didn't need to get rid of the body. In fact he would need it later. For the first time he wondered who it was. He directed the first robot to put its extensor eye against the body's right wrist, and read with its magnetic imager. It took a long time for the eye to hit the right spot on the wrist. Then it held fast. The minute tag that everyone had implanted on a wristbone held information in the standard dot language, and it only took a minute for Pauline to get an ID. Yashika Mui, UNOMA auditor, based at Underhill, arrived 2050. An actual person. A man who might have lived a thousand years.

John began to shiver. He leaned against the glazed blue brick wall of Underhill. It would be an hour before he could go inside, or a little less. Impatiently he pushed off and walked around the quadrant. It took about fifteen minutes to walk around it usually, but now he found he was doing it in ten. After the second turn he walked over to the trailer park.

Only two of the old trailers were still there, and they were apparently abandoned or used only for storage. Figures loomed out of the night dust between them, and for a second he was afraid, but they passed on by. He returned to the quadrant and circled it again, then walked out the path to the Alchemists' Quarter. He stood looking at the antiquated complex of tubes and piping and squat white buildings, all covered with their black calligraphic equations. He thought of their first years. And now it had come to this, in what seemed the blink of an eye. In the gloom of the Great Storm. Civilization, corruption, crisis. Murder on Mars. He gritted his teeth.

An hour had passed, it was nine p.m. He went back to the lock and went inside, took off his helmet and walker and boots in the changing room and stripped, went into the showers and showered, dried off and put on a jumper, combed his hair. He took a deep breath and walked around the south side of the quadrant and up through the vaults to the one with his room. As he was opening his door he was not surprised to see four of the UNOMA investigators appear, but he tried to act surprised when they ordered him to stop: "What's this?" he said.

It wasn't Houston or Chang, but rather three men, with one of the women from that first group at Low Point. The men clustered at his sides without really responding to him, and pulled his door completely open and two of them went inside; John controlled the urge to punch them, or shout at them, or laugh at the expressions that came over their faces when they saw that his room was empty; he merely stared curiously at them, and tried to limit himself to the irritation he would have shown had he been ignorant of what was going on. This irritation would have been considerable of course, and once he opened that door inside himself it was hard indeed to keep all his fury from banging through, hard to keep it to an innocent's level; they had to be snapped at as if they were overzealous policemen, rather than assaulted as murderous functionaries; and that was extremely hard to hold to.

In their confusion at the unexpected situation he managed to drive them off with a few biting sentences, and when he had closed the door on them he stood in the middle of his room. "Pauline, transmit what's happening on the security system to yourself, please, and record. Show me whatever cameras have them."

So Pauline tracked them. It only took a couple of minutes for them to go to the security control room, where they were joined by Chang and others. They went after the camera packs. John sat at Pauline's screen and watched right along with them as they ran the loops back and found that they were only an hour long, and that the events of the afternoon had been erased. That would give them something to think about. He smiled grimly and told Pauline to get off the system.

A wave of exhaustion swept through him. It was only eleven, but all adrenalin and the morning's dose of omegendorph had drained out of him, and he was tired. He sat on his bed, but then remembered what had last been there, and got up. In the end he slept on the floor.

He was awakened in the timeslip by Spencer Jackson, with news of a body discovered in a robot hopper. He went and stood wearily beside Spencer in the clinic, staring at the body of Yashika Mui while several of the investigators eyed him warily. The diagnostic machinery was as good at autopsy as anything else, maybe better; tests of minute samples were indicating a blood coagulant. Somberly John ordered a full criminal autopsy; Mui's body and clothes had to be scanned, and all microscopic particles read against his genome, and all foreign particles read against the list of people who were currently in Underhill. John stared at the UNOMA investigators as he gave this instruction, but they didn't blink. Probably they had been wearing gloves and walkers, or teleoperated the whole thing as he had. He had to turn away to hide his disgust; he couldn't let on that he knew!

But then of course they knew that they had put the body there; and so they must suspect that he was the one who had removed it, and erased the camera tapes. So they already knew that he knew, or suspected he did. But they couldn't be sure; and there was no reason to give anything away.

An hour later he went back to his room, and lay on the floor again. Although he was still exhausted, he could no longer sleep. He stared at the ceiling, thinking it over. Thinking over everything that he had learned.

Near dawn he felt he had things sorted out. He gave up on sleep, and got up to go out for another walk; he needed to be outside, away from the human world and all its sickening corruption, out into the great rush of the wind, made so dramatically visible by the storm's flying dust.

But when he got out of the lock door, there were stars overhead. The complete net of them – all the thousands burning as of old, without the slightest twinkle or flicker, the faint ones so dense that the black sky itself appeared slightly whitish, as if the whole sky were the Milky Way.

When he had recovered from his astonishment, and the almost-forgotten wonder of the stars, he got on his intercom and called in the news.

It caused pandemonium; people heard and woke their friends, and rushed down to the changing rooms to grab a walker before the supply was exhausted. And the lock doors started opening and spewing out crowds.

The sky to the east turned a blackish red, and then lightened quickly. The whole sky shifted to a dark rose shade, and then began to glow. The stars disappeared by the hundreds, until only Venus and the Earth hung in the east, over a growing intensity of light. The sky in the east grew brighter, and brighter again, until it seemed brighter than day could ever get; even behind faceplates their eyes watered, and some cried out over the common band at the sight. There were figures scampering around, the intercom babbling, the sky growing impossibly brighter, and brighter, and brighter yet, until it seemed it would burst: it pulsated with glowing pink light, the dots that were Venus and Earth overwhelmed by it. And then the sun cracked the horizon and fountained across the plain like a thermonuclear bomb, and the people roared and jumped up and down and ran among the long black shadows of the rocks and the buildings. All east-facing walls were great blocks of Fauvist color, their glaze mosaics stunning, hard to look at directly. The air was clear as glass and indeed seemed a solid substance, imbuing the things stuck in it with razor-edged clarity.

John walked out away from the crowds, east toward Chernobyl. He turned his intercom off. The sky was a darker

423

pink than he remembered, with a touch of purple at the zenith. Everyone in Underhill was going crazy; many of the people there had never seen the sun shine on Mars, and no doubt it felt like they had lived their whole lives in the Great Storm. And now it was over, and they were wandering out in the sunshine drunk with it, slipping on pink ice left and right, getting in yellow snowball fights, climbing the frosted pyramids. When John saw that he turned, and went up the steps of the last pyramid himself, to have a look at the tors and hollows around Underhill. They were somewhat frosted and silted over, but otherwise just the same. He turned on the common band, but turned it back off; people still inside were howling for walkers, and no one outside was paying any attention to them. It had been an hour since sunrise, one cried, though John found that hard to believe. He shook his head; the raucous voices, and the memory of the body on his bed, made it hard to feel much joy in the end of the storm.

Eventually he went back inside, and gave his walker over to a pair of women his size who were squabbling over who got to use it next, went down to the comm center and called Sax in Echus Overlook. When he got him he congratulated him on the end of the storm.

Sax waved this away brusquely, as if it had happened years before. "They've boarded Amor 2051B," he said. This was the ice asteroid they had found for insertion into Martian orbit. They were in the process of installing rockets on it, which would knock it onto a course that would bring it in on a trajectory similar to the *Ares'*; without a heat shield the aerobraking would burn it up. All looked well for a MOI ETA about six months away. *That* was the big news, Sax implied in his blinking, calm way. The Great Storm was history.

John had to laugh. But then he thought of Yashika Mui, and he told Sax about it because he wanted someone else's celebration to be ruined as well. Sax only blinked. "They're

424

getting serious," he finally said. Disgusted, John said good-bye and got off.

He wandered back out through the vaults, disturbed by a fiercely clashing mix of good and bad emotions. He returned to his room and took an omegendorph and one of the new pandorphs Spencer had given him, and then he went out into the quadrant's central atrium, and wandered among the plants, all skinny storm spawn, troping toward the light bulbs running overhead. The sky was still a clear dark pink, still very bright. A lot of the people who had gone out first were now back and in the atrium between the rows of crops, partying. He ran into a few friends, some acquaintances, mostly strangers. He went back into the vaults, through rooms full of strangers who sometimes cheered when he walked in. If they yelled "Speech!" long enough he would stand on a chair and rattle something off, feeling the endorphins, which today were rendered unpredictable in their effect by the thought of the murdered man. Sometimes he was pretty vehement, and he never knew what he was going to say until it came out of him. We saw John Boone drunk on his ass, they would say, the day the Great Storm ended. Fine, he thought, let them say what they wanted. It never mattered what he did anymore anyway, as far as the legend was concerned.

One room contained a crowd of Egyptians, not like his Sufis but orthodox Moslems, talking like the wind and drinking cups of coffee, high on caffeine and sunlight, flashing white smiles under their moustaches, extremely cordial for once, in fact pleased to see him there. He warmed to that, and flying on the momentum of the day he said, "Look, we're part of a new world. If you don't base your actions on Martian reality then you become a kind of schizophrenic, with your body on one planet and your spirit on another. No society split like that can function for long."

"Well, well," one of them said with a smile. "You must understand we have traveled before. We are a traveling

425

people. But wherever we are, Mecca is our spirit's home. We could fly to the other side of the universe and that would still be true."

Nothing to say to that; and in fact such direct honesty was so much cleaner than what he had been dealing with through the night that he nodded, and said, "I see. I understand." Compare that after all to the hypocrisy of the West, where people talked of profit at prayer breakfasts, people who couldn't articulate a single belief they had; people who thought their values were physical constants, who would say "That's just the way things are," like Frank so often did.

So John stayed and talked with the Egyptians for a while, and when he left them he was feeling better. He wandered back to his vault, listening to the rowdy voices pouring into the hallway from every room; shouts, shrieks, happy scientist talk, "these things are such halophytes that they don't like brine because there's too much water in it," peals of laughter.

He had an idea. Spencer Jackson lived in the vault next door to John's, and was passing through when John hurried in, so John told him the idea. "We ought to gather everyone we can for a big celebration of the storm's end. All the sort-of Mars-centered groups, you know, or really everyone who can possibly make it. Anyone who wants to be there."

"Where?"

"Up on Olympus Mons," he said without considering it. "We could probably get Sax to time the arrival of his ice asteroid so that we could watch it from there."

"Good idea!" Spencer said.

Olympus Mons is a shield volcano, and therefore a cone that is not steep in most places, its great height resulting from its even greater breadth; it is twenty-five kilometers higher than the surrounding plain, but eight hundred kilometers across, so its slope averages about six degrees. But around the circumference of its great bulk there is a circular escarpment some seven kilometers high, and this spectacular cliff, twice as tall as that at Echus Overlook, is in many places close to vertical. Sections of it had already lured the few climbers on the planet, but no one had yet succeeded in climbing it, and for most of the inhabitants of the planet it remained merely a spectacular impediment on the way to the summit caldera. Travelers on the ground made it up the escarpment by way of a wide ramp on the north side, where one of the last lava flows had overrun the cliff – areologists told tales of what it must have been like, of a river of molten rock a hundred kilometers wide, too bright to look at, falling seven thousand meters onto the black lava-crusted plain, piling higher and higher and higher. This spill of lava had left a rampway with nothing more than a slight jog in it where the escarpment had been overrun; it was an easy ascent, and after it, an uphill drive of some two hundred kilometers took one to the rim of the caldera.

The summit rim of Olympus Mons is so broad and flat that while it has an excellent view down into the many-ringed caldera, the rest of the planet cannot be seen from it; looking outward one sees only the outer edge of the rim, and then the sky. But on the south side of the rim there is a small meteor crater, with no name but its map designation, THA-Zp. The interior of this little crater is somewhat sheltered from the thin jet stream rushing over Olympus Mons, and standing on the southern arc of its fresh spiky rim, an observer finally has a view down the slope of the volcano,

and then over the vast rising plain of west Tharsis:
like looking down at the planet from a platform in low
space.

It took almost nine months before the asteroid was brought
to a rendezvous with Mars, and word of John's celebration
had had time to get around. So they came in scattered rover
caravans, in twos and fives and tens, up the north ramp and
around to the southern outer slope of Zp; and they erected
a number of big crescent-shaped clear-walled tents; with
rigid clear floors that stood two meters off the ground, resting on clear entry stalks. They were the very latest thing in
temporary shelter, in fact, and all set with their inner arcs
facing uphill, so that when they were done they had a row
of crescents stacked like stairs, like greenhouse gardens on a
terraced hillside, overlooking the immense sweep of a bronze
world. Every day for a week the caravans arrived, and dirigibles labored up the long slope, and were tethered inside
Zp, filling it so that the interior of the little crater looked
like a bowl of birthday balloons.

The size of the crowd surprised John, as he had expected
only a few friends to travel to such a remote site. It was yet
another proof of his inability to comprehend the planet's
current population; there were nearly a thousand people
gathered there together, it was amazing. Although many
were faces he had seen before, and quite a few he knew by
name. So it was a collection of friends, in a way. It was as
if a home town that he hadn't known existed had suddenly
sprung up around him. And since so many of the first hundred had come, forty of them in all, including Maya and Sax,
Ann and Simon and Nadia and Arkady, Vlad and Ursula and
the rest of the Acheron group, Spencer, Rya, Alex and Raul
and Janet and Mary and Dmitri and Elena and the rest of the
Phobos group, and Arnie and Sasha and Yeli and several
more, some of whom he hadn't seen in twenty years – everyone he was close to, in fact, except for Frank, who had said

he was too busy, and Phyllis, who hadn't replied to the invitation at all.

And it wasn't just the first hundred; many of the others were old friends as well, or friends of friends: a lot of Swiss, including the roadbuilding gypsies; Japanese from all over; most of the Russians on the planet; his Sufi friends; and all of them scattered up and down the terraced crescent tents, in collections of caravan groups and dirigible teams, rushing from time to time to the locks to greet the latest arrivals.

During the days many of them wandered around outside the tents, collecting loose rock from the great curved slope. The Zp meteor's impact had scattered chunks of brecciated lava everywhere, including shishtovite shattercones like pottery shards, some dead black, others a bright blood red, or flecked with impact diamonds. An areological team from Greece started laying these in a pattern on the ground under the raised floor of their tent, and they had brought a little kiln with them, so they could glaze some shards yellow or green or blue, to accent their designs. This idea caught on as soon as others saw it, and within two days each clear tent floor stood over a flagged parquet with a mosaic design: circuitry maps, pictures of birds and fish, fractal abstracts, Escher drawings, the Tibetan calligraphy spelling *Om Mani Padme Hum*, maps of the planet and of smaller regions, equations, people's faces, landscapes, and so on.

John spent his time wandering from tent to tent, talking with people and enjoying the carnival atmosphere – an atmosphere which did not preclude arguments, there were a lot of those – but most people spent the time partying, talking, drinking, going out on excursions on the wavy surface of the old lava flows, making mosaic floors, dancing to music made by various amateur bands. The best of these was a magnesium drum band, the instruments local, the players from Trinidad and Tobago, a notorious transnational flag of convenience with a vigorous local resistance movement of which the band were representatives. There was also a country and western group with a good slide guitar player, and an Irish band with home-made instruments and a large shifting membership, which allowed it to play more or less non-stop. These three bands were all surrounded by crowds of dancers, and indeed the tents they occupied had all of their movement transformed into a kind of pulsing dance, as just getting from here to there was suddenly stuffed with the grace and exuberance of the music, the gravity, the view.

So it was a great festival, and John was pleased, partying hard in every waking moment. He didn't need any omegendorph or pandorph; once when Marian and the Senzeni Na crowd hustled him in a corner and started passing tabs around, he could only laugh; "I don't think so right now," he said to the young hotheads, waving a hand weakly. "It'd be carrying coals to Newcastle at this point, really it would."

"Carrying coals to Newcastle?"

"He means it'd be like taking permafrost to Borealis."

"Or pumping more CO_2 into the atmosphere."

"Bringing lava to Olympus."

"Putting more salt in the goddamn soil."

"Putting any more ferric oxide anywhere on the whole damn planet!"

"Exactly," John said, laughing. "I'm already full red."

"Not as red as these folks," one of them said, pointing down to the west. A string of three sand-colored dirigibles floated up the slope of the volcano. They were small and antiquated, and did not answer radio inquiries. By the time they had scraped over Zp's rim and anchored among the larger and more colorful dirigibles in the crater, everyone was waiting to hear from the observers at the lock who they might be. When their gondolas popped open, and twenty or so figures in walkers stepped out, a silence fell. "That's Hiroko," Nadia said suddenly over the common band. The first hundred made their way quickly to the upper tent, looking up at the walktube that ran over the rim. And then the new visitors were walking down the tube to the tent lock, and were through and inside, and yes, it was Hiroko – Hiroko, Michel, Evgenia, Iwao, Gene, Ellen, Rya, Raul, and a whole crowd of youngsters.

Shrieks and shouts pierced the air, people were embracing, a few crying, and there were a good number of angry accusations; John himself couldn't help it when he got a chance to hug Hiroko, all those hours in his rover worrying about things, wishing he could have talked to her; now he took her shoulders in his hands and almost shook her, ready for hot words to pour from his throat; but her grinning face was so much like his memory of her and yet not – her face thinner and more lined, not her and yet clearly her – that her face blurred and flowed in his vision, from what he expected to see to what he saw. He was confused enough by this hallucinatory smear (in his feelings too) that he only said, "Oh, I've wanted to talk to you so!"

"And me to you," she said, although it was hard to hear her in the din; Nadia was intervening between Maya and Michel, for Maya was shouting "Why didn't you tell me?" again and again, before bursting into tears. John was distracted by this, and then he saw Arkady's face over Hiroko's shoulder, bunched in an expression that said there's going to be questions answered later, and he lost his train of thought. There were going to be some hard things said – but still, here they were! Here they were. Down in the tents the noise level had jumped twenty decibels. People were cheering their reunion.

Late in the afternoon John convened the first hundred, now numbering almost sixty. They gathered in the highest tent by themselves, and looked out over those below, and the land beyond.

It was all so much huger than Underhill and the tight rocky plain around it. Everything had changed, it seemed; the world and its civilization all grown vastly larger and more complicated. And yet there they stood nevertheless, all the oh-so-familiar faces changed, aged in all the ways human faces age: time texturing them with erosion as if they had lived for geological ages, giving them a knowing look, as if one could see the aquifers behind their eyes. They were in their seventies now, most of them. And the world was indeed larger – in many different ways: after all it was now quite possible that they were destined to watch each other age a lot more, if they were lucky. It was a strange sensation.

So they milled about, looking at the people in the tents below, and beyond them to the variegated orange carpet of the planet; and the conversations rushed this way and that in quick chaotic waves, creating inteference patterns, so that sometimes they all went still at once and stood there together, stunned or bemused or grinning like dolphins. In the tents below, people occasionally looked up through the plastic arcs at them, curious to catch a glimpse of such a historic meeting.

Finally they sat in a scattering of chairs, passing around cheese and crackers and bottles of red wine. John leaned back in his chair and looked around. Arkady had one arm over Maya's shoulders, the other over Nadia's, and the three of them were laughing at something Maya had said; Sax was blinking his owlish pleasure, and Hiroko was beaming. John had never seen that look on her face in the early years. It was a shame to disturb such a mood, but there would never be a good time; and the mood would return. So in a quiet moment he said to Sax in clear loud tones, "I can tell you who's behind the sabotages."

Sax blinked. "You can?"

"Yes." He looked Hiroko in the eye. "It's your people, Hiroko."

That sobered her, though she still smiled: but it was the contained, private smile of old. "No no," she said mildly, and shook her head. "You know I wouldn't do that."

"I figured not. But your people are doing it without your

knowledge. Your children, in fact. Working with the Coyote."

Her eyes narrowed, and she threw a quick glance down at the tents below.

When she looked at John again he went on. "You grew them, right? Fertilized a bunch of your eggs, and grew them in vitro?"

After a pause she nodded.

"Hiroko!" Ann said. "You don't have any idea how well that ectogene process works!"

"We tested it," Hiroko said. "The kids have turned out all right."

Now the whole group was silent, and watching Hiroko and John. He said, "Maybe so, but some of them don't share your ideas. They're doing things on their own, like kids will. They have eyeteeth made of stone, isn't that right?"

Hiroko wrinkled her nose. "They're crowns. A composite rather than true stone. A silly fashion."

"And a kind of badge. And there are people out on the surface who have picked it up, people in contact with your kids, helping them with the sabotages. I almost got killed by some of them in Senzeni Na. My guide there had a stone eyetooth, although it took me a long time to remember where it was I had seen it. I assume it was an accident that we were down there at the time the truck fell. I hadn't given them any warning I was going to visit, so I assume the whole thing was planned before I got there, and they didn't know to stop it. Okakura probably went down the hole thinking he was going to get squished like a bug for the cause."

After another pause Hiroko said, "Are you sure?"

"I'm pretty sure. It was confusing for a long time, because it's not just them — there's more than one thing going on. But when I remembered where I had seen that first stone tooth I looked into it, and I found out that a whole shipment of dental equipment from Earth arrived empty, back in 2044.

433

A whole freighter ripped off. It made me think I was onto something. And then, the sabotages kept happening in places and at times when no one who was in the net could possibly have done it. Like that time I visited Mary at the Margaritifer aquifer, and the well housing was blown up. It was clear it hadn't been done by anyone stationed there, it just wasn't possible. But that's a really isolated station, and there was no one else anywhere nearby at the time. So it had to be someone outside the net. And so I thought of you."

He shrugged apologetically. "When you check it out, you find that about half the sabotages simply couldn't have been done by anyone in the net. And in the other half, someone with a stone tooth was usually spotted in the area. It's becoming a pretty widespread fashion now, but still. I figured it was you, and I had my AI do an analysis which showed that about three-quarters of the cases have happened in the lower southern hemisphere, that or else inside a three thousand kilometer circle with the chaotic terrain at the east end of Marineris as its center point. That's a circle that holds a lot of settlements, but even allowing for that it seemed to me the chaos was a logical place for the saboteurs to hide. And we've all figured for years that that was where you folks went when you left Underhill."

Hiroko's face revealed nothing. Finally she said, "I will look into this."

"Good."

Sax said, "John, you said there was more than one thing going on?"

John nodded. "It hasn't just been sabotage, you see. Someone's been trying to kill me."

Sax blinked, and the rest of them looked shocked. "At first I thought it was the saboteurs," John said, "trying to stop my investigation. It made sense, and the first incident really was an act of sabotage, so it was easy to get confused. But now I'm pretty sure that time was a mistake. The saboteurs aren't interested in killing me – they could have done

434

it and they didn't. One night a group of them stopped me, including your son Kasei, Hiroko, and the Coyote, who I take it is the same as the stowaway that you were hiding on the *Ares*—"

This caused an uproar; it looked like a fair number of them had had suspicions about this stowaway, and Maya was on her feet pointing a dramatic finger at Hiroko, crying out. John shouted them all down, forged on: "Their visit – their visit! – that was the best proof of my theory about the sabotages, because I managed to get a few skin cells off one of them, and I was able to get his DNA read and compared with some other samples found at some of the sabotage sites, and this person had been there. So those were the saboteurs, but they weren't trying to kill me, obviously. But one night at Hellas Low Point I was knocked down, and my walker cut open."

He nodded at his friends' exclamations. "That was the first intentional attack on me, and it came pretty soon after I went up to Pavonis, and talked to Phyllis and a bunch of transnational types about internationalizing the elevator and so on."

Arkady was laughing at him, but John ignored him and forged on. "After that, I was harassed several times by UNOMA investigators that Helmut allowed to come up, and he did that under pressure from those same transnationals. And in fact I found out that most of those investigators had worked for Armscor or Subarashii on Earth, rather than for the FBI like they told me. Those are the transnationals most involved with the elevator project and the mining on the Great Escarpment, and now they've got their own security people established everywhere, and this roving team of so-called investigators. And then, just before the big storm ended, some of those investigators tried to get me accused of that murder that happened at Underhill. Yes they did! It didn't work, and I can't absolutely prove it was them, but I saw two of them working on the set-up. And I think they killed that man, too, just to get me in trouble. To get me out of their way."

"You should tell Helmut," Nadia said. "If we present a united front and insist that these people be sent back to Earth, I don't think he could deny us."

"I don't know how much real power Helmut has anymore," John said. "But it would be worth a try. I want these people kicked off the planet. And those two in particular I've got recorded by the Senzeni Na security system, both going into the med clinic and messing with the cleaning robots before I did. So the circumstantial evidence against them is about as strong as it could be."

The others didn't know quite what to make of this, but it turned out that several of them had also been harassed by other UNOMA teams — Arkady, Alex, Spencer, Vlad and Ursula, even Sax — and they quickly agreed that an attempt to get the investigators deported was a good idea. "Those two in particular ought to be deported *at best*," Maya said hotly.

Sax simply tapped at his wristpad, and called Helmut up on the phone right then and there: he laid the situation out to Helmut, and the angry group pitched in from time to time. "We'll take this to the Terran press if you don't act on it," Vlad declared.

Helmut frowned, and after a pause he said, "I'll look into it. Those agents that you complain about in particular will be rotated back home, for sure."

"Check their DNA again before you let them go," John said. "The murderer of that man in Underhill is among them, I'm sure of it."

"We will check," Helmut said heavily.

Sax cut the connection, and John looked around at his friends again. "Okay," he said. "But it'll take more than a call to Helmut to make all the changes we need. The time has come to act together again, across a whole range of issues, if we want the treaty to survive. That as a minimum, you know. A start on the rest of it. We need to form a coherent political unit no matter what kind of disagreements we might have."

"It won't matter what we do," Sax said mildly, but he was jumped on immediately, in an incomprehensible babble of competing protests.

"It does matter!" John cried. "We've got as much chance as anyone does of directing what happens here."

Sax shook his head, but the others were listening to John, and most seemed to agree with him: Arkady, Ann, Maya, Vlad, each from their different perspective . . . It could be done, John could see it in their faces. Only Hiroko he could not read; her face was a blank, closed in a way that brought back a sharp pang of recollection. She had always been that way to John, and suddenly it made him ache with frustration and remembered pain, and he got annoyed.

He stood, and waved a hand outward; it was nearing sunset, and the enormous curved plate of the planet was dappled with an infinite texture of shadows. "Hiroko, can I have a word with you in private? Just for a second. We can go down into the tent below here. I just have a couple questions, and then we can come right back up."

The others stared at them curiously. Under that gaze Hiroko finally bowed, and walked ahead of John to the tube down to the next tent.

They stood at one tip of that tent's crescent, under the gazes of their friends above, and the occasional observer below. The tent was mostly empty; people were respecting the first hundred's privacy by leaving a gap.

"You have suggestions for how I can identify the saboteurs?" Hiroko said.

"You might start with the boy named Kasei," John said. "The one that is a mix of you and me."

She would not meet his eye.

John leaned toward her, getting angry. "I presume there's kids from every man in the first hundred?"

Hiroko tilted her head at him, and shrugged very slightly. "We took from the samples everyone gave. The mothers are all the women in the group, the fathers all the men."

"What gave you the right to do all these things without our permission?" John asked. "To make our children without asking us – to run away and hide in the first place – why? Why?"

Hiroko returned his gaze calmly. "We have a vision of what life on Mars can be. We could see it wasn't going to go that way. We have been proved right by what has happened since. So we thought we would establish our own life—"

"But don't you see how *selfish* that is? We *all* had a vision, we *all* wanted it to be different, and we've been working as hard as we can for it, and all that time you've been *gone*, off creating a little pocket world for your little group! I mean we could have used your help! I wanted to talk to you so often! Here we have a kid between us, a mix of you and me, and you haven't talked to me in twenty years!"

"We didn't mean to be selfish," Hiroko said slowly. "We wanted to try it, to show by experiment how we can live here. Someone has to show what you mean when you talk about a different life, John Boone. Someone has to live the life."

"But if you do it in secret then no one can see it!"

"We never planned to stay secret forever. The situation has gotten bad, and so we've stayed away. But here we are now, after all. And when we are needed, when we can help, we will appear again."

"You're needed every day!" John said flatly. "That's how social life works. You've made a mistake, Hiroko. Because while you've been hiding, the chances for Mars remaining its own place have gone way down, and a lot of people have been working to speed that disappearance, including some

438

of the first hundred. And what have you done to stop them?''

Hiroko said nothing. John went on: ''I suppose you've been helping Sax a little in secret. I saw one of your notes to him. But that's another thing I object to – helping out some of us and yet not others.''

''We all do that,'' Hiroko said, but she looked uncomfortable.

''Have you had the gerontological treatments in your colony?''

''Yes.''

''And you got the process from Sax?''

''Yes.''

''Do these kids of yours know their parentage?''

''Yes.''

John shook his head, exasperated and more. ''I just can't believe you would do these things!''

''We do not ask for your belief.''

''Obviously not. But aren't you the least bit concerned about stealing our genes and making kids by us without our knowledge or consent? About bringing them up without giving us any part in their upbringing, any part in their childhood?''

She shrugged. ''You can have your own kids if you want. As for these, well. Were any of you interested in having children twenty years ago? No. The subject never came up.''

''We were too old!''

''We were not too old. We chose not to think of it. Most ignorance is by choice, you know, and so ignorance is very telling about what really matters to people. You did not want children, and so you did not know about late birth. But we did, and so we learned the techniques. And when you meet the results, I think you will see it was a good idea. I think you will thank us. What have you lost, after all? These children are ours. But they have a genetic link to you, and

439

from now on they will exist for you, as an unexpected gift, say. As a quite extraordinary gift." Her Mona Lisa smile appeared and disappeared.

The concept of the gift, again. John paused to think about it. "Well," he finally said. "We'll be talking about that for a long time, I suspect."

Twilight had turned the atmosphere below them into a dark purple band, running like a velvet border around the black star-studded bowl which had appeared over their heads. In the tents below they were singing, led by the Sufis: "Harmakhis, Mangala, Nirgala, Aquakuh; Harmakhis, Mangala, Nirgala, Aquakuh," and around again, time after time, adding grace notes that were other names for Mars, and encouraging the bands already there to add instrumental accompaniments of all kinds, until every tent was filled with this song, all of them singing together. The Sufis then began their whirling, and little knots of dancers swirled all through the crowds.

"Will you at least stay in contact with me now?" John said intently to Hiroko. "Will you give me that?"

"Yes."

They returned to the upper tent and the group went down together into the general party and joined the celebration. John made his way slowly to the Sufis, and tried the spins he had learned from them on their mesa, and people cheered and caught him when he spun out of control into the spectators. After one fall he was helped to his feet by the thin-faced man with dreadlocks who had led the midnight visit to his rover. "Coyote!" John cried.

"It's me," the man said, and his voice caused a ripple of electricity down John's spine. "But no reason for alarm."

He offered John a flask; after a moment's hesitation John took it and drank. Fortune favors the bold, he thought. Tequila, apparently. "You're Coyote!" he shouted over the music of the magnesium drum band.

The man grinned widely and nodded once, took the flask back and drank.

"Is Kasei with you?"

"No. He doesn't like this meteor." And then with a friendly slap to the arm the man moved off into the swirling crowd. He looked over his shoulder and shouted, "Have fun!"

John watched him disappear among the faces in the crowd, feeling the tequila burn in his stomach. The Sufis, Hiroko, now Coyote; the gathering was blessed. He saw Maya and hurried over to her and threw an arm over her shoulder, and they walked through the tents and the connecting tunnels, and people toasted them as they passed. The semi-rigid tent floors were gently bouncing up and down.

The countdown reached two minutes, and many people ascended to the upper tents, and then pressed against the clear walls of the south-facing arcs. The ice asteroid would probably burn up in a single orbit, its injection trajectory was so steep; an object a quarter the size of Phobos burned to steam and then, as it got hotter, to oxygen and hydrogen molecules; and all in a matter of minutes. No one could be sure what it would look like.

So they stood there, some of them still singing the chords of the name round. And then a final countdown was picked up by more and more of them, until they were all into the last ten, shouting out the reversed sequence of numbers at the top of their lungs, in the astronaut's primal scream. They roared out *"zero!"*, and for three breathless heartbeats nothing happened; then a white ball trailing a blazing fan of white fire came shooting up over the southwestern horizon, as big as the comet in the Bayeux Tapestry, and brighter than all the moons and mirrors and stars combined. Burning ice, bleeding across the sky, white on black, hurtling fast and low, so low that it was not much higher than they were on Olympus, so low that they could see white chunks bursting back through the tail and falling away like giant sparks. Then about halfway across the sky it broke into fragments, and the whole collection of incandescent blazes tumbled east, scattering like buckshot. All the stars suddenly shuddered; it was the first sonic boom, striking the tents and shaking them. A second boom followed, and the phosphor chunks bounced wildly for a moment as they tumbled down the sky and disappeared over the southeast horizon. Their firebrake tails followed them into Mars, and disappeared, and it was suddenly dark again, the ordinary night sky standing overhead as if nothing had happened. Except the stars were twinkling.

After all that anticipation, the passage had taken no more than three or four minutes. The celebrants had mostly gone silent at the sight, but many had cried out involuntarily at the sight of the breakup, as during a fireworks show; and again at the impact of the two sonic booms. Now, in the old dark, the silence was complete, and people stood in their tracks. What could you do after something like that?

But there was Hiroko, making her way down through the tents to the one where John and Maya and Nadia and Arkady were standing together. As she walked she chanted, in a tone that was quiet but carried throughout each tent she crossed: "Al-Qahira, Ares, Aquakuh, Bahram. Harmakhis, Hrad, Huo Hsing, Kasei. Ma'adim, Maja, Mamers, Mangala. Mawrth, Nirgal, Shalbatanu, Simud, Tiu." She walked through the crowd right to John, and facing him she plucked up his right hand and pulled it aloft, and suddenly shouted, "John Boone! John Boone!"

And then everyone was cheering and yelling "Boone! Boone! Boone! Boone!" and others were shouting "Mars! Mars! Mars!"

John's face blazed like the meteor had, and he felt stunned, as if a piece of it had pinged him on the head. His old friends were laughing at him, and Arkady yelled "Speech!" in what he imagined was an American accent: "Speech! Speech! Speeeeeeeeeech!"

Others picked this up, and after a time the noise died down, and they watched him expectantly, laughter rippling through them at the sight of his slack-faced astonishment. Hiroko released his hand, and he raised the other one helplessly, holding both overhead with hands outstretched.

"What can I say, friends?" he cried. "This is the thing itself, there are no words for this. This is what words ask for."

But his blood ran high with adrenalin, with tequila and omegendorph and happiness, and without willing it the words spilled out of him as they so often had before. "Look," he said, "here we are on Mars!" (Laughter) "That's our gift and a great gift it is, the reason we have to keep giving all our lives to keep the cycle going, it's like in eco-economics where what you take from the system has to be balanced by what you give in to it, balanced or exceeded to create that anti-entropic surge which characterizes all creative life and especially this step across to a new world, this place that is neither nature nor culture, transformation of a planet into a world and then a home. Now we all know that different people have different reasons for being here and just as important the people who sent us up had different reasons for sending us, and now we're beginning to see the conflicts caused by those differences, there are storms brewing on the horizon, meteors of trouble flying in and some of them are going to strike dead on rather than skip overhead like that blaze of white ice just did!" (Cheers). "It may get ugly, at times it almost certainly will get ugly, so we have to remember that just as these meteor strikes enrich the atmosphere, thicken it and add the elixir oxygen to the poison soup outside these tents, the human conflicts coming down may do the same, melting the permafrost at our social base, melting all those frozen institutions away and leaving us with the *necessity of creation*, the imperative to invent a new social order that is purely Martian, as Martian as Hiroko Ai, our own Persephone now come back up out of the regolith to announce the start of this new spring!" (Cheers) "Now I know I used to say that we had to invent it all from scratch but in these last few years traveling around and meeting you all I've seen that I was wrong to say that, it's not like we have nothing and are being forced to conjure forms godlike out of the vacuum – we have the genes you might say, the memes as Vlad says meaning our cultural genes, so that it's in the nature of an act of genetic engineering what we do here, we have the DNA pieces of culture all made and broken and mixed by history, and we can choose and cut and clip together from what's best in that gene pool, knit it all together the way the Swiss did their constitution, or the Sufis their worship, or the way the Acheron group made their latest fast lichen, a bit from here and there, whatever's appropriate, keeping in mind the seven generation rule, thinking seven generations back and seven generations forward, and seven times seven if you ask me because now it's our lives we're talking about extending way off into the years, we don't know how that will affect us yet, but it's certainly true that altruism and self-interest have collapsed together more tightly than ever before. But also it's still and always our children's lives and our children's children and on down forever that we have to think of, we must act in a way that gives them just as many chances as we have been given and hopefully more, channeling the sun's energy in ever more ingenious ways to reverse the flow of entropy in this little pocket of the universal flow. And I know that's an awfully general way of putting it when this treaty that orders our lives here is coming up for renewal so soon, but we have to keep that level in mind because what's coming is not just a treaty but more a kind of constitutional congress, because we're dealing with the genome of our social organization here – you can do this, you can't do that, you have to do this, to eat or to give. And we've been living by a set of rules established for empty land, the Antarctic treaty so fragile and idealistic which has held that cold continent free of intrusion for so long, up until the last decade in fact when it's been chipped away at, and that's a sign of what's beginning to happen here too. The encroachment on that set of rules has begun everywhere, like a parasite feeding on the edges of its host organism, because that's what the replacement set of rules is: the old parasitic greed of the kings and their henchmen — this system we call the transnational world order is just feudalism all over again, a set of rules that is anti-ecologic — it does *not* give back but rather enriches a floating international elite while impoverishing *everything* else, and so of course the so-called rich elite are in actuality poor as well, disengaged from real human work and therefore from real human accomplishment, parasitical in the most precise sense, and yet powerful too as parasites that have taken control can be, sucking the gifts of human work away from their rightful recipients which are the seven generations, and feeding on them while increasing the repressive powers that keep them in place!" (Cheers)

"So it's democracy versus capitalism at this point, friends, and we out on this frontier outpost of the human world are perhaps better positioned than anyone else to see this and to fight this global battle, there's empty land here, there's scarce and non-renewable resources here, and we're going to get swept up into the fight and we cannot choose not to be part of it, we are one of the prizes and our fate will be decided by what happens throughout the human world. That being the case, we had better band together for the common good, for Mars and for us and for all the people on earth and for the seven generations, it's going to be hard it's going to take years, and the stronger we are the better our chances, which is why I'm so happy to see that burning meteor in the sky pumping the matrix of life into our world, and why I'm so happy to see you all here to celebrate it together, a representative congress of all that I love in this world, but look I

445

think that steel drum band is ready to play, aren't you?"
(shouts of assent) "so why don't you folks start and we'll
dance till dawn and tomorrow scatter on the winds and down
the sides of this great mountain, to carry the gift
everywhere."

Mad cheers. The magnesium drum band picked them up
into its staccato flurry of plinks and plonks, and the crowd
heaved into motion again.

They partied all night long. John spent the time wandering
from tent to tent, shaking hands and hugging people,
"Thanks, thanks, thanks. I don't know, I don't remember
what I said. But this is what I meant all along, this right
here." His old friends laughed at him. Sax, drinking coffee
and looking supremely relaxed, said to him, "Syncretism is
it? Very interesting, very well put"—with the tiniest of
smiles. Maya kissed him, Vlad and Ursula and Nadia kissed
him; Arkady lifted him up and with a great roar swirled him
around in the air, giving him a hairy kiss on each cheek and
shouting, "Hey, John, could you repeat that please?" hooting
at the very thought. "You amaze me, John, you always
amaze me!" And Hiroko with her private smile, with Michel
and Iwao flanking her, grinning at him . . .

Michel said, "I think this is what Maslow meant by the
term peak experience," and Iwao groaned and elbowed him,
while Hiroko reached out and touched John on the arm with
her forefinger, as if to pass along a certain animating touch,
a power, a gift.

They next day they sorted and bagged the party wreckage
and took down the tents, leaving the flagstone terraces
behind, like strands of cloisonné necklace draped down the
side of the old black volcano. They said good-bye to the
dirigible crews, and the dirigibles drifted down the slope like
balloons slipped from a child's fist; the sand-colored ones of
the hidden colony got hard to see very quickly.

As he got in his rover with Maya John said good-byes,

and as they drove around the rim of Olympus Mons they caravaned with rovers containing Arkady and Nadia, and Ann and Simon and their son Peter. In conversations that day John said, "We need to talk to Helmut, and get the UN to accept us as speakers at large for the local population. And we need to present the UN with a draft of the revised treaty. Around Ls ninety I'm scheduled to go to a dedication ceremony for a new tent city on east Tharsis. Helmut is supposed to be there, maybe we could meet then?"

Only a few of them could make it, but they were named delegates for the rest, and the plan was agreed on. After that they talked about what the contents of the draft treaty should be, calling around to all the caravans and the dirigibles. The next day they came to the ramp down the northern escarpment, and at its foot they took off each in every direction. "That was a good party!" John said over the radio to each in turn. "See you at the next one!"

The Sufis rolled by while they were stopped, and they waved from their windows came on the radio to say good-bye as well. John recognized the voice of the old woman who had tended him at the toilet after his dance in the storm; as he was waving at their caravan she said over the radio,

"Whether it be of this world or of that,
Your love will lead us yonder at the last."

PART SIX

Guns Under the Table

The day John Boone was assassinated we were up on east Elysium and it was morning and this meteor shower came raining down on us, there must have been thirty streaks or so and they were all black, I don't know what those meteorites were made of but they burned black instead of white. Like smoke from crashing planes except straight and fast as lightning. It was so strange to see that we all were amazed and we hadn't even yet heard the news, but when we did we figured back, and it happened at exactly the same time.

We were down in Hellas Lakefront and the sky went dark and a sudden wind whipped over the lake and blew every walktube in that town away, and then we heard.

We were in Senzeni Na where he worked a lot, and it was night and lightning started hammering us, giant bolts of lightning shooting right down into the mohole – no one could believe it, and it was so loud you couldn't hear. And there was a picture of him down in the workers' quarters, up on the wall of one suite, and a lightning bolt hit the concourse window and everyone was blinded for a second, and when our sight returned the frame of that picture was busted and the glass cracked and it was smoking. And then we heard the news.

We were in Carr and we couldn't believe it. All the first hundred there were crying, he must have been the only one in that whole gang that everyone liked, if most of them were killed a good half of the rest would be cheering. Arkady was out of his mind, he cried for hours and it was so scary because it was so unlike him, Nadia kept trying to comfort him and she was saying, It's all right, it's all right and Arkady kept saying It's not all right, it's not all right, and roaring and throwing things and then falling into Nadia's arms again, even Nadia was freaked. And that was when he ran off to his room and came back with one of the ignition transmitter boxes, and when he explained what it was Nadia got really furious at all of us, she said Why would you ever do a thing like that? And Arkady was crying and yelling What do you mean why? Because of this, because of what just happened to John, they killed him, they killed him! Who knows which of us will be next! They'll kill all of us if they can! And Nadia kept trying to give the transmitter back and he got so upset, he kept making her hold it saying Please Nadia please, just in case, just in case, please, until finally she had to keep it to get him to calm down. I never saw anything like it.

We were in Underhill and the power went off, and when it came back on every plant in the farm had frozen solid. The lights and heat came back on and the plants all began to wilt. We sat around all night telling stories about him. I remembered what it was like when he first touched down back in the twenties, a lot of us did. I was just a kid at the time but I remember everyone laughing at his first words, I thought it was funny myself but I remember being very surprised that all the adults were laughing too, everyone was so tickled, I think everyone fell in love with him at that moment, I mean how could you not like someone who was the first person on another planet walking out there and saying Well, here we are. It was impossible not to like him.

Oh I don't know. I saw him punch a man once, it was on the Burroughs train and he was in our car obviously high, and there was this woman who had some kind of deformity, a big nose and no chin and when she went down to the toilets some guy said My Lord, that woman has really been beat hard with the ugly stick, and Boone bam! knocks him into the next seat and says, There is no such thing as an ugly woman.

That's what he thought.

That is what he thought, why he slept with a different woman every night, and he didn't care what they looked like. Or how old they were — he had to talk fast when

452

they found him with that fifteen-year-old. I don't suppose Toitovna ever heard of that one or it would have been his balls, and hundreds of women would have gone wanting. He used to like to do it in two-person gliders with the woman on top of him while he piloted.

Oh man once I saw him pull a glider out of a downdraft that would have killed anyone else — it was a shear-off and it would have ripped the glider apart if he'd tried to resist it, but he just went with it and the plane dropped like a Rickover a thousand meters in a second, three or four times terminal velocity, and then when it was about to go smash he just tweaked it to the side and up and pancaked it in about twenty meters. Came out with his nose and ears bleeding. He was the best pilot on Mars, he could fly like an angel. Hell the whole first hundred would've been dead if he hadn't hand flown them into their orbital insertion, that's what I heard.

There were people who hated him. And with good reason too. He stopped the mosque on Phobos from being built. And he could be cruel, I've never met a man more arrogant.

We were on Olympus Mons and the whole sky went black.

Well, back before the beginning, Paul Bunyan came to Mars, and he brought his blue ox Babe with him. He walked around looking for lumber and his every footprint cracked the lava and left a rift canyon. He was so tall that he could reach into the asteroid belt while he walked around, and he chewed those rocks like Bing cherries and spit the pits out and boom there would be another crater.

And then he ran into Big Man. It was the first time Paul had ever seen anyone bigger than himself, and believe me Big Man was bigger — the usual two magnitudes, and that ain't just twice as big let me tell you. But Paul Bunyan didn't care. When Big Man said let's see what you can do with that axe of yours Paul said sure, and with one stroke he hit the planet so hard that all the cracks of Noctis appeared at once. But then Big Man scratched the same spot

453

with his toothpick, and the entire Marineris system yawned open. Let's try bare fists, Paul said, and he landed a right cross on the southern hemisphere and there was Argyre. But Big Man tapped a spot nearby with his pinky and there was Hellas. Try spitting, Big Man suggested, and Paul spat and Nirgal Vallis ran as long as the Mississippi. But Big Man spat and all the big outflow channels ran at once. Try shitting! Big Man said, and Paul squatted and pushed out Ceraunius Tholus — but Big Man threw back his butt and there was the Elysium massif right next to it, steaming hot. Do your worst, Big Man suggested. Take a shot at me. And so Paul Bunyan picked him up by the toe and swung his whole bulk around and slammed him into the North Pole so hard that that whole northern hemisphere is depressed to this day. But without even getting up Big Man grabbed Paul by the ankle, and caught up his blue ox Babe in that same fist, and swung them into the ground and slammed them right through the planet and almost out the other side. And that's the Tharsis bulge — Paul Bunyan, almost sticking out — Ascraeus his nose, Pavonis his cock, and Arsia his big toes. And Babe is off to one side, pushing up Olympus Mons. The blow killed Babe and Paul Bunyan both, and after that Paul had to admit that he was beat.

But his own bacteria ate him, naturally, and they crawled all around down on the bedrock and under the megaregolith, down there going everywhere, sucking up the mantle heat, and eating the sulfides, and melting down the permafrost. And everywhere they went down there, every one of those little bacteria said I am Paul Bunyan.

It's a matter of will, Frank Chalmers said to his face in the mirror. The phrase was the only residue of the dream he had been having when he awoke. He shaved with quick decisive strokes, feeling tense, crammed with energy ready to be unleashed, wanting to get to work. More residue: Whoever wants it the most wins!

He showered and dressed, padded down to the dining hall. It was just after dawn. Sunlight flooded Isidis with horizontal beams of red-bronze light, and high in the eastern sky cirrus clouds looked like copper shavings.

Rashid Niazi, the Syrian representative to the conference, passed by and gave Chalmers a cool nod. Frank returned it and walked on. Because of Selim el-Hayil, the Ahad wing of the Moslem Brotherhood had gotten blamed for Boone's assassination, and Chalmers had always been quick and public in defending them from all such accusations. Selim had been a lone assassin, he always asserted, a mad murder-suicide. This underlined the Ahads' guilt while at the same time commanding their gratitude. Naturally Niazi, an Ahad leader, was a bit frustrated.

Maya came into the dining room and Frank greeted her cordially, automatically covering the discomfort he always felt in her presence.

"May I join you?" she said, watching him.

"Of course."

Maya was perceptive, in her way; Frank concentrated on the moment. They chatted. The subject of the treaty began to come up, and so Frank said, "How I wish John were here now. We could use him." And then: "I miss him." This kind of thing would distract Maya instantly. She put her hand over his; Frank scarcely felt it. She was smiling, her arresting gaze full on him. Despite himself he had to look away.

The TV wall was showing the news package beamed up from Earth, and he tapped on the table console and turned up the sound. Earth was in bad shape. The video was of a massive protest march in Manhattan, the whole island packed with a crowd the protesters would call ten million and the police five hundred thousand. The helicopter images were quite arresting, but there were a lot of places these days that, although less visual, were much more dangerous. In the advanced nations people were marching because of draconian birth reduction acts, laws that made the Chinese look like anarchists, and the young had erupted in fury and dismay, feeling their lives pulled out of their hands by a great crowd of ancient unnatural undead, by history itself come alive. That was bad, sure. But in the developing countries they were rioting over "inadequate access" to the treatments themselves, and that was far worse. Governments were falling; people were dying by the thousands. Really these images of Manhattan were probably meant to reassure; everything's still orderly! they said. People conducting themselves in a civil manner, even if it be civil disobedience. But Mexico City and São Paulo and New Delhi and Manila were in flames.

Maya looked at the screen and read aloud one of the Manhattan banners: "'Send the Old To Mars.'"

"That's the essence of a bill someone's introduced in Congress. Reach a hundred and you're off, to retirement orbitals, the moon, or here."

"Especially here."

"Maybe," he said.

"I suppose that explains their stubbornness about emigration quotas."

Frank nodded. "We'll never get those. They're under too much pressure down there, and we're seen as one of the few escape valves. Did you see that program aired on Eurovid about all the open land on Mars?" Maya shook her head. "It was like a real estate ad. No. If the UN delegates gave us any say in emigration, they'd be crucified."

"So what do we do?"

He shrugged. "Insist on the old treaty at every point. Act like every change is the end of the world."

"So that's why you were so crazy about the preface material."

"Sure. That stuff may not be all that important, but we're like the British at Waterloo. If we give at any point the whole line collapses."

She laughed. She was pleased with him, she admired his strategy. And it was a good strategy, although it was not the one he was pursuing. For they were not like the British at Waterloo; they were if anything like the French, making a last-ditch assault which they had to win if they wanted to survive. And so he had been very busy giving in on many points in the treaty, hoping to thrust forward and hold on to what he really wanted in other areas. Which certainly included some remaining role for the American Martian Department, and its Secretary; after all, he needed a base from which to work.

So he shrugged, dismissing her pleasure. On the TV wall the crowds boiled up and down the great avenues. He clenched his teeth a few times. "We'd better get to it again."

Upstairs the conferees were milling about in a sequence of long high rooms that were divided by tall partitions. Sunlight streamed into the big central room from the eastern meeting chambers, throwing a ruddy glare over the white pile carpet and the squarish teak chairs and the dark pink stone of the long table top. Knots of people were chatting casually against the walls. Maya went off to confer with Samantha and Spencer. The three of them were now the leaders of the MarsFirst coalition, and as such had been invited to the conference as non-voting representatives of the Martian population: the people's party, the tribunes, and the only ones there actually elected to their positions, although they were there only at Helmut's sufferance. Helmut had been as inclusive as anyone could ask; he had allowed Ann to attend as a non-voting member representing the Reds, even though they were part of the coalition; Sax was there observing for the terraforming team; and any number of mining and development executives were observing as well. There was a whole crowd of observers, in fact; but the voting members were the only ones to sit at the central table, where Helmut was now ringing a small bell. Fifty-three national representatives and eighteen UN officials took their seats; another hundred continued to wander in the eastern rooms, watching the discussion through the open portals or on small TVs. Outside the windows, Burroughs crawled with figures and vehicles, moving around in the clear-walled mesas, and the tents on and between the mesas, and in the network of connecting clear walktubes that lay on the ground or arched through the air, and in the huge valley tent with its wide streetgrass boulevards and its canals. A little metropolis.

Helmut called the session to order. In the eastern rooms people clustered around the TVs. Frank glanced through a portal into the east room nearest him; there would be rooms like that all over Mars and Earth, thousands of them, with millions of observers. Two worlds watching.

The day's topic, as it had been for the past two weeks, was emigration quotas. China and India had a joint proposal to make; the head of the Indian office rose and read it in his musical Bombay English. Stripped of camouflage it came down to a proportional system, of course. Chalmers shook his head. India and China between them had forty percent of the world's population, but they were only two votes of fifty-three at this conference and their proposal would never pass. The Brit in the European delegation rose to point out this fact, not in so many words of course. Wrangling began. It would go on all morning. Mars was a real prize, and the rich and poor nations of Earth were struggling over it as they were over everything else. The rich had the money but the poor had the people, and the weapons were pretty evenly distributed, especially the new viral vectors that could kill everyone on a continent. Yes, the stakes were high, and the situation existed in the most fragile of balances, the poor surging up out of the south and pressing the northern barriers of law and money and pure military force. Gun barrels in their faces, in essence. But now there were so many faces; a human wave attack might explode at any instant, it seemed, just from the expansive pressure of sheer numbers — attackers shoved over the barricades by the press of babies in the rear, raging for their chance at immortality.

At the midmorning break, with nothing more accomplished, Frank rose from his seat. He had heard little of the wrangle, but he had been thinking, and his lectern's sketchpad was marked up with a rough schematic. Money, people, land, guns. Old equations, old trade-offs. But it wasn't originality he was after: it was something that would work.

Nothing would happen at the long table itself, that was certain. Someone had to cut the knot. He got up and wandered over to the Indian and Chinese delegation, a group of about ten conferring in a camera-free side room. After the usual exchange of pleasantries he invited the two leaders, Hanavada and Sung, to take a walk on the observation bridge. After a glance at each other, and quick conversations in Mandarin and Hindi with their aides, they agreed.

So the three delegates walked out of the rooms and down the corridors to the bridge, a rigid walktube which began at the wall of their mesa and arched out over the valley and into the side of an even taller mesa to the south. The bridge's height gave it an airy flying magnificence, and there were quite a few people walking its four kilometers, or just standing midway and taking in the view of Burroughs.

"Look," Chalmers said to his two colleagues, "the expense of emigration is so great that you will never ease your population problems by moving them here. You know that. And you already have lots more reclaimable land in your own countries. So what you want from Mars isn't land but resources, or money. Mars is leverage to get your share of resources back home. You're lagging behind the North because of resources that were taken from you without payment during the colonial years, and you should have repayment for that now."

"I am afraid that in a very real sense the colonial period never ended," Hanavada said politely.

Chalmers nodded. "That's what transnational capitalism means: we're all colonies now. And there's tremendous pressure on us here, to alter the treaty so that most of the profits from local mining become the property of the transnationals. The developed nations are feeling that very strongly."

"This we know," Hanavada said, nodding.

"Okay. And now you've made the pitch for proportional emigration, which is just as logical as allotting profits proportional to investment. But neither of these proposals is in your best interest. The emigration would be a drop in the bucket to you, but the money wouldn't. Meanwhile the developed nations have a new population problem, so a chance at a larger share of emigration would be welcome. And they can spare the money, which would mostly go to transnationals anyway and become free-floating capital, outside any national control. So why shouldn't the developed nations give you more of it? It wouldn't really be coming out of their pocket anyway."

Sung nodded quickly, looking solemn. Perhaps they had foreseen this response, and had made their proposal to stimulate it, and were waiting for him to play his part. But that just made it easier. "Do you think your governments will agree to such a trade?" Sung asked.

"Yes," Chalmers said. "What is it but governments reassserting their power over the transnationals? Sharing the profits resembles in a way your old nationalization movements, only this time all countries would benefit. Internationalization, if you will."

"It will cut down on investments by the corporations," Hanavada noted.

"Which will please the Reds," Chalmers said. "Please most of the MarsFirst group, in fact."

"And your government?" Hanavada asked.

"I can guarantee it." Actually the administration would be a problem. But Frank would deal with them when the time came, they were a bunch of Chamber of Commerce kids these days, arrogant but stupid. Tell them it was this or a third world Mars, a Chinese Mars, a Hindu Chinese Mars, with little brown people and cows unmolested in the walk-tubes. They would come around. In fact they would hide behind his knees yelling for protection, Grandpa Chalmers please save me from the yellow horde.

He watched the Indian and the Chinese look at each other, in a completely scrutable consultation. "Hell," he said, "this is what you were hoping for, right?"

"Perhaps we should work on some figures," Hanavada said.

It took much of the next month to implement the compromise, as it entailed a whole set of corollary compromises to get the all voting delegations to accept it. Every nation's delegate had to get a cut to show the folks back home. And there was Washington to be convinced as well; in the end Frank had to go over the heads of the kids right to the President, who was only a bit older than them, but could see a deal when it was poking him in the sternum. So Frank was busy, meetings nearly sixteen hours a day in his old pattern, as familiar as the sunrise. In the end, mollifying transnat lobbyists like Andy Jahns was the hardest part – essentially impossible, as the deal was being made at their expense and they knew it. They put all the pressure they could on the northern governments and on their flags of convenience, and that was considerable, as evidenced by the President's scared irritability, and the defection of Singapore and Sofia from

461

the deal. But Frank convinced the President, even across all that space, even across the deep psychological barrier of the time lag. And he used the same arguments with every other northern government. If you give in to the transnationals, he would say, then they're the real government of the world. This is the chance to assert the interests of you and your population over those free-floating accumulations of capital which are very near to holding the ultimate power on earth! You need to get them on the leash somehow!

And it was the same at the UN, for every official there. "Who do you want to be the real world government? You or them?"

Still, it was a close thing. The pressures the transnats could bring to bear were awesome, it was impressive to watch. Subarashii and Armscor and Shellalco were each bigger than all but the ten largest countries or commonwealths, and they really put out the funds. Money equals power; power makes the law; and law makes government. So that the national governments in trying to restrain the transnats were like the Lilliputians trying to tie down Gulliver. They needed a great network of tiny lines, staked into place along every millimeter of the circumference. And as the giant heaved to free itself and start trampling about, they had to rush from side to side, throw new lines over the monster, hammer new little pin stakes into place. Rush around making quarter-hour pin-stake appointments, for sixteen hours a day. Mad Dutch boy juggling.

Andy Jahns, one of Frank's oldest corporate contacts, took him to dinner one night. He was angry with Chalmers, naturally, but tried to hide it, as the evening's business consisted of the offer of a bribe thinly disguised, accompanied by threats thinly veiled. Business as usual, in other words. He offered Chalmers a position as head of a foundation which was being set up by the Earth-to-Mars transport consortium – the old aerospace industries, with their old Pentagon stash still sloshing around in their pockets. This new foundation would assist the consortium to make policy, and advise the UN on Mars-related matters. The position was to begin after his tenure as Secretary for Mars was over, to avoid any appearance of conflict of interest.

"It sounds marvelous," Chalmers said. "I'm very interested indeed." And over the course of the dinner he convinced Jahns he was sincere. Not only about taking the position in the foundation, but in working for the consortium immediately. This was work indeed, but he was good at it; he could see the suspicion slowly leak out of Jahns as the evening wore on. The weakness of businessmen: the belief that money was the point of the game: they worked fourteen hour days in order to earn enough of it to buy cars with leather interiors, they thought it was a sensible recreation to play around with it in casinos – idiots, in short, but useful idiots. "I'll do what I can," Chalmers promised energetically, and outlined some strategies he would start to pursue at once. Talk to the Chinese about their need for land, get Congress back to the idea of a fair return on investments. Certainly. Make promises here and some of the pressure would subside; meanwhile the work could go on. There was no pleasure like double-crossing a crook.

So he went back to the conference table and carried on as before. The walk on the bridge, as it was now being called (others called it the Chalmers Shift), had broken the impasse. February 6th, 2057; Ls=144, M-15; a red-letter date in the history of diplomacy. Now it was a matter of giving everyone else a piece, and fixing the actual numbers. As this process ground along Chalmers talked with all the first hundred observers there, reassuring them and checking their opinions. Sax, it turned out, was upset with him, because he thought that if the transnats ceased investment his terraforming would have to slow considerably. He saw all the arriving business as heat. And yet Ann too was upset with him, because a new treaty based on the shift would allow both emigration and investment, and she and the Reds had been hoping for a treaty that would give Mars a kind of world park status. That kind of disconnection from reality made him crazy. "I've just saved you fifty million Chinese immigrants," he yelled at her, "and you bitch at me because I haven't managed to send everyone back home. You bitch because I didn't work a miracle and turn this rock into a holy shrine, right next door to a world that's beginning to look like Calcutta on a bad day. Ann, Ann, Ann. What would *you* have done? What would you have done except stalk around glaring at every single fucking thing people said, and convincing everyone that you're from Mars? Jesus Christ. Go out and play with your rocks and leave the politics to people who can think."

"Remember what thinking is, Frank," she said. Somehow he had made her smile for a second there, in the middle of his tirade. But she laid the same old wild glare on him before she left.

But Maya, now; Maya was pleased with him. He could feel her gaze on him when he talked in the public meetings. Millions of people watching, and he felt only that gaze. It made him angry. She was full of admiration for the bridge walk, and he told her only what she would be pleased to hear about the backstage compromises he was making in order to get it accepted. She began joining him every evening during the cocktail hour, approaching him when the first press of critics and supplicants had ebbed, standing by his side through the second and third waves, watching and easing things along with her laugh, and extricating him from time to time with reminders that they had to go out and eat. Then they would go out onto restaurant terraces under the stars, and eat and then sip coffee, looking over the orange tiles and roof gardens under one of the big mesa-topping tents, feeling the evening breeze just as if they were out in the open. The MarsFirst crowd had committed themselves to his plan; so he had most of the locals, and he had the home office, and those were the two most important single parties in the whole process, he judged, aside from the transnational leadership, which he could do little about. So it was only a matter of time before he would work the deal. As he would tell her, sometimes, late in the evenings when he had fallen a bit under her spell. Been calmed by her. "Between us we'll get it done," he would say as he looked up at the vivid stars in the sky, unable to meet her penetrating gaze.

And one night she kept returning to his side during the cocktail gathering. With all the others they watched the Terran news reports of the day's progress, and saw again how oddly distorted and flattened they appeared, like tiny players in an incomprehensible soap opera. And then they left together, and ate, and then went walking down the wide grassy boulevards, eventually coming to his room in the lower town. And she accompanied him inside. Without explanation or comment, in Maya's usual way. As if she always did this. It just happened, was happening. She was in his room, and then in his arms, hugging him. They lay on his bed and she kissed him. The shock of it was such that Frank felt completely removed from his body, his flesh like rubber. This was beginning to worry him when the sheer animal presence of her broke through the shock, body spoke to body and suddenly he could feel her again; sensation flooded back into him, and he responded to it with animal intensity. It had been a long time.

Afterward she walked around with a white sheet draped over her like a cape, getting a glass of water. "I like the way you work those people," she said, her back to him. She drank from the glass, looked over her shoulder with her old affectionate grin, with that full and open gaze of hers, a gaze that seemed so insightful, like lazed light shining right through him, that suddenly he felt not only naked, but exposed. He pulled the remaining sheet up over his hip, then felt that he had given himself away. Surely she would see, see the way the air turned to cold water in his lungs, the way his stomach knotted, the way his feet froze. He blinked,

465

returned her smile. He knew it was a wan and crooked smile; but feeling his face like a stiff mask over his real flesh, he took comfort. No one could accurately read emotions from facial expressions, that was all a lie, a bogus relationship as in palm reading or astrology. So he was safe.

But after that night she began spending a lot of time with him, both in public and private. She joined him at the receptions given every night by one or another of the national offices; she sat beside him at many of the group dinners; she sailed the hot sea of conversation with him afterward, as they watched the bad news from Terra, or sat in the close knot of the first hundred. And she went with him to his room at night, or even more disturbing, took him to hers.

And all without any sign of what she wanted from him. He could only conclude that she knew she did not have to speak of it. That just being with him was enough, that he would know what she wanted, and try his best to do it without her ever having to say a word. That she would get what she wanted. For of course it was impossible that she was doing it all without cause. That was the nature of power; when you had it no one was ever again simply a friend, simply a lover. Inevitably they all wanted things you could give them – if nothing else, the prestige of friendship with the powerful. That was prestige that Maya did not need, but she knew what she wanted. And wasn't he doing it, after all? Infuriating a large part of his power base, to forge a treaty that would please no one but a handful of locals? Yes, she was getting what she wanted. And all without a word, or without a direct word. Nothing but praise and affection.

So that as he talked in the endless caucus conferences, carefully hammering out the wording of each clause of the new treaty, playing James Madison to this strange simulacrum of a constitutional convention, Spencer and Samantha and Maya would wander around helping him, and Maya would watch him with the most fractional smile, which revealed to him alone her approval, her pride in him. And then, energized by the day's work, he would roam the evening reception, and she would laugh at him and stand at his side and chatter with all the rest, a kind of consort. Hell, a consort! And at night shower him with kisses, until it was impossible to imagine that she did not like him.

Which was intolerable. That it should be so easy to deceive even the people who knew you best . . . that she should be so stupid . . . it was shocking to realize these things more strongly than ever before. How hidden the true self is, he thought, under the phenomenological mask. In reality they were all actors *all the time*, playing their video parts, and there was no chance of contact with the true selves inside others, not anymore: over the long years their parts had hardened into shells and the selves inside had atrophied, or wandered off and gotten lost. And now they were all hollow.

Or perhaps it was just him. Because she seemed so real! Her laughter, her white hair, her passion, my God: her sweaty skin and the ribs underneath it, ribs that slid back and forth under his fingers like the slats of a fence, ribs that clamped down on the paroxysms of orgasm. A true self, didn't it have to be so? Didn't it? He could hardly believe otherwise. A true self.

But sadly deceived. One morning he awoke from a dream of John. It was from their time together on the space station, when they had been young. Except in the dream they had been old, and John had not died and yet he had; he spoke as a ghost, aware that he had died and that Frank had killed him, yet aware also of everything that had happened since, and free of all anger or blame. It was just something that had happened, like the time John had gotten the first landing assignment, or had taken Maya away on the *Ares*. A lot of things had happened between them one way and another, but they were still friends, still brothers. They could talk, they understood each other. Feeling the horror of that Frank had groaned through the dream, and tried to fold in on himself, and awakened. It was hot, his skin was sweaty.

Maya was sitting up, her hair wild, her breasts swinging loosely between her arms. "What's wrong!" she was saying. "What's wrong!"

"Nothing!" he cried, and got up and padded to the bathroom. But she came after him, put her hands on him. "Frank, what was it?"

"Nothing," he shouted, involuntarily jerking out of her grip. "Can't you leave me alone!"

"Of course," she said, hurt. A flush of anger: "Of course I can." And she walked out of the bathroom.

"Of course you can!" he shouted after her, suddenly furious at her stupidity, to be so ignorant of him, so vulnerable to him, when it was all an act anyway. "Now that you've got what you want from me!"

"What does that mean?" she said, reappearing instantly in the bathroom doorway, a sheet around her.

"You know what I mean," he said bitterly. "You've got what you wanted from the treaty, haven't you. And you never would have, without me."

She stood there, hands on her hips, watching him. The sheet was loose around her hips and she looked like the French figure of Liberty, very beautiful and very dangerous, her mouth a tight line. She shook her head in disgust and walked away. "You don't have the faintest idea, do you?" she said.

He followed her. "What do you mean?"

She threw the sheet away and stepped violently into her underwear, yanked it up over her bottom. As she dressed she hurled short sentences at him. "You don't know anything about what other people think. You don't even know what you think. What do *you* want out of the treaty? You, Frank Chalmers? You don't know. It's only what I want, what Sax wants, what Helmut wants. What any of them want. You yourself have no opinion. Whatever is easiest to manage. Whatever leaves you in control at the end.

"And as for *feelings*!" She was dressed, standing at the

468

door. She stopped to glare at him, a look like a lightning strike: he had been standing there too stunned to move and so now he stood there naked before her, exposed to the full blast of her scorn. "You don't have any feelings, do you. I've tried, believe me, but you just—" She shuddered, apparently unable to think of words vile enough to describe him. Hollow, he wanted to say. Empty. An act. And yet—

She walked out.

So when they signed the new treaty, Maya was not at his side; not even in Burroughs. Which was a relief in many ways, really. And yet he could not help but feel empty, and cold in the chest; and certainly the others of the first hundred (at least) knew something had happened between them (again), which was infuriating, or so he told himself.

They signed the thing in the same conference room they had hammered it out in, with Helmut doing the honors with a big smile and each delegate coming up in turn, in penguin suit or black evening gown, to say a few words for the cameras and then put their hand to "the document", a gesture that only Frank seemed to see as bizarrely archaic, like scratching a petroglyph. Ridiculous. When it was his turn he went up and said something about striking a balance, which was exactly it; he had arranged the competing interests to strike together at angles that matched their momentum exactly, arranging a traffic accident so that all the vehicles would collide into a single solidified mass. The result was something not all that dissimilar to the previous version of the treaty, with both emigration and investment, the two main threats to the status quo (if there was such a thing on Mars), mostly blocked, and (this was the clever part) *blocked by each other*. It was a good piece of work, and he signed with a flourish, "for the United States of America," he announced emphatically, glaring around the world intently. That would play well on vid.

So he strode through the subsequent parade with the cold

469

satisfaction of work well done. The grass-floored tents and walktubes of the city were crowded with thousands of spectators, and the parade wound through them, wandering down the big canalside tent with diversions up into the mesas, coming back down and crossing every canal bridge to cheers, and proceeding up to Princess Park for a great street party. The weather people had set for cool and crisp, with brisk downslope winds. Kites duelled under the tent roofs like raptors, their colors bright against the dark pink afternoon sky.

Frank found the party in the park unsettling, there were too many people watching him, too many who wanted to approach him and talk. That was fame: you talked to groups. So he turned around and walked back up the canalside tent.

Two parallel rows of white pillars ran down the sides of the canal; each pillar was a Bareiss column, semicircular at top and bottom but with the hemispheres rotated 180° to each other. This simple maneuver created pillars that looked completely different depending on where you were when you looked at them, and the two rows of these pillars had a strange tumbledown look, as if they were already ruins, although the smoothness and whiteness of their diamond-coated salt belied that; they stood off the grass as white as sugar cubes, and gleamed as if wet.

Frank walked between the rows, touching each pillar in turn. Above them on each side the valley slopes rose to the window-walled bluffs of mesas. Massed greenery shone behind these cliffs of untinted glass, so that it looked as if the city were rimmed by enormous terrariums. A really elegant ant farm. The part of the valley slope under tenting was dotted with trees and tile roofs, and cut by broad grassy boulevards. The uncovered part was still a red rocky plain. A great number of buildings were just being finished, or still under construction; there were cranes everywhere rearing up toward the tent roofs, a kind of odd colorful skeletal statuary. Also scores of scaffolded buildings, so that Helmut had said the tented hillsides reminded him of Switzerland, no surprise since most of the construction was being done by Swiss. "They scaffold a house to replace a window box."

Sax Russell was standing at the foot of one of these scaffolded buildings, looking up at it critically. Frank turned and walked up a tube to him, said hello.

"There's twice as much support as they need," Sax said. "Maybe more."

"The Swiss like that."

Sax nodded. They stared at the building.

"Well?" Frank said. "What do you think?"

"The treaty? It will reduce support for terraforming," Sax said. "People are more inclined to invest than to give."

Frank scowled. "Not all investment is good for terraforming, Sax, you have to remember that. A lot of that money is spent on other things entirely."

"But terraforming is a way to reduce overheads, you see. A certain percentage of the total investment will always be devoted to it. So I want the total as high as possible."

"Real benefits can only be calculated using real costs," Frank said. "All the real costs. Terran economics never bothered to do that, but you're a scientist and you should. You have to judge the environmental damage from higher population and activity, as well as the benefits to terraforming that go along with it. Better to up the investment devoted to pure terraforming, rather than compromising and taking a percentage of a total that in some ways is working against you."

Sax twitched. "It's funny to hear you speak against compromise after the last four months, Frank. Anyway, I say it's better to up both the total and the percentage. The environmental costs are negligible. Managed right they can mostly be turned to benefits. An economy can be measured in terrawatts or kilocalories, like John used to say. And that's energy. And we can use energy here in any form, even a lot

471

of bodies. Bodies are just more work, very versatile, very energetic."

"Real costs, Sax. All of of them. You're still trying to play at economics, but it isn't like physics, it's like politics. Think what will happen when millions of displaced Terran emigrants arrive here, with all their viruses, biological and psychic. Maybe they'll all join Arkady or Ann, ever thought of that? Epidemics, running through the mob's body and mind – they could crash your whole system! Look, hasn't the Acheron group been trying to teach you biology? You should pay attention! This isn't mechanics, Sax. It's ecology. And it's a fragile, managed ecology, so it has to *be* managed."

"Maybe," Sax said. It was one of John's mannerisms, that phrase. Frank missed what Sax was saying for a minute, then his attention was captured again:

". . . this treaty isn't going to make all that much difference anyway. The transnationals that want to invest will find a way. They'll make a new flag of convenience and it'll look like a country staking its claim here, exactly according to the treaty's quotas. But behind it will be transnational money. There'll be all kinds of that stuff happening, Frank. You know how it is. Politics, right? Economics, right?"

"Maybe," Frank said harshly, upset. He walked away.

Later he found himself in an upper valley district, still being built. The scaffolding was extreme, as Sax had said, especially for Martian g. Some of it looked like it would be hard to bring down. He turned and looked out over the valley. The city was nicely placed, that was indisputable. The two sides of the valley meant there was going to be a lot visible from any point. Everywhere in town would have a view.

Suddenly his wristpad beeped, and he answered. It was Ann, staring up at him. "What do you want?" he snapped. "I suppose you think I sold you out too. Let in the hordes to overrun your playground."

She grimaced. "No. You did the best that could be done,

472

given the situation. That's what I wanted to say." She clicked off and his pad went blank.

"Great," he said aloud. "I've got everyone on two worlds mad at me except *Ann Clayborne.*" He laughed bitterly, took off walking.

Back down to the canal and the rows of Bareiss columns. Lot's wives. There were knots of celebrants scattered over the canalside sward, and in the late afternoon light their shadows were long. The sight took on a somehow ominous cast, and Frank turned, uncertain where to go. He didn't like the aftermath of things. Everything seemed finished, done, revealed as pointless. It was always this way.

A group of Terrans were standing under one of the more magnificent new office blocks in the Niederdorf tent. There was Andy Jahns among them.

If Ann was pleased, Andy would be furious. Frank walked up to him, wanting to witness that.

Andy saw him, and his face went still for a moment. "Frank Chalmers," he said. "What brings you down here?"

His tone was amiable, but his eyes were unamused, even cold. Yes, he was angry. Frank, feeling better every second, said, "I'm just walking around, Andy, getting the blood flowing again. What about you?"

After the briefest of hesitations Jahns said, "We're looking at office space."

He watched as Frank digested the implications of the statement. His smile took on an edge, became a genuine smile. He went on: "These are friends of mine from Ethiopia, from Addis Ababa. We're thinking of moving our home office there next year. And so—" his smile broadened, no doubt in response to the look on Frank's face, which Frank could feel hardening over the front of his skull— "we have a lot to discuss."

Al-Qahira is the name for Mars in Arabic and Malaysian and Indonesian. The latter two languages got it from the former; look at a globe and see how far the Arabs' religion spread. The whole middle of the world, from West Africa to the West Pacific. And most of that in a single century. Yes, it was an empire in its time; and like all empires, after death it had a long half-life.

The Arabs who live out of Arabia are called Mahjaris, and the Arabs who came to Mars, the Qahiran Mahjaris. When they arrived on Mars a good number of them began to wander Vastitas Borealis ("The Northern Badia") and the Great Escarpment. These wanderers were mostly Bedouin Arabs, and they traveled in caravans, in a deliberate recreation of a life that had disappeared on Earth. People who had lived in cities all their lives went to Mars and moved around in rovers and tents. The excuses for their ceaseless travel included the hunt for metals, areology, and trade; but it seemed clear that the important thing was the travel, the life itself.

Frank Chalmers joined old Zeyk Tuqan's caravan a month after the treaty was signed, in the northern autumn of M-15 (July 2057). For a long time he wandered with this caravan over the broken slopes of the Great Escarpment. He worked on his Arabic, and helped with their mining, and took meteorological observations. The caravan was composed of actual Bedouins from Awlad 'Ali, the western coast of Egypt. They had lived north of the area that the Egyptian government had named the New Valley Project, after a search for oil discovered a water aquifer holding an amount equal to a thousand years of the Nile's flow. Even before the discovery of the gerontological treatment, the Egyptian population problem had been severe; with 96 percent of the country

474

desert, and 99 percent of the population in the Nile Valley, it was inevitable that the hordes relocated in the New Valley Project would overwhelm the Bedouins and their entirely distinct culture. The Bedouins wouldn't even call themselves Egyptians, and despised the Nile Egyptians as spineless and immoral; but that did not keep the Egyptians from crowding north from the New Valley Project into Awlad 'Ali. Bedouins in the other Arab countries had taken the side of these overwhelmed outposts of their culture, and when the Arab commonwealth started a Mars program, and bought space on the continuous Earth-to-Mars shuttle fleet, they asked Egypt to give preference to their western Bedouins. The Egyptian government had been only too happy to oblige, and clear the region of its troublesome minority. So here they were, Bedouins on Mars, wandering the world-wrapping northern desert.

The weather observations piqued Frank's interest in climatology like none of the scientists' talk ever had. The weather on the Escarpment was often violent, with katabatic winds rushing downslope and colliding with the Syrtis trade winds to create tall fast red tornadoes, or onslaughts of gritty hail. Currently the atmosphere was at around 130 millibars in the summer, in a mix about 80 percent carbon dioxide and 10 percent oxygen, the remainder mostly argon. It wasn't clear yet whether they were going to be able to overwhelm the CO_2 with oxygen and the other gases, but Sax seemed satisfied with their progress so far. Certainly on a windy day on the escarpment it was clear that the air was thickening; it had some real heft to it, it threw heavy sand, and darkened the afternoons to the color of a scab. And in the hardest gales the gusts could knock you down quite easily. Frank timed one katabatic gust at six hundred kilometers an hour; luckily it was part of such a hard general blow that everyone was in the rovers when it happened.

*

The caravan was a mobile mining operation. Metals and ore-bearing minerals were being discovered in all kinds of locations and concentrations on Mars, but one thing the Arab prospectors were discovering was that a lot of sulfides were very lightly scattered on the Great Escarpment and the flats immediately below it. Most of these deposits were in concentrations and total quantities that would not justify the use of conventional mining methods, and so the Arabs were engaged in pioneering new extraction and processing procedures; they had built an array of mobile equipment, altering construction vehicles and exploration rovers to suit their purpose. The resulting machines were big, segmented, and distinctly insectile, looking like things out of a truck mechanic's nightmare. These creatures wandered the Great Escarpment in loose caravans, seeking the diffuse surface areas of stratiform copper deposits, preferably those with high amounts of tetrahedrite or chalcocite in them, so that they could recover silver as a byproduct of the copper. When they located one of these, they would stop for what they called the harvesting.

While they did this, prospector rovers would range ahead along the Escarpment, on expeditions of a week or ten days, following the old flows and rifts. When Frank had arrived he had been welcomed by Zeyk, who told him to do whatever work he chose; so Frank commandeered one of the prospector rovers, and took it out on solo expeditions. He would spend a week out, puttering around on automatic search, reading the seismograph and the samplers and the weather instruments, doing an occasional boring, watching the skies.

All over both worlds, Bedouin settlements looked drab from the outside; when they abandoned tents, their neighborhoods took on a windowless thick-walled look, as if perpetually hunched over to protect themselves from the desert heat. Only when you got inside their homes did one see what was protected, the courtyards, the gardens, the fountains, the birds, the staircases, the mirrors, the arabesques.

The Great Escarpment was strange country, cut by north-south canyon systems, marred by old craters, overrun by lava flows, broken into hummocks and karsts and mesas and ridges; and all of them on a steep slope, so that on top of any rock or prominence one could see far down to the north. In his days of solitary travel, Frank let the prospector program make most of the decisions, and sat watching the land roll by: silent, stark, huge, torn like the dead past itself. Days would pass, and the shadows wheel. The winds swirled upslope in the mornings, and downslope in the late afternoons. Clouds stacked the sky, from low fog balls bouncing over the rocks to high cirrus shavings, with the occasional thunderhead spanning the whole distance, solid masses of cloud twenty thousand meters high.

Occasionally he would turn on the TV and watch the Arabic news channel. Sometimes in the silence of the mornings he would talk back to the TV. There was a part of him that was outraged at the stupidity of the media, and of the events they packaged. The stupidity of the human race, playing out its spectacle. Except that the vast bulk of humanity never appeared on video, never once in their lives, not even in the crowd scenes when a camera swept the mob. Back there the Terran past still lived on in enormous regions, where village life was plodding on as it always had. Maybe that was wisdom, held to by old wives and shamans. Maybe. But it was hard to believe, because look what happened when they gathered in cities. Idiots on video, history in the making. "One can say that the lengthening of human life must, by definition, be a great boon." These things made him laugh. "Haven't you ever heard of secondary effects, you asshole!"

One night he watched a report on the fertilization of the Antarctic Ocean with iron dust, which was to act as a dietary supplement to phytoplankton, a population that was shrinking at an alarming rate for no obvious reason. The iron dust was dumped out of planes, it looked like they were fighting some kind of submarine fire; the project would cost ten billion dollars a year, and would have to be continued in perpetuity, but it had been calculated that a century's worth of fertilization would reduce the global concentration of carbon dioxide by fifteen percent plus or minus ten percent, and given the ongoing warming and subsequent threat to the coastal cities, not to mention the death of most of the world's coral reefs, the project had been judged worth it. "Ann's going to love this," Frank muttered. "Now they're terra-forming Earth."

Each vocal outburst he made untied a knot in his chest. He came to realize that no one was watching him, no one was listening. The tiny imaginary audience inside his head did not exist; no one watches our life movies. No friend or enemy would ever know what he did here, he could do whatever he liked and normalcy be damned. Apparently this was what he had been craving, what he had instinctively sought. He could go out and kick stones down the side of a karst for a whole afternoon; or cry; or write aphorisms in the sand; or scream abuse at the moons, careening across the southern sky. He could talk back to himself over meals, he could talk back to the TV, he could have conversations with his parents or his lost friends, with the President, or John, or Maya. He could dictate long rambling entries into his lectern: bits of a sociobiological history of the world, a journal, a philosophical treatise, a pornographic novel (he could masturbate), an analysis of the Arab culture and their history. He did all these things, and when he and his prospector rolled back to the caravans, he would feel better: emptier, calmer. More truly hollow. "Live," as the Japanese said helpfully, "as if you were already dead."

But the Japanese were aliens. And living with the Arabs sharpened his sense of how alien they were too. Oh, they were part of twenty-first century humanity, no doubt about it; they were sophisticated scientists and technicians, cocooned like everyone else in a protective shell of technology at every moment of their lives, and busy making and watching their own life movies. And yet they prayed three to six times a day, bowing toward Earth when it was the morning or evening star. And the reason their techno-caravans gave them such great and obvious pleasure was because the caravans were an outward manifestation of this bending of the modern world to their ancient goals. "Man's work is to actualize God's will in history," Zeyk would say. "We can change the world in ways that help to actualize the divine pattern. It's always been our way: Islam says the desert does not remain desert, the mountain does not remain mountain. The world must be transformed into a semblance of the divine pattern, and that is what constitutes history in Islam. Al-Qahira gives us the same challenge as the old world, except in a purer form."

He would say these things to Frank as they sat around in his rover, in its tiny courtyard. These family rovers were transformed into private preserves, spaces that Frank was seldom invited into, and then only by Zeyk. Each time he visited he was surprised anew: the rover was nondescript from the exterior, big, with darkened windows, one of several parked in a bunch with walktubes between them. But then one ducked through a doorway and inside, and stepped into space filled with sunlight pouring down through skylights, illuminating couches and elaborate rugs, tiled floors, green-leafed plants, bowls of fruit, a window with the Martian view tinted and framed like a photo, low couches, silver coffee urns, computer consoles of inlaid teak and mahogany, running water in pools and fountains. A cool wet world, green and white, intimate and small. Looking around, Frank had the powerful sensation that rooms like this had existed for centuries, that the chamber would be instantly recognized for what it was by people living in the Empty Quarter in the tenth century, or across Asia in the twelfth.

479

Often Zeyk's invitations would come in the afternoon, when a group of men would convene in his rover for coffee and talk. Frank would sit in his spot near Zeyk, and sip his muddy coffee and listen to the Arabic with all the attention he could muster. It was a beautiful language, musical and intensely metaphoric, so that all their modern technical terminology resonated with desert imagery because of the root meanings of all the new words, which like most of their abstract terms had concrete physical origins. Arabic, like Greek, had been a scientific language early on, and this showed in many unexpected cognates with English, and in the organic and compact nature of the vocabulary.

The conversations ran all over, but they were guided by Zeyk and the other elders, who were deferred to by the younger men in a way Frank found incredible. Many times the conversation became an overt lesson for Frank on Bedouin ways, which allowed him to nod and ask questions, and occasionally to offer comments or criticism. "When you have a strong conservative streak in your society," Zeyk would say, "which detaches itself from the progressive streak, that's when you get the worst kinds of civil wars. As in the conflict in Colombia that they called La Violencia, for instance. A civil war that became a complete breakdown of the state, a chaos that no one could understand, much less control."

"Or like Beirut," said Frank innocently.

"No, no." Zeyk smiled. "Beirut was much more complex than that. It was not only civil war, but also had a number of exterior wars impinging on it. It was not a matter of social or religious conservatives detaching from the normal progress of culture, as in Colombia or the Spanish Civil War."

"Spoken like a true progressive."

"All Qahiran Mahjaris are progressive by definition, or we would not be here. But Islam has avoided civil war by remaining a whole: we have a coherent culture, so that the Arabs here are still devout. This is understood even by the most conservative elements back home. We will never have civil war, because we are united by our faith."

Frank let his expression alone speak the fact of the Shiite heresy, among many other Islamic "civil wars". Zeyk understood the expression, but ignored it and forged on: "We all move together through history, one loose caravan. You could say that we here on Al-Qahira are like one of our prospecting rovers. And you know what a pleasure it is to be in one of those."

"So . . ." Frank thought hard about how to word his question; his inexperience with Arabic would only give him a certain amount of leeway before they got offended. "Is there really the idea of social progress in Islam?"

"Oh, certainly!" Several of them had replied in the affirmative, and were nodding still. Zeyk said, "Don't you think so?"

"Well . . ." Frank let it pass. There still was not a single Arab democracy. It was a hierarchical culture with a premium put on honor and freedom; and for the many who were low down in the hierarchy, honor and freedom were only achievable by deference. Which reinforced the system and held it static. But what could he say?

"The destruction of Beirut was a disaster for progressive Arab culture," another man said. "It was the city where intellectuals and artists and radicals went when they were attacked by their local governments. The national governments all hated the pan-Arab ideal, but the fact is we speak one language across these several countries, and language is a powerful unifier of culture. Along with Islam it makes us one, really, despite the political borders. Beirut was always the place to affirm that position, and when the Israelis destroyed it, that affirmation became more difficult. The destruction was calculated to splinter us, and it did. So here we begin the work again."

And that was their social progress.

*

481

The stratiform copper deposit that they had been raking up ran dry and it was time for another *ráhla*, the movement of the *hejra* to the next site. They traveled for two days, and arrived at another stratiform deposit that Frank had found. Frank went out again on another prospecting trip.

For days he sat in the driver's seat, feet on the dash, watching the land roll by. They were in a region of *thulleya* or little ribs, parallel ridges running downslope. He never turned on the TV anymore; there was a lot to think about. "The Arabs don't believe in original sin," he wrote in his lectern. "They believe that man is innocent, and death natural. That we do not need a saviour. There is no heaven or hell, but only reward and punishment, which take the form of this life itself and how it is lived. It is a humanist correction of Judaism and Christianity, in that sense. Although in another sense they have always refused to take responsibility for their destiny; it's always Allah's will. I don't understand that contradiction. But now they are here. And the Mahjaris have always been an intimate part of Arab culture, often its leading edge; Arabic poetry was revived in the twentieth century by poets who actually lived in New York or Latin America. Perhaps it will be the same here. It is surprising to find how much their vision of history corresponds to what Boone believed; I don't think either understood that at all. Very few people ever bother to find out what other people really think. They are willing to accept whatever they are told about anyone sufficiently distant."

He came on a find of porphyry copper, unusually dense, and with high concentrations of silver in it as well. That would be welcome. Copper and silver were both only somewhat scarce metals on earth, but silver was used in massive quantities in a great number of industries, and they were running low on easy sources of it. And here was more of it, right on the surface, in good concentrations; not as much as in Silver Mountain on the Elysium massif, of course, but the

Arabs would not care. Harvest it, and then they would get to move again.

He moved on himself. Days passed, the shadows wheeled. The wind went downslope, upslope, downslope, upslope. Clouds formed and storms broke, and sometimes the sky was spangled with icebows and sundogs and dust devils made of hail, sparkling like mica in the pink sunlight. Sometimes he would see one of the aerobraking continuous shuttles, like a blazing meteor running steadily across the sky. One clear morning he saw Elysium Montes bulking over the horizon like a black Himalaya: the view bent a thousand kilometers over the horizon by an inversion layer in the atmosphere. He stopped turning on the lectern as he had the TV. Nothing but the world and him. Winds caught at the sand, and tossed clouds of it against the rover. Khála, the empty land.

But then dreams began to plague him, dreams that were memories, intense and full and accurate, as if he were reliving his past while he slept. One night he dreamed of the day he had found out for sure that he would lead the American half of the first Martian colony. He had driven from Washington out to the Shenandoah Valley, feeling very odd. He walked for a long time in the great Eastern hardwood forest. He came on the limestone caves at Luray, now a tourist attraction, and on a whim he took the tour. Every stalactite and stalagmite was lit by lurid colored lights. Some had had mallets attached to them, and an organist could play them like the plates of a glockenspiel; the well-tempered cavern! He had to walk out into the peripheral blackness and stuff his sleeve in his mouth so the other tourists wouldn't hear him laugh.

Then he parked in a scenic overlook and walked off into the forest, and sat down between the roots of a big tree. No one around, a warm fall night, the earth dark, and furry with trees. Cicadas cycling through their alien hum, crickets creaking their last mournful creaks, sensing the frost that

483

would kill them. He felt so *odd* . . . could he really leave this world behind? Sitting there on the earth he had wished he could slide down a crack like a changeling and re-emerge something else, something better, something mighty, noble, long-lived — something like a tree. But nothing happened, of course; he lay on the ground, cut off from it already. A Martian already.

And he woke, and was disturbed all the rest of that day.

And then, even worse, he dreamed of John. He dreamed of the night he had sat in Washington and watched John on TV, stepping out onto Mars for the first time, closely followed by the other three. Frank left the official celebration at NASA and walked the streets, a hot DC night, summer of 2020. It had been part of his plan for John to make the first landing, he had given it to him as one sacrifices a queen in chess, because that first crew would be fried by the voyage's radiation, and according to the regs grounded for good on their return. And then the field would be cleared for the next trip out, for the colonists who would stay for good. That was the real game; and that was the one Frank planned to lead.

Still, on that historic night he found himself in a foul mood. He went back to his apartment near Dupont Circle and then went out and lost his FBI tag and slipped into a dark bar and sat there watching the TV over the bartenders' heads, drinking bourbon like his father, with Martian light pouring out of the TV and reddening the whole dark room. And as he got drunk and listened to John's inane talk his mood got worse and worse. It was hard to focus on his plan. He drank hard. The bar was noisy, the crowd inattentive; not that the landing hadn't been noticed, but here it was just another entertainment, on a par with the Bullets game that one bartender kept cutting to. Then blip, back to the scene on Chryse Planitia. The man next to him swore at the switch. "Basketball's gonna be a hell of a game on Mars," Frank said in the Florida accent he had long ago eradicated.

"Have to move the hoop up, or they be breaking their heads."

"Sure, but think of the jumps. Twenty foot dunks, easy."

"Yeah even you white boys'll jump high there, or so you say. But you better leave the basket alone, or you got the same trouble you got here."

Frank laughed. But outside it was hot, a muggy DC summer night, and he walked home in a plummeting foul mood, blacker and blacker with every step; and coming upon one of Dupont's beggars, he pulled out a ten-dollar bill and threw it at the man, and as the bum reached for it Frank shoved him away shouting "Fuck you! Get a job!" But then people came up out of the Metro and he hurried off, shocked and furious. Beggars slumped in the doorways. There were people on Mars and there were beggars in the streets of the nation's capital, and all the lawyers walked by them every day, their freedom-and-justice talk no more than a cover for their greed. "We're gonna do it *different* on Mars," Frank said viciously, and all of a sudden he wanted to be there immediately, no careful years of waiting, of campaigning — "Get a fucking *job!*" he shouted at another homeless man. Then on to his apartment building, with its bored security team behind the foyer desk, people wasting their whole lives sitting there doing nothing. Upstairs his hands shook so hard that he couldn't at first get his door open; and once inside he stood frozen, horrified at the sight of all the bland executive's furniture, all of it a theater set, built to impress infrequent visitors, really just NASA and the FBI. None of it his. *Nothing his.* Nothing but a plan.

And then he woke up, alone, in a rover on the Great Escarpment.

Eventually he returned from this horrid expedition of dreams. Back in the caravan he found it hard to talk. He was invited to Zeyk's for coffee, and he swallowed a tablet of an opiate complex to relax himself in the company of men. In

485

Zeyk's rover he sat in his spot, and waited for Zeyk to pass around little cups of clove-dosed coffee. Unsi Al-Khal sat on his left, speaking at length about the Islam vision of history, and how it had begun in the Jahili or pre-Islam period. Al-Khal had never been friendly, and when Frank tried to pass him the cup that came his way in a standard gesture of politeness, Al-Khal curtly insisted that the honor was Frank's, that Al-Khal would not be prevailed upon to usurp it. Typical insult by over-politeness, the hierarchy again: one could not do favors for one higher in the system, favors only went downward. Alpha males, pecking orders; really they might as well have been back on the savannah (or in Washington), it was nothing more than primate dominance tactics again.

Frank ground his teeth, and when Al-Khal began pontificating again he said, "What about your women?"

They were taken aback, and Al-Khal shrugged. "In Islam men and women have different roles. Just as in the West. It is biological in origin."

Frank shook his head and felt the sensuous buzz of the tabs, the black weight of the past. The pressure on a permanent aquifer of disgust at the bottom of his thinking increased, and something gave, and suddenly he didn't care about anything and was sick of pretending he did. Sick of all pretense everywhere, the glutinous oil that allowed society to run on in its gnashing horrible way.

"Yes," he said, "but it's slavery, isn't it?"

The men around him stiffened, shocked by the word.

"Isn't it?" he said, helplessly feeling the words bubble up out of his throat. "Your wives and daughters are powerless, and that is slavery. You may keep them well, and they may be slaves with peculiar and intimate powers over their masters, but the master-slave relationship twists everything to it. So that all these relations are twisted, pressured to the bursting point."

Zeyk's nose was wrinkled. "This is not the lived

experience of it, I can assure you. You should listen to our poetry."

"But would your women assure me?"

"Yes," Zeyk said with perfect confidence.

"Maybe. But look, the most successful women among you are modest and deferent at all times, they are scrupulous in honoring the system. Those are the ones that aid their husbands and sons to rise in the system. So to succeed, they must work to enforce the same system that subjugates them. This is poisonous in its effects. And the cycle repeats itself, generation after generation. Supported by both masters and slaves."

"The use of the word *slaves*," Al-Khal said slowly, and paused, "is offensive, because it presumes judgement. Judgement of a culture you do not really know."

"True. I only tell you what it looks like from the outside. This can only be of interest to a progressive Moslem. Is this the divine pattern you are struggling to actualize in history? The laws are there to read, and to watch in action, and to me it looks like a form of slavery. And, you know, we fought wars to end slavery. And we excluded South Africa from the community of nations for arranging its laws so that the blacks could never live as well as the whites. But you do this all the time. If any men in the world were treated like you treat your women, the UN would ostracize that nation. But because it is a matter of women, the men in power look away. They say it is a cultural matter, a religious matter, not to be interfered with. Or it is not called slavery because it is only an exaggeration of how women are treated elsewhere."

"Or not even an exaggeration," Zeyk suggested. "A variation."

"No, it is an exaggeration. Western women choose much of what they do, they have their lives to live. Not so among you. But no human submits to being property, they hate it, and subvert it, and have what revenge they can against it.

That's how humans are. And in this case it is your mother, your wife, your sisters, your daughters."

Now the men were glaring at him, still more shocked than offended; but Frank stared at his coffee cup, and went on regardless. "You must free your women."

"How do you suggest we do this?" Zeyk said, looking at him curiously.

"Change your laws! Educate them in the same schools in which you educate your sons. Make them the equal in rights to any Moslem of any kind anywhere. Remember, there is much in your laws that is not in the Koran, but was added in the time since Mohammed."

"Added by holy men," Al-Khal said angrily.

"Certainly. But we choose the ways we enforce our religious beliefs in the behavior of daily life. This is true of all cultures. And we can choose new ways. You must free your women."

"I do not like to be given a sermon by anyone but a mullah," Al-Khal said, mouth tight under his moustache. "Let those who are innocent of crime preach what is right."

Zeyk smiled cheerily. "This is what Selim el-Hayil used to say," he said.

And there was a deep, charged silence.

Frank blinked. Many of the men were smiling now, looking at Zeyk with appreciation. And it came to Frank in a flash that they all knew what had happened in Nicosia. Of course! Selim had died that night just hours after the assassination, poisoned by a strange combination of microbes; but they knew anyway.

And yet they had accepted him, taken him into their homes, into their private enclosures where they lived their private lives. They had tried to teach him what they believed.

"Perhaps we should make them as free as Russian women," Zeyk said with a laugh, extricating Frank from the moment. "Crazed by overwork, don't they say? Told they are equal, but actually not?"

Yussuf Hawi, a high-spirited young man, leered and cackled: "Bitches, I can tell you! But no more or less than any other woman! Isn't it true that in the home the power always goes to the strong? In my rover *I* am the slave, I can tell you that. I kiss snake's butt daily with my Aziza!"

The men roared with laughter at him. Zeyk took their cups, and poured another round of coffee. The men patched up the conversation as best they could; they covered for Frank's gross assault, either because it was so far beyond the pale that it only indicated ignorance, or because they wanted to acknowledge and support Zeyk's sponsorship of him. But only about half of them looked at Frank anymore.

He withdrew and listened again, profoundly angry at himself. It was a mistake to speak one's mind at any time, unless it perfectly matched your political purpose; and it never did. Best to strip all statements of real content, this was a basic law of diplomacy. Out on the Escarpment he had forgotten that.

Disturbed, he went out in a prospector again. The dreams became less frequent. When he came back in, he did not take any drugs. He sat silently in the coffee circles, or spoke about minerals and groundwater, or the comfort of the newly-modified prospecting rovers. The men regarded him cautiously, and only included him in the conversation again because of Zeyk's friendliness, which never flagged – except for that one moment, when he had most effectively reminded Frank of one of the basic facts of the situation.

One night Zeyk invited him over for a dinner with Zeyk and his wife Nazik only. Nazik wore a long white dress cut in the traditional Bedouin style, with a blue waist band and bare-headed, her thick black hair drawn back into a flat comb and then left to fall down her back. Frank had read enough to know that this was all wrong; among the Bedouin of the Awlad 'Ali, women wore black dresses and red sashes, to indicate their impurity, sexuality, and moral inferiority; and they kept their heads covered, and used the veil in an

489

elaborate hierarchical code of modesty. All in deference to male power; so that Nazik's clothes would be deeply shocking to her mother and grandmothers, even if she was, as now, wearing them before an outsider who didn't really matter. But if he knew enough to understand, then it was a sign.

And then at one point, when they were all laughing, Nazik rose at Zeyk's request to get them dessert, and she said to Zeyk with a laugh, "Yes, master."

Zeyk scowled and said, "Go, slave," and took a swipe at her, and she snapped her teeth at him. They laughed at Frank's fierce blush, and saw that he understood: they were mocking him, and also breaking the Bedouin taboo against showing marital affection of any kind, to anyone. Nazik came over and put her fingertip on his shoulder, which shocked him further. "We are only joking with you, you know," she said. "We women heard about your declaration to the men, and we love you for it. You could have as many wives among us as an Ottoman sultan. Because there is some truth to what you said, too much." She nodded seriously, and pointed a finger at Zeyk, who wiped the grin from his face and nodded as well. Nazik went on: "But so much depends on the people within the laws, don't you find? The men in this caravan are good men, smart men. And the women are even smarter, and we have taken over entirely." Zeyk's eyebrows shot up, and Nazik laughed. "No, really, we have only taken our share. Seriously."

"But where are you, then?" Frank said. "I mean where are the caravan's women, during the day? What do you do?"

"We work," Nazik said simply. "Take a look, you'll see us."

"Doing all the kinds of work?"

"Oh yes. Perhaps not where you can see us much. There are still some — habits, customs. We are reclusive, separate, we have our own world — it is perhaps not good. We Bedu tend to group together, men and women. We have our traditions, you see, and they endure. But there is much that is changing here, changing fast. So that this is the next stage of the Islamic way. We are . . ." She searched for the word.

"Utopia," Zeyk suggested. "The Moslem utopia."

She waggled a hand doubtfully. "History," she said. "The *hadj* to utopia."

Zeyk laughed with pleasure. "But the *hadj* is the destination," he said. "That is what the mullahs always teach us. So we are already there, no?" And he and his wife smiled at each other, a private communication with a high density of information exchange, a smile which they shared, for a moment, with Frank. And their talk veered elsewhere.

In practical terms Al-Qahira was the pan-Arab dream come alive, as all the Arab nations had contributed money and people to the Mahjaris. The mix of Arab nationalities on Mars was complete, but in the individual caravans it separated out a bit. Still, they mixed; and whether they came from the oil-rich nations or the oil-poor ones didn't seem to matter. Here among the foreigners they were all cousins. Syrians and Iraqis, Egyptians and Saudis, Gulf Staters and Palestinians, Libyans and Bedouins. All cousins here.

Frank began to feel better. He slept deeply again, refreshed by the timeslip in every day, a little slack in the circadian rhythm, the body's own time off. Indeed all life in the caravan had an altered duration, as if the moment itself had dilated: he felt there was time to spare, that there was never a reason to hurry.

And the seasons rolled by. The sun set in almost the same spot every night, shifting ever so slowly; they lived entirely by the Martian calendar now, it was the only new year they noticed or celebrated: Ls=0, the start of northern spring in the year 16. Season after season, each six months long, and each passing in the absence of the old sharp sense of mortality: it was like living in the eternal now, in an endless round of works and days, in the continuous cycle of prayer to the oh-so-distant Mecca, in the ceaseless wandering over the land. In the always-cold. One morning they woke to find it had snowed in the night and the whole landscape was pure white. And mostly water ice. The whole caravan went crazy for the day, all of them, men and women, outside in walkers, giddy at the sight, kicking snow, making snowballs that did not cohere satisfactorily, trying to pile snowmen that likewise did not stick together. The snow was too cold.

Zeyk laughed hard at these efforts. "What an albedo," he said. "It's astonishing how much of what Sax does rebounds against him. Feedbacks naturally adjust toward homeostasis, don't you think? I wonder if Sax shouldn't have first made things so much colder that the whole atmosphere froze out onto the surface. How thick would it be, a centimeter? Then line up our harvesters pole to pole, and run them around the world like latitude lines, processing the carbon dioxide into good air and fertilizer. Ha, can't you see it?"

Frank shook his head. "Sax probably considered it, and rejected it for some reason we don't see."

"No doubt."

The snow sublimed away, the red land returned, they traveled on their way. Occasionally they passed nuclear reactors, standing like castles on the top of the Escarpment; not just Rickovers but giant Westinghouse breeders, with frost plumes like thunderheads. On Mangalavid they saw programs about a fusion prototype in Chasma Borealis.

Canyon after canyon. They knew the land in a way that even Ann didn't; every part of Mars interested her equally, so she could not have this focused knowledge of a single region, this way they had of reading it like a story, following its leads through the red rock to a patch of blackish sulfides, or the delicate cinnabar of mercury deposits. They were not so much students of the land as lovers of it; they wanted something from it. Ann, on the other hand, asked for nothing but answers. There were so many different kinds of desire.

Days passed, and then more seasons. When they ran into other Arab caravans they celebrated long into the night, with music and dance, coffee and hookahs and talk, in meeting tents covering an octagon of parked rovers. Their music was never recorded, but played with great facility on flutes and electric guitars, and mostly sung, in quarter-tones and wails so strange to Frank's ear that for a long time he couldn't tell if the singers were accomplished or not. The meals lasted hours, and afterwards they talked till dawn, and made a point of going out to watch the furnace blast of sunrise.

When they met with other nationalities, however, they were naturally more reserved. Once they passed a new Amex mining station manned mostly by Americans, perched on one of the rare big veins of mafic rock rich in platinoids, in Tantalus Fossae near Alba Patera. The mine itself was down on the long flat floor of the narrow rift canyon, but it was mostly robotic, and the crew lived up in a plush tent, on the rim overlooking the rift. The Arabs circled next to this tent, made a brief guarded visit inside, and retreated into their insectile rovers for the night. It would have been impossible for the Americans to learn a thing about them.

But that evening Frank went back over into the Amex tent by himself. The folks inside were from Florida, and their voices brought up memories in him like nets filled with coelacanths; Frank ignored all the little mental explosions, and asked question after question, concentrating on the black and Latino and redneck faces that answered him. He saw that this group was imitating an earlier form of community just like the Arabs did; this was a wildcat oil field crew, enduring harsh conditions and long hours for big paychecks, all saved for the return to civilization. It was worth it even if Mars sucked, which it did. "I mean even on the ice you can go outside, but here, fuck."

They didn't care who Frank was, and as he sat among them listening they told stories to each other that astonished him even though they were somehow deeply familiar. "There was twenty-two of us prospecting with this little mobile habitat with no rooms to it, and one night we got to partying and took all our clothes off, and all the women got in a circle on the floor with their heads in the middle, and the guys went in a circle around the outside, and there were twelve guys and ten gals so the two guys out kept the rotation going pretty fast, and we actually got all the way around the circle in the timeslip. We tried to all come at once at the end of the timeslip and it worked pretty good, once a few couples got going it was like a whirlpool and it sucked everyone down into it. Felt so *good*."

And then, after the laughter and the shouts of disbelief: "We was killing and freezing these hogs in Acidalia, and those humane killers are like shooting a giant arrow into their heads so we figured why not kill and freeze them both at once and see what happens. So we got them all handicapped, and bet on which ones would get the furthest, and we open the outer lock door and those pigs all dash out outside and *wham*, they all keeled over inside of fifty yards of the door, except for one little gal that got almost *two hundred yards*, and froze *standing upright*. I won a thousand dollars on that hog."

Frank grinned at their howls. He was back in America. He asked them what else they had done on Mars. Some had been building nuclear reactors up on top of Pavonis Mons, where the space elevator would touch down. Others had worked on the water pipe running up eastern Tharsis bulge from Noctis to Pavonis. The parent transnational for the elevator, Praxis, had a lot of interests at the bottom end, as they called it. "I worked on a Westinghouse on top of the Compton aquifer under Noctis, which is supposed to have as much water in it as the Mediterranean, and this reactor's entire job was going to be to power a bunch of humidifiers.

Fucking two hundred megawatts of *humidifier*, they're the same as the humidifier I had in my bedroom when I was a kid, except they take fifty kilowatts apiece! Gigantic Rockwell monsters with single molecule vaporizers and jet turbine engines that shoot the mist out of thousand meter stacks. Fucking unbelievable. A million liters a day of H and O added to the air."

Another of them had been building a new tent city in the Echus channel, below Overlook: "They've tapped an aquifer there and there's fountains all over town, statues in the fountains, waterfalls, canals, ponds, swimming pools, you name it, it's a little Venice up there. Great thermal retention too."

The conversation removed itself to the gym, which was well-stocked with machines designed to enable their users to stay Earth-ready. "He's buffed, look at that, must be short time." Almost everyone kept to a rigorous workout schedule, three hours a day minimum. "If you give up you're stuck here, right? And then what good is that savings account?"

"Eventually it'll be legal tender," another one of them said. "Where people go, the American dollar is sure to follow."

"You got it backwards, assbite."

"As we are the proof of."

Frank said, "I thought the treaty blocked the use of Terran money here?"

"The treaty's a fucking joke," said one doing lat pulls.

"Dead as Bessy the Long Distance Hog."

They stared at Frank, all of them in their twenties and thirties, a generation he had never talked to much; he didn't know how they had grown up, what had shaped them, what they might believe. The oh-so-familiar accents and faces might be deceptive, in fact probably were. "You think so?" he asked.

Some of them seemed more aware than the rest that he might be connected to the treaty, along with all his other

historical associations. But the man doing lat pulls was oblivious: "We're here on a deal that the treaty says is illegal,
man. And it's happening all over. Brazil, Georgia, the Gulf
States, all the countries that voted against the treaty are
letting the transnats in. It's a contest among the flags of
convenience as to how convenient they can be! And
UNOMA is flat on its back with its legs spread, saying,
More, more. Folks are landing by the thousands and most are
employed by transnats, they've got their government visas
and five year contracts, including rehab time to get you Earth
buffed, things like that."

"By the thousands?" Frank said.

"Oh yeah! By the tens of thousands!"

He hadn't looked at TV, he realized, for . . . For a long
time.

A man doing military presses spoke between lifts of the
whole stack of black weights. "It's gonna blow pretty soon
– A lot of people don't like it – Not just oldtimers like you
– A whole bunch of newtimers too – They're disappearing
in droves – Whole operations – whole towns sometimes –
Came on a mine in Syrtis – completely empty – Everything
useful gone – Completely stripped – Even stuff like inner
lock doors – Oxygen tanks – Toilets – Stuff that'd take hours
– to pull loose."

"Why did they do that?"

"Going native!" a bench presser exclaimed. "Won over
by your comrade Arkady Bogdanov!"

From flat on his back this man met Frank's gaze; a tall,
broad-shouldered black man with an aquiline nose. He said,
"They get up here and the company tries to look good, gyms
and good food and rec time and all, but what it comes down
to is them telling you everything you can do and can't do,
it's all scheduled, when you wake up, when you eat, when
you shit, it's like the Navy has taken over Club Med, you
know? And then here comes your bro Arkady, saying to us,
You're Amurricans, boys, you got to be free, this Mars is the

496

new frontier, and you should know some of us are treating it that way, we ain't no robot software, we're free men, making our own rules on our own world! And that's it, man!" The room crackled with laughter, everyone had stopped to listen: "That does the trick! Folks get up here and they see they're schedule software, they see they can't keep Earth-buffed without they spend their whole time in here sucking the air hose, and even then I spect it's impossible, they lied to us I'll bet. So the pay means nothing, really, we're all software and maybe stuck here for good. Slaves, man! Fucking slaves! And believe you me, that's pissing a lot of folk off. They're ready to strike back, I mean to tell you. And that's the folks who are disappearing. Gonna be a whole lot of them before it's all over."

Frank stared down at the man. "Why haven't you disappeared?"

The man laughed shortly and began pumping weights again.

"Security," someone else called from the Nautilus machine.

Military Press disagreed. "Security's lame – But you got to have – Somewhere to go. Soon as Arkady shows – Gone!"

"One time," Bench Press said, "I saw a vid of him where he talked about how folk of color are better suited for Mars than white folk, how we do better with the UV."

"Yeah! Yeah!" They were all laughing at that, both skeptical and amused at once.

"It's bullshit, but what the hell," Bench Press said. "Why not? Why not? Call it our world. Call it Nova Africa. Say no boss is gonna take it away from us this time." He was laughing again, as if everything he had said was no more than a funny idea. Or else a hilarious truth, a truth so delicious that just saying it made you laugh out loud.

And so very late that night Frank went back to the Arab rovers, and he continued on with them, but it wasn't the same. He had been yanked back into time, and now the long days in the prospector only made him itch. He watched TV; he made some calls. He had never resigned as Secretary; the office had been run in his absence by Assistant Secretary Slusinski, and he had done just enough by phone for them to cover for him, telling Washington that he was working, then that he was doing deep research, then that he was taking a working vacation, and that as one of the first hundred he needed to be out there wandering around. It wouldn't have lasted much longer, but when Frank called Washington directly the President was pleased, and in Burroughs the exhausted-looking Slusinski looked happy indeed. In fact the whole Burroughs office sounded pleased that he planned to come back, which surprised Frank quite a bit. When he had left Burroughs, disgusted at the treaty and depressed about Maya, he had been, he thought, a bastard of a boss. But here they had covered for him for almost two years, and seemed happy to hear he was coming back. People were strange. The aura of the first hundred, no doubt. As if that mattered.

So Frank returned from his final prospecting trip and sat that evening in Zeyk's rover, sipping his coffee, watching them talk, Zeyk and Al-Khan and Yussuf and the rest, and, wandering in and out of the room, Nazik and Aziza. People who had accepted him; people who in some sense understood him. By their code he had done the necessary things. He relaxed in the flow of Arabic, still and always awash with ambiguity: lily, river, forest, lark, jasmine, words that might refer to a waldo hand, a pipe, a kind of talus, robot parts; or perhaps just to lily, river, forest, lark, jasmine. A beautiful, beautiful language. The speech of the people who had taken him in, and let him rest. But he would have to leave.

They had arranged things so that if you spent half the year in Underhill you were assigned a permanent room of your own. Towns all over the planet were adopting similar systems, because people were moving around so much that no one felt at home anywhere, and this arrangement seemed to mitigate that. Certainly the first hundred, who were among the most mobile Martians of all, had started spending more time in Underhill than they had in the years before, and this was mostly a pleasure, to most of them. At any given time twenty or thirty would be around, and others came in and stayed for a while between jobs, and in the constant come and go they had a chance to carry on a more-or-less continuous conference on the state of things, with newcomers reporting what they had seen firsthand, and the rest arguing about what it meant.

Frank, however, did not spend the required twelve months a year in Underhill, and so he did not have a room there. He had moved the department's head offices to Burroughs back in 2050, and before joining the Arabs in '57 the only room he had kept was there in the offices.

Now it was '59 and he was back, in a room one floor down from his old one. Dropping his bag on the floor and looking around at the room, he cursed aloud. To have to be in Burroughs in person — as if one's physical presence made any difference these days! It was an absurd anachronism, but that's the way people were. Another vestige of the savannah. They lived like monkeys still, while their new god powers lay around them in the weeds.

Slusinski came in. Though his accent was pure New York, Frank had always called him Jeeves, because he looked like the actor in the BBC series. "We're like dwarves in a waldo," Frank said to him angrily. "One of those really big waldo excavators. We're inside it and supposed to be moving a mountain, and instead of using the waldo capabilities we're leaning out of a window and digging with teaspoons. And complimenting each other on the way we're taking advantage of the height."

"I see," Jeeves said carefully.

But there was nothing to be done about it. He was back in Burroughs, hurrying around, four meetings an hour, conferences that told him what he already knew, which was that UNOMA was now using the treaty for toilet paper. They were approving accounting systems which guaranteed that mining would never show any profits to distribute to the general assembly members, even after the elevator was working. They were handing out "necessary personnel" status to thousands of emigrants. They were ignoring the various local groups, ignoring MarsFirst. Most of this was done in the name of the elevator itself, which provided an endless string of excuses, thirty-five thousand kilometers of excuses, a hundred and twenty billion dollars of excuses. Which was not all that expensive, actually, compared to the military budgets of the past century – less than a year of the global military budget of those days, in fact, and most of the elevator funds had been needed in the first years of finding the asteroid and getting it into proper orbit, and setting up the cable factory. After that the factory ate the asteroid and spat out the cable, and that was that; they only had to wait for it to grow long enough, and nudge it down into position. A bargain, a real bargain!

And also a great excuse for breaking the treaty whenever it seemed expedient. "God damn it," Frank shouted at the end of a long day in the first week back. "Why has UNOMA caved like this?"

Jeeves and the rest of his staff took this as a rhetorical question and offered no theories. He had definitely been away too long; they were afraid of him now. He had to answer the question himself: "It's greed I guess, they're all getting paid off in one cosmeticized way or another."

At dinner that night, in a little café, he ran into Janet Blyleven and Ursula Kohl and Vlad Taneev. As they ate they watched the news from Earth on a bar TV. Really it had gotten to be almost too much to watch. Canada and Norway were joining the plan to enforce population growth slowdown. No one would say population control, of course, it was a forbidden phrase in politics, but that's what it was and it was turning into the tragedy of the commons all over again: if one country ignored the UN resolutions, then nearby countries were howling for fear of being overwhelmed – another monkey fear, but there it was. Meanwhile Australia, New Zealand, Scandinavia, Azania, the United States, Canada, and Switzerland had all proclaimed immigration illegal. While India was growing by eight percent a year. Famine would solve that, as it would in a lot of countries. The Four Horsemen were good at population control. Until then . . . the TV cut to an ad for a popular diet fat, which was indigestible and went right through the gut unchanged. "Eat all you want!"

Janet clicked off the TV. "Let's change the subject."

They sat around their table and stared at their plates. It turned out Vlad and Ursula had come from Acheron because there was an outbreak of resistant tuberculosis in Elysium. "The cordon sanitaire has fallen apart," Ursula said. "Some of the emigrant viruses will surely mutate, or combine with one of our tailored systems."

Earth again. It was impossible to avoid it. "Things are falling apart down there!" Janet said.

"It's been coming for years," Frank said harshly, his tongue loosened by the faces of his old friends. "Even before the treatment life expectancy in the rich countries was nearly double that in the poor. Think about that! But in the old days the poor were so poor they hardly knew what life expectancy was, the day itself was their whole concern. Now every corner shop has a TV and they can see what's happening – that they've got AIDS while the rich have the treatment. It's gone way beyond a difference in degree, I mean they die young and the rich live forever! So why should they hold back? They've got nothing to lose."

"And everything to gain," Vlad said. "They could live like us."

They huddled over cups of coffee. The room was dim. The pine furniture had a dark patina; stains, nicks, fines rubbed in by hand . . . It could have been one of those nights in that distant time when they were the only ones in the world, a few of them up later than the rest, talking. Except Frank blinked and looked around, and saw in his friends' faces the weariness, the white hair, the turtle faces of the old. Time had passed, they were scattered over the planet, running like he was, or hidden like Hiroko, or dead like John. John's absence suddenly seemed huge and gaping, a crater on whose rim they huddled glumly, trying to warm their hands. Frank shuddered.

Later Vlad and Ursula went to bed. Frank looked at Janet, feeling immobilized as he sometimes did at the end of a long day, incapable of ever moving again. "Where's Maya these days?" he asked, to keep Janet from retiring too. She and Maya had been good friends in the Hellas years.

"Oh, she's here in Burroughs," Janet said. "Didn't you know?"

"No."

"She's got Samantha's old rooms. She may be avoiding you."

"What?"

"She's pretty mad at you."

"Mad at me?"

"Sure." She regarded him across the dim, faintly humming room. "You must have known that."

While he was still considering how open to be with her, he said "No! Why should she be?"

"Oh Frank," she said. She leaned forward in her chair. "Quit acting like you've got a stick up your ass! We know

502

you, we were there, we saw it all happen!" And as he was recoiling she leaned back, and said calmly, "You must know that Maya loves you. She always has."

"Me?" he said weakly. "It's John she loved."

"Yeah, sure. But John was easy. He loved her back, and it was glamorous. It was too easy for Maya. She likes things hard. And that's you."

He shook his head. "I don't think so."

Janet laughed at him. "I know I'm right, she's told me as much! Ever since the treaty conference she's been angry at you, and she always talks when she's mad."

"But why is she angry?"

"Because you rejected her! Rejected her, after pursuing her for years and years, and she got used to that, she loved it. It was romantic, the way you persisted. She took it for granted, sure, but she loved you for it. And she liked how powerful you were. And now John is dead, and she could finally say yes to you, and you sent her packing. She was furious! And she stays mad a long time."

"This . . ." Frank struggled to collect himself. "It just doesn't match with my understanding of what's happened."

Janet stood up to go, and as she walked by him she patted him on the head. "Maybe you ought to talk to Maya about it then." She left.

For a long time he sat there, feeling stunned, examining the shiny grain of his chair arm. It was hard to think. Eventually he stopped trying and went to bed.

He slept poorly, and at the end of a long night he had another dream about John. They were in the long drafty upcurved chambers of the space station, spinning at Martian gravity, in their long stay of 2010, six weeks together up there, young and strong, John saying I feel like Superman, this gravity's great, I feel like Superman! Running laps around the big ring of the station hallway. Everything's going to change on Mars, Frank. Everything!

No. Each step was like the last jump of a triple jump. Boing, boing, boing, boing.

Yes! The whole question will be learning to run fast enough.

A perfect interference pattern of cloud-dots lay pasted over the western coast of Madagascar. The sun bronzing the ocean below.

Everything looks so fine from up here.

Get any closer and you begin to see too much, Frank murmured.

Or not enough.

It was cold, they argued over the temperature, John was from Minnesota and had slept as a boy with his window open. So Frank shivered, a down coverlet draped over his shoulders, his feet blocks of ice. They played chess and Frank won. John laughed. How stupid, he said.

What do you mean?

Games don't mean anything.

Are you sure? Sometimes life seems like a kind of game to me.

John shook his head. In games there are rules, but in life the rules keep changing. You could put your bishop out there to mate the other guy's king, and he could lean down and whisper in your bishop's ear, and suddenly it's playing for him, and moving like a rook. And you're fucked.

Frank nodded. He had taught these things to John.

A confusion of meals, chess, talk, the view of the rolling Earth. It felt like the only life they had ever lived. The voices from Houston were like AIs, their concerns absurd. The planet itself was so beautiful, so intricately patterned by its land and its clouds.

I never want to go down. I mean this is almost better than Mars'll be, don't you think?

No.

Huddled, shivering, listening to John talk of boyhood. Girls, sports, dreams of space. Frank responded with tales of

Washington, lessons from Machiavelli, until it occurred to him that John was formidable enough as it was. Friendship was just diplomacy by other means, after all. But later, after a vague blur . . . talking, halting, shivering, talking about his father, coming home drunk from the Jacksonville bars, Priscilla and her white blond hair, her fashion magazine face. How it meant nothing to him anymore, a marriage for the resumé, for looking normal to the shrinks without holding him down. And not his fault. Abandoned, after all. Betrayed.

That sounds bad. No wonder you think people are so fucked.

Frank waved at their big blue lamp. But they are. Waving by coincidence at the Horn of Africa. Think about what's happened down there.

That's history, Frank. We can do better than that.

Can we? Can we?

You just wait and see.

He woke up, his stomach knotted, his skin sweaty. He got up and took a shower; already he could remember no more than a single fragment of the dream: John, saying "Wait and see." But his stomach was like wood.

After breakfast he clicked his fork on the table, thinking. All that day he spent distracted, wandering as if still in a dream, wondering from time to time how one told the difference. Wasn't this life dreamlike in every significant respect? Everything overlit, bizarre, symbolic of something else?

That evening he went looking for Maya, feeling helpless, in the grip of a compulsion. The decision had been made the night before, when Janet said "she loves you, you know." And he turned a corner to the dining commons and there she was, her head thrown back in the middle of her pealing laugh, vividly Maya, her hair as white as it had once been black, her eyes fixed on her companion; a man, dark-haired, handsome, perhaps in his fifties, smiling at her. Maya put a hand to his upper arm, a characteristic gesture, one of her

505

usual intimacies, it meant nothing and in fact indicated that he was not her lover but rather someone she was in the process of enchanting; they could have met just minutes before, although the look on his face indicated he knew her better than that.

She turned and saw Frank, blinked with surprise. She looked back at the man and continued to speak, in Russian, her hand still on his arm.

Frank hesitated and almost turned and left. Silently he cursed himself; was he no more than a schoolboy, then? He walked by them and said hello, did not hear if they replied. All through the dinner she stayed glued to the man's side, not looking his way, not coming over. The man, pleasant-enough looking, was surprised at her attention, surprised but pleased. Clearly they would leave together, clearly they would spend the night together. That foreknowledge always made people pleasant. She would use people like that without a qualm, the bitch. Love . . . The more he thought about it the angrier he got. She had never loved anyone but herself. And yet . . . that look on her face when she first saw him; for a split second hadn't she been pleased, and then wanted him angry at her? And wasn't that a sign of hurt feelings, of a desire to hurt back, meaning a certain (incredibly child-ish) desire *for* him?

Well, the hell with her. He went back to his room and packed his bag, and took the subway to the train station, and got on a night train west, up Tharsis to Pavonis Mons.

In a few months' time, when the elevator was maneuvered into its remarkable orbit, Pavonis Mons was going to become the hub of Mars, superceding Burroughs as Burroughs had once superceded Underhill. And as the elevator's touchdown was not far off, signs of the area's coming predominance were already everywhere. Paralleling the train piste as it ascended the steep eastern slope of the volcano were two new roads and four thick pipelines, as well as an array of cables,

506

a line of microwave towers, and a continuous litter of stations, loading tracks, warehouses, and dumps. And then, on the last and steepest upcurve of the volcano's cone, there was a vast congregation of tents and industrial buildings, thicker and thicker until up on the broad rim they were everywhere, and between them immense fields of insolation capture sheets, and receivers for the energy microwaved down from the orbiting solar panels. Each tent along the way was a little town, stuffed with little apartment blocks; and each apartment block was stuffed with people, their laundry hanging from every window. The tents nearest the piste had very few trees in them, and looked like commercial districts; Frank caught quick glimpses of food stands, video rentals, open-front gyms, clothing stores, laundromats. Litter piled in the streets.

Then he was into the train station on the rim, and out of the train and into the spacious tent of the station. The south rim had a tremendous view over the great caldera, an immense, nearly circular hole, flawless except for a single giant scoop bursting out of the rim to the northeast. This scoop formed a great gap across the caldera from the station, the mark of a truly huge sideways explosion. But that was the only flaw in the design; otherwise the cliff was regular, and the floor of the caldera was almost perfectly round, almost perfectly flat. And sixty kilometers across and a full five thousand meters deep. Like the start of the mohole to end all moholes. The few signs of human presence on the caldera floor were on an ant's scale, almost invisible from the rim.

The equator ran right across the southern rim, and that was where they were going to secure the lower end of the elevator. The attachment point was obvious: a massive tan and white concrete blockhouse, located a few kilometers west of the big tent town around the train station. Running west along the rim beyond the blockhouse was a line of factories and earthmovers and cones of feedstock materials, all gleaming with photographic clarity in the clear dustless thin high air, under a sky that was a kind of plum black. There were a number of stars near the zenith that were visible by day.

The day after his arrival, the staff of the local department office took him out to the elevator base; apparently technicians were going to capture the leader line from the cable that afternoon. This turned out to be unspectacular, but it was a peculiar sight nevertheless. The end of the leader line was marked by a small guidance rocket, and this rocket's eastern-facing jets flared continuously, while the north and south jets added occasional spurts. The rocket thus descended slowly into the grasp of a gantry, looking like any other landing vehicle, except that there was a silver line extending up from it, a straight fine line that was only visible for a couple of thousand meters above the rocket. Looking at it Frank felt as if he were standing on a sea floor observing a fishing line dropped down among them from the plum sea surface – a fishing line tied to a bright colorful lure, in the process of snagging on a bottom wreck. His blood burned in his throat, and he had to look down and breathe deep. Very peculiar.

They toured the base complex. The gantry that had captured the leader line was located inside a big hole in the concrete block, a concrete crater with a thick ring of a rim. The walls of this concrete crater were studded by curved silver columns, which held magnetic coils that would fix the cable butt in a shock-cushioning collar. The cable would float well off the concrete floor of the chamber, suspended there by the pull of the outer half of the cable; an exquisitely balanced orbit, an object extending from a moonlet down into this room, thirty-seven thousand kilometers in all. And only ten meters across.

With the leader line secured, the cable itself could be guided down fairly easily; but not rapidly, as it had to drift down into its final orbit very gently indeed, in an asymptotic approach. "It's going to be like Zeno's paradox," Slusinski said.

So it was many days after that visit when the butt of the cable finally appeared in the sky, and hung there. Over the next few weeks it descended ever more slowly, always there in their sky. A very odd sight indeed; it gave Frank a touch of vertigo, and every time he saw it the image of standing on an ocean floor returned to him. They were looking up at a fishing line, a black thread hanging down from the plum sea surface.

Frank spent this time setting up the head Department of Mars offices in the town, which one day was christened Sheffield. The Burroughs staff protested the move, but he ignored them. He spent his time meeting with American executives and project managers, all at work on various aspects of the elevator or Sheffield, or the outlying Pavonis towns. Americans represented only a fraction of the workforce on hand, but Chalmers was kept busy nevertheless, because the overall project was so huge. And Americans appeared to be dominating the superconducting, and the software involved with the actual elevator cars, a coup that was worth billions and which many people gave Frank credit for, though it was in fact his AI and Slusinski who were responsible, along with Phyllis.

Many of the Americans lived out in a tent town east of Sheffield called Texas, sharing the space with internationals who liked the idea of Texas, or had just ended up there randomly. Frank met with as many of them as he could, so that by the time the cable touched down they would be organized and working with a coherent policy – or under his thumb, as some of them put it. But happy to be there, as long as it gave them any clout. They knew they were less powerful than the East Asian commonwealth, which was building the elevator car shells, and less powerful than the EEC, which had constructed the cable itself. And less powerful than Praxis, and Amex, and Armscor, and Subarashii.

*

Eventually the day came when the cable was going to touch down. A giant crowd gathered in Sheffield to see it; the train station concourse was jammed to well over capacity, as it had a good view along the rim to the base complex, popularly referred to as the Socket.

As the hours passed, the end of the black column drifted downward, moving more and more slowly as it approached its target. There it hung, not that much bigger than the leader line guiding it down; smaller in fact than the business end of an Energia rocket. It stood up into the sky perfectly vertically, but it was so thin and the foreshortening was so severe that it looked not much longer than a tall skyscraper. A very skinny tall skyscraper, walking on air. A black tree trunk, taller than the sky. "We ought to be right under it, down on the floor of the socket," one of his staff said. "There'd be headroom when it stops, right?"

"Magnetic field might scramble you a bit," Slusinski replied, never taking his gaze from the sky.

As it got closer they saw that the cable was knobbed with various protrusions, and filigreed with silver lines. The gap under it got smaller. Then the end of it disappeared into the base complex, and the seashell roar of the crowd in the concourse grew louder. People watched the TVs closely; cameras inside the socket showed the cable come to a slow halt, still ten meters above the concrete floor. After that came the tweezerlike movement of gantries, and the clamping of a physical collar around the cable, a few meters up from its end. Everything happened in dreamlike slow motion, and when it was done it looked like the round socket room had suddenly gained an ill-fitting black roof.

Over the loudspeaker system a woman's voice said, "The elevator is secured." There was a brief cheer. People moved away from the TVs and looked out the tent walls again. Now the object looked much less strange than it had when hanging out of the sky; now it was nothing more than the *reductio ad absurdum* of Martian architecture, a very slender, very tall black spire. A beanstalk. Peculiar, but not so unsettling. The crowd burst into a thousand conversations, and scattered.

And not long after that, the elevators were working. During the years when the cable was extruding from Clarke, robots had been spidering along it, constructing the power lines, safety cables, generators, superconducting pistes, maintenance stations, defense stations, position adjustment rockets, fuel tanks, and emergency shelters that marked the cable every few kilometers. This work had proceeded at the same pace as the cable construction itself, so that soon after touchdown the cars were running up and down, up and down, four hundred of them going in each direction, like parasites on a strand of hair. And a few months after that, you could take an elevator into orbit. And you could take another elevator down out of orbit, to the surface.

And down they came, transported from Earth by the fleet of continuous shuttles, those big spaceships that boomed around the Earth-Venus-Mars system, using the three planets and Luna as gravity handles, fielding madly accelerating ferry packets from Earth and Mars. Each of the thirteen operating ships held a thousand people, and they were full every trip out. So there was a continuous stream of people docking on Clarke, descending in elevator cars, and debarking in the socket. And then pouring into Sheffield's concourses, wild and unsteady and bug-eyed with gawking, as they were herded with some difficulty to the train station, and onto trains outbound. Most of these trains then emptied their loads into the Pavonis tent towns; robot crews were building the tents just fast enough to house the influx, and the completion of two new pipelines had secured the water supply on Pavonis, which was being pumped up from the Compton Aquifer beneath Noctis Labyrinthus. So the emigrants settled in.

And back in the socket, on the other side of the cable,

upbound elevator cars were being loaded with refined metals, platinum, gold, uranium, silver; and then the cars swung in and locked onto the piste, and up they rose again, accelerating slowly to their full speed of three hundred kilometers an hour. Five days later they arrived at the top of the cable, and decelerated into locks inside the ballast asteroid Clarke, now a much-tunneled chunk of carbonaceous chondrite, so filigreed with exterior buildings and interior chambers that it seemed more a spaceship or a city than Mars's third moon. It was a busy place: there was a continuous procession of incoming and outgoing ships, and crews perpetually in transit, as well as a large force of local traffic controllers, using some of the most powerful AIs in existence. Though most of the operations involving the cable were computer controlled and robotically accomplished, entire human professions were springing up to direct and oversee all these efforts.

And of course media coverage of all the new imagery was immediate and intense; and all in all, despite the decade of waiting, it seemed that on touchdown the elevator had sprung into being like Athena.

But there was trouble. Frank found that his staff was spending more and more time dealing with men and women from the tents, who had come in to Sheffield and right into their offices, new arrivals who were sometimes nervous, sometimes loud and angry, rattling on about crowded living conditions or insufficient police or bad food. One bulky red-faced man wearing a baseball cap shook a finger at them and said, "Private security companies come in from tents higher up and offer protection, but they're just gangs, it's just extortion! I can't even give you my name or our security might find out I came here! I mean I believe in the black economy as much as the next guy, but this is crazy! This isn't what we came here for."

Frank paced his office, seething. These kinds of allegations were clearly true, but difficult to verify without a security team of one's own, a big police force in fact. When the man left, he grilled his staff, but they could tell him nothing new, which made him even angrier. "You're paid to find these things out for me, that's your job! What are you doing sitting around in here all day watching Terran news!"

He cancelled a day's appointments, thirty-seven meetings in all. "Lazy incompetent bastards," he said loudly as he stalked out of the door. He went to the train station and caught a local downslope to have a look for himself.

The local train now stopped every kilometer of the descent, in small stainless steel locks that served as stations for the tent towns. He got out in one; signs in the lock identified it as El Paso. He walked through the open doors of the passage lock.

At least these tents had a view, there was no denying that. Down the great eastern slope of the volcano ran the train piste and the pipelines, and on either side of them tent after tent, like blisters. The clear fabric of the older ones upslope was already turning a bit purple. Ventilators hummed loudly from the physical plant next to the station, and from somewhere a hydrazine generator was adding its high hum. People were conversing in Spanish and English. Frank called his office and got them to ring the apartment of a man from El Paso who had dropped in to complain; the man answered, and Frank arranged to meet him at a cafe next to the station, then walked over and sat at an outer table. Men and women sat around tables eating and talking like anywhere else. Little electric cars hummed up and down the narrow streets, most piled high with boxes. The buildings near the station were three stories tall and appeared prefab, steel-reinforced concrete painted bright blue and white. There was a line of young trees in tubs running away from the station down the main thoroughfare. Small groups sat on the astroturf, or walked aimlessly from shop to shop, or hurried with shoulderbags and daypacks toward the station. All of them looked a bit disoriented or uncertain, as if they had no habits, or had not yet learned to walk properly.

The man showed up with a whole crowd of his neighbors, all in their twenties, too young to be on Mars or so it used to be said; perhaps the treatment could fix damage from radiation, allow them to reproduce accurately, who could say for sure till they tried? Laboratory animals, that's what they were. What they had always been.

It was strange to stand among them like some ancient patriarch, treated with a mixture of awe and condescension, like a grandpa. Irritably he told them to take him on a walk and show him around. They guided him down narrow streets away from the station and the taller buildings, between long rows of what turned out to be AG huts, designed for temporary shelter in the outlands: research outposts, or water stations, or refugee huts. Now lined up by the score. The slope of the volcano had been hastily graded, and a lot of the huts were on a two or three degree slope, so that they had to be careful in the kitchens, they said, and make sure to align their beds properly.

Frank asked them what they did. Stevedores in Sheffield, most replied; offloading the elevator cars and getting the stuff on trains. Robots were supposed to do it, but it was surprising how much labor remained in the process for human muscle. Heavy equipment operations, robot programmers, machine repairmen, waldo dwarves, construction workers. Most of them had rarely gotten out onto the surface; some of them never had. They had done similar kinds of work back home, or had been unemployed. This was their chance. Most wanted to return to Earth someday, but the gyms were crowded and expensive and time-consuming, and they were all losing their tone. They had southern accents that Frank hadn't heard since childhood; it was like hearing voices from a previous century, like listening to Elizabethans. Did people still talk that way? TV never revealed it. "Y'all been here so long you don't mind being indoors, but I can't stand it." *Ah caint stayun det.*

Frank glared into a kitchen. "What do you eat?" he demanded.

Fish, vegetables, rice, tofu. It all came in bulk packages. They had no complaints: they thought it was good. Americans, the most degraded palates in history. Somebody gimme a cheeseburger! No, what they minded was the confinement, the lack of privacy, the teleoperation, the crowding together. And the resulting problems: "All my stuff got stole the day after I got here." "Me too." "Me too." Theft, assault, extortion. The criminals all came from other tent towns, they said. Russians, they said. White folks with strange talk. Some black folks too, but not so many here as at home. A woman had been raped the previous week. "You're kidding!" Frank said.

"What do you mean *you're kidding*," one woman said, disgusted at him.

Eventually they led him back to the station. Pausing in the door, Frank didn't know what to say to them. Quite a crowd had gathered, people had recognized him or been called or drawn to the group. "I'll see what I can do," he muttered, and ducked through the passage lock.

Thoughtlessly he stared into tents as he rode a train back up. There was one fitted with coffin hotels, Tokyo style. That would be much more crowded than El Paso, but did its occupants care about that? Some people were used to being treated like ball bearings. A lot of people, in fact. But on Mars it was supposed to be different!

Back in Sheffield he stalked the rim concourse, staring out at the thin vertical line of the elevator, ignoring other people and forcing some of them to jump out of his way as he paced. Once he stopped and looked around at the crowd; there were perhaps five hundred people in view at that moment, living their lives. When had it gotten like this? They had been a scientific outpost, a handful of researchers, scattered over a world with as much land surface as the Earth: a whole Eurasia, Africa, America, Australia, and Antarctica, all for them. All that land was still out there, but what percentage of it was under tents and habitable? Much less than one percent. And yet what was UNOMA saying? A million people here already, with more on the way. And so police, and crime – or rather, crime without police. A million people and no law, no law but corporate law. The bottom line. Minimize expenses, maximize profits. Run smoothly on ball bearings.

The next week a set of tents on the south slope went on strike. Chalmers heard about it on his way to the office, Slusinski actually breaking in on his walk with a call. The striking tents were mostly American, and his staff was in a panic. "They've closed the stations and aren't allowing anyone off the trains, so they can't be controlled unless their emergency locks are stormed—"

"Shut up."

Frank went down the south piste to the striking tents, ignoring Slusinski's objections. In fact he ordered several of the staff down to join him.

A team from Sheffield security was standing in the station, but he ordered them to get on the train and leave, and after a consultation with the Sheffield administrators, they did. At the passage lock he identified himself and asked to come in alone. They let him through.

He emerged in the main square of another tent, surrounded by a sea of angry faces. "Kill the TVs," he suggested. "Let's talk in private."

They killed the TVs. It was the same as in El Paso, different accents but the same complaints. His earlier visit gave him the ability to anticipate what they were going to say, to say it before they did. He watched grimly as their faces revealed how impressed they were by this ability. They were young.

"Look, it's a bad situation," he said after they had talked for an hour. "But if you strike for long, you'll only make it worse. They'll send in security and it won't be like living with gangs and police among you, it'll be like living in prison. You've made your point already, and now you've got to know when to let off and negotiate. Form a committee to represent you, and make a list of complaints and demands. Document all the incidents of crime, just write them down and get the victims to sign the statements. I'll make good use of them. It's going to take work at UNOMA and back home, because they're breaking the treaty."

He paused to get control of himself, relax his jaw. "Meanwhile, get back to work! It'll pass the time better than sitting around cooped up in here, and it'll make you points for the negotiation. And if you don't, they'll maybe just cut off your food and make you. Better to do it of your own free will, and look like rational negotiators."

So the strike ended. They even gave him a ragged round of applause when he went back out into the station.

He got on the train in a blinding fury, refusing to acknowledge any of his staff's questions or their mute looks of idiot inquiry, and savaging the head of the security team, who was an arrogant fool: "If you corrupt bastards had any integrity this wouldn't have happened! You're nothing but a protection racket! Why are people getting assaulted in the tents? Why are they paying protection, where *are* you when all this is happening!"

"It's not our jurisdiction," the man said, white-lipped.

"Oh come on, what *is* your jurisdiction? Your pocket is your only jurisdiction." He went on until they got up and left the car, as angry at him as he was at them, but too disciplined or scared to talk back.

In the Sheffield offices he strode from room to room, shouting at the staff and making calls. Sax, Vlad, Janet. He told them what was happening, and they all eventually offered the same suggestion, which he had to admit was a

517

good one. He would have to go up the elevator, and talk to Phyllis. "See if you can manage the reservations," he said to his staff.

The elevator car was like an old Amsterdam house, narrow and tall, with a light-filled room at the top, in this case a clear-walled and domed chamber that reminded Frank of the bubble dome of the *Ares*. On the second day of the trip he joined the car's other passengers (only twenty on this one, there weren't too many people going this way) and they took the car's own little interior elevator up the thirty stories to this clear penthouse, to see Phobos pass. The outer perimeter of the room was set out over the elevator proper, so there was a view down as well. Frank gazed down at the curved line of the planet's horizon, much whiter and thicker than the last time he had seen it. Atmosphere at one hundred fifty millibars now, really quite impressive, even if it was composed of poison gas.

While they were waiting for the little moon's appearance Frank stared at the planet below. The gossamer arrow of the cable pointed straight down at it; it looked like they were rising on a tall slender rocket, a strange attenuated rocket which stretched some kilometers above and below them. That was all they would ever see of the cable. And below them the round orange floor of Mars looked just as blank as it had on their first approach so long ago, unchanged despite all their meddling. One only had to get far enough away.

Then one of the elevator pilots pointed out Phobos, a dim white object to the west. In ten minutes it was upon them, flashing past with astonishing speed, a large gray potato hurtling faster than the head could turn. Zip! Gone. The observers in the penthouse hooted, exclaimed, chattered. Frank had caught only the merest glimpse of the dome on Stickney, winking like a gem in the rock. And there had been a piste banding the middle like a wedding ring, and some bright silver lumps; that was all he could recall of the blurred image. Fifty kilometers away when it passed, the pilot said. At seven thousand kilometers an hour. Not all that fast, actually; there were meteors that hit the planet at fifty thousand kilometers an hour. But fast enough.

Frank went back down to the dining floor, trying to fix the hurtling image in his mind. Phobos: people at the dining table next to him talked of shoving it up into a braided orbit with Deimos. It was out of the loop now, a new Azores, nothing but an inconvenience to the cable. And Phyllis had argued all along that Mars itself would have suffered the same fate in the solar system at large, unless the elevator were built to climb its gravity well; they would have been bypassed by miners going to the metal-rich asteroids, which had no gravity wells to contend with. And then there were the moons of Jupiter, Saturn, the outer planets . . .

But there was no danger of that now.

On the fifth day they approached Clarke and slowed down. It had been an asteroid about two kilometers across, a carbonaceous hunk now shaped to a cube, with every centimeter of its Mars-facing surface graded and covered with concrete, steel, or glass. The cable plunged right into the center of this assemblage; there were holes on both sides of the joint where cable met moon, just big enough to allow passage to the elevator cars.

They slid up into one of these holes and came to a smooth stop. The interior space they slid into was like a vertical subway station. The passengers got out and went their ways into the tunnels of Clarke. One of Phyllis's assistants met him and drove him in a little car through a warren of rock-walled tunnels. They came to Phyllis's offices, which were rooms on the planet side of the moon, walled with mirrors and green bamboo. Though they were in microgravity and pulling themselves around, they stood on a consensus floor as established by the furniture, rip-ripping around in velcro shoes. A rather conservative practice, but to be expected in such an Earth-regarding place. Frank exchanged his shoes for some velcro slippers by the door and followed suit.

Phyllis was just finishing talking to a couple of men: "Not only a cheap and clean lift out of the gravity well, but a propulsion system for slinging loads all over the solar system! It's an extraordinarily elegant piece of engineering, don't you think?"

"Yes!" the men replied.

She looked about fifty years old. After fulsome introductions – the men were from Amex – the others left. When Phyllis and Frank were the only ones left in the room, Frank said to her, "You'd better stop using this extraordinarily elegant piece of engineering to flood Mars with emigrants, or it'll blow up in your face and you'll lose your anchoring point."

"Oh Frank." She laughed. She really had aged well: hair silver, face handsomely lined and taut, figure trim. Neat as a pin in a rust jumpsuit and lots of gold jewelry, which together with her silver hair gave her an overall metallic sheen. She even looked at Frank through gold wire-rimmed glasses, an affectation that distanced her from the room, as if she were focusing on flat video images on the insides of her spectacles.

"You can't send down so many so fast," he insisted. "There's no infrastructure for them, physically or culturally. What's developing are the worst kind of wildcat settlements, like refugee camps or forced labor camps, and it'll get reported like that back home, you know how they always use analogies to Terran situations. And that's bound to hurt you."

She stared at a spot about three feet in front of him. "Most people don't see it that way," she proclaimed, as if the room were full of listeners. "This is just a step on the path to full human use of Mars. It's here for us and we're going to use it. Earth is desperately crowded, and the mortality rate is still dropping. Science and faith will continue to create new

521

opportunities as they always have. These first pioneers may suffer some hardships, but those won't last long. We lived worse than they do now, when we first arrived."

Startled at this lie, Frank glared at her. But she did not back down. Scornfully he said, "You're not paying attention!" But the thought frightened him, and he paused.

He brought himself back under control, stared through the clear floor at the planet. As they were rotating with it they always looked down on Tharsis, of course, and from this high it looked like one of the old photographs, the orange ball with all the familiar markings of its most famous hemisphere: the great volcanoes, Noctis, the canyons, the chaos, all unblemished. "When was the last time you went down?" he asked her.

"LS 60. I go down regularly." She smiled.

"Where do you stay when you descend?"

"In UNOMA dorms." Where she worked busily to break the UN treaty.

But that was her job, that was what UNOMA had assigned her to do. Elevator manager, and also the primary liaison with the mining concerns. When she quit the UN, she could take all the jobs she could handle from them. Queen of the elevator. Which was now the bridge for the greater part of the Martian economy. She'd have at her disposal all the capital of whatever transnationals she chose to associate with.

And all this showed, of course, in the way she rip-ripped around the brilliant glassine room, in the way she smiled at all his withering remarks. Well, she always had been a little stupid. Frank gritted his teeth. Apparently it was time to start using the good old USA like a sledgehammer, see if it had any heft remaining in it.

"Most of the transnationals have giant holdings in the States," he said. "If the American government decided to freeze their assets, because they were breaking the treaty, it would slow down all of them, and break some."

"You could never do that," Phyllis said. "It would bankrupt the government."

"That's like threatening a dead man with hanging. A couple more zeroes on the figure are just one more level of unreality, no one can really imagine it anymore. The only ones who even think they can are exactly your transnational executives. They hold the debt, but no one else cares about their money. I could convince Washington of this in a minute, and then you just see how it blows up in your face. Whichever way it does, it wrecks your game." He waved a hand angrily. "At which point someone else will occupy these rooms, and," a sudden intuition, "you'll be back in Underhill."

That got her attention, no doubt about it. Her easy contempt took on a sudden edge. "No single person can convince Washington of anything. It's quicksand down there. You'll have your say and I'll have mine, and we'll see who has more influence." And she rip-ripped across the room and opened the door, and loudly welcomed a gang of UN officials.

So. A waste of time. He wasn't surprised; unlike those who had advised him to come, he had had no faith in the idea of Phyllis being rational. As with many religious fundamentalists, business for her was part of the religion; the two dogmas were mutually reinforcing, part of the same system. Reason had nothing to do with it. And while she might still believe in America's power, she certainly didn't believe in Frank's ability to wield it. Fair enough; he would prove her wrong.

On the trip back down the cable, he scheduled video appointments on the half hour, for fifteen hours a day. His messages to Washington quickly got him into complex, transmission-delayed conversations with his people in the State and Commerce departments, and with the various cabinet heads who mattered. Soon the new president would give him a meeting as well. Meanwhile message after message, back and forth, leapfrogging around in the various arguments, replying to whichever correspondent got back to him first. It was complicated, exhausting. The case down on Earth had to be built like a house of cards, and a lot of them were bent.

Near the end, with the cable visible all the way down into the Sheffield socket, he suddenly felt really odd: it was a physical wave that passed through him. The sensation passed, and after a bit of thought he decided it must have been that the decelerating car had passed momentarily through one g. An image came to him: running along a long pier, wet uneven boards splashed with silver fish scales; he could even smell the salt fish stink. One g. Funny how the body remembered it.

Once resettled in Sheffield he went back to the continuous round of recording messages and analyzing the incoming replies, dealing with old cronies and with upcoming powers, all the talk patched together into a crazy quilt of arguments proceeding at different rates. At one point, late in the northern autumn, he was engaged in about fifty conferences simultaneously; it was like those people who play chess blind with a room full of opponents. Three weeks of this, however, and it began to come around, basically because President Incaviglia himself was extremely interested in getting any leverage he could over Amex and Mitsubishi and Armscor. He was more than willing to leak to the media his intent to look into allegations of treaty violations.

He did that, and stocks fell sharply in the relevant quarters. And two days later, the elevator consortium announced that enthusiasm for Martian opportunities had been so great that demand had exceeded supply for the time being. They would raise prices, of course, as their creed required; but also they would have to slow down emigration temporarily, until more towns and robotic townbuilders had been constructed.

Frank first heard this on a bar TV news report, one evening in a café over his solitary dinner. He grinned wolfishly as he chewed. "So we see who's better at wrestling in quicksand, you bitch." He finished eating and went for a walk along the rim concourse. It was only one battle, he knew. And it was going to be a bitter long war. But still, it was nice.

Then in the northern middle winter the occupants of the oldest American tent on the east slope rioted and threw out all the UNOMA police inside, and locked themselves in; and the Russians next door did the same.

A quick conference with Slusinski gave Frank the background. Apparently both groups were employed by the road-building subdivision of Praxis, and both tents had been invaded and attacked in the middle of the night by Asian toughs, who had slashed the tent fabric, killed three men in each tent and knifed a bunch of others. The Americans and Russians both claimed the attackers were *yakuza* on a race rage, although it sounded to Frank like Subarashii's security force, a small army that was mostly Korean. In any case, UNOMA police teams had arrived on the scene and found the attackers gone, and the tents in a turmoil: they had sealed the two tents, then denied permission for those inside to leave. The inhabitants had concluded they were prisoners, and enraged by this injustice they had burst out of their locks and destroyed the piste running through in their stations with welders, and several people on both sides had been killed. The UNOMA police had sent in massive reinforcements, and the workers inside the two tents were more trapped than ever.

Enraged and disgusted, Frank went down again to deal with it in person. He had to ignore not only the standard objections of his staff, but also the new factor's prohibition (Helmut had been called back to Earth); and once at the station he also had to face down the UNOMA police head, no easy task. Never before had he tried to rely so heavily on the charisma of the first hundred, and it made him furious. In the end he had to simply walk through the policemen, a

525

crazy old man striding through all civilized restraint. And no one there cared to stop him, not this time.

The crowd inside the tent looked ugly indeed on the monitors, but he banged on their passage lock door and finally was let in, into a crush of angry young men and women. He walked through the inner lock door and breathed hot stale air. So many people were shouting he could make nothing out, but the ones in front recognized him and were clearly surprised to see him there. A couple of them cheered.

"All right! I'm here!" he shouted. Then: "Who speaks for you?"

They had no spokesman. He swore viciously. "What kind of fools are you? You'd better learn to operate the system, or you'll be in bags like this one forever. Bags like this or else bodybags."

Several people shouted things at him, but most wanted to hear what he would say. And still no sign of a spokesman, so Chalmers shouted, "All right, I'll talk to all of you! Sit down so I can see who's speaking!"

They would not sit; but they did stand without moving, in a group around him, there on the tattered astroturf of the tent's main square. Chalmers balanced himself on an upturned box in the middle of them. It was late afternoon and they cast shadows far down the slope to the east, into the tents below. He asked what had happened, and various voices described the midnight attack, the skirmish in the station.

"You were provoked," he said when they were done. "They wanted you to make some fool move and you did, it's one of the oldest tricks in the book. They've gotten you to kill some third parties that had nothing to do with the attack on you, and now you're the murderers the police have caught! You were stupid!"

The crowd murmured and swore at him angrily, but some were taken aback. "Those so-called police were in on it too!" one of them said loudly.

"Maybe so," Chalmers said, "But it was corporate troops that attacked you, not some random Japanese on a rampage. You should have been able to tell the difference, you should have bothered to find out! As it is you played into their hands, and the UNOMA police were happy to go along, they're on the other side right now, at least some of them. But the national armies are shifting over to *your* side! So you've got to learn to co-operate with them, you've got to figure out who your allies are, and act accordingly! I don't know why there are so few people on this planet capable of doing that. It's like the passage from Earth scrambles the brain or something."

Some laughed a startled laugh. Frank asked them about conditions in the tents. They had the same complaints as the others had, and again he could anticipate, and say it for them. Then he described the result of his trip to Clarke. "I got a moratorium on emigration, and that means more than just time to build more towns. It means the start of a new phase between the US and the UN. They finally figured it out in Washington that the UN is working for the transnationals, and so they need to enforce the treaty themselves. It's in Washington's best interest, and they're the only ones that'll do it. The treaty is part of the battle now, the battle between people and the transnationals. You're in that battle and you've been attacked, and you have to figure out who to attack back, and how to connect up with your allies!"

They were looking grim at this, which showed sense, and Frank said, "Eventually we're going to win, you know. There's more of us than them."

So much for the carrot, such as it was. As for the stick, that was always easy with people as powerless as these. "Look, if the national governments can't calm things down quick, if there's more unrest here and things start coming apart, they'll say the hell with it — let the transnats solve their labor problems themselves, they'll be more efficient at it. And you know what that means for you."

"We're sick of this!" one man shouted.

"Of course you are," he said. He pointed a finger. "So do you have a plan to bring it to an end, or not?"

It took a while to ratchet them into agreement. Disarm, co-operate, organize, petition the American government for help, for justice. Put themselves in his hands, in effect. Of course it took a while. And along the way he had to promise to address every complaint, to solve every injustice, to right every wrong. It was ridiculous, obscene; but he pursed his lips and did it. He gave them advice in media relations and arbitration technique, he told them how to organize cells and committees, to elect leaders. They were so ignorant! Young men and women, educated very carefully to be apolitical, to be technicians who thought they disliked politics, making them putty in the hands of their rulers, just like always. It was appalling how stupid they were, really, and he could not help lashing into them.

He left to cheers.

Maya was out there in the station. Exhausted, he could only stare at her in disbelief. She had been watching him over the video, she said. Frank shook his head; the fools inside hadn't even bothered to disable the interior cameras, were possibly even unaware of their existence. So the world had seen it all. And Maya had that certain look of admiration on her face, as if pacifying exploited laborers with lies and sophistry were the highest heroism. Which to her it no doubt was. In fact she was off to employ the same techniques in the Russian tent, because there had been no progress there, and they had asked for her. The MarsFirst president! So the Russians were even more foolish than the Americans, apparently.

She asked him to accompany her, and he was too exhausted to run a cost/benefit analysis of the act. With a twist of the mouth he agreed. It was easier just to tag along.

They took the train down to the next station, made their way through the police and inside. The Russian tent was packed like a circuit board. "You're going to have a harder job of it than I did," Frank said as he looked around.

"Russians are used to it," she said. "These tents aren't that different from Moscow apartments."

"Yes, yes." Russia had become a kind of immense Korea, sporting the same brutal streamlined capitalism, perfectly Taylorized and with a veneer of democracy and consumer goods covering the junta. "It's amazing how little you need to keep starving people strung along."

"Frank, please."

"Just remember that and it will go okay."

"Are you going to help or not?" she demanded.

"Yes, yes."

The central square smelt of bean curd and borscht and electrical fires, and the crowd was much more unruly and loud than in the American tent, everyone there a defiant leader, ready to unleash a declamation. A lot more of them were women than in the American tent. They had unpisted a train and this had galvanized them, they were anxious for more action. Maya had to use a hand megaphone, and all the time that she stood on a chair and talked, the crowd swirled around them and participants in several loud arguments ignored her, as if she were a cocktail lounge pianist.

Frank's Russian was rusty, and he couldn't understand most of what the crowd shouted at Maya, but he followed her replies pretty well. She was explaining the emigration moratorium, the bottleneck in town robot production and in water supplies, the necessity for discipline, the promise of a better life to come if all was enacted in an orderly fashion. He supposed it was a classic babushka harangue, and it had the effect of pacifying them somewhat, as there was a strong reactionary streak in many Russians now; they remembered what social unrest really meant, and were justifiably afraid of it. And there was a lot to promise, it all seemed plausible: big world, few people, lots of material resources, some good

529

robot designs, computer programs, gene templates . . .

In one really loud moment of the discussion he said to her in English, "Remember the stick."

"What?" she snapped.

"The stick. Threaten them. Carrot and stick."

She nodded. Into the megaphone again: the never-to-be-taken-for-granted fact of the poisonous air, the deadly cold. They were alive only because of the tents, and the input of electricity and water. Vulnerable in ways they hadn't fully thought out, in ways that didn't exist back home.

She was quick, she always had been. Back to promises. Back and forth, stick and carrot, a jerk on the leash, some niblets. Eventually the Russians too were pacified.

Afterward on the train up to Sheffield Maya gabbled with nervous relief, face flushed, eyes brilliant, hand clutching his arm as she threw her head back abruptly and laughed. That nervous intelligence, that arresting physical presence . . . he must have been exhausted himself, or more shaken than he had realized by the time in the tents, or maybe it was the encounter with Phyllis; because he felt himself warming to her, it was like stepping into a sauna after a freezing day outside, with that same sense of relief from vigilance, of penetrating ease. "I don't know what I would have done without you," she was saying rapidly, "really you are so good in those situations, so clear and firm and sharp. They believe you because you don't try to flatter them or soften the truth."

"That's what works best," he said, looking out the window at the tents running by. "Especially when you're flattering them and lying to them."

"Oh Frank."

"It's true. You're good at it yourself."

This was an example of the trope under discussion, but Maya didn't see it. There was a name for that in rhetoric, but he couldn't recall it. Metonymy? Synecdoche? But she only laughed and squeezed his shoulder, leaning against him.

As if the fight in Burroughs had never happened, not to mention everything before that. And in Sheffield she ignored her stop, and got off the train with him at his stop, walking at his shoulder through the spaciousness of the rim station, and then to his rooms, where she stripped and showered and put on one of his jumpers, chattering all the while about the day and the situation at large, as if they did this all the time: went out to dinner, soup, trout, salad, a bottle of wine, every night sure! Leaning back in their chairs, drinking coffee and brandy. Politicians after a day of politics. The leaders.

She had finally wound down, and was poured into her chair, content just to watch him. And for a wonder it didn't make him nervous, it was as if some force field protected him from all that. Perhaps the look in her eye. Sometimes it seemed you really could tell if someone liked you.

She spent the night. And after that she divided her time between her quarters at the MarsFirst office and his rooms, without ever discussing what she was doing, or what it meant. And when it was time for bed, she would take off her clothes and roll in next to him, and then onto him, warm and calm. The touch of a whole body, all at once . . . And if he ever started things, she was so quick to respond; he only had to touch her arm. Like stepping into a sauna. She was so easy these days, so calm. Like a different person, it was amazing. Not Maya at all; but there she was, whispering Frank, Frank.

But they never talked about any of that. It was always the situation, the day's news; and in truth that gave them a lot to talk about. The unrest on Pavonis had gone into abeyance temporarily, but the troubles were planetwide, and getting worse: sabotages, strikes, riots, fights, skirmishes, murder. And the news from Earth had plummeted through even the blackest of gallows humor, into just plain awfulness; Mars was the picture of order in comparison, a little local eddy spun away from the vortex of a giant maelstrom, which looked to Frank like a death spiral for everything that fell

531

into it. Little wars like matchheads were flaring everywhere. India and Pakistan had used nuclear weapons in Kashmir. Africa was dying, and the north bickered over who should help first.

One day they got word that the mohole town Hephaestus, west of Elysium, manned by Americans and Russians, had been entirely deserted. Radio contact had stopped, and when people went down from Elysium to look, they had found the town empty. All Elysium was in an uproar, and Frank and Maya decided to see if they could do something in person. They took the train down to Tharsis together, back down into the thickening air and across the rocky plains now pie-bald with snowdrifts that never melted, with snow that was a dirty granular pink, conforming tightly to the north slope of every dune and rock, like colored shadows. And then onto the glistening crazed black plains of Isidis, where the permafrost melted on the warmest summer days, and then refroze in a bright black craquelure. A tundra in the making, maybe even a marsh. Flying by the train windows were tufts of black grass, perhaps even arctic flowers. Or maybe it was just litter.

Burroughs was quiet and uneasy, the broad grassy boulevards empty, their green as shocking as hallucination or an afterimage of looking into the sun. While waiting for the train to Elysium, Frank went to the station's storage room and reclaimed the contents of his Burroughs room, which he had left behind. The attendant returned with a single large box, containing a bachelor's kitchen equipment, a lamp, some jumpers, a lectern. He didn't remember any of it. He put the lectern in his pocket and tossed the rest of it in a trash dumper. Wasted years; he couldn't remember a day of them. The treaty negotiation, now revealed as pure theater, as if someone had kicked a backstage strut and brought down the whole backdrop, revealing real history on the back steps, two men exchanging a handshake and a nod.

The Russian office in Burroughs wanted Maya to stay and

deal with some business there, and so Frank took a train on to Elysium by himself, and then joined a rover caravan out to Hephaestus. The people in his car were subdued by his presence, and irritably he ignored them and glanced through his old lectern. A standard selection for the most part, a great book series only slightly augmented by some political philosophy packages. A hundred thousand volumes; lecterns today beat that a hundredfold, although it was a pointless improvement, as there was no longer time to read even a single book. He had been fond of Nietschze in those days, apparently. About half the marked passages were from him, and glancing through them Frank couldn't see why, it was all windy drivel. And then he read one that made him shudder: "The individual is, in his future and his past, a piece of fate, one law more, one necessity more for everything that is and everything that will be. To say to him 'change yourself' means to demand that everything should change, even in the past . . ."

In Hephaestus a new mohole crew was settling in, old timers for the most part, tech and engineering types, but much more sophisticated than the newcomers on Pavonis. Frank talked with quite a few of them, asking about those who had disappeared, and one morning at breakfast, next to a window that looked out on the mohole's solid white thermal plume, an American woman who reminded him of Ursula said, "These people have seen the videos all their life, they're students of Mars, they believe in it like a grail, and organize their lives around getting here. They work for years, and save, and then sell everything they have to get passage, because they have an idea of what it will be like. And then they get here and they're incarcerated, or at best back in the old rut, in indoor jobs so it's all just like it's still on TV. And so they disappear. Because they're looking for more of the kind of thing they came here for."

"But they don't know how the disappeared live!" Chalmers objected. "Or even if they survive at all!"

The woman shook her head. "Word gets around. People come back. There are one-play videos that show up occasionally." The people around her nodded. "And we can see what's coming up from Earth after us. Best to get into the country while the chance is still there."

Frank shook his head, amazed. It was the same thing the benchpresser in the mining camp had been saying, but coming from this calm middle-aged woman it was somehow more disturbing.

That night, unable to sleep, he put out a call for Arkady, and got him half an hour later. Arkady was on Olympus Mons of all places, up at the observatory. "What do you *want*?" Frank said. "What do you imagine will happen if everyone here slips away into the highlands?"

Arkady grinned. "Why then we will make a human life, Frank. We will work to support our needs, and do science, and perhaps terraform a bit more. We will sing and dance and walk around in the sun, and work like maniacs for food and curiosity."

"It's *impossible*!" Frank exclaimed. "We're part of the world, we can't escape it."

"Can't we? It's only the blue evening star, the world you speak of. This red world is the only real one for us, now."

Frank gave up, exasperated. He had never been able to talk to Arkady, never. With John it had been different; but then he and John had been friends.

He trained back to Elysium. The Elysium Massif rose over the horizon like an enormous saddle dropped on the desert; the steep slopes of the two volcanoes were pinkish white now, deep in snows that had packed down to firn, and would become glaciers before too long. He had always thought of the Elysium cities as a counterweight to Tharsis; older, smaller, more manageable and sane. But now people there were disappearing by the hundreds; it was a jump-off point into the unknown nation, hidden out there in the cratered wilderness.

534

In Elysium they asked him to give a speech to a group of American newcomers, on the first evening of their orientation. A formal speech, but there was an informal gathering before, and Frank wandered around asking questions as usual. "Of course we'll get out if we can," one man said to him boldly.

Others chipped in immediately. "They told us not to come here if we wanted to get outdoors much. It's not like that on Mars, they said."

"Who do they think they're fooling?"

"We can see the video you sent back as well as they can."

"Hell, every other article you read is about the Mars underground, and how they're communists or nudists or Rosicrucians—"

"Utopias or caravans or cave-dwelling primitives—"

"Amazons or lamas or cowboys—"

"What it is, is everyone's projecting their fantasies out here because it's so bad back there, do you understand?"

"Maybe there's a single co-ordinated counterworld—"

"That's another big fantasy, the totalizing fantasy—"

"The true masters of the planet, why not? Hidden away, maybe led by your friend Hiroko, maybe in contact with your friend Arkady, maybe not. Who knows? No one knows for sure, not on Earth they don't."

"It's all stories. It's the best story going right now, and millions of people on Earth are into it, they're addicted to it. A lot of them want to come, but only a few of us get to. And a good percentage of those of us who got chosen went through the whole selection process lying through our teeth to get here."

"Yes, yes," Frank interjected gloomily. "We all did that." It reminded him of Michel's old joke; since they were all going to go crazy anyway . . .

"Well there you are! What did you expect?"

"I don't know." He shook his head unhappily. "But it's *all* fantasy, do you understand? The need to stay hidden would hamper any community in a crippling way. It's all stories, when you get right down to it."

"Then where are all the disappeared going?"

Frank shrugged uneasily, and they grinned.

An hour later he was still thinking about it. Everyone had moved out into an open-air amphitheater, built from fixed salt blocks in classical Greek style. The semi-circle of rising white benches was filled with bodies topped by attentive faces, waiting for his speech, curious to see what one of the first hundred would say to them; he was a relic of the past, a character out of history, he had been on Mars ten years before some of the people in the audience were born, and his memories of Earth were of their grandparents' time, on the other side of a vast and shadowy chasm of years.

The classical Greeks had certainly gotten the size and proportions right for a single orator: he hardly had to raise his voice, and they all heard him. He told them some of the usual things, his standard address, all chopped and censored, as it was sadly tattered by current events. It didn't sound very coherent, even to him. "Look," he said, desperately revising as he spoke, ad libbing, searching through the faces in the crowd, "when we came up here we came to a different place, to a new world, and that necessarily makes us different beings than we were before. None of the old directives from Earth matter. Inevitably we will make a new Martian society, just in the nature of things. It comes out of the decisions we make together, by our collective action. And they are decisions that we're making in our time, in these years, right now at this very instant. But if you dodge off into the outback and join one of the hidden colonies, you isolate yourself! You remain whatever you were when you came, never metamorphosing into a Martian human. And you also deprive the rest of us of your expertise and your input. I know this personally, believe me." Pain lanced through him, he was astonished to feel it: "As you know, some of the first hundred were the first to disappear, presumably under the

536

leadership of Hiroko Ai. I still don't understand why they did it, I really don't. But how we have missed her genius for systems design in the years since, I can hardly tell you! Why, I think you can accurately say that part of our problems now result from her absence these many years." He shook his head, tried to gather his thoughts. "The first time I saw this canyon we're in, I was with her. It was one of the first explorations to this area, and I had Hiroko Ai at my side, and we looked down into this canyon, its floor bare and flat, and she said to me, It's like the floor of a room." He stared at the audience, trying to remember Hiroko's face. Yes . . . no. Strange how one remembered faces until you tried to look at them in your mind, when they turned away from you. "I've missed her. I come here, and it's impossible to believe it's the same place, and so . . . it's hard to believe I ever really knew her." He paused, tried to focus on their faces. "Do you understand?"

"No!" someone bellowed.

A flicker of his old anger boiled through his confusion. "I'm saying we have to make a new Mars here! I'm saying we're completely new beings, God dammit, that nothing is the same here! Nothing is the same!"

He had to give up, go sit down. Other speakers took over, and their droning voices floated over him as he sat, stunned, looking out the open end of the amphitheater into a park of wide-set sycamore trees. Slender white buildings beyond, trees growing on their roofs and balconies. A green and white vision.

He couldn't tell them. No one could tell them. Only time, and Mars itself. And in the meantime they would act in obvious contradiction to their own best interests. It happened all the time, but how could it, how? Why were people so stupid?

He left the amphitheater, stalked through the park and the town. "How can people act against their own obvious material interests?" he demanded of Slusinski over his wristpad. "It's crazy! Marxists were materialists, how did they explain it?"

"Ideology, sir."

"But if the material world and our method of manipulating it determine everything else, how can ideology happen? Where did they say it comes from?"

"Some of them defined ideology as an imaginary relationship to a real situation. They acknowledged that imagination was a powerful force in human life."

"But then they weren't materialists at all!" He swore with disgust. "No wonder Marxism is dead."

"Well, sir, actually a lot of people on Mars call themselves Marxists."

"Shit! They might as well call themselves Zoroastrians, or Jansenists, or Hegelians."

"Marxists are Hegelian, sir."

"Shut up," Frank snarled, and broke the connection.

Imaginary beings, in a real landscape. No wonder he had forgotten the carrot and the stick, and wandered off into the realm of new being and radical difference and all that crap. Trying to be John Boone. Yes, it was true! He was trying to do what John had done. But John had been good at it; Frank had seen him work his magic time after time in the old days, changing everything just by the way he talked. While for Frank the words were like rocks in his mouth. Even now, when it was just what they needed.

Maya met him at the Burroughs station, gave him a hug. He endured it stiffly, his bags hanging from his hand. Outside the tent low chocolate thunderheads billowed in a mauve sky. He couldn't meet her eye. "You were wonderful," she said. "Everyone is talking about it."

"For an hour." After which the emigrants would disappear as before. It was a world of acts, and words had no more influence on acts than the sound of a waterfall has on the flow of the stream.

He hurried off to the mesa offices. Maya came along and chattered at him as he checked into one of the yellow-walled rooms on the fourth floor. Bamboo furniture, flowery sheets and couch cushions. Maya was full of plans, cheery, pleased with him. She was pleased with him! He crushed his teeth together until they hurt. Bruxism was giving him headaches and all kinds of facial pain, wearing through his crowns and the cartilage in his jaw joints.

Finally he stood and walked to the door. "I have to go for a walk," he said. As he left he saw her face in his peripheral vision: hurt surprise. As usual.

He walked quickly down to the sward, and paced off the long row of Bareiss columns, their disarray like bowling pins caught flying. On the other side of the canal he sat at a round white table at the edge of a sidewalk café, and nursed a Greek coffee for an hour.

Suddenly Maya was standing before him.

"What do you mean by this?" she said. She gestured at the table, at his own annoyed scowl. "What is wrong now?"

He stared at his coffee cup, looked up at her; back down at the cup. It was impossible. A sentence was pronouncing itself in his mind, each word equally weighted: I killed John.

"Nothing's wrong," he said. "What do you mean?"

The corners of her mouth tightened, making her glare look contemptuous, and her face old. Nearly eighty now. They were too old for this. After a long silence she sat down across from him.

"Look," she said slowly. "I don't care what happened in the past." She stopped speaking, and he risked a glance at her; she was staring down, looking inward. "What happened in the *Ares*, I mean, or in Underhill. Or any of it."

His heart beat inside him like a child trying to escape. His lungs were cold. She was still talking, but he hadn't caught it. Did she know? Did she know what he had done in Nicosia? It was impossible, or she would not have been here (would she?); but she ought to have known.

539

"Do you understand?" she asked.

He hadn't heard what she was referring to. He continued to stare at his coffee cup, and suddenly she slapped it away with the back of her hand. It clattered under a nearby table and broke. The white ceramic semi-circle of the handle spun on the ground.

"I said *do you understand?*"

Paralyzed, he continued to stare at the empty table top. Overlapping rings of brown coffee stains. Maya leaned forward and put her face in her hands. She was hunched tight over her stomach, not breathing.

Finally she breathed, pulled her head up. "No," she said, so quietly that at first he assumed she was addressing herself. "Don't speak of it. You think I care, and so you do all this. As if I would care more about then than now." She looked up at him and caught his gaze. "It was thirty years ago," she said. "Thirty-five since we met, and thirty since all that happened. I am not that Maya Katarina Toitovna. I don't know her, I don't know what she thought or felt, or why. That was a different world, another life. It doesn't matter to me now. I have no feeling for it. Now I am here, and this is me." She poked herself between the breasts with a thumb. "And look; I love you."

She let the silence stretch, her last words drifting out like ripples on a pond. He couldn't stop looking at her; then he pulled his gaze away, he glared up at the faint twilight stars overhead, let their position seep into his memory. When she said I love you, Orion stood tall in the southern sky. The metal chair under you was hard. Your feet were cold.

"I don't want to think about anything but that," she said.

She didn't know; and he did. But everyone has to assume their past somehow. They were eighty-odd years old, and healthy. There were people who were now a hundred and ten years old, healthy, vigorous, strong. Who knew how long it would last? They were going to have a lot of past to assume. And as it went on, and those years of their youth

540

receded into the distant past, all those searing passions that had cut so deep . . . could they really be only scars? Weren't they crippling wounds, a thousand amputations?

But it wasn't a physical thing. Amputations, castrations, hollowing out; they were all in the imagination. An imaginary relationship to a real situation . . .

"The brain is a funny animal," he muttered.

She cocked her head, looked curiously at him. Suddenly he was afraid: they *were* their pasts, they had to be or they were nothing at all, and whatever they felt or thought or said in the present was nothing more than an echo of the past; and so when they said what they said, how could they know what their deeper minds were really feeling, thinking, saying? They didn't know, not really. Relationships were for that reason utterly mysterious; they took place between two subconscious minds, and whatever the surface trickle thought was going on could not be trusted to be right. Did that Maya down at the deepest level know or not know, remember or forget, swear vengeance or forgive? There was no way of telling, he could never be sure. It was impossible.

And yet there she was, sitting there miserably, looking as if he could shatter her like a coffee cup, shatter her with a single flick of his finger. If he didn't at least pretend to believe her, what then? What then? How could he shatter her like that? She would hate him for it — for forcing her to remember the past, to care about it. And so . . . one had to go on, to act.

He lifted his hand, so frightened that the movement felt like teleoperation. He was a dwarf in a waldo, a waldo that was stiff, touchy, unfamiliar: lift, quick modulate! To the left, hold; return, hold; steady. Down gently. Gently gently onto the back of her hand. Clasp, very gently. Her hand was really very cold; and so was his.

She looked wanly at him.

"Let's—" He had to clear his throat. "Let's go back to our rooms."

*

For weeks after that he remained physically clumsy, as if he had withdrawn into some other space, and had to operate his body from a distance. Teleoperation. It made him aware of how many muscles he had. Sometimes he knew them so well he could snake through the air; but most of the time he jerked across the landscape like Frankenstein's monster.

Burroughs was flooded with bad news; life in the city seemed fairly normal, but the video screens piped in scenes of a world Frank could scarcely believe. Riots in Hellas; the domed crater New Houston declaring itself an independent republic; and that same week, Slusinski sent tape of an American orientation in which all five dorms had voted to leave for Hellas without the proper travel permits. Chalmers contacted the new UNOMA factor, and got a detachment of UN security police to go there; and ten men arrested five hundred, by the simple expedient of overriding the tent's physical plant computer and ordering the helpless occupants to board a series of train cars, before the tent's air was released. They had then been trained off to Korolyov, which was now in effect a prison city. Its transformation into a prison had become general knowledge sometime recently; it was hard to recall exactly when, as it had an air of already-always about it, perhaps because the parts of a prison system had existed for several years, scattered planetwide.

Chalmers interviewed some of the prisoners over their room videos, two or three at a time. "You see how easy it was to detain you," he told them. "That's the way it will be all over. The life support systems are so fragile that they're impossible to defend. Even on Earth advanced military technology makes a police state much more possible to implement than ever before, but here it's absurdly easy."

"Well, you got us when it was easiest," replied a man in his sixties. "Which was smart. Once we get free I'd like to see you catch us. At that point your life support system is as vulnerable to us as ours is to you, and yours is more visible."

542

"You should know better than that! All life support here is hooked back ultimately to Earth. But they have a number of vast military powers at their disposal, and we don't. You and all your friends are trying to live out a fantasy rebellion, some kind of sci-fi 1776, frontiersmen throwing off the yoke of tyranny, but it isn't like that here! The analogies are all wrong, and deceptively wrong because they mask the reality, the true nature of our dependence and their might. They keep you from seeing that it's a fantasy!"

"I'm sure there was many a good Tory neighbor arguing the same case in the colonies," the man said with a grin. "Actually the analogy is in many ways a good one. We're not just cogs in the machine here, we're individual people, most of us ordinary, but there's some real characters too — we're going to see our Washingtons and Jeffersons and Paines, I guarantee you. Also the Andrew Jacksons and Forrest Mosebys, the brutal men who are good at getting what they want."

"This is ridiculous!" Frank cried. "It's a false analogy!"

"Well, it's more metaphor than analogy anyway. There are differences, but we intend to respond to those creatively. We won't be hefting muskets over rock walls to take potshots at you."

"Hefting mining lasers over crater walls? You think that's different?"

The man flicked at him, as if the camera in his room were a mosquito. "I suppose the real question is, will we have a Lincoln?"

"Lincoln is dead," Frank snapped. "And historical analogy is the last refuge of people who can't grasp the current situation." He cut the connection.

Reason was useless. Also anger, also sarcasm, not to mention irony. He could only try to match them in fantasyland. So he stood up in meetings and did his very best, haranguing them about what Mars was, how it had come to be, what a fine future it could have as a collective society, specifically and organically Martian in its nature, "with the dross of all those Terran hatreds burnt away, all those dead habits that keep us from really living, from the creation that is the world's only real beauty, damn it!"

Useless. He tried to arrange meetings with some of the disappeared, and once he talked with a group by phone, and asked them to pass the word along to Hiroko if possible, that he urgently needed to talk to her. But no one seemed to know where she was.

Then one day he got a message from her, in print faxed down from Phobos. He'd be better off talking to Arkady, it said. But Arkady had disappeared while down in Hellas, and was no longer taking calls. "It's like playing fucking hide and seek," Frank exclaimed bitterly to Maya one day. "Did you have that game in Russia? I remember playing with some older kids one time, it was around sunset and a storm over the water making it really dark, and there I was, wandering around empty streets knowing I'd never find any of them."

"Forget the disappeared," she advised. "Concentrate on who you can see. The disappeared will be monitoring you anyway. It doesn't matter if you can't see them or if they don't reply."

He shook his head.

Then there was a new wave of emigration. He shouted for Slusinski and ordered him to get an explanation from Washington.

"Apparently, sir, the elevator consortium has been bought in a hostile takeover by Subarashii, so its assets are in Trinidad Tobago and it is no longer interested in responding to American concerns about the matter. Infrastructure construction capability is now in line with a moderate emigration rate, they say."

"Damn them!" Frank said. "They don't know what they're doing with this!"

He walked in a circle, grinding his teeth. The words spilled

544

quietly out of him, in a monologue of their own making;
"You see but you don't understand. It's like John used
to say, there's parts of Martian reality that don't make it
across the vacuum, not just the feel of the gravity, but the
feel of getting up in a dorm and going down to the baths,
and then across the alley to a dining hall. And so you're
getting it all wrong, you arrogant, ignorant, stupid sons
of bitches . . ."

He and Maya took the train from Burroughs back up to
Pavonis Mons. All during the trip he sat by the window and
watched the red landscape rise and fall, contract in to the
flatland five kilometers and then, as they rose, extend out to
forty kilometers, or a hundred. Such a big bulge in the
planet, Tharsis. Something inside, breaking out. As in the
current situation. Yes, they were stuck on the side of the
Tharsis bulge of Martian history, with the big volcanoes
about to pop.

And then there one was, Pavonis Mons, an enormous
dream mountain, as if the world were a print by Hokusai.
Frank found it difficult to talk. He avoided looking at the TV
at the front of the car; news flashed up and down the train
almost instantly anyway, in snatches of overheard conversation or the looks on people's faces. It was never necessary
to watch the video to find out the really important news.
The train ran through a forest of Acheron pines, tiny things
with bark like black iron, and cylindrical bushes of needles;
but the needles were all yellow and drooping. He had heard
about this, there was some kind of problem with the soil, too
much salt or too little nitrogen, they weren't sure. Helmeted
figures stood around one on a ladder, plucking specimens of
the sick needles. "That's me," Frank said to Maya under his
breath, as she was asleep. "Playing with needles when the
roots are sick."

In the Sheffield offices he started meeting with the new
elevator administrators, at the same time beginning another
round of simultaneous meetings with Washington. It turned

545

out Phyllis was still in control of the elevator, having aided Subarashii in the hostile takeover.

Then they heard that Arkady was in Nicosia, just down the slope from Pavonis, and that he and his followers had declared Nicosia a free city like New Houston. Nicosia had become a big jump-off point for the disappeared: you could slip into Nicosia and never be heard of again – it had happened hundreds of times, so many that it was clear there was some system there, of contact and transmission, an underground railroad kind of thing that no undercover agent had yet been able to penetrate, or at least to return from. "Let's go down there and talk to him," Frank said to Maya when he heard. "I really want to confront him in person."

"It won't do any good," Maya said darkly. But Nadia was supposed to be there as well, and so she came along.

All down the slope of Tharsis they rode in silence, watching the frosted rock fly by. At Nicosia the station opened for their train as if there was not even a question of refusing them. But Arkady and Nadia were not in the small crowd that greeted them; instead it was Alexander Zhalin, and Raul. Back at the city manager's offices, they called up Arkady on a vidlink: judging by the sunlight behind him, he was already many kilometers to the east. And Nadia, they said, had never been in Nicosia at all.

Arkady looked the same as ever, expansive and relaxed. "This is madness," Frank said to him, furious that he had not gotten him in person. "You can't hope to succeed."

"But we can," Arkady said. "We do." His luxuriant red-and-white beard was an obvious revolutionary badge, as if he were the young Fidel about to enter Havana. "Of course it would be easier with your help, Frank. Think about it!"

Then before Frank could say more, someone offscreen got Arkady's attention. A muttered conversation in Russian, and then Arkady faced him again. "Sorry, Frank," he said. "I must attend to something. I'll get back to you as soon as possible."

"Don't you go!" Frank shouted, but the connection was gone. "God *damn* it!"

Nadia came on the line. She was in Burroughs, but had been linked into the exchange, such as it was. In contrast to Arkady she was taut, brusque, unhappy. "You can't support what he's doing!" Frank cried.

"No," Nadia said grimly. "We aren't talking. We still have this phone contact, which is how I knew where you were, but we don't use it direct anymore. No point."

"You can't influence him?" Maya said.

"No."

Frank could see that this was hard for Maya to believe, and it almost made him laugh: not influence a man, not manipulate him? What was Nadia's problem?

That night they stayed at a dorm near the station. After supper Maya went back to the city manager's office, to talk to Alexander and Dmitri and Elena and Raul; Frank wasn't interested, it was a waste of time. Restlessly he walked the circumference of the old town, through alleys running against the tent wall, remembering that night so long ago. Only nine years, in fact, though it felt like a hundred. Nicosia looked little these days. The park at the western apex still had a good view of the whole, but a blackness filled things so that he could scarcely see.

In the sycamore grove, now mature, he passed a short man hurrying the other way. The man stopped and stared at Frank, who was under a streetlamp. "Chalmers!" the man exclaimed.

Frank turned. The man had a thin face, long tangled dreadlocks, dark skin. No one he knew. But seeing him, he felt a chill. "Yes?" he snapped.

The man regarded him. He said, "You don't know me, do you?"

"No I don't. Who are you?"

The man's grin was asymmetrical, as if his face had been

547

cracked at the point of the jaw. Underneath the streetlight it looked warped, half-crazed.

"Who are you?" Frank said again.

The man raised a finger. "The last time we met, you were bringing down the town. Tonight it's my turn. Ha!" He strode off laughing, each sharp "ha!" higher than the last.

Back at the city manager's, Maya clutched his arm. "I was worried, you shouldn't be walking around alone in this town!"

"Shut up." He went to a phone and called the physical plant. Everything was normal. He called the UNOMA police, and told them to mount an armed guard at the plant and the train station. He was still repeating the order to someone higher up the chain of command, and it seemed likely it would go all the way up to the new factor for final confirmation, when the screen went blank. There was a tremor underfoot, and every alarm bell in town went off at once. A concerted, adrenal *brinnnnng!*

Then there was a sharp jolt. The doors all hissed shut; the building was sealing, meaning pressures outside had made a rapid drop. He and Maya ran to the window and looked out. The tent over Nicosia was down, in some places stretched over the tallest rooftops like saran wrap, in others blowing away on the wind. People down on the street were pounding on doors, running, collapsing, huddled in on themselves like the bodies in Pompeii. Frank wheeled away, his teeth bursting with hot pain.

Apparently the building had sealed successfully. Below all the noise Frank could hear or feel the hum of a generator. The video screens were blank, which had the effect of making it hard to believe the view out the window. Maya's face was pink, but her manner calm. "The tent is down!"

"I know."

"But what happened?"

He didn't reply.

548

She was working away at the video screens. "Have you tried the radio yet?"

"No."

"Well?" she cried, exasperated by his silence. "Do you know what's going on?"

"Revolution," he said.

PART SEVEN

Senzeni Na

Suspects

On the fourteenth day of the revolution Arkady Bogdanov dreamed he and his father sat on a wooden box, before a small fire at the edge of the clearing: a kind of campfire, except that the long low tin-roofed buildings of Ugoly were just a hundred meters behind their backs. They had their bare hands extended to the radiant heat, and his father was once again telling the story of his encounter with the snow leopard. It was windy and the flames gusted. Then a fire alarm rang out behind them.

It was Arkady's alarm, set for 4 a.m. He got up and took a hot sponge bath. An image from the dream re-occurred to him. He had not slept much since the revolt's beginning, just a few hours snatched here or there, and his alarm had awakened him from several deep sleep dreams, the kind one normally did not remember. Almost all had been undistorted memories of his childhood, memories never once recalled before. It made him wonder just how much the memory held, and if its storage might not be immensely more power-ful than its retrieval mechanism. Might one be able to remember every second of one's life, but only in dreams that were always lost on waking? Might this be necessary, somehow? And if so, what would happen if people started living for two or three hundred years?

Janet Blyleven came by, looking worried. "They've blown up Nemesis. Roald has analyzed the video, and guesses they hit it with a bunch of hydrogen bombs."

They went next door to Carr's big city offices, where Arkady had spent most of the previous two weeks. Alex and Roald were inside watching the TV. Roald said, "Screen, replay tape one for Arkady."

An image flickered and held: black space, the thick net of stars, and midscreen a dark irregular asteroid, visible mostly as a patch of occluded stars. For a few moments the image

553

held, and then a white light appeared on the side of the asteroid. The expansion and dispersal of the asteroid was immediate. "Fast work," Arkady remarked.

"There's another angle from a camera farther away."

This clip showed the asteroid as oblong, and it was possible to make out the silver blisters of its mass driver. Then there was a white flash, and when the black sky returned the asteroid was gone; a shimmering of stars to the right of the screen indicated the passage of fragments, then they steadied and it was over. No fiery white cloud, no roar on the soundtrack; just a reporter's tinny voice, chattering about the end of the Martian rioters' doomsday threat, and the vindication of the concept of strategic defense. Although apparently the missiles had come from the Amex lunar base, launched by rail gun.

"I never did like the idea," Arkady said. "It was mutual assured destruction all over again."

Roald said, "But if there's mutual assured destruction, and one side loses the capability . . ."

"We haven't lost the capability here, though. And they value what's here as much as we do. So now we're back to the Swiss defense." Destroy what they wanted and take to the hills, for resistance forever. It was more to his liking.

"It's weaker," Roald said bluntly. He had voted with the majority, in favor of sending Nemesis on its course toward the Earth.

Arkady nodded. It couldn't be denied that one term had been erased from the equation. But it wasn't clear if the balance of power had changed or not. Nemesis had not been his idea; Mikhail Yangel had proposed it, and the group in the asteroids had carried it out on their own. Now a lot of them were dead, killed by the big explosion or by smaller ones out in the belt; while Nemesis itself had created the impression that the rebels would countenance mass destruction on Earth. A bad idea, as Arkady had pointed out.

But that was life in a revolution. No one was in control,

no matter what people said. And for the most part it was better that way, especially here on Mars. Fighting had been severe in the first week, UNOMA and the transnationals had beefed up their security forces in the previous year. A lot of the big cities had been instantly seized by them, and it might have happened everywhere except that there turned out to be so many more rebel groups than they or anyone else had known about. Over sixty towns and stations had gotten on the net and declared independence, they had popped out of the labs and the hills and simply taken over. And now with Earth on the far side of the sun, and the nearest continuous shuttle destroyed, it was the security forces who were looking under siege, big cities or not.

A call came from the physical plant. They were having some trouble with the computers, and wanted Arkady to come have a look.

He left the city offices and walked across Menlo Park to the plant. It was just after sunrise, and most of Carr Crater was still in shadow; only the west wall and the tall concrete buildings of the physical plant were in sunlight at this hour, their walls all yellow in the raw morning light, the pistes running up the crater wall like gold ribbons. In the shadowed streets the city was just waking. A lot of rebels had come in from other towns or the cratered highlands, and they slept on the park grass. People sat up, sleeping bags still draped over their legs, eyes puffy, hair wild. Night temperatures were being kept up, but it was still cool at dawn, and those out of their bags crouched around stoves, blowing into their hands and puttering with coffee pots and samovars, and checking to the west to see how close the line of sunlight had crept. When they saw Arkady they waved, and more than once he was stopped by people who wanted to get his opinion of the news, or give him advice. Arkady answered them all cheerfully. Again he felt that difference in the air, the sense that they were all in a new space together, everyone facing the same problems, everyone equal, everyone

(seeing a heating coil, glowing under a coffe pot) incandescent with the electricity of freedom.

He walked feeling lighter, chattering into his wristpad's
diary file as he went. "The park reminds me of what Orwell
said about Barcelona in the hands of the anarchists; it is the
euphoria of a new social contract, of a return to that child's
dream of fairness we all began with—"

His wristpad beeped and Phyllis's face appeared on the
tiny screen, which was annoying. "What do you want?" he
asked.

"Nemesis is gone. We want you to surrender before any
more damage is done. It's simple now, Arkady. Surrender
or die."

He almost laughed. She was like the wicked witch in the
Oz movie, appearing unexpectedly in his crystal ball.

"It's no laughing matter!" she exclaimed. Suddenly he
saw that she was scared.

"You know we had nothing to do with Nemesis," he said.
"It is irrelevant."

"How can you be such a fool!" she cried.

"It is not foolishness. Listen, you tell your masters this;
if they try to subdue the free cities here, we will destroy
everything on Mars." That was the Swiss defense.

"Do you think that matters?" She was white-lipped, her
tiny image like a primitive fury mask.

"It matters. Look, Phyllis, I'm only the polar cap of this,
there's a massive underground lens that you can't see; it's
really vast, and they've got the means to strike back at you
if they want."

She must have let her arm fall, because the image on his
little screen swung wildly, then showed a floor. "You were
always a fool," her disembodied voice said. "Even back on
the Ares."

The connection went dead.

Arkady walked on, the city's bustle no longer as exhilarat-
ing as it had been. If Phyllis were frightened . . .

556

At the physical plant they were busy running a malfunction search. A couple of hours before, oxygen levels in the city had begun to rise, and no warning lights had gone off; a tech had discovered it accidentally.

Half an hour's work and they found it. A program had been substituted. They replaced it, but Tati Anokhin was not happy. "Look, that had to be sabotage, and there's still more oxygen than even this accounts for. Look, it's nearly forty percent out there right now."

"No wonder everyone is in such a good mood this morning."

"I'm not. Besides that mood thing is a myth."

"Are you sure? Go through the programming again, and look at the encryption IDs, and see if there are any other substitutions hidden under this one."

He headed back to the city offices. He was halfway there when there was a loud pop overhead. He looked up and saw a small hole in the dome. The air suddenly took on an iridescent shimmer, as if they were inside a great soap bubble. A bright flash and a loud boom knocked him off his feet. Struggling back up, he saw everything ignite simultaneously; people were burning like torches; and right before his eyes his arm caught fire.

557

It was not hard to destroy Martian towns. No harder than breaking a window, or popping a balloon.

Nadia Cherneshevsky discovered this while holed up in the city offices of Lasswitz, a tent town which had been punctured one night just after sunset. All the surviving occupants were now huddled in the city offices or the physical plant. For three days they had spent their time going out to try to repair the tent, and watching TV to try and figure out what was going on. But the Terran news packages were concerned with its own wars, which seemed to be coalescing into one. Only infrequently was there a brief report on the wrecked Martian towns. One said that many domed craters had been hit by missiles from over the horizon, usually in a sequence where oxygen or aerated fuels were introduced and then quickly followed by an ignitor that caused explosions of varying severity – from anti-personnel fires, to blasts that blew the domes off, to really big explosions that in effect re-excavated the crater. Anti-personnel oxygen fires appeared to be the most common; these left the infrastructure intact, for the most part.

Tent towns were simpler still. Most of them had been punctured by Phobos-based lasers; some had had their physical plants targeted by guided cruise missiles; others had been invaded by troops of one kind or another, their spaceports seized, armored rovers crashing through city walls, and in rare cases rocketpack paratroopers descending from above.

Nadia watched the jiggling video images that so clearly revealed the fear of the camera operators, her stomach collasping to a tight walnut inside her. "What are they doing, testing methods?" she cried.

"I doubt it," said Yeli Zudov. "It's probably just a matter of different groups using different methods. Some look like they're trying to do as little damage as possible, others seem to want to kill as many of us as they can. Make more room for emigration."

Nadia turned away, sickened. She got up and took off for the kitchen, bent slightly over her collapsed stomach, desperate to do something. In the kitchen they had turned on a generator and were microwaving frozen dinners. She helped hand them out, moving up and down a line of people sitting in the hall outside. Unwashed faces, splashed with black frostnip blisters: some people talked animatedly, others sat like statues, or slept leaning against each other. Most of them had been residents of Lasswitz, but a good number had driven in from tents or hideouts that had been destroyed from space, or attacked by ground forces. "Is stupid," an old Arab woman was saying to a gnarled little man. "My parents were Red Crescent in Baghdad when the Americans bombed it, if they have the sky is nothing you can do, nothing! We have to surrender. Surrender as soon as possible!"

"But to whom?" the little man asked wearily. "And for whom? And how?"

"To anyone, from everybody, and by radio, of course!" The woman glared at Nadia, who shrugged.

Then her wristpad beeped, and Sasha Yefremov babbled in a tinny wristphone voice; the water station north of town had gone up in an explosion, and the well it had capped was now fountaining in an artesian eruption of water and ice.

"I'll be right there," Nadia said, shocked. The town's water station tapped the lower end of the Lasswitz aquifer, which was a big one; if any significant part of the aquifer broached the surface, the water station and the town and the entire canyon they lay in would disappear in a catastrophic flood – and worse, Burroughs was located only two hundred kilometers down the slope of Syrtis and Isidis, and the flood could very conceivably run that far. Burroughs! Its population was far too large to evacuate, especially now that it had become a refuge for people escaping the war; there was simply no other place to go.

"Surrender!" the Arab woman insisted from the hall. "All surrender!"

"I don't think that will work anymore," Nadia said, and ran for the building's lock.

A part of her was immensely relieved to be able to do something, to stop huddling in a building watching disasters on TV, and *do something*. And Nadia had planned and overseen the construction of Lasswitz, only six years before, so now she had an idea what to do. The town was a Nicosia-class tent, with the farm and physical plant in separate structures, and the water station well off to the north. All the structures were down on the floor of a big east-west rift called Arena Canyon, the walls of which were nearly vertical and half a kilometer high. The water station was located only a couple hundred meters from the canyon's north wall, which in that area had an impressive overhang at the top. As Nadia drove with Sasha and Yeli to the water station, she quickly outlined her plan: "I think we can bring down the cliff onto the station, and if we can, the landslide ought to be enough to cap the leak."

"Won't the flood just carry the landslide's rock away?" Sasha asked.

"It will if it's a full aquifer outbreak, sure. But if we cover it when it's still just an uncapped well, then the escaping water will freeze in the landslide, and hopefully form a dam heavy enough to hold it. Hydrostatic pressure in this aquifer is only a bit greater than the lithostatic pressure of the rock over it, so the artesian flow isn't all that high. If it were we'd be dead already."

She braked the rover. Out of the windshield they could see the remains of the water station, under a cloud of thin frost steam. A rover came bouncing full speed toward them, and Nadia flashed their headlights and turned the radio to the common band. It was the water station crew, a couple named Angela and Sam, rabid with the adventures of the last hour. When they had driven alongside and finished their story, Nadia explained to them what she had in mind. "It could work," Angela said. "Certainly nothing else will stop it now, it's really pumping."

"We'll have to hurry," Sam said. "It's eating the rock at an unbelievable rate."

"If we don't cap it," Angela said with a certain morbid enthusiasm, "it'll look like when the Atlantic first broke through the Straits of Gibraltar and flooded the Mediterranean basin. That was a waterfall that lasted ten thousand years."

"I never heard of that one," Nadia said. "Come on with us to the cliff and help us get the robots going."

During the ride over she had directed all the town's construction robots from their hangar to the foot of the north wall, next to the water station; when the two rovers got there, they found a few of the faster robots had already arrived, and the rest were grinding over the canyon floor toward them. There was a small talus slope at the foot of the cliff, which towered over them like an enormous frozen wave, gleaming in the noon light. Nadia linked into the earthmovers and bulldozers and gave them instructions to clear paths through the talus; when that was done, tunnelers would bore straight into the cliff. "See," Nadia said, pointing at an areological map of the canyon that she had called onto the rover's screen, "there's a big fault there behind that whole overhanging piece. It's causing the lip of the wall to slump a bit, see that slightly lower shelf at the top? If we set off all the explosives we've got at the bottom of that fault, it's sure to bring down the overhang, don't you think?"

"I don't know," Yeli said. "It's worth a try."

The slower robots arrived, bringing an array of explosives left over from the excavation of the town's foundation. Nadia went to work programming the vehicles to tunnel into the bottom of the cliff, and for most of an hour she was lost to the world. When she was finished she said, "Let's get back to town and get everyone evacuated. I can't be sure how much of the cliff might come down, and we don't want to bury everyone. We've got four hours."

"Jesus, Nadia!"

"Four hours." She typed in the last command and started up their rover. Angela and Sam followed with a cheer.

"You don't seem very sorry to leave," Yeli said to them.

"Hell, it was boring!" Angela said.

"I don't think that's going to be much of a problem anymore."

"Good."

The evacuation was difficult; a lot of the town's occupants didn't want to leave, and there was barely room for them in the rovers at hand. Finally they were all stuffed into one vehicle or another, and off on the transponder road to Burroughs. Lasswitz was empty. Nadia spent an hour trying to contact Phyllis by satellite phone, but the comm channels were disrupted by what sounded like a number of different jamming efforts. Nadia left a message on the satellite itself: "We're non-combatants in Syrtis Major, trying to stop the Lasswitz aquifer from flooding Burroughs. So leave us alone!" A surrender of sorts.

Nadia and Sasha and Yeli were joined in their rover by Angela and Sam, and they drove up the steep switchbacks of the cliff road, onto the south rim of Arena Canyon. Across from them was the imposing north wall; below to the left lay the town, looking almost normal; but to the right it was clear something was wrong: the water station was broken in the middle by a thick white geyser, which plumed like a broken fire hydrant, and then fell into a jumble of dirty red-white ice blocks. This weird mass shifted even as they watched, briefly exposing black flowing water which frost-steamed madly, white mists pouring out of the black cracks and then whipping downcanyon on the wind. The rock and fines of the Martian surface were so dehydrated that when water splashed onto them they seemed to explode in violent chemical reactions, so when the water ran over dry ground, great clouds of dust fired off into the air and joined the frost steam swirling off the water.

"Sax will be pleased," Nadia said grimly.

At the appointed hour, four plumes of smoke shot out of the base of the northern wall. For several seconds nothing else happened, and the observers groaned. Then the cliff face jerked, and the rock of the overhang slipped down, slowly and majestically. Thick clouds of smoke shot up from the bottom of the cliff, and then sheets of ejecta shot out, like water from under a calving iceberg. A low roar shook their rover, and Nadia cautiously backed it away from the south rim. Just before a massive cloud of dust cut off their view, they saw the water station covered by the swift tumbling edge of the landslide.

Angela and Sam had been cheering. "How will we tell if it's worked?" Sasha asked.

"Wait till we can see it again," Nadia said. "Hopefully the flood downstream will have gone white. No more open water, no more movement."

Sasha nodded. They sat looking down into the ancient canyon, waiting. Nadia's mind was mostly blank; the thoughts that did occur to her were bleak. She needed more action like the last few hours', the kind of intense activity that gave her no time to think; even a moment's pause and the whole miserable situation crashed back in on her, the wrecked cities, the dead everywhere, Arkady's disappearance. And no one in control, apparently. No plan to any of it. Police troops were wrecking towns to stop the rebellion, and rebels were wrecking towns to keep the rebellion alive. It would end with everything destroyed, her whole life's work blown up before her eyes; and for no reason! No reason at all.

She couldn't afford to think. Down there a landslide had overrun a water station, hopefully, and the water rushing up the well had been blocked and frozen, making a composite dam. After that it was hard to say. If the hydrostatic pressure in the aquifer was high enough, a new breakout might be forced. But if the dam were thick enough . . . well, nothing to be done about it. Although if they could create some kind of escape valve, to take the pressure off the landslide dam . . .

Slowly the wind tattered the dust away. Her companions cheered; the water station was gone, covered by a fresh black landslide that spilled out from the northern wall, which now had a big new arc in its rim. But it had been a close thing, not anywhere near as big a landslide as she would have hoped; Lasswitz itself was still there, and it appeared that the layer of rock over the water station was not all that thick. The flood seemed to have stopped, it was true; it was motionless, a chunky, dirty white swath, like a glacier running down the middle of the canyon. And there was very little frost steam rising from it. Still . . .

"Let's go back down to Lasswitz and look at the aquifer monitors," Nadia said.

They drove back down the canyon wall road and into Lasswitz's garage. They walked down the empty streets in walkers and helmets. The aquifer study center was located next to the city offices. It was odd to see their refuge of the last few days empty.

Inside the aquifer center they studied the readouts from the array of underground sensors. A lot of them were no longer functioning, but those that were showed that hydrostatic pressure inside the aquifer was higher than ever before, and increasing. As if to emphasize the point a small trembler shook the ground, vibrating the soles of their boots. None of them had ever felt such a thing on Mars before. "Shit!" Yeli said, "it's going to blow again for sure!"

"We have to drill a runoff well," Nadia said. "A kind of pressure valve."

"But what if it breaks out like the main one?" Sasha asked.

"If we put it at the upper end of the aquifer, or midway

564

so that it takes some flow, it should be fine. Just as good as the old water station, which someone probably blew up, or else it would still be working fine." She shook her head bitterly. "We have to risk it. If it works, it works. If it doesn't, then maybe we cause an outbreak. But if we don't do something, it looks like there'll be an outbreak anyway."

She led the little group down the main street to the robot warehouse in the garage, and sat down in the command center to begin programming again. A standard drilling operation, with maximum blowout baffling. The water would come to the surface under artesian pressure, and then they would direct it into a pipeline, which they would instruct a robot crew to lay in some direction that would take it out of the Arena canyon region. She and the others studied topographic maps, and ran simulated floods down several canyons paralleling Arena to north and south. They found that the watershed was huge – everything on Syrtis drained down toward Burroughs, the land was a big bowl here. They would have to pipe the water north for nearly three hundred kilometers to get it into the next watershed. "Look," Yeli said, "released into the Nili Fossae, it will run straight north onto Utopia Planitia, and freeze on the northern dunes."

"Sax must be *loving* this revolution," Nadia said again. "He's getting stuff they *never* would have approved."

"But a lot of his projects must be getting wrecked too," Yeli pointed out.

"I bet it's still a net gain, in Sax's terms. All this water on the surface . . ."

"We'll have to ask him."

"If we ever see him again."

Yeli was silent. Then he said, "Is it that much water, really?"

"It's not just Lasswitz," Sam said. "I saw a news bit a while ago – they've broken the Lowell aquifer, a big breakout like the ones that cut the outflow channels. It'll rip billions

565

of kilos of regolith downslope, and I don't know how much water. It's unbelievable."

"But *why?*" Nadia said.

"It's the best weapon they have, I guess."

"Not much of a weapon! They can't aim it or stop it!"

"No. But neither can anyone else. And think about it – all the towns downslope from Lowell are gone – Franklin, Drexler, Osaka, Galileo, I imagine even Silverton. And all those were transnational towns. A lot of channel mining towns are vulnerable, I should think."

"So both sides are attacking the infrastructure," Nadia said dully.

"That's right."

She had to work, there was no other choice. She got them going again on robot programming, and they spent the rest of that day and the next getting the robot teams out to the drilling site, and making sure the start-up went right. The drilling was straightforward; it was only a matter of making sure that pressures in the aquifer didn't cause a blowout. And the pipeline to transfer the water north was even simpler, an operation that had been fully automated for years; but they doubled up on all the equipment, just to make sure. Up the north canyon road bed, and on northward from there. No need to include pumps; artesian pressure would regulate the flow quite nicely, because when the pressure dropped low enough to stop pushing water out of the canyon, the danger of a breakout at the lower end would presumably be past. So when the mobile magnesium mills were grinding along, scooping up fines and making pipe, and when the forklifts and frontloaders were taking these pipe segments to the assembler, and when that great moving building was taking in the segments and extruding pipe behind it as it rolled slowly along up the road, and when another mobile behemoth was going over the completed pipe, and wrapping it in aero-lattice insulation made from tailings from the refinery; and when the first segment of the pipeline was

heated and running – then they declared the system operational, and hoped it would make it three hundred kilometers
farther. The pipeline would be built at about a kilometer an
hour, for twenty-four and a half hours a day; so if all went
well, about twelve days to Nili Fossae. At that rate the pipeline would be done very soon after the well was drilled and
ready. And if the landslide dam held that long, then they
would have their pressure valve.

So Burroughs was safe, or as safe as they could make it
by their efforts. They could go. But it was a question what
their destination should be. Nadia sat slumped over a microwaved dinner, watching a Terran news show, listening to her
companions debate the issue. Horrible how the revolution
was being portrayed on Earth: extremists, communists, van-
dals, saboteurs, reds, terrorists. Never the words rebel or
revolutionary, words of which half the Earth (at least) might
approve. No, they were isolated groups of insane, destructive
terrorists. And it didn't help Nadia's mood that there was,
she felt, some truth to the description; it only made her
angrier.

"We should join whoever we can, and help fight!" Angela
said.

"I'm not fighting anyone," Nadia said mulishly. "It's
stupid. I won't do it. I'll fix things where I can, but I won't
fight."

A message came over the radio. Fournier Crater, about
eight hundred and sixty kilometers away, had a cracked
dome. The populace was trapped in sealed buildings, and
running out of air.

"I want to go there," Nadia said. "There's a big central
warehouse of construction robots there. They could fix the
dome, and then be set to other repairs down on Isidis."

"How will you get there?" Sam asked.

Nadia thought it over, took a deep breath. "Ultralite, I
guess. There's some of those new 16Ds up on the south rim
airstrip. That would be the fastest way for sure, and maybe

567

even the safest, who knows?" She looked at Yeli and Sasha. "Will you fly with me?"

"Yes," Yeli said. Sasha nodded.

"We want to come with you," Angela said. "It'll be safer with two planes anyway."

They took two planes that had been built by Spencer's aeronautic factory in Elysium, the latest things, called simply
16Ds, ultralite delta-winged four-seat turbojets, made
mostly of aerogel and plastics, dangerous to fly because they
were so light. But Yeli was an expert flier and Angela said
she was too, so they climbed into two of them the next
morning, after spending the night in the empty little airport,
and taxied out to the packed dirt runway and took off directly
into the sun. It took them a long time to rise to a thousand
meters.

The planet below looked deceptively normal, its old harsh
face only a bit whiter on the north faces, as if aged by its
parasite infestation. But then they flew out over Arena
Canyon, and saw running down it a dirty glacier, a river of
broken ice blocks. The glacier widened frequently where the
flood had pooled for a time. The ice blocks were sometimes
pure white, but more often stained one Martian shade or
other, then broken and tumbled into a mix, so that the glacier
was a shattered mosaic of frozen brick, sulfur, cinnamon,
coal, cream, blood . . . spilling down the flat bed of the
canyon all the way to the horizon, some seventy-five kilometers away.

Nadia asked Yeli if they could fly north and inspect the
land that the robots were going to build the pipeline over.
Soon after they turned they received a weak radio message
on the first hundred band, from Ann Clayborne and Simon
Frazier. They were trapped in Peridier Crater, which had lost
its dome; it was to the north also, so they were already on
the right course.

The land they crossed that morning appeared negotiable
to the robot team; it was flat, and though littered with ejecta,
there were no little stopper escarpments. Farther on in this
region the Nili Fossae began, very gradually at first, just four

very shallow depressions, curving down to the northeast like the fingertips of a faint handprint. A hundred kilometers farther north, however, and they were parallel chasms each five hundred meters deep, separated by dark land that had been heavily bashed by craters — a kind of lunar configuration, reminding Nadia of a messy construction site. Farther north still, they got a surprise: where the easternmost canyon debouched onto Utopia, there was another aquifer outbreak. At its upper end it was simply a new slump, a big bowl of land shattered like a broken plate of glass; lower down, patches of frosting black and white water surged right out of the broken land, ripping at the new blocks and carrying them away even as they watched, in a steaming flood that caused the land it touched to explode. This shocking wound was at least thirty kilometers across, and ran right over the horizon to the north, with no sign of dissipating.

Nadia stared at the sight and asked Yeli to fly nearer. "I want to avoid the steam," Yeli said, absorbed in the sight himself. Most of the white frost cloud was blowing east and falling down onto the landscape, but the wind was fitful, and sometimes the thin white veil would rise straight up, obscuring the swath of black water and white ice. The outflow was as big as one of the big Antarctic glaciers, or even bigger. Cutting the red landscape in two.

"That is a hell of a lot of water," Angela said.

Nadia switched to the first hundred band, and called Ann down in Peridier. "Ann, do you know about this?" She described what they were flying over. "And it's still running, the ice is moving, and we can see patches of open water, it looks black or sometimes red, you know."

"Can you hear it?"

"Just sort of like a ventilator hum, and some cracks and pops from the ice, yeah. But we're pretty loud up here ourselves."

"Hell of a lot of water!"

570

"Well," Ann said, "That aquifer isn't very big compared to some."

"How are they breaking them open? Can people really break those open?"

"Some of them," Ann said. "The ones with hydrostatic pressure greater than lithostatic pressure are in essence lifting the rock up, and it's the permafrost layer that is forming a kind of dam, an ice dam. If you drilled a well and blew it up, or if you melted it . . ."

"But how?"

"Reactor meltdown."

Angela whistled.

"But the radiation!" Nadia cried.

"Sure. But have you looked at your counter lately? I figure three or four of them must have gone."

"Wow!" Angela cried.

"And that's just so far." Ann's voice had that distant, dead tone it took on when she was angry. She answered their questions about the flood very briefly. A flood that big caused extreme pressure fluctuations; bedrock was smashed then plucked away, and it was all swept downstream in a pulverizing rush, a ripping, gaseous, boulder-filled slurry. "Are you going to come over to Peridier?" she asked when their questions trailed off.

"We're just turning east now," Yeli replied. "I wanted to get a visual fix on Crater Fv first."

"Good idea."

They flew on. The astounding roil of the flood dropped beneath the horizon, and they flew over the familiar old stone and sand again. Soon Peridier appeared over the horizon ahead, a low, much-eroded crater wall. Its dome was gone, tattered sheets of the fabric thrown aside, still rolling this way and that over the crater rampart, as if a seed pod had burst. The piste running south reflected the sun like a silver thread. They flew over the arc of the crater wall, and Nadia peered down at the dark buildings through binoculars, cursing in a low Slavic chant. How? Who? Why? There was no way to tell. They flew on to the airstrip out on the far crater rampart. None of the hangars were working, and they had to suit up and drive some little cars over the rim into town.

All the surviving occupants of Peridier were holed up in the physical plant. Nadia and Yeli went through its lock and gave Ann and Simon a hug, and then they were introduced to the others. There were about forty of them, living off emergency supplies, struggling to balance the gas exchange in the sealed buildings. "What happened?" Angela asked them, and they told the story in a kind of Greek chorus, interrupting each other frequently: a single explosion had burst the dome like a balloon, causing an instantaneous decompression that had also blown up many of the town's buildings. Luckily the physical plant was reinforced, and had withstood the internal pressures of its own air supply; and those inside had survived. Those out on the streets, or in the other buildings, had not.

"Where's Peter?" Yeli asked, startled and fearful.

"He's on Clarke," Simon said quickly. "He called us right after this all began. He's been trying to get a spot on one of the elevators down, but it's all police at this point, I guess there were a lot of them in orbit. He'll get down when he can. It's safer up there right now anyway, so I'm not in that much of a hurry to see him."

This made Nadia think of Arkady again. But there was nothing to be done; and quickly she set herself to the task of rebuilding Peridier. She first asked the survivors what their plans were, and when they shrugged, she suggested that they start by setting up a much smaller tent than the dome had been, using tenting material stored in the construction warehouses out at the airport. There were a lot of older robots mothballed out there, and so reconstruction would be possible without too much preliminary tooling. The occupants were enthusiastic; they had not known about the contents of the airport warehouses. Nadia shook her head at this. "It's in all the records," she said to Yeli later, "they only had to ask. They just weren't thinking. They were just watching the TV, watching and waiting."

"Well, it's a shock to have a dome go like that, Nadia. They had to make sure the building was secure first."

"I guess."

But there were very few engineers or construction specialists among them. They were mostly escarpment areologists, or miners. Basic construction was something that robots did, or so they seemed to think. It was hard to say how long they would have gone before they would have started in on the reconstruction themselves, but with Nadia there to point out what could be done, and drive them with a brief burst of withering scorn at their inactivity, they were soon under way. Nadia worked eighteen and twenty hours a day for a few days, and got a foundation wall laid, and tenting cranes into action over the rooftops; after that it was mostly a matter of supervision. Restlessly Nadia asked her companions from Lasswitz if they would join her in the planes again, and move on. They agreed; and so about a week after their arrival they took off again, with Ann and Simon joining them in Angela and Sam's plane.

As they flew south, down the slope of Isidis toward Burroughs, a coded message clittered abruptly over their radio speakers. Nadia dug through her pack and found a bag of stuff Arkady had given her, including a bunch of files; she found the one she wanted and plugged it into the plane's AI, and they ran the message through Arkady's decryption program. After a few seconds the AI spoke the message in its even tones:

"UNOMA is in possession of Burroughs, and detaining everyone who comes here."

There was silence in the two planes, winging south

through the empty pink sky. Below them the plain of Isidis sloped down to the left.

Ann said, "Let's go there anyway. We can tell them in person to stop the assaults."

"No," Nadia replied. "I want to be able to work. And if they lock us up . . . Besides, why do you think they'd listen to what we tell them about the assaults?"

No answer from Ann.

"Can we make it to Elysium?" Nadia asked Yeli.

"Yes."

So they turned east and ignored radio queries from Burroughs air traffic control. "They won't come after us," Yeli said with assurance. "Look, the satellite radar shows there's a lot of planes up and around, too many to go after all of them. And it would be a waste of time anyway, because I suspect most of them are decoys. Someone's sent up a whole lot of drones, which confuses the issue nicely as far as we're concerned."

"Someone really put a lot of effort into this," Nadia muttered as she looked at the radar image. Five or six objects were glowing in the southern quadrant. "Was it you, Arkady? Did you hide that much from me?"

She thought of that radio transmitter of his, which she had just run across in her bag. "Or maybe it wasn't hidden. Maybe I just didn't want to see it."

They flew to Elysium, and landed next to South Fossa, the largest roofed canyon of them all. They found that the roof was still there; but only, it turned out, because the city had been depressurized before it had been punctured. So the inhabitants were trapped in any number of intact buildings, and trying to keep the farm alive. There had been an explosion at the physical plant, and several others in the town itself. So there was a lot of work to be done, but there was a good base for a quick recovery, and a more enterprising population than the group in Peridier. So Nadia threw herself

574

into it as before, determined to fill every waking moment with work. She could not stand to be idle; she worked every moment she was awake, her old jazz tunes running through her mind — nothing appropriate, there was no jazz or blues appropriate to this — it was all completely incongruous, "On the Sunny Side of the Street", "Pennies From Heaven", "A Kiss To Build a Dream On" . . .

And in those hectic days on Elysium she began to realize just how much power the robots had. In all her years of construction she had never really tried to exert that power to the full; there simply had been no need. But now there were hundreds of jobs to be done, more than could be accomplished even with a total effort, and so she took the system right out to the bleeding edge as programmers would say, and saw just how much that effort could do, even as she tried to figure out how to do more. She had always considered teleoperation to be a basically local procedure, for instance, but it wasn't necessarily so; using relay satellites she could drive a bulldozer in the other hemisphere, and now, whenever she could establish a good link, she did so. She did not stop working for even a single waking second; she worked as she ate, she read reports and programs in the bathroom, and she never slept except when exhaustion knocked her out. While in this timeless state she told anyone and everyone she worked with what to do, without regard for their opinion or comfort; and in the face of her monomaniacal concentration, and the authority of her grasp of the situation, people obeyed her.

Despite all this effort, they could not do enough; so that it always came back to Nadia, and she alone through the sleepless hours gave the system a full stretch, out on the bleeding edge all the time. And Elysium had a huge fleet of construction robots already built, so that it was possible to attack most of the pressing problems simultaneously. Most of those were located among the canyons on Elysium's western slope. All the roofed canyons had been broken open

575

to one degree or another, but most of their physical plants were untouched, and there were a great number of survivors hunkered down in individual buildings running on emergency generators, as in South Fossa. When South Fossa was covered and heated and pumped up, she directed teams to go out and find all the survivors on the western slope, and they were pulled out of the other canyons and brought to South, and then sent back out with jobs to do. The roofing crews moved from canyon to canyon, and their ex-occupants went to work underneath, readying for the pump-ups. At that point Nadia turned her attention to other matters, programming toolmakers, starting robot linemen along the broken pipelines from Chasma Borealis. "Who *did* all this?" she said with disgust, staring one night at the TV's image of burst water pipes.

The question was torn out of her; in reality she didn't want to know. She didn't want to think about the bigger picture, about anything but that pipeline there, broken on the dunes. But Yeli took her at her word, and said, "It's hard to tell. The Terran news programs are all about Earth now, there's only an occasional clip from here, and they don't know what to make of it either. Apparently the next few shuttles are bringing UN troops, who are supposed to restore order. But most of the news is about Earth – the Middle East war, the Black Sea, Africa, you name it. A lot of the Southern Club is bombing flag of convenience countries, and the Group of Seven has declared they're going to defend them. And there's a biological agent loose in Canada and Scandinavia — "

"And maybe here too," Sasha interrupted. "Did you see that clip of Acheron? Something happened there, the windows of the habitat are all blown out, and the land underneath the fin is covered with these growths of God knows what, no one wants to get near enough to find out . . ."

Nadia closed her mind to their talk, and concentrated on the problem of the pipeline. When she returned to real time, she found that every single robot she could find was in action reconstituting the towns, and the factories were busily pumping out more bulldozers, earthmovers, dump trucks, backhoes, frontloaders, steamrollers, framers, foundation diggers, welders, cement makers, plastic makers, roofers, everything. The system was at full pump, and there wasn't enough to occupy her anymore. And so she told the others she wanted to take off again, and Ann and Simon and Yeli and Sasha decided to accompany her; Angela and Sam had met friends in South Fossa, and were going to stay.

So the five climbed into their two planes, and took off again. This was the way it would happen everywhere, Yeli asserted; whenever members of the first hundred encountered each other, they would not separate.

They headed in the two planes south, toward Hellas. Passing over Tyrrhena Mohole, next to Hadriaca Patera, they landed briefly; the mohole town was punctured, and needed help to start the rebuilding. There were no robots on hand, but Nadia had found she could start an operation with as small a seed as her programs, a computer, and an air miner. That kind of spontaneous generation of machinery was another aspect of their power. It was slower, no doubt of that; still, within a month these three components together would have conjured obedient beasts out of the sand: first the factories, then the assembly plants, then the construction robots themselves, vehicles as big and articulated as a city block, doing their work in their absence. It really was confounding, their new power.

And yet all of it was as nothing in the face of human destructiveness. The five travelers flew from ruin to ruin, becoming numb to the damage and to the dead. Not that they were insensible to their own danger; after passing over a number of wrecked planes in the Hellas-Elysium flight corridor, they switched to night flights. These flights were more dangerous than day flights in many ways, but Yeli was more comfortable with their level of stealth. The 16Ds were nearly invisible to radar, and would leave only the faintest traces on the most powerful tight-focus IR detectors. All of them were willing to take the risk of that minute exposure. Nadia didn't care at all, she would have been happy to fly by day. She lived in the moment as much as she could, her thoughts ran in circles as she kept trying to drag them back to the moment; stunned by the waste of all that had been destroyed, she was becoming far distanced from her emotions. She only wanted to work.

And Ann, some part of Nadia noticed, was worse. Of course she must have been worried about Peter. And then all the destruction as well; for her it was not the structures but the land itself, the floods, the mass wasting, the snow, the radiation. And she had no work to distract her. Her work would have been the study of the damage. And so she did nothing, or tried to help Nadia when she could, moving around like an automaton. Day after day they worked at initiating the repair of one ruined structure or another, a bridge, a pipeline, a well, a power station, a piste, a town. They lived in what Yeli called Waldo World, ordering robots about as if they were slavemasters or magicians, or gods; and the machines went to work, trying to reverse the film of time and make broken things fly back together. With the luxury of haste they could be sloppy, and it was incredible how fast they could initiate construction, and then fly on. "In the beginning was the word," Simon said wearily one evening, punching at his wristpad. A bridge crane swung across the setting sun. And then they were off again.

They started up containment and burial programs for three blown reactors, staying safely over the horizon and working by teleoperation. While watching the operations, Yeli sometimes switched channels and had a look at the news. Once the shot was from orbit: a full disk shot of the Tharsis hemisphere, in daytime for all but the western limb. From that height they could see no sign of the outflows. But the voiceover claimed they had occurred in all the old outflow channels that ran north from Marineris into Chryse; and the image jumped to a telescopic shot, which showed whitish pink bands in that region. Canals at last, of a sort.

Nadia snapped the TV back to their work. So much destroyed, so many people killed, people who might have lived a thousand years – and, of course, no word of Arkady. It had been twenty days now. People were saying he might have been forced into complete hiding, to avoid being killed by a strike from orbit. But Nadia no longer believed this, except in moments of extreme desire and pain, the two emotions surging up through the obsessive work mode in a brand-new mixture, a new feeling that she hated and feared: desire causing pain, pain causing desire – a hot fierce desire, that things not be as they were. How painful such a desire was! But if she worked hard enough, there was no time for it. No time to think or feel.

They flew over the bridge spanning Harmakhis Vallis, on the eastern border of Hellas; it was down. Repair robots were cached in endhouses on all major bridges, and these could be adapted to total reconstruction of the spans, although they would be slow at it. The travelers got them going, and that evening, after finishing the last programs, they sat down to microwaved spaghetti in the plane's cabins, and Yeli turned on the Terran TV channel again. There was nothing but static and a snaking, destroyed image. He tried switching channels, but all the channels were the same. Dense, buzzing static.

"Have they blown up Earth too?" Ann said.

"No no," Yeli said. "Someone's jamming it. The sun is between us and it, these days, and you would only have to interfere with a few relay satellites to cut contact."

They stared glumly at the fizzing screen. In recent days the local areosynchronous communications satellites had been going down left and right; shut down or sabotaged, it was impossible to say. Now, without the Terran news, they would really be in the dark. Surface-to-surface radio was limited indeed, given the tight horizons and the lack of an ionosphere; not much more range than walker intercoms, really. Yeli tried a variety of stochastic resonance patterns, to see if he could cut through the jamming. The signals were scrambled beyond repair. He gave up with a grunt, punched out a search program. The radio oscillated up and down through the hertz, gathering static and stopping at the occasional faint punctuation: coded clicking, irretrievable snatches of music. Ghost voices gabbling in unrecognizable languages, as if Yeli had succeeded where SETI had failed, and finally, now that it was pointless, gotten messages from the stars. Probably just stuff from the asteroid miners. In any case incomprehensible, useless. They were alone on the face of Mars, five people in two small airplanes.

It was a new and very peculiar sensation, which only became more acute in the days that followed, when it didn't go away, and they understood that they were going to have to proceed with all their TVs and radios blanked by white noise. It was an experience unique not only in their Martian experience, but in their whole lives. And they quickly found that losing the electronic information net was like losing one of their senses; Nadia kept glancing down at her wristpad, on which, until this breakdown, Arkady could have appeared any second; on which any of the first hundred might have showed up, and declared themselves safe; and then she would look up from the little blank square at the land around her, suddenly so much bigger and wilder and emptier than it had ever been before. It was frightening, truly. Nothing but jagged rust hills for as far as the eye could see, even when flying in the airplanes at dawn and looking for one of the little landing strips marked on the map, which when spotted would resemble little tan pencils. Such a big world! And they were alone in it. Even navigation could no longer be taken for granted, no longer be left to the computers; they had to use road transponders, and dead reckoning, and visual fixes, peering down anxiously in the dawn twilight to spot the next airstrip in the wilderness. Once it took them well into the morning to find a strip near Dao Vallis; after that Yeli began to follow pistes, flying low through the night and watching the silvery ribbon snake below them through the starlight, checking transponder signals against the maps.

And so they managed to fly down in the broad lowland of Hellas basin, following the piste to Low Point Lakefront. Then in the horizontal red light and long shadows of sunrise, a sea of shattered ice came over the horizon into view. It filled the whole western part of Hellas. A sea.

The piste they had been following ran right into ice. The frozen shoreline was a jagged tangle of ice plates that were black or red or white or even blue, or a rich jade green — all piled together, as if a tidal wave had crushed Big Man's butterfly collection, and left it strewn over a barren beach. Beyond it the frozen sea stretched right over the horizon.

After many seconds' silence, Ann said, "They must have broken the Hellespontus aquifer. That was a really big one, and it would drain down to Low Point."

"So the Hellas mohole must be flooded!" Yeli said.

"That's right. And the water at the bottom of it will heat up. Probably hot enough to keep the surface of the lake from freezing. Hard to say. The air is cold, but with the turbulence there might be a clear spot. If not, then right under the surface it will be liquid for sure. Must be some strong convection currents in fact. But the surface . . ."

Yeli said, "We'll see pretty soon, we're going to fly over it."

"We should be landing," Nadia observed.

"Well, we will when we can. Besides, things seem to be calming down a bit."

"That's just a function of being cut off from news."

"Hmm."

As it turned out they had to fly all the way across the

lake, and land on the other side. It was an eerie morning, flying low across a shattered surface reminiscent of the Arctic Sea, except here the ice flows were frosting like an open freezer door, and they were colored across the whole spectrum, heavy on the reds of course, but this only made the occasional blues and greens and yellows stand out more vividly, the focal points of an immense, chaotic mosaic.

And there at its center — where, even flying as high as they were, the ice sea still extended to the horizon in every direction — there was an enormous steam cloud, rising thousands of meters into the air. Circling this cloud cautiously, they saw that the ice underneath it was broken into bergs and floes, floating tight-packed in roiling, steaming black water. The dirty bergs rotated, collided, turned turtle and caused thick walls of red-black water to splash upward; when these walls fell back down, waves expanded out in concentric circles, bobbing all the bergs up and down as they passed.

There was silence in the two planes as they stared down at this most unMartian spectacle. Finally, after two mute circumnavigations of the steam column, they flew on westward over the shattered waste. "Sax must be *loving* this revolution," Nadia said as she had before, breaking the silence. "Do you think he's part of it?"

"I doubt it," Ann said. "He probably wouldn't risk his Terran investment. Nor an orderly progression to the project, or some kind of control. But I'm sure he's evaluating it in terms of how it affects the terraforming. Not who's dying, or what's getting wrecked, or who's taking over here. Just how it affects the project."

"An interesting experiment," Nadia said.

"But hard to model," Ann said. They both had to laugh.

Speak of the devil — they landed west of the new sea (Lakefront was drowned), and spent the day resting; and the next night as they followed the piste northwest toward Marineris, they flew over a transponder that was blinking

S.O.S. in Morse code. They circled the transponder until dawn, and landed on the piste itself, just beyond a disabled rover. And next to it was Sax, in a walker, fiddling with the transponder to send his manual S.O.S.

Sax climbed into their plane and slowly took off his helmet, blinking and purse-mouthed, his usual bland self. Tired, but looking like the rat that ate the canary, as Ann said to Nadia later. He said little. He had been stuck on the piste in the rover for three days, unable to move; the piste was dead, and the rover had no emergency fuel. Lakefront had indeed drowned: "I was leaving for Cairo," he said, "to meet with Frank and Maya, because they think it would help to have the whole first hundred together, to form some kind of authority to negotiate with the UNOMA police, and get them to stop." He had taken off, and was in the Hellespontus foothills when the Low Point mohole's thermal cloud had suddenly turned yellow, and plumed twenty thousand meters into the sky. "It turned into a mushroom cloud like a nuclear explosion, but with a smaller cap," he noted. "The temperature gradient isn't so steep in our atmosphere."

After that he had turned back, and gone to the edge of the basin to see some of the flooding. The water running down the basin from the north had been black but kept going white, icing over in big segments almost instantaneously, except around Lakefront, where it had bubbled "like water on the stove. Thermodynamics were pretty complex there for a while, but the water cooled the mohole pretty fast, and—"

"Shut up, Sax," Ann said.

Sax lifted his eyebrows, and went to work improving the plane's radio receiver.

They flew on, six of them now, Sasha and Yeli, Ann and Simon, Nadia and Sax: six of the first hundred, gathered together as if by magnetism. There was a lot to talk about that night, and they exchanged stories, information, rumors, speculations. But Sax could add little concrete to the overall picture. He had been cut off from the news just like they had. Again Nadia shuddered as if at a lost sense, realizing that this was a problem that wasn't going to go away.

The next morning at sunrise they landed at Bakhuysen's airstrip, and were met by a dozen people carrying police stun guns. This little crowd kept their gun barrels down, but escorted the six with very little ceremony into the hangar inside the crater wall.

There were more people in the hangar, and the crowd grew all the time. Eventually there were about fifty of them, about thirty of them women. They were perfectly polite, and, when they discovered the travelers' identities, even friendly. "We just have to make sure who we're dealing with," one of them said, a big woman with a strong Yorkshire accent.

"And who are you?" Nadia asked boldly.

"We're from Korolyov Prime," she said. "We escaped."

They took the travelers into their dining hall, and treated them to a big breakfast. When they were all seated, people took up magnesium jugs and reached across the table to pour their neighbor's apple juice, and their neighbors did likewise, until everyone was served. Then over pancakes the two groups exchanged stories. The Bakhuysen crowd had escaped from Korolyov Prime in the first day of the revolt, and had made their way this far south, with plans to go all the way down to the southern polar region. "That's a big rebel location," the Yorkshire woman (who it turned out was really Finnish) told them. "There are these stupendous bench terraces with overhangs, you see, so in effect they're these long open-sided caves, a couple klicks long most of the time, and quite wide really. Perfect for staying out of satellite view but having a bit of air. A kind of a Cro-Magnon cliff-dweller life they're setting up down there. Lovely, really." Apparently these long caves had been famous in Korolyov, and a lot of the prisoners had agreed to rendezvous there if a breakout ever occurred.

"So are you with Arkady?" Nadia asked.

584

"Who?"

It turned out they were followers of the biologist Schnelling, who from the sound of it had been a kind of red mystic, held in Korolyov with them, where he had died a few years before. He had given wrist lectures that had been very popular on Tharsis, and after his incarceration many of the prisoners in Korolyov had become his students. Apparently he taught them a kind of Martian communalism based on principles of the local biochemistry; the group at Bakhuysen wasn't very clear about it, but now they were out, and hoping to contact other rebel forces. They had succeeded in establishing contact with a stealthed satellite, programmed to operate in directed microbursts; they had also managed briefly to monitor a channel being used by security forces on Phobos. So they had a little news. Phobos, they said, was being used as a surveillance and attack station by transnational and UNOMA police forces, recently arrived on the latest continuous shuttle. These same forces had control of the elevator, of Pavonis Mons, and of most of the rest of Tharsis; the Olympus Mons observatory had rebelled, but been firestormed from orbit; and transnational security forces had occupied most of the Great Escarpment, effectively cutting the planet in two. And the war on Earth appeared to be continuing, although they had the impression it was hottest in Africa, Spain, and the US-Mexican border.

They thought it was useless to try going to Pavonis: "They'll either lock you up or kill you," as Sonja put it. But when the six travelers decided to try anyway, they were given precise directions to a refuge a night's flight to the west; it was the Southern Margaritifer weather station, the Bakhuysen people told them. Occupied by Bogdanovists.

Nadia's heart leaped when she heard that word, she couldn't help it. But Arkady had a lot of friends and followers, and none of them seemed to know where he was. Still, she found herself unable to sleep that day, her stomach again tied in a knot. That night at sunset she was happy to return the planes and take off. The rebels in Bakhuysen sent them on their way so laden with hydrazine and gases and freeze-dried food that their planes had a hard time getting off the ground.

Their night flights had taken on a strangely ritual aspect, as if they were in the process of inventing a new and exhausting pilgrimage. The two planes were so light that they were buffeted hard by the prevailing western winds, sometimes bouncing wildly ten meters up or down, so that it was impossible to sleep for long even when one was not flying; a sudden drop or lift and one was awake again, in the dark little cabin, staring out the window at the black sky and stars above, or the starless black world below. They spoke hardly at all. The pilots hunched forward, expending their energy on keeping a visual fix on the other plane. The planes hummed along, winds keening over their long flexible wings. It was sixty degrees below zero outside, the air only 150 millibars and poisonous; and there was no shelter on the black planet below, for many kilometers in every direction. Nadia would pilot for a while, then move to the back, and twist and turn, and try to sleep. Often the click of a transponder over the radio, combined with the general aspect of their situation, would remind her of the time she and Arkady had ridden the storm in the *Arrowhead*. She would see him then, striding red-bearded and naked through the broken interior of the dirigible, tearing away paneling to throw overboard, laughing, fines floating in a nimbus around him – then the 16D would jerk her awake, and she would twist with the discomfort of her fear. It would have helped to pilot again, but Yeli wanted to as much as she, at least for the first couple of hours of his watch. There was nothing for it but to help him watch for the other plane, always a kilometer to the right if all was well. They had occasional radio contact with the other plane, but microbursted the calls, and kept them to a minimum; hourly checks, or inquiries if one fell behind.

586

Everything had taken on ritualistic qualities, and in the dead of night it sometimes seemed this was all any of them had ever done, it was hard to recall what life had been like before the revolt. And what had it been, twenty-four days? Three weeks, though it felt like five years.

And then the sky would begin to bleed behind them, high cirrus clouds turning purple, rust, crimson, lavender, and then swiftly to metal shavings, in a rosy sky; and the incredible fountain of the sun would pour over some rocky rim or scarp, and they would search anxiously as they ghosted over the pocked and shadowed landscape, looking for some sign of an airstrip by the piste. After the eternal night it seemed impossible that they would have navigated successfully to anything at all, but there lay the gleaming piste below, which they could land on directly in an emergency. And the transponders being all individually identifiable, and pegged to the map, their navigation was always more sure than it seemed; so every dawn they would spot a strip down in the shadows ahead, a welcome blond pencil strip of perfect flatness. Down they would glide, thump against the ground, slow down, taxi to whatever facilities they could find; stop the engines, slump back in the seats. Feel the strange lack of vibration, the stillness of another day.

That morning they landed at the strip by the Margaritifer station, and were met at their planes by a dozen men and women who were extravagantly enthusiastic in their welcome, hugging and kissing the six travelers countless times, and laughing as they did so. The six clumped together, more alarmed by this than by the wary greeting of the day before. Their welcomers did not neglect to run laser readers over their wrists to identify them, which was reassuring; but when the AI confirmed that they were indeed receiving six of the first hundred, they burst into cheers, and carried on in the very highest of spirits. In fact when the six were led through a lock into a commons, several of their hosts went over immediately to some small tanks, and breathed in hits of what proved to be nitrous oxygen and a pandorphin aerosol, after which they laughed themselves silly.

One of them, a slender fresh-faced American, introduced himself. "I'm Steve, I trained with Arkady on Phobos in 12, and worked with him on Clarke. Most of us here worked with him on Clarke. We were in Schiaparelli when the revolution began."

"Do you know where Arkady is?" Nadia asked.

"Last we heard he was in Carr, but now he's out of the net, which is the way it should be."

A tall skinny American shambled up to Nadia, and put his hand on her shoulder and said, "We're not always like this!" and laughed.

"We're not!" Steve agreed. "But it's a holiday today! You haven't heard?"

A giggling woman scraped her face off the table and cried, "Independence Day! Fourteen the Fourteenth!"

"Watch, watch this," Steve said, and pointed at their TV.

An image of space flickered onto the screen, and suddenly the whole group was yelling and cheering. They had locked onto a coded channel from Clarke, Steve explained, and though they could not decode its messages, they had used it as a beacon to aim their station's optical telescope. The image from the telescope had been transferred onto the commons TV, and there it was, the black sky and the stars blocked at the center by the shape they had all learned to recognize, the squared-off metallic asteroid with the cable extending out of it. "Now watch!" they yelled at the puzzled travelers. "Watch!"

They howled again, and some of them began a ragged countdown, starting at one hundred. Some of them were inhaling helium as well as nitrous oxide, and these stood below the big screen singing, "We're off to see the wizard, the wonderful wizard of Oz! Because, because, because, because, because of the wonderful things he does! We're off

588

to see the wizard, the wonderful wizard of Oz! We're . . . *off* to see the *wizard*! . . ."

Nadia found herself shivering. The shouted countdown got louder and louder, reached a shrieked "*Zero.*"

A gap appeared between the asteroid and the cable. Clarke disappeared from the screen instantly. The cable, gossamer among the stars, dropped out of view almost as fast.

Wild cheers filled the room, for a moment at least. But it caught, as if on a hitch, as some of the celebrants were distracted by Ann leaping to her feet, both fists at her mouth.

"He's sure to be down by now!" Simon cried to Ann over their din. "He's sure to be down! It's been weeks since he called!"

Slowly it got quiet. Nadia found herself at Ann's side, across from Simon and Sasha. She didn't know what to say. Ann was rigid, her eyes bugged out horribly.

"How did you break the cable?" Sax asked.

"Well, the cable's pretty much unbreakable," Steve replied.

"You *broke* the *cable*?" Yeli exclaimed.

"Well, no, we separated the cable from Clarke, is what we did. But the effect is the same. That cable is on its way down."

The group cheered again, somewhat more weakly. Steve explained to the travelers over the noise: "The cable itself was pretty much impervious, it's graphite whisker with a diamond sponge-mesh gel double-helixed into it, and they've got smart pebble defense stations every hundred kilometers, and security on the cars that was intense. So Arkady suggested we work on Clarke itself. See, the cable goes right through the rock to the factories in the interior, and the actual end of it was physically as well as magnetically bonded to the rock of the asteroid. But we landed with a bunch of our robots in a shipment of stuff from orbit, and dug into the interior and placed thermal bombs outside the cable casing, and around the magnetic generator. Then today we set them all off at once, and the rock went liquid at the same time the magnets were interrupted, and you know Clarke is going like a bullet, so it slipped right off the cable end just like that! And we timed it so that it's going directly away from the sun, and twenty-four degrees out of the plane of the ecliptic as well! So it'll be damned hard to track it down. At least we hope so!''

"And the cable itself?" Sasha said.

It got loud with cheers again, and it was Sax who answered her, in the next quiet moment: "Falling," he said. He was at a computer console, typing as fast as he could, but Steve called out to him, "We have the figures on the descent if you want them. It's pretty complex, a lot of partial differential equations."

"I know," Sax said.

"I can't believe it," said Simon. He still had his hands on Ann's arm, and he looked around at the revelers, his face grim. "The impact's going to kill a lot of people!"

"Probably not," one of them replied. "And those it does kill will mostly be UN police, who have been using the elevator to get down and kill people here on the ground."

"He's probably been down a week or two," Simon repeated emphatically to Ann, who was now white-faced.

"Maybe," she said.

Some people heard this, and quieted down; others did not want to hear, and continued to celebrate.

"We didn't know," Steve said to Ann and Simon. His expression of triumph was gone, he was frowning with concern. "If we had known, I guess we could have tried to contact him. But we didn't know. I'm sorry. Hopefully —" he swallowed. "Hopefully he wasn't up there."

Ann walked back to their table, sat down. Simon hovered anxiously at her side. Neither of them appeared to have heard anything Steve had said.

*

Radio traffic increased somewhat, as those in control of the remaining communications satellites got the news about the cable. Some of the celebrating rebels got busy monitoring and recording these messages; other continued to party.

Sax was still absorbed by the equations on the screen. "Going east," he remarked.

"That's right," Steve said. "It'll make a big bow in the middle at first, as the lower part pulls down, and then the rest will follow."

"How fast?"

"That's hard to say, but we think about four hours for the first time around, and then an hour for the second time around."

"Second time around!" Sax said.

"Well, you know, the cable is 37,000 kilometers long, and the circumference at the equator is twenty-one thousand. So it'll go around almost twice."

"The people on the equator had better move fast," Sax said.

"Not exactly the equator," Sam said. "The Phobos oscillation will cause it to swerve away from the equator to a certain extent. That's actually the hardest part to calculate, because it depends where the cable was in its oscillation when it began to fall."

"North or south?"

"We should know in the next couple of hours."

The six travelers stared helplessly at the screen. It was quiet for the first time since their arrival. The screen showed nothing but stars. No vantage point existed from which to view the elevator's fall; the cable, never visible for more than a fraction of its length to any single observer, would stay invisible to the end. Or visible only as a falling line of fire.

"So much for Phyllis's bridge," Nadia said.

"So much for Phyllis," said Sax.

The Margarifiter group re-established contact with the satellite transmissions they had located, and they found they were also able to poach a number of security satellites. From all these channels they were able to piece together a partial account of the cable's fall. From Nicosia, a UNOMA team reported that the cable had fallen north of them, crumpling down vertically while yet still rapidly covering ground, as if it were cutting through the turning planet. Though north of them, they thought it was south of the equator. A staticky, panicky voice from Sheffield asked them for confirmation of this; the cable had already fallen across half the city and a line of tents east of it, all the way down the slope of Pavonis Mons and across east Tharsis, flattening a zone ten kilometers wide with its sonic boom; it would have been worse, but the air was so thin at that elevation that it did not carry much force. Now the survivors in Sheffield wanted to know whether to run south to escape the next wrapping, or try to get around the caldera to the north.

They got no reply. But more escapees from Korolyov, on the south rim of Melas Chasma in Marineris, reported over one of the rebel channels: the cable was now falling so hard it was shattering on impact. Half an hour later an Aureum drilling operation called in; they had gone out after the sonic booms, and found a mound of glowing brecciated debris, stretching from horizon to horizon.

There was an hour's absence of any new hard information, nothing but questions and speculation and rumor. Then one of the headphoned listeners leaned back and showed thumbs up to the rest of them, and clicked on the intercom, and an excited voice came on yelling through the static: "It's exploding! It came down in about four seconds, it was burning top to bottom and when it hit the ground everything jumped right under our feet! We're having trouble with a leak here. We figure we're about eighteen kilometers south of where it hit, and we're twenty-five south of the equator, so you should be able to calculate the rest of the wrap from that, I hope. It was burning from top to bottom! Like this white line cutting the sky in half! I've never seen anything like it. I've still got afterimages in my vision, they're bright green. It was like a shooting star had stretched . . . Wait, Jorge is on the intercom, he's out there and saying it's only about three meters high where he is. It's soft regolith here, so the cable's in a trench it smashed for itself. He says it's so deep in places you could bury it and have a level surface. Those'll be like fords, he says, because in other places it stands five or six meters high. I guess it'll do that for hundreds of kilometers at a stretch! It'll be like the Great Wall of China.''

Then a call came in from Escalante Crater; it was right on the equator, and they had evacuated immediately on news of the break with Clarke, but had gone south, so that the arrival of the cable had turned out to be a close thing. The cable was now exploding on impact, they reported, and sending sheets of molten ejecta into the sky, lava-esque fireworks that arced up into their dawn twilight, and were dim and black by the time they fell back to the surface.

During all this time Sax never left his screen, and now he was muttering through pursed lips as he typed and read the screen. The second time around the speed of the fall would accelerate to 21,000 kilometers an hour, he said, almost six kilometers a second; so that for anyone within sight of it – a dangerous place to be, deadly if you were not up on a prominence and many kilometers away – it would look like a kind of meteor strike, and cross from horizon to horizon in less than a second. Sonic booms to follow.

"Let's go out and have a look," Steve suggested with a guilty glance at Ann and Simon. A lot of them suited up and went outside. The travelers contented themselves with a video image piped in from the exterior camera, alternating that with video clips gleaned from the satellites. Clips shot from the night side surface were spectacular; they showed a blazing curved line, cutting down like the edge of a white scythe that was trying to chop the planet in two.

Even so they found it hard to concentrate, hard to focus

on what they were seeing and understand it, much less feel anything about it. They had been exhausted when they had landed, and now they were even more exhausted, and yet it was impossible to sleep; more and more video clips were being passed along, some from robot cameras flying in drones on the day side, showing a blackened steaming swath of desolation – the regolith blasted to the side in two long parallel ejecta dikes, banking a canal full of blackness, black all studded with a brecciated mix of stuff which got more exotic as the impact became more severe, until finally a drone camera sent along a clip of a horizon-to-horizon trench of what Sax said must be rough black diamonds.

The impact in the last half hour of the fall was so strong that everything far to north and south was flattened; people were saying that no one close enough actually to see the cable hit survived it, and most of the drone cameras had been smashed as well. For the final thousands of kilometers of the fall, there were no witnesses.

A late clip came in from the west side of Tharsis, from the second pass up that great slope. It was brief but powerful: a white blaze in the sky, and a explosion running up the west side of the volcano. Another shot, from a robot in West Sheffield, showed the cable blasting by just to the south; then an earthquake or sonic blast struck, and the whole rim district of Sheffield fell off the rim in a mass, dropping slowly to the caldera floor five kilometers below.

After that there were any number of video clips bouncing around the fragmented system, but they proved to be only repeats, or late arrivals, or film of the aftermath. And then the satellites began to shut down again.

It had been five hours since the fall began. The six travelers slumped in their chairs, watching or not watching the TV, too tired to feel anything, too tired to think.

"Well," Sax said, "now we've got an equator just like the one I thought the Earth had when I was four years old. A big black line running right around the planet."

Ann glared at Sax so bitterly that Nadia worried she would get up and hit him. But none of them moved. The images on the TV flickered, and the speakers hissed and crackled.

They saw the new equator line in person, the southernmost one anyway, on the second night of their flight toward Shalbatana Vallis. In the dark it was a broad straight black swath, leading them west. As they flew over it Nadia stared down somberly. It hadn't been her project, but it was work, and work destroyed. A bridge brought down; and bringing down a bridge was always a dubious proposition.

And that black line was also a grave. Not many people on the surface had been killed, except on the east side of Pavonis, but most if not all of those on the elevator must have been, and that in itself meant several thousand people. Most of whom had probably been all right until their part of the cable hit the atmosphere and burned up.

As they flew over the wreckage Sax intercepted a new video of the fall. Someone had already stitched up a chronological montage from all the images that had been sent onto the net live or in the hours immediately afterward. In this montage, a very effective bit of work, the final clip was of the last section of the cable, exploding into the landscape. The impact zone was never anything but a moving white blob, like a flaw in the tape; no video was capable of registering such illumination. But as the montage continued the images had been slowed down and processed in every way possible, and one of these processed images was the final clip, an ultra-slow motion shot in which one could see details that would have been impossible to spot live. And so they could see that as the line had crossed the sky, the burning graphite had stripped away first, leaving an incandescent double helix of diamond, flowing majestically out of a sunset sky.

All a gravestone, of course, the people on it already dead at that point, burned away; but it was hard to think of them when the image was so utterly strange and beautiful, a vision of some kind of fantasy DNA, DNA from a macroworld made of pure light, plowing into our universe to germinate a barren planet . . .

Nadia stopped watching the TV, moved into the copilot's seat to help spot the other plane. All that long night she stared out the window, unable to sleep, unable to get the image of that diamond descent out of her mind's eye. It was the longest night of their trip so far, for her. It seemed a kind of eternity before the dawn.

But time passed, another night of their lives, and at last dawn came. Soon after sunrise they landed at a pipeline service airstrip above Shalbatana, and stayed with a group of refugees who had been working on the pipeline, and were now caught there. This group had no political stance in common, and wanted only to survive until things got back to normal. Nadia found their attitude only partly refreshing, and tried to get them to go out and repair pipelines; but she did not think they were convinced.

That evening they took off once more, again laden with supplies given to them by their hosts. And the following dawn they landed on the abandoned airstrip of Carr Crater. Before eight, Nadia and Sax and Ann and Simon and Sasha and Yeli were out in walkers, and up to the crater rim.

The dome was gone. There had been a fire below. All the buildings were intact but scorched, and almost all their windows had been broken or melted. Plastic walls were bent or deformed; concrete was blackened. There were splashes of soot scattered everywhere, and piles of soot scattered here and there on the ground, little heaps of blackened carbon. Sometimes they looked like Hiroshima shadows. Yes, they were bodies. The outlines of people trying to claw down through the sidewalks. "The city's air was hyperoxygenated," Sax ventured. In such an atmosphere human skin and flesh were combustible and flammable. That was what had happened to those early Apollo astronauts, stuck in a test capsule filled with an atmosphere of pure oxygen; when the fire started they had burnt like paraffin.

And so here. Everyone on the streets had caught fire and rushed around like torches, one could see that by the placement of the soot piles.

The six old friends walked down together into the shadow of the eastern crater wall. Under a circular dark pink sky they stopped at the first clutch of blackened bodies, and then walked quickly on. They opened doors in buildings when it was possible, and knocked on all the jammed doors, and listened at the walls with a stethoscope device Sax had brought along. No sound but their own heartbeats, loud and fast at the backs of their coppery throats.

Nadia stumbled around, her breath harsh and ragged. She forced herself to look at the bodies she passed, trying to estimate heights from the black piles of carbon. Like Hiroshima, or Pompeii. People were taller now. They still burnt to the bone, though, and even the bones were thin black sticks.

When she came to a likely-sized pile, she stood staring at it. After a while she approached, and found the right arm, and scraped with her four-fingered glove at the back of the charred wristbones, looking for the dotcode tag. She found it, cleaned it. Ran her laser over it like a grocery clerk pricing goods. Emily Hargrove.

She moved on, did it again with another likely-sized pile. Thabo Moeti. It was better than checking teeth against dental records; but she wouldn't have done that.

She was light-headed and numb when she came to a soot pile near the city offices, alone, its right hand splayed out so that she only had to check. She cleaned the tag and checked. Arkady Nikolayevich Bogdanov.

They flew west for eleven more days, hiding through the daylight hours under stealth blankets, or taking shelter with people they encountered en route. During the nights they followed transponders, or the directions of the last group with which they had stayed. Though these groups often knew of each other's existence and location, they were definitely not parts of a single resistance, or coordinated in any way: some hoped to make it to the south polar cap like the prisoners from Korolyov, others had never heard of this refuge; some were Bogdanovists, others were revolutionaries following different leaders; some were religious communes or utopian experiments, or nationalist groups trying to contact their governments back home; and some were merely collections of survivors without a program, orphaned by the violence. The six travelers even stopped at Korolyov itself, but they did not attempt to enter when they saw the naked frozen bodies of guards outside the locks, some of them propped in standing positions like statues.

After Korolyov, they encountered no one. The radios and TVs went dead as satellites were shot out; the pistes were empty; the Earth was on the other side of the sun. The landscape seemed as barren as before their arrival, except for the spreading patches of frost. They flew on as if they were the only people in the world, the sole survivors.

White noise buzzed in Nadia's ear, something to do with the plane's ventilators no doubt. She checked the ventilators, but they were okay. The others gave her chores to do, let her go on walks by herself before take-off, and after landing. They were stunned themselves by what they had found at Carr and Korolyov, and unable to bring much to the effort of cheering her up, which she found a relief. Ann and Simon were still worried about Peter. Yeli and Sax were worried about their food supplies, dropping all the time; the plane's cabinets were nearly bare.

But Arkady was dead, and so none of that mattered. The revolt seemed to Nadia more a waste than ever, an unfocused spasm of rage, the ultimate cutting off one's nose to spite one's face. The whole world, wrecked! She told the others to send out a radio message on one of the general channels, announcing that Arkady was dead. Sasha agreed, and helped convince the others to do it. "It will help stop things more quickly," Sasha said.

Sax shook his head. "Insurrections don't have leaders," he said. "Besides, no one is likely hear it."

But a couple days later, it was clear some people had heard it. They received a microburst in response from Alex Zhalin. "Look, Sax, this isn't the American Revolution, or the French or the Russian or the English. It's all the revolutions at once, and everywhere! A whole world in revolt, with a land area equal to Earth's, and only a few thousand people trying to stop it, and most of those still in space, where they have a good view but are very vulnerable. So if they manage to subdue a force in Syrtis, there is another in the Hellespontus. Imagine space-based forces trying to stop a revolution in Cambodia, but also in Alaska, Japan, Spain, Madagascar. How do you do it? You can't. I only wish that Arkady Nikoleyevich had lived to see it, he would have—"

The microburst ended abruptly. Perhaps a bad sign, perhaps not. But even Alex hadn't been able to keep a note of discouragement out of his voice, when he talked about Arkady. It was impossible; Arkady had been so much more than a political leader – everybody's brother, a natural force, the voice of one's conscience. One's innate sense of what was fair and just. One's best friend.

Nadia stumped through her grief, helping to navigate their flights by night, sleeping as much as she could through the days. She lost weight. Her hair turned pure white, all the remaining gray and black hairs coming out in her brush. She

599

found it hard to speak. It felt like her throat and guts had petrified. She was a stone, it was impossible to weep. She went about her business instead. No one they met had any food to spare, and they were running out themselves. They set a strict rationing schedule, dividing meals in half.

And on the thirty-second day of their journey from Lasswitz, after a journey of some ten thousand kilometers, they came to Cairo, up on the southern rim of Noctis Labyrinthus, just to the south of the southernmost strand of the fallen cable.

Cairo was under the de facto control of UNOMA, in that no one in the city had ever claimed otherwise, and like all the rest of the big tent cities it lay helpless under the orbiting lasers of UNOMA police ships, which had burned into orbit sometime in the last month. Also most of the inhabitants of Cairo at the beginning of the war had been Arab and Swiss, and in Cairo, at least, people of both nationalities seemed only to be trying to stay out of harm's way.

Now, however, the six travelers were not the only refugees arriving; a flood of them had just come down Tharsis from the devastation in Sheffield and the rest of Pavonis; others were driving up from Marineris, through the maze of Noctis. The city was at quadruple capacity, with crowds living and sleeping in the streets and parks, the physical plant strained to the breaking point, and food and gases running out.

The six travelers were told this by an airstrip worker who was still stubbornly doing her job, although none of the strip shuttles were running any more. After guiding them into parking places among a great fleet of planes at one end of the strip, she told them to suit up and walk the kilometer to the city wall. It made Nadia unreasonably nervous to leave the two 16Ds behind and walk into a city; and she was not reassured once through the lock, when she saw that most people inside were wearing their walkers and carrying their helmets with them, ready for depressurization if it came.

They went to the city offices, and there found Frank and Maya, as well as Mary Dunkel and Spencer Jackson. They all greeted each other with relief, but there was no time for catching up on their various adventures; Frank was busy before a screen, talking to someone in orbit by the sound of it, and he shrugged off their hugs and kept talking, waving once later to acknowledge their appearance. Apparently he was hooked into a functioning communications system, or even more than one, because he stayed in front of the screen talking to one face or another for the next six hours straight, pausing only to sip water or make another call, not sparing another glance for his old compatriots. He seemed to be in a permanent fury, his jaw muscles bunching and unbunching rhythmically; other than that he was in his element, explaining and lecturing, wheedling and threatening, inquiring and then commenting impatiently on the answers he got. Wheeling and dealing in his old style, in other words, but with an angry, bitter, even frightened edge, as if he had walked off a cliff and was trying to argue his way back to ground.

When he finally clicked off, he leaned back in his seat and sighed histrionically, then rose stiffly from his seat and came over to greet them, putting a hand briefly on Nadia's shoulder. Aside from that he was brusque with all of them, and completely uninterested in how they had managed to make it to Cairo. He only wanted to know whom they had met, and where, and how well these scattered parties were doing, and what they intended. Once or twice he went back to his screen and contacted these groups immediately upon being informed of their location, an ability that stunned the travelers, who had assumed that everyone was as cut off as they had been. "UNOMA links," Frank explained, running a hand over his swarthy jaw. "They're keeping some channels open for me."

"Why?" Sax said.

"Because I'm trying to stop this. I'm trying for a cease-fire, then a general amnesty, then a reconstruction joined by all."

"But under whose direction?"

"UNOMA's, of course. And the national offices."

"But UNOMA agrees only to the cease-fire?" Sax ventured. "While the rebels only agree to the general amnesty?"

Frank nodded curtly. "And neither like the reconstruction joined by all. But the current situation is so bad they may go for it. Four more aquifers have blown since the cable came down. They're all equatorial, and some people are saying it's cause and effect."

Ann shook her head at this, and Frank looked pleased to see it. "They were broken open, I was pretty sure. They broke one at the mouth of Chasma Borealis, it's pouring out onto the Borealis dunes."

"The weight of the polar cap probably puts that one under a good bit of pressure," Ann said.

"Do you know what happened to the Acheron group?" Sax asked Frank.

"No. They've disappeared. It might be like with Arkady, I'm afraid." He glanced at Nadia, pursed his lips unhappily. "I should get back to work."

"But what's happening on Earth?" Ann demanded. "What does the UN have to say about all this?"

" 'Mars is not a nation but a world resource'," Frank quoted heavily. "They're saying that the tiny fraction of humanity that lives here can't be allowed to control the resources, when the human material base as a whole is so deeply stressed."

"That's probably true," Nadia heard herself say. Her voice was harsh, a croak. It felt like she hadn't spoken in days.

Frank shrugged.

Sax said, "I suppose that's why they've given the transnationals such a free hand. It seems to me there's more of their security here than UN police."

"That's right," Frank said. "It took the UN a while to agree to deploy their peacekeepers."

"They don't mind having the dirty work done by someone else."

"Of course not."

"And Earth itself?" Ann asked again.

Frank shrugged. "The Group of Seven seems to be getting things under control." He shook his head. "It's hard to say from here, it really is."

He went to his screen to make more calls. The others went off to eat, to clean up, to sleep, to catch up on friends and acquaintances, on the rest of the first hundred, on what news there was from Earth. The flags of convenience had been destroyed by attacks from the have-nots in the south, but apparently the transnationals had fled to the Group of Seven, and had been taken in and defended by the seven's giant militaries. The twelfth attempt at a cease-fire had held for several days now.

So, a bit of time to try and recover. But when they went through the comm room, Frank would still be there, shifting ever more surely into a bitter black fury, snapping his way through what seemed an endless nightmare of screen diplomacy, talking on and on in an urgent, scornful, biting tone. He was past cajoling anyone into anything, now; it was purely an exertion of will. Trying to move the world without a fulcrum, or with the weakest of fulcrums, his leverage consisting mainly of his old American connections and his current personal standing with a variety of insurrection leaders, both nearly severed by events and the TV blackouts. And both becoming less important daily on Mars itself, as UNOMA and the transnational forces took over town after town. It seemed to Nadia that Frank was now trying to muscle the process along by the sheer force of his anger at his lack of influence. She found she could not stand to be around him; things were bad enough without his black bile.

But with Sax's help, he got an independent signal to Earth,

by contacting Vega and getting the technicians there to transmit messages back and forth. That meant a few hours between transmission and reception, but in a long couple of days after that, he got in five coded exchanges with Secretary of State Wu, and while waiting through the night for return messages, the people on Vega filled the gaps with tapes of Terran news programs that they had not seen. All these reports, when they referred to the Martian situation at all, portrayed the insurrection as a minor disruption caused by criminal elements, principally by escaped prisoners from Korolyov, who had gone on a rampage of senseless property damage, in the process killing great numbers of innocent civilians. Clips of the frozen naked guards outside Korolyov were featured prominently in these reports, as were satellite telephotos of the aquifer outbursts. The most skeptical programs mentioned that these and all other clips from Mars were provided by UNOMA; and some stations in China and the Netherlands even questioned the accuracy of the UNOMA accounts. But they provided no alternative explanation of events, and for the most part, the Terran media disseminated the transnationals' version of things. When Nadia pointed this out, Frank snorted. "Of course," he said contemptuously. "Terran news *is* a transnational." He turned off the sound.

Behind him Nadia and Yeli leaned forward instinctively on the bamboo couch, as if that might help them to hear the silent clip better. Their two weeks of being cut off from outside news had seemed like a year, and now they watched the screen helplessly, soaking in whatever information they could. Yeli even stood to turn the sound back up, but Frank was asleep in his chair, his chin on his chest. When a message from the State Department came in he jerked awake, turned up the sound, stared at the tiny faces on the screen, snapped out a reply in a hoarse rasp. Then he closed his eyes and slept again.

At the end of the second night of the Vega link, he had

gotten Secretary Wu to promise to press the UN in New York to restore communications, and halt all police action until the situation could be assessed. Wu was also going to try to get transnational forces ordered back to Earth, though that, Frank noted, would be impossible.

The sun had been up for a couple of hours when Frank sent a final acknowledgment to Vega, and shut down. Yeli was asleep on the floor. Nadia stood up stiffly and went for a walk around the park, taking advantage of the light to have a look around. She had to step over bodies sleeping in the grass, in groups of three or four spooned together for warmth. The Swiss had set up big kitchens, and rows of outhouses lining the city wall; it looked like a construction site, and suddenly she found tears running down her face. On she walked. It was nice to be able to walk around in the open light of day.

Eventually she returned to the city offices. Frank was standing over Maya, who was asleep on a couch. He stared down at her with a blank expression, then looked up bleary-eyed at Nadia. "She's really out."

"Everyone's tired."

"Hmph. What was it like at Hellas?"

"Under water."

He shook his head. "Sax must be loving it."

"That's what I kept saying. But I think it's too out of control for him."

"Ah yes." He closed his eyes, appeared to sleep for a second or two. "I'm sorry about Arkady."

"Yes."

Another silence. "She looks like a girl."

"A little." Actually Nadia had never seen Maya look older. They were all pushing eighty, they couldn't keep the pace, treatments or not. In their minds they were old.

"The folks on Vega told me that Phyllis and the rest of the people on Clarke are going to try to get across to them in an emergency rocket."

"Aren't they out of the plane of the ecliptic?"

"They are now, but they're going to try to push down to Jupiter, and use it to swing back downsystem."

"That'll take a year or two, won't it?"

"About a year. Hopefully they'll miss entirely, or fall into Jupiter. Or run out of food."

"I take it you're not happy with Phyllis."

"That bitch. She's responsible for a lot of this. Pulling in all those transnats with promises of every metal ever put to use — she figured she would be queen of Mars with all those folks backing her, you should have seen her up there on Clarke, looking down at the planet like a little tin god. I could have strangled her. How I wish I could have seen her face when Clarke took off and went flying!" He laughed harshly.

Maya stirred at the sound, woke. They pulled her up and went out into the park in search of a meal. They got in a line of people huddled in their walkers, coughing, rubbing their hands together, blowing out plumes of frost like white cotton balls. Very few talked. Frank surveyed the scene with a disgusted look, and when they got their trays of roshti and tabouli he devoured his and began conversing to his wristpad in Arabic. "They say Alex and Evgenia and Samantha are coming up from Noctis with some Bedouin friends of mine," he told them when he shut down.

That was good news; Alex and Evgenia had been heard from last in Aureum Overlook, a rebel bastion that had destroyed a number of orbiting UN ships before being incinerated by missile fire from Phobos. And no one had heard from Samantha the whole month of the war.

So all the first hundred in town went to the north gate of Cairo that afternoon to greet them. Cairo's north gate looked down a long natural ramp that ran into one of the southernmost canyons of Noctis; the road rose up from the canyon floor on this ramp, and they could see all the way down it to the canyon bottom. There, in the early afternoon, came a rover caravan, churning up a small dust cloud and moving slowly.

It was nearly an hour before the cars rolled up the last part of the ramp. They were no more than three kilometers away when great gouts of flame and ejecta burst into being among them, knocking some rovers into the cliff wall, some over the ramp into space. The rest twisted to a halt, shattered and burning.

Then an explosion rocked the north gate, and they dove for the wall. Cries and shouts over the common band. Nothing more; they stood back up. The fabric of the tent still held, although the gate lock was apparently stuck fast.

Down on the road thin plumes of tan smoke lofted into the air, tattering to the east, pulled back down into Noctis on the dusk wind. Nadia sent a robot rover down to check for survivors. Wristpads crackled with static, nothing but static, and Nadia was thankful for that; what could they have hoped for? Screams? Frank was cursing into his wristpad, switching between Arabic and English. Trying vainly to find out what had happened. But Alexander, Evgenia, Samantha . . . Nadia looked fearfully at the little images on her wrist, directing the robot cameras with dread. Shattered rovers. Some bodies. Nothing moved. One rover still smoked.

"Where's Sasha?" Yeli's voice cried. "Where's Sasha?"

"She was in the lock," someone said. "She was going out to greet them."

They went to work opening the inner lock door, Nadia at the front punching all the codes and then working with tools and finally a shape charge that someone handed to her. They moved back and the lock blew out like a crossbow bolt, and then they were there, crowbarring the heavy door back. Nadia rushed in and dropped to her knees by Sasha, who was huddled head-in-jacket, in the emergency posture; but she was dead, the flesh of her face Martian red, her eyes frozen.

Feeling that she had to move or else turn to stone on the

spot, Nadia broke and ran back to the town cars they had come in. She jumped in one and drove away; she had no plan, and the car seemed to choose the direction. Her friends' voices cut through the crackle on her wristpad, sounding like crickets in a cage, Maya muttering viciously in Russian, crying, only Maya was tough enough to keep feeling in all of this: "That was Phobos again!" her little voice cried. "They're psychotic up there!"

The others were in shock, their voices like AIs'. "They're not psychotic," Frank said. "It's perfectly rational. They see a political settlement coming and they're getting in as many shots as they can."

"Murderous bastards!" Maya cried. "KGB fascists . . ."

The town car stopped at the city offices. Nadia ran inside, to the room where she had stashed her stuff, at this point no more than her old blue backpack. She dug in it, still unaware of what she was looking for until her claw hand, still the strong one, reached into a bag and pulled it out. Arkady's transmitter. Of course. She ran back to the car and drove to the south gate. Sax and Frank were still talking, Sax sounding the same as always, but saying, "Every one of us whose location is known is either here, or else has been killed. I think they're after the first hundred in particular."

"Singling us out, you mean?" Frank said.

"I saw some Terran news that said we were the ring-leaders. And twenty-one of us have died since the revolt began. Another forty missing."

The town car arrived at the south gate. Nadia turned off her intercom, got out of the car, went into the lock and put on boots, helmet, gloves. She pumped up and checked out, then slammed the open button and waited for the lock to empty and open. As it had on Sasha. They had lived a life-time together in just the last month alone. Then it was out onto the surface, into the glare and push of a windy hazy day, feeling the first diamond bite of the cold. She kicked through drifts of fines and red puffs blew out ahead of her.

The hollow woman, kicking blood. Out of the other gate were the bodies of her friends and others, their dead faces purplish and bloated, as after construction accidents; Nadia had seen several of those now, seen death several times, and each had been a horror – and yet here they were deliberately creating as many of these horrible accidents as they could! That was war; killing people by every means possible. People who might have lived a thousand years. She thought of Arkady and of a thousand years, and hissed. They had quarreled so in recent years, mostly about politics. Your plans are all anachronism, Nadia had said. You don't understand the world. Ha! he had laughed, offended. This world I understand. With an expression as dark as any she had ever seen from him. And she remembered when he had given her the transmitter, how he had cried for John, how crazy he had been with rage and grief. Just in case, he had said to her refusals, pleading. Just in case.

And now it had happened. She couldn't believe it. She took the box from her walker's thigh pocket, turned it over in her hand. Phobos shot up over the western horizon like a gray potato. The sun had just set, and the alpenglow was so strong that it looked like she was standing in her own blood, as if she were a creature as small as a cell standing on the corroded wall of her heart, while around her swept the winds of her own dusty plasma. Rockets were landing at the spaceport north of the city. The dusk mirrors gleamed in the western sky like a cluster of evening stars. A busy sky. UN ships would soon be descending.

Phobos crossed the sky in four and a quarter hours, so she didn't have to wait long. It had risen as a half moon, but now it was gibbous, almost full, halfway to the zenith, moving at its steady clip across the coagulating sky. She could make out a faint point of light inside the gray disk: the two little domed craters, Semenov and Leveykin. She held the radio transmitter out and tapped in the ignition code, MANGALA. It was like using a TV remote.

And then a bright light flared on the leading edge of the little gray disk. The two faint lights went out. The bright light flared even brighter. Could she really perceive the deceleration? Probably not; but it was there.

Phobos was on its way down.

Back inside Cairo, she found that the news had already spread. The flare had been bright enough to catch people's eyes, and after that they had clumped together around the blank TV screens, by habit, and exchanged rumors and speculation, and somehow the basic fact had gotten around, or been worked out independently. Nadia strolled past group after group, and heard people saying "Phobos has been hit! Phobos has been hit!" And someone laughed, "They brought the Roche limit up to it!"

She thought she was lost in the medina, but almost directly she came to the city offices. Maya was outside: "Hey Nadia!" she cried. "Did you see Phobos?"

"Yes."

"Roger says when they were up there in year One, they built a system of explosives and rocketry into it! Did Arkady ever tell you about it?"

"Yes."

They went in to the offices, Maya thinking aloud: "If they manage to slow it down very much, it'll come down. I wonder if it'll be possible to calculate where. We're pretty damn close to the equator right here."

"It'll break up, surely, and come down in a lot of places."

"True. I wonder what Sax thinks."

They found Sax and Frank bunched before one screen, Yeli and Ann and Simon before another. A UNOMA satellite was tracking Phobos with a telescope, and Sax was measuring the moon's speed of passage across the Martian landscape to get a fix on its velocity. In the image on the screen Stickney's dome shone like a Fabergé egg, but the eye was drawn away from that to the moon's leading edge, which was blurry and

610

streaked with white flashes of ejecta and gases. "Look how well balanced the thrust is," Sax said to no one in particular. "Too sudden a thrust and the whole thing would have shattered. And an unbalanced thrust would have set it spinning, and then the thrust would have pushed it all over the place."

"I see signs of stabilizing lateral thrusts," his AI said.

"Attitude jets," Sax said. "They turned Phobos into a big rocket."

"They did it in the first year," Nadia said. She wasn't sure why she was speaking, she still seemed out of control, observing her actions from several seconds behind. "A lot of the Phobos crew was from rocketry and guidance. They processed the ice veins into liquid oxygen and deuterium, and stored it in lined columns buried in the chondrite. The engines and the control complex were buried centrally."

"So it is a big rocket." Sax was nodding as he typed. "Period of Phobos, 27, 547 seconds. So it's going . . . 2.146 kilometers per second, approximately, and to bring it down it needs to decelerate to . . . to 1.561 kilometers per second. So, .585 kilometers per second slower. For a mass like Phobos . . . wow. That's a lot of fuel."

"What's it down to now?" Frank asked. He was black-faced, his jaw muscles pulsing under the skin like little biceps – furious, Nadia saw, at his inability to predict what would happen next.

"About 1.7. And those big thrusters still burning. It'll come down. But not in one piece. The descent will break it up, I'm sure."

"The Roche limit?"

"No, just stress from aerobraking, and with all these empty fuel chambers . . ."

"What happened to the people on it?" Nadia heard herself ask.

"Someone came on and said it sounded like the whole population had bailed out. No one stuck around to try and stop the firing."

"Good," Nadia said, sitting down heavily on the couch.

"So when will it come down?" Frank demanded.

Sax blinked. "Impossible to say. Depends on when it breaks up, and how. But pretty soon, I'd guess. Within a day. And then there'll be a stretch somewhere along the equator, probably a big stretch of it, in big trouble. It's going to make a fairly large meteor shower."

"That will clear away some of the elevator cable," Simon said weakly. He was sitting beside Ann, watching her with concern. She stared at Simon's screen bleakly, showed no sign of hearing any of them. There never had been word of their son Peter. Was that better or worse than a soot pile, a dot code name coming up on your wristpad? Better, Nadia decided. But still hard.

"Look," Sax said. "It's breaking up."

The satellite telescopic camera gave them an excellent view: the dome over Stickney bursting outward in great shards, the crater pit lines that had always marked Phobos suddenly puffing with dust, yawning open; and then the little potato-shaped world blossomed, fell apart into a scattering of irregular chunks. A half a dozen large ones slowly spread out, the largest one leading the way. One chunk flew off to the side, apparently powered still by one of the rockets that had lain buried in the moon's interior. The rest of the rocks began to spread out in an irregular line, tumbling each at a different speed.

"Well, we're kind of in the line of fire," Sax remarked, looking up at the rest of them. "The biggest chunks will hit the upper atmosphere soon, and then it'll happen pretty quickly."

"Can you determine where?"

"No, there's too many unknowns. Along the equator, that's all. We're probably far enough south to miss most of it, but there may be quite a scatter effect."

"People on the equator ought to head north or south," Maya said.

"They probably know that. Anyway the fall of the cable probably cleared the area pretty effectively already."

There was little to do but wait. None of them wanted to leave the city and head south, it seemed they were past that kind of effort, too hardened or too tired to worry about longshot risks. Frank paced the room, his swarthy face working with anger; finally he couldn't stand it, and got back on his screen to send off a sequence of short pungent messages. One came back in, and he snorted. "We've got a grace period, because the UN police are afraid to come down here until after the shit falls. After that they'll be on us like hawks. They're claiming that the command initiating the Phobos explosions originated here, and they're tired of a neutral city being used as a command center for the insurrection."

"So we've got until the fall is over," Sax said.

He clicked into the UNOMA network, and got a radar composite of the fragments. After that there was nothing to do. They sat; they stood and walked around; they looked at the screens; they ate cold pizza; they napped. Nadia did none of these things. She could only manage to sit, hunched over her stomach, which felt like an iron walnut in her. She waited.

Near midnight and the timeslip, something on the screens caught Sax's attention, and with some furious typing on Frank's channels he got through to the Olympus Mons observatory. It was just before dawn there, still dark, and one of the observatory cameras gave them its low space view southward, the black curve of the planet blocking the stars. And then there were shooting stars blazing down at an angle out of the western sky, as fast and bright as if they were perfectly straight lightning bolts, or titanic tracer bullets, spraying in a sequence eastward, breaking apart in the last moments before impact, causing phosphor blobs to burst into existence at every impact point, like the first moments of a whole string of nuclear explosions. In less than ten seconds the strike was over, leaving the black field dotted with a line of glowing yellow smoke-obscured patches.

Nadia closed her eyes, saw swimming afterimages of the strike. She opened them again, looked at the screen. Clouds of smoke were surging up into the pre-dawn sky over west Tharsis, pouring so high that they got up out of the shadow of the planet and were lit by the rising sun; they were mushroom clouds, their heads a bright pale pink, their dark gray stalks illuminated by reflection from above. Slowly the sunlight moved down the tumultuous stalks, until they were all burnished by the new morning sun. Then the lofty line of yellow and pink mushroom clouds drifted across a sky that was a delicate shade of indigo pastel: it looked like a Maxfield Parrish nightmare, too strange and beautiful a sight to believe. Nadia thought of the cable's last moment, that image of the incandescent double helix of diamonds. How was it that destruction could be so beautiful? Was there something in the scale of it? Was there some shadow in people, lusting for it? Or was it just a coincidental combination of the elements, the final proof that beauty has no moral dimension? She stared and stared at the image, focused all her will on it; but she could not make it make sense.

"That may be enough particulate matter to trigger another global dust storm," Sax observed. "Although the net heat addition to the system will surely be considerable."

"Shut up, Sax," Maya said.

Frank said, "It's about our turn to get hit, right?"

Sax nodded.

They left the city offices and went out into the park. Everyone stood facing northwest. It was silent, as if they were performing some religious ritual. It felt completely different from waiting for bombardment by the police. By now it was mid-morning, the sky a dull dusty pink.

Then over the horizon lanced a painfully bright comet. There was a collective indrawn gasp, punctuated by scattered cries. The brilliant white line curved down toward them, then shot over their heads in an instant, disappearing over the eastern horizon. There hadn't even been time to catch one's breath as it passed. A moment later the ground trembled slightly under their feet, and the silence was broken by exclamations. To the east a cloud shot up, redefining the height of the sky's pink dome; it must have plumed twenty thousand meters.

Then another brilliant white blaze crossed the sky overhead, trailing comet tails of fire. Then another, and another, and a whole blazing cluster of them, all crossing the sky and dropping over the eastern horizon, down into great Marineris. Finally the shower stopped, leaving the witnesses in Cairo half-blinded, staggering, afterimages bouncing in their sight. They had been passed over.

"Now comes the UN," Frank said. "At best."

"Do you think we ought to . . ." Maya said. "Do you think we're . . ."

"Safe in their hands?" Frank said acidly.

"Maybe we should take to the planes again."

"In daylight?"

"Well, it might be better than staying here!" she retorted. "I don't know about you, but I don't want to just get lined up against a wall and shot!"

"If they're UNOMA they won't do that," Sax said.

"You can't be sure," Maya said. "Everyone on Earth thinks we're the ringleaders."

"There aren't any ringleaders!" Frank said.

"But they want there to be ringleaders," Nadia said.

This stilled them.

Sax said mildly, "Someone may have decided things will be easier to control without us around."

More news of impacts in the other hemisphere came in, and Sax settled down before the screens to follow it. Helplessly Ann stood over his right shoulder to observe it as well;

these kinds of strikes had happened all the time back in the Noachian, and the chance to see one live was too much for her to pass up, even if it was the result of human agency.

While they watched, Maya continued to urge them to do something – to leave, to hide, whatever, just *something*. She swore at Sax and Ann when they didn't respond. Frank left to see what was happening at the spaceport. Nadia accompanied him to the door of the city offices, afraid that Maya was right, but unwilling to listen anymore. She said goodbye to Frank and stood before the city building, looking at the sky. It was afternoon, and the prevailing westerlies were beginning to sweep down the slope of Tharsis, bringing with them dust from the impacts; it looked like smoke in the sky, as if there were a forest fire on the other side of Tharsis. The light inside Cairo dimmed as the dust clouds obscured the sun, and the tent's polarization created short rainbows and sundogs, as if the very fabric of the world were unraveling into kaleidoscopic parts. Huddled masses, under a burning sky. Nadia shivered. A thicker cloud covered the sun like an eclipse. She went indoors, out of its shadow, back into the offices. Sax was saying, "Very likely to begin another global."

"I hope it does," Maya said. She was pacing back and forth like a great cat in a cage. "It will help us escape."

"Escape where?" Sax asked.

Maya sucked air in through her teeth. "The planes are stocked. We could go back to the Hellespontus Montes, to the habitats there."

"They'd see us."

Frank came onto Sax's screen. He was staring into his wristpad, and the image quivered. "I'm at the west gate with the mayor. There's a bunch of rovers outside. We've locked all the gates because they won't identify themselves. Apparently they've surrounded the city, and are trying to broach the physical plant from the outside. So everyone should get their walkers on, and be ready to go."

"I told you we should have left!" Maya cried.

"We couldn't have," Sax said. "Anyway, our chances may be just as good in some sort of mêlée. If everyone makes a break for it at once, they might be overwhelmed by numbers. Now look, if anything happens, let's all meet at the east gate, okay? You go ahead and go. Frank," he said to the screen. "You should get over there too when you can. I'm going to try some things with the physical plant robots that should keep those people out until dark at least."

It was now three p.m., although it seemed like twilight, as the sky was thick with high, rapidly-moving dust clouds. The forces outside identified themselves as UNOMA police, and demanded to be let in. Frank and Cairo's mayor asked them for authorization from UN Geneva, and declared a ban on all arms in the city. The forces outside made no reply.

At 4:30 alarms went off all over the city. The tent had been broached, apparently catastrophically, because a sudden wind whipped west through the streets, and pressure sirens went off in every building. The electricity went off; and just that quick it went from a town to a broken shell full of running figures in walkers and helmets, crowding toward the gates, knocked down by gusts of wind or by each other. Windows popped out everywhere, the air was full of clear plastic shrapnel. Nadia, Maya, Ann and Simon and Yeli left the city building and fought their way through crowds toward the east gate. There was a great crush of people around it because the lock was open, and some people were squeezing through: a deadly situation for anyone who fell underfoot, and if the lock were blocked in any way, it could turn deadly for everyone. And yet it all happened in silence, except for helmet intercoms and some background impacts. The first hundred were tuned to their old band, and over the static and exterior noises Frank's voice came on. "I'm at the east gate now. Get out of the crush so I can find you." His voice was low, businesslike. "Hurry up, there's something happening outside the lock."

They worked their way out of the crowd, and saw Frank just inside the wall, waving a hand overhead. "Come on," the distant figure said in their ears. "Don't be such sheep, there's no reason to join the toothpaste when the tent's lost its integrity, we can cut through anywhere we want. Let's go straight for the planes."

"I told you," Maya began, but Frank cut her off: "Shut up, Maya, we couldn't leave like this until something like this happened, *remember*?"

It was near sunset now, the sun pouring through a gap between Pavonis and the dust cloud, illuminating the clouds from below in a garish display of violent Martian tones, casting a hellish light over the milling scene. And now figures in camouflaged uniforms were pouring in through rents in the tent. There were big spaceport shuttle buses parked outside, with more troops emerging from them.

Sax appeared out of an alley. "I don't think we'll be able to get to the planes," he said.

A figure in walker and helmet appeared out of the murk. "Come on," it said on their band. "Follow me."

They stared at this stranger. "Who are you?" Frank demanded.

"Follow me!" The stranger was a small man, and behind his faceplate they could see a bright ferocious grin. Brown thin face. The man took off into an alley leading to the medina, and Maya was the first to follow. Helmeted people ran everywhere; those without helmets were sprawled on the ground, dead or dying. They could hear sirens through their helmets, very faint and attenuated, and there were sounds like vibrations underfoot, seismic booms of some kind; but other than that all the hectic activity occurred in silence, broken only by the sounds of their own breathing, and their voices in each other's ears, "Where to?" "Sax are you there?" "He went down that one," and so forth, a strangely intimate conversation, given the dusky chaos they

618

ran through. Looking around Nadia almost kicked the body of a dead cat, lying in the streetgrass as if asleep.

The man they were following appeared to be humming a tune over their band, an absorbed little *bum, bum, ba-dum-dum dum* – Peter's theme from *Peter and the Wolf*, perhaps. He knew the streets of Cairo well, making turns in the medina's tight warren without a moment's pause for thought, and leading them to the city wall in less than ten minutes.

At the wall they peered through the warped tenting; outside in the murk, anonymous suited figures were running off alone or in groups of two or three, in a kind of Brownian dispersion onto the south Noctis rim. "Where's Yeli?" Maya exclaimed suddenly.

No one knew.

Then Frank pointed. "Look!"

Down the road to the east, a number of rovers had appeared out of Noctis Labyrinthus. They were very fast cars of an unfamiliar shape, coming up out of the dusk without headlights.

"Who now?" Sax said. He turned to look at their guide for an answer; but the man was gone, disappeared back into the alleyways.

"Is this still the first hundred's frequency?" a new voice said.

"Yes!" Frank replied. "Who is this?"

Maya cried, "Isn't that Michel?"

"Good ear, Maya. Yes, it's Michel. Look, we're here to take you away if you want to go. It appears they are systematically eliminating any of the first hundred they can get their hands on. So we thought you would be willing to join us."

"I think we are all ready to join you," Frank said. "But how?"

"Well, that's the tricky part. Did a guide show up and lead you to the wall?"

"Yes!"

"Good. That was Coyote, he's good at things like that. So, wait there; we will create some diversions elsewhere, and then come right to your section of the wall."

In only a matter of minutes, though it seemed like an hour, explosions rocked the city. They saw flashes of light to the north, toward the spaceport. Michel came back on: "Shine a headlamp east for just a second."

Sax put his face to the tent wall and turned on his headlamp, briefly illuminating a cone of smoke-choked air. Visibility had dropped to a hundred meters or less, and seemed to be still diminishing. But Michel's voice said, "Contact. Now, cut through the wall and step outside, we're almost there. We'll take off again when you're all in our rover locks, so be prepared. How many are you?"

"Six," Frank said after a pause.

"Wonderful. We have two cars, so it won't be too bad. Three of you in each, okay? Get ready, let's do this fast."

Sax and Ann cut at the tent fabric with little knives from their wristpad tool kits. They looked like kittens clawing at drapes, but quickly made holes big enough to crawl through, and they all clambered over the waist-high coping, and out onto the smoothed regolith of the wall skirt. Behind them explosions were blowing the physical plant into the sky, illuminating the wrecked city in flashes that cut through the haze like photographic strobes, freezing individual moments before they disappeared in the murk.

Suddenly the strange rovers they had seen appeared out of the dust and skidded to a halt before them. They yanked open the outer lock doors and piled in, Sax and Ann and Simon in one, Nadia with Maya and Frank in the other, and they were tumbled head over heels when the rover jerked into motion and accelerated away. "Ow!" Maya cried.

"All aboard?" Michel asked.

They called out their names.

"Good. I'm glad we have you!" Michel said. "It's getting

620

pretty hard. Dmitri and Elena are dead, I just heard. Killed at Echus Overlook.''

In the silence that ensued they could hear the tires, grinding over the gravel of the road.

"These rovers are really fast," Sax remarked.

"Yes. And great shock absorbers. Made for just this kind of situation, I'm afraid. We'll have to abandon them once we get down into Noctis; they're much too visible."

"You have invisible cars?" Frank asked.

"In a manner of speaking."

After half of hour of bouncing in the lock they stopped briefly, and transferred into the rovers' main rooms. And there in one was Michel Duval, white-haired, wrinkled − an old man, gazing at Maya and Nadia and Frank with tears in his eyes. He embraced them one by one, laughing an odd, choked laugh.

"You're taking us to Hiroko?" Maya said.

"Yes, we will try. But it's a long way, and conditions are not good. But I think we can do it. Oh, I am so glad we have found you! You don't know how horrible it has been to look and look, and find only bodies."

"We know," Maya said. "We found Arkady, and Sasha was just killed today, and Alex and Edvard and Samantha, and I guess Yeli too, just now . . ."

"Yes. Well. We will try to make sure there aren't any more."

The rover's TV showed the interior of the following car, where Ann and Simon and Sax were being greeted stiffly by a young stranger. Michel turned to look over his shoulder out of the windshield and hissed. They were at the head of one of the many box canyons leading down into Noctis, a rounded canyon end that dropped rapidly away. The road that descended this headwall had followed an artificial ramp which had been built to support it; but now the ramp was gone, blasted away, and the road with it.

"We will have to walk," Michel said after a while. "We

621

would have had to abandon these cars at the bottom anyway. It's only about five kilometers. Are your suits fully supplied?"

They refilled their tanks from the rover, and put their helmets back on. Then it was back out through the locks.

When they were all out, they stood staring at each other: the six refugees, Michel and the younger driver. The eight of them set off on foot, in darkness, using headlamps only during the tricky climb down the broken-off section of the road ramp. Once back on the road, they turned their head-lamps off and strode down the steeply sloping gravel path, falling naturally into the long lope that was the most comfortable pace in this angle of descent. The night was starless, and the wind whistled downcanyon around them, sometimes in gusts so strong that it felt like they were being shoved in the back. It felt like another dust storm was indeed beginning; Sax muttered about equatorial versus global, but it was impossible to tell what it would be. "Let's hope it goes global," Michel said. "We can use the cover."

"I doubt it will," Sax said.

"What's our destination?" Nadia asked.

"Well, there is an emergency station in Aureum Chaos."

So they had to thread the entire length of Valles Marineris – five thousand kilometers! "How will we do it!" Maya cried.

"We have canyon cars," Michel said briefly. "You'll see."

The road was a steep one, and they kept up the fast pace, punishing their joints. Nadia's right knee began to throb, and her ghost finger itched for the first time in years. She was thirsty, and cold in the old diamond pattern. It got so dusty and dark that they turned on their headlamps; each bobbing cone of yellow light barely reached to the road surface, and glancing back up Nadia thought they looked like a string of deep sea fish, their luminous spots glowing on a great ocean floor. Or like miners in some fluid smoky tunnel. Some part of her began to enjoy the situation; it was a tiny stirring, a sensation mostly physical, but still, the first positive feeling she could remember since finding Arkady. Pleasure like the ghost itching of her lost finger, faint and slightly irritating.

It was still the middle of the night when they came to the bottom of the canyon, a broad U, very common to all the Noctis Labyrinth canyons. Michel approached a boulder, pushed its side with a finger; then lifted a hatch in the boulder's side. "Get in," he said.

There were two of these boulder cars: big rovers, shelled by a thin layer of actual basalt. "What about their thermal signals?" Sax asked as he ducked into one.

"We direct all the heat into coils and bury the coils. So there's no signal to speak of."

"Good idea."

The young man who had driven Michel's fast rover helped them into the new cars. "Let's get out of here," he said brusquely, almost shoving them through the outer lock doors. Light from the lock illuminated his face, framed by his helmet: Asian, perhaps twenty-five, he aided the refugees without meeting their eye, appearing disgruntled, disgusted, perhaps frightened. He said to them scornfully, "Next time you have a revolution you'd better try some other way."

PART EIGHT

Shikata Ga Nai

When the occupants of the elevator car Bangkok Friend learned that Clarke had broken away and the cable was falling, they hurried to the foyer and the locker room and pulled on emergency spacesuits as fast as they could, and for a wonder there was no general panic, it all happened in the heart, on the surface everyone was businesslike and attentive to the small group at the lock door who were trying to determine where exactly they were, and when they should abandon the car. This steadiness amazed Peter Clayborne, whose own blood was hammering through his body in great adrenal shocks; he wasn't sure he could have spoken if he had to. A man in the group at the front told them in level tones that they were approaching the areosynchronous point and so they all pulled into the lock together until they were jammed in like the suits had been in the storage closet, and then they locked the lock and sucked the air. The outer door slid open and there it was, a big rectangle of starry death black space. It was daunting indeed to launch into it in an untethered spacesuit, it felt to the young man like suicide; but the ones at the front pulled out and the rest followed, like spores from an exploding seed pod.

The car and the elevator dwindled eastward and quickly disappeared. The cloud of spacesuits began to disperse. Many of them stabilized with their feet toward Mars, which lay below them like a dirty basketball: when steady, they ignited their main rockets and lofted upward. The group doing the calculations was still on the common band, talking it over as if it were a chess problem. They were near the areosynchronous orbit, but with a downward velocity of several hundred kilometers an hour; burning half their main packs' fuel would counteract most of that, and then they would be in an orbit much more stable than would be strictly necessary, given their air supplies. In other words they would die later of asphyxiation rather than sooner of re-entry heat. But then that had been the whole point of bailing out in the first place. It was possible rescuers might appear in the grace period, one never knew. Clearly most people were willing to give it a try.

The young man pulled his rocket control rods out of his wrist consoles and put his fingers and thumbs on the buttons and got the world between his boots, and shot away from it for a while. Some of the others were trying to stay together, but he judged it impossible and a waste of fuel, and let them drift off above him until they were just more stars. He wasn't as frightened as he had been in the locker, but he was angry and sad: he didn't want to die. A spasm of grief for his lost future shook through him and he cried aloud, and wept. After a while the physical manifestations went away, even though he felt just as miserable as before. He stared dully at the stars. Occasional gusts of fright or despair shuddered through him, but they became less frequent as the minutes dragged on and then the hours. He tried to slow his metabolism but the effort had the opposite effect, and he decided to forget about it, although first he did call up his pulse rate on his wrist console: 108 beats a minute. Lucky he hadn't checked when they were suiting up and bailing out. He grimaced and tried identifying constellations. Time dragged by.

He woke up, and when he realized he had fallen asleep he was both appalled and amused, and promptly fell back asleep. Then after a time he was awake again, this time for good. The other refugees from the car were out of sight, though some stars seemed to move against the backdrop, and could have been them. No sign of the elevator, in space or down on the planet's surface.

It was an odd way to go. Something like the night before a date with the firing squad, perhaps, spent in a dream of space. Death would be like space, except without the stars or the thinking. It was a tedious wait in some ways; it made him impatient and he considered turning off his heating system and having done with it. Knowing he could do that made the wait easier, and he figured he would do it when the air supply was about to run out. The thought put his pulse up to 130, and he tried to concentrate on the planet below. Home sweet home. He was still in almost areosynchronous orbit, it had been hours and Tharsis was still below, though a bit further west. He was over Marineris.

Hours passed and without intending to, he fell asleep again. When he woke there was a small silver spacecraft hanging before him like a UFO and he shouted with surprise, and started tumbling helplessly. He worked the rockets feverishly to bring himself under control, and when he managed it the craft was still there. There was a woman's face in a side window port, talking to him and pointing to her ear. He turned on the common band but she wasn't on it; he couldn't find her. He rocketed over toward the craft and scared the woman by nearly crashing into it. He managed to arrest and draw back a bit. The woman was gesturing; did he want in? He made a clumsy circle with gloved forefinger and thumb, nodding so vigorously that he started tumbling again. As he spun he saw a bay door open behind the window, on top of the craft. He got the suit stabilized and puffed toward the bay, wondering if it would be real when he got to it. He touched the open doorway and tears sprang to his eyes; he blinked and the teardrop spheres floated into his faceplate as he flattened against the bottom of the bay. He had an hour of air left.

When the bay was closed and pumped he unsealed his helmet and lifted it off. The air was thin and oxygen-rich, and cool. The bay lock door opened and he pushed through.

Women were laughing. There were two of them aboard, and they were in high spirits. "What were you going to do, land in that?" one asked.

"I was on the elevator," he said, voice cracking. "We had to jump off. Have you picked up anyone else?"

629

"You're the only one we've seen. Want a ride down?"

He could only gulp. They laughed at him.

"We're amazed to run into anyone out here, boy! How many gs are you comfortable with?"

"I don't know — three?"

They laughed again.

"Why, how many can you take?"

"A lot more than that," said the woman who had looked out at him.

"A lot more," he scoffed. "How many more can a person take?"

"We'll find out," the other woman said, and laughed. The little craft began to accelerate down toward Mars. The youth lay exhausted in a chair behind the two women, asking questions and sucking down water and cheddar cheese from a tube. They had been on one of the mirror complexes and had hijacked this emergency descender after sending the mirrors tumbling in a tangle of molecule-thin sheets. They were complicating their descent by shifting into a polar orbit; they were going to land near the south polar cap.

Peter absorbed this in silence. Then they were bouncing wildly and the windows went white, then yellow, then a deep angry orange. Gravity forces jammed him back in his chair, his vision blurred and his neck hurt. "What a lightweight," one of the women said, and he didn't know if she meant him or the descender.

Then the forces let off and the window cleared. He looked out; they were dropping toward the planet in a steep dive, and were only a few thousand meters above the surface. He couldn't believe it. The women kept the craft in its radical stoop until it seemed they were going to spear the sand, and then at the last minute they flattened out and again he was shoved back into his chair. "Sweet," one of the women commented, and then boom, they were down and running over the layered terrain.

Gravity again. Peter clambered out of the descender after

630

the two women, down a walktube and into a big rover, feeling stunned and ready to cry. There were two men in the rover, shouting greetings and hugging the women. "Who's this?" they cried. "Oh, we picked him up up there, he jumped off the elevator. He's a bit spaced still. Hey," she said to him with a smile, "we're down, it's okay."

Some mistakes you can never make good.

Ann Clayborne sat in the back of Michel's rover, sprawled across three seats, feeling the wheels rise and fall over the rocks. Her mistake had been in coming to Mars in the first place, and then falling in love with it. Falling in love with a place everyone else wanted to destroy.

Outside the rover, the planet was being changed forever. Inside, the main room was lit by floor-level windows, which gave a snake's eye view out under the skirt of the rover's stone roof. Rough gravel road, scattered rockfall in the way. They were on the Noctis Highway, but a lot of rock had fallen on it. Michel wasn't bothering to drive around the smaller samples; they rolled along at about 60 kph, and when they hit a big one they all jounced in their seats. "Sorry," Michel said. "We have to get out of the Chandelier as soon as possible."

"The Chandelier?"

"Noctis Labyrinthus."

The original name, Ann knew, given to it by the Terran geologists staring at Mariner photos. But she didn't speak. The will for speech had left her.

Michel talked on, his voice low and conversational, reassuring. "There's several places where if the road were cut it would be impossible to get the cars down. Transverse scarps that run from wall to wall, giant boulder fields, that kind of thing. Once we get into Marineris we'll be okay, there's all kinds of cross-country routes there."

"Are these cars supplied for a drive down the whole canyon?" Sax asked.

"No. We've got caches all over the place, though." Apparently the great canyons had been some of the principal transport corridors for the hidden colony. When the official

632

Canyon Highway was built it had caused them problems, cutting off a lot of their routes.

From her corner Ann listened to Michel as attentively as the rest; she couldn't help being curious about the hidden colony. Their use of the canyons was ingenious. Rovers designed to stay down in them were disguised to look like one of the millions of boulders that lay in great talus piles sloping out from the cliffs. The roofs of the cars actually were boulders, hollowed out from below. Heavy insulation kept the rock roof of the car from heating up, so there was no IR signal, "especially since there's still any number of Sax's windmills scattered around down here, and they confuse the picture." The rover was insulated on its underside as well, so that it left no snail's track of heat to reveal its passing. The heat from the hydrazine motor was used to warm the living quarters, and any excess was directed into coils for later use; if they built up too much while moving, the coils were dropped into holes dug under the car, and buried with regolith mixed with liquid oxygen. By the time the ground over the coil warmed up, the rover was long gone. So they left no heat signal, never used the radio, and moved only at night. During the day they sat in place among other boulders, "and even if they compared daily photos and saw we were new in the area, we would just be one in a thousand new boulders that had fallen off the cliffs that night. Mass wasting has really accelerated since you started the terraforming, because it's freezing and thawing every day. In the mornings and evenings there's something coming down every few minutes."

"So there's no way they can see us," Sax said, sounding surprised.

"That's right. No visual signal, no electronic signal, no heat signal."

"A stealth rover," Frank said over the intercom from the other car, and laughed his harsh bray.

"That's right. The real danger down here is the very

633

rockfall that's hiding us." A red light on the dash went off, and Michel laughed. "We're going so well we'll have to stop and bury a coil."

"Won't it take a while to dig a hole?" Sax said.

"There's one already dug, if we can get to it. Another four kilometers. I think we'll make it."

"You have quite a system here."

"Well, we've been living underground for fourteen years now, fourteen Martian years I mean. Thermal disposal engineering is a big thing for us."

"But how do you do it for your permanent habitats, assuming you have any?"

"We pipe it down into the deep regolith, and melt ice for our water. Or else we pipe it out to vents disguised as your little windmill heaters. Among other methods."

"Those were a bad idea," Sax said. From the next car Frank laughed at him. Only thirty years late with that realization, Ann would have said if she were speaking.

"But no, an excellent idea!" Michel said. "They must have added millions of kilocalories to the atmosphere by now."

"About an hour from any of the moholes," Sax said primly.

He and Michel began to discuss the terraforming projects. Ann let their voices drift into glossolalia; it was amazingly easy, conversations these days were always right on the edge of meaninglessness for her, she had to exert herself to understand, rather than the reverse. She relaxed away from them, and felt Mars bounce and jumble under her. They stopped briefly to bury a heating coil. The road got smoother when they started again. They were deep in the labyrinth now, and in a normal rover she would have been looking through the skylights at tight steep canyon walls. Rift valleys, enlarged by slumping; there had been ice in this ground, once upon a time, now all migrated down to the Compton aquifer at the bottom of Noctis, presumably.

Ann thought of Peter and shuddered helplessly. One

couldn't assume things, but the fear gnawed at her. Simon watched her surreptitiously, the worry plain on his face, and suddenly she hated his doggy loyalty, his doggy love. She didn't want anyone to care for her like that, it was an unbearable burden, an imposition.

At dawn they stopped. The two boulder rovers parked at the edge of a patch of similar boulders. All day they sat in one of the cars together, lingering over small rehydrated or microwaved meals, trying to find TV or radio transmissions. There weren't any to speak of, only the occasional burst in a number of languages and encryptions. An ether junkyard, adding up to an incoherent mash. Harsh blasts of static seemed to indicate electromagnetic pulses. But the rover's electronics were hardened, Michel said. He sat in a chair as if meditating. A new calm for Michel Duval, Ann thought. As if he were used to waiting out his days in hiding. His companion, the youth driving the other car, was named Kasei. His voice had a permanent tone of grim disapproval. Well, they deserved it. In the afternoon Michel showed Sax and Frank where they were, on a topo map he clicked onto both cars' screens. Their route through Noctis was to run a course southwest to northeast, along one of the biggest canyons of the labyrinth. Emerging from that it zigzagged eastward, dropping steeply until they were at the big area between Noctis and the heads of Ius and Tithonium Chasms. Michel called this area the Compton Break. It was chaotic terrain; and until they had crossed it and gotten down into Ius Chasm, Michel would not feel comfortable. For without their surreptitious road, he said, the area was basically impassable. "And if they figure we went this way out of Cairo, they may bomb the route." They had traveled nearly five hundred kilometers the previous night, almost the whole length of Noctis; another good night and they would be down into Ius, and beyond their complete reliance on a single route.

It was a dark day, the air thick with brown fines, the winds

635

high. Another dust storm, no doubt about it. Temperatures were plummeting. Sax sniffed at a radio voice which claimed the dust storm was going global. Michel, however, was pleased. It meant they could travel during the day as well, cutting their travel time in half. "We've got five thousand kilometers to go, and most of it off-road. It will be wonderful to be able to travel by day, I haven't done that since the Great Storm."

So he and Kasei began driving round the clock, taking shifts of three hours at the wheel followed by a half-hour off. Another day and they were down the Compton Break, and into tight-walled Ius Chasm, and Michel relaxed.

Ius was the narrowest of all the canyons in the Marineris system, only twenty-five kilometers wide when it left the Compton Break, dividing Sinai Planum from Tithania Catena. The canyon was a deep slash between these two plateaus, its side cliffs a full three kilometers high; a long, narrow giant of a rift. But they only saw the walls in glimpses, through bubbles of open air in the blowing dust. They continued to follow a level but rockstrewn route, making good progress through all of a long dim day. It was quiet in the car, the radio turned down to decrease the irritation of the static. The cameras' views, higher than the windows, were of dust whipping past them so that it seemed they hardly moved. Often it looked as if they were slewing sideways. It was hard driving, and Simon and Sax spelled Michel and Kasei, following their directions. Ann was still not talking, and they did not ask her to drive. Sax drove with one eye on his AI screen, which was giving him atmospheric readouts. She could tell from across the car that the AI was indicating that the impact of Phobos was thickening the atmosphere a great deal, projected to as much as a fifty milli-bar addition, an extraordinary amount. And the newly smashed craters were still outgassing. Sax noted this change with his owlish satisfaction, oblivious to the death and destruction that came with it. He noticed her glare and said,

"Like the Noachian Age, I suppose." He nearly added more, but Simon silenced him with a look, and changed the subject.

In the next car Maya and Frank passed the hours by calling over and asking Michel questions about the hidden colony, or discussing with Sax the physical changes occurring, or speculating about the war. Hashing it all over endlessly, trying to make sense of it, to figure out what had happened. Talking talking talking. On Judgement Day, Ann thought, as all the quick and the dead staggered around together, Maya and Frank would still be talking, trying to figure out what had happened. Where they had gone wrong.

Their third night out, the two cars ran down the lower end of Ius, and came to a long lemniscate fin dividing the canyon. They followed the official trans-Marineris Highway down the south fork. In the last hour before dawn, they caught sight of some clouds overhead, and the dawn was much lighter than those of the previous days. It was enough to send them to cover, and they stopped in a fall of boulders stacked against the foot of the canyon's south wall, and gathered in the lead car to wait out the day.

Here they had a view out over the broad expanse of Melas Chasma, the biggest canyon of them all. Ius's rock was rough and blackish in comparison to the smooth red floor of Melas; it seemed to Ann possible that the two canyons were made of rock from ancient tectonic plates, once moving past each other, now juxtaposed forever.

They sat through a long day, talked out, tense, exhausted, their hair oily and uncombed, their faces grimy with the ubiquitous red fines of a dust storm. Sometimes there were clouds, sometimes haze, sometimes sudden pockets of clarity.

In mid-afternoon, without any warning at all, the rover rocked on its shock absorbers. Startled to attention, they jerked up to look at the TVs. The rover's rear camera was pointed back up Ius, and suddenly Sax tapped the screen displaying its view. "Frost," he said. "I wonder . . ."

The camera showed the frost steam thickening, moving downcanyon toward them. The highway was up on a bench above the main floor of Ius's south fork; and this was lucky, because with a roar that shook the rover, that main floor disappeared, overwhelmed by a low wall of black water and dirty white mush. It was a juggernaut of ice chunks, tumbling rocks, foam, mud and water, a slurry throwing itself down the middle of the canyon. The roar was like thunder, even inside the car; it was too loud to talk, and the car trembled under them.

Below their bench, the canyon floor proper was perhaps fifteen kilometers across. The flood filled this whole expanse in a matter of minutes, and promptly began to rise against a long talus slope that ran out from the cliff downcanyon from them. The surface of the flood settled as it pooled against this dam, and froze solid as they watched: a lumpy discolored chaos of ice, strangely stilled. Now they could hear themselves shout over the cracks and booms and omnipresent roaring, but there was nothing to say: they only stared out the low windows or at the TVs, stunned. The frost steam coming off the flood's surface lessened to a light fog. But no more than fifteen minutes later the ice lake burst at its lower end, rupturing in a surge of black steaming water that tore the talus dam away, with an explosive roar of avalanching rock. The flood poured downcanyon again, its leading edge beyond their view, down the great slope from Ius into Melas Chasma.

Now there was a river running down Valles Marineris, a broad, steaming, ice-choked deluge. Ann had seen videotape of the outbreaks in the north, but she hadn't been able to get to one, to see it in person. Here in the flesh, she found it almost impossible to grasp. The landscape itself was now speaking a kind of glossolalia. The inchoate roar smashed at the air, and quivered their stomachs like some bass tearing of the world's fabric; and it was visual chaos as well, a meaningless jumble that she couldn't seem to focus on, to distinguish near from far, or vertical from horizontal, or moving from still, or light from dark. She was losing the ability to read meaning from her senses. Only with great difficulty could she understand her companions in the car. She wasn't sure if it was her hearing or not. She couldn't stand to look at Sax, but then Sax she at least understood. He was trying to hide it from her, but it was clear he was excited by what was happening. That calm dead exterior had always been a mask over a passionate nature, and she had always known it. Now he was high-colored as if he had a fever, and he never met her eye; he knew that she knew what he felt. She despised his shirking inability to confront her, even if it did arise from some kind of consideration for her. And the way he stayed always busy at his screen. She had never seen him get down and actually looked out of the low floor windows of the rover, to see the flood with his own eyes. The cameras have a better view, he would say mildly when Michel urged him to have a look. And after only a half hour of watching the first arrival of the flood on the TVs, he had gone to his AI screen to work out what it might mean to his project. Water rushing down Ius, freezing, breaking up and rushing down again; certainly into Melas; whether there would be enough water to make it into Coprates, and then down into Capri and Eos, and then down into the Aureum chaos . . . it seemed unlikely on the face of it, but the Compton Aquifer had been big, one of the biggest ever found. Marineris very likely owed its existence to outbreaks from earlier incarnations of the same aquifer, and the Tharsis Bulge had never stopped outgassing . . . She found she was lying on the floor of the rover, watching the flood, trying to comprehend it. She tried to calculate its flow in her head, just as a way to focus better on what she saw, to bring it back out of the meaninglessness that threatened to overwhelm her. Despite herself she felt the fascination of the calculation, and of the view, and even of the flood itself; this had happened on Mars before, billions of years ago, and probably just like this. There were signs of catastrophic floods all over, beach terraces, lemniscate islands, channel beds, scablands . . . And the old broken aquifers had refilled, from the Tharsis upwelling and all the heat and outgassing that that engendered. It would have been slow, but give it two billion years . . .

She forced herself to focus, to see. The near edge of the flood was about a kilometer away, and two hundred meters below them. The foot of the northern wall of Ius was about fifteen kilometers away, and the flood stretched right to it. The flood was perhaps ten meters deep, judging by the giant boulders that rolled downstream like Big Man's bowling balls, smashing ice to shards and leaving steaming black polynaps in their wake. The water in the open patches seemed to be moving at perhaps thirty kilometers an hour. So (punching figures into her wristpad) perhaps four and a half million cubic meters per hour. That was about a hundred Amazons out there, but running irregularly, freezing and bursting in a perpetual series of ice dams building and failing, whole steaming lakes leaping downhill over whatever channel or slope they found themselves on, stripping the land down to bedrock and then tearing the bedrock away . . . Lying on the floor of the rover, Ann could feel that assault in her cheekbones, vibrating the ground in a rapid pounding. Such tremors hadn't been felt on Mars in millions of years, which explained something else that she had seen but not been able to comprehend; the northern wall of Ius was moving. The rock of the cliffs was flaking off and falling into the canyon, which shook the ground, and triggered more collapses, and giant waves that washed out into the flood, water pouring back upstream over the ice, the rock bursting apart in explosions of hydration, the frost steam pouring so thickly into the dust-choked air that she could see the northern wall only in snatches.

And without a doubt the southern wall would be collapsing in a similar way, although their view of this wall, which loomed over their road to the right, was foreshortened and cut off. But it had to be falling. And if it flaked off above them, then they were dead for sure. It was quite possible – very possible. Judging by her glimpses of the north wall, the chances might be as high as fifty percent. But then it was probably worse over there; the northern wall appeared to be undercut by the flood, while the south wall was removed from it by the bench they were driving over. So the southern cliffs should be a bit more stable—

But then something drew her eye forward, downstream from them. Up there the south wall was indeed collapsing, falling in great sheets of rock. The base of the cliff exploded in a cloud of dust that bloomed over the talus, and the upper sections of the cliff slid down into this new cloud of dust and disappeared. After a second the whole mass reappeared flying horizontally out of the cloud, a strange sight. The noise was painfully loud, even inside the car; then it was just a long, slow landslide, down into the flood, the rocks crushing the ice and blocking the flow beneath. An instant dam, cutting off much of the flow downcanyon; and so the banks of the flood began to rise. Ann watched the icy sheet of the shoreline below her rupture, and then it was chunks of ice, jostling in a sea of black smoking fizzing water, rising swiftly toward the rover. It would engulf them if the landslide dam lasted long enough. Ann peered at the long black spill of rock ahead of them; only a strip of it was still visible above the flood. But the slush beneath her continued to rise. It was a race of sorts. Big Man's bathtub, draining while he poured new bucketfuls in. The speed of the lake's ascent caused Ann to raise her estimate of the flow rate. She felt paralyzed, disconnected, in some curious sense serene; it was a matter of indifference to her whether or not the dam broke before the flood reached them. And in the overwhelming roar she felt no need to communicate with the others about this; it was impossible. She found that in a way she was cheering the flood on. It would serve them all right.

But then the landslide dam disappeared under the discolored slurry, and it all rolled off downstream in a stately collapse, the short-lived lake dropping as she watched, ice blocks on its surface clattering together, shrieking and booming as they collided and jumbled around and shot high into the air, all fantastically loud, every audible pitch roaring at once. It had to be well over a hundred decibels. She had her fingers in her ears, but couldn't remember for how long. The car was bouncing up and down. She could see more landslides from the cliffs farther downstream, no doubt undercut by the sudden surge of the flood; and the tremors they caused were triggering further collapses, until it looked like the whole canyon would fill. It seemed impossible in all the noise and vibration that their little cars would survive. The travelers clutched their chair arms or lay there on the floor like Ann, isolated by the roar, their veins pumping with an awful mix of ice and adrenalin; even Ann, who did not care, found her breath short, her muscles tensed against the kinetic assault.

When they could hear each other's shouts again, they asked Ann what had happened. Dully she stared out the window, ignoring them. Apparently they were going to survive, for the moment at least. The flood surface was now the most shattered chaotic terrain she had ever seen, the ice pulverized to a plain of wicked shards. The high point of the lake had climbed their bench until it had been only a hundred meters downslope from them; the re-exposed wet ground down there had turned from rusty black to dirty white in less than twenty seconds. Freezing time on Mars.

Sax had stayed in his seat through all that, absorbed by the flickering on his screen. A lot of water would evaporate, or rather freeze and sublime, he muttered to no one as he worked. It was a heavily carbonated saline brine, but it would end up as dust-filled snow, falling somewhere else. The atmosphere might get hydrated enough so that it would snow

642

several times, or even on a regular basis, in cycles of precipitation and sublimation. Thus the floodwater would get distributed pretty evenly planetwide, except perhaps at the highest altitudes. Albedo would rise dramatically. They would have to lower it, presumably by encouraging the snow algae that the Acheron group had created. (But there was no more Acheron, Ann said to him in her mind.) Black ice would melt by day, then freeze at night. Sublimate and precipitate. And thus they would have a waterscape: streams collecting, pooling, running downstream, freezing and expanding in cracks in the rock, subliming and snowing and melting and running again. A glaciated or muddy world, most of the time. But a waterscape nevertheless.

And every single feature of the primal Mars would melt away. Red Mars was gone.

Ann lay there on the floor by the window. Her tears poured out of her to join the flood; over the dam of her nose, downstream until her right cheek and ear and the whole side of her face was wet.

"This will complicate the process of getting downcanyon," Michel said with a little Gallic smile, and from the next car Frank laughed. In fact it looked as if it would be impossible for them to proceed even five kilometers. Directly before them the canyon highway was buried under the great landslide, completely gone. The new spill of rock was shattered and unstable, sapped from below by the flood, pounded from above by subsequent mass wasting of the new slope.

For a long time the others debated even making a try. They had to speak loudly to be heard over the jet engine roar of the flood, which still swept past with no sign of a let-up. Nadia considered the slope suicidal, but Michel and Kasei were pretty sure they could find a way, and after a long day's reconnaissance on foot they managed to convince Nadia to agree to try it, and the rest were willing if Nadia was. And so the day after that, protected from surveillance by the general dust storm and the flood's steam, they divided into the two cars and drove slowly out onto the slide.

It was a rough mass of gravel and sand, liberally sprinkled with boulders. There was, however, a zone corresponding to the bench below it, which was relatively level. This zone was the only thing that made passage possible; it was a matter of finding an unobstructed way over a surface like poorly mixed cement, around boulders and past the occasional gaping hole. Michel drove the lead car boldly, with a stubbornness verging on the reckless. "Desperate measures," he declared cheerily. "Can you imagine getting on this kind of ground in the normal course of things? It would be insane."

"It's insane now," Nadia said sourly.

"Well, what can we do? We can't go back, and we can't give up. These are the times that try men's souls."

"Women, however, do fine."

"I was quoting. You know what I mean. There's simply no possibility of going back. The head of Ius will be flooded wall to wall. I suppose it's this that makes me somehow happy. Have we ever been so free of choices? The past is wiped out, all that matters is now. The present and the future. And the future is this field of stones, and here we are. And, you know, you never really summon all of your strength until you know that there's no way back, no way to go but onward."

And so onward they went. But Michel's sanguinity was sharply reduced when the second car collapsed into a hole that had been concealed by a kind of trapdoor arrangement of boulders. With some work they were able to open the front lock and pull out Kasei, Maya, Frank and Nadia. But there was no chance whatsoever of freeing the second car, they didn't have the lift or the leverage. So they transferred all the supplies out of it, until the lead car was absolutely stuffed. And they moved on, eight of them and their supplies, all now in a single car.

*

Beyond the landslide, however, it got easier. They followed the canyon highway down into Melas Chasma, and found that the road had been built close to the south wall, and as Melas was such broad a canyon, the flood had had room to spread out, and had bowed off some ways to the north. It still sounded like air miners were running at full capacity right outside their lock, but the road was well above and to the south of the flood, which was releasing veils of frost steam that filled the chasm, and obscured any views farther north.

So they proceeded without difficulty for a couple of nights, until they came to the Geneva Spur, which stuck out from the gigantic south wall nearly to the edge of the flood. Here the official road had swung out into what was now the course of the deluge, and they had to find a higher route. The rocky traverses they made around the lower slopes of the Spur were really difficult for the rover. Once they were nearly hung up on an obtruding rounded rock, and Maya shouted at Michel, accusing him of recklessness. She took over the driving while Michel and Kasei and Nadia went out in walkers. They jacked them off the rock, and then walked ahead to reconnoiter the route of the traverse.

Frank and Simon helped Maya look for obstructions as she drove. Sax continued to spend all his time at his screen. From time to time Frank would turn on the TV and run a search for signals, trying to piece together news from the occasional staticky voices the radio found in the jamming. On the very spine of the Geneva Spur, as they were crossing the absurdly thin concrete thread of the Transcanyon Highway, they were far enough out from the south wall to get some transmissions, something about it not becoming a global dust storm after all. And indeed the days were sometimes only hazy, rather than clotted with the dust. Sax claimed this as proof of the relative success of the dust-fixing strategies pursued since the Great Storm. No one responded to this. The haze that was in the air, Frank observed, seemed actually to help clarify weak radio signals. That was stochastic resonance, Sax said. The phenomenon was counterintuitive, and Frank questioned Sax closely for an explanation of it. When he understood, the room rang with his mirthless bray: "Maybe all the emigration was stochastic resonance, enhancing the weak signal of the revolution."

"I don't think it helps to make analogies between the physical and social worlds," Sax said primly.

"Shut up, Sax. Go back to your virtual reality."

Frank was still angry, still filled with bitter bile; it sublimed from him like the frost steam off the flood. He snapped questions at Michel about the hidden colony, his curiosity bursting out two or three times a day. Ann was happy to think she would not be Hiroko when Frank first met her. Michel answered these accusing questions calmly, ignoring the sarcasm and the furious gleam in Frank's eye. Maya's attempts to cool Frank only increased his rage, but she kept at it; Ann was impressed at how persistent she was, how insensitive to Frank's brusque rejections. It was a side of Maya that Ann had never seen before; Maya was usually the most volatile person around. But not now, not when the pressure was really on.

Eventually they rounded the Geneva Spur, and got back on the bench under the southern escarpment. The way east was often interrupted by landslides, but they always had room to veer left around them. Progress was good.

But then they came to the eastern end of Melas. Here the greatest chasm of them all narrowed, and dropped several hundred meters down into the two parallel canyons of Coprates, which were separated by a long narrow plateau. South Coprates dead-ended in a cliffy headwall some two hundred and fifty kilometers away; North Coprates connected with the lower canyons farther east, and therefore was the one they wanted to take. North Coprates was the longest single segment of the Marineris system: Michel called it La Manche, and it, like the English Channel, narrowed as it progressed eastward, until at around 60° longitude it narrowed and reared into a gigantic gorge: sheer cliffs four kilometers high, facing each other across a gap only twenty-five kilometers across. Michel called this gorge the Dover Gate; apparently the cliff walls in this gap were whitish, or had been.

So they made their way down North Coprates, and the cliffs closed in on them more every day. The flood filled almost the whole width of the canyon floor, and its flow was so rapid that the ice on its surface had broken into small bergs, which flew off the lips of standing waves and crashed back into the cascade: a furious whitewater rapid with the flow of a hundred Amazons, topped by icebergs. The canyon floor was being ripped away, torn free of its bed and rushing down in red jolts of water like massive pulses of rusty blood, as if the planet were bleeding to death. The noise was incredible, a roar so continuous and pervasive that it dulled thought, and made talk almost impossible; they had to shout everything at the top of their lungs, which quickly reduced them to communicating only the basic necessities.

But then there was a very basic necessity to shout about, for when they came to the Dover Gate they found that the canyon floor was almost completely covered by the flood; their bench below the southern wall of the gorge was no more than two kilometers wide, and diminishing every minute. It seemed possible the whole bench might be torn away in a flash. Maya cried that it was too dangerous to go on, and argued for a retreat. If they circled around and drove up to the dead end of south Coprates, she shouted, and managed to climb to the plateau above, then they could drive past the pits of Coprates Catena, and proceed onward to Aureum.

Michel shouted his insistence that they press forward, and get through the Gate on the bench. "If we hurry we can make it! We must try!" And when Maya continued to protest, he added forcefully: "The head of south Coprates is steep! The car would never get up it, it's a cliff like these! And we don't have the supplies to add so many extra days to our trip! We can't go back!"

The insane roar of the flood was his only answer. They sat in the car, in their separate thoughts, separated by the roar as if by many kilometers of space. Ann found herself wishing the bench would slide from under them, or a piece of the south wall fall onto them, and put an end to their indecision, and to the awful, maddening noise.

They drove on. Frank and Maya and Simon and Nadia stood behind Michel and Kasei, watching them drive; Sax sat at his screen, stretching like a cat, staring myopically at the little picture of the deluge. The surface calmed for a moment, and froze over, and the explosive noise reduced to a violent low rumble. "It's like the Grand Canyon on a kind of super-Himalayan scale," Sax said, apparently to himself, although only Ann would be able to hear him. "The Kala Gandaki Gorge is like three kilometers deep, isn't it? And Dhalagiri and Annapurna only forty or fifty kilometers apart, I think. Fill that with a flood like . . . " He failed to recall any comparable flood. "I wonder what all that water was doing so high on the Tharsis bulge."

Cracks like gunshots announced another surge. The white surface of the flood blew apart and tumbled downstream. White noise suddenly enveloped them, battening everything they said or thought, as if the universe were vibrating. A bass tuning fork . . .

"Outgassing," Ann said. "Outgassing." Her mouth was stiff, she could feel in her face how long it had been since she had last spoken. "Tharsis rests on an upwelling of magma. Rock alone couldn't sustain the weight; the bulge would have subsided if it weren't being supported by an upwelling current in the mantle."

"I thought there was no mantle." She could just hear him through the noise.

"No no." She didn't care if he could hear her or not. "It's

just slowed down. But currents are still there. And since the last great floods, they have refilled the high aquifers on Tharsis. And kept aquifers like Compton warm enough to stay liquid. Eventually the hydrostatic pressures were extreme. But with less vulcanism, and fewer big meteor strikes, nothing set it off. It might have been full for a billion years."

"Do you think Phobos broke it open?"

"Maybe. More likely a reactor meltdown."

"Did you know Compton was this big?" Sax asked.

"Yes."

"I never heard of it."

"No."

Ann stared at him. Had he heard her say that?

He had. Concealing data: he was shocked, she could tell. He couldn't imagine any reason good enough to conceal data. Perhaps this was the root of their inability to understand each other. Value systems based on entirely different assumptions. Completely different kinds of science.

He cleared his throat. "Did you know it was liquid?"

"I thought so. But now we know."

Sax twitched, and called up on his screen the image from the left side camera. Black fizzing water, gray debris, shattered ice, boulders like great tumbling dice; standing waves freezing in place, collapsing and sweeping away in clouds of frost steam . . . the noise had risen back to its crackling jet howl.

"I wouldn't have done it this way!" Sax exclaimed.

Ann stared at him. He steadfastly regarded the TV.

"I know," she said. And then she was tired of talk again, tired of its uselessness. It had never been any more than it was now: whispers against the great roar of the world, half-heard and less understood.

They drove as quickly as they could through the Dover Gate, following the Calais Ramp as Michel called their bench.

Progress was nerve-rackingly slow, it was a bitter struggle to get the rover over the rockfall covering this narrow terrace; boulders were scattered everywhere, and the flood ate away at the land to their left, narrowing the bench at a perceptible rate. Landslides from the cliff walls fell ahead and behind them, and more than once individual rocks crashed into the car's roof, making them all jump. It was perfectly possible that a bigger rock would hit them and smash them like bugs, without a single bit of warning. That possibility subdued them all, which was fine by Ann. Even Simon left her alone, throwing himself into the navigational effort and going out on scouting trips with Nadia or Frank or Kasei, happy, she thought, to have some excuse to get away from her. And why not?

They bumped along at a couple kilometers per hour. They traveled through a night and then the following day, even though the haze had diminished to the point where it was possible they were visible from satellites. There was no other choice.

And then finally they were through the Dover Gate, and Coprates opened up again, giving them some leeway. The flood veered a few kilometers to the north.

At dusk they stopped the car. They had been driving for some forty hours straight. They stood up and stretched, shuffled around, and then sat back down and ate a micro-waved meal together. Maya, Simon, Michel and Kasei were in good spirits, cheerful to have gotten through the Gate; Sax was the same as always; Nadia and Frank a bit less grim than usual. The surface of the flood was frozen over for the moment, and it was possible to speak without hurting one's throat, and still be heard. And so they ate, concentrating on the small portions of food, talking in a desultory manner.

Late in this quiet meal Ann looked around curiously at her companions, suddenly awed by the spectacle of human adaptability. Here they were eating their dinner, talking over the low boom from the north, in a perfect illusion of dining room conviviality: it might have been anywhere anytime, and their tired faces bright with some collective success, or merely with the pleasure of eating together – while just outside their chamber the broken world roared, and rockfall could annihilate them at any instant. And it came to her that the pleasure and stability of dining rooms had always occurred against such a backdrop, against the catastrophic background of universal chaos; such moments of calm were things as fragile and transitory as soap bubbles, destined to burst almost as soon as they blew into existence. Groups of friends, rooms, streets, years, none of them would last. The illusion of stability was created by a concerted effort to ignore the chaos they were imbedded in. And so they ate, and talked, and enjoyed each other's company; this was the way it had been in the caves, on the savannah, in the tenements and the trenches and the cities huddling under bombardment.

And so, in this moment of the storm, Ann Clayborne exerted herself. She stood up, she went to the table. She picked up Sax's plate, Sax who had first drawn her out; and then Nadia's and Simon's. She carried the plates over to their little magnesium sink. And as she cleaned the dishes, she felt her stiff throat move; she croaked out her part of the conversation, and helped, with her little strand, to weave the human illusion. "A stormy night!" Michel said to her as he stood beside her drying plates, smiling. "A stormy night indeed!"

The next morning she woke before the rest, and looked at the faces of her sleeping companions, now revealed in the daylight to be utterly disheveled – grimy, puffy, black with frostnip, open-mouthed in the total sleep of exhaustion. They looked dead. And she had been no help to them – on the contrary! She had been a drag on the group; every time they had come back in the car they had had to step by the madwoman on the floor, lying there refusing to speak, often crying, clearly in the throes of severe depression. Just what they had needed!

Ashamed, she got up and quietly finished cleaning up the main room and the drivers' area. And later that day she took her turn driving the rover, doing a six hour shift, and ending up exhausted. But she got them well east of the Dover Gate.

Their troubles, however, were not over. Coprates had opened up a bit, yes, and the south wall had for the most part held; but in this area there was a long ridge, now an island, running down the middle of the canyon, dividing it into north and south channels; and unfortunately the southern channel was lower than the northern one, so that the bulk of the flood was running down it, and crowding them tight against the southern wall. Happily the bench terrace gave them some five kilometers between the deluge and the wall proper; but with the flood so close on their left, and the steep cliffs on their right, they never lost the sense of danger. And they had to raise their voices to talk at least half the time; and the crackling roar of the surges seemed to invade their heads, making it harder than ever to concentrate, or to pay attention, or indeed to think at all.

One day Maya crashed her fist against the table and cried, "Couldn't we wait for the island ridge to get torn away?"

After an awkward pause Kasei said, "It's a hundred kilometers long."

"Well, shit – couldn't we just wait until this flood *stops*? I mean, how long can it go *on* like this?"

"A few months," Ann said.

"Can't we wait that long?"

"We're running low on food," Michel explained.

"We have to keep going," Frank snapped at Maya. "Don't be stupid." She glared at him and turned away, clearly furious. The rover suddenly seemed much too small, as if a bunch of tigers and lions had been thrown together in a dog's kennel. Simon and Kasei, oppressed by the tension, suited up and went out to scout what lay ahead.

*

Beyond what they called Island Ridge, Coprates opened up like a funnel, with deep troughs under the diverging canyon walls. The northern trough was Capri Chasma, the southern trough was Eos Chasma, which ran on as a continuation of Coprates. Because of the flood they had no choice but to follow Eos, but Michel said it was the way they would have wanted anyway. Here the southern cliff finally lowered a bit, and was cut with deep embayments, and shattered by a couple of good-sized meteor craters. Capri Chasma curved out of their sight to the northeast; between the two trough canyons was a low triangular mesa, now a peninsula dividing the course of the flood in two. Unfortunately the great bulk of the water ran into the somewhat lower Eos, so that even though they were out of the tight constriction of Coprates, they were still pressed against a cliff, and moving slowly, off any road or trail, and with diminishing supplies of food and gases. The cupboards were nearly bare.

And they were tired, very tired. It had been twenty-three days since they had escaped from Cairo, now 2500 kilometers upcanyon; and all that time they had been sleeping in shifts, and driving almost constantly, and living in the aural assault of the flood, the roar of a world falling down in pieces on their heads. They were too old for this, as Maya said more than once, and nerves were frayed; they were fudging things, making little mistakes, falling into little microbursts of sleep.

The bench that was their road between cliff and flood became an immense boulder field, the boulders mostly ejecta from nearby craters, or detritus from really extensive mass wasting. It looked to Ann like the big fluted and scalloped embayments in the southern cliff were sappings that would initiate tributary subsidence canyons; but she didn't have the time to look very closely. Often it seemed that they were going to have their way blocked entirely by boulders, that after all these days and kilometers, after negotiating most of Marineris in the midst of a most violent cataclysm, they were going to be halted just short of the tremendous washes leading out of its lower end.

But then they found a way; and were stopped; and found a way; and were stopped; and found a way; and so on, for day after day after day. They went to half rations. Ann drove more than anyone else, as she seemed to be fresher than the rest, and was the best driver there anyway with the possible exception of Michel. And she felt she owed it to them after her shameful collapse during the greater part of their journey. She wanted to do everything she could, and when she wasn't driving, she went out to scout the way. It was still numbingly loud outside, and the ground trembled underfoot. It was impossible to get used to that, though she did her best to ignore it. Sunlight burned through the mist and haze in broad lurid splashes, and in the sunset hour icebows and sundogs appeared in the sky, along with rings of light around the dulled sun; often the whole sky seemed afire, a Turner vision of the apocalypse.

Soon enough Ann too wore down, and the work became exhausting. She understood now why her companions had been so tired, why they had been so short with her and with each other. Michel had been unable to locate the last three caches they had passed; buried or drowned, it didn't matter. The half rations were 1200 calories a day, much less than they were expending. Lack of food, lack of sleep: and then, for Ann at least, the same old depression, persistent as death, rising in her like a flood, like a black slurry of mud, steam, ice, shit. Doggedly she kept at the work, but her attention kept blinking out and the glossolalia kept returning, washing everything away in the white noise of despair.

The way got harder. One day they made only a kilometer. The following day they seemed completely stopped, the boulders arrayed across the bench like tankstoppers in Big Man's Maginot Line. It was a perfect fractal plane, Sax remarked, of about 2.7 dimensions. No one bothered to answer him.

Kasei, wandering on foot, found a passage right down on

the bank of the flood. For the moment the whole visible expanse of the deluge was frozen, as it had been for the last couple of days. It stretched out to the horizon, a jumbled surface like Earth's Arctic Sea, only much dirtier, a great mix of black and red and white lumps. The ice just offshore was flat, however, and in many places clear. They could look down into it, and see that it appeared to be only a couple meters deep, and frozen right down to the bottom. So they drove down to this icy shore and ran along it, and when rocks in the way forced her to, Ann put the left wheels of the rover out onto the ice, and then the entire car; and it held like any other surface. Nadia and Maya snorted at the others' nervousness about this course: "We spent all winter driving on the rivers in Siberia," Nadia said. "They were the best roads we had."

So for an entire day Ann drove along the ragged edge of the flood, and out onto its surface, and they made a hundred and sixty kilometers, their best day in two weeks.

Near sunset it began to snow. The west wind poured out of Coprates, driving big gritty clumps of snow past them as if they weren't moving at all. They came to a fresh slide zone, which spilled right out onto the ice of the flood. Big boulders scattered over the ice gave it the air of an abandoned neighborhood, old houses half demolished. The light was dusky gray. They needed a foot guide through this maze, and in an exhausted conference Frank volunteered, and went out to do the job. At this point he was the only one of them with any strength left, more even than the younger Kasei; still burning with the force of his anger, a breeder fuel that would never give out.

Slowly he walked ahead of the car, testing routes and returning, either shaking his head or waving Ann on. Around them thin veils of frost steam lofted into the falling snow, the two mixing and gusting off together on the powerful evening wind, off into the murk. Watching the dark spectacle of one hard gust, Ann misread the configuration of the ice's meeting with the ground, which was hard to see in any case; and the rover ran up onto a round rock right at the frozen shoreline, lifting the left rear wheel off the ground. Ann gunned the front wheels to roll them over the rock, but they dug into a patch of sand and snow, and suddenly both rear wheels were barely touching the ground, while the front two merely spun in the holes they had dug. She had run the rover aground.

It had happened before several times, but she was annoyed with herself for getting distracted by the irrelevant spectacle of the sky.

"What the fuck are you doing?" Frank shouted over the intercom. Ann jumped in her chair; she would never get used to Frank's biting vehemence. "Get going!" he shouted.

"I ran it onto a rock," she said.

"Damn you! Why don't you watch where you're going! Here, stop the wheels, stop them! I'm gonna put the grip cloths under the front wheels and lever you forward, and then you get it off this rock and up the slope as quick as you can, understand? There's another surge coming!"

"Frank!" Maya cried. "Get inside!"

"Soon as I get the fucking pads down! Be ready to go!"

The pads were strips of spiked metal mesh, set under wheels that had dug holes into sand, and then pegged out ahead so that the wheels had something to grip. An ancient desert method, and Frank ran around the front of the rover cursing under his breath and snapping directions to Ann, who obeyed with her teeth clenched and her stomach knotted.

"Okay go!" Frank shouted. "Go!"

"Get in first!" Ann cried.

"There's no time, go, it's almost here! I'll hang on the side, go, damn it, *go*!"

So Ann gently accelerated the front wheels, and felt them catch on the grips and scrape the car forward over the rock, until the rear wheels touched down again and they scraped off and were free. But the roar of the flood suddenly doubled and redoubled behind them, and then there were chunks of ice bounding past the car, bursting along with a hideous cracking, and then the ice was overwhelmed by a dark wave of steaming bubbling slurry, a surge that washed up over the windows of the car; Ann floored the accelerator and held the wheel with a death grip as it bounced in her hands. Mixed with the crashing of the surge wave she heard Frank's voice shouting "Go, idiot, go!" and then they were hit hard and the car slewed off to the left, out of control. Ann hung onto the wheel as it threw her from side to side. Her left ear throbbed with pain, she had hit something with it. She held on to the wheel and kept her foot jamming the accelerator to the floor. The wheels caught on something and the rover ground through water, they were rolling through water, it poured from right to left and there was a dull banging against the side of the car. "Go!" She kept the accelerator floored and turned uphill, bouncing wildly in the driver's seat, all the windows and TV screens liquid madness. Then the water ran under the rover, and the windows were clear. The rover's headlights showed rocky ground, falling snow, and ahead a bare flat area. Ann kept it floored and jounced wildly toward it, the flood still roaring behind them. When she reached the flat rise she had to pull her leg and foot away from the accelerator with her hands. The car stopped. They were above the flood, on a narrow bench terrace. It looked like the surge was already receding. But Frank Chalmers was gone.

Maya insisted that they return and look for him, and as it was likely that the initial surge would be the largest one they did so, but it was futile. In the twilight the headlights cut fifty meters into the snowfall, and in the two intersecting yellow cones, and the dark gray world outside them, they saw only the ragged surface of the flood, a pouring sea of flotsam and jetsam without the slightest hint of any regular shape; in fact it looked like a world in which such shapes were impossible. No one could survive in such madness. Frank was gone, either knocked off the car in its jouncing, or swept off it in its brief and nearly fatal encounter with the wave.

His final curses still seemed to bubble out of the static on the intercom, out of the roar of the flood. His final imprecations rang in Ann's ears like the judgement they were: Go, idiot, go! It had been her fault, all her fault —

Maya was weeping, choking on sobs, doubling over her stomach as if cramping, "No!" she cried. "Frank, Frank! We have to look for him!" Then she was crying too hard to speak. Sax went over and dug into the medicine chest, and walked over to her and crouched by her side. "Here, Maya, do you want a sedative?" And she uncoiled and dashed the pills from his hand, "No!" she screamed, "they're *my* feelings, they're *my* men, do you think I'm a coward, do you think I would want to be a zombie like *you*!"

She collapsed into helpless, involuntary, racking sobs. Sax stood over her, blinking, face twisted with a stricken look; Ann found herself cut to the quick by that look, "Please," she said. "Please, please." She got up from the driver's seat, went back to them and held Sax briefly by the arm. She crouched to help Nadia and Simon pick Maya up off the floor, and get her to her bed. Already Maya was quieter, withdrawing from them, her eyes red and her nose running, off in her own grief, one hand clenched in a death grip over Nadia's wrist. Nadia looked down at her with a doctor's detached expression, withdrawn in her own way, murmuring in Russian.

"Maya, I'm sorry," Ann said. Her throat was cramped, it hurt to talk. "It was my fault. I'm sorry."

Maya shook her head. "It was an accident."

Ann couldn't bring herself to say aloud that she had stopped paying attention. The words stuck in her throat, and another spasm of sobs racked Maya, and the chance to speak was gone.

Michel and Kasei took over the drivers' seats, and started the rover along the bench again.

Not far east of that, the southern canyon wall finally sank down into the surrounding plain, and they were free to move away from the flood, which was in any case following Eos Chasma in a swing to the north, off to a distant reunion with Capri Chasma. Michel ran across the hidden colony's trail, but lost it again, as the trail ducks were often buried in snow. He tried throughout all one day to locate a cache he thought was nearby, but failed. Rather than waste more time they decided to drive on at full speed, a bit north of east, toward the refuge they had been trying to reach, which Michel said was in the broken terrain just south of Aureum Chaos. "It's not our main colony anymore," he explained to the others. "It's where we went first, after we left Underhill. But Hiroko wanted to leave for the south, and after a few years we did. She said she didn't like this first shelter because Aureum is a sink, and she thought it might become a lake someday. I thought that was crazy, but I see now that she was right. It looks like Aureum may even be the final drainage for this flood, I don't know. But the refuge is at a higher elevation than we are now, so it will be okay. It may be empty of people, but it will be stocked with supplies. And any port in a storm, yes?"

No one had the spirit to reply.

On the second day of hard driving the flood disappeared over the horizon to the north. The roar of it went away soon after. The ground, covered with a meter of dirty snow, no longer trembled underfoot; the world seemed dead, strangely silent and still, shrouded in white. When it wasn't snowing the sky was still hazy, but it seemed clear enough for them to be spotted from above, so they stopped traveling by day. They moved at night without headlights, across a snowscape that glowed faintly under the stars.

Ann drove through these nights. She never told anyone

about her moment of inattention at the wheel. And she never even came close to doing it again; she stayed focused with a desperate concentration, biting the inside of her mouth till it bled, oblivious to everything but what lay in the cones of light before her. She usually drove all night, forgetting to wake the next watch's driver, or deciding not to. Frank Chalmers was dead, and it was her fault; desperately she wished she could reach back and change things, but it was hopeless. Some mistakes you can never make good. The white landscape was marred by an infinity of stones, each capped with its own cake of snow, and the salt-and-pepper landscape was such a patchwork that it was hard at night for the eye to make sense of it; sometimes they seemed to be plowing underground, or floating five meters over it. A white world. Some nights she understood she was driving a hearse, across the body of the deceased. The widows Nadia and Maya in back. And now she knew that Peter was dead too.

Twice she heard Frank calling out to her over the intercom, once asking for her to turn back and help him; the other crying, Go, idiot, go!

Maya was bearing up well. She was tough, somehow, despite all her moods. Nadia, whom Ann used to think of as the tough one, was silent most of the time. Sax stared at his screen and worked. Michel tried to talk to his old friends, and gave up unhappily when it was clear no one wanted to talk back. Simon watched Ann anxiously as always, with unbearable concern; she couldn't stand it, and avoided his gaze. Poor Kasei must have felt like he was trapped in an asylum for the aged insane, it was almost funny to think of it, except that his spirit seemed to be somehow broken, she did not know why, perhaps the waste, perhaps the increasing likelihood that they would not survive; perhaps simple hunger, there was no way of telling. The young were odd. But he reminded her of Peter, and so she didn't look at him either.

The snow made each night glow and pulse. All of it would

660

melt eventually, carve new streambeds and carry her Mars away. Mars was gone. Michel sat beside her through the second shifts of the night, looking for signs of the way. "Are we lost?" Maya asked him once, just before dawn.

"No, not at all. It's just . . . we're leaving tracks in the snow. I don't know how long they'll last, or how visible they are, but if . . . well, just in case they do last, I want to leave the car, and walk the last part of the way. So I want to be precisely sure of where we are before we do that. We've got some standing stones and dolmens erected that will tell us for sure, but I have to find one of those first. They'll show on the horizon, you know. Boulders a bit taller than usual, or columns."

"It will be easier to see those by day," Simon said.

"True. We'll have a look around tomorrow, and that should do it – we'll be in an area of them. They were designed to help people lost like us. We'll be okay."

Except that their friends were dead. Her only child was dead. And their world was gone for good. Lying down by the windows at dawn, Ann tried to imagine life in the hidden shelter. Underground for years and years. She couldn't do it. Go, idiot, go! Damn you!

At dawn Kasei hooted with hoarse triumph: out there on the northern horizon was a trio of standing stones. A lintel bridging two pillars, as if a single fragment of Stonehenge had flown here. Home was that way, said Kasei.

But first they would wait through the day. Michel was becoming extremely cautious about being seen from satellites, and wanted to continue on by night. They settled down to get some sleep.

Ann couldn't sleep, finding herself energized by a new resolve. When the rest were out cold, Michel snoring happily, all of them asleep for the first time in about fifty hours, she tugged into her walker and tiptoed into the lock. She looked back and surveyed them; a hungry, ragged lot. Nadia's crippled hand stuck out from her side. Getting out

661

of the lock made some unavoidable noise, but everyone was used to sleeping through noise, and the whirrs and clicks of the life support system partially covered her exit. She got out without waking anyone.

The planet's basal chill. She shuddered in it, and set off west, walking in the rover's tracks so she couldn't be followed. The sun was cutting through the mist. Snow was falling again, tinted pink in shafts of sunlight. She trudged along until she came on a little drumlin ridge, with its steep side clear of snow. She could traverse along the bare rock without leaving tracks. She did so until she got tired. It was really cold out, the snow falling straight down in tiny flakes, probably accreted around sand grains. At the end of the drumlin was a fat low boulder. She sat in its lee. She turned off her walker's heating unit, and covered the blinking alarm light on her wristpad with a clump of snow.

It got colder fast. The sky was an opaque gray now, tinged with faint pink. Snow fell out of the pinkness onto her faceplate.

She had just stopped shivering, and was getting comfortably chill, when a boot kicked her hard in the helmet, and she was dragged up to her knees with her head ringing. A suited figure banged its faceplate into hers, hard. Then hands with a vise's grip took her by the shoulders and flung her down to the ground. "Hey," she cried weakly. She was yanked by her shoulders to her feet, and her left arm was pulled back and held up high behind her back. Her assailant worked at her wristpad, and then shoved her painfully forward, her arm still held high. She couldn't fall without breaking her arm. She could feel the diamond pattern of her suit's heating elements begin to flare against her skin, burning their pattern into her. Every few steps she was slapped hard in the helmet.

The figure marched her right back to their own rover, which astonished her. She was shoved into the lock, and the figure tumbled in after her, and closed and pumped the

662

chamber, and tore off her helmet, and then his, and to her utter amazement it was her Simon, purple-faced and shouting at her, striking her still, his face soaking wet with tears – this her Simon, the quiet one, now yelling at her, "Why? Why? Damn you, you *always* do this, it's always just you you you, off in your own world, you are so *selfish*!" Voice rising to a final painful shriek, her Simon who never said anything, never raised his voice, never spoke more than a word, now striking her and shrieking in her face, literally spitting, gasping with fury; and suddenly it made her mad. Why not before, why not when she had needed someone with some life in him? Why had it taken this to rouse him? She punched him right in the chest, hard, and he fell back. "Leave me alone!" she shouted. "Leave me alone!" And then the anguish shuddered through her, the chilled shiver of Martian death: *"Why didn't you leave me alone?"*

He regained his balance, lunged forward and seized her by both shoulders, shook her. She had never noticed how powerful his hands were. "Be*cause*," he shouted, and paused to lick his lips and catch his breath — "Because—" And his eyes bugged out, and his face darkened even further, as if a thousand sentences had all jammed in his throat at once, this her mild Simon! – and then he gave up on saying it, and roared, and shook her in his arms, shouting *"Because! Because! Because!"*

Snow fell. Though it was early afternoon, it was dim. Wind whipped across the chaos, swirling the spindrift over the shattered land. Boulders as big as city blocks lay jumbled against each other, and the landscape was broken in a million little cliffs, holes, mesas, ridges, peaks – also many peculiar spikes, and towers, and balancing rocks, held in place by *kami* alone. All the steep or vertical stone in this chaotic terrain was still black, while flatter areas were now white with snow, so that the landscape was a densely variegated black and white, all swirling in and out of visibility as billows and veils of snow gusted by.

Then the snow stopped. The wind died. The black verticals and white horizontals gave the world a definition it didn't usually have. In the overcast there were no shadows, and the landscape glowed as if light were pouring up through the snow onto the bottoms of the dusky low clouds. Everything was sharp-edged and distinct, as if captured in glass.

Over the horizon appeared moving figures. One by one they appeared, until there were seven of them, in a ragged line. They moved slowly, their shoulders slumped, their helmets bent forward. They moved as if they had no destination. The two in front looked up from time to time, but they never paused, or pointed the way.

The clouds gleamed like mother of pearl, the only sign on that dull day that the sun was lowering. The figures walked up a long ridge that emerged from the blasted landscape. From the upper slopes of the ridge one could see a long way in every direction.

It took a long time for the figures to climb the ridge. Finally they approached a peak, a bouldery knob where the ridge began to descend again. At the summit of the knob was a curious thing: a big flat-bottomed boulder standing high in the air, balanced on six slender stone pillars.

The seven figures approached this megalith. They stopped and regarded it for a time, under the dark bruised clouds. Then they stepped between the pillars, and under the boulder. It stood well over them, a massive roof. The circular floor beneath it was flat, made of cut polished stone.

One of the figures walked to a far column, and touched it with a finger. The others looked out at the motionless snowy chaos. A trapdoor slid open in the floor. The figures went to it, and one by one stepped down into the ridge.

When they were gone the six slender columns began to sink into the floor, and the great dolmen that they held aloft descended on them, until the columns disappeared and the great rock rested on the ridge, returned to its ancient existence as an impressive peak boulder. Beyond the clouds the sun had set, and the light leaked out of the empty land.

It was Maya who kept them going, Maya who drove them into heading south. The refuge under the dolmen was just that, a sequence of small caves in the ridge, stocked with emergency rations and gas supplies, but otherwise empty. After a few days to rest and catch up on sleep and food, Maya began to complain. It was no way to live, she said, it was no more than a kind of death-in-life; where were all the others? Where was Hiroko? Michel and Kasei explained again that the hidden colony was in the south, that they had moved down there long ago. All right, Maya said, then we will go south too. There were other boulder cars in the refuge's garage, they could caravan down by night, she said, and out of the canyons they would be safe. The refuge was no longer self-sustaining in any case, its supplies were large but limited, so they would have to go sooner or later. Best to go while the dust storm would still provide some cover for the trip. Best to go.

So she drove the tired little group to action. They loaded two cars, and took off again, south across the great rumpled plains of Margarifiter Sinus. Free from the restrictions of Marineris, they made hundreds of kilometers per night and slept through the days, and in a nearly speechless journey of several days they passed between Argyre and Hellas, through the endless craterland of the southern highlands. It began to seem that they had never done anything but drive onward in their little cars, that the journey would last forever.

But then one night they drove onto the layered terrain of the polar region, and near dawn the horizon ahead gleamed, and then became a dim white bar, which thickened and thickened as they proceeded, until it was a white cliff standing before them. The southern polar cap, evidently. Michel and Kasei took over the two drivers' seats, and conferred over the intercom in low voices. They drove on until they reached the white cliff, and they continued to drive straight at it, until they were on frozen crusted sand that was under the bulk of the ice. The cliff was an enormous overhang, like a wave stopped in the moment it was about to crash onto a beach. There was a tunnel cut into the ice at the bottom of the cliff, and a figure in a walker appeared, and directed the two rovers into it.

The tunnel led them straight into the ice for what must have been a kilometer at least. The tunnel was wide enough for two or three rovers, and had a low ceiling; the ice around them was a pure white, dry ice only lightly streaked by stratification. They passed through two locks filling the tunnel; and in the third lock Michel and Kasei stopped the rovers, and opened the locks, and climbed down. Maya, Nadia, Sax, Simon and Ann followed them out of the cars. They walked down the tunnel in silence. Then the tunnel opened up and they all stopped, stilled by the sight that met them.

Overhead was an enormous dome of gleaming white ice. They stood under it as if under a giant overturned bowl. The dome was several kilometers in diameter, and at least a kilometer high, maybe more; it rose swiftly from the perimeters, and then bowled gently across the center. The light was diffuse but fairly strong, as if on a cloudy day, and it seemed to come from the white dome itself, which gleamed.

The ground under the dome was gently rolling reddish sand, grassy in the hollows, with frequent stands of tall bamboo and gnarled pine. There were some small hillocks to the right, and clustered in these hills was a little village, one and two-story houses painted white and blue, interspersed with large trees which had bamboo rooms and staircases set in their thick branches.

Michel and Kasei were walking toward this village, and the woman who had guided their cars into the tunnel lock was running ahead, shouting "They're here, they're here!"

Under the other side of the dome there was a lake of faintly steaming open water, its surface a white sheen lined by waves that broke on the near shore. On the far shore stood the blue bulk of a Rickover, its reflection a smear of blue across the white water. Gusts of cold damp wind nipped at their ears.

Michel came back and retrieved his old friends, who were standing like statues. "Come on, it's cold out," he said with a smile. "There's a water-ice layer stuck to the dome, so we have to keep the air below freezing all the time."

People were spilling out of the village, calling out. Down by the little lake a young man appeared sprinting toward them, gazelling over the dunes in great leaps. Even after all their years on Mars such a flying run still looked dreamlike to the first hundred, and it took a while before Simon clutched Ann by the arm and cried "That's Peter! That's Peter!"

"Peter," she said.

And then they were in a crush of people, many of them young folk and children, strangers, but with familiar faces everywhere making their way to the fore, Hiroko and Iwao, Raul, Rya, Gene, Peter crashing in to hug Ann and Simon, and there were Vlad and Ursula and Marina and several others from the Acheron group, all clustered around them, reaching to touch them.

"What is this place?" Maya cried.

"This is home," Hiroko said. "This is where we start again."

MY THANKS TO:

Lou Aronica, Adam Bridge, Michael H. Carr, Robert Craddock, Bruce Faust, Bill Fisher, Hal Handley, Cecilia Holland, Fredric Jameson, Jane Johnson, Steve McDow, Beth Meacham, Tom Meyer, James Edward Oberg, Ralph Vicinanza, and John B. West.

A special thanks to Charles Sheffield.

CHRONOLOGY

2010: John Boone and Frank Chalmers spend six weeks together on US space station.

2020: John Boone, age 38, lands on Mars in group of 4; he steps out first.

2026: *Ares* leaves Earth orbit for Mars.

2027: First hundred land on Mars.

2032: Japanese and other groups arrive on Mars.

2035: Hiroko and farm team depart.

2046: John Boone begins sabotage investigation.

2047: Birth of Peter Clayborne.

2048: First applications of gerontological treatment.

2049: Beginning of Great Storm.

2051: End of Great Storm.

2052: First Olympus Mons festival.

2053: Death of John Boone.

2057: Revision and re-signing of the Mars Treaty.

2062: Revolution.